The United States Service Magazine, Volume 5, issue 3 - Primary Source Edition

Henry Coppée

Nabu Public Domain Reprints:

You are holding a reproduction of an original work published before 1923 that is in the public domain in the United States of America, and possibly other countries. You may freely copy and distribute this work as no entity (individual or corporate) has a copyright on the body of the work. This book may contain prior copyright references, and library stamps (as most of these works were scanned from library copies). These have been scanned and retained as part of the historical artifact.

This book may have occasional imperfections such as missing or blurred pages, poor pictures, errant marks, etc. that were either part of the original artifact, or were introduced by the scanning process. We believe this work is culturally important, and despite the imperfections, have elected to bring it back into print as part of our continuing commitment to the preservation of printed works worldwide. We appreciate your understanding of the imperfections in the preservation process, and hope you enjoy this valuable book.

THE

UNITED STATES SERVICE

MAGAZINE.

VOL. III.

NEW YORK:
CHARLES R. RICHARDSON, 540 BROADWAY.
LONDON: TRÜBNER & CO
1865.

Entered according to Act of Congress, in the year 1865,

By C. B. RICHARDSON,

In the Clerk's Office of the District Court of the United States for the Southern District of New York.

ALVORD, PRINTER.

TABLE OF CONTENTS OF VOL. III.

	PAGE
Amazons, The	102
Ana of the War........C. G. Leland	16, 143
Army Directory	87
Army Movements........Lieut.-Colonel C. W. Tolles	540
Breech-Loading Musket........Major T. T. S. Laidley	67
Burnside, Major-General A. E.	384
Campaign in Missouri against Price, The	39
Captures and Prize Money	260
Chloroform........Dr. C. C. Bombaugh	323
Correspondence	82, 179, 285, 477
Day's March, A........Chaplain R. Ross	180
Editor's Special Department	76, 174, 281, 372, 470, 565
Farragut........Lieut.-Colonel B. B. Irwin	5
Foreign and International	81, 178, 570
Fort Fisher, with Plan	334
Grant........Editor	401
Great Battles in History. No. IV........Prof. H. Vethake, LL.D.	330
Gun, A New	82
How shall Boys be selected for the Military and Naval Academies?	476
Justice to our Gallant Defenders	206
Justice to our Officers	110
Literary Intelligence, and Notes on New Books	72, 171, 277, 377, 469, 566
May Campaign on the James River, Notes on the	23, 245
Military Espionage........General George W. Cullum	150
Military Notes and Queries	285, 479
Military Reading........Prof. George Allen	524
Military Situation, with a View to Peace, The........De B. B. Keim	45
Military Surrenders and Paroles	456
My Capture and Escape from Mosby........Captain W. W. Badger	548
Napoleon I.—A Bibliographical Sketch........Lloyd P. Smith	218
Napoleon, The Field Eloquence of........Colonel J. G. Wilson	560
Naval Staff Rank........Dr. W. N. S. Ruschenberger	356
New York State Militia—Its Services in 1861	283
Obituary.—Brigadier-General James St. Clair Morton	286
" Brigadier-General T. E. G. Ransom	389

TABLE OF CONTENTS OF VOL. III.

	PAGE
Official Intelligence.—The Army	89, 184, 289, 390, 482, 572
" " Regular Navy	96, 191, 296, 392, 484, 579
" " Volunteer Navy	100, 195, 299, 394, 489, 583
Our Moral Weakness................De R. B. Keim....................	369
Pay of Officers..	288
Personal Items...................................65, 184, 376, 496, 571	
Quartermaster's Department, A Word for the. Captain J. F. Rusling, A. Q. M., 57, 133, 255, 446	
Reorganization of the Army..................................	200
Richmond and the End................Editor....................	404
Romance of a Raid...................C. D. Gardette................	28
Seeking the Bubble.................Lieut.-Colonel R. B. Irwin..... 128, 345, 415, 515	
Sherman's Atlanta Campaign.........Colonel S. M. Bowman...........	305
Sherman's Georgia Campaign ....Colonel S. M. Bowman...........	426
Sherman, Letter from Major-General W. T...............................	1
Sherman's Sixty Days in the Carolinas......Captain J. E. P. Doyle........	511
Sherman's Truce...................Editor............................	497
Sherman's Winter Campaign through Georgia. Captain J. E. P. Doyle......	164
Sheridan, Major-General Philip Henry.....L. P. Brockett, M. D........	406
Slang, A Word about................R. W. McAlpine..................	585
Victory at Nashville, The.............Captain J. F. Rusling. A. Q. M........	113
What the Coast Survey has done for the War. R. Meade Bache............	499
Willcox, Major-General O. B..	295
Women in the War.................C. G. Leland........................	270

POETRY.

Army of the Dead, The................Mrs. Lucy H. Hooper................	276
Hetty McEwen.....................Mrs. Lucy H. Hooper................	467
Home from the War................George Cooper.....................	565
Laurea Denandus..................Mrs. Lucy H. Hooper................	565
On the Threshold...................C. D. Gardette.....................	170
Relieved Guard....................Henry P. Leland....................	363
Soldier's Love, The.................George Cooper.....................	468
Third of April 1865, The.............Mrs. Lucy H. Hooper................	466
To Goldwin Smith..................Rev. E. A. Washburn, D. D.........	71
Vision of Death, A ....C. D. Gardette.....................	468
Wind and the Weathercock, The..	232

STEEL PORTRAITS.

Vice-Admiral D. G. Farragut.   Major-General Philip Henry Sheridan.

THE UNITED STATES SERVICE MAGAZINE.

VOL. III.—JANUARY, 1865.—NO. I.

THE BATTLE OF PITTSBURG LANDING.

A LETTER FROM GENERAL SHERMAN.

HEAD-QUARTERS MILITARY DIVISION OF THE MISSISSIPPI.

PROF. HENRY COPPÉE, *Philadelphia:*

DEAR SIR:—In the June number of the UNITED STATES SERVICE MAGAZINE I find a brief sketch of Lieutenant-General U. S. Grant, in which I see you are likely to perpetuate an error, which General Grant may not deem of sufficient importance to correct. To General Buell's noble, able, and gallant conduct you attribute the fact that the disaster of April 6th, at Pittsburg Landing, was retrieved, and made the victory of the following day. As General Taylor is said in his later days to have doubted whether he was at the battle of Buena Vista at all, on account of the many things having transpired there, according to the historians, which he did not see, so I begin to doubt whether I was at the battle of Pittsburg Landing of modern description. But I was at the battles of April 6th and 7th, 1862. General Grant visited my division in person about ten A. M., when the battle raged fiercest. I was then on the right. After some general conversation, he remarked, that I was doing right in stubbornly opposing the progress of the enemy; and, in answer to my inquiry as to cartridges, told me he had anticipated their want, and given orders accordingly: he then said his presence was more needed over at the left. About two P. M. of the 6th, the enemy materially slackened his attack on me, and about four P. M. I deliberately made a new line behind McArthur's drill-field, placing batteries on chosen ground, repelled easily a cavalry attack, and watched the cautious approach of the enemy's infantry, that never dislodged me there. I selected that line in advance of a bridge across Snake Creek, by which we had all day been expecting the approach of Lew. Wallace's Division from Crump's Landing. About five P. M., before the sun set, General Grant came again to me, and after hearing my report of matters, explained to me the situation of affairs on the left, which were not as favorable; still, the enemy had failed to reach the landing of the boats. We agreed that the enemy had expended the *furore* of his attack, and we estimated our loss, and approximated our then strength, including Lew. Wallace's fresh division, expected each minute. He then ordered me to get all things ready, and at daylight the next day to assume the offensive. That was before General Buell had arrived, but he was known to be near at hand. General Buell's troops took no essential part in the first day's fight, and Grant's army, though collected together hastily, green as militia, some regiments arriving without cartridges even, and nearly all hearing the dread sound of battle for the first time, had successfully withstood and repelled the first day's terrific onset of a superior enemy, well commanded and well handled. I know I had orders from General Grant to assume the offensive before I knew General Buell was on the west side of the Tennessee. I think General Buell, Colonel Fry, and others of General Buell's staff, rode up to where I was about sunset, about the time General Grant was leaving me. General Buell asked me many questions, and got of me a small map, which I had made for my own use, and told me that by daylight he could have eighteen thousand fresh men, which I knew would settle the matter.

I understood Grant's forces were to advance on the right of the Corinth Road, and Buell's on the left, and accordingly at daylight I advanced my division by the flank, the resistance being trivial, up to the very spot where the day before the battle had been most severe, and then waited till near noon for Buell's troops to get up abreast, when the entire line advanced and recovered all the ground we had ever held. I know that, with the exception of one or two severe struggles, the fighting of April 7th was easy as compared with that of April 6th.

I never was disposed, nor am I now, to question any thing done by General Buell and his army, and know that approaching our field of battle from the rear, he encountered that sickening crowd of laggards and fugitives that excited his contempt, and that of his army, who never gave full credit to those in the front line, who did fight hard, and who had, at four P. M., checked the enemy, and were preparing the next day to assume the offensive. I remember the fact the better from General Grant's anecdote of his Donelson battle, which he told me then for the first time—that, at a certain period of the battle, he saw that either side was ready to give way if the other showed a bold front, and he determined to do that very thing, to advance on the enemy, when, as he prognosticated, the enemy surrendered. At four P. M. of April 6th, he thought the appearances the same, and he judged, with Lew. Wallace's fresh division and such of our startled troops as had recovered their equilibrium, he would be justified in dropping the defensive and assuming the offensive in the morning. And, I repeat, I received such orders before I knew General Buell's troops were at the river. I admit that I was glad Buell was there, because I knew his troops were older than ours, and better systematized and drilled, and his arrival made that certain, which before was uncertain. I have heard this question much discussed, and must say, that the officers of Buell's army dwelt too much on the stampede of some of our raw troops, and gave us too little credit for the fact that for one whole day, weakened as we were by the absence of Buell's army, long expected, of Lew. Wallace's Division, only four miles off, and of the fugitives from our ranks, we had beaten off our assailants for the time. At the same time, our Army of the Tennessee have indulged in severe criticisms at the slow approach of that army which knew the danger that threatened us from the concentrated armies of Johnston, Beauregard, and Bragg, that lay at Corinth. In a war like this, where opportunities for personal prowess are as plenty as blackberries, to those who seek them at the front, all such criminations should be frowned down; and were it not for the military character of your journal, I would not venture to offer a correction to a very popular error.

I will also avail myself of this occasion to correct another very common mistake in attributing to General Grant the selection of that battle-field. It was chosen by that veteran soldier, Major-General Charles F. Smith, who ordered my division to disembark there, and strike for the Charleston Railroad. This order was subsequently modified, by his ordering Hurlbut's Division to disembark there, and mine higher up the Tennessee, to the mouth of Yellow Creek, to strike the railroad at Burnsville. But floods prevented our reaching the railroad, when General Smith ordered me in person also to disembark at Pittsburg Landing, and take post well out, so as to make plenty of room, with Snake and Lick Creeks the flanks of a camp for the grand army of invasion.

It was General Smith who selected that field of battle, and it was well chosen. On any other we surely would have been overwhelmed, as both Lick and Snake Creeks forced the enemy to confine his movement to a direct front attack, which new troops are better qualified to resist than where the flanks are exposed to a real or chimerical danger. Even the divisions of that army were arranged in that camp by General Smith's order, my division forming, as it were, the outlying picket, whilst McClernand and Prentiss's were the real line of battle, with W. H. L. Wallace in support of the right wing, and Hurlbut of the left; Lew. Wallace's Division being detached. All these subordinate dispositions were made by the order of General Smith, before General Grant succeeded him to the command of all the forces up the Tennessee—head-quarters, Savannah. If there were any error in putting that army on the west side of the Tennessee, exposed to the superior force of the enemy also assembling at Corinth, the mistake was not General Grant's; but there was no mistake. It was necessary that a combat, fierce and bitter, to test the manhood of the two armies, should come off, and that was as good a place as any. It was not then a question of military skill and strategy, but of courage and pluck, and I am convinced that every life lost that day to us was necessary, for otherwise at Corinth, at Memphis, at Vicksburg, we would have found harder resistance, had we not shown our enemies that, rude and untutored as we then were, we could fight as well as they.

Excuse so long a letter, which is very unusual from me; but of course my life is liable to cease at any moment, and I happen to be a witness to certain truths which are now beginning to pass out of memory, and form what is called history.

I also take great pleasure in adding, that nearly all the new troops that at Shiloh drew from me official censure, have more than redeemed their good name; among them, that very regiment which first broke, the 53d Ohio, Colonel Appen. Under another leader, Colonel Jones, it has shared every campaign and expedition of mine since, is with me now, and can march, and bivouac, and fight as well as the best regiment in this or any army. Its reputation now is equal to that of any from the State of Ohio. I am, with respect,

Yours, truly,

W. T. SHERMAN, *Major-General.*

FARRAGUT.

BY THE AUTHOR OF "THE RED RIVER EXPEDITION," "THE MILITIA," ETC.

"FEAR, Grandmother?" said little Nelson; "*fear*, Grandmother? I never saw fear!" And in this childish prattle sprouted the germ of Trafalgar.

I begin by striking the key-note of the character of the man whose name heads this sketch. What Nelson's achievements and Collingwood's character were to England, and more, Farragut is to America. Of that large class of mankind which refuses to believe in the contemporaneous existence of greatness, in the possibility of shaking hands with genius, it is perhaps useless to request a comparison of the actual present, seen in the raw daylight, with the mythical mezzotint past of their imaginations. But to the careful reader of history, not merely of the past, but of all times, the name of our Admiral must stand out in bold relief on the roll of the great naval heroes of the world. He has carved his own name with his sword. No noble relatives pushed him forward; no influence at Court spiced commonplaces, till, in the nostrils of the people, they had the flavor of heroism. If his entry into the service now justly proud to claim him as its own was not exactly through the hawse-hole, it certainly was not through the cabin window, in the sense of the old saw. We have no moral parallax to calculate—no angle of apparent and true position to determine. We are to judge him as he is, his achievements as they were.

If, in the historical perspective, the naval hero necessarily casts a shorter shadow than that of the leader of armies, the student of character may find some compensation for the absence of the bold outlines and high coloring that belong to the figures which monopolize the foreground, in the perfect details, the matchless simplicity, the delicate finish, the harmony of the accessories. The Admiral can never occupy so large a space in the public mind as the General; but he appeals more nearly to the popular heart of all maritime nations.

Many of those particulars as to the Admiral's parentage and early years, which would serve so materially to illuminate his character, and to show those of us the man, who now see only the admiral, are unfortunately wanting, or at best rare or of somewhat doubtful authenticity. His father, George Farragut, a native of Citadella, the capital of the Island of Minorca, and a descendant of an ancient Catalonian house, came to this country in 1776 and entered the American army, rising, it is said, to the rank of major. After the peace, he married Miss Elizabeth Shine, of North Carolina, a member of the old Scotch family of McIven, and settled down, to fight the Indians and subdue the soil, at Campbell's Station, near Knoxville, Tennessee. Here on the 5th of July, 1801, was born to this fortunate pair a son, DAVID GLASCOE FARRAGUT, destined, under Providence, to become the great naval hero of the century. As early as the 17th of December, 1810, being then little more than nine years of age, he became seized with the boyish thirst for salt water that makes the sailor, and that hankering for the smell of villainous saltpetre that makes the hero. His desire was probably gratified without much difficulty, through the influence of Captain Porter, between whose father and young Farragut's, then sailing-masters in the Navy together, a warm friendship had sprung up; and a midshipman's warrant—there were midshipmen in those days!—was procured for him. The War of 1812 broke out, and his gallant patron began to fit out the "Essex" for her famous cruise under the flag of Free Trade and Sailors' Rights, which it pleased his fancy to fly in the faces of the Englishmen, more to the annoyance of the latter by reason of association of ideas than for any intrinsic meaning of the phrase in the ears of to-day. Midshipman Farragut was ordered to her. The now historic vessel sailed from the Delaware on the 28th of October, 1812, carrying as fair a freight of immortals as has, perhaps, fallen to the share of most ships since that one, bearing the kernels of mankind and his animal kingdom, bumped ashore on Ararat.

The "Essex" shaped her course successively for Port Praya, Fernando de Noronho, and Cape Frio, and after cruising for a while off the coasts of Brazil and Buenos Ayres, with the object of meeting Commodore Bainbridge, who was just then making our little navy famous in those waters, made the best of her way to the Pacific, arriving at Valparaiso on the 14th of March, 1813. And now began that career of destruction of British commerce, which, after effectually extinguishing it during nearly a year, was to terminate on the 28th of March, 1814, by the capture of the "Essex" and her consort, the armed prize ship "Essex, junior," in the neutral port of Valparaiso, by the British ships-of-war "Phœbe" and "Cherub." The "Cherub" carried twenty-eight guns, viz., eighteen thirty-twos, eight twenty-fours, and two long nines; and the "Phœbe" mounted fifty-three guns, including thirty long eighteens, sixteen thirty-twos, one howitzer, and six three-pounders—the complement of the former being one hundred and eighty, and that of the latter three hundred and twenty men. Opposed to this force, Captain Porter had the "Essex," forty-six, and the "Essex, junior," twenty, while the united crews of the two ships amounted to but three hundred and thirty-five men. In spite of these odds, the fight was bravely maintained for over two and a half hours, until the "Essex," on fire for the third or fourth time, the flames at length threatening the magazine, her decks swept, her rigging shot away, her hull in a sinking condition, from the effect of the enemy's superior fire, her guns disabled by the number of killed and wounded, was forced to strike her flag. Our loss was indeed "dreadfully severe," as Captain Porter says: fifty-eight killed, sixty-six wounded (thirty-nine severely), and thirty-one missing—the missing apparently consisting of those who availed themselves of the permission to jump overboard and swim ashore, when the progress of the flames and a terrible explosion between decks first showed that there was no hope. But among those who stuck to the ship till the last was, quite as a matter of course to us of 1864, Midshipman D. G. Farragut, then a boy of scarce fourteen years of age. Those who are curious in the history of those times, in tracing the dawn of greatness, or in studying historic parallels, will find plenty of food for their digestion in the "Journal of a Cruise made to the Pacific Ocean, by Captain DAVID PORTER, in the United States Frigate ESSEX, in the Years 1812, 1813, and 1814," a book which made stir enough in its day, but rests quietly enough now in the back alcoves of our great libraries. In it appears, with his name mis-spelled, at the head of the list of slightly wounded, "D. G. Faragut, midshipman." And a page or two further on, we find him, with improved orthography this time, as one of those sent home in the "Essex, junior," on their parole. Of his conduct during these perilous hours, his commander says: "Midshipmen Isaacs, Farragut, and Ogden exerted themselves in the performance of their respective duties, and gave an earnest of their value to the service. * * They are too young to be recommended for promotion." How that earnest was fulfilled in the life of one of the trio—whether the lessons thus burned upon the youthful brain were soon effaced, we shall see.

Captain Porter now had the young midshipman put to school at Chester and taught military tactics, among other things; but he soon found himself afloat again in new waters, in the Mediterranean this time. In 1816, he was attached to the ship-of-the-line, and there had the good fortune to meet in the capacity of chaplain a gentleman to whom he himself in a moment of generous exuberance has attributed all that he knows and all that he is. This was before the days of the Naval Academy, when the chaplain in addition to his spiritual functions was expected to perform the duties of schoolmaster. Between the worthy chaplain and one of his young charges, now our Admiral, sprang up an interest which was to continue, afloat and ashore, for the next three years. When Mr. Charles Folsom, for that worthy member of the University of Harvard was then our chaplain, was appointed Consul at Tunis, young Farragut was sent with him. I wish there were space in this article to quote more than these few words from the excellent letter which Mr. Folsom has recently given to the public, speaking of this interesting period in the Admiral's life: "I describe him as he now appeared to me by one word, 'ARIEL.' * * * All needed control was that of an elder over an affectionate younger brother.

"He was now introduced to entirely new scenes, and had social advantages which compensated for his former too exclusive sea-life. He had found a home on shore, and every type of European civilization and manners in the families of the consuls of different nations. In all of them my young countryman was the delight of old and young. This had always been among his chief moral dangers; but here he learned to be proof against petting and flattery. Here, too, he settled his definition of true glory—glory, the idol of his profession,—if not in the exact words of Cicero, at least in his own clear thought. Our familiar walks and rides were so many lessons in ancient history; and the lover of historical parallels will be gratified to know that we possibly sometimes stood on the very spot where the boy Hannibal took the oath that consecrated him to the defence of his country."

We pass over the piping times of peace that succeeded with their routine of sea service, shore duty, other duty, leave, and waiting orders; years of idleness for some, of preparation for others, when the true Navy growl, that luxury of the professional sailor, reaches its perfection, and a good practicable grievance is above par; when a cruise lasts three years and insures a long holiday in pleasant pastures. Were they years of indolence or years of rest? Let the history of this war decide. We have only space to notice the heads of our Admiral's progress during the long peace; how he was promoted to be lieutenant in 1825, commander in 1841, and captain in 1855; how he served afloat in the Brandywine, Vandalia, Decatur, Saratoga, and Brooklyn; in the Brazil and in the Home Squadrons; at the Norfolk Navy Yard; in command of the Navy Yard at Mare Island in San Francisco Bay; as Assistant Inspector of Ordnance for three years. This last service especially must have been an invaluable addition to his thorough training. In early life, when a lieutenant, he was married to a young lady, the daughter of a highly respectable family of Norfolk, to whom, through the years of suffering that attended her in consequence of a physical malady, he was always fondly attached, ever exhibiting, it is said, those thousand marks of exquisite tenderness that the strong and the brave, especially of the sailor race, are wont to show to the weak and helpless. Having had the misfortune to lose the wife to whom he had been so devoted, he was subsequently married again, this time to Miss Virginia Loyall, the accomplished daughter of a prominent citizen of Norfolk. By her he has one son, now a promising cadet at West Point, under the promising name of

LOYALL FARRAGUT. *Noblesse oblige.* The youthful cadet has a harder task before him than any laid down in the stony course of West Point mathematics, to wear his father's name so that it will not seem too big for him.

All this time Farragut was constantly enlarging the sphere of his professional and general knowledge. He has always been a zealous student, and is said to read and speak several languages with fluency. He was ripening in the sun, for the great and stormy work before him.

In 1860, he had been eighteen years and ten months afloat, eighteen years and four months on shore duty, and ten years and ten months unemployed. Of his fifty-eight years he had spent forty-eight years in the navy. And all these years of preparation seemed likely to lead to no great practical result. There was nothing but peace.

But at last came the rebellion. Convinced by Mr. Lincoln's election that the days of Southern rule were almost run, the leaders of the Southern party made haste to resort to that desperate expedient for which they had so long been educating the Southern people. One after another the slave States passed their ordinances of secession, assumed to be independent, seized the forts, arsenals, and navy yards of the United States within their limits, and prepared for war. One after another, in dozens at last, the Southern officers of the Army and Navy sedulously educated in the school of State rights were doing what they called "going with their States." Scores of others catching the fever, and deceived by the conciliatory policy of the new Administration into the belief that the power of the Union was dead, were following their example every day; the tide set all one way. Men who declared they meant to stand by the flag to the last, deserted it among the first. Men who had solemnly declared they must go with their States, refused to *stay* with their States. Whole messes resigned, whole stations were deserted. The panic seemed universal. But through it all there were some stout hearts that never faltered, some minds that never saw a double allegiance; some true men, Southern by birth, Southern by connection, Southern by association, Southern in every thing but treason, who never wavered in their fidelity to the flag they had sworn to uphold. Foremost among these was Farragut. He was living at Norfolk at the time. Fort Sumter had just fallen. The attack on the Norfolk Navy Yard was being hatched. Farragut was told that his opinions freely and decidedly expressed, as usual, scarcely suited that locality. He would go, he informed those selected to convey this delicate hint, where he could live with just such sentiments. And so on the night of the 18th of April, 1861, accompanied by his family, he left his home and came to reside upon the Hudson. The next day the Navy Yard was burned, the Baltimore mob fired upon our soldiers, and the war, inaugurated a week before at Sumter, was fairly installed.

The Government now stood fairly aghast at the rottenness discovered among its supporters. Every day some new prop was giving way. Even after the battle of Bull Run the desertions continued, unchecked by any act of ours. What wonder that the Administration knew not whom to trust, when those heretofore supposed the most honorable had failed to stand the test? What wonder that all were distrusted alike? So far as Captain Farragut was concerned, his course had been too decidedly loyal, his character was too decidedly loyal and too well known to leave any doubt. But the Navy was inactive. It had no tools to work with, no ships to put in commission, until our scattered squadrons were recalled from foreign waters, and their thin numbers increased by degrees by purchased merchant steamers, ferry-boats, tugs, or what not, good, bad, or indifferent, that could or could not carry guns. In the autumn of 1861, the battle of Bull Run having by this time roused the people and Government to the tardy conviction that we were going to have a war, the capture of New Orleans was resolved upon. The West Gulf Blockading Squadron, a fleet of armed steamers, and twenty bomb-schooners were to constitute the naval force, and military co-operation being deemed essential, the War Department was to furnish eighteen thousand men, under Major-General Butler, to occupy the city when taken, and to reap the fruits of the expected conquest. The preparations of the fleet were considerably advanced before its commander was selected. Happily the choice fell upon Captain Farragut. He received his orders on the 20th of January, 1862, and sailed from Hampton Roads in the Hartford on the 3d of the following month. Commander David D. Porter was to command the bomb-fleet, and was to report to Flag-officer Farragut and be under his orders.

The Hartford arrived at Ship Island, in the Gulf of Mexico, on the 20th of February, and the flag-officer immediately began the work of collecting, arranging, and preparing his squadron for its great task. It was new work for our Navy, getting a large fleet ready to fight formidable shore batteries, but it was undertaken and executed with zeal. Great difficulties had to be surmounted or set aside. Much valuable time and thought was expended in trying to get the steam-frigate Colorado, drawing twenty-two feet, over the bars at the Pass à l'Outre and Southwest Pass, giving respectively twelve and fifteen feet of water. The Mississippi and Pensacola were not got over the bar without much trouble. In spite of drawbacks, things progressed steadily. The fleet was moved up the river to the head of the passes, the forts were reconnoitred, a hospital was established at Pilot-Town, the ships were put in trim for fighting the shore batteries as well as the enemy's rams. The most minute details were arranged by the flag-officer, with a care which might well astonish that portion of the public which persists in believing him a creature of impulse, fearless but nothing more. Coal, not arriving from the North, had to be borrowed from General Butler, until the naval supplies at last came to hand.

On the 16th of March, 1862, the bombardment of Fort Jackson was commenced, and was continued with little intermission by the fleet and the mortar-boats, or *bummers*, as they got to be called, until the morning of April 24th. Every thing began to run out, or run short: shells, fuzes, grape, canister, cartridge-bags, coal, hospital stores. Nothing seemed to come from the North at the time it was expected. The bombardment was severe, as may well be fancied. The citadel of Fort Jackson was set on fire. The cannoneers were driven from their guns to take refuge in the bomb-proofs. But the forts still held out, and a lull in the fire of the fleets was sure to wake up the land batteries again. A council of war was held on board the flagship. The captains had their say. We are left to imagine the usual diversity of opinion; the doubters, the bulgers, the non-committal men, the men who knew no opinion but their orders; and the flag-officer fingering his sword impatiently, full of answers for every one, implying chiefly and always that result alarming to the nerves of every well-conducted council of war, *Fight!* Hear the clear ring of his General Order of April 20th, 1862: "The flag-officer, *having heard all the opinions expressed by the different commanders, is of the opinion that* WHATEVER IS TO BE DONE WILL HAVE TO BE DONE QUICKLY." "When, in the opinion of the flag-officer, the propitious time has arrived, the signal will be made to weigh and advance to the conflict. * * He will make the signal for close action, No. 8, *and abide the result—conquer or be conquered.*"

Of the preliminary arrangements, the flag-officer says: "Every vessel was as well prepared as the ingenuity of her commander and officers could suggest, both for the preservation of life and of the vessel, and perhaps there is not on record such a display of ingenuity as has been evinced in this little squadron. The first was by the engineer of the Richmond, Mr. Moore, by suggesting that the sheet cables be stopped up and down on the sides in the line of the engines, which was immediately adopted by all the vessels. Then each commander made his own arrangements for stopping the shot from penetrating the boilers or machinery, that might come in forward or abaft, by hammocks, coal, bags of ashes, bags of sand, clothes bags, and, in fact, every device imaginable. The bulwarks were lined with hammocks by some, by splinter nettings made with ropes by others. Some rubbed their vessels over with mud, to make their ships less visible; and some whitewashed their decks, to make things more visible by night during the fight. In the afternoon I visited each ship, in order to know positively that each commander understood my orders for the attack, and to see that all was in readiness. I had looked to their efficiency before. Every one appeared to understand his orders well, and looked forward to the conflict with firmness, but with anxiety, as it was to be in the night, or at two o'clock A. M."

At five minutes before the appointed time, the signal to advance was given, but some of the vessels having trouble in weighing anchor, the fleet did not get under-way until about half-past three. The great chain which obstructed the channel had been previously broken. The mortar-fleet moved up and anchored ready to pour in its fire as soon as the forts should open. The fleet moved up in two columns, the Cayuga leading the right column, under Captain Bailey, consisting of the first division of gunboats and the second division of ships, and the Hartford leading the left column, which was under the flag-officer's personal command, and consisted of the first division of ships and the second division of gunboats. The left column was composed of the Hartford, Brooklyn, Richmond, Sciota, Iroquois, Kennebec, Pinola, Itasca, and Winona; the right, of the Cayuga, Pensacola, Mississippi, Oneida, Varuna, Katahdin, Kineo, and Wissahickon. The right was to engage Fort St. Philip; the left, Fort Jackson. Scarcely had the advance begun when the forts opened. The fleet replied hotly; the mortars belched and bellowed; the smoke rolled down upon the rushing water; the ships fired at the flash from the forts, the forts fired at the flash from the ships. In the midst of it all comes down through the dense smoke a fire-raft, the ram Manassas pushing it against the helpless side of the Hartford. In trying to avoid it, the flag-ship runs ashore. The fire mounts half way to the tops; the ship is aground and in flames. An awful moment, and but for discipline a fatal one. The powerful engine backs off; the fire department, thoroughly organized, works like mad, and presently masters the flames, and all the while the great guns are never silent! The forts find things too hot for them, and begin to slacken their fire. And now comes down the great and terrible mosquito fleet of thirteen gunboats and two iron-clad rams—name of terror in those days, especially in the newspapers, for there is nothing so terrible as your *paper-clad*—and of these the flag-officer says simply: "We took them in hand, and in the course of a short time destroyed eleven of them." The Hartford was now past the forts. The Varuna had been sunk by two of the enemy's gunboats, destroying them in the operation. What had become of the other vessels? All but the Itasca, Winona, and Kennebec turned up, one after another. These three unfortunately became disabled, and had to turn back. And thus on the morning of the 24th of April, 1862, the sun rose through the yellow Mississippi mist upon the greatest naval triumph of the century. Of a fleet of seventeen vessels, thirteen had safely passed through the concentric fire of two formidable forts—in spite of obstructions and incendiary rafts, had partially silenced the land batteries, and had destroyed thirteen of the enemy's gunboats and rams, and driven the four remaining ones to shelter. Surprising to state, our entire loss in this glorious achievement was but thirty-six killed and one hundred and thirty-five wounded.

Farragut now steamed up the river, encountering slight opposition from a battery at English Turn, and arrived off the city of New Orleans by noon on the 25th of April. On the 29th the forts surrendered to Captain Porter, and General Butler came up the river to arrange for landing his troops and possessing the conquered city.

It is impossible for us here to follow the plucky flag-officer through the very interesting details of his career during the rest of 1862 and the following year; to note his straightforward, dignified, terse correspondence, with the peppery, blatant, and long-winded petty officers of the hostile municipal governments; to describe the gallant passage of the bluff batteries at Vicksburg on the 27th of June, 1862, and the repassage on the 15th of July, in the attempt to destroy the ram Arkansas; to speak of the frequent guerrilla attacks, and the necessary destruction of their haunts; to recount the intrepid attempt of the fleet to pass the formidable batteries at Port Hudson, in which only the Admiral's ship, and her consort, the Albatross, succeeded; to detail the subsequent fights at various points on the river, and the Admiral's share in the bombardment and reduction of Port Hudson. These things, great in themselves, illustrating the indomitable pluck, the careful preparation, the "conquer or be conquered" spirit of our Admiral, are thrown in the shade by his own achievements at New Orleans, and still later at Mobile. And we have not space for all.

Indeed it seems to me that Mobile was New Orleans *sublimed*. For here again we have the spectacle of a fleet of wooden ships, —aided by iron-clads this time, it is true,—running the gauntlet of two powerful forts, regardless of torpedoes and obstructions, and destroying a powerful fleet, but this time the deed is done in broad daylight, under the eye of the Admiral who has had himself lashed "in an elevated position in the main rigging near the top." The Admiral gave the lead this time, under pressure, to the Brooklyn, but, much after the fashion of Nelson at Trafalgar (who, after ordering the fleet to pass the flag-ship, crowded on all sail so that obedience became impossible!) took the first chance to run by and resume his old place at the head of the fleet. The story of the historic fight with the rebel ram Tennessee, can hardly be better told than in the words of the Admiral's graphic dispatch:

"From the moment I turned to the northwestward to clear the middle ground, we were enabled to keep such a broadside fire upon the batteries of Fort Morgan that their guns did us comparatively little injury. Just after we passed the fort, which was about ten minutes before eight o'clock, the ram Tennessee dashed out at this ship, as had been expected, and in anticipation of which I had ordered the monitors on our starboard side. I took no further notice of her than to return her fire.

"The rebel gunboats Morgan, Gaines and Selma, were ahead, and the latter particularly annoyed us with a raking fire, which our guns could not return. At two minutes after eight o'clock I ordered the Metacomet to cast off and go in pursuit of the Selma. Captain Jouett was after her in a moment, and in an hour's time he had her as a prize. She was commanded by P. N. Murphy, formerly of the United States Navy. He was wounded in the wrist. His executive officer, Lieutenant Comstock, and eight of the crew were killed, and seven or eight wounded. Lieutenant-Commander Jouett's conduct during the whole affair commands my warmest commendations. The Morgan and Gaines succeeded in escaping under the protection of the guns of Fort Morgan, which would have been prevented had the other gunboats been as prompt in their movements as the Metacomet. The want of pilots, however, I believe, was the principal difficulty. The Gaines was so injured by our fire that she had to be run ashore, where she was subsequently destroyed; but the Morgan escaped to Mobile during the night, though she was chased and fired upon by our cruisers.

"Having passed the forts and dispersed the enemy's gunboats, I had ordered most of the vessels to anchor, when I perceived the ram Tennessee standing up for this ship; this was at forty-five minutes past eight. I was not long in comprehending his intentions to be the destruction of the flag-ship. The monitors and such of the wooden vessels as I thought best adapted for the purpose, were immediately ordered to attack the ram, not only with their guns but bows on at full speed. And then began one of the fiercest naval combats on record. The Monongahela, Commander Strong, was the first vessel that struck her, and in doing so carried away his own iron prow, together with the cutwater, without apparently doing his adversary much injury. The Lackawanna, Captain Marchand, was the next vessel to strike her, which she did at full speed, but though her stern was cut and crushed to the plank ends for the distance of three feet above the water's edge to five feet below, the only perceptible effect on the ram was to give her a heavy lift. The Hartford was the third vessel which struck her, but as the Tennessee quickly shifted her helm, the blow was a harmless one, and as she rasped along our side, we poured our whole port broadside of nine-inch solid shot within ten feet of her casemate. The monitors worked slowly, but delivered their fire as opportunity offered. The Chickasaw succeeded in getting under her stern, and a fifteen-inch shot from the Manhattan broke through her iron plating and heavy wooden backing, though the missile itself did not enter the vessel.

"Immediately after the collision of the flag-ship, I directed Captain Drayton to bear down for the ram again. He was doing so at full speed, when, unfortunately, the Lackawanna ran into the Hartford just forward of the mizzen-mast, cutting her down to within two feet of the water's edge. We soon got clear again, however, and were fast approaching our adversary, when she struck her colors and ran up the white flag. She was at this time sore beset; the Chickasaw was pounding away at her stern, the Ossipee was approaching her at full speed, and the Monongahela, Lackawanna and this ship were bearing down upon her, determined upon her destruction. Her smoke-stack had been shot away, her steering chains were gone, compelling a resort to her relieving tackles, and several of the port-shutters were jammed. Indeed, from the time the Hartford struck her until her surrender, she never fired a gun. As the Ossipee, Commander Le Roy, was about to strike her, she hoisted the white flag, and that vessel immediately stopped her engine, though not in time to avoid a glancing blow.

* * * * * * *

"As I had an elevated position in the main rigging near the top, I was able to overlook not only the deck of the Hartford, but the other vessels of the fleet. I witnessed the terrible effects of the enemy's shot and the good conduct of the men at their guns; and although no doubt their hearts sickened, as mine did, when their shipmates were struck down beside them, yet there was not a moment's hesitation to lay their comrades aside and spring again to their deadly work."

The fight began a few minutes before seven o'clock A. M. By ten, the fleet floated in triumph in the bay of Mobile. Our losses had been heavy, including the monitor Tecumseh, sunk, with her officers and crew, by a torpedo. It is related that at the moment of the collision between the Hartford and Lackawanna, when the men called to each other to save the Admiral, Farragut, finding the ship would float at least long enough to serve his purpose, and thinking of that only, cried out to his fleet captain, "Go on with speed! Ram her again!" The anecdote ought to be true, if it is not.

The lustre which Farragut's achievements has spread upon

our arms is not confined to America. The authentic exponent of the navy of naval England,—"Russell's Army and Navy Gazette,"—in an article which seems to have the editor's earmarks, speaks of him as "the doughty Admiral whose feats of arms place him at the head of his profession, and certainly constitute him the first naval officer of the day as far as actual reputation, won by skill, courage, and hard fighting goes."

When his biography cómes to be written, the public, who now see only high courage and indomitable vigor, rewarded by great and brilliant victories, will recognize the completeness and harmony of a character that has so far appeared to them only in profile. The stainless honor, the straightforward frankness, the vivacity of manner and conversation, the gentleness, the flow of good humor, the cheerful ever-buoyant spirit of the true man: these will be added to the complete education, the thorough seamanship, the careful preparation, the devotion to duty, and lastly, the restless energy, the disdain of obstacles, the impatience of delay or hesitation, the disregard of danger, that stand forth in such prominence in the portrait, deeply engraven on the loyal American heart, of the GREAT ADMIRAL.

May he long be preserved, to emulate his own example; to set forth to the youth the model of a true man, an accomplished gentleman, and a brave sailor; and in the fulness of his years and honors to enjoy, in ease and dignity, the gratitude of his countrymen.

Young gentlemen: he *lived* the words of little Nelson: "Fear, Grandmother? I never saw fear!"

ANA OF THE WAR.

PICKINGS AND PICKETINGS.

I.

THE correspondent of a rebel newspaper once wrote: "The war is a huge frolic to the Yankees. Soldiers and officers are enjoying themselves. They want nothing. There is no sorrow in their camps or longing for home, and a bloody field is looked on joyously as opening the door of promotion."

However this may be, it is very certain that there has long been a wide difference between Rebel and Union camps as regards cheerfulness. The Indian-like gloom, or at least that sullen gravity, which was always peculiar to every Southerner, below the rank of an F. F., has not disappeared in a long and wearying war "where hunger was much more frequent than *enough*," as a rebel letter once said. It is well worth noting, that, despite all that has been said of "psalm-singing Yankees" and "canting curs"—and I have before me an article on this very text, from a Southern newspaper—there has always been in our camps much more of that healthy cheerfulness which Confederate writers, oddly enough, claim as one of their own characteristics, than is to be found anywhere among the enemy.

What the Union soldier is, "as a general thing," and in his own opinion, has been amusingly set forth in *The Crutch*, a newspaper published by the patients at the United States General Hospital, Annapolis:

"The model American soldier is patient and enduring; likes camp-life; is good-natured and jolly, and makes fun for his comrades; is always ready for any duty; does all the cooking for his tent-mates and himself; washes a shirt occasionally for tent-mate; has his knapsack always ready to start at a moment's notice; spends all day Sunday *cleaning his gun;* can eat raw pork on a march; don't drink much water on a march; don't consider it healthy; sleeps with his boots and cap on; carries his pockets full of ammunition; has his tent up and supper cooked just ten minutes after a halt; knows where to find plenty of rail fences; always has plenty of straw to sleep on; don't have a high opinion of officers; wouldn't do any thing for the Colonel if 'twas to save his life; thinks the Major ought to have something to do to prevent him from getting lazy; thinks his Captain a first-rate fellow, and helps to put up his tent; won't stand any nonsense from the Lieutenant; don't like battles better than anybody else, but is ready to do his duty; tries to take care of his health; has re-enlisted, and intends to see the thing through; sends home all his pay; intends to buy land and settle down when the war is over; considers it foolish to get drunk; never spends money at the sutler's; helps the new recruit strap on his knapsack; advises him not to eat much grease; wants him to take care of his health; never gets angry except when talking about rebels; swears a little then; can't help it; is willing to sacrifice his life to put down the rebellion; believes Abe Lincoln an honest man; will vote for him or any other man that will put down this rebellion; thinks army contractors and officers with big salaries have kept the war going too long; is willing to do his duty any way, and hopes, when the war is over, to see Jeff Davis and the Copperheads go to destruction together."

"'To take it coolly' is an old lesson of soldier life, which was in all probability the test of *savoir faire* and social supremacy among the camps of the primeval Aryans or antediluvian Celts, as well as with the 'Feds' and 'Johnny Rebs' of the present day. And they have certainly attained to great excellence in the art. 'I have seen soldiers chase hares,' says the writer of an army letter, 'and pick blackberries, when a shower of the leaden messengers of death was falling thick and fast around them, and do many other cool and foolish things. But the following, which actually took place at Mine Run, surpasses any thing I remember to have ever seen or heard; One of those biting cold mornings, while the armies of Meade and Lee were staring at each other across the little rivulet known as Mine Run, when moments appeared to be hours and hours days, so near at hand seemed the deadly strife, a solitary sheep leisurely walked along the run on the rebel side. A rebel vidette fired and killed the sheep, and, dropping his gun, advanced to remove the prize. In an instant he was covered by a gun in the hands of a Union vidette, who said: "Divide is the word, or you are a dead Johnny." This proposition was assented to, and there, between the two skirmish lines, Mr. Rebel skinned the sheep, took one half and moved back with it to his post, when his challenger, in turn, dropping his gun, crossed the run, got the other half of the sheep, and resumed the duties of his post, amidst the cheers of his comrades, who expected to help him eat it.'"

The old story which attributed to General Putnam extraordinary coolness—in the opinion at least of the British officer—because he sat at his ease on a barrel of gunpowder with a smoking fuze—but which proved after all to contain mere onions or onion seed, has undoubtedly been re-enacted in more than one form since his day. Since it is so very easy to "make believe," and pass off an empty revolver for a loaded one, as was done by an excellent and pious friend of mine, Captain C——, in the Southwest. Having been ordered to drive in certain pickets, the captain, with a small band, proceeded to "drive"—which he did with such success as to frighten into flight a larger body of men than his own. Unfortunately, his horse was "just a little too good," and, excited by the headlong chase, bore him into the centre of the "Johnnies."

"I hadn't a shot left in my revolver, but I made the best of things, and riding up to a gentlemanly-looking officer who was somewhat separated from the others, put my pistol in his face, and told him to surrender. He held a carbine in one hand, and his only answer was to begin to search in his pocket for something. He did this twice—when I cried in a great rage: 'Surrender at once, or you're a dead man!' So he surrendered, but when I brought him into camp he remarked: 'It was lucky for you I couldn't find a percussion-cap just when I wanted one.' I replied: 'It was luckier for you that my pistol was not loaded at all.' Our Colonel recognized in him an old friend from New Orleans—so they paroled him."

Apropos of *minus* powder and General Putnam, I find the following:

"'THPIT ON IT.'—A good story is told of a lisping officer in the army having been victimized by a brother officer (noted for his cool deliberation and strong nerves), and his getting square with him in the following manner. The cool joker, the Captain, was always quizzing the lisping officer, a lieutenant, for his nervousness.

"'Why,' said he, one day, in the presence of his company, 'nervousness is all nonsense; I tell you, Lieutenant, no brave man will be nervous.'

"'Well,' inquired his lisping friend, 'how would you do, thpose a shell with an inch futhe thould drop itthelf into a walled angle, in which you had taken thelter from a company of tharpthootherth, and where it wath thertain, if you put your nose, you'd get peppered.'

"'How?' said the Captain, winking at the circle; 'why take it cool and spit on the fuze.'

"The party broke up, and all retired except the patrol. The next morning, a number of soldiers were assembled on the parade and talking in clusters, when along came the lisping lieutenant. Lazily opening his eyes, he remarked:

"'I want to try an experiment thith morning, and thee how exceedingly cool you can be.'

"Saying this, he walked deliberately into the Captain's quarters, where a fire was burning on the hearth, and, placing in the hottest centre a powder canister, instantly retreated. There was but one mode of egress from the quarters, and that was upon the parade-ground, the road being built up for defence. The occupant took one look at the canister, comprehended the situation, and in a moment dashed at the door, but it was fastened on the outside.

"'Charley, let me out, for your love of me,' shouted the Captain.

"'Thpit on the canithter!' shouted he, in return.

"Not a moment was to be lost. He had first caught up a blanket to cover his egress; but now, dropping it, he raised the window and out he bounded, sans culottes, sans every thing but a very short under-garment; and thus, with hair almost on end, he dashed upon a full parade-ground. The shouts which hailed him called out the whole barracks to see what was the matter, and the dignified Captain pulled a sergeant in front of him to hide himself.

"'Why didn't you thpit on it?' inquired the Lieutenant.

"'Because there were no sharpshooters in front to stop a retreat,' answered the Captain.

"'All I got to thay, then, ith,' said the Lieutenant, 'that you might thafely have done it, for I'll thware there wasn't a thingle grain of powder in it.'

"The Captain has never spoken of nervousness since."

The coolness acquired in the field, and amid the ups and downs of army life, seldom deserts the veteran, even in the sad trials of the hospital. Those who visit the sick and wounded, occasionally see a flash of fun among all the sad scenes—for any wag who has been to the wars seldom loses his humor, although he may have lost all else, save that and honor. Witness the sketch from life of "A little heavy," for which I am indebted to a well-known writer:

"C——, good soul, after taking all the little comforts he could afford to give to the wounded soldiers, went into the hospital for the fortieth time the other day, with his mite, consisting of several papers of fine-cut chewing-tobacco, Solace for the wounded, as he called it. He came to one bed, where a poor fellow lay cheerfully humming a tune, and studying out faces on the papered wall.

"'Got a fever?' asked C——.

"'No,' answered the soldier.

"'Got a cold?'

"'Yes, cold—*lead*—like the d—l!'

"'Where?'

"'Well, to tell you the truth, it's pretty well scattered. First, there's a bullet in my right arm—they hau't dug that out yet. Then there's one near my thigh—it's sticking in yet: one in my leg—hit the bone—*that* fellow *hurts!* One through my left hand—that fell out. And I tell you what, friend, with all this lead in me, I feel, gin'rally speaking, *a little heavy all over!*'

"C—— lightened his woes with a double quantity of Solace."

C—— was a good fellow, and the soldier deserved his "Solace." Many of them among us are poor indeed. "Boys!" exclaimed a wounded volunteer to two comrades, as they paused the other day before a tobacconist's and examined with the eyes of connoisseurs the brier or bruyère-wood pipes in his window, "Boys! I'd give fifty dollars, if I had it, for four shillins to buy one of them pipes with!"

Time was when the hardships of a sailor's life were considered a first-class subject for sympathy. Since those days, we have learned that men may suffer inconceivably more than Jack Tar is ever expected to do, and yet be jolly. Take in illustration a description of "how the soldier sleeps," which to-day is applicable to hundreds of thousands of men:

"You would, I think, wonder to see men lie down in the dusty road, under the full noon sun of Tennessee and Alabama, and fall asleep in a minute. I have passed hundreds of such sleepers. A dry spot is a good mattress, the flap of a blanket quite a downy pillow. You would wonder, I think, to see a whole army corps, as I have, without a shred of a tent to bless themselves with, lying anywhere and everywhere in all-night rain, and not a growl or a grumble. I was curious to see whether the pluck and good nature were washed out of them, and so I made my way out of the snug dry quarters I am ashamed to say I occupied, at five in the morning, to see what water had done with them. Nothing! Each soaked blanket hatched out as jolly a fellow as you would wish to see—muddy, dripping, half floundered, forth they came, wringing themselves out as they went, with the look of a troop of 'wet down' roosters in a full rain-storm, plumage at half-mast, but hearts trumps every time. If they swore—and some did—it was with a laugh; the sleepy fires were stirred up; then came the coffee, and they were as good as new. 'Blood is thicker than water.'"

Many of my readers have found, with the writer, that three fence rails constitute an "elegant bed" of a rainy night and that the little incident of a T-rail across and under the small of the back, is not necessarily a cause of grief. Ill-bred horses pawing around a patriot's head, are not to be regarded as either annoying or alarming—not nearly so horrible, in fact, as mosquitos are to those civilians who wonder why soldiers in a chase do not "keep on," after a trifling run of seventy or eighty hours, with nothing to eat, "and less to sleep," as I once heard an old cavalry-ite say. Well—if the war had done nothing else, it would be a blessing for having taught so many young men what they can do.

"Hard-tack," or army biscuit, has risen, in ordinary American parlance, to the dignity of an institution—that is to say, it is talked about, and has been joked over, to a degree which would fill many a volume like this, were all the Hard-Tack-iana collected. Perhaps the best unspoken pun—one devised by no human brain, but strangely moulded by nature or chance, once presented itself to me under this popular name for military bread. On breaking open a specimen of the article, I found a large iron *tack*, which had been baked in, by accident, and was, I need not say, several degrees harder even than the tack in which it was imbedded.

A good song, on the hardships of soldier life, setting them forth very much in the spirit in which they are accepted, is the following, which first appeared in the "War Songs for Freemen," edited by that warm friend of the Union, F. J. Child, professor at Cambridge, Mass.:—

"Would you be a soldier, laddy?
 Come and serve old Uncle Sam!
He henceforth must be your daddy,
 And Columbia your dam.
Do you like salt-horse and beans?
Do you know what hard-tack means?
Jolly hard-tack, tack, tack, tack,
That's the stuff you have to crack;
Do you like salt-horse and beans?
Do you know what hard-tack means?
That's the jolly stuff we soldiers have to crack.
Hard-tack, hard-tack, and hard-tack.

"Do you want to be a soldier?
   Now's the time to put in play
What your good old granny told you
   Of the Revolution day!
What had their brave jaws to chew?
Sometimes nothing—what have you?
Jolly hard-tack, tack, tack, tack,
That's the stuff you have to crack;
What had their brave jaws to chew?
Sometimes nothing—what have you?
What's the jolly stuff we soldiers have to crack?
Hard-tack, hard-tack, and hard-tack!

"Want to be a soldier, do you?
   You must march through swamps and sludge,
And, though balls go through and through you,
   Blaze away, and never budge!
But when muskets go crack, crack,
Bite your cartridge and hard-tack!
Jolly hard-tack! tack, tack, tack,
That's the stuff you have to crack;
When the muskets go crack, crack,
Bite your cartridge and hard-tack!
That's the jolly stuff we soldiers have to crack,
Hard-tack, hard-tack, and hard-tack!"

The tack in question is always packed in square wooden boxes—generally bearing a date, as well as the brand of the maker or baker; anent which the following is told:—

"One day a lot of boxes, of peculiarly hard crackers, arrived in the camp of the Vth Excelsior. Several of the boys were wondering at the meaning of the brand upon the boxes, which was as follows:

'B C.
603.'

"Various interpretations were given, but all were rejected, until one individual declared it was all plain enough—couldn't be misunderstood.

"'Why, how so?' was the query.

"'Oh!' he replied, 'that is the date when the crackers were made—six hundred and three years before Christ—(603 B. C.)'"

"McClellan pies," was at one time the name generally applied to hard-tack. Of late, another variety of pie has come forth—as appears from a rather recent anecdote:

"Army pies are so terribly tough, that soldiers call them leather pies. A poor fellow of Grant's army, whose arm had just been amputated, was being carried past a stand the other day where an old woman was selling pies, when he raised himself in the ambulance, and called out: 'I say, old lady, are those pies sewed or pegged?'"

"Monitors" is a name sometimes applied by our men to hard-tack, and sometimes to the abominable and tough pies sold by sutlers, or camp-followers. During the great Central Sanitary Fair, held in Philadelphia, June, 1864, an invalid soldier, who was selling a book called "The Haversack," for the benefit of the boys in hospital, was asked by one who bought a copy:

"Is there any thing in this haversack?"

He replied to this question:

"Yes, sir—lots of hard-tack—the real old iron-clads."

Apropos to pies, I find in a letter from the army, the following story of General Nelson, who succeeded to the command of General Mitchells Division:

"General Nelson, the commander of our division, occasionally comes dashing through camp, bestowing a gratuitous cursing on some offender, and is off like a shot. He is a great, rough, profane, old fellow,—he 'followed the seas' for many years. He has a plain, good, old-fashioned fireplace kindness about him, that is always shown to those who do their duty, but offenders meet with no mercy at his hands. The General hates peddlers, and there are many that come about the camp, selling hoe-cakes, pies, milk, &c., at exorbitant prices. Cracker-fed soldiers are free with their money; they will pay ten times the value of an article—if they want it. The other day the General came across a peddler, selling something that he called pies, not the delicious kind of pies that our mothers make,—the very thought of which even now makes me home-sick,—but an indigestible combination of flattened dough and woolly peaches, minus sugar, minus spice, minus every thing that is good—any one of which the General swore 'would kill a hyena deader than the d—l.' 'What do you charge for those pies?' roared he. 'Fifty cents a-piece,' responded the pie-man. 'Fifty cents a-piece for *such* pies!' was the reply. 'Now, you infernal swindling pirate,' cried he, letting fly one of his great rifled oaths, that fairly made the elbow tremble, 'I want you to go to work and cram every one of those pies down you as quick as the Lord will let you—double quick, you villain!' Expostulations, appeals, or promises, were of no avail, and the peddler was forced, to the great amusement of the soldiers, to 'down' half a dozen of his own pies—all he had left. 'Now,' said the General, looking at the fellow, after he had finished his repast, and stood looking as deathlike as the doctor who was forced to swallow his own medicine, 'leave!—and if ever I catch you back here again, swindling my men, *I'll hang you!*' The man departed."

But the writer has a friend in the army who once ate of even worse pies than those, the bad quality of which so excited the mingled pity and wrath of General Nelson. The gentleman of whom I speak, had been taken prisoner by the rebels at Murfreesboro, was conveyed by them to Alabama, and sent thence as a prisoner to Richmond. While on the route, at a stopping-place on the railroad in Georgia, certain female rebels made their appearance with sundry "rice pies," so badly made, that nearly all the prisoners, starved as they were, refused to touch them, though freely offered as a gift. "Imagine," said my friend, "the worst of rice spread on a dark and disgusting crust of hardened flour—the rice itself but quarter softened. I was however *very* hungry, and had, in common with a friend, filled my pockets with some refuse sugar, which we had, unseen by the guard, scraped from the outside of some sugar-barrels stored at a way-station. This sugar we spread on one of the rice-pies—and contrived to worry it down. During the night, in the cattle car, in which we were shut, we were attacked by terrible pains, but were finally relieved by nausea. Among our fellow-prisoners was an eminent medical man and expert chemist. Firstly from the symptoms, and subsequently from an examination of the pie, he declared that we had been deliberately poisoned with arsenic, and that nothing but the large quantity of the nauseous mess which we had swallowed, had saved our lives. "If you had eaten only a little," said he, "you would have died."

NOTES ON THE MAY CAMPAIGN ON THE JAMES RIVER.

As a part of the grand campaign against the rebel capital, it was determined to move a large force up the James River, simultaneously with the movement of Meade from the Rapidan.

This force was gathered at Yorktown and Gloucester Point, during the month of April. The Tenth Corps was brought from the Department of the South, under command of Major-General Gillmore. It had been previously reorganized—or rather its organization was completed at Gloucester—and consisted of three divisions, commanded respectively by Brigadier-Generals Terry, Ames, and Turner. There were seven brigades in the corps, all commanded by colonels. The troops in the Department of Virginia and North Carolina, were concentrated, and the Eighteenth Corps was reorganized, and placed under command of Major-General W. F. Smith. There were two divisions, commanded by Brigadier-Generals Brooks and Weitzell, and four brigades, with Brigadier-Generals Heckman, Wistar, Burnham, and Marston as commanders. There was a fine force of artillery attached to each corps. A division of colored troops, under Brigadier-General Hinks, was organized at Hampton, and a magnificent division of cavalry, consisting of both white and colored troops, at Norfolk and Portsmouth, under command of General Kautz. This army was a splendid body of men, containing some of the best disciplined troops in the service, and all eager to have a share in giving the grand finishing stroke to the great Rebellion. Our destination was kept a profound secret. Whether we were to proceed up the York River to White House or West Point, or march up the Peninsula, or through Gloucester county to threaten the flank and rear of Lee's army, or whether we were to steam up the James to Harrison's Landing or City Point, none could tell. The rebels, of course, were as much puzzled as our own people, in regard to the point to be aimed at by this formidable force, which they knew was concentrating at Yorktown. On the 1st of May, one brigade of Turner's Division, under command of Colonel Henry, of the 4th Massachusetts, embarked on transports, and proceeded up the York River, and landed at West Point the next day. This was intended to conceal our real destination. This brigade remained there in rear of the earthworks erected by Gordon's Division in the spring of 1863, which were still in good condition, until the night of the 4th, when they re-embarked, descending the York on the 5th. An incident occurred illustrating the murderous spirit of secessionism. A small party of men appeared near a house on the left bank of the river, and made signals to one of the gunboats accompanying the expedition. A boat was promptly lowered and sent to the shore. As it neared the landing, the party which had signalled fired a volley into the boat, killing one man instantly.

The main force was embarked during the day of the 4th, and that night dropped down the river, passed Fort Monroe and entered the James, convoyed by the fleet, under command of Rear-Admiral Lee. In the afternoon of the 5th, the expedition reached a landing at the junction of the James and Appomattox Rivers, a mile or two above City Point, and about twenty-two miles from Richmond, and twelve miles from Petersburg. There is no village there, and but two or three houses in the vicinity, but the tract of country is called Bermuda Hundreds. The troops were rapidly disembarked, and a portion of them moved out into the country. The signal stations of the enemy were captured, with the men of the signal corps, at several points. The colored troops of Hinks's Division were landed at two or three points on the north side of the James, and at City Point on the south side. The disembarkation of the troops at Bermuda Hundreds was completed on the 6th, the whole having arrived.

The Eighteenth Corps had advanced on the afternoon of the 5th, five or six miles toward the Richmond and Petersburg Railroad, its left resting on or near the Appomattox. In the morning of the 6th, one brigade from that corps moved on, and struck the railroad, a little north of the junction of the Walthal road with the Petersburg. Here a small body of the enemy was encountered, and a sharp skirmish ensued, in which the advantage was with the Union troops. The whole army, that evening, had taken up its position within about three miles of the railroad, and its lines reached from the James to the Appomattox, the Tenth Corps on the right and the Eighteenth on the left.

This was the position on the morning of the 7th—thirty-six hours after landing. The force had advanced but about seven or eight miles. There were many speculations and wonderings as to why we had not advanced rapidly, and struck vigorously all the points near us.

No intelligent person had the slightest suspicion that the main purpose of this formidable expedition was accomplished by merely securing a landing at Bermuda Hundreds, and possessing the little neck of land between the James and Appomattox, because this could have been done at any time by the naval forces.

It was thought, in well-informed circles, that the objects of the movement were: to interrupt the enemy's communications, thereby retarding, and, if possible, preventing the advance of his troops coming up from the South; to threaten Richmond; to seize any opportunity that might offer for damaging the enemy, and at the same time to furnish a *point d'appui* for Meade's army, if it should be judged best to move it across the Peninsula, in its efforts to capture Richmond.

It was also thought by many that there was little danger in a rapid advance, for it was well known that there were very few troops at either Richmond or Petersburg. Sober-minded and intelligent officers asked in all seriousness, "Is not Petersburg within our grasp?" and some, more sanguine, affirmed their conviction that Fort Darling and Richmond could be taken by a prompt and vigorous movement upon them.

It was also feared that these advantages would be ours but a very few days; for undoubtedly the enemy would move troops as rapidly as possible to confront this formidable force, threatening him in a vital point. How well-founded were these opinions as to the number of troops at Richmond and Petersburg, and fears as to the dangers of delay, may be inferred from the fact, since definitely ascertained, that ten thousand of the best troops, intended for the defence of Richmond, had been sent to North Carolina to operate against Newbern, and in anticipation of the supposed purpose of the gathering of Burnside's force at Annapolis, in addition to the troops sent to Lee's army.

These forces were hastening toward Richmond, and with them several brigades which had been stationed in North Carolina; and not far behind was the command of Beauregard, from Charleston, Savannah, and Florida, numbering about twenty thousand men, thus making an aggregate of nearly forty thousand; a force equal to that under command of General Butler. On the morning of the 7th, five brigades, three from the Eighteenth and two from the Tenth Corps, under command of General Brooks, advanced, and found the enemy posted along the railroad between Chester Station and Walthal Junction, and drove them from their position. They, however, rallied, and showing considerable force, pushed back our right, and finally both parties withdrew.

Our loss was quite severe, the 8th Connecticut losing heavily. In the mean time, working parties were diligently occupied fortifying the line between the two rivers, the distance being less than three miles, with a deep ravine in front of both the right and left. On the morning of the 9th, nearly the whole force was put in motion, on the different roads leading to the railroad. Terry's and Turner's Divisions of the Tenth Corps, struck the railroad at Clover Hill Junction, thirteen miles from Richmond. Terry left one brigade there, faced toward Richmond, its right toward the James, and its left crossing the railroad, and with the other brigade followed Turner, who had turned to the left and moved along the railroad toward Petersburg. Ames's Division of the same corps reached the railroad between Chester Station and Walthal Junction, and crossing it, marched some distance to the west, then faced to the southeast. The right of the Eighteenth Corps had previously reached the railroad at Walthal Junction, and made a left wheel toward Petersburg, and was advancing in that direction, when Ames joined his left to it, and thus our line of battle was formed. Heckman's Brigade had the right of the Eighteenth Corps, and came upon the advanced posts of the enemy, about a mile from Walthal Junction.

Brisk skirmishing at once began, and they were driven, from point to point, across Bakehouse Creek, and finally to Swift Creek, about three miles from Petersburg. They had, before crossing the latter stream, made a determined resistance, their line of battle along a road about a hundred rods north of, and parallel with it, near Arrowfield Church. From this position they were dislodged, by an impetuous charge of a portion of Heckman's Brigade, and retired across the creek to a line of strong earthworks, about five hundred yards beyond it, their skirmishers occupying the bank, and covered by slight breastworks, and the bushes along the stream. Turner's Division supported Weitzell. The troops passed over the field of the contest two days before, and found quite a number of rebel, and some of our own dead, unburied.

We found on this field instances of the horrid barbarities practised by some rebel soldiers.

The bodies of Union soldiers were found shamefully mutilated, and the parts that had been sewered placed in their mouths.

These fiendish operations were committed by South Carolinians. There is not the shadow of a doubt that such things occurred on that field. I heard of this that day, and made diligent inquiry in relation to it at the time, and afterwards, thinking the story too horrible for belief, and am perfectly satisfied of its truthfulness. There was a singular coincidence in the affair at Arrowfield Church. The 23d, 25th, and 27th Massachusetts Regiments, encountered the 23d, 25th, and 27th South Carolina Regiments. The prowess of the despised Yankees was too much for the pluck of these Carolinians—the flower of Southern chivalry—who fled in great confusion, making very fast time in their efforts to reach the friendly shelter of their intrenchments. Our troops rested that night on the field where the contest had been during the afternoon. It was a beautiful moonlight night. Some made their ambrosial couches on the sharp edges of rails, and others on the damp ground, but we, like Homer's Immortal Gods having their dwellings in Olympus, had not sweet sleep *all night* long. Occasionally a shell crashing through the trees, would disturb our repose.

The shrill steam-whistle was heard at intervals—a rebel ruse to make us believe their troops were arriving from the South—then about midnight a rifle-shot or two, and then a volley rang out into the clear air, followed by the dog-like rebel yell, and answered by the full-toned Union shout, pealing in our ears. We spring to arms. We wait a few minutes in eager attitude. The affair is soon ended. The rebels have made a desperate charge on the line in front of us, and a few hundred yards to the left, and have been driven back with severe loss. After this all is quiet till the morning.

In the mean time the enemy had advanced a force from the direction of Richmond, and attacked the brigade of Terry's Division left to guard that point. The rest of the division, and a brigade of the Eighth Corps, were moved rapidly in that direction.

There was some severe fighting participated in by two of Terry's brigades and one brigade of the Eighteenth Corps.

From the batteries across Swift Creek, an irregular fire was kept up during the forenoon, doing however no damage, as the troops were covered by the woods. At about noon, orders were given to withdraw our force from the direction of Petersburg. Just at the moment the movement began, two rebel officers, a lieutenant-colonel and a captain, came to our skirmish line on the turnpike at Swift Creek, with a flag of truce. The object was transparent—it was a device to find out if possible the precise position of our troops, so that their batteries might fire to some purpose. But they came on a bootless errand.

They were taken along with the retiring column, about four miles, and then permitted to return under escort. The enemy attacking Terry were repulsed after a contest of an hour or two, and retired. The same evening the whole force returned to camp.

The net results of the operations up to the night of the 10th, were: the railroad temporarily obstructed; an aggregate loss of between twelve and fifteen hundred men; the enemy having lost about the same number; and the possession of a fortified position, likely to be of value in further operations.

The damage done to the railroad was slight indeed. The culverts were not blown up, as they might have been very easily, and much of what was done consisted in simply prying up the track, and turning it over, the rails adhering to the ties so that, in repairing the damage, it was only necessary to pry it over again, and with a little adjustment it was in running order.

If the condition of this railroad is an indication of the state of railroads throughout the South, another delusion which we have cherished, has been swept away. It has been again and again declared, and published, that Southern railroads are worn out; and we have thought that they must be, in the nature of things, nearly destroyed by the wear of war. But the rails on the Richmond and Petersburg road are of the very best quality of iron, and nearly new.

The force of the enemy confronting us toward Petersburg and Richmond, on the 9th and 10th, could not have been large, as but few of their troops from the South had arrived; they were, however, near at hand. A large portion of them passed along the front of our line on the turnpike during the 11th, and by the morning of the 12th, it is probable that nearly the whole force had reached Richmond. Though they passed so near to our lines, the turnpike on which one column moved being little more than two miles from our main defences, they were not molested.

[To be continued.]

THE ROMANCE OF A "RAID."

I.

For various reasons—"too numerous to mention"—I shall disguise the names, rank, and all other specialties of person, place, and time, connected with this otherwise veracious episode of the war.

This, if it do no other good, will, at least, allow me to tell my story, unencumbered by topographical, or other professional technicalities, save such as I may choose to give for the purpose of preserving what the French call the *couleur locale*.

And even these—if I indulge in any—may not be very accurate, for I give you notice, that I belong to the civil branch of the service, and have not received a military education. What little I know about tactics and the "art of war," I have picked up on the march, or at the camp-fire, and "mighty" superficial it is, I confess! However, there is more than one general officer, in the volunteer service, who could not——but I had better let that subject alone. "Comparisons are odorous," saith Mrs. Malaprop. And so, *andiamos!*

We were sitting round the stove—a "confiscated" rebel stove, part of the "*spolia opima*" of a recent "advance"—in Captain Buff's quarters: three of us, namely: Captain Buff (of the Eleventh Fusileers, but then serving on the staff of General Dash), our host for the moment, as just mentioned; Lieutenant Bead (of the mounted Sharpshooters, but at that time commanding a corps of Independent Scouts), and myself.

It was a raw, cold evening in March (or November, or any other raw, cold month you please), 1860-61-62, or 63, and a glass of good cognac, or bourbon, would have been extremely comforting—if we had had any such cordial. But we hadn't.

The canteens were empty, and it so happened——it is unnecessary to enter into details of the whys and wherefores here—but it did so happen that we could not conveniently replenish our stock at the moment.

"Never mind," said Bead; "we're going on a little expedition to-night, you know; and if I'm not much mistaken, there will be a splendid chance for a cheerful raid on the enemy's 'store of wines and liquors.' You'll go along, Doctor?" (I may as well state at once, that my grade in the army was simply that of acting assistant surgeon, and that I had just obtained a ten days' leave, which it was my purpose to act upon in a few hours, *i. e.*, to go home and see the ladye of my love.) "Come, you can postpone your wooing trip for 'this night only,' and I promise you a treat; something in your line, perhaps—the lover's line, I mean, not the surgeon's: we *hope* to get off without broken bones or 'trenched gashes.'"

I demurred, very naturally, thinking the loss, even of a few hours, under the circumstances, a serious sacrifice to make to any thing short of necessity.

"Tell me just what the thing is to be," said I finally, "and I'll see about volunteering."

"Just this," replied Captain Buff, anticipating the Lieutenant: "One of Bead's scouts has brought in an 'intelligent contraband,' who, among other miscellaneous information, has told us that his master's daughter is to be wedded to-night to one of the chivalry,—a guerrilla officer, I believe,—and that the ceremony, including the feast, of course, takes place at the said master's country mansion, which is just within the rebel lines. Now, Bead, with his usual heartless cruelty and fiendish malice, proposes to swoop down like the wolf on the fold, and tear the amorous bridegroom from the arms of his lady love, to cast him into a foul and reeking dungeon, where—and so forth—eh, Bead?"

"Not exactly," quoth the Lieutenant; "I only propose to be an uninvited guest at the wedding-feast, and forbearing to reproach the fair bride with her want of courtesy in omitting said invitation, gallantly to drink her health in her father's champagne, or whatever other nectar may be on hand, and giving her three times three, to insist upon the bridegroom and his male friends, seeing us back to our quarters by way of *amende honorable*. What say you, Doctor, won't you volunteer now, as the Captain has done?"

"But, my dear fellow, if the house is within the enemy's lines, and the bridegroom an officer who will probably bring an escort of his friends and comrades to give dignity to the scene—I don't exactly see how you are going to avoid——"

"Pooh! pooh! there's no danger, man!—don't look savage; I didn't mean to asperse your courage, my boy; I've seen you under fire, you know;—the place is beyond the rebel lines, it is true; but on their extreme flank, which does not reach to the river, within a stone's throw of which the house stands, and we will drop quietly down the stream, land pleasantly in the belt of timber on the bank, walk comfortably up to the back veranda, and enter with graceful serenity upon the brilliant scene,— having properly posted a small but efficient band of sentinels outside,—and thus give a new zest to the party, by an unexpected and somewhat dramatic surprise! It is not likely that the *guerrilleros* will sport their sabres, carbines, and revolvers in the 'festive hall.' We shall find them only armed with the courage of despair, and guarded by the smiles or tears of beauty, which last, by the way, you will find harder to resist than the cold steel or 'blue bullet' of the male foe. Thus we——"

"There! that will do, Bead!" cried the Captain. "If your action was as deliberate and Grandisonian as your speech, you wouldn't surprise a tortoise. I see in the Doctor's eye that he'll be of our party, and so, I'd advise you to give the necessary orders at once. Be careful how you pick your men. Don't take more than twenty at the outside."

"I shall only take seventeen; these, with us three, will complete the score, which will just leave room for a dozen prisoners, or so, in the two skiffs. Time is nine, sharp!"

"All right!" said the Captain; and Lieutenant Bead and myself departed to our respective quarters.

As I stood fully committed to the adventure, I prepared myself accordingly. "As it is a wedding," said I to myself, "we must go *en grande tenue;* but as it is cold, and there will doubtless be plenty of sable lackeys in the vestibule to relieve us of our cumbrous outer-wrappings, we will cover our 'neat but not gaudy' uniform with an ample *capote* of sombre hue." Thus soliloquizing, cheerfully, I followed the suggestions of my other self; and moreover, fancying there might be occasion, spite of Bead's confidence, for their use, I slipped a small wallet of surgical instruments into my pocket. These, with a pair of capital "Derringers" (which I prefer to Colt's, Sharp's, and all other *belt* pistols, for sure and effective service), and a very superfluous bowie-knife—seeing that it required no little effort to make the blade part company with the sheath—completed my equipment. At nine o'clock I was at the rendezvous with the others; the men were told off, ordered to fall in, and we marched silently and swiftly to the river bank.

II.

The night was dark, and a thick mist hung over the river. On the further shore we could see the camp-fires of the Confederates glimmering hazily, but those that stretched along a low line of hills on our left flank as we faced South, we could not see for the intervening belts of wood, though we knew they extended for several miles inland in an arc of a circle, on our side of the stream. They did not touch the river, however, at any point between ourselves and our destination, and their chief communication with the outlying force on the other side was by a ford, nearly twelve or fifteen miles further down. The river itself, though broad and rapid, was only navigable for boats of very light draught, and not very easily so, even for them.

Our own army lay, somewhat similarly disposed, and also on both sides of the river, though we had both a ford and a fragment of bridge between us, about eight miles above. If the reader does not think these positions lucidly given, we can't help it, and can only comfort him with the information that the story will probably be quite as interesting to him, even if he omits these, and similar details—should there be any further such—altogether.

The "point" of the thing does not lie in its military situations; but simply in the rather unusual and somewhat romantic character of the "episode."

In a short time we were in the boats, and going steadily down stream, close under the hither shore.

Captain Buff and myself were in the same boat, the other leading, under the command of the Lieutenant, and piloted—under difficulties, in the shape of a cocked revolver and a promise of its contents in case he proved false—by the "intelligent contraband."

After dropping down in silence for a while, an idea suddenly occurred to me, coupled with a wonder that it had not suggested itself to either of the two shrewd and experienced officers who led the foray.

"Captain," I whispered; "a thought strikes me! Isn't it quite probable that the expectant bridegroom has friends across the river, and has notified them of the affair on hand; and that they will take advantage of this fog to drop down on *their* side and then cross over in *their* boats, so that we shall perhaps have the unexpected pleasure of——."

"By Jove! Doctor! That is shrewdly thought. We'll signal Bead, and confer."

So said, so done.

"What's the row?" asked the Lieutenant, as we came alongside.

"Tell him, Doctor!" I did so.

"Is that all? I hope you give me credit for more wit than would suffice to forget such a possible accident as that! I think with you, Doctor, that Captain Crow—that's his name, Sambo says—has, possibly, *cronies* over the river. And that it's very likely he may have invited them to his nuptials."

"Well, then, and if they come——"

"Why, even let 'em come! But they won't be likely—at least not very many, I fancy—to come. And, at any rate, they won't come in their boats!"

"Why not?"

"Simply because they haven't any boats to come in! And though it is quite natural that you, Doctor, might not be aware of this, yet, I own, it does astonish me that the Captain, who is in the regular line of service, and even——"

"Confound your impudence! Bead! I only came down from Whatsisname day before yesterday, as you know. How should I know——"

"All right! I accept your apology, Captain: move on, men!" And once more the Lieutenant took the lead.

"I recollect, now," whispered I to Buff, "that I heard we had swept off every boat, skiff, raft and floating thing from the Rebs across the way, t'other day. And, as Bead says, it isn't likely many of his cronies will ride twenty-five miles or more, in such a night, to attend any wedding but their own, is it?"

"No!" replied the Captain rather gruffly; then added: "Bead's a humbug! What the devil did he mean by saying he accepted my apology? I'll be hanged if I apologized; or had any thing to apologize for, for that matter!"

"Why, it was a joke, Captain!"

"It was a very bad one, then!" growled the "touchy" officer. But, in another moment, his wonted good humor returned, and he whispered: "Don't tell Bead I was 'huffed,' Doctor. It's of no consequence; he's a capital fellow, and I can't bear malice for his jokes, no matter how bad they are. More especially to-night, when perhaps one or both of us may——"

"Hist! here we are! Pull in, men! Quickly! So! Step this way, Captain. Sergeant, see to the landing, and draw up the men yonder, in the grove to the left. Leave four with the boats. Not a word above a whisper, for your lives! Come here, Sambo!"

We stood with Bead, under a gigantic dead tree of some sort, impossible to make out then, and agreed upon the final details of our plan.

"Now, then," said the Lieutenant, "be good enough, Captain, to take eight men, and Sambo, and let him show you where to post them to cut off fugitives. I think he is to be trusted, but don't lose sight of him. The Doctor and I, with the other five, will push a reconnoissance to the front, and surprise the garrison, either by a direct or flank movement, as shall be found most convenient. When you have posted the men and given the Sergeant his instructions, you can join our festive party at your leisure. *Au revoir!*"

The two squads separated, and were instantly lost to sight of each other in the misty shadows. The lights, however, gleamed with sufficient distinctness from the mansion, toward which we cautiously advanced. It was evident, from the confused murmur of voices that reached us as we approached, that the festivity was in full blast, and all the servants had apparently gathered into the house to " assist ;" so that we were in no danger of being prematurely discovered.

"Halt!" said Bead, in a whisper: "Close up! Corporal Jukes, advance!" The Corporal, who was the captor of the contraband, came forward.

"Jukes, take a couple of men, and get round to the stables— you know where they are, I think you said? Yes? Well, see how many horses there are—troopers' horses, you know; cut their girths and bridles, and 'hobble' them securely. Then return here. Be silent, and quick!"

"And if there is a guard, sir?"

"No bloodshed, if you can help it: but above all, no noise. Gag him, and tie him to something. Go!"

In a few moments, Jukes returned. "Only seven horses, sir, and a black boy, asleep. We gagged him first, and then woke him. He's all right, and the nags too."

"Very well. Let each man draw his revolver, but not cock it, and follow, single file, close order. No one to fire, or use violence without my command. Each to do as he sees me do, after we enter the house."

We crossed the open space in front of the house, and advanced toward the veranda by the flank.

Suddenly a figure started out of the mist, and a low but distinct challenge followed.

"Who goes there? Halt!"

"Friends!"

"Advance, and give the countersign!"

It was the voice of Captain Buff.

"My fellows are all posted, and the Sergeant has Sambo with him. Is all right?"

"Yes! come on."

The lower windows of the house were all closed with outside wooden shutters, but the gleam of lights was very perceptible through the chinks. Above, all was dark. The sounds of mirth were now quite distinct and cheering. Not a living creature save ourselves, without; not even a dog.

"It is plain they don't expect us," whispered Bead, "or they would have waited, I hope."

In another moment we were under the piazza, and at the broad heavy door.

"It would be polite to knock," murmured the Lieutenant, " but that would diminish the pleasure of the surprise. Let us open it quietly; that is, if it isn't locked. We shall, probably, find no one in the hall; the party is at supper; I hear the clinking of glass. Jukes, keep a sharp lookout for the servants. I give you the charge of the kitchen entrance. Take two men with you the moment we are in, and see that no one passes in or out. They may howl as much as they please. Now, are you all ready? Then here goes!" Bead quietly put his hand on the latch; it turned; the door swung gently back; and we passed into the long dim hall, which ran directly through the house, and was lighted by a single lamp, hung from a cross-beam in the centre. The outside fog seemed to have affected this lamp, for it burned low, and the globe round it was covered with a film.

The hall was perfectly empty, so far as we could see.

The company were evidently assembled in the back room, on the left; there were four, two on each side of the hall, but though those on the right seemed lit up, no sound came from them; they were probably the parlors, where the ceremony had taken place. The third room was dark as well as silent, and we supposed it to be the library.

The Lieutenant softly approached the door of the banquet-room, closely followed by the rest of us. At this instant we perceived a black man sitting asleep on the bottom step of the stairs. Bead beckoned Jukes, and silently pointed to the negro. The Corporal nodded, and placed himself close to the man, but did not touch him. The sleep of the black is lethargic generally. This one never moved. Bead's hand glided toward the knob of the fateful door.

III.

"I drink your health, Captain, and success to our sacred cause!" exclaimed a feminine voice, above the various murmurs of the feast.

The door suddenly swung wide open: "Permit my friends and myself to join the toast, fair lady!" said Lieutenant Bead, making a graceful bow. And the gallant companions of the Lieutenant, each gravely repeated his chivalric salutation.

The male guests sprang to their feet—the ladies screamed—the hurly-burly was terrible for an instant.

"Sit down, or I fire!" said Bead, sternly and quickly; cocking, and pointing his pistol, with one movement, full at the breast of the bridegroom, who was nearest him.

"Down, or I fire!" said each of his comrades, imitating their commander, and each covering his man promptly. One of the guests had drawn a small revolver, but he did not use it. By a simultaneous impulse, and, under the circumstances, an extremely natural one, they all sat down.

The bride had fainted, and the other ladies clustered about her, some in tears and terror, others with side looks of defiance at the "Yankee Vandals."

"Ladies and gentlemen," said Bead, "I beg you to believe that I sincerely regret the necessity which compels me thus to disturb your genial festivity. But it is your own fault; for, had you not thrown down the gauntlet——"

"Drop Grandison!" exclaimed the Captain, "and come to the point, Bead. Time flies."

"My friend justly, perhaps, rebukes me," resumed the Lieutenant, though he was evidently a little nettled at the interruption. "I was about, then, briefly to say, that I was really sorry to cause you—that is, the ladies—sorrow or fear, but that it was my duty to request these gentlemen to accompany me back to my quarters:—resistance is useless, sirs," said he quickly, as he saw signs of a fresh disposition to make a sortie. "The first man that rises, falls to rise no more! Remember the ladies! My force outnumbers yours, even here, and I have sentinels at every outlet. Your arms are in the custody of my men: your horses and accoutrements useless. You *must* surrender at discretion. Be reasonable, and you shall receive courtesy. Do you surrender?"

They looked sullenly at one another. Then the bridegroom spoke:

"We *must* surrender, as you say, or—yes, sir! we surrender! If you have any honorable feelings, you will allow me to attend to my——" he looked toward the bride, who had recovered, and was lying on a sofa at the end of the room, surrounded by her female friends.

"Go! my dear sir! I have your word to attempt no escape? Very well! cheer and comfort your bride, by all means. I give you and the ladies, as well as this gentleman, whom I take to be the fair bride's father, free permission to retire. In half an hour, however, sir, you must hold yourself in readiness to bear me company. It is hard, I know; but, as I said before——no matter: I cannot help it. So go, and make the most of your time! Meanwhile, we will partake of our host's unintentional, but welcome hospitality. Corporal Jones! (to one of his men) wait upon Captain Crow—yes! I have the pleasure of knowing your name, sir!—as a guard of honor, and to prevent accidents, which happen, even in the 'first families,' you know, sometimes."

The two "gentlemen" and the ladies went out of the room, looking as little as possible like a bridal party. Bead, the Captain, and myself sat down gayly, and helped ourselves to edibles and fluids.

"Gentlemen," said the Lieutenant, "a lady was proposing a toast as I entered. Suffer me to repeat it, and join me, if you will, in giving it a bumper." He filled the glass of each guest—now prisoner—and gave one also to each of the soldiers, in his left hand—his right still holding the ready revolver; then, doing the same by us, he rose, and we followed his example.

"I drink," said he, "to the health of *my* friend, the Captain, here present, and to the success of *our* sacred cause!" and he drained the glass. Of course, we did likewise; the Captain, however, not exactly knowing whether to feel complimented or not.

"I gave him one, when I stopped his speech, at all events," muttered he in my ear.

The rebel guests sat silent, and touched not their glasses.

"What!" cried Bead, "you refuse to do honor to such a toast! Upon my soul, I pity you!"

"Is it not enough to break into a private house like a burglar?" cried one of the rebels, suddenly—"but you must insult us with ribald scoffs."

Bead's brow darkened, but ere he could reply, or the other finish his sentence, Captain Buff anticipated one, and interrupted the other, by saying:

"Silence, sir! and Bead, for God's sake, let's be serious!" and he whispered something in the Lieutenant's ear.

"You are right, Captain!" said Bead. "Doctor, be good enough to take a couple of men, and escort these gentlemen of susceptible feelings to the boats; relieve the Sergeant as you pass him, and—hold! Smith, go and send Corporal Jukes to me; he's in the kitchen. * * * Jukes, all safe in your department?"

"Quiet as lambs, sir. Only four of 'em: three women and the sleepy chap. They want to go back with us—at least 'sleepy' does; but there'll hardly be room, sir."

"We'll find room! Send in the Sergeant, and four men; take the others with you, Doctor! We'll join you in half an hour or so, as soon as we have attended to a little business here, with our host."

I politely signified to the prisoners my readiness to wait on them. They rose doggedly, and in a few moments we left the house, and wended our way through the fog to the river side.

"What will be done with us, sir?" asked one of the prisoners of me, as he marched gloomily along by my side.

"Upon my word, I don't know. If you are officers in the regular Confederate army, you will be treated as prisoners of war; if you are guerrillas, I suppose—that is, I think it very likely——"

"Well, sir?"

"That you will be——hanged!"

He started aside, and in so doing nearly ran against the barrel of the revolver, in the hand of the soldier on his other flank.

This seemed to steady him, for he said, quickly, "We are commissioned officers, sir: and any outrage upon our persons will be followed by speedy and terrible retaliation!"

I made no reply, and in a few moments more we reached the boats, and found every thing all right.

IV.

Somewhat more than half an hour later, Lieutenant Bead and his party joined us.

Each of his men seemed laden with mysterious looking packages, and behind them came the "sleepy chap," as Jukes called him, with Sambo, both also bearing burdens. These, and the prisoners, safely stowed in the boats, we pushed off, and pulled stoutly up the river.

"I had a devil of a time with the bride," whispered Bead, in whose boat I now was. "She was resolved to go with her new-wedded lord. In fact, I had to threaten to shoot him on the spot, in order to bring her to reason."

"What have you got in all those bundles?"

"Contraband of war, my boy. Aid and comfort to the enemy."

"But what?"

"Well, firstly, half a dozen revolvers; ditto, sabres; two or three rifles and fowling-pieces; ditto——"

"I saw them. I mean the things wrapped up, and the boxes."

"Ah! Why, the old gentleman was so grateful that we did not cut his throat, and those of all his guests, male and female, as Yankees generally do, you know; nor set fire to his house and out-buildings, as perhaps we ought to have done, he being a 'noted malignant'—that he forced on our acceptance—when I say forced, &c., I speak metaphorically, and with poetic license, you know—quite a large quantity of champagne, claret, and other costly wines, besides a store of delicious hams, of rice, and of other edibles, and even wished us to take a considerable sum in gold, which he had intended bestowing on his son-in-law, for recruiting the somewhat diminished ranks of his guerrilla legion, or for some other equally patriotic purpose."

"But you did not take it, eh?"

"Certainly not! That is, we made an equitable exchange with him for the dross; giving him crisp, loyal, authentic greenbacks for his rebel bullion, dollar per dollar! It was magnanimous—it was even weak! Nay! it was almost criminal, perhaps! But his forlorn daughter's eyes were so soft and bright through her tears, and she called me 'an accursed Yankee robber' so sweetly, that I was melted almost to forgetfulness of my duty!"

"Bead, you are incorrigible!" I exclaimed, laughing, in spite of myself, at his mock heroics. "What did the Captain say?"

"He! Why, it was he who suggested the idea. Didn't you see him whisper to me, just before I detached you to escort the rebels to the boat? Well, he said—'I think, Bead, you ought to search the premises for contraband of war; and our wine-cellar is very low, you know, just now.' And, of course, I took the hint."

"Is Captain Crow an officer in the regular line, or a guerrilla chief?"

"O! *ne plus ultra* guerrilla! . Though, no doubt, he has a commission of some sort, which will save him from the 'Tristan L'hermite' of our division. And, to tell the truth, I shall really rejoice, for his bride's sake, if he has a safeguard of the kind. For, in spite of her peculiar style of complimenting my friends and myself, she was a real beauty. You sympathize with my sentiments, I fancy, Sir Lover, eh?"

* * * * * * *

It was nearly three o'clock when we landed within our own lines, and almost four, before I threw myself on my mattress, where slumber profound speedily descended upon me.

Having to leave for home, that same morning, however, I was afoot before seven, and while making a hasty toilet, Corporal Jukes was admitted, by special request, to an audience. He brought a small pile of sandwiches on a tin plate, and a bottle of Clicquot; also a neat pasteboard box, carefully tied.

"Lieutenant Bead's compliments, sir," said he, saluting with the bottle, "and ordered me to say that sandwich and champagne is excellent to travel on; also begs you will accept this little *souvenir*—I'm repeating the Lieutenant's own words, sir—of last night, and hand it to your fair nam—namer—I didn't exactly catch *that* foreign word, sir; but it means the lady you——"

"I understand, Corporal: *inamorata* was the word, probably. Thank you! Give my compliments, and thanks also, to Lieutenant Bead. Hand me the box."

"I forgot to mention, sir," said Jukes, "that the Lieutenant told me to ask you, as a special favor, not to open the box till—that is—to present it just as it is to—— the lady."

"Ha! Perhaps it's an infernal machine! No matter. I'll humor him, and you may tell him, that, in case of the worst, I forgive him with my latest breath."

The Corporal grinned, and departed.

V.

Upon my honor, it was really too bad! Bead was certainly a flinty-hearted and perfidious wretch, as the Captain asserted so emphatically. "Or words to that effect." For—what do you think was the *souvenir* in the mysterious box?

Sympathizing, and about-to-become indignant reader; it was nothing more nor less than the *Bridal-Wreath of Mrs. Captain Crow!*

C. D. G.

THE CAMPAIGN IN MISSOURI AGAINST PRICE.

The invasion of Missouri by the rebel General Price, with the troops of his command, had been long predicted by Southern sympathizers of this State, and long expected by the various murderous bands of guerrillas and bushwhackers who infested its border districts. These bands of marauders grew more formidable and daring as the season advanced, their numbers being augmented by those disloyal citizens who were ready to hail Price as their deliverer, and who confidently looked forward to his permanent occupation of the State as soon as the crops should be harvested and the leaves should fall. The atrocities committed by these predatory bands during the season of expectancy, have never been equalled, even in the records of barbarous nations, and the blackest page in the history of this rebellion will set forth the massacres and outrages committed by these bush-ranging fiends. Price, the deliverer of Missouri, as he delighted to call himself, and to be called, crossed the State line from Arkansas *via* Pocahontas, and Poplar Bluff, about the 15th of September. His force, according to our best information, consisted of about fifteen thousand men, nearly all mounted, and eighteen pieces of artillery. This force was divided into three divisions, commanded respectively by Major-Generals Shelby, Marmaduke, and Fagan. From Poplar Bluff, Price advanced, *via* Bloomfield, to Pilot Knob, driving before him the various outpost garrisons, and threatening Cape Girardeau. His advance was slow, from the fact that he stopped to plunder the towns, and conscript the citizens along his line of march. He seemed especially anxious to procure horses to mount such of his command as were on foot, and for this purpose had foraging parties scouting the country in every direction; no animal capable of bearing a saddle escaped their rapacity.

There were troops enough and to spare within the State to have whipped this boastful invader on its southern border, but had they been concentrated there, the fairest portions of the department would have been left to the tender mercies of such outlaws as Bill Anderson, Todd, Thrailkill, and other notorious guerrillas. Price, therefore, advanced without opposition to his attack on Pilot Knob, to which point the gallant General Ewing had been previously sent. This point was partially fortified, and garrisoned by a trifle less than one thousand men. On the morning of the 26th, the attack on the town commenced, and for several hours the battle raged fiercely outside the works. The fighting continued for two days, Ewing finally retiring to the fortifications, and defending them most pertinaciously, notwithstanding the rebels assaulted him several times in force. Finding that the works could not be carried by assault, the rebels planted their artillery upon a commanding hill, and would have soon compelled the stubborn garrison to surrender had not night fallen upon them. Seeing that his position was untenable, Ewing resolved to evacuate the place. Accordingly, about three o'clock A. M. of the 28th, the small band of Federals marched out of the fortifications, taking the road towards Harrison, on the southwest branch of the Pacific Railroad. Although the enemy had troops on all sides of the town, Ewing's retreat was not discovered by them until the explosion of a magazine in the fort, which occurred some time after his departure, and when he was well on his way to Harrison. Pursuit was immediately commenced, and for two or three days the Federals were sorely pressed and compelled to fight for every mile they made in their retreat. A small force of cavalry, sent out from Rolla, met Ewing's forces at Harrison, and with them Ewing continued to retreat to Rolla, where he arrived safely on the 1st of October with upwards of eight hundred of his men.

During the attack on Pilot Knob, and the subsequent five days, the rebel loss amounted to about five hundred, exceeding ours by more than three hundred men, which fact may be attributed to the over-confidence of the rebels, who thought they had but to threaten the place to secure it.

From Pilot Knob one division of the enemy marched to Franklin, on the Pacific Railroad, where they burned the depot, and were engaged in plundering the town when a small brigade of General A. J. Smith's Infantry marched in on the double quick, and speedily put the pillagers to rout.

The enemy was unmolested for several days following this, during which time he marched toward the Missouri River, reaching that stream at a point a little below Hermann, with his left extending toward Jefferson City, the capital of the State, which place he seemed determined to occupy. Our commanders and troops were not idle meantime, although the unusually low stage of water in the Missouri River rendered the transportation of troops a slow and tedious task. This fact alone may be said to have protracted the Missouri campaign at least two weeks, inasmuch as the rebels had destroyed the railroad so effectually that troops and supplies had to be transported by water, and no headway could be made with any boat drawing over twenty-six inches of water. However, the cavalry from the various districts were concentrated at Jefferson City, and fortifications were erected. On the 6th the city may be said to have been besieged, the enemy having moved up the Pacific Railroad, destroying all the bridges, depots, and supplies along the route, and swarming on the hills overlooking the town. Price, seeing the preparations made to receive him, evidently feared to attack, and so quietly marched past the place, unmolested, on his way to the north and west.

At this juncture Major-General Pleasonton was sent from St. Louis to take command of the troops in the field, and arrived at Jefferson City in time to witness the rear of Price's column moving westward. Pleasonton immediately organized the cavalry—about five thousand—into a temporary division, selecting Brigadier-General J. B. Sanborn as its commander, and started it in pursuit. Sanborn harassed Price's rear for several days, avoiding a general engagement, but acting, according to his instructions, as a corps of observation. Every nerve was being strained by the commanding officers to concentrate the forces at their disposal, but it seemed almost impossible to overcome the difficulties of transportation. Price finally entered Booneville, and was attacked by Sanborn, who caused great consternation in the rebel ranks, but was compelled, from inferiority of numbers, to fall back. At this point the position was such that Price could have been annihilated had he been attacked by an adequate force, and even the little fight made by Sanborn came very near demoralizing his entire army. From here Price moved to the vicinity of Marshall, where he manœuvred and pillaged for several days with but little interruption.

On the 17th, the cavalry was reorganized into four brigades, commanded by Brigadier-Generals Brown, McNeil, Sanborn, and Colonel Winslow, the latter having just reported with his command from Memphis, Tennessee, the whole forming a provisional division, commanded by Major-General Pleasonton. General Pleasonton joined his command, numbering now about six thousand men, and eight rifled guns, at once, and immediately started after Price who had by this time moved to Lexington.

Major-General Blunt, with a force of two thousand Kansas cavalry and nine guns, having entered Missouri by the southern line of Jackson County, also moved toward Lexington, meeting Price's advance in the town. A brisk fight ensued, resulting in Blunt's being driven back to Westport, beyond the Big Blue. Price occupied Lexington one day, and then moved in the direction taken by Blunt, Pleasonton's advance reaching Lexington in time to have a slight skirmish with the rebel rearguard. A vigorous pursuit was instituted by Pleasonton, and the enemy were forced to make a stand at Independence. After a severe contest, lasting two or three hours, the enemy were driven through the town in confusion. The 13th Missouri here made a gallant charge, and captured two brass six-pounder rifled guns, and a number of prisoners. Without halting, Pleasonton's command pushed on, driving the enemy from every position, by a series of vigorous charges, until he arrived at Byron's Ford on the Big Blue River, where the natural advantages of the position seemed to bid defiance to any ordinary attack. From Independence to this position the fighting done by Colonel Winslow's Brigade was superb, most of it being done through the woods, and after dark, the enemy stubbornly contesting every inch of the way. Winslow never ceased skirmishing until nearly midnight, by which time the enemy were all across the river. At daylight on Sunday morning, the 23d, slight skirmishing was resumed, and at nine o'clock, Pleasonton sent the First Brigade to Winslow's assistance. The ball speedily opened in earnest, artillery being used to advantage on both sides. The rebs had made a good selection of position, and seemed determined "to fight it out on that line," but Colonel Philips—now commanding the First Brigade—and Winslow threw their whole force in as dismounted skirmishers, and after three hours' hard fighting, had crossed the stream and were rapidly pushing the enemy through the woods to the prairie beyond. That the fight at this point was a severe one, was clearly shown by the great numbers of killed and wounded, particularly of the enemy, who fell into our hands. Winslow received a bullet in the calf of his leg, and ten of Philips's officers were placed *hors de combat.*

Entering upon the immense prairie, beyond the Big Blue, Marmaduke and Fagan's Divisions were found in line of battle, to oppose our further progress, while, six miles to our right, Shelby could be seen contending with Blunt for the possession of Westport, which town was plainly visible. On the previous day, McNeil, with his brigade, had been sent from Independence to Little Santa Fé, to intercept the enemy's wagon train, which was moving south on the military road, towards Fort Scott. Finding himself thus struck in the flank, Price abandoned the attack on Westport, and Shelby fell back, passing south, on the military road, in rear of the lines, confronting Pleasonton. Blunt followed Shelby, and soon united with Pleasonton. The eight thousand cavalry thus united, rushed at the charge with vociferous yells, across the broad open prairies, driving before them a greater number of astonished rebs, forming, probably, one of the most exciting scenes of this war. The chase continued at this gait for about four miles, the enemy losing many small arms, horses, and men. Arriving at Little Santa Fé, at dark, our forces were compelled to halt for rest and forage, the enemy continuing the retreat twelve miles further.

General Curtis, commanding the Department of Kansas,

who, with an infantry force of militia, had been co-operating with Blunt, here came up. The militia were sent back to Westport by General Curtis, the cavalry alone being equal to the pursuit of the enemy. On the morning of the 24th the troops were put in motion at daylight, Blunt having the advance, and pressed forward rapidly, followed by Pleasonton. The enemy having twelve miles the start, and having marched rapidly all day, considered himself out of danger, and so quietly went into camp on the *Maris des Cygnes*. At dark, however, Pleasonton's Division took the advance, and after a fatiguing march of fifty-two miles, through darkness, rain, and mud, without food or rest for man or horse, the enemy's pickets were encountered about one o'clock at night. At daylight, on the morning of the 25th, the enemy was startled from his slumber by the vigorous attack of our advance, shelling their camp, and in a very short time was again in full retreat, leaving a strong rear-guard to impede our progress. This force was speedily driven across the river, and so hastily had they left their camp, that a number of wagons, and one little three-pounder rifled gun, were abandoned. Coming upon the prairie again, Pleasonton's Cavalry pressed forward, driving the rebs at every charge, and capturing many prisoners. At the Little Osage every preparation had been made by the enemy to change the order of pursuit, and he confidently expected to administer to us a sound thrashing. Marmaduke's and Fagan's entire divisions were formed in line of battle, supported by seven pieces of artillery. Colonel Philips, commanding the First Brigade, and Lieutenant-Colonel Benteen, commanding the Fourth (*vice* Winslow, wounded), soon arrived upon the ground, and hastily prepared for action, while the enemy, with his artillery, endeavored to prevent any formation. Scarcely was the line of battle formed, when the order to charge was given, and our little force, of scarcely three thousand men, was hurled against more than three times their number. Across the prairie they went, filling the air with their enthusiastic yells, and carrying consternation and death to the rebel ranks. A hand-to-hand sabre-fight ensued, which lasted, however, but a few moments, as the enemy broke, and fled in every direction. The results of this charge were seven pieces of artillery, two battle-flags, Major-General Marmaduke, Brigadier-General Cabell, five colonels, over fifty other commissioned officers, upwards of six hundred enlisted men, and two thousand stand of small arms. Without stopping to gather up the spoils, Pleasonton crowded on in pursuit of the now completely demoralized enemy, who scattered his munitions and equipments on all sides. For the next fifteen miles the route was complete, the enemy making a little show occasionally, but never waiting to receive another charge, which our enthusiastic and victorious men were most anxious to make.

Late in the afternoon, however, Price attempted to make another stand, to cover his crossing of the Marmaton River, throwing the greater part of his force into line of battle in his rear. Pleasonton's command, having marched ninety-two miles in two days, and fought thirty-two miles of that distance, without a grain of food for the horses, or rations for the men, and many of the animals having fallen by the roadside from sheer exhaustion, it was impossible to follow him after driving him from his position. Neither General Curtis's nor General Blunt's forces, from Kansas, had any participation in the fighting of this day. Price departed during the night, first blowing up his ammunition train, and burning a large number of his wagons. Pleasonton's Division was then marched to Fort Scott, three miles distant, where forage and rations were obtained. To save this fort, and the large accumulation of Government stores concentrated here, from capture by Price, had been the object for which Pleasonton had made his forced marches, and persistent fighting for the past two days, and this object was now satisfactorily achieved.

The campaign may be said to have ended here, although Blunt continued the chase on the following day, supported by McNeil and Sanborn. Price, however, had too good a start to be materially affected by further pursuit, and but small results ensued. A little skirmishing followed, wherein Blunt and Sanborn participated, and Price burned a few more wagons, but no general engagement followed, Price being south of the Missouri line, in the State of Arkansas.

The results of Price's invasion were exceedingly disastrous to him, notwithstanding the fact that he appeared to have matters pretty much his own way for a week or two. He came with the assurance that twenty thousand men would flock to his standard, and with this addition to his force, he designed occupying the State for the winter. He scouted the idea of his being on a raid, and assured his command that his was an army of occupation. Instead of twenty thousand men, he obtained about six thousand armed men, and this number will not cover his loss in killed, wounded, and missing. He lost every gun he opened on the Missouri troops, ten in all, besides abandoning three others, and retired from the State with fewer wagons and horses than he brought into it, and without sufficient plunder to indemnify him for the loss of even one gun. His army retires demoralized and dispirited, and on returning to the barren wastes of Arkansas, will leave him by hundreds. His rout has destroyed the confidence of his army in him, and disheartened the guerrillas who infested the State, and they have nearly if not quite all followed his retreating footsteps; and we anticipate that Missouri will be less disturbed for the future than at any time during the war.

The last hope has thus been banished forever from the Southern mind of possessing the State of Missouri.

While Price devastated the country as he passed it, it is a consolation to know that he robbed the Southern sympathizer with as keen a relish as he did the Union man.

THE MILITARY SITUATION WITH A VIEW TO PEACE.

It is indeed cheering to contemplate the important successes that have attended the campaigns and labors of our armies, since the opening of spring and during the past summer. We are evidently, allowing full scope for possibilities, rapidly approaching the last stages of the war. How it will terminate, viewed in relation to the present situation of the two armies, admits of no mistake. The decided advantage of position, superiority of numbers, and unexhausted and untouched resources, point towards the speedy and most complete triumph in the field, of the national arms. The theatre of war is fast being reduced to the smallest possible compass, and the forces of the contending hosts are concentrating upon particular points. The fighting is now almost that of two individuals, and the general success of dexterity, watchfulness, weight, and muscular power, will apply in this case as well to armies as to men. The finishing struggle lies between Generals Grant and Lee in the East, Generals Sherman, Thomas, and Hood in the division of the Mississippi, and Rosecrans and Price in Missouri. There are, it is true, other points of active operations, but these are secondary to, though part of, the great centres of action, and figure only in the general results of the closing scenes now being enacted.

Let us particularize briefly upon the relative conditions of the two armies, considered according to the resources of the two powers which they represent. And first, in point of men:

Superiority of numbers has but little to do with hastening the ultimate success of the national cause, by the mere display and triumph of brute force. We labor under disadvantages, which enable the enemy with a much less force to compete with us successfully. For instance, at Richmond we act on the circumference of a circle, and are subject to the inconveniences of extended lines and large spaces to be operated upon, while the enemy launches himself against threatened or weak points from a single centre. In other localities, large forces are required to keep open long lines of communication, guard the flanks, observe the antagonist's movements, and conduct necessary raids. In some cases, too, it is necessary to hold points of little immediate value to the army, but that have a contingent importance, which it might be fatal to overlook. To accomplish all this and to keep up the numeric standard and efficiency of the body of the army in actual contest, requires an immense number of men, and unless we design to create an army to overwhelm and crush the South, we have little to expect from numbers. The disparity between the two armies at Richmond is doubtless nearly three to one. It is position and a strict defensive that has enabled the enemy so long to hold his own. It is admitted by military minds that offensive armies, to be successful, accepting every thing else as equal, should possess extra numbers, if for no other reason, to perform that incidental duty, always attendant upon initiative operations. How much more, then, is this necessary where the enemy has had several years to fortify his central positions and train his armies up to an equal efficiency with our own. Unless, as we have already said, we break down the South beneath the weight of overwhelming numbers, we can expect very little except through the genius and good fortune of our commanders.

But this case supposes that each army has a proportionately equal fund of men to draw from, and fill up all depletion of numbers. Here lies an advantage, and a very valuable one, in our favor. Every action in which the contending parties now engage, is unavoidably attended with more or less losses, from the inevitable casualties of battle. Unless one party has a marked advantage, in open battle, the losses generally are nearly equal. At Richmond, against the strong works of the enemy, the losses of the Northern army, until recently, have been vastly greater than those of the enemy, and were the population of the two sections the same, the North would soon be obliged to desist in its attacks upon well erected fortifications, be more chary of life, and resort more to strategy, or else ultimately find its fighting material exhausted. The difference of male population, however, in favor of the North, admits, if necessary, of larger losses, and, even then, the North will come off triumphant. The stage of the game is such, that this policy now seems to be the best. We are determined that the nation shall be an integer. The fighting population of the South has been reduced, through the large losses attending their army in its numerous defeats in the open field, in a most appalling degree. They admit that their armies are rapidly falling away with hardly a single able-bodied man left in the country to fill up their ranks. Their uneasiness at this insurmountable deficiency has become a matter of positive remark, and, as our Commander-in-chief has well said, they are now obliged alike to "rob the cradle and the grave" to keep up their numerical display. Such is not the case with us. The impetus given the national cause by the victories of the last few months, has called out large numbers of new men, and our armies to-day have almost as full numbers as at any time during the war. The South loses not less than a thousand men per day, by desertion, killed, wounded, and deaths by disease. The North is receiving accessions daily of far greater numbers. The consequence of such a condition of things is easily to be seen. Time, if no more accelerating agency were used, would soon terminate open hostilities on the part of the South, and the North be indisputably the triumphant power. Pride, overruling the better judgment of the people of the South, may, and perhaps will, prolong the struggle to the last possible moment, but that the present defence of their mistaken views must soon cease in subjugation or honorable submission, is beyond all reasonable question.

Not only, further, are the flesh and muscle—the men—of the rebellion fast giving out, but its bone and sinew—money—was exhausted long ago. Our Army and our Navy have cut the South off from the outer world, and the valuable staples of the country have now become so much useless wealth. The fleece of the fields, in the great struggle for life, whether it be national or individual, must bow before the autocracy of corn. An army can fight without money, or its representative, but it must have food. Cotton, through open ports, is readily convertible into money, and money will soon attract the surplus cereals of foreign markets. But a people dependent upon this precarious and slow means of supply, must surely suffer in case of war. There is no doubt the commissaries of the Southern armies are not unfrequently badly pinched for want of supplies. Their armies have often been obliged to live upon the inhabitants who have been obliged to suffer the consequences of the demand upon them. We are hardly of the opinion that the whole South will be starved into submission, but garrisoned posts may be. The universal scarcity of food has prevented the accumulation of large depots of food for long periods at any one point. It is probable Richmond in this particular is better off than any other town in the South, and yet, by every deserter, we learn that they are becoming shorter every day. Nor do we need wholly the testimony of deserters to show this fact. The great importance placed upon the possession of the railroads ramifying through the country in all directions around Richmond, confirms it. The possession of the Weldon Railroad, called forth the next day one of the most determined efforts to oblige us to abandon it. Failing in the attempt, the sudden apprehension of the inhabitants of Petersburg and Richmond could not be mistaken. The South-Side Railroad, now menaced, is watched by the enemy with all the vigilance and held with all the strength that can be spared from the simple defence of the two cities. In fact, the possession of the railroads is all that enables the enemy to exist in his present position. For without them, food and material would grow so rapidly in arrears, that the whole rebel army would be obliged to evacuate in a very short time.

Next to the rapid exhaustion of men, money, and food, is the growing scarcity, in the South, of the *matériel* of war, such as cannon, muskets, ammunition, wagons, medical supplies, &c. Without the precarious assistance of the blockade-runners, the first three of these necessary instruments of war would be much less in quantity than they are; in fact, had it not been for this contraband traffic, it would have been impossible, considering the terrible destruction incident to a battle, and the large excess of captured material in our favor, for the South to have held out thus long. The closing of the port of Mobile will have a tendency to lessen the supplies, but the possession, by us, of the North and South Carolina coasts, particularly of the port of Wilmington, would cut them off entirely. How much material the South has on hand, we do not pretend to know, but surmise it must be getting very small. We have been told by persons resident in the South until a very recent period, that the scarcity of ammunition, particularly powder, has caused much embarrassment, and in several instances their armies have been obliged to refrain from pressing advantages gained, on account of its entire exhaustion or inadequacy in quantity to accomplish the full object. As regards wagon transportation, the South has always been deficient, and the scarcity of medical supplies has occasioned an immense suffering among their sick and wounded. It is very certain that the recent operations of our armies have not increased the supply of these materials.

We hardly think it necessary to add that in men, food, and material, our armies all over the country are abundantly supplied. Our financial schemes answer our purpose, for our armies being furnished mainly by home manufacture, confidence in ultimate success keeps them up. If we were dependent upon foreign ingenuity, capital, and production for what we consume, the case would be quite different.

Let us next view the situation in its strictly military features, and first of all, note a few generalities. In glancing in a rapid manner at the aspect presented by the great theatre of operations, we observe that both armies are actively employed, the one in directing attacks, and the other using its best endeavors to repel them, or the one initiating a desperate, broken, and unsupported offensive, while the other, as strong as ever, and in unity of action, marshals its hosts for the finishing blow. Everywhere the great machine is moving. The enemy, reduced to desperate circumstances, has adopted desperate measures. Emboldened by illusory advantages, he strikes out with the incident paroxysm of ebbing vigor. These appearing signs of recuperated strength should be to us a theme of agreeable rejoicing, rather than gloomy despair. A sudden change from the defensive to the offensive, unless the change be based upon overwhelming numbers or some fatal blunder of the enemy, is critical and hazardous. In the West and Southwest, the enemy has undertaken the initiative, and with what chances of ultimate success? Before, he was scarcely able to survive the tide of opposition which flowed from our armies; how much less are his prospects when he exposes himself to the innumerable dangers of the offensive? The enemy certainly has received no recent accessions to his numbers, nor has the *morale* of his troops been much benefited by late disasters. On the other hand, we have lost nothing of the prestige of victory, and we have thousands of new volunteers by the draft and filled quotas. Supposing the numbers of each army were the same as six weeks since, the chances of success would be decidedly in our favor. That which could not be held in Georgia and Missouri by a determined defensive, with the same numbers, cannot reasonably be recovered by an imperfect offensive. The enemy had better look to the defence of his own soil, instead of seeking to invade the soil of others.

One of the best grounds of our success and encouragement for the future, is the present contracted sphere of operations to which the South is reduced. At one time it covered, by official enactment or popular control, all the large extent of territory south of the Ohio and Potomac Rivers, including Delaware and Maryland, with the exception of a small District in the latter State. Where true Union sentiment did exist in these States in the beginning, it was hushed by the lawless and threatening acts of the opposite sentiment. On the west side of the Mississippi River, for a time it controlled all that extensive region within the limits of Missouri, Arkansas, West Louisiana, and Texas, and even extended to the uprising of numerous tribes of Indians in the Territories. What are now the limits of this great insurrection? Its Government and the proud army which for three years has combated the strength of three opposing armies, is at length cooped up in Richmond and Petersburg, with but two lines of railroads out of eight in its possession, and a speedy probability of losing these. On the coast, Charleston and Wilmington still maintain a sullen defence. In Georgia, Hood has fled northward from Sherman's army, while Sherman moves southward like the "scourge of God" through Georgia to the coast. In Missouri, Price was on a raid, butchering defenceless women and children, but he has gone like a fog before the sun. There is not a State all over the land in which the national flag does not now float. Out of fifteen States at one time in rebellion, or undecided, eleven are now controlled by the national army, and three out of the remaining four are open to an easy submission.

In view of the armies in the field, the military situation and prospects all over the land are favorable. The army operating against Richmond is, without a single doubt, more resolutely and firmly fixed in its purpose, and with more prospects of success, than has characterized any that has preceded it. Cut off from the South Atlantic, and the roads north and east destroyed, Richmond is certainly in a desperate predicament. The only communication with the other insurrectionary States is on the west and northwest. All the successes here gained by the national army have been followed by an unsparing use of the spade, until both the cities of Petersburg as well as Richmond have been reduced almost to a complete investment. On the left, Grant is gradually extending the left of the Army of the Potomac towards the South-Side Railroad, at this moment is within a few miles of the road, and it will not be surprising if the next movement places it in our possession. Nor, while these movements have been going on, on the left, has the Army of the James been idle on the right. The past week has witnessed successes on the north side of the James River which, the enemy admits, are not very flattering to his cause. Our army now lies within seven miles of Richmond, by the old Osborn Pike. The enemy has been forced back from his powerful positions in front of Deep Bottom. We command the principal roads leading to the city. The new positions of our forces are now strengthened by powerful field-works, and the army is determined to hold them at all hazards. The operations against the rebel capital are full of encouragement, and the day seems not far distant when Lee will be obliged to evacuate or capitulate.

In the Shenandoah Valley, the success of Sheridan's army, as far as it extended, has been an important and a decisive one. The numerous defeats of Early's army, which had for some time diverted a strong force from the army now contending against Richmond, and kept the Border States continually in a fever of apprehension, cannot be over-estimated. As the operations of the enemy in the Shenandoah Valley have always been secondary to, and part of, the defence of Richmond, so the presence and operations of a large army on our side must be considered part of the grand combination against that strong position. Accordingly, our success in the Shenandoah Valley has contributed vastly to increase the fears and uneasiness of the rebel leaders. Unfortunately, General Sheridan was not in a condition to prosecute his advantage farther than Port Republic, Staunton, and the vicinity of Charlottesville. Had he been able to push his cavalry on to Lynchburg, and destroy the railroad at that point, the results of his campaign would have had a crowning consummation. The possession of Lynchburg would cut off one of the most important remaining lines of communication now in the hands of the enemy, and one which, for its remoteness, will require time and labor for us to secure.

It is probable from the policy adopted in rendering the Shenandoah Valley a barren waste, inadequate to the supply of a large army, that we will experience in the future very little trouble from regular armies in this section. The large force, therefore, operating here, can be considerably reduced, and the surplus veteran troops sent to the armies under Butler and Meade. However, the Shenandoah Valley will still, in all probability, require close watching. Implacable guerrilla bands will infest the mountains and make frequent descents upon unprotected or small parties. Sudden incursions across the Potomac borders must be prevented, but in view of the great end, the capture of Richmond, we shall very probably never experience any further trouble from the Shenandoah Valley.

Next in importance to the campaign in Virginia, is Sherman's campaign in Georgia. While the former still combats the stronger army of the rebellion, the latter with his great resources has succeeded in dislodging his antagonist, and attaining the final purpose of the campaign. Sherman, from his position at Atlanta, held the three States of Georgia, Alabama, and Tennessee, under his feet. Hood's army hardly dares to claim a foot beyond the area upon which it stands. And while he makes a show of marching northward, he trembles in prospect of the uncoiling of Sherman's hosts for the approaching fall campaign. During the repose of his army, Sherman, with his customary deep foresight, prepared for all contingencies. Atlanta is to be used exclusively for military purposes. The same embarrassment experienced at Vicksburg, Chattanooga, and elsewhere, is not to be repeated at Atlanta. Military roads are to be used for military purposes. The Division of the Mississippi, in its present campaign, is to have its base of supplies in the field. The precarious situation of an army five hundred miles from its base, will be secured in its safety by having a large store of supplies on hand. The line of communication, which has always been more or less threatened, will not then figure with so much importance, and a few days' interruption of intercourse will not threaten such serious results.

The army, unembarrassed, can prosecute its finishing work, and not be diverted by conducting the double duties of a defence of its rear, and initiative in front. The opening of the approaching campaign in Georgia will be an auspicious one. Augusta, Savannah, Montgomery, and Macon will make fine points of attack, Hood's army will be pressed and broken up, and the rebellion in the whole Southwest, as a military power, will be dissipated. This will, no doubt, be the culmination of a short campaign. Already the people of the three named States seem to be taking action tending to peace. Sherman will soon rivet these intentions by the hard knocks of another season of war.

It is hardly necessary to mention the unmistakable advantages of position and numbers which we possess on the Mississippi River. From Cairo to New Orleans, that great stream is garrisoned by strong posts and patrolled by numerous light-draught gunboats. By the ready and unlimited facilities of steamboat transportation, a force can easily be moved to threatened or occupied points along its banks. Or the river furnishes a desirable base for expeditions into the interior by land or by its numerous tributaries. Although the possession of the river, from this standpoint, is not objectionable, its effect upon crippling the enemy, as a whole, lies in the fact that it cuts off a large range of insurrectionary territory and no inconsiderable army from harmonious participation in the efforts of the rebellion. Re-enforcements are unable to cross, and supplies of beef and grain, which hitherto had an undisputed passage to the east from western Louisiana and Texas, are now confined to the west side. The general aspect of affairs on the river, since our possession of it, has always been the same—conducting raids, dispersing guerrillas, and allowing legitimate trade to follow in the wake of successful conquest.

From the capitulation of Vicksburg and Port Hudson until last spring, the military operations in the trans-Mississippi region have formed a monotonous chapter in the history of the war; but the failure of the Red River expedition opened a new era. The enemy, massed to oppose our advance, finding Banks's army driven back to the Mississippi, assumed an offensive attitude, and at one time threatened a very serious advantage, such as the crossing to the east side of the river. This, however, was defeated; but, still strong, the enemy has now undertaken another movement, the invasion of Missouri. But, fortunately, the invasion cannot last long. The very first advance of Price's army has been a mistake and a failure. Instead of moving his entire force on one line, or two within easy supporting distance, he undertook to ravage the State by entering it in three columns. One of these columns, although not more than ten days since it crossed the borders, has already met a check. The national forces are now moving, under Generals Smith and Mower, and will soon compel the enemy to action, the result of which cannot fail to break the power of the invasion, and soon hurl the whole force back into Arkansas. Here, then, it will find another, and have to contend with the forces of General Steele, from Little Rock. Affairs in Missouri are looked upon as serious only to the extent of damage done to the people. That Price can long remain in the State, is no more believed than is the ability of Forrest to control

General Sherman's line of communication, or Early to recover the Valley of the Shenandoah.

In taking a view of other less conspicuous points on the theatre of war, we find the possession of the forts commanding the entrance to Mobile Bay in our possession. This will have the desired effect of keeping out blockade-runners. The possession of the city can at present have but a prospective advantage, which, in fact, is very remote. The design of the recent demonstration was nothing more than to control and prevent the contraband commerce of the city, which has been quite considerable, particularly in the shipment of cotton. In this we have succeeded, and Mobile is no longer a harbor of the blockade-runners.

In Texas, the entire coast has been evacuated by the Union forces, with the exception of a single post, the holding of which has also a prospective value. The larger part of the troops, which, as a whole, were too few for the subjection of the State, have wisely been withdrawn to press greater advantages on more important fields.

On the Gulf coast of Florida, and several points on the Atlantic coast, our armies have a foothold from which to operate at the proper time. Little is now expected from these garrisons, except to hold their own, alarm the country, and make occasional raids into the enemy's territory. Success at the centres of contest, will soon place us in possession of the territory which is controlled by the presence or contiguity of a large rebel force.

Having taken this general view, let us make the natural deductions. In the first place, the rapid and irreparable consumption of men has reduced the armies of the South to mere garrisons. The large extent of territory for a long time held by them has been necessarily abandoned, in order to preserve the standard of numbers necessary to combat the armies of the North. This has opened to the Union armies numerous strategic points, the continued possession of which by the enemy would be attended with great delay in driving him to the end; but, in the hands of the armies of the North, presage a speedy breaking up of the military power of the rebellion.

In the next place, the scarcity of material is no less than in the item of men. Without material, an army must give up the contest, or submit itself to be butchered, with a great disparity of advantages. To destroy the arsenals and producing cities of the South, which is now engaging the attention of the military, will add no trifling results in favor of the North. The South, through the entire war, has been much embarrassed by its deficiency in the particular of war supplies. A few months will find its armies entirely cut off from the manufacturing portions of their territory, and their military strength crippled beyond recuperation.

The want of money, thus far, has shown itself one of the least of the embarrassments of the South. This cannot remain so long. The patriotism of an army cannot long endure, amid the unanswered cries of suffering and want from those at home. Though this, perhaps, will have but little effect to hasten the closing of the war, so long as the army of the South remains an organized and disciplined aggregation, the demoralization of that army, and the failure of the cause, will create a storm of passion and turbulence which no one will be able to check, and the leaders will meet, at the hands of their dupes, the merited punishment of their misdeeds. Men will have their earnings. Where will they be able to get them? Blood will have to wash out the indebtedness.

Men, money, and supplies, no one can doubt, are absolutely necessary to the prosecution of war. The South, there is no question, is now reduced to the last resort in all these particulars. But while all these considerations accelerate the end, there is something more necessary before that can be wholly reached. The armies of the rebellion in the field must be defeated, captured, and destroyed. We have already seen the great advantages of position which we possess. Our commanders fully appreciate this, and all the skill and energy in their power is being applied to irrecoverably destroy the armies of the rebellion. Another campaign promises this desired result, and if the next six months be attended with the same fortune we have experienced in the same duration in the past, the blooming spring that succeeds the approaching winter will also be the spring-time of the new era of this great nation. Vindictive men may prosecute their desire for revenge by organizing into lawless bands, and occasion some disturbances in particular sections, but can effect little in the general termination of hostilities. Let peace be proclaimed, and the people—the masses —of the South convinced of their interest in the preservation of that sacred boon, and they will not long permit themselves to be annoyed and cut off by desperadoes.

Peace, after all, is nothing but the result of self-interest. Armies may break up armies, but they can never dictate nor bring about a lasting peace. You can never conquer the spirit of a people, but you can convince. Durable peace is a conviction of error on the part of one and magnanimity on the part of the other. To effect peace, it is necessary to come back to the instruments of peace. The substantial weapons of war answer their purpose to open negotiations, though never to prosecute them. But the time for the cessation of military operations has not yet come. The way is not yet sufficiently cleared for conventions, conferences, or a settlement. There is much yet to be done by the army. Richmond must be taken and Lee's army broken up. The South must be at the mercy of the North. The leaders of the rebellion captured, and punished or driven out of the land, and the people convinced of their deception and the pre-eminent benefits and privileges which they can secure under the old Government. But with all this yet to perform, the military promises to be a short work. The military situation is certainly tending to the opening and securement of a durable peace. Whether we will make proper use of the advantages thus placed before us, remains to be seen.

POSTSCRIPT.—The events of the past few weeks have brought out developments in military operations, which are still more convincing of the desperate character of the rebel fortunes, and the brightening prospects of our own. We have already alluded to Grant's strong hold upon the great force of the enemy at Richmond, the situation of affairs in the Shenandoah Valley, in Georgia, and in Missouri. We will summarize what has taken place since the time of writing. The long quiet which had prevailed along Grant's lines on both sides of the James, was broken October 27th, by a strong reconnoissance, or rather movement, towards the South-Side Railroad, meanwhile the Army of the James making a demonstration against the immediate defences of Richmond. The object designed by the commanding general, was, no doubt, to discover the strength of the enemy, and to invite an action. Portions of the Army of the Potomac reached the vicinity of Hatcher's Run; a brisk engagement ensued, the enemy being strongly intrenched, and not disposed to accept the challenge; the army withdrew, locating its left on an advantageous position, three miles nearer the South-Side Railroad. While these events were taking place on the south side of the James, General Butler advanced his troops from their old camps on the north, and pressed the enemy into his heavy works, and held him there; and upon the withdrawal of the Army of the Potomac, also fell back, very cautiously pursued. It is evident, judging from the affairs of October 27th and 28th, that Lee is so weak that he can scarcely maintain his position. Three months ago he would have readily accepted the liberal opportunity of a fight extended by General Grant.

The rebel army is now so weak, that Lee trembles to stir a hair's-breadth from his fortified lines, for fear of an engagement, and its inevitable results. Grant, meanwhile, is growing stronger in his position, and the return of the soldier voters will consummate the end.

In the Shenandoah Valley the enemy attempted to initiate a kind of semi-offensive, defensive, or some other undefinable movement. A series of persistent and unsuccessful efforts found him with one piece of artillery, and minus nearly twenty thousand men, and the rest advancing by the rear with unparalleled velocity. Rebel power in the Shenandoah region is now unquestionably broken. The irregular warfare of guerrillas alone disturbs the quiet. Early is said to be recuperating, but he will never recover—what he has lost.

In Georgia, we last witnessed Wheeler and Forrest threatening, in their own opinions, wonderful results, meantime attacking very useless and unimportant posts, and giving plenty of room to the great ones. A few hours' entertainment at Big Shanty cured Mr. Forrest of his offensive schemes. Mr. Davis came to Georgia, made a few speeches, and ordered Hood on the offensive. Sherman's three hundred miles of communication were to be wiped out. Atlanta was to be starved into capitulation. Hood thought he fully mastered the movement. He obeyed. His army ragged, hungry, and exhausted, has already been defeated by a fraction of Sherman's army, in the neighborhood of Blue-Water Creek, Tennessee River. Sherman, meanwhile, is preparing a larger force at Atlanta, to sweep the region abandoned by Hood, and to open a new base of supplies, from which he will be able to provision his army with greater economy of time and men. Hood has undoubtedly committed an irretrievable blunder, and Sherman is taking advantage of it. Under the impulses of this greater failure of the Confederacy, the lukewarmness of Georgia and Alabama, will doubtless soon be transformed into incipient, and ultimately, full measures of peace. Price, too, in Missouri, has met his usual fate. After a few weeks of almost unopposed depredations and bloodshed, by the combined action of the Missouri and Kansas militia, together with the volunteer troops, and General Pleasonton's Provisional Cavalry Division, the enemy has been routed, losing largely in killed, wounded, prisoners, artillery, wagons, and plunder. He is now fleeing from the State, vigorously pursued by our troops. Under reasonable circumstances, this closes the last raid into Missouri.

Thus the three great schemes of the enemy have been disposed of. His offensive-defensive campaigns, which but a few weeks ago gave him so much encouragement, have most disastrously failed in every quarter. The national army, improving by its success, has arrived at the highest degree of efficiency. The choice of the next President, the strong political feeling attendant upon great elections, being subdued, and the whole nation will again turn its attention to the war, and hurry it to its close.

A WORD FOR THE QUARTERMASTER'S DEPARTMENT.

I.

The nation is now well into the fourth year of the War *for* the Union. Of the causes that led to the war, we do not propose here to speak; neither particularly of its progress or results. All of these topics have been widely, not to say searchingly discussed, both from the rostrum and by the press, and they all occupy already a full share of the public mind. For the purposes of this paper, it suffices to say that, three years ago, the armies of the Republic, scarcely certain at that time of either themselves or their leaders, were marshalling for combat on the banks of the Potomac and the Ohio; to-day, our victorious legions, under such unmistakable chieftains as Grant and Sherman, have passed the James and the Chattahoochie, and ere long, let us hope, the tramp of their march will resound from the streets of Richmond and Mobile.

It matters not that paltry politicians, for party's sake, "giving up to mere party what was meant for mankind," have agreed to call the war thus far "a failure." There stands the record of Antietam and Gettysburg, Vicksburg and Chattanooga, Atlanta and Winchester; and there it will stand forever! But, as we have said, we do not propose in this paper specially to recount the achievements of our arms, or to trace the flight of our triumphant eagles. We purpose rather to give some notice of the *forethought*, the *preparation*, and the *organization*, that have backed our armies in their vast operations, and without which the best of armies, though led by the greatest of captains, would soon achieve only disaster and defeat, retreat and ruin. Few people, in ordinary civil life, conceive of what an army really is. They look upon it merely as so many men, massed together for hostile purposes, and estimate its worth and its renown solely by its battles fought and victories won. They forget, that it is in fact a vast community on legs, with all its institutions and appointments complete, here one day and the next day gone, bearing within itself all the elements of life and motion, and that its fights and sieges are only the net products of long weeks and months of anxious and laborious preparation beforehand. With a view to correct these false ideas, and to vindicate somewhat the worth and dignity of bureau work, we have selected the Quartermaster's Department, as the subject of this paper, because the most abused and the least understood of any in the army, though the most important by far of all the staff departments. We say this advisedly, in view of the vast responsibilities devolving upon it, and believe a candid consideration of its many, its complex, and its very onerous duties, will make good the assertion. Let us begin with the Regulations, the *vade mecum* of the quartermaster, and the *Code Napoléon* of the army. It coolly defines the Quartermaster's Department (see page 159, Revised United States Army Regulations, 1863) as the one that "provides the barracks, quarters, hospitals, storehouses, offices, stables, and transportation (horses, oxen, mules, wagons, harness, &c.) of the army; storage and transportation for all army supplies; army clothing; camp and garrison equipage; cavalry and artillery horses; fuel; forage; straw; material for bedding; and stationery." A common man would be likely to think that this was about enough for one department to do, and that it would require a busy hand and active brain to be architect and carpenter, jockey and wheelwright, forwarding and commission merchant, shipper and teamster, tailor and tent-maker, farmer and stationer,—all at the same time. And yet, not content with this, the next paragraph turns the unlucky quartermaster into a tolerable paymaster also, by requiring him to pay "the incidental expenses of the army," such as "per diem to extra duty men; postage on public service; the expenses of courts-martial, of the pursuit and apprehension of deserters, of the burials of officers and soldiers, of hired escorts, of expresses, interpreters, spies, and guides, of veterinary surgeons and medicines for horses, and of supplying posts with water." One would naturally suppose, that the duties of a quartermaster would end here, at least; but, as if determined to overwhelm and crush him, the Regulations next proceed to heap remorselessly upon him the shortcomings and failures of everybody else, by making him responsible also for "generally the proper and authorized expenses for the movements and operations of an army, not *expressly* assigned to *any other* department!" Those who condemn the Quartermaster's Department for occasional failure, should not talk about "riding a free horse to death," after this. In truth, from this statement in the rough, it is easy to be seen, that one would have to be a Jack-of-all-trades and Master-of-all—a veritable Admirable Crichton, in order to be even a tolerable quartermaster. To be a great one, or even a good one, would require both the brain of Apollo, and the brute force of Hercules, and even then some aide-de-camp or doctor would be continually finding fault with and badgering him, though he performed the twelve labors of Hercules every day of his life, and every hour in the day.

The truth is, in the army, everybody (and his wife too, if he has one) goes to the Quartermaster's Department for every thing he wants; and if he does not get it right off, *instanter*, and of the very best quality, no matter what the situation, the quartermaster is straightway branded as an imbecile or a thief, and oftentimes as both. Nevertheless, the Quartermaster's Department, as we have already shown, houses and nurses the army; makes its fire and furnishes its bed; shoes and clothes it; follows it up, with its outstretched and sheltering arms, dropping only mercies, wherever it goes; carries, even to its most distant and difficult camps, the food it eats, the clothing it wears, the cartridges it fires, the medicines it consumes; and finally, when "life's fitful fever" is over, constructs its coffin, digs its grave, conducts its burial, nay, even erects a head-board to mark the spot where "sleeps well" the departed hero, and keeps besides, by special Act of Congress, a record of the time and place of his interment, for future reference of his friends or others.

Pleasantry aside, it will be seen at once that the duties of this staff department, from the very nature of the case, are vast and almost overwhelming; for, in addition to its own legitimate duties, it also has to provide transportation and storage for all the other departments, Pay, Subsistence, Ordnance, Medical, &c.; in fact, in many instances, it has to carry all these other departments literally on its shoulders, and to take good care of them first, before it dare spare time or labor to look after its own affairs proper at all. True, there is an old saw in the army, attributed to a former Quartermaster-General, that the first duty of a quartermaster is to make himself comfortable; that his second duty is to make himself *more* comfortable; his third duty, to make himself as comfortable as he *can;* and his fourth duty, to make everybody else uncomfortable! But the story, if not apocryphal, is nevertheless so opposed to ordinary facts, that it is scarcely worth refuting. At the opening of the war, of course, the Quartermaster's Department was struck with the same paralysis and had the same difficulties to encounter that then beset the Government everywhere. It was literally bankrupt, and its head gone. Though not among the first of the old army officers to resign, yet long before the commencement of active hostilities, the Quartermaster-General threw up his commission and went over to rebeldom. He was no less a personage than the present rebel Lieutenant-General Joe. Johnston, whom we all remember as the able opponent of Sherman at first in his Atlanta campaign. The question at once arose, who was to succeed him? A most grave and momentous question it was, too, in view of the great operations about to be undertaken. Our army heretofore had mustered but some thirteen thousand men, rank and file, all told; now half a million of men were soon to take the field. Except the brief raid on Mexico, for half a century our troops had operated only within narrow and peaceful bounds; now vast regions were to be penetrated, inhabited by a brave and hostile people, and long lines of communication, by both rail and river, were to be opened up and maintained. We were without forage, clothing, animals, and means of transportation, to begin with; without accoutrements and equipage; without transports and storehouses; without barracks and hospitals; without depots and magazines; and, worst of all, almost entirely without officers fit for the arduous and responsible duties soon to be assumed. To comprehend the importance, and to master the details of the vast business thus soon to be thrust upon him, and especially to select proper officers, and effect the necessary organization to carry affairs forward, there was need of a man of high qualities, with a physical frame to back them, that no work could weary or break down. None but a broad and capacious brain could grasp the operations about to commence, and none but a Titan of endurance could bear the fret, and worry, and work, and ceaseless stretch of mind that were soon to begin.

The required conditions were thought to centre in Captain M. C. Meigs, of the Engineer Corps, who for some time had superintended the construction of the Public Works at Washington, and Mr. Lincoln accordingly soon called him to the post just vacated by Johnston. It was no child's play that the Quartermaster-General now sat down to, and although Meigs stripped himself for the work, we may well believe that he was oft beset by "heavy fears and forebodings dire." Over a half million of men, fresh from civil life, unused to the hardships and economies of the soldier, were to be shod, clothed, and put in the field; were to be equipped with tools, tentage, and transportation; furnished with subsistence, ammunition, and medicines; and when it was decided to move, were to be followed up along their lines of march, over mountain and stream, through valley and plain, with almost the anxious care of Providence, and the inevitable certainty of fate. To assist him, he had—he knew not *whom*, until he had tried them; for treason was yet rife everywhere in the public service, and traitors in all the Staff Departments still "went unwhipt of justice." Even his course since then, too, must have been largely tentative; for his officers were few, if any, of them experienced in great affairs, and he himself originally could have known but little of the vast and intricate department committed to his hands. And yet, with all this, it must be frankly acknowledged, he has "filled the bill;" has always, so far, sustained the army; has never failed to meet promptly all just and reasonable demands, in this the greatest war of modern times; and the verdict of impartial history will be, that he has throughout exhibited a breadth of view, a fertility of resource, and a genius for hard work that justly entitle him to the thanks of the Nation.

As grounds for this judgment of Meigs and his department, let us consider somewhat how the Quartermaster's Department has borne itself, in connection with the chief movements of the war thus far. The war once begun, it will be remembered that all interest in the North soon centred in two chief points— Washington, in the East, and St. Louis, in the West. First of all, of course, the Government was bound, by the most sacred of obligations—its fealty to a free people—to defend its own seat. Hence, at the first news from Charleston Harbor, troops at once began to collect in and about Washington, and with their first coming, the work of the Quartermaster's Department arduously commenced. We shall not attempt to portray its operations during the *quasi*-campaign that ended so gloomily at Bull Run. We prefer rather to draw a veil over that brief period, which appears to have had no organization anywhere, except a magnificent system of *sauve qui peut*, from beginning to end. In the Quartermaster's Department, especially, clothing, equipage, transportation, all seem to have been issued quite *ad libitum*, on the principle of "Keep all you have, and get all you can," and the outfit of a single regiment at Bull Run, it is well authenticated, in many instances, equalled and surpassed the total equipment of a brigade or division, as they now move and fight under Grant and Sherman. Coming then at once to the advent of McClellan, it was obvious from the start that two chief officers of the Quartermaster's Department would be immediately required; one to provide and issue supplies, in charge of the depot at Washington; the other to prescribe and regulate the kind and the amount, in charge of the troops in the field. Fortunately for the Government, the first of these officers was already in Washington, with some faults of manner, it is true, but with his heart in the right place; and the other was soon found, and ordered to duty without delay. Both of these officers took hold of business with a will, and in spite of the ignorance and chaos that then reigned supreme, as was to be expected from such raw and unformed material as the volunteer force at first, soon succeeded in reducing things at least to somewhat of order and system. The troops were adequately supplied, and no more; the allowance of tentage and transportation was regulated; and a system of reports was inaugurated, that promised data most valuable for the future. The chief object, at first, of course, was to regulate the army, and to accumulate stores at Washington and about there sufficient to warrant a forward movement. The supplies, of course, lay in the North, and from there but two lines of communication were open to Washington—the Potomac River, by far the best, and the Baltimore Railroad. Soon these two were reduced to one, the railroad, the rebels sealing up the river with their audacious batteries, not long after Bull Run; and over this slender line of iron, liable to be cut at any moment, all the vast supplies of the army, fuel, forage, clothing, tentage, subsistence, ammunition, &c., for months had to come. From Baltimore, however, three great lines of railroad, seeming no doubt to the Government at times almost like the beneficent arms of Providence, stretched away throughout the teeming and abundant North, and the Chesapeake Bay, besides, was always ready to bear to her ample wharves the commerce of the seas. By all these channels, though for the last few miles on a single line of railway, the resources of the North were poured into Washington during the fall and winter of 1861-2, until supplies everywhere were piled mountain high, and the city and its environs became one enormous magazine. Thus passed the fall and winter of 1861-2, in organization and preparation, as we have said, with the Army of the Potomac still encamped about Washington.

But with the spring of '62, there came one day a General Order from the President, and soon the grand army was at last thoroughly in motion. As preliminary thereto, there was of course a general peeling for the campaign. Transportation was cut down to the lowest figure, and camp equipage and private baggage were reduced from the luxurious and comfortable to the absolutely essential. Then came the transfer of the army bodily, by the Quartermaster's Department, from Alexandria to Yorktown. If anybody supposes this a light job, to embark an army, horse, foot, and artillery, over a hundred thousand strong, with all its appliances for living, moving, and fighting complete, then to transport it a hundred and fifty miles down a fretful bay and up an uncertain river, and again disembark it in safety, in the midst of a Virginia wilderness of quicksands and mud, he is simply vastly mistaken. It required foresight and forethought of the highest order, and an organization Argus-eyed and Briarean-handed. At that time the Army of the Potomac was reputed to consist of at least one hundred and twenty thousand men, of all arms of the service; this would give, at the ratio of about two-thirds animals to the men, which has proven to be the usual ratio in American armies in this war, full seventy thousand animals of all grades—cavalry, artillery, private, and draught. To this must also be added fully thirty thousand men more of all classes, such as employés of the various staff departments, servants, camp-followers, and hangers-on generally. To move quickly such a prodigious multitude, with all their necessary appurtenances, and to keep up the necessary supplies from day to day of subsistence, clothing, forage, and ammunition, laid even the vast shipping of the commercial North under heavy contribution, and from April to

July the lower Chesapeake, the York, and the James, literally swarmed with craft of all descriptions. At all points where it became necessary to debark troops or supplies, floating wharves were extemporized by means of canal-boats or barges; pontoon-boats also came into good play for the same purpose, and there were instances, such as at Cheeseman's Creek, where the service thus rendered was, so to speak, incalculable. Yorktown evacuated, the army was at last fairly afoot, and then came the race for Richmond. Of the movement up the Peninsula, and the affairs at Williamsburg and Fair Oaks, as well as the so-called Seven Days' Fight, resulting in the retreat to James River, it is foreign to our purpose here to speak. We have only to say that, during all these operations, supplies met the troops regularly at all points, usually at a distance of but a few miles from the line of march, and that extraordinary as was the march to Harrison's Landing, the trains of the army, nevertheless, nowhere impeded or embarrassed the movement, and were all substantially gotten off safe, huge and unwieldy as they necessarily were. The movement of the trains June 29th and 30th, from the line of Fair Oaks to James River, was an experience never to be forgotten, we venture to say, by those who participated in it, as did the writer. The movement began, properly speaking, on Saturday night, June 28th, and continued on into Tuesday, July 1st. At times portions of the trains were badly under fire, as at White Oak Swamp on Sunday morning, and the enemy did not fail to pay the laggards his usual compliment of shot and shell. But notwithstanding this, scarcely a serviceable wagon, if any, was destroyed or left behind; and when at last they had all fairly debouched into the plain by Harrison's Bar—ammunition, ambulance, subsistence, and baggage-trains all complete—there was, stretching away in all directions, a perfect ocean of billowy wagon-covers, among which stray donkeys here and there, after their kind, went cavorting about like porpoises "on a bender," with an occasional forlorn performance on their infernal horns of "Whee-haugh," "Whee-haugh," which, being interpreted, means, we suppose, "Here's your mule! Here's your mule!" The march of the trains, subsequently, from Harrison's Landing to Yorktown, though excessively hot and dusty, was made without incident, as the enemy scarcely pursued, being well after Pope; and then came the transfer of the army again by water to Aquia Creek and Alexandria. Much as the army was reduced in numbers, this re-embarkation at Yorktown seemed almost interminable, although a large amount of its equipage and baggage had previously been sent by boat down James River, before leaving Harrison's Landing. The artillery and land transportation, especially, seemed as if they never *would* get off. They came in very slowly and chaotically at Alexandria and Washington, and doubtless much of McClellan's hesitation and delay in moving to the relief of Pope, after landing at Alexandria, arose from the fact that both his artillery and wagons, in the main, were yet down the Potomac. The Quartermaster's Department, to be entirely candid, was here no doubt considerably to blame. How far the Commanding General was responsible for this failure, by omitting to give timely notice to his staff of his intended movement, may well be considered. But the result was a deal of unkind censure of the original Chief Quartermaster—much of it clearly unjust—who had just been relieved, with scarcely time for his successor to arrange for the pending movement in view of the vastness of the project, and the multitudinousness of its details.

The Pope and Antietam campaigns were quickly over, with nothing especially noteworthy in the Quartermaster's Department except the great loss of teams and supplies "gobbled up," chiefly by Jeb Stuart and Stonewall Jackson. There was a story rife at the time about General Rucker, the Chief Quartermaster at Washington, which is too good a commentary on the Pope campaign to be lost to history. It seems one day, when in a particularly ursine humor, he was presented by an officer with a requisition for one hundred teams to go to Warrenton, or Culpepper, or somewhere about there; the General read it slowly over, and then looking stormily up, over his glasses, at the unlucky Quartermaster, growled fiercely out, as only Rucker can growl, "What do you *want* of these teams?" The meek reply was, "For General Pope's army." "For Pope, do you? Well, you can have 'em! Take 'em along! Don't want your receipts either!" The officer, astonished, inquired what he meant by not wanting receipts. The answer was, in the same ursine growl, "Where's the use of taking your receipts for what I know you won't keep? Jeb Stuart will have them all, to the last tar-pot and jackass, in less than a week, and so I shall instruct Captain Dana to invoice them to Bob Lee or Jeff. Davis direct!"

After this, late in the fall, came the Burnside campaign, and the fiasco at Fredericksburg for want of the pontoons. Some people, only too eager to blame others for their own shortcomings, and wholly ignorant of army routine, at the time charged the non-arrival of the pontoons to the Quartermaster-General. The truth is, however, as will be seen on a moment's reflection, that neither Meigs nor Halleck, indeed, had any thing whatever to do with the pontoons, nor will either of them be held so responsible by an impartial future. The duties of both were, and now are, of a general, supervisory, administrative nature, at general head-quarters, Washington, and therefore they had, properly, no more to do with the particular job of getting pontoons to Fredericksburg for the Army of the Potomac, than they would have had with pitching tents at Nashville for the Army of the Cumberland, or driving a six-mule team, with one line, along the levee at New Orleans, for the Army of the Gulf. No; the Major-General Commanding had his own Chief Quartermaster, and should have looked to him, and to nobody else—had no right to look to anybody else—to get up his pontoon-train in time. Disagreeable as it is to say it, unfortunately for the country, the pontoon-failure at Fredericksburg was of an exact piece with the failure of the mine at Petersburg, a year and a half afterwards—twin blunders of the same brain,—"Somebody *else* was expected to attend to it,"—and the unerring voice of history will not fail to so pronounce them.

The long halt of the Army of the Potomac, in front of Fredericksburg, and the subsequent campaign to Chancellorsville and return, passed without matter of moment to the Quartermaster's Department. The depots of the army at first were at Belle Plain and Aquia Creek, but a few miles away at worst, and the railroad to Aquia Creek being speedily reconstructed, supplies were conveyed by it almost into the very camps, at least into the very heart of the army. But subsequently, in June, '63, when Lee crossed the Potomac, and advanced boldly into Pennsylvania, Hooker within twelve hours set his whole army in motion, and then to Gettysburg and back again to Culpepper there came a time that "tried men's souls" in the Quartermaster's Department to the utmost. The march across the country and return necessitated a constant change of depots and lines of supplies, and it required all the consummate vigilance and energy of the Chief Quartermaster to keep things going. Considerable forage, and some animals, it is true, were picked up in Pennsylvania; yet, after all, it was found that the resources of the country availed but little in supplying such a prodigious multitude. The army was never less than one hundred thousand strong, and generally more, with an average of from fifty to sixty thousand animals; and then, besides, the seesaw movement—first north, and then south—was, much of it, over almost identically the same line of march. When the army got back about Warrenton and Culpepper, so far as supplies are concerned it might as well have been in the middle of the Great Sahara. All that region had been campaigned over by both armies since the spring of '61, each side alternately seesawing east or west, north or south, as the fortune of war demanded, until the whole region was literally stripped bare of every thing available for either man or beast. The Gettysburg campaign, as we have said, was a hard one; nevertheless, the army was kept well supplied, and when at last it located at Culpepper, there was soon an abundance of every thing essential.

The subsequent campaign of the Army of the Potomac, beginning with the movement from Culpepper last spring, and continuing down to the present writing, has been a severe one in all respects, for all branches of the service. From the outset, General Grant cut boldly loose from his line of supplies—the Orange and Alexandria Railroad—and trusted to luck and hard blows to find another. Loading up his wagons, he turned his army, though more numerous than ever before, into a movable column, fighting as it marched, and resolved to depend for supplies on a base equally movable. His first change of base was from Culpepper to Fredericksburg or rather Belle Plain, next to Port Royal, next to the White House, and then to City Point, or at least it is still there at this writing. All of these changes involved gigantic work on the part of the Quartermaster's Department, which was all the more onerous and harassing because no one could say how long it would prove available. Nevertheless, no sooner was Fredericksburg occupied, than men were set to work to rebuild and reopen the railroad to Aquia Creek. In less than a fortnight, the road was in working order, though it involved the construction of wharves at Aquia Creek, and the building of a bridge across Potomac Creek four hundred and twenty-two feet long, by eighty-two feet high, which was finished, it is said, in two and a half days, or forty working hours. The road was run for barely a week or so, when Grant cut loose from Fredericksburg, and the base of operations was switched to Port Royal. A few days sufficed for that line, when again the base was transferred to the White House. Scarcely twenty-four hours after our advance reached Bottom's Bridge, so as to cover the necessary work, locomotives were whistling on the York River Railroad, and in less than a week the road to the White House, for all army purposes, was in full working condition. Then came the crossing of the James, and the halt at Petersburg; and, more recently, the attack on the Weldon Road, and the tenacious holding of it. This last move so lengthened his lines, that Grant called for a railroad to bring up his supplies, and almost before the country had fairly heard of the commencement of the work, a railroad ten miles long was in full blast from City Point to his extreme left. From this statement in the rough, hasty and imperfect as it necessarily is, it may well be believed that the work of thus following up and sustaining the Lieutenant-General's army has been no mere child's play. Half the job would be sufficient to engross the attention, and to tax to the utmost the energies of most men; and none but a really able man—of stout heart and fertile brain—could possibly have succeeded when assigned the whole. Any ordinary brigadier, such men as usually find their way into the command of brigades and divisions, would have broken down the campaign and starved the army long ago. That the army has *not* been starved, but well fed, and the campaign throughout stoutly maintained, let the country, in thanking others—alas, but too often far less deserving!—forget not also to thank, at least half-way, the long-suffering, much-abused, but in most instances, hard-working officers of the Quartermaster's Department.

In our next article we will consider the operations in the West.

BREECH-LOADING MUSKET.

BY MAJOR T. T. S. LAIDLEY, U. S. ORD. DEPT.

THAT the soldier should be armed and equipped in such a manner as to render him in the highest possible degree efficient, is a general proposition which will be readily acceded to by all. The nation which neglects this principle, or is slow to perceive and adopt those improvements (which, if adopted, would materially add to the efficiency of its troops), either from some mistaken idea of economy, or from a blind adherence to that which has gained a hold upon the affections by time and by valuable service, must soon or late pay dearly for its supineness or infatuation.

At no time in the history of the world has greater activity been displayed by all nations than at the present, in searching out and adopting new improvements in arms and *materiél*, and whatever may tend to add to their power of attack and of defence.

During the last few years the merits of the rifle-musket have been generally conceded, and this improved arm has been adopted by all nations.

Rifled cannon for field-service are used exclusively in all services except our own, to our discredit it must be said: for siege and harbor defence, they are rapidly working their way into general use. Guns of monster size are deemed not only practicable, but necessary: new explosive materials are sought: the balloon and telegraph are applied to military uses: war vessels propelled by steam have been generally introduced, and navies are regarded as incomplete, and incapable of performing their expected duties, if they have not their fleet of iron-clad vessels.

There is still another improvement that is now attracting much attention, one that has already been partially adopted, and must soon be generally introduced by all nations,—I mean the adoption of breech-loading, in place of muzzle-loading arms, for all foot, as well as mounted troops.

The advantages of the breech-loading system have long been acknowledged, in the abstract; and there are to be found in the Artillery Museums of Europe arms constructed, more than two hundred years ago, on this principle—efforts made at this early age to solve this important but difficult problem.

Great stress has been laid by military writers, of all times, and even by recent writers of our own service, on the great waste of ammunition that takes place in all battles—the large number of cartridges fired, for the number of men disabled—and have founded on this an argument against the breech-loading arm, on account of the increased facility it gives for rapid firing.

That accuracy of fire is a consideration of the first importance, and that it should be increased to its greatest possible extent, no one will pretend to deny. That there is a vast deal of ammunition thrown away uselessly, by both infantry and artillery troops, is equally evident—our own experience confirms the fact. It has been estimated that from three thousand to ten thousand balls were fired in European armies, to place one man *hors de combat*, and though the percentage of balls that prove effective, to those fired, has doubtless been very much decreased in our recent battles, it is not to be gainsaid, that there is still, in all engagements, a great waste of ammunition. But why lay such special stress on this waste of ammunition? In war, of what is there not a great waste? a waste of men, of arms, of ammunition, of supplies of all kinds; so that it may be properly designated as in itself a great waste.

Increase the accuracy of fire to its utmost possible extent, but let it not be pretended that it is not desirable to deliver a greater number of shots in a given time than the enemy. This is one of the fallacies that belong to the past—one that our recent battles have effectually exploded.

There are in our service those, to whom if you speak of the advantages of a breech-loading arm for infantry, they will urge, in addition to the objection of the waste of ammunition just referred to, that the breech-loading apparatus is liable to get out of order, and then the gun is worthless. They will, probably, wind up their argument by telling you, as conclusive on the subject, of the report of Major C——, on the first crude breech-loading arm offered to our service: "That it shot well, and was a very good gun, but it was such a pity that the barrel was made in two parts;" or, of Colonel F——'s remark on the same gun, "that if the muzzle-loading arm had then been known for the first time, it would be regarded as a great invention."

Norway was the nation which first acknowledged the importance of abolishing the inconvenient and troublesome mode of loading with a ramrod, by adopting for the infantry a breech-loading musket. No change, however, was made in the manner of firing, but the percussion-cap was used, and put on in the usual way, by hand. In 1851, a different arm, also breech-loading, was given to the Swedish Marine. Soon after, Prussia took a great stride in advance of the other nations, by doing away with the two most difficult and troublesome operations in loading,—the use of the ramrod to send the cartridge home, and putting the cap on the cone,—by the introduction into service of the *needle-gun*, as it is called, which is breech loading, and has the cap in the cartridge. The efficiency of this arm in the hands of the Prussian infantry, has proved so striking, in the recent campaign in Denmark, that England, for almost the first time, has taken a lesson from a war, in which she has not been engaged, and has, by a formal decision of the War Department, ordered that her infantry shall, in future, be armed with breech-loading muskets. The particular model which is to be adopted remains yet to be determined.

The Emperor Napoleon has also adopted the breech-loading system, in arming his special corps, the Cent-Gardes.

In determining this question for ourselves, whether there are any advantages to be gained by adopting the breech-loading system for the musket, we are not left entirely to the deductions of theory, but are enabled to call to our aid the voice of experience, that umpire, from whose decisions theorists cannot appeal.

The examination of the muskets, picked up on the battlefield of Gettysburg, reveals a fact that few would be prepared to admit, and speaks in terms which should not pass unheeded, as to the inherent defects of the muzzle-loading system.

Of the twenty-seven thousand five hundred and seventy-four muskets collected after the battle, it was found that twenty-four thousand were loaded: twelve thousand contained each two loads, and six thousand (over twenty per cent.), were charged with from *three* to *ten loads* each.

One musket had in it *twenty-three loads*, each charge being put down in regular order. Oftentimes the cartridge was loaded without being first broken, and in many instances it was inserted, the ball down first.

What an exhibit of useless guns does this present!—useless for that day's work, and from causes peculiar to the system of loading.

But experience has spoken out yet more unmistakably in favor of the advantages of the breech-loading musket. There have been several instances where a single regiment, armed with breech-loading, self-capping rifles, has held in check a whole brigade armed with the ordinary musket; and in a line of skirmishers, repelling an attack, the portion of the troops armed with the breech-loading rifle, is readily distinguished by their advanced position. They are not so easily driven in.

To those who oppose the introduction of the breech-loading musket on the ground that it is liable to get out of order, by a derangement of the breech-loading parts, we would point to the large number of muzzle-loading guns which are rendered unserviceable by causes which would be inoperative with breech-loading arms.

To those who oppose its adoption on the ground that men fire too rapidly already, and throw away, uselessly, too much ammunition, we would recommend the remedy of introducing into the Manual of Arms certain motions, having for their object to retard the loading; such, for instance, as wiping out and lubricating the bore after each shot. Besides accomplishing the object which they have in view, this operation would have a decidedly beneficial effect, in increasing the accuracy of fire, and might be omitted when deemed advisable by the officers.

It is understood that the question of changing the system of loading the musket to breech loading, has claimed the attention of the indefatigable Secretary of War, who is ever ready to lend an ear to proposals for increasing the efficiency of his Department, and he has directed a Board of officers to be convened, for the purpose of determining whether it is advisable to make any change in the present musket, and if so, what they would recommend.

It cannot, of course, be known for some time, perhaps for months, what will be the action of this Board; but whatever it may be, it can hardly be doubted that the order appointing the Board may be regarded as the death-warrant of the rammer and the percussion-cap. They have had their day, and must now soon be numbered among the things of the past, to be seen only in the museums of arms, indices of the age in which they were used, mile-stones on the pathway of progressive improvement.

TO GOLDWIN SMITH,

ON READING HIS LETTER TO A WHIG MEMBER OF THE SOUTHERN INDEPENDENCE ASSOCIATION.

BY E. A. W.

A PEOPLE welcomes thee across the sea,
Thou manliest Briton! who above the crowd
Of narrow islanders, hast dared aloud
Speak such clear, ringing words for Liberty
Beyond the Channel. With an eye how true
Fixed on the Northern lights wild flashing, high
Upon the forehead of our crimson sky,
Thou read'st the fates binding the Old and New;
A nation battling in this Titan strife
For the world's hopes, knit with its deathless life.

O England! mother great, whose life-blood still
Thro' our young veins back to the well-head runs;
Once mother of a race of stalwart sons!
Where sleeps thy Hampden now, whose dauntless will
No falsehood bribed? where Milton's sunlit flame,
That fed our torches? Fallen, ah! fallen to-day!
A land of shopmen bartering away
The best crown-jewel of thy stately name!
Methinks thy Clarkson shivers in his grave,
To see thee love the Cotton, scorn the Slave!

Yet no! recall the taunts that rashly light
The mines of hate; and help us, friend, to trust
In souls like thine, as generous, as just;
A people's heart yet pulsing with the right:
Nor blear-eyed prophets, nor a hireling press
Unteach our olden faith in Englishmen.
Better than iron fleets, be thy wise pen
To quench our fires, and wake our nobleness,
From Pilgrim rock to where the queenly West
Wears her blue lakes as sapphires on her breast.

December, 1864.

LITERARY INTELLIGENCE
AND
NOTES ON NEW BOOKS.

FIRST in order, as of importance on our monthly list of books, stands "Webster's Unabridged Dictionary," for a splendid copy of which we are indebted to the publishers, Messrs. G. & C. Merriam, of Springfield, through the hands of Messrs. Mason, Brothers, New York. This truly great work, acknowledged in England and America as the best, most authoritative, and most complete Lexicon of the English Language now in existence, again appears to the public with new and more paramount claims. It has been thoroughly revised and much enlarged, is illustrated with over three thousand fine engravings, which present more surely to the eye the forms of certain objects than the best definitions can offer to the mind, and contains ten thousand words and meanings not to be found in any other dictionary. Begun on purely philological principles, and the product literally of the author's lifetime, it has since subsidized the labors of the best American, English, and Continental scholars, with a determination on the part of all concerned to make it—as it now is—*facile princeps* among dictionaries. The "battle of the books" may now be considered as over: the palm, *non sine pulvere*, remains with Webster. Among the great features, which we can only notice briefly, are the Introduction, an admirable text-book of English philology in itself, and numerous tables, one of which is quite unique, and quite invaluable: we refer to that of *names in fiction of persons, places, and phrases*, by which those allusions to standard literature, in constant use among cultivated people, may be explained and verified. It is an admirable feature, and is entirely original with this work. We shall have occasion to call the attention of our readers to the minuter excellences of Webster's Unabridged, when we have time to give it that detailed examination which it so richly deserves and so fully repays. 1 vol. royal quarto, 1840 pp. A splendid New Year's gift. $12 00.

Messrs. Ticknor & Fields have issued, in a beautiful little blue and gold edition, "Twice Told Tales, by Nathaniel Hawthorne." These charming little essays, stories, and cloister reveries, were, most of them, written while the author was not known to fame. Other and greater works established him as a favorite writer wherever English readers are found; and the earlier efforts of his "prentice hand" are now brought into proper relations with those which wrought his fame. They are worthy the companionship: refined taste, delicate humor, touching pathos, real sympathy, and pure English, characterize them all, and their brevity, simplicity, and variety will find them readers among those who might yawn over the art criticisms and curious fancies of *Monte Beni*. 2 vols. 32mo, of about 400 pp. each. $3.00.

The same house has issued, in similar sumptuous form, "Sacred and Legendary Art, by Mrs. Jameson," in two volumes. Volume I. contains Legends of the Angels and Archangels, the Evangelists, the Apostles, the Doctors of the Church, and St. Mary Magdalene, as represented in the fine arts. Volume II. treats of the Patron

Saints, the Martyrs, the early Bishops, the Hermits, and the Warrior Saints of Christendom.

A supplementary third volume presents "Legends of the Monastic Orders," and thus forms the second series of "Sacred and Legendary Art." We have nothing but words of admiration and recommendation of and for these beautiful volumes. They contain, presented with all the exquisite taste of this gifted lady, the best instruction in art, at and before the *renaissance*, and thus touch one of the most attractive pages of history. Beside this, they show how in the ages of ignorance, superstition, and unbelief, art was the glorious handmaiden of religion, presenting to the people models, albeit ideal, of faith, purity, fervor—in a word, of "the beauty of holiness." Her authorities are very numerous, and her study has been intense and assimilative. Among the works from which she has procured her legends, are mentioned "Legenda Aurea," "Flos Sanctorum," "Vies des Saints," and numerous others. Such a work as this would attract, interest, and instruct young persons and imbue them with a desire for more extended art-studies—the most satisfying as well as refining of all forms of intellectual culture. Blue and gold, 32mo. $1.50 each.

"Clever Stories of Many Nations, rendered into Rhyme, by John G. Saxe," is a holiday book, just issued by Messrs. Ticknor & Fields. The beautiful illustrations, one to each story, on the same page with the letter-press, are by W. L. Champney. Perhaps the best comment we can make upon this book, is the following very practical one. Taking it to our home last night, we released it from the bundle of books, and, with wife and children around us, began to read the "clever stories." Laughter and applause were loud and constant, satisfaction marked even the smallest faces, and the only interruption was "to see the pictures," which also came in for their share of praise. Not an "olive-branch" would go to bed until the book was finished, and then the author was maligned because there were no more stories to read—the book was too small. If any reader doubts our word, let him try the experiment on his own people, if he is fortunate enough to have any, or still more fortunate, if, in these war-times, he can get an occasional home-sitting with them. The "Snake in the Glass" is an admirable temperance lecture. A beautiful gift-book, from the University Press of Cambridge. Small quarto, 192 pp. $3.50.

Among the new juvenile books, containing also much matter for older heads—comprehensive views of great campaigns, and good acquaintance with the military principles upon which the war is conducted—we give our hearty commendation to Major Penniman's attractive little volume, "Winfield, the Lawyer's Son, and how he became a Major-General." This is a great improvement upon all the "Tanner-Boys," "Errand-Boys," *et hoc genus omne*, which a fair trial has shown to be unsatisfactory to the American public—democratic as it is. That the father of General Hancock is a gentleman, distinguished in the legal profession, in short, that the General had the most respectable antecedents, has not interfered with his rapid rise in a glorious career. This splendid soldier will have numerous biographies, but this touches points upon which later history may be silent. The author, Rev. C. W. Denison, late a chaplain in our Army, has been in immediate communication with General Hancock's family, and has the entire approval of his father and brother. The book is a recital of *facts*, and owes its chief interest to these. They have been skilfully interwoven and most attractively told. Its moral tone, as might be expected, is excellent, and its didactic value in putting forward the high traits of Hancock's character for the imitation and emulation of the young, cannot be too highly commended. The portrait of the General is pronounced "a good one" by his father. The illustrations are from designs by White—a most admirable artist in his branch—and by Hancock himself while a cadet. The book must have a large sale, adding, as it does, to its intrinsic merits, the fine paper, clear type, and beautiful appearance, which make it a handsome gift for boys at this holiday season. Ashmead & Evans, Philadelphia. 12mo, 323 pp. $1.50.

We do not often take sudden fancies, but Gail Hamilton was one of them, and we have never been called upon to withdraw our first favor. "A New Atmosphere," just published, is a good book; one to read at a sitting, and then to put by for further reading; to turn over with a friend, to talk about, and to act upon. Her judgment of men and women, is as like that of the sensational novels as "Hyperion to a Satyr." Humanely satirical, she does not lash, but reasons with the culprits. *Men* may take lessons from her writings, which will tend to the production of a new and purer atmosphere: and if she championizes women occasionally in a partial manner, the spirit of a true chivalry is not yet extinct, and so we fairly range ourselves on her side. Would it not be well to give us an occasional opportunity to differ with her? She is real, startling, fearless, and original. We like Gail Hamilton more and more, and in spite of all polemics, we commend her books as excellent moral teachers. Such writings do much towards purging the moral atmosphere of the miasms arising around the swamp-bedded feet of the "Old Dagons," and killing their worshippers while in the act of swinging their censers. Ticknor & Fields. 12mo, 310 pp. $2.00.

"Hymns of the Ages," is a second pure, sparkling stream from a perennial wellhead. Splendid in typography, it contains gems of holy thought, worthy of all splendor of setting. Among the "Hymns in Time of War," are some of the best of Whittier's, the magnificent "Marching On" of Mrs. Julia Ward Howe, the finest of Koerner, and a spirited version of Luther's grand "Ein Feste Burg." There are divisions of poems upon "Old Age," "Love," "Praise," "Prayer," and "Self-Examination." One of the great values of such a collection, is that it contains the best poems, and only the best, on these various topics, and in this regard imparts to its readers an eclectic power, by which to judge of poetry at large. Ticknor & Fields. Gilt top, 328 pp. $2.50.

We omitted to mention in our notice last month of the History of Duryee's Brigade, that a few of the copies (only three hundred in all), could be had at D. Van Nostrand's, 192 Broadway, to whom we are indebted for our copy. Every brigade should emulate such a chronicle, and thus lay up not only the record of its own glory, but minute materials for a future history of the war.

We have received from Messrs. Barnes & Burr, of New York, the "Elements of Descriptive Geometry, with its Application to Spherical Projections. By Albert E. Church, LL. D., Professor of Mathematics in the United States Military Academy at West Point." 1 vol. 8vo, 138 pp., and 1 vol. of plates. This important branch of geometry, not as much studied as it should be in our colleges, is here offered in a clear and admirable manner, and is divested, by the lucid presentation of Professor Church, of many of the difficulties and obscurities found in former treatises. It contains all descriptive problems from the projections of right lines to those of the most complicated intersections of continent surfaces. All principles and systems of mapography are laid down and explained. Having been among the first to profit by his volumes on Analytical Geometry and the Calculus, the first of which was as easy, and far more pleasant than arithmetic, and the second the only truly clear and succinct treatment of the differential bugbear in existence, we have examined the present work to find, and have not been disappointed in finding, the same plate-glass distinctness in his teaching. No cadet of that day, who had the honor of being in the first section of the third class (then taught by the Professor himself), will forget how Mr. Church took the last fifteen minutes of a recitation hour to demonstrate upon the blackboard the lesson of the next day, and did it with such logical accuracy and sequence, that it needed but little study that evening to prepare it for the morrow. Mr. Church's mathematical pen is entirely *en rapport* with his mind and tongue. His books are transcripts of these prelections, and, in our judgment, should supersede all others on the subjects of which they treat. $3.00.

"The Bohemians of London," just published by Messrs. T. B. Peterson & Brothers, of Philadelphia, reminds us of the Disinherited Knight, who appears upon the scene at an unexpected moment, to have a dash at all comers. His Bohemians are not mere gypsies of art, or "chevaliers d'industrie;" many of them are rich and titled, but all of them more or less bad. The book is powerfully written; the command of language is something marvellous; several of the scenes are literally "thrilling." But the satirists, whom we admire, are those who whip rascals, in the hope of making them better. Our great objection to this satire is that it believes man irretrievably bad, and only lashes to destroy, not to reform. The author is Mr. J. M. Whitty, an English journalist, who died recently in Australia. Dr. R. Shelton McKenzie supplies a notice of him as an introduction. 12mo, 432 pp.

THE MANIFOLD FIELD ORDER BOOK, invented by Colonel IRWIN, formerly Adjutant-General of the Department of the Gulf, and made and sold by Messrs. Philp & Solomons, Washington, D. C., is, to our minds, the handiest contrivance in the way of army stationery we have yet seen. We agree with Colonel Townsend, Acting Adjutant-General of the army, in pronouncing it "one of the most complete and useful articles which an officer can carry about him in the field, in the way of writing apparatus."

We acknowledge with thanks the receipt of copies of Adjutant-General's reports from the following officers :—

Adjutant-General N. Baker, of Iowa, 1861-2-3.
      "   A. Gaylord, of Wisconsin, 1861-2-3.
      "   Wm. C. Kibbe, of California, 1861-2-3.
      "   Cyrus A. Reed, of Oregon, 1863.

From Adjutant-General John T. Sprague, of New York, two valuable volumes of Muster-in Rolls, being for regiments 1 to 67, N. Y. Volunteers, inclusive; and from Inspector-General J. T. Miller, of New York, a copy of his interesting report for 1864; also, copies of the reports of the Secretary of the Navy, and the Chief of the Bureau of Ordnance.

EDITOR'S SPECIAL DEPARTMENT.

THE MOVEMENTS OF GENERAL SHERMAN: THE ANABASIS REVERSED.—We could only refer, when our last number went to press, to the initiation of a movement, just then indeed on the eve of its execution, which astonished the whole country, fell like a stroke of lightning upon the rebel commanders and their strategic plans, and will make the most brilliant closing chapter to the most brilliant campaign ever recorded in history. If any thing was needed to stamp General Sherman as the most able captain of the *age*, it was the conception and attempt of this daring plan; its complete success will cause us to look in vain in other times for his superior as the commander of a great army.

The principal facts, which we can only state briefly, are these:—Tired of running after Hood, who had waged unrelenting war against his communications, he determined to cut loose from his old northern base, and move his army—a large, well-equipped, compact, veteran force—immediately into the heart of the Confederacy; to live upon the country; devastate it as to the enemy's supplies; and take one or more of his strong sea-board fortresses, already blockaded and pressed by our fleets, in rear. The plan was so daring that it was not anticipated or provided for; it was fairly begun while Beauregard and Hood were daily awaiting his discomfited march in retreat from Atlanta. He took with him four corps, condensed into two wings. The right wing, under General Howard, was composed of the Fifteenth Corps under General Osterhaus, and the Seventeenth under General Blair; the left wing, under General Slocum, was formed by the Fourteenth under Jefferson C. Davis, and the Twentieth, General Slocum's own corps.

The cavalry, comprising two divisions, was under General Kilpatrick. The artillery, thoroughly organized by General Barry, the Chief of Artillery, just before a serious sickness snatched him, at the moment of starting, from the glory of this march, was properly distributed among these corps, excellent horse artillery moving with the cavalry. The entire force numbered from forty thousand to fifty thousand men: and General Sherman said he had every man, every gun, and all the *matériel* he desired.

The great movement towards the coast having been decided upon, the columns were put in march without delay, keeping pace with each other.

A glance at the railroad map discloses the lines of march. From Atlanta, passing through Decatur and running nearly eastward to Augusta, on the Savannah River, is the *Georgia Railroad*, on or near which the principal places mentioned are,—Covington, Social Circle, Madison, Union Point, Camak, and Dearing. From Augusta there is a continuation of the railroad to Charleston.

Southward from Atlanta is a railroad to Macon, which there meets the *Georgia Central Railroad*. This latter road, nearly two hundred miles long, connects Macon and Savannah. It is met by a railroad from Augusta, at Millen. The general direction of the Georgia Central Railroad is eastward, parallel to the Georgia Railroad, but at Millen it turns southeastwardly to Savannah.

These two main lines of rail form the double route of Sherman to the coast. As means of transportation, they contain the enemy's dépôts of supplies, the larger numbers of towns and people; and on every account they manifestly present the most advantageous routes.

Starting on the 14th and 15th of November, Howard moved upon the Georgia Central; Slocum upon the Georgia Road. The former marched down the Macon and Atlanta Road, to East Point, to Rough and Ready, and to Jonesboro, brushing away Iverson's rebel brigade, which was going to take Atlanta. On the 18th of November Howard was at Griffin; and, then, threatening and terrifying Macon, but giving it the go-by, he cut the Georgia Central at Griswoldsville, near Gordon Station, thus severing Macon from Savannah. He then sent a strong force to take Milledgeville, the capital of the State. We need not stop to laugh at the rapid flight of the Legislature in search of a new base. They fulminate paper-bolts far better than the thunder-bolts of war, and report says that they are among the "derelicts" in the emergency. The capture of Milledgeville and the burning of its public buildings was but an episode, and did not alter nor delay Howard's march, which was directed upon Millen.

Pari passu moved Slocum, through Decatur and Covington and Madison, stopping and making, here and there, offsets on his road to Augusta. On the 19th he was at Madison, and on the 20th he crossed the Oconee, near Greensboro. The interruptions he met from the enemy amounted to nothing: they did not delay his march. Meantime the cavalry was ubiquitous. The eyes of the army, upon them rested the responsibility of finding and holding roads, bridges, fords; of disclosing what was in the front; of guarding front, flanks, and rear of these great compact bodies, as they moved through a hostile, an unexplored country, in which the dangers grew and multiplied at every step. What a glorious chapter in the history of that campaign will the conduct and services of the cavalry make! And how fortunate shall we esteem ourselves, if some officer who can truly say *magna pars fui*, would choose our pages in which to offer it to the world.

Thus moving, it seemed to be General Sherman's policy to avoid pitched battles, to pass by and get in rear of those towns where hasty intrenchments were thrown up, and where women and boys of thirteen have been pressed into digging. He does not want them at all, and he must not delay; and as for leaving them in his rear, he has no rear nor front proper, but only an aim with which these cannot interfere. So Macon draws a long breath, while Sherman sweeps by and is gone.

The grand divisions moving along their lines of railway concentrate at Millen, and there we may suppose the short but striking experience of the march leads to the final determination. The railroads destroyed, the Confederacy again cut in two, only seventy or eighty miles to Savannah. Savannah it is.

Again the cavalry take long marches in front, and while we write are reported only six miles from Savannah, which now seems the prime objective of the movement. Then Sherman marches along in the narrow but secure pathway between the Savannah and Ogeechee Rivers, his flanks strongly *appuyée* on both streams, at once to the siege of Savannah and to a secure base on the Atlantic.

To resist this march of Sherman, the people of Georgia, stricken with a great panic, call out men of all ages, women, and children. Not content with "robbing the cradle and the grave," they also rob the domestic hearth; the Governor issues proclamations in rapid succession, pardons and releases convicts who will fight, and all talk exceedingly large, but with exceeding vagueness, about Sherman's defeat and final destruction. They have had, as Sherman predicted they would say, victories all along the route; but strangely enough our columns would move directly forward, although so often defeated. If they still have time to concentrate men at Savannah, they cannot now make and man inland forts, where it was never expected they would be needed; they cannot at once fill the place with proper supplies; and they cannot long resist the iron circle which completes the investment by sea and land. At the latest moment we hear that he is in line of battle at Savannah, and before our ink (printer's) is dry, the great battle will doubtless be fought.

A few words of comment must close this brief summary of Sherman's movement.

1st. It is a *great strategic movement.* Suddenly cutting loose from his base, when that was threatened, he moves a large and well appointed army, without a premonition, upon the enemy's rear, upon the weak and unprotected points of those strongholds which have defied all maritime inventions and ingenuity. He thus makes war support war, cuts the enemy in two, invades his rich depot of supplies, renders Hood additionally anxious and desperate; further isolates Richmond, and "out of the nettle danger, plucks the flower safety."

2d. It is a *mammoth raid;* a broad path of desolation marks his track; the railroad communications are severed and destroyed; most of the towns in his rear are rendered useless to the enemy, should he again attempt to occupy them, and his chief, almost his only opposition is found in the form of declaiming generals (almost as numerous as their soldiers), and proclaiming Governors, whose cry of "wolf" is unheeded, even now that the peril has come.

3d. It is the boldest movement of its kind known in history. By some it has been likened to Napoleon's march to Moscow. But although the great Emperor carried "five hundred thousand men and more" into the heart of Russia, he may be said never to have entirely abandoned his base, for until he crossed the Niemen, all Europe was at his back in the shape of the strongest alliances. Poles and Prussians, Saxons and Austrians were in his ranks, and he left garrisons in the conquered towns, as he advanced; and, although his supplies sometimes miscarried, it was provided that they should always follow in his train. But Sherman has no base, and no supplies, and the Moscow he will reach will never burn to compel a disastrous retreat.

To us it has more in common with the famous Anabasis. But the Greeks were fleeing homeward from Persian treachery, in great anxiety, if not in terror, after the fall of Cyrus at Cunaxa. Their glad shout, "The sea! the sea!" when they beheld the sunlit waves of the distant Euxine, was a cry of thanksgiving for their safety. Sherman reverses all this; he seeks the sea indeed, but with a triumphant advance; and although his glorious veterans will hail it as eagerly as did the ten thousand, it is because it is the sign not only of perils over, but of new conquests.

The boldness of the plan, and the responsibility of its arduous execution are his. Let the great glory be his and that of his famous army. As for his destruction, to speak of it is ridiculously absurd; he is not only perfectly safe in any event, but he cannot now fail of his purpose.

Such being the great cardinal movement, let us look at the collaterals. Hood, angry and desperate, too late to intercept or harass Sherman, his thorn in the flesh, establishes his base on the Tennessee, from Florence to Decatur, and thence moves rapidly, with numbers superior to Thomas, along the Nashville and Decatur Railroad, to overwhelm Nashville, and, in event of success, to invade Kentucky. Thus he advances upon Pulaski, crosses the Duck River at Columbia, and, not entirely unopposed or unchecked, at last reaches Franklin.

Who, for a moment, doubts the true policy of Thomas? It is as clear as noonday. He has a vast region to protect: he must retire on Nashville and receive strong re-enforcements. Who, then, will misunderstand his cautious and well-conducted retreat as Hood attacks and flanks him, admirably aided by Forrest with his cavalry? This brings us to a brief consideration of

GENERAL SCHOFIELD'S VICTORY AT FRANKLIN.—Following out the policy we have indicated, it became necessary for General Schofield, the commander of the troops in the field, to check the enemy from time to time, until he could get his trains and *matériel* safely to Nashville. So there was fighting at Columbia, and a sharp action at Spring Hill, about twelve miles south of Franklin, on the 29th of November, after which our troops retired to Franklin.

Here Hood pressed Schofield so fiercely that it became necessary to fight a battle. The danger was great; the town was filled with our trains, and time must be gained for them to cross the Big Harpeth, and hurry on to Nashville. On this river, in a bend with the concavity southward, thus forming a close re-entering, is the town of Franklin. On the north bank is a well constructed fort, with heavy guns in barbette, commanding the town and the country southward, and also protecting the railroad and turnpike to Nashville, on the north bank.

Schofield rapidly formed his line of battle south of the town, across the bend, in semicircular form, both wings resting on the river. Stanley's Corps formed his right, and Cox his left; the head-quarters, from which every point of the field was to be seen, were in the fort. Numerous batteries were posted in front of our entire line, and Wilson's cavalry was disposed on the flanks.

The rebel order of battle placed Cheatham on their left, Stewart on the right, and Lee in reserve opposite the right centre. The ranks were ranged four deep on the wings. They were about to try their old system of tactics, first to crush our centre and then to attack the right wing. Meantime our trains were using all possible expedition to get away.

The battle opens; the irregular firing of the skirmishers merges into the roar of cannon and the drum-like rattle of musketry. Hood, ever valiant but never wise, had personally inspected our lines, and then riding along each brigade of his own army, had repeated a little speech prepared and conned for the occasion: "These lines must be broken, boys; break them, and you have finished the campaign; break them, and nothing can impede your march to the Ohio." These words were the prologue to one of the most splendid and sanguinary battle scenes of the war. The rebels rushed forward in a magnificent charge upon our centre, designed to crush it, sever the two wings, beat them in detail, gain the town, and destroy our trains. On came the long lines of gray and steel, with an unflinching valor always the most admirable in war. But the sweeping fire of our batteries in front, and the terrible barbettes from the fort kept up a *feu d'enfer* which they could not breast. Line after line was melted, and poured back. Lee's reserves came to the rescue, and with fresh vigor succeeded at last in piercing our centre; it swung wide open like a human gateway, and their purpose seemed to be effected. Not so. Behind our centre lay Opdyke's brigade in reserve. This was the critical moment. General Stanley, who had moved like Mars upon the field, the bravest of the brave and the coolest, too, is said to have called out, "Opdyke, I want that line restored." "Conclude it done, General," was the calm reply, which, unless we are mistaken, will pass into proverbial history. It was done. Opdyke springs upon the advancing rebels; Wagner and Riley, who had given way under the tremendous strain, rally behind him and charge again, recapture the guns and the line, and take a thousand prisoners; a brilliant *riposte*.

There was desultory fighting elsewhere—a feeble effort on our right, but thus the battle ended in our favor. The enemy's loss was more than double ours; we captured eighteen battle-flags, our trains were in safety, and our army, true to its original purpose, left the barren field and retired to Nashville.

Of course Hood claims a victory, although he knows far better. We heartily wish him many such. We condemn him out of his own mouth. The campaign in Tennessee is not ended; the road to the Ohio is still slightly obstructed, and his own situation seems to grow more aimless and desperate every day. We are fond of "old saws," especially when we can apply them to "modern instances." Hood realizes more than any other rebel general, the apophthegm of Horace:

"Vis consili expers mole ruit sua."

The more he displays such *vim*, the better for us. General Schofield deserves great praise for his forecast, skill, resolution, and judgment, and his name will have a permanent and brilliant reputation in history as the hero of Franklin.

Of other movements our space will only permit a brief mention of the action of General Foster at Grahamsville, and the destruction of the railroad, seventy miles from Charleston, and thirty-four from Savannah. This was manifestly intended as a diversion in favor of Sherman; and although it seems to have been made too soon, the force still remains in observation on the Broad River. Our troops did not succeed in taking the works, which were defended by General G. W. Smith, with five thousand rebel troops, but they maintained their position on the Broad River, and by a later account are said to have again attacked the rebels with greater success.

The advance of General Burbridge from Cumberland Gap to Bean Station, in East Tennessee, has caused Breckinridge to retire northward towards Western Virginia. He will, doubtless, be confirmed in his retreat by the advance of Stoneman, and will find it difficult to join Hood, if such be his purpose.

From the Army of the Potomac, there is comparatively little to chronicle. The men are made comfortable in "winter quarters," which, however, may be vacated at a moment's warning. The rebels announce that Grant is going to make an attack at an early day.

Gregg's raid on the Weldon Railroad was preparatory to a greater movement. He moved out on Thursday, December 1st, marched to Duvall's, Rowanty, and Stony Creek Stations (the latter being the terminus of the Petersburg and Weldon Road), destroyed these stations, and numerous mills, and depots of supplies. Taking advantage of Gregg's march, General Warren, with the Fifth Corps and a portion of the Second, a strong force of artillery and a division of cavalry moved down the Jerusalem plank road, crossed the Nottoway on pontoons, and proceeded as far as the bridge over the Meherrin River, where, finding the enemy in force, he returned, having thoroughly destroyed twenty miles of the railroad, numerous station houses and bridges, and thus cut off one means and the most important of supplies for Petersburg and Richmond. On his return he burned Sussex Court-House in retaliation for the murder and mutilation of some of our stragglers; and was back in his old quarters before the rebels were sufficiently aware of his expedition to offer the slightest resistance.

Every thing remains quiet in Sheridan's Army, except an occasional raid which the rebels make upon the Baltimore and Ohio Railroad.

Southern unanimity is once more seriously endangered. South Carolina is again about to secede: a series of resolutions, presented to her legislature by R. Barnwell Rhett, complains of the usurpation of the Confederate Government; declares that she is not amenable to Jefferson Davis; that he has no right to emancipate the slaves, or restrict the freedom of the press, and calls on the other States not to submit. We can only admire—her consistency.

GENERAL MEADE.

In recognition and recompense of his brilliant and faithful services, General

Meade has been appointed a major-general in the regular army, to date from the 10th of August last.

The immediate presence of the Lieutenant-General, who is commander-in-chief of all our armies, has caused the world sometimes, nay most of the time, to forget that from the crossing of the Rapidan to the present moment, General Meade has been the commander of the Army of the Potomac, its chief in every bloody battle, and has been unsparing, heroic, and self-sacrificing in his labors and service. We rejoice at this promotion; it is his due; it calls public attention to his real high position; it silences all cavils, and adds another chaplet to the crown whose laurels were plucked at Gettysburg.

FOREIGN AND INTERNATIONAL.

Mexico is at length declared pacificated. Maximilian is a fixture. If she is satisfied with this almost bloodless submission, she deserves nothing better; we have no more sympathy to waste upon her.

The capture of the Florida, about which our President maintains a dignified silence in his message, has given rise to a correspondence between the Brazilian Secretary of State, and our Minister, General Webb. Blaming Brazil—as well as France and England—for recognizing the rebels as belligerents, our ambassador accepts the fact, and half promises restitution. The accidental destruction of the Florida—for of course it was accidental—does not complicate the question in reality, while it certainly renders any restitution we may deem it proper to make less painful to us.

An English nobleman without a title has been visiting us, and deserves public recognition and thanks. We mean Goldwin Smith, Regius Professor of Modern History in the University of Oxford. He has clearer, more practical, more philosophic views of the war and of American slavery, than any man who has written upon it.

Lord Lyons has left Washington, ostensibly on the score of his health. But the sale of his wines, horses, &c., seems to indicate no intention of return.

The application of Lord Wharncliffe to our Government to permit the distribution of the money realized by the Anglo-Rebel Bazaar, among the Southern prisoners, was made through our minister, Mr. Adams. It has called forth an able and trenchant letter from Mr. Seward. The New York *Herald* thus presents the correspondence:—

"Lord Wharncliffe informs Mr. Adams that the Liverpool Bazaar produced about seventeen thousand pounds, and asks permission for an accredited agent to visit the military prisons within the Northern States and distribute aid to their inmates. He denies that any political aid is aimed at, or any imputation that rebel prisoners are deprived of such attentions as the ordinary rules enjoin. He says:—

"'The issues of the great contest will not be determined by individual suffering, be it greater or less, and you, whose family name is interwoven with American history, cannot view with indifference the sufferings of American citizens, whatever their State or opinions.'

"Mr. Adams replied that it has never been the desire of the Government to treat with unnecessary or vindictive severity any of the misguided individual parties in this deplorable rebellion who have fallen into its hands in the regular course of the war, and that he should greatly rejoice if the effects of such sympathy could be extended to ministering to their mental ailment as well as their bodily suffering, thus contributing to put an end to a struggle which otherwise is too likely to be only procrastinated by their English sympathizers.

"Mr. Seward replies as follows to the application received through Mr. Adams:

"'DEPARTMENT OF STATE, WASHINGTON, Dec. 5, 1864.

"'SIR—I have received your dispatch of the 18th of November, No. 807, together with the papers therein mentioned, viz., a copy of a letter which was addressed to you on the 12th of November last by Lord Wharncliffe, and a copy of your answer to that letter. You will now inform Lord Wharncliffe that permission for an agent of the committee described by him to visit the insurgents detained in the military prisons of the United States, and to distribute among them seventeen thousand pounds of British gold, is disallowed. Here it is expected that your correspondence with Lord Wharncliffe will end. That correspondence will necessarily become public. On reading it, the American public will be well aware that while the United States have ample means for the support of prisoners as well as for every other exigency of the war in which they are engaged, the insurgents who have blindly rushed into that condition, are suffering no privations that appeal for relief to charity, either at home or abroad. The American people will be likely to reflect that the sum thus insidiously tendered in the name of humanity, constitutes no large portion of the profits which its contributors may be justly supposed to have derived from the insurgents, by exchanging with them arms and munitions of war for the coveted productions of immoral and enervating slave labor. Nor will any portion of the American people be disposed to regard the sum thus ostentatiously offered for the relief of captured insurgents, as a too generous equivalent for the devastation and dissolution which a civil war, promoted and protracted by British subjects, has spread throughout the States, which before were eminently prosperous and happy. Finally, in view of this last officious intervention in our domestic affairs, the American people can hardly fail to recall the warning of the Father of our Country, directed against two great and intimately connected public dangers, namely, sectional faction and foreign intrigue. I do not think the insurgents have become debased, although they have sadly wandered from the ways of loyalty and patriotism. I think that, in common with all our countrymen, they will rejoice in being saved by their considerate and loyal Government from the grave insult which Lord Wharncliffe and his associates, in their zeal for the overthrow of the United States, have prepared for the victims of this unnatural and hopeless rebellion. I am, sir, your obedient servant,

"'WILLIAM H. SEWARD.'"

CORRESPONDENCE.

A NEW GUN.

[Translated from the "Militär Zeitung."]

THE Darmstadt "Universal Military Journal" contained in the first number of the current volume a correspondence dated New York, that stated, at some expense of words, that the Parrott gun, which has proved so excellent at the bombardment of Fort Sumter and on several other occasions, was not an original idea, but an invention of Mr. Lindner, and that the merits of that gentleman, who through his inventions was about to reform, or rather had already reformed the whole system of artillery, had never been recognized or rewarded as they deserved. We might doubt whether this letter was really written in New York, though the humbug might require the acknowledgment of a Barnum himself.

Even though the "Military Journal" should publish the communications sent to it, without entering into a strict investigation of their truth and justice, yet it is scarcely to be blamed therefor, since there is not always time for such investigations, and in a case like the present, where the subject in question was one almost unknown in Europe, an examination was not possible, and the Darmstadt "Military Journal" naturally accepted the communication in good faith.

But since we happen to possess a somewhat closer acquaintance with the subject, we cannot forbear, while we reprint the letter at length, adding some explanatory notes, hoping to do a favor to that considerable portion of our readers who have been mystified by the correspondence.

The letter is as follows:

"NEW YORK, December 6, 1863.

"The Parrott cannon is not the discovery of Mr. Robert Parrott, of New Hampshire, but of Mr. Edward Lindner, of Berlin.* Lindner urged Parrott, some years ago, to make the attempt to strengthen cast-iron cannon by an iron ring forged to the breech.† Parrott said very decidedly that this would be an impossibility, for such a ring would never be solid to the cast iron; and he declined to make the attempt.‡ A year after this interview, Parrott took out his patent, which set forth especially, that he strengthened the breech of his cannon by an iron ring, exactly as Lindner had suggested to him.§ This fact was related to me by Lindner himself,‖ and I have no reason to doubt, indeed I steadfastly believe that Parrott played him a trick. Lindner's last invention, however, far surpasses the Parrott, and every other gun.¶ This cannon is breech loading, is cast altogether 'in the block,' then drilled and rifled, and is in every respect of remarkable construction.** Lindner made a 12-pounder of this description at his own expense, which I myself proved about a year ago at Manchester, N. H. The trial was favorable beyond all expectation;†† and a marked distinction of this cannon is the prevention of the recoil, which makes it peculiarly fitted for sea-service.‡‡ This gun was exhibited at West

---

* We must confess that the correspondent does not long leave us in doubt as to his drift.

† Even were this statement true, Mr. Lindner would have no right to lay claim to the Parrott invention, for the peculiarity of that invention lies in something very different from the strengthening of the breech through an iron ring. Besides this gun-ring is not an original idea of Lindner's, for it has been used many times, in many places, first in Belgium, then in England, Spain, Russia, and, if we do not mistake, by way of experiment on some Austrian naval guns.

‡ If Lindner really did make this proposal, Parrott was certainly not bound on that account to accede to it, since he believed in the propriety of the construction of his own cannon and the ammunition belonging to it, and he was not disposed to allow his work to be improved (?) by others who were probably totally ignorant of his invention.

§ We have already remarked, how little the gun-ring proves, and how far Mr. Lindner is from a right of priority in its invention.

‖ Perhaps there would have been yet more to hear from Parrott's rival, if we had heard less in praise of his system, but the correspondent should have the more considered the "audiatur et altera pars."

¶ We wish Mr. Lindner, for his own sake, a favorable result to this attempt, and that his gun may not be brought to trial and then prove a miserable fiasco (as may have happened not long ago!) but we wish, at this moment, that the Prussian artillery were furnished with the corresponding number of Parrotts one hundred or two hundred pounders (*which have been already proved*) during the attack on the fortifications at Düppel, and we could then prove that much depends not only on the practice of arms, but also on the system. It should not be difficult to decide, whether the fault at Missunde, where seventy-four cannon of different calibre (but none over twenty-four pounds) were used, is due to the practice or to the system (and perhaps to the size of the calibres).

** This is more than unlikely, since Mr. Lindner ascribed the peculiarity and the consequent excellence of the Parrott gun only to the iron ring already mentioned, and appears to have no opinion of the arrangement of the rifling and the shot, or at least ignores it entirely.

†† We know how easy it is, to calculate the effect produced by the tests so as to obtain results at once dazzling and deceptive. Is it only private individuals who so mislead their customers, or do official corporations deceive their commissioners and themselves by showy productions and illusions?

‡‡ This seeming advantage may be bought very dear by the early destruction of the gun-car-

Point, tried by an authorized commission, and submitted to many tests.* The commission pronounced itself entirely in favor of this new invention, which is not an improvement on those already in existence, but the embodiment of an original idea.† That the Lindner gun was not accepted by the United States Government, may be ascribed to the fact that Parrott and Dahlgren combined to keep up the market value of their own productions‡. Lindner's offer, to compete with Dahlgren and Parrott, was civilly declined,§ and he was allowed to retire with his cannon,‖ although it is the best, the most original, the most complete, and the most serviceable production of the new knowledge of artillery."

If the Lindner cannon is really "the best, the most original, the most complete, and the most serviceable production of the new knowledge of artillery" (we see the New York (?) correspondent knows how to lay the colors on thickly), then Mr. Lindner would only have to congratulate himself, and we are convinced that the representatives of the science of artillery would everywhere give the greatest pains to the examination of so superior an invention, and would grant it the fullest recognition.

We have only to remark, in addition, that in the course of the present war the Americans have had sufficient occasion to know and value the worth of superior arms, and especially to discriminate the good from the bad, and it is not to be believed that they would throw away good and useful weapons to replace them by useless and expensive ones.

PIEDMONT.
[From our own Correspondent.]

Turin, March 4.

The Army Register for the year 1864 gives the following statistics with relation to the corps of officers in the Piedmontese Army:

Generals (on and off duty)	252	Officers of Infantry		9,415
Guards	223	" " Cavalry		1,013
General Staff	168	" " Artillery		994
Officers attached to bureaux and posts	1,585	" " Engineers		451
Officers of Carabineers	513	" " Artillery-trains		192
			Total,	14,806

officers of all grades, besides the corresponding Sanitary Corps, the medical branch the chaplains, the military intendancy, and a host of military employés.

---

riage. In Schleswig, where the firing was on soft ground, and the recoil was consequently prevented, many evil consequences ensued.

* After these many tests, it is still possible that the fitness of the gun was but partially proved and judged. After all, as far as we know, we cannot believe that Mr. Lindner has hit the right nail on the head, and that the conditions that attach to the breech-loading system where small arms are concerned, can be more easily fulfilled in a cannon, where great rapidity of firing is required.

† This originality can only be shown in the arrangement of the breech, and whether this arrangement have a practical value, can only be ascertained by continuous trial. The arrangement of the lock of the Lindner gun is besides no particularly favorable sign for the originality of the gun.

‡ The practical Americans are certainly much too wise not to find out the most serviceable.

§ Probably they despised the easy victory that might and must have been theirs in a contest with Mr. Lindner.

‖ Under the present circumstances, while so much money is spent in America on munitions of war, this dismissal might be considered significant.

PERSONAL ITEMS.

LIEUTENANT-GENERAL GRANT arrived in New York November 19th, and remained until the 21st, when he returned to the front.

Brigadier-Generals Rufus Ingalls and Henry J. Hunt have been brevetted as major-generals of volunteers. Major Biddle, aide to General Meade, has received the brevet of colonel.

Major-General W. S. Hancock has been relieved from the command of the Second Corps, at his own request, and has been assigned to the command of the new veteran "First Corps," now being organized, with head-quarters in Washington.

Major-General A. A. Humphreys assumed command of the Second Corps November 26th.

Major-General D. N. Couch has been transferred from the Department of the Susquehanna, and ordered to report to Major-General Thomas at Nashville.

Major-General George Cadwalader succeeds General Couch in command of the Department of the Susquehanna.

Major-General Q. A. Gillmore has been ordered to report to Major-General Canby, to perform an inspection tour of the defences and fortifications in the West.

Major-General N. J. T. Dana has been appointed to the command of the District of West Tennessee and Vicksburg, with head-quarters at Vicksburg.

Major-General C. C. Washburne has been assigned to the command of the Post and District of Vicksburg, with its present limits.

Major-General F. Steele has been relieved from the command of the Seventh Army Corps and the Department of Arkansas, and ordered to report to General Canby. Major-General J. J. Reynolds succeeds him in command.

Major-General Alexander McDowell McCook has been ordered to report to Major-General Sheridan, and left Dayton, Ohio, November 29, to do so.

Major-General John Newton is in command at Key West.

Major-General P. H. Sheridan has been elected an associate member of the United States Sanitary Commission.

Major-General Emory has been assigned to the permanent command of the Nineteenth Corps.

Major-General T. F. Meagher has reported for duty to Major-General Steedman at Chattanooga.

Major-General W. S. Rosecrans was relieved from the command of the Department of Missouri December 6th, and Major-General G. M. Dodge has been appointed to the command in his stead.

Major-General William B. Franklin is ordered as president of a retiring board at Wilmington, Del.

Major-General W. F. Smith is temporarily ordered to New Orleans.

Brigadier-General Egan has been made major-general for services before Petersburg.

Brevet Major-General S. G. Burbridge has been relieved from the command in Kentucky, and Maj.-Gen. George Stoneman has been appointed in his stead.

Brevet Major-General M. C. Meigs has been assigned to duty according to his brevet, to date from July 5, 1864.

General F. C. Barlow sailed for Europe Nov. 9, hoping to restore his shattered health. The Secretary of War gave him his leave in a most complimentary order.

Brigadier-General John A. Rawlings, chief of General Grant's staff, was in New York November 13th, staying at the residence of Colonel Hillyer.

Brigadier-General Truman Seymour, has returned to the Sixth Corps.

Brigadier-General Morgan L. Smith has been assigned to command at Vicksburg.

Brigadier-General Ashboth has been compelled by his wounds, received in West Florida, to go to New Orleans for medical attendance. Brigadier-General Bailey succeeds him in command.

Brigadier-General John P. Hatch has been relieved from the command of the District of Florida and ordered to take command of the Northern District, relieving Brigadier-General E. E. Potter, who takes command of the Hilton Head District.

Brigadier-General E. P. Scammon has been relieved from the command of the Hilton Head District, and ordered to take command of the District of Florida.

Brigadier-General H. N. Wessels has been appointed commissary-general of prisoners east of the Mississippi, and Brevet Brig.-Gen. Hoffman, west of that river.

Brigadier-General W. F. Barry, who is prevented by severe illness from accompanying General Sherman in his present campaign, is temporarily with his family at Buffalo, New York.

Brigadier-General George J. Stannard has been promoted to be brevet major-general of volunteers, for gallant services at Fort Harrison (Chapin's Farm), where he lost his right arm.

Brigadier-General Nelson A. Miles has been appointed a major-general by brevet. He is the youngest general officer in the service.

Brigadier-General Robert B. Porter has been brevetted major-general for distinguished and gallant conduct in the several actions since crossing the Rapidan, to rank from August 1st, 1864.

Colonel Guy V. Henry, 40th Massachusetts, has been brevetted Brigadier-General for gallantry in the engagements before Richmond and Petersburg.

Colonel S. M. Bowman, who was relieved from the command of the District of Delaware, and ordered to report to Major-General Wallace, at Baltimore, has, at the request of the Executive, been returned to the former command.

Captain W. V. Hutchins has been appointed chief quartermaster of the Tenth Corps, with the rank of lieutenant-colonel.

The President has accepted the resignations of Major-General John A. McClernand and Brigadier-Generals E. A. Payne and Neal Dow, to date from Nov. 30.

The Tenth and Eighteenth Corps have been discontinued. The white troops of both corps have been reformed into the Twenty-fourth Corps, Major-General E. O. C. Ord commanding. And all the black troops of the Ninth, Tenth, and Eighteenth Corps have been organized into a Corps d'Afrique, designated the Twenty-fifth Corps, under Major-General G. Weitzel.

Rear-Admiral S. F. Dupont was in New York November 16, and visited the Brooklyn Navy Yard.

Rear-Admiral S. P. Lee assumed command of the Mississippi Squadron Nov. 1.

Acting Rear-Admiral C. H. Bell was relieved from the command of the Pacific Squadron October 25, and arrived in New York Nov. 4, in U. S. S. Rhode Island.

Captain John A. Winslow, of the Kearsarge, landed in Boston November 8.

OFFICIAL INTELLIGENCE.

Army Directory.

The following is published for reference (future changes will be noticed as they occur):—

SECRETARY OF WAR.

Hon. Edwin M. Stanton—Office, second floor War Department.

ASSISTANT SECRETARIES OF WAR.

Hon. P. H. Watson and Hon. C. A. Dana—Offices, third floor War Department.

GENERAL-IN-CHIEF.

Office in charge of Captain G. K. Leet, Assistant Adjutant-General, No. 29, Winder's Buildings, second floor.

CHIEF OF STAFF.

Major-General H. W. Halleck—Office, corner F and Seventeenth streets.

ADJUTANT-GENERAL.

Brigadier-General L. Thomas—Office, War Department.

BUREAU OF MILITARY JUSTICE.

Brigadier-General Joseph Holt, Judge-Advocate General—Office, Winder's Building, corner F and Seventeenth streets.

JUDGES-ADVOCATE.

Major L. C. Turner, Judge-Advocate, Department of Washington, &c.—Office, 539 Seventeenth street.

Theophilus Gaines, Major and Judge-Advocate, Twenty-Second Army Corps—Office, 534 Fourteenth streets.

SOLICITOR OF THE WAR DEPARTMENT.

Hon. William Whiting—Office, Rooms Nos. 29 and 31, War Department.

INSPECTOR-GENERAL'S DEPARTMENT.

Office, 537 Seventeenth street.

BUREAU OF THE SIGNAL CORPS.

Lieutenant-Colonel W. J. L. Nicodemus, Acting Chief Signal Officer—Office, 167 F street.

PROVOST-MARSHAL GENERAL.

Brigadier-General James B. Fry—Office, War Department.

QUARTERMASTER'S DEPARTMENT.

Brevet Major-General M. C. Meigs, Quartermaster-General—Office, Art Union Building, corner of Pennsylvania Avenue and Seventeenth street.

Brigadier-General D. H. Rucker, Dépôt Quartermaster—Office, corner G and Eighteenth streets.

Captain J. M. Moore, Chief Assistant Quartermaster—Office, corner Twenty-First and F streets.

Colonel ——— ———, Chief Quartermaster Department of Washington—Office, 534, 536, 538, and 540 Fourteenth street, near New York Avenue.

Captain H. L. Thayer, Assistant Quartermaster Volunteers, Post Quartermaster—Office, 232 G street.

Captain D. G. Thomas, Military Storekeeper—Office, 304 H, near Seventeenth street.

SUBSISTENCE DEPARTMENT.

Brigadier-General A. B. Eaton, Commissary-General—Office, on La Fayette Square, corner H street and Jackson Place.

Lieutenant-Colonel G. Bell, Dépôt Commissary—Office, 223 G street.

MEDICAL DEPARTMENT.

Brigadier-General J. K. Barnes, Surgeon-General—Office, corner Fifteenth street and Pennsylvania Avenue.

Lieutenant-Colonel John M. Cuyler, Acting Medical Inspector-General, United States Army—Office, 302 H street, corner of Seventeenth street, first floor.

Lieutenant-Colonel A. C. Hamlin, Medical Inspector Department of Washington—Office, No. 4 Louisiana Avenue.

Lieutenant-Colonel John Wilson, Medical Inspector United States Army, Inspector of the Army of the Potomac—Office, at Rev. Dr. Samson's, Columbian College, Washington, D. C.

Surgeon R. O. Abbott, Medical Director, Department of Washington—Office, 132 Pennsylvania Avenue.

Surgeon Basil Norris, to attend officers of the Regular Army—Office, corner Fourteenth and G streets.

Surgeon Thomas Antisell, to attend officers of the Volunteer Army—Office, in a frame building on the space between Eighteenth and Nineteenth streets, south side Pennsylvania Avenue.

Surgeon C. Sutherland, U. S. A., Medical Purveyor—Office, 212 G street, near Eighteenth.

General Hospitals are under the charge of Surgeon R. O. Abbott.

UNITED STATES ARMY MEDICAL MUSEUM,

H street, between Fourteenth street and New York Avenue. Open daily, except Sundays, from 9 A. M. until 4 P. M.

EXAMINING BOARD FOR ASSISTANT SURGEONS OF VOLUNTEERS.

Thomas Antisell, President—Office, in a frame building on the space between Eighteenth and Nineteenth streets, south side Pennsylvania Avenue.

PAY DEPARTMENT.

Colonel T. P. Andrews, Paymaster-General, detached on special duty. Major B. M. Brice, Acting Paymaster-General, in charge of the department—Office, corner F and Fifteenth streets.

Chief Clerk E. H. Brooke, Examination of Accounts—Office, 211 F street.

Major Hutchins—Discharge Office of all Officers, corner F and Fifteenth streets.

Major Rochester—Discharge Office of all Officers, corner F and Fifteenth streets.

Major Potter—Discharge office of Regulars, corner F and Fifteenth streets.

Major Taylor—Discharge Office of Volunteer Soldiers, corner Thirteenth street and New York Avenue.

ENGINEER DEPARTMENT.

Brigadier-General R. Delafield, Chief Engineer—Office, Winder's Building, corner F and Seventeenth streets.

ORDNANCE DEPARTMENT.

Brigadier-General A. B. Dyer, Chief—Office, Winder's Building, corner F and Seventeenth streets.

MILITARY DEPARTMENT OF WASHINGTON.

Major-General C. C. Augur, commanding department—Head-quarters, corner of Fifteenth-and-a-half street and Pennsylvania Avenue.

Brigadier-General J. A. Haskin, Chief of Artillery, Department of Washington—Office with Major-General C. C. Augur, corner Fifteenth-and-a-half street and Pennsylvania Avenue.

Captain H. W. Smith, Assistant Adjutant-General, Discharge Office for Department—Office, 536 Fourteenth street.

Colonel T. Ingraham, Provost-Marshal, District of Washington—Office, corner Nineteenth and I streets.

DEFENCES OF WASHINGTON.

Brevet Major-General J. G. Barnard, Chief Engineer—Office, northwest corner Pennsylvania Avenue and Nineteenth streets.

MISCELLANEOUS.

Major-General E. A. Hitchcock, Commissioner for Exchange of Prisoners—Office 28 Winder's Building, second floor.

Brevet Brigadier-General William Hoffman, Commissary-General of Prisoners—Office 148 F street, corner of Twentieth street.

Brevet Brigadier-General D. C. McCallum, Superintendent of Military Railroads—Office, 250 G street, near Seventeenth street.

Brigadier-General A. P. Howe, Inspector of Artillery, U. S. A.—Office, corner of Pennsylvania Avenue and Nineteenth street.

Cavalry Bureau—302 H street, under command of Major-General Halleck, Chief of Staff; Lieutenant Colonel Ekin, in charge of Purchase and Inspection of Horses, and Quartermaster duties—Office, No. 374 H street.

Captain Henry Keteltas, 15th United States Infantry, Commissary of Musters—Office, corner Nineteenth and G streets.

Brevet Colonel C. W. Foster, Assistant Adjutant-General, Chief of Colored Bureau—Office, 531 Seventeenth street, opposite War Department.

The Army.

Resignation of Gen. McClellan—Promotion of Gen. Sheridan.

[General Orders No. 282.]

War Department,
Adjutant-General's Office,
Washington, Nov. 14, 1864.

Ordered by the President,

I. That the resignation of GEORGE B. McCLELLAN, as Major-General in the United States Army, dated November 8, and received by the Adjutant-General on the 10th instant, be accepted as of the 8th of November.

II. That for the personal gallantry, military skill, and just confidence in the courage and patriotism of his troops, displayed by PHILIP H. SHERIDAN on the 19th day of October, at Cedar Run, whereby, under the blessing of Providence, his routed army was reorganized, a great national disaster averted, and a brilliant victory achieved over the rebels for the third time in pitched battle, within thirty days, PHILIP H. SHERIDAN is appointed Major-General in the United States Army, to rank as such from the 8th day of November, 1864.

By order of the President of the United States.

E. D. TOWNSEND, *Assist. Adj.-Gen.*

Insignia of Rank Dispensed with.

[General Orders, No. 286.]

War Department,
Adjutant-General's Office,
Washington, Nov. 22, 1864.

Officers serving in the field are permitted to dispense with shoulder-straps and the prescribed insignia of rank on their horse equipments. The marks of rank prescribed to be worn on the shoulder-straps will be worn on the shoulder in place of the strap. Officers are also permitted to wear overcoats of the same color and shape as those of the enlisted men of their command. No ornaments will be required on the overcoats, hats, or forage caps; nor will sashes or epaulettes be required.

By order of the Secretary of War.

E. D. TOWNSEND, *Assist. Adj.-Gen.*

Dismissals,

For the Week ending November 5, 1864.

Colonel H. L. Potter, 7th New York Volunteers, to date November 2, 1864, for conduct unbecoming an officer and a gentleman, and involving complicity on his part in an attempt to defraud a soldier of his bounty.

Captain William Neussil, 82d Ohio Volunteers, to date October 29, 1864, for having presented and certified to a fraudulent claim against the United States.

Captain Edwin M. Newcomb, 16th Iowa Volunteers, to date October 29, 1864, for absence without leave.

Captain John T. Croff, 16th unattached company Massachusetts Volunteer Militia, to date October 29, 1864, for conduct unbecoming an officer and gentleman.

Captain James Cullen, 1st Michigan Cavalry, to date November 1, 1864, for drunkenness when in the presence of the enemy.

Second Lieutenant Robert Harper, 5th New York Cavalry, to date November 1, 1864, for misconduct before the enemy, and drunkenness while on duty.

Second Lieutenant G. B. Smith, 4th United States Infantry, to date September 26, 1864, for absence without leave, having been published officially and failed to appear before the Commission.

The following officers, to date October 4, 1864, for the causes mentioned, having been published officially and failed to appear before the Commission:

For being in the City of Washington without authority, and failing to report at Headquarters Military District of Washington, under arrest, as ordered.

Second Lieutenant Charles B. Oliver, Battery C, Independent Pennsylvania Artillery.

Desertion.

First Lieutenant Michael Dempsey, 24th Michigan Volunteers.

For gross intoxication, and conduct scandalous, disgraceful, and unbecoming an officer and gentleman.

Captain Michael Gleason, 23d Illinois Volunteers.

For the Week ending November 12, 1864.

Major J. M. Daily, 14th Pennsylvania Cavalry, to date November 10, 1864, for absence without leave.

Captain T. J. Manning, 73d New York Volunteers, to date November 10, 1864, for breach of arrest, and absence without leave while under charges for trial by court-martial.

Captain Joseph W. Hall, 14th Pennsylvania Cavalry, to date November 7, 1864, for inefficiency, utter worthlessness, and absence without leave.

Captain A. J. Ralph, 6th Michigan Volunteers (1st Heavy Artillery), to date November 7, 1864, for robbing and swindling enlisted men under his command, and neglect of duty in allowing them to desert.

Captain Joseph M. Kirk, 39th Kentucky Volunteers, to date March 31, 1864.

Captain Charles C. Smith, 13th United States Infantry, to date November 5, 1864.

First Lieutenant A. C. Salisbury, 14th United States Colored Troops, to date November 11, 1864, for insolent and insubordinate conduct toward his commanding officer.

First Lieutenant Alexander Anderson, 14th New York Cavalry, to date November 10, 1864, for absence without leave, in going to a private house to receive medical treatment when he was ordered to report at a general hospital.

First Lieutenant Henry H. Weaver, 28th Iowa Volunteers, to date November 9, 1864, for protracted absence without leave from his regiment.

First Lieutenant Martin Mahan, 16th United States Infantry, to date November 8, 1864, with loss of all pay and allowances that may be due him, for repeatedly enlisting minors contrary to law.

First Lieutenant James O. Christie, Regimental Quartermaster 13th New York Cavalry, to date November 7, 1864.

First Lieutenant H. F. Armstrong, 13th New York Cavalry, to date November 7, 1864.

Second Lieutenant Jacob S. Parker, 115th United States Colored Infantry, to date November 7, 1864, for having tendered his resignation while under charges.

Second Lieutenant Frank C. Kinnicutt, 34th Massachusetts Volunteers, to date November 8, 1864, for neglect of duty, and wanton abuse of a horse, the property of the United States, with loss of pay to the amount of $75, the depreciated value of said horse since in his possession.

For the Week ending November 19, 1864.

Colonel Thomas Stevens and Major George N. Richmond, 2d Wisconsin Cavalry, to date November 17, 1864, for general worthlessness, and for the good of the service.

Captain J. P. Wagner, 202d Pennsylvania Volunteers, to date November 12, 1864, for drunkenness, and desertion of his command while on picket guard.

Captain Judson Haycock, 1st United States Cavalry, to date November 12, 1864, for cowardice, drunkenness on duty, and absence without leave.

Captain Benjamin F. Craig, 14th New Jersey Volunteers, to date November 12, 1864, for cowardice, and utter worthlessness as an officer.

Captain Carswell McClellan, Assistant Adjutant-General United States Volunteers, to date November 16, 1864.

Captain William H. Vallance, Assistant Quartermaster United States Volunteers, to date November 16, 1864, with loss of all pay and allowances.

Captain Simpson Hamburger, 91st New York Volunteers, to date November 17, 1864, for neglect of duty, and absence without leave, to the prejudice of good order and military discipline.

Assistant Surgeon John Jassay, 124th Illinois Volunteers, to date November 17, 1864, for repeated disobedience of orders.

Assistant Surgeon J. A. Vervais, 2d Minnesota Cavalry, to date November 15, 1864, for absence without leave, gross disobedience of orders, and general inefficiency.

The following officers, to date October 17, 1864, for the causes mentioned, having been published officially and failed to appear before the Commission:—

For being in the City of Washington without authority, and failing to report under arrest at Head-quarters Military District of Washington, as ordered.

Lieutenant Adam Schrant, 21st United States Colored Troops.

Absence without leave.

Assistant Surgeon Charles E. Goldsborough, 5th Maryland Volunteers.

Second Lieutenant G. W. Cunningham, 14th West Virginia Volunteers, to date November 12, 1864, with loss of all pay and allowances since July 26, 1864, for absence without leave, and utter worthlessness as an officer.

For the Week ending November 26, 1864.

Captain Jehu Evans, 4th New Jersey Volunteers, to date November 22, 1864, for conduct prejudicial to good order and military discipline.

Captain David Cain, 10th Missouri Cavalry, to date November 23, 1864, for absence without leave, and conduct prejudicial to good order and military discipline.

The following officers, to date October 24, 1864, for the causes mentioned, having been published officially, and failed to appear before the Commission:—

Absence without leave.

Captain Ruthven W. Houghton, 3d New Hampshire Volunteers.
Second Lieutenant Justus Shiebler, 15th New York Artillery.

The following officers, to date November 21, 1864, for absenting themselves from their commands during the engagement of October 19, 1864:—

Captain James Humes, 15th West Virginia Volunteers.
Lieutenant Martin Park, 11th West Virginia Volunteers.
Lieutenant Philip T. Poe, 11th West Virginia Volunteers.

The following officers, to date November 22, 1864, for absenting themselves from their commands during the engagement of October 19, 1864:

Captain James W. Myers, 11th West Virginia Volunteers.
Second Lieutenant Harry Hinckley, 15th West Virginia Volunteers.

Surgeon W. H. Tanner, 178th New York Volunteers, to date November 22, 1864, for absence without leave.

First Lieutenant George T. Curvan, 148th Pennsylvania Volunteers, to date November 21, 1864, with loss of all pay and allowances, for misapplication of company funds, and conduct prejudicial to good order and military discipline, while Acting Adjutant of Camp Biddle, Carlisle, Pennsylvania.

First Lieutenant S. L. Barnes, Veteran Reserve Corps, to date November 22, 1864.

First Lieutenant Anton Meyer, 12th United States Infantry, to date November 23, 1864, for absence without leave.

Second Lieutenant C. S. Chapman, 9th Michigan Cavalry, to date November 21, 1864, for want of due appreciation of his position as an officer of the United States service in having requested a dishonorable discharge from the same.

Second Lieutenant J. W. Runyan, 129th Indiana Volunteers, to date November 22, 1864, for cowardice, and for straggling from his command while it was in front of the enemy, August 19, 1864.

Assistant Surgeon John J. Saunders, 1st Iowa Cavalry, to date November 10, 1864, for being a drunkard, and useless to the service.

First Lieutenant Joseph C. Johns, 10th Illinois Cavalry, to date October 12, 1864, for drunkenness, repeated disobedience of orders, associating and drinking with private soldiers, conduct unbecoming an officer and gentleman, and absence without leave.

Lieutenant A. V. Burnham, 1st Connecticut Cavalry, to date November 14, 1864, for disobedience of orders.

Captain J. W. Peabody, 2d Louisiana Volunteers, to date October 20, 1864, on account of physical disability arising from a loathsome disease disqualifying him from duty and the result of his own imprudence and immorality.

Second Lieutenant W. H. Mathews, 5th New York Heavy Artillery, to date August 7, 1864, for habitual drunkenness.

Dropped from the Rolls.

By direction of the President, Captain Frederic G. Larned, 12th United States Infantry, has been dropped from the rolls of the Army, to date from August 31, 1863, for having disappeared and having remained absent since August, 1863.

The name of Captain James S. Hall, Signal Corps, United States Army, has been dropped from the rolls of the Army, to take effect December 7, 1863, for absence without leave.

Dishonorably Discharged.

The orders heretofore issued mustering out of service Colonel T. W. Cahill and Captain William Wright, 9th Connecticut Volunteers, have been so amended as to dishonorably discharge them for disobedience of orders and neglect of duty.

Exempt from Dismissal.

WAR DEPARTMENT,
ADJUTANT-GENERAL'S OFFICE,
WASHINGTON, Nov. 8, 1864.

The following-named officers, charged with offences, and heretofore published, are exempt from being dismissed the service of the United States, the Military Commission instituted by Special Orders, No. 53, series of 1863, from the War Department, having reported that satisfactory defence has been made in their respective cases, viz.:—

Major J. E. Williams, 1st New York Cavalry.
Major George V. Boutelle, 21st New York Cavalry.

Nov. 21, 1864.

Lieutenant D. M. Jones, 51st Ohio Volunteers, is exempt from being dismissed the service of the United States, the Military Commission instituted by Special Orders, No. 53, series of 1863, from the War Department, having reported that satisfactory defence has been made in his case.

Nov. 28, 1864.

Lieutenant William W. Webb, 7th Rhode Island Volunteers, charged with offences, and heretofore published, is exempt from being dismissed the service of the United States, the Military Commission instituted by Special Orders, No. 53, series of 1863, from the War Department, having reported that satisfactory defence has been made in his case.

Captain Henry C. Gapen, 15th United States Infantry, heretofore published for failing to report at Cincinnati, Ohio, as ordered, is exempt from dismissal from the service of the United States, satisfactory explanation to the charges against him having been received at this office.

E. D. TOWNSEND,
Assistant Adjutant-General.

Dismissals Revoked.

The orders of dismissal heretofore issued, in the following cases, have been revoked:—

Captain J. E. Erickson, 24th Regiment Veteran Reserve Corps.

Captain Samuel Barry, 67th Pennsylvania Volunteers, with a view to his trial by court-martial.

Assistant Surgeon S. A. Grimes, 32d Ohio Volunteers.

First Lieutenant Charles D. Root, "Merrill's Horse" Missouri Volunteers, and he is honorably discharged the service of the United States as of date of the order of dismissal.

Captain Byron C. Ketcham, 64th New York Volunteers, and he is restored to his command, provided the vacancy has not yet been filled by the Governor of his State.

Assistant Surgeon G. W. H. Kemper, 17th Indiana Volunteers, and he is honorably discharged as of the date of the order of dismissal.

Captain F. B. Holt, 1st New Jersey Volunteers, and he has been honorably discharged, to date September 12, 1864.

Second Lieutenant Mortier L. Norton, Veteran Reserve Corps.

Dismissal Amended.

The order heretofore issued dismissing First Lieutenant George S. Hutting, 96th United States Colored Infantry, has been so amended as to read First Lieutenant George S. Nutting, 96th United States Colored Infantry.

Dishonorable Discharge Revoked.

The order heretofore issued dishonorably discharging First Lieutenant Charles T. Baroux, 119th Pennsylvania Volunteers, has been revoked, and he has been honorably discharged as of the date of the former order.

Restored to Commission.

Major Timothy Quinn, 1st New York Lincoln Cavalry, heretofore dismissed, has been restored, with pay from the date at which he rejoins his regiment for duty, provided the vacancy has not been filled by the Governor of the State.

Captain William T. Cummings, 19th Kentucky Volunteers, heretofore dismissed, has been restored, with pay from the date at which he rejoins his regiment for duty, provided the vacancy has not been filled by the Governor of his State.

Captain J. M. Adams, 1st Missouri Cavalry, heretofore dismissed, has been restored, with pay from the date at which he rejoins his regiment for duty, provided the vacancy has not been filled by the Governor of the State.

Disability Removed.

The disability to receive another appointment in the military service of the United States, imposed by sentence of a general Court-Martial, "to be dismissed the service of the United States," in the case of Captain C. J. Dietrich, Commissary of Subsistence of Volunteers, has been removed.

Publication Recalled.

WAR DEPARTMENT,
ADJUTANT-GENERAL'S OFFICE,
WASHINGTON, Nov. 21, 1864.

The official publication of Second Lieutenant R. B. Humphrey, 13th United States Infantry, for failing to report at Cincinnati, Ohio, as ordered, is hereby recalled, evidence having been furnished this office of the decease of that officer on the 4th ultimo.

E. D. TOWNSEND,
Assistant Adjutant-General.

Presentation of Captured Rebel Flags.

The following rebel flags, were delivered at the War Department November 12, 1864, by their captors, who received medals of honor for their gallantry:—

Battle-flag of the 47th North Carolina Regiment, captured at Hatcher's Run, Virginia, October 27, 1864, by Sergeant Daniel Murphy, 19th Massachusetts Volunteers, General Egan's command, First Brigade, Second Division, Second Army Corps, Army of the Potomac; residence, Woburn, Massachusetts.

Battle-flag of the 26th North Carolina Regiment, captured at Hatcher's Run, Virginia, October 27, 1864, by Sergeant Alonzo Smith, 7th Michigan Volunteers, General Egan's command, First Brigade, Second Division, Second Army Corps, Army of the Potomac; residence, Allen, Michigan.

Medals of Honor.

Medals of honor have been awarded the following men, for gallantry in capturing rebel flags, in the engagement near Nineveh, West Virginia, November 12, 1864, in which General Powell's Division, of General Sheridan's Army, captured two pieces of artillery and two colors:—

Sergeant Levi Shoemaker, Company A, 1st Virginia Cavalry, who captured the flag of the 22d Virginia Cavalry.

Private James F. Adams, Company D, 1st Virginia Cavalry, who captured the flag of the 14th Virginia Regiment.

Record of Courts-Martial.

Second Lieut. Mandeville J. Fogg, Battery E, 1st Reg. W. Va. Vol. Light Art., sentenced to be dismissed the service of the United States.

First Lieut. Patrick S. Early, 13th Pa. Cav., sentenced to be cashiered, with forfeiture of all pay and allowances now due, and be imprisoned at hard labor in Fort Delaware for the term of two years.

Capt. Henry Troll, Battery A, 2d Mo. Art., sentenced to be cashiered.

Capt. A. A. Guest, 2d U. S. Sharpshooters, sentenced to be dishonorably dismissed the United States service, with the forfeiture (to the United States) of all pay and allowances.

First Lieut. Joseph S. Oakley, 120th N. Y. Vols., sentenced to refund to the United States two hundred and fourteen dollars and ninety-four cents; to be reduced to the rank of a private soldier, then be dishonorably discharged the United States service, and to be confined in such penitentiary as the proper authorities may appoint for the term of three years;* the order promulgating this sentence to be published in at least one newspaper in the county in which he resides.

First Lieut. Frank H. Boyd, 8th N. Y. Heavy Art., sentenced to forfeit all pay and allowances due or to become due him to the amount of five hundred and thirty-seven dollars, to be dishonorably dismissed the service of the United States, and to be confined for the term of three years in the State prison at Auburn, New York, or at such other place of confinement as may be designated by the proper authority.

First Lieut. John Knoppel, 1st Md. Vet. Vols., sentenced to forfeit all pay and allowances that are or may become due him, and that he be dishonorably dismissed the service of the United States.

Capt. J. J. Wakefield, Co. K, 27th Regt. U. S. Col'd Troops, sentenced to be cashiered the service.

Second Lieut. Thomas B. Campbell, 30th Regt. U. S. Col'd Troops, sentenced to be dismissed the service of the United States.

Second Lieut. Nelson Mitchell, 10th N. Y. Cav. sentenced to be cashiered.

Capt. David Thompson, 2d D. C. Vols., sentenced to be cashiered.

First Lieut. E. F. Wenckeback, 4th N. Y. Cav., sentenced to be reprimanded publicly by the commander of the Twenty-Second Army Corps.

First Lieut. John W. Peck, 2d D. C. Vols., sentenced to be dismissed the military service of the United States.

Capt. E. M. Warren, Ind. Mounted Co. one hundred days' Pa. Vols., sentenced to be dishonorably dismissed from the service of the United States.

Capt. William McNally, 77th N. Y. S. N. G., sentenced to be cashiered, to forfeit all pay and allowances due and to become due, and to be imprisoned at hard labor in the penitentiary at Albany, N. Y., or in such other place as the Commanding General may direct, for the period of one year.

First Lieut. B. J. Ashley, 7th N. Y. Heavy Art., sentenced to be dismissed the

---

* So much of the sentence in this case as directs confinement "in such penitentiary as the proper authorities may appoint for the term of three years" is remitted.

service of the United States, and to forfeit all pay and allowances which are now due or may become due him.

Capt. John H. Devine, 93d N. Y. S. N. G., sentenced to be cashiered and utterly disabled to have or hold any office or employment in the service of the United States; sentence mitigated to dismissal from the military service of the U. States.

Captain Absalom B. Selheimer, 195th Pa. Vols., sentenced to be dismissed the service of the United States.

First Lieut. Samuel B. Marks, 195th Pa. Vols., sentenced to be dismissed the service of the United States.

First Lieut. Richard H. See, 16th Pa. Cav., sentenced to be dismissed the service.

Surgeon Robert L. Waterbury, 93d N. Y. S. N. G., sentenced to be dismissed the service of the United States.

First Lieut. Robert Russell, Jr., 43d N. Y. Vols., sentenced to be reprimanded by the General commanding, in General Orders.

Capt. John L. Jefferies, 110th Pa. Vols., sentenced to be cashiered.

Second Lieut. L. A. Waldo, 50th N. Y. Engineers, sentenced to be cashiered.

Second Lieut. A. M. Herrick, 1st Pa. Cav., sentenced to be dismissed the service of the United States.

Capt. T. A. Byrens, 13th Pa. Cav., sentenced to be cashiered; sentence commuted to forfeiture of pay proper for six months.

First Lieut. Alex. Buchannan, 96th N. Y. Vols., sentenced to be cashiered.

First Lieut. Zeno I. Downing, 98th N. Y. Vols., sentenced to be cashiered.

Lieut. Paul Buchmeyer, Battery H, 3d N. Y. Art., sentenced to be dismissed the service of the United States.

Capt. Jesse W. Peabody, 2d La. Mounted Inf., sentenced to forfeit one-half of one month's pay, and be reprimanded in General Orders.

Act. Asst. Surgeon E. Herwig, U. S. A., sentenced to be dismissed from the service of the United States.

Major John C. Febles, 7th Cav., 119th Ind. Vols., sentenced to be cashiered; sentence mitigated to a public reprimand by his commanding officer.

Lieut. F. G. Drieskill, 48th Ky. Vols., sentenced to be dishonorably dismissed the service of the United States.

Second Lieut. Wm. G. Gabhart, 13th Ky. Cav., sentenced to be dismissed the service.

First Lieut. Charles A. McCue, 37th Ky. Mounted Inf., sentenced to be cashiered.

Capt. Barry H. Lynch, 86th U. S. Col'd Inf., sentenced to be dismissed the service; sentence mitigated to forfeiture of pay and emoluments for three months.

Capt. John C. Gosman, 86th U. S. Col'd Inf., sentenced to be dismissed the service.

Lieut.-Col. J. B. Leake, 20th Iowa Vols., sentenced to be reprimanded in orders by the Commanding Officer Department of the Gulf.

Capt. Orin A. Avery, 3d R. I. Cav., sentenced to be dismissed the service; sentence mitigated to a forfeiture of two months' pay and emoluments.

First Lieut. George L. Cross, 13th Wis. Battery, sentenced to be dismissed the service of the United States.

Second Lieut. James B. Moore, 43d Regt. U. S. Col'd Troops, sentenced to be cashiered the service, with the loss of all pay and emoluments except so much as may be due the sutler and laundress.

Lieut.-Col. N. H. Hixon, 13th Ohio Cav., sentenced to be cashiered, with loss of all pay and allowances from September 30, 1864.

Major N. Ward Cady, 2d N. Y. Mounted Rifles, sentenced to be dismissed the service, with loss of all pay due or to become due.

Major Jacob Szink, First Battalion one hundred days' Pa. Vols., sentenced to be dishonorably dismissed the service of the United States.

Second Lieut. William A. C. Ryan, 132d N. Y. Vols., sentenced to be dishonorably dismissed the service of the United States, with the loss of all pay and allowances and to be forever disqualified from receiving or holding a commission in the Army or volunteeer forces of the United States of America.

First Lieut. Joseph Roberts, 13th Pa. Cav., sentenced to be cashiered.

First Lieut. Elias Gibbs, 11th Kansas Cav., sentenced to be cashiered.

Capt. Jerome Kunkle, 11th Kansas Cav., sentenced to be cashiered, to forfeit all pay and allowances now due him or that may become due, and pay a fine of one hundred dollars to the Government of the United States.

Regular Navy.

Orders, &c.

Nov. 23.—Commodore J. L. Lardner, ordered to report to Rear-Admiral Goldsborough at Washington, D. C., for duty.

Nov. 30.—Commodore James L. Lardner, ordered to report to Rear-Admiral Gregory for such duty as he may assign.

Nov. 10.—Captain William M. Walker, on completion of duty as member of Court of Inquiry at Portsmouth, N. H., to report to Rear-Admiral Gregory for duty.

Nov. 11.—Captain G. H. Scott, detached from command of the Vermont, on the reporting of his relief, and ordered to command the Canandaigua. Captain Joseph F. Green, detached from command of the Canandaigua, on the reporting of his relief, and ordered North.

Nov. 16.—Captain John M. Berrien, detached from command of the Monadnock, and ordered to command the Navy Yard at Norfolk, Va.

Nov. 21.—Captain John P. Gilliss, ordered to the Navy Yard at Philadelphia.

Nov. 23.—Captain John A. Winslow, detached from the Kearsarge, and waiting orders.

Nov. 7.—Commander Paul Shirley ordered to command the Suwanee.

Nov. 9.—Commander Fabius Stanley, detached from ordnance-duty at Cairo, Ill., and ordered to command the State of Georgia. Commander A. J. Drake, detached from command of the Iosco, on the reporting of his relief, and granted sick leave. Commander S. Nicholson, detached from command of the State of Georgia, and ordered to command the Galatea. Commander John Guest, detached from command of the Galatea, and ordered to command the Iosco.

Nov. 11.—Commander Charles H. Baldwin, ordered to ordnance-duty at Navy Yard, Mare Island, California. Commander John C. Carter, detached from the command of the Michigan, on the reporting of his relief, and ordered to command the Receiving-Ship Vermont.

Nov. 17.—Commander Peirce Crosby, ordered to command the Muscoota.

Nov. 21.—Commander Reed Werden, detached from the Navy Yard, Philadelphia, on the reporting of his relief, and ordered to duty as Fleet-Captain of the East Gulf Squadron.

Nov. 22.—Commander John J. Almy, ordered to report to Rear-Admiral Gregory for temporary duty.

Nov. 5.—Lieutenant-Commander John S. Barnes, ordered to command the Bat.

Nov. 8.—Lieutenant-Commander William G. Temple, detached from special duty at Cold Spring, N. Y., and ordered to command the Pontoosuc. Lieutenant-Commander George A. Stephens, detached from command of the Pontoosuc, and waiting orders.

Nov. 11.—Lieutenant-Commander Francis A. Roe, detached from ordnance-duty at New York, and ordered to command the Michigan.

Nov. 12.—Lieutenant-Commander Richard L. Law, detached from command of the Cyane, on the reporting of his relief, and ordered home. Lieutenant-Commander John H. Russell, ordered to command the Cyane.

Nov. 17.—Lieutenant-Commander C. S. Norton, ordered to the Lackawanna.

Nov. 19.—Lieutenant-Commander E. Simpson, detached from the Isonomia, and ordered North.

Nov. 21.—Lieutenant-Commander William M. Gamble, detached from ordnance-duty at New York, and ordered to the Naval Rendezvous at Brooklyn. Lieutenant-Commander Ralph Chandler, detached from rendezvous duty at Brooklyn, on the reporting of his relief, and ordered to command the Maumee. Lieutenant-Commander James Parker, detached from command of the Maumee, on the reporting of his relief, and ordered to the Minnesota.

Nov. 22.—Lieutenant-Commander William Gibson, ordered to command the Mahaska. Lieutenant-Commander S. L. Breese, ordered to the Navy Yard, Philadelphia.

Nov. 23.—Lieutenant-Commander James S. Thornton, detached from the Kearsarge, and waiting orders.

Nov. 7.—Lieutenant S. W. Preston, detached from the South Atlantic Squadron, and waiting orders. Lieutenant Louis Kempff, ordered to the Suwanee.

Nov. 9.—Lieutenant Henry D. H. Manley, ordered to the State of Georgia.

Nov. 18.—Lieutenant Stephen A. McCarty, detached from the Lackawanna, on the reporting of his relief, and ordered North. Lieutenant A. Dexter, detached from the Navy Yard at New York, and ordered to the St. Mary's.

Nov. 21.—Lieutenant C. S. McDonough, detached from the Receiving-Ship North Carolina, and ordered to the Receiving-Ship Vandalia.

Nov. 22.—Lieutenant William B. Cushing, ordered to the North Atlantic Squadron.

Nov. 25.—Lieutenant John H. Rowland, ordered to the St. Mary's. Lieutenant John W. Phillip, detached from the South Atlantic Squadron, on the reporting of his relief, and ordered North. Lieutenant Edwin T. Brower, ordered to the South Atlantic Squadron.

Nov. 29.—Lieutenant Charles D. Jones, ordered to the Lackawanna.

Nov. 4.—Ensign John C. Pegram, detached from the South Atlantic Squadron, and granted leave.

Nov. 7.—Acting Ensign J. D. Graham, Jr., detached from the Jamestown and ordered home.

Nov. 12.—Ensign B. H. Porter, ordered to final examination.

Nov. 18.—Ensign Edward Shepard, ordered to final examination. Acting Ensign W. S. Dana, ordered to the Lancaster.

Nov. 22.—Ensign E. M. Shepard, detached from the Wachusett, and waiting orders.

Nov. 26.—Ensign James H. Sands, ordered to the Shenandoah.

Nov. 29.—Ensign B. H. Porter, ordered to physical examination at Philadelphia. Ensign Edwin M. Shepard, ordered to physical examination at Philadelphia.

Nov. 23.—Surgeon John M. Brown, detached from the Kearsarge, and waiting orders.

Nov. 25.—Surgeon John A. Lockwood, ordered to duty at Navy Yard, Mare Island, California. Passed Assistant Surgeon William S. Bishop, detached from Navy Yard, Mare Island, California, on the reporting of his relief, and ordered home.

Nov. 29.—Surgeon W. S. W. Ruschenberger, ordered to duty, as member of Board of Examiners at Philadelphia.

Nov. 14.—Assistant Surgeon George D. Slocum, ordered to the Naval Hospital at New York.

Nov. 17.—Assistant Surgeon William K. Van Reypen, detached from the East Gulf Squadron, on the reporting of his relief, and ordered North. Passed Assistant Edward S. Matthews, detached from Naval Rendezvous at Providence, Rhode Island, and ordered to the East Gulf Squadron.

Nov. 18.—Assistant Surgeon George W. Woods, detached from the Naval Hospital at Norfolk, Virginia, and ordered to the Receiving-Ship Alleghany.

Nov. 14.—Paymaster A. H. Gilman, detached from duty in charge of money, stores, and accounts at Mound City, Illinois, but will continue his duties as Paymaster of the Station. Paymaster C. C. Jackson, detached from duty as Purchaser of Flour, &c., at New York, and ordered to Mound City, Illinois, as Purchasing Paymaster. Paymaster J. C. Eldridge, ordered to duty as Purchaser of Flour, &c., and Instructor of Pay-Officers at New York.

Nov. 16.—Paymaster J. C. Eldridge's orders of the 14th instant revoked, and waiting orders. Paymaster James Hoy, Jr., ordered to temporary duty at New York, as Purchaser of Flour and Instructor of Pay-Officers.

Nov. 18.—Paymaster T. T. Caswell, detached from the Pawtuxet, on the reporting of his relief, and ordered to settle his accounts.

Nov. 19.—Paymaster W. W. Williams, detached from the Wachusett, on the reporting of his relief, and waiting orders.

Nov. 23.—Paymaster Joseph A. Smith, detached from the Kearsarge, on the transfer of her crew, and ordered to settle his accounts.

Nov. 25.—Paymaster James Hoy, Jr., ordered to examination at New York.

Nov. 30.—Paymaster James Hoy, Jr., relieved from duty, as Superintendent of Baking, and Purchasing of Flour, and Instructor of Pay Officers, at New York. Paymaster Joseph C. Eldredge, ordered to duty, as Superintendent of Baking, and Purchasing of Flour, and Instructor of Pay Officers, at New York.

Nov. 23.—Chief Engineer William H. Cushman, detached from the Kearsarge, and awaiting orders.

Nov. 25.—Chief Engineer J. W. Thompson, Jr., detached from Naval Rendezvous at New York, on the reporting of his relief, and ordered to duty, as a member of the Board of Examiners at Philadelphia. Chief Engineer William S. Stamm, ordered to special duty at New York.

Nov. 26.—Chief Engineer Francis C. Dade, detached from duty, as member of Board of Examiners, at Philadelphia, and ordered to resume the duties previously assigned him.

Nov. 12.—First Assistant Engineer Henry W. Robie, detached from the Sangamon, on the reporting of his relief, and ordered to the Shamokin. First Assistant Engineer R. H. Fitch, ordered to Portsmouth, New Hampshire, Navy Yard.

Nov. 25.—First Assistant Engineer N. B. Littig, detached from special duty, at Newburg, N. Y., and ordered to temporary duty at the Naval Rendezvous at New York.

Nov. 1.—Second Assistant Engineer Philip Miller, detached from the Canandaigua, and waiting orders.

Nov. 2.—Second Assistant Engineer Henry Snyder, and ordered to the Muscoota.

Nov. 4.—Second Assistant Engineer Charles W. Breaker, ordered to Experimental duty at New York. Second Assistant Engineer John Pemberton, ordered to the Naval Academy.

Nov. 11.—Second Assistant Engineer George W. Rogers, ordered to the Glaucus.

Nov. 14.—Second Assistant Engineer Thomas H. Bordley, ordered to examination for promotion at Philadelphia. Second Assistant Engineer B. C. Gowing, ordered to the Hibiscus.

Nov. 15.—Second Assistant Engineer B. F. Wood's orders to the Albatros revoked, and ordered to the Mohongo.

Nov. 17.—Second Assistant Engineer H. C. McIlvaine, detached from the Ticonderoga, on the reporting of his relief, and ordered to the Winnipec. Second Assistant Engineers William A. Dripps and W. W. Heaton, ordered to the Winnipec.

Nov. 23.—Second Assistant Engineer William H. Badlam, detached from the Kearsarge, and ordered to examination at Philadelphia.

Nov. 25.—Second Assistant Engineer John P. Kelley, detached from the Tallapoosa, and ordered to the Wando.

Nov. 29.—Second Assistant Engineer George W. Roche, detached from the Lackawanna, and ordered North.

Nov. 30.—Second Assistant Engineer Ezra J. Whittaker, ordered to the Pontoosuc.

Nov. 11.—Third Assistant Engineer H. Webster, detached from the Manhattan, and waiting orders.

Nov. 14.—Third Assistant Engineer Joseph H. Thomas, ordered to the Pontoosuc.

Nov. 17.—Third Assistant Engineer Harrie Webster, ordered to the Winnipec.

Nov. 23.—Third Assistant Engineers Frederick L. Miller, Sydney L. Smith, and Henry McConnell, detached from the Kearsarge, and ordered to examination at Philadelphia.

Nov. 26.—Third Assistant Engineer J. H. Harmany, ordered to examination at Philadelphia. Third Assistant Engineer G. W. Hall, detached from the Saugus, and ordered to examination at Philadelphia.

Nov. 28.—Third Assistant Engineer J. H. Harmany, detached from the South Atlantic Squadron, and waiting orders.

Nov. 4.—Boatswain Charles Fisher, detached from the Vermont, and ordered to the Canandaigua. Boatswain Charles A. Bragden, ordered to the Vermont. Boatswain Thomas Smith, detached from the Canandaigua, on the reporting of his relief, and ordered North.

Nov. 10.—Boatswain George C. Abbott, ordered to temporary duty on board the Receiving-Ship Vandalia.

Nov. 23.—Boatswain James C. Walton, detached from the Kearsarge, and waiting orders.

Nov. 18.—Gunner Burgess P. Allen, ordered to the Lancaster. Gunner T. Bascom, detached from the Lancaster, on the reporting of his relief, and ordered home. Sailmaker John Joins, ordered to the Naval Station at Baltimore. Boatswain Francis McCloud, ordered to the Naval Station at Baltimore.

Nov. 23.—Gunner Franklin A. Graham, detached from the Kearsarge, and waiting orders.

Nov. 5.—Sailmaker Stephen Seaman, detached from the Naval Academy, and ordered to the Lancaster. Sailmaker Francis Boom, detached from the Lancaster, on the reporting of his relief, and ordered North.

Nov. 19.—Carpenter Joseph Cox, detached from the Navy Yard, Portsmouth, New Hampshire, and waiting orders. Sailmaker John Joins's orders to Baltimore revoked, and ordered to the Receiving-Ship Vermont. Sailmaker J. G. Gallaher, detached from the Receiving-Ship Vermont, and ordered to the Naval Station at Baltimore. Carpenter William M. Laighton, ordered to the Naval Academy. Carpenter Joseph G. Myers, detached from the Naval Academy, and ordered to the Navy Yard at Portsmouth, New Hampshire.

Nov. 23.—Carpenter William F. Laighton, detached from the Sabine, and ordered to the Hartford. Carpenter Joseph Cox, ordered to the Sabine.

Nov. 25.—Sailmaker Richard Van Voorhes, detached from the Navy Yard, New York, and ordered to the Receiving-Ship North Carolina. Sailmaker George C. Boerum, detached from the North Carolina, and ordered to the Navy Yard, New York.

Nov. 29.—Sailmaker David Bruce, ordered to the Receiving-Ship Ohio. Sailmaker John H. Birdsall, detached from the Receiving-Ship Ohio, and ordered to the Naval Academy.

Nov. 30.—Carpenter H. M. Griffiths, detached from special duty, and ordered to the Chattanooga.

Placed on the Retired List.

Nov. 15.—Lieutenant Commander S. Livingston Breese.

Suspended.

Nov. 16.—Midshipman Edward N. Roth, suspended on half-pay for one year.

Resigned.

Nov. 4.—Midshipman Joseph P. Yerkes.
Nov. 7.—Midshipman Frederick W. Gardner.
Nov. 9.—Midshipman H. L. Mansfield; Midshipman Wm. B. Buckminster.
Nov. 12.—Midshipman H. W. Wessels, Jr.
Nov. 15.—Midshipman Charles M. Mott. Midshipman Frederick Klapp.
Nov. 16.—Assistant Paymaster William H. Sells.
Nov. 22.—Midshipman John F. Gay.
Nov. 23.—Lieutenant Adolphus Dexter.

Dismissed.

Nov. 9.—Gunner James Thayer.

Dropped from the List.

Nov. 17.—Midshipmen Alexander H. Cofforth and C. H. E. Stockbridge.

Miscellaneous.

Nov. 7.—Assistant Surgeon Edmund C. Vermeulen, restored to his original position on the list, to take rank next after Assistant Surgeon Samuel N. Brayton.

Volunteer Navy.

Orders, &c.

Nov. 8.—Acting Volunteer Lieutenant J. S. French, detached from the Wilderness, and ordered to the Mississippi Squadron.

Nov. 9.—Acting Volunteer Lieutenant J. B. Breck, detached from the Niphon, and granted sick leave.

Nov. 11.—Acting Volunteer Lieutenant W. G. Saltonstall, ordered to Ordnance duty at Boston Navy Yard. Acting Volunteer Lieutenant G. W. D. Patterson, placed on waiting orders.

Nov. 19.—Acting Volunteer Lieutenant Charles P. Clark, to regard himself as waiting orders.

Nov. 21.—Acting Volunteer Lieutenant G. W. D. Patterson, ordered to the Mississippi Squadron.

Nov. 25.—Acting Volunteer Lieutenant D. A. Campbell, detached from the Stepping-Stones, and ordered to report to Rear-Admiral Porter for duty.

Appointed Acting Master.

Nov. 17.—Gustavus Percival, waiting orders.

Appointed Acting Masters and Pilots.

Nov. 4.—D. V. N. Wrights, Henry North, and John Dorey, and ordered to the North Atlantic Squadron.

Nov. 5.—A. F. Davis, and ordered to the North Atlantic Squadron.

Nov. 7.—Thomas Smith, James T. Stover, Henry Stevens, Marcus Brower, Hankerson Vanderveer, and William Nelson, and ordered to the North Atlantic Squadron. S. W. Hadley, John Bolles, George Look, and Charles Cook, and ordered to the South Atlantic Squadron.

Nov. 8.—Isaac Sofield, and ordered to the North Atlantic Squadron.

Nov. 9.—David M. Abbott, John P. Foote, Thomas A. Wyatt, Samuel J. White, and James Fountain, and ordered to the North Atlantic Squadron.

Nov. 10.—Amos Rainer, and ordered to the North Atlantic Squadron.

Nov. 15.—Charles M. Lane, North Atlantic Squadron.

Nov. 17.—John Price, North Atlantic Squadron.

Nov. 21.—William H. Albury, Courtland P. Williams, Nathaniel Thrift, and William Richardson, and ordered to the East Gulf Squadron.

Nov. 22.—D. K. Kennison, Silas Blunt, Ethan A. Elliot, Charles Lookee, and ordered to the North Atlantic Squadron. William Reed, and ordered to the South Atlantic Squadron.

Nov. 26.—Alfred Everett, and ordered to the North Atlantic Squadron.

Nov. 7.—Acting Master Samuel B. Gregory, detached from the Potomac Flotilla, and ordered to the Minnesota. Acting Master Samuel Very's, orders to command the Casco revoked, and he is ordered to the North Carolina. Acting Master W. L. Martine, ordered to command the Hibiscus. Acting Master Franklin Hokkius, Jr., ordered to the Hibiscus. Acting Master J. F. Winchester, ordered to command the Gemsbok.

Nov. 8.—Acting Master Henry Lelar, detached from the North Carolina and ordered to the Suwanee. Acting Master H. K. Lapham, detached from the North Carolina, and ordered to the Suwanee. Acting Master W. R. Newman, ordered to the North Carolina.

Nov. 9.—Acting Master Charles Courtney, ordered to Medical Survey at Boston.

Nov. 10.—Acting Master Samuel Hall, detached from the Aster, and ordered to the Mississippi Squadron.

Nov. 11.—Acting Master O. B. Warren, on the expiration of leave, ordered to the South Atlantic Squadron.

Nov. 14.—Acting Master Charles C. Wells, detached from the Farallones, and ordered home. Acting Master William Rogers, detached from the Mary Sandford, and waiting orders.

Nov. 15.—Acting Master Franklin Hopkins, Jr., orders to the Hibiscus revoked, and ordered to Medical Survey at Boston. Acting Master W. B. Newman's orders to the North Carolina revoked, and waiting orders. Acting Master Allen M. Newman, ordered to the North Carolina.

Nov. 16.—Acting Master J. P. Carr, ordered to command the Horace Beals.

Nov. 17.—Acting Master Henry D. Edwards, detached from the Ohio, and ordered to the Albatross.

Nov. 18.—Acting Master C. A. Crocker, ordered to the command of the Casco. Acting Master J. P. Carr, ordered to command the Horace Beals. Acting Master Frederick T. King, detached from the Horace Beals, and waiting orders.

Nov. 22.—Acting Masters George Cables and Allen Hoxie, detached from the St. Louis, on the reporting of their relief, and ordered North. Acting Master Frederick T. King, ordered to command the Wando. Acting Master Gustavus Percival, ordered to the Mahaska.

Nov. 23.—Acting Master J. N. Rowe, detached from the St. Louis, on the reporting of his relief, and ordered North. Acting Masters James R. Wheeler and Eben M. Stoddard, detached from the Kearsarge, and waiting orders. Acting Master William Watson, ordered to command the J. S. Chambers. Acting Master David H. Sumner, detached from the Kearsarge, and waiting orders.

Nov. 25.—Acting Master E. L. Haines, ordered to the Nereus. Acting Master Samuel Curtis, detached from the Nereus, and ordered to command the Rachel Seaman. Acting Master Charles Potter, detached from command of the Rachel Seaman, and waiting orders. Acting Master L. Bartholomew, ordered to the Mississippi Squadron.

Nov. 29.—Acting Master H. S. Borden, detached from the Niphon, and waiting orders. Acting Masters George E. Nelson and Joseph Marthon, detached from the Mobile, and waiting orders.

Nov. 30.—Acting Master Eliphalet Brown, Jr., detached from special duty at Navy Yard, New York, and ordered to special duty, under Rear-Admiral Gregory. Acting Master Henry Lelar, detached from the Suwanee, and ordered to the North Carolina. Acting Master John A. French, detached from the Mercedita, and ordered to command the Sophronia. Acting Master R. Platt, detached from the U. S. Coast Survey Steamer Bibb, and ordered North, to report to the Superintendent of the Coast Survey for such duty as he may assign.

Appointed Acting Ensigns.

Nov. 1.—Rufus N. Miller, U. S. S. Metacomet.

Nov. 4.—William C. Williams, North Atlantic Squadron; William L. Baker, U. S. S. Hendrick Hudson; A. W. Harvey, U. S. S. Fah-Kee.

Nov. 5.—Harry P. Arbecam, U. S. S. Rachel Seaman.

Nov. 7.—G. C. Mendall, John Denson, and W. Lamie (for special duty as Pilots), South Atlantic Squadron.

Nov. 8.—James C. Greene, U. S. S. Wyalusing.

Nov. 9.—David C. Kierstead, U. S. S. Aitu; John Brennan, U. S. S. Onondaga.

Nov. 11.—Edward Hiller (for special service as Pilot), North Atlantic Squadron.

Nov. 12.—John H. Moore, U. S. S. Home.

Nov. 14.—Samuel Lomax (special service as Pilot), North Atlantic Squadron.

Nov. 15.—Jacob G. Hudson (special service as Pilot), North Atlantic Squadron.

Nov. 18.—Francis Tuttle, U. S. S. Morse.

Nov. 19.—Daniel W. Andrews, U. S. S. Orvetta; Walter N. Smith, U. S. S. Braziliera; George Delaps, U. S. S. Oleander.

Nov. 21.—H. G. Bunker, U. S. S. Hendrick Hudson; William R. Cox, Jr., U. S. S. Amaranthus; G. H. Rexford, U. S. S. Philadelphia; Sydney N. Gray, Navy Yard, Washington, D. C.

Nov. 22.—Edmund Parys, U. S. S. Powhatan; S. E. Willets, U. S. S. Tuscarora; John C. Oakley, U. S. S. Sabine; L. H. White, U. S. S. Shenandoah.

Nov. 23.—Charles H. Danforth and Ezra Bartlett, U. S. S. Kearsarge; C. L. Weeden, U. S. S. Ohio.

Nov. 26.—Thomas V. Parker, U. S. S. Ino; Samuel Carpenter, Navy Yard, Boston; Thomas Welch, U. S. S. St. Lawrence; H. M. Pishon, U. S. S. Poppy; Jarvis Wilson (for special duty as Pilot), North Atlantic Squadron.

Nov. 28.—Levi L. Odiorne, U. S. S. Queen.

Nov. 29.—Gorham S. Johnson and P. W. Fagan, U. S. S. John Adams.

Nov. 1.—Acting Ensigns Adolphus Dennett and Robert M. Wagstaff, detached from the Morse, and ordered to the Potomac Flotilla.

Nov. 2.—Acting Ensign Joseph Hadfield, detached from the Monticello, and ordered to report to Rear-Admiral Gregory at New York.

Nov. 3.—Acting Ensign George Anderson's orders to the New Hampshire revoked, and waiting orders.

Nov. 5.—Acting Ensign John Daley, ordered to Medical Survey at Philadelphia.

Nov. 7.—Acting Ensign L. R. Chester, ordered to the Hibiscus. Acting Ensign F. W. Sanborn, ordered to the Gemsbok. Acting Ensign C. R. Scoffin, detached from temporary duty at New York, and ordered to the Hibiscus. Acting Ensign J. G. Koehler, detached from the Naval Rendezvous at New York, and ordered to the Hibiscus. Acting Ensign Charles Moore, detached from the Casco, and ordered to the Ohio. Acting Ensign J. H. Ankers, ordered to the Gemsbok.

Nov. 8.—Acting Ensign Jeremiah Potts, detached from the Casco, and ordered to the Suwanee. Acting Ensign Arthur J. Hider, detached from the National Guard, and ordered to the Casco.

Nov. 10.—Acting Ensign David Stephen, detached from the Potomac Flotilla, and ordered to the North Atlantic Squadron.

Appointed Acting Ensigns, and ordered to the School-Ship Savannah.

Nov. 1.—Robert Adair.
Nov. 4.—J. B. Edwards (Acting Ensign and Coast Pilot). Lewis P. Delan.
Nov. 15.—John G. Lloyd, Ralph E. Peck, Elias Lawson.
Nov. 19.—Herman Fischer.
Nov. 22.—George B. Lowell.
Nov. 23.—Joseph Estes.
Nov. 25.—H. N. Crockett and Thomas J. Cannon.
Nov. 29.—Gorham P. Tyler.
Nov. 30.—William White.

Nov. 11.—Acting Ensign Joshua Simmonds, ordered to Medical Survey at Norfolk, Virginia.

Nov. 12.—Acting Ensign Charles D. Duncan, detached from the Union, and ordered to the South Atlantic Squadron. Acting Ensign William P. Burke, detached from the Montgomery, and ordered to the Snow-Drop.

Nov. 14.—Acting Ensign Daniel Lester, ordered to Medical Survey at New York.

Nov. 15.—Acting Ensign John Daley, detached from the Howquah, and granted sick leave. Acting Ensign J. C. Vandeventer, ordered to the Hibiscus.

Nov. 17.—Acting Ensign M. S. Porter, ordered to the Albatross.

Nov. 18.—Acting Ensign Charles F. Moore, ordered to the Morse.

Nov. 21.—Acting Ensign J. H. Delano, detached from the Galena, and ordered to the Morse. Acting Ensign Adolphus Dennett, detached from the Potomac Flotilla, and ordered to the Morse. Acting Ensign Charles F. Moore, orders to the Morse revoked, and ordered to the Potomac Flotilla. Acting Ensign Sanford S. Miner, detached from the Galena, and ordered to the Neptune.

Nov. 22.—Acting Ensign Henry Taylor, detached from the Crusader, and waiting orders. Acting Ensign Henry Pease, Jr., detached from the Galena, and ordered to the St. Louis. Acting Ensign Robert M. Wagstaff, detached from the Potomac Flotilla, and granted leave. Acting Ensigns George E. Mills and W. B. Arey, detached from the Grand Gulf, and ordered to the Mahaska.

Nov. 23.—Acting Ensign Sanford S. Miner, orders to the Neptune revoked, and ordered to the St. Louis. Acting Ensign William Jennings, detached from the Calypso, and ordered to the J. S. Chambers. Acting Ensign E. K. Smith, detached from the Grand Gulf, and ordered to the Wando. Acting Ensign John Williams, detached from the Fah-kee, and ordered to the Receiving-Ship North Carolina. Acting Ensign M. A. Nickerson, detached from the Niphon, and ordered to the Wando. Acting Ensign Edward A. Sawyer, detached from the Sassacus. Acting Ensign Charles A. Hodgdon, to await orders.

Nov. 25.—Acting Ensign E. G. Drayton, ordered to the Nereus. Acting Ensign E. D. Pettengill, detached from the Mercedita, and ordered to the Sophronia. Acting Ensigns George Anderson and G. M. Smith, ordered to the Nereus. Acting Ensign F. H. D'Estimeauville, ordered to Medical Survey at New York.

Nov. 26.—Acting Ensign Charles A. Hodgdon, ordered to the South Atlantic Squadron. Acting Ensign F. P. Center, detached from the Shenandoah, and ordered to report to Rear-Admiral Porter for duty. Acting Ensign S. S. Bissell, detached from the Shenandoah, and ordered to report to Rear-Admiral Porter for duty.

Nov. 29.—Acting Ensigns Neil Larsen and E. N. Seaman, detached from the Niphon, and waiting orders. Acting Ensign E. T. Strong, detached from the Rachel Seaman, and ordered to instruction at New York.

Appointed Acting Master's Mates.

Nov. 4.—Enoch M. Reed, U. S. S. Sabine; Harry C. Norton, U. S. S. Sabine; James W. Hanaway, U. S. S. Sabine; John C. Parker, U. S. S. Sabine.

Nov. 5.—John McGee, U. S. S. Harvest Moon; William W. Hunter, North Atlantic Squadron.

Nov. 7.—Andrew Baker, U. S. S. Young Rover.

Nov. 8.—William W. Harding, U. S. S. Ohio; Henry Gardner, U. S. S. Eutaw.

Nov. 9.—C. G. Brown, U. S. S. Fort Donelson; Thomas Harris, U. S. S. Fort Donelson; Henry J. Buckless, U. S. S. Miami.

Nov. 12.—Henry P. Diermanse, U. S. S. Harvest Moon; James Williams, U. S. S. Harvest Moon; R. W. Robins, U. S. S. Glaucus.

Nov. 15.—David Leavis, U. S. S. Lockwood.

Nov. 18.—L. P. Cook, John S. Sinclair, and John Foster, U. S. S. Colorado; J. H. Gilley, U. S. S. General Putnam; Henry J. Bentley, Pacific Squadron.

Nov. 19.—Nathan Brown, U. S. S. John Adams.

Nov. 21.—Collins J. Andrews, U. S. S. Gem of the Sea.

Nov. 22.—James B. Raynor, U. S. S. Shenandoah.

Nov. 23.—Francis P. Vultee, U. S. S. Shenandoah; Roger Connolly, U. S. S. Acacia.

Nov. 29.—Samuel H. Gardner, U. S. S. Harvest Moon; A. C. Watts, Potomac Flotilla.

Nov. 7.—Acting Master's Mate George A. Johnson, ordered to instruction at Navy Yard, New York. Acting Master's Mate John G. Brown, ordered to temporary duty on board the Receiving-Ship Ohio.

Nov. 9.—Acting Master's Mate R. H. Eldridge, detached from the Owasco and granted sick leave.

Nov. 10.—Acting Master's Mate William H. Yeaton, ordered to the Receiving-Ship Vandalia.

Nov. 11.—Acting Master's Mate Sydney B. Cline, ordered to the Potomac Flotilla.

Nov. 15.—Acting Master's Mate George A. Thompson, detached from the West Gulf Squadron, and ordered to instruction on board the Savannah.

Nov. 17.—Acting Master's Mate John G. Brown's orders to the Ohio revoked, and waiting orders.

Nov. 19.—Acting Master's Mate E. D. W. Parsons, ordered to report to Rear-Admiral Paulding. Acting Master's Mate Charles C. Jones, ordered to instruction on board the Savannah.

Nov. 22.—Acting Master's Mate J. C. Boteler, detached from the Grand Gulf, and ordered to the Mahaska. Acting Master's Mates J. C. Foster and J. W. Sanderson, detached from the Calypso, and ordered to the Mahaska.

Nov. 23.—Acting Master's Mate R. M. Cornell, detached from the Mercedita, and ordered to the Sophronia. Acting Master's Mate P. M. Topham, detached from the Calypso, and ordered to the J. S. Chambers. Acting Master's Mates William Smith and John F. Bickford, detached from the Kearsarge, and waiting orders. Acting Master's Mate G. W. Barnes, detached from the Niphon, and ordered to the Wando. Acting Master's Mate A. K. Baylor, detached from the Galena, and ordered to the J. S. Chambers.

Nov. 25.—Acting Master's Mates W. B. Spencer, W. K. Engall, and W. Cromack, ordered to the Nereus.

Nov. 26.—Acting Master's Mate Charles C. Jones, ordered to Medical Survey at Portsmouth, N. H.

Nov. 28.—Acting Master's Mate W. C. N. Sandford, detached from the Niphon, and ordered to the Wando. Acting Master's Mate William K. Engall, orders to the Nereus revoked, and ordered to temporary duty at Navy Yard, Philadelphia.

Nov. 29.—Acting Master's Mate W. D. Giles, detached from the Niphon, and ordered to the Wando. Acting Master's Mate C. C. Chamberlain, detached from the Neptune, and ordered to the Suwanee. Acting Master's Mate H. E. Geraud, detached from the Mobile, and ordered to the Nereus.

Appointed Acting Master's Mates, and ordered to the School-Ship Savannah.

Nov. 4.—Eugene McCarty.
Nov. 5.—Henry M. Upham.
Nov. 8.—Charles J. Murphy.
Nov. 9.—Thomas G. Underdown.
Nov. 14.—George A. Woodbury, Benjamin S. Reed.
Nov. 18.—John Gilmore.
Nov. 30.—Edwin H. Richardson.

Appointed Acting Assistant Surgeons.

Nov. 1.—Benjamin F. Hamell, and ordered to the North Carolina.
Nov. 3.—John R. Latson, and ordered to the Ohio.
Nov. 14.—John Blackmer, and ordered to the Montgomery.

Nov. 5.—Acting Assistant Surgeon B. F. Hamell, detached from the North Carolina, and ordered to the Shockokon. Acting Assistant Surgeon W. H. Pierson, ordered to Washington, to report to the Department.
Nov. 7.—Acting Assistant Surgeon S. B. Doty, detached from the North Carolina, and ordered to the West Gulf Squadron. Acting Assistant Surgeon J. G. Park, ordered to the West Gulf Squadron.
Nov. 10.—Acting Assistant Surgeon W. J. Donor, detached from the Casco, and ordered to the Galatea.
Nov. 12.—Acting Assistant Surgeon, W. H. Pierson, detached from the Chimo, and ordered to the Pontoosuc.
Nov. 21.—Acting Assistant Surgeon Charles S. Eastwood, ordered to the State of Georgia. Acting Assistant Surgeon J. G. Park, ordered to the West Gulf Squadron. Acting Assistant Surgeon Joseph R. Layton, ordered to the Stars and Stripes.
Nov. 23.—Acting Assistant Surgeon John R. Latson, detached from the Ohio, and ordered to the Massasoit.

Appointed Acting Assistant Paymasters.

Nov. 1.—H. T. B. Harris, waiting orders; Joseph L. Terrell, waiting orders.
Nov. 3.—Albert B. Clark, waiting orders; Gerrett L. Hoodless, waiting orders.
Nov. 11.—John Macmahon, and waiting orders.
Nov. 14.—George Rock, and waiting orders.
Nov. 15.—Charles W. Seeley, and waiting orders.
Nov. 16.—W. D. Walker, and waiting orders.
Nov. 17.—William L. G. Thayer, and waiting orders.
Nov. 18.—George H. Griffing, and waiting orders.
Nov. 19.—Joseph G. Morton, and waiting orders; George A. Ferree, and waiting orders.
Nov 25.—Edwin Boss, and waiting orders.

Nov. 2.—Acting Assistant Paymaster Charles F. Guild, ordered to the North Atlantic Squadron.
Nov. 4.—Acting Assistant Paymaster S. T. Savage, ordered to the Casco. Acting Assistant Paymaster Charles S. Park, ordered to the Chimo. Acting Assistant Paymaster William A. Purse, ordered to the Bat. Acting Assistant Paymaster William M. Good, ordered to the Naubuc.
Nov. 7.—Acting Assistant Paymaster William H. Palmer, ordered to the Nahant. Acting Assistant Paymaster D. A. Smith, detached from the Nahant, on the reporting of his relief, and to settle accounts. Acting Assistant Paymaster J. W. McLellan, ordered to the Bat. Acting Assistant Paymaster H. T. B. Harris, ordered to the Naubuc. Acting Assistant Paymaster William A. Purse's orders to the Bat revoked, and waiting orders. Acting Assistant Paymaster William M. Good's orders to the Naubuc revoked, and waiting orders.
Nov. 9.—Acting Assistant Paymaster E. H. Brink, ordered to the Gemsbok. Acting Assistant Paymaster H. M. Rogers, ordered to the "Wilderness."
Nov. 12.—Acting Assistant Paymaster C. B. Gold, ordered to the Vincennes. Acting Assistant Paymaster Samuel Anderson, detached from the Jacob Bell, on the reporting of his relief, and ordered to settle his accounts. Acting Assistant Paymaster J. C. Hatch, ordered to the Hibiscus. Acting Assistant Paymaster A.

J. Greeley, ordered to the Jacob Bell. Acting Assistant Paymaster David Davis, Jr., ordered to the Exchange (Mississippi Squadron).

Nov. 16.—Acting Assistant Paymaster J. Appleton Berry, to the Suwanee.

Nov. 17.—Acting Assistant Paymaster D. W. Hale, ordered to settle his accounts.

Nov. 18.—Acting Assistant Paymaster G. A. Emerson, ordered to the Pawtuxet. Acting Assistant Paymaster George Rack, ordered to the Mathew Vassar. Acting Assistant Paymaster J. L. Ferrell, ordered to the Albatross.

Nov. 19.—Acting Assistant Paymasters G. L. Hoodless and Albert B. Clark, ordered to the West Gulf Squadron. Acting Assistant Paymaster E. H. Sears, ordered to the Wachusett.

Nov. 23.—Acting Assistant Paymaster C. D. Harvey, ordered to the Mahaska.

Nov. 26.—Acting Assistant Paymaster Lysander C. Tripp, ordered to the Otsego. Acting Assistant Paymaster Joseph G. Morton, ordered to the Mahaska. Acting Assistant Paymaster George H. Griffing, ordered to the Hibiscus. Acting Assistant Paymaster C. D. Harvey, orders to the Mahaska revoked, and ordered to Medical Survey at New York. Acting Assistant Paymaster W. L. G. Thayer, ordered to the Wando. Acting Assistant Paymaster William D. Walker, ordered to the J. S. Chambers.

Nov. 30.—Acting Assistant Paymaster Charles H. Lockwood, detached from the Mobile, on the transfer of her crew, and ordered to settle his accounts. Acting Assistant Paymaster Theodore Barker, detached from the Niphon, and settling accounts.

Nov. 3.—Acting Chief Engineer Henry Waite, ordered to the Miantonomah.

Appointed Acting First Assistant Engineers.

Nov. 11.—Theodore D. Coffer, East Gulf Squadron.
Nov. 16.—Daniel C. Stillson, U. S. S. Queen.
Nov. 23.—William P. Nolan, U. S. S. Honduras.
Nov. 30.—Robert Mulready, U. S. S. Philadelphia.

Nov. 12.—Acting First Assistant Engineer John Tallon, detached from the Glaucus, and ordered to the Sangamon.

Nov. 19.—Acting First Assistant Engineer Frank A. Bremon, ordered to the North Atlantic Squadron.

Appointed Acting Second Assistant Engineers.

Nov. 1.—William W. Collier, U. S. S. Ossipee.
Nov. 2.—Joseph H. Mathews, U. S. S. Quaker City; John W. Wall, U. S. S. Morse.
Nov. 3.—Robert J. Middleton, U. S. S. Wyoming.
Nov. 4.—John F. Fitzpatrick, U. S. S. Agamenticus.
Nov. 7.—Newton Champion, U. S. S. Galatea.
Nov. 9.—Alfred E. Chipendale, U. S. S. Hibiscus.
Nov. 10. William Ray, U. S. S. Hibiscus.
Nov. 12.—Charles B. Wright, U. S. S. Western World.
Nov. 14.—Philip Eckenroth, U. S. S. Nereus.
Nov. 18.—Reuben Riley, U. S. S. Honeysuckle.
Nov. 22.—Francis R. Shoemaker, U. S. S. Western World.
Nov. 23.—George E. Burwell, U. S. S. Mahaska.
Nov. 30.—Frank Marsh, U. S. S. E. B. Hale.

Nov. 1.—Acting Second Assistant Engineer Edward F. McGinniss, ordered to the Bat.

Nov. 2.—Acting Second Assistant Engineer John W. Dexter, detached from the Cœur de Lion, on the reporting of his relief, and ordered to the Morse.

Nov. 11.—Acting Second Assistant Engineer John A. Patterson's orders to the San Jacinto revoked, and ordered to the Nereus.

Nov. 12.—Acting Second Assistant Engineer William Campbell, released from arrest, and directed to await orders. Acting Second Assistant Engineer James W. Smyth, detached from the Muscoota, and ordered to the Rhode Island.

Nov. 15.—Acting Second Assistant Engineer William Campbell, ordered to the Pontoosuc.

Nov. 16.—Acting Second Assistant Engineers William H. Smith and James H. Plunkett, to the Miantonomah.

Nov. 17.—Acting Second Assistant Engineer Robert J. Middleton, detached from the Wyoming, and ordered to the Ticonderoga.

Nov. 22.—Acting Second Assistant Engineer William A. Leavitt, detached from the Morse, and ordered to the Wyoming. Acting Third Assistant Engineer Raimond F. Roswald, detached from the Grand Gulf, and ordered to the Nereus.

Nov. 25.—Acting Second Assistant Engineer Theodore O. Reynolds, ordered to Medical Survey at New York.

Nov. 29.—Acting Second Assistant Engineers Thomas Fitzgerald and F. D. Stuart, detached from the Mobile, and waiting orders.

Appointed Acting Third Assistant Engineers.

Nov. 1.—Jarvis B. Edson, U. S. S. Fah-kee; Frank Rivers, U. S. S. Bat; Charles H. Crawford, U. S. S. Bat; Reuben G. Watson, U. S. S. Nyanza.

Nov. 2.—Charles J. Price, U. S. S. Michigan.

Nov. 3.—Byron W. Worsley, U. S. S. Dictator; Francis Withers, U. S. S. Morse.

Nov. 5.—George Hall, U. S. S. State of Georgia.

Nov. 8.—George West, U. S. S. Hibiscus.

Nov. 9.—Solon C. Smith, U. S. S. Hibiscus; Isaac P. Davis, Jr., U. S. S. Galatea.

Nov. 11.—Russell Warner, U. S. S. Nereus; Thomas Tilton, U. S. S. Nereus.

Nov. 14.—John K. Foster, U. S. S. Nereus; Henry F. Allen, U. S. S. Nereus.

Nov. 17.—William H. Walters, U. S. S. Albatross.

Nov. 18.—Jeremiah Barringer, Picket-Boat, No. 6.

Nov. 19.—Reid R. Throckmorton, U. S. S. Nereus.

Nov. 21.—John Slack, U. S. S. Albatross; George W. Hughes, North Atlantic Squadron.

Nov. 22.—John H. Wilson, U. S. S. Saco.

Nov. 23.—Edward Collins, U. S. S. Glaucus; Edward Schwartz, North Atlantic Squadron; Robert A. Inglis, North Atlantic Squadron.

Nov. 26.—James D. Wallin, U. S. S. Saugus; Peter Smith, U. S. S. Michigan; James H. Groves, U. S. S. Michigan.

Nov. 28.—M. J. Wallace, U. S. S. Commodore Read.

Nov. 1.—Acting Third Assistant Engineer James Campbell, ordered to the Bat. Acting Third Assistant Engineer Charles H. Lawrence, ordered to the Bat.

Nov. 2.—Acting Third Assistant Engineer William Baas, detached from the Michigan, on the reporting of his relief, and ordered to the Galatea.

Nov. 3.—Acting third Assistant Engineer James E. Smith, ordered to the Cœur de Lion. Acting Third Assistant Engineer Bernard Rice, detached from the Dictator, on the reporting of his relief, and ordered to the Galatea.

Nov. 8.—Acting Third Assistant Engineer James B. German, detached from the Mingoe, and granted sick leave.

Nov. 12.—Acting Third Assistant Engineer John A. Frank, detached from the Ceres, on the reporting of his relief, and ordered to the Don. Acting Third Assistant Engineer Lawrence J. Lyons, detached from the Don, and ordered to the Ceres.

Nov. 15.—Acting Third Assistant Engineer George C. Brown, ordered to the Pontoosuc.

Nov. 16.—Acting Third Assistant Engineer William S. Rainier, ordered to the Miantonomah.

Nov. 18.—Acting Third Assistant Engineer Alfred O. Tilden, ordered to the Mohongo. Acting Third Assistant Engineer William C. Woods, detached from the Agamenticus, and ordered to the Albatross. Acting Third Assistant Engineers Russell Wheeler and Reuben W. Burlingame, detached from the Merrimack, and ordered to the Albatross.

Nov. 22.—Acting Third Assistant Engineers John K. Foster and Patrick J. McMahon, detached from the Nereus, and ordered to the Mahaska. Acting Third Assistant Engineer Patrick Burns, detached from the Galena, and ordered to the Morse.

Nov. 25.—Acting Third Assistant Engineers William Noire, Thomas F. Sanborn, and James J. Sullivan, detached from the Niphon, and ordered to the Wando. Acting Third Assistant Engineer George W. Wakefield, detached from the Tallapoosa, and ordered to the Wando. Acting Third Assistant Engineer David Walsh, ordered to Medical Survey at New York.

Nov. 26.—Acting Third Assistant Engineer William Moran, detached from the Michigan, on the reporting of his relief, and ordered to the Grand Gulf. Acting Third Assistant Engineer Robert Reilly, detached from the Michigan, on the reporting of his relief, and ordered to the Grand Gulf.

Nov. 28.—Acting Third Assistant Engineer Thomas M. Jenks, ordered to Medical Survey at Washington, D. C. Acting Third Assistant Engineer William C. Wynn, detached from the O. M. Pettit, and ordered North.

Nov. 29.—Acting Third Assistant Engineer Wesley J. Phillips, detached from the Commodore Read, on the reporting of his relief, and ordered to the O. M. Pettit. Acting Third Assistant Engineers Thomas Campbell and G. W. Kiersted, detached from the Mobile, and waiting orders.

Appointed Acting Gunners, Boatswains, &c.

Nov. 12.—J. H. Baker, U. S. S. Nereus.
Nov. 18.—Albert Baxter, U. S. S. Pontoosuc; John Sullivan, U. S. S. Saranac.
Nov. 22.—Robert Knox, U. S. S. Mahaska.

Nov. 18.—Acting Gunner Herman Peters, detached from the Pontoosuc, and ordered to command the Picket-Boat, No. 6.

Promoted for Good Conduct, &c.

Nov. 1.—Acting Ensign John Utter, to Acting Master.
Nov. 4.—Acting Ensign Henry C. Neilds, to Acting Master.
Nov. 5.—Acting Master L. D. D. Voorhees, to Acting Volunteer Lieutenant. Acting Ensigns S. R. Luce, Ira Bursley, and David W. Carral, to Acting Masters. Acting Volunteer Lieutenant William Budd, to Acting Volunteer Lieutenant-Commander.
Nov. 7.—Acting Master L. G. Vassals, to Acting Volunteer Lieutenant. Acting Ensigns L. B. King, Joseph B. Wells, and S. B. Davis, to Acting Masters. Acting Volunteer Lieutenant Thomas P. Ives, to Acting Volunteer Lieutenant-Commander.
Nov. 8.—Acting Ensigns Charles A. Pettit and Warren Porter, to Acting Masters.
Nov. 9.—Acting Master Felix McCurley, to Acting Volunteer Lieutenant. Acting Ensigns Henry S. Lambert, F. M. Paine, and J. H. Porter, to Acting Masters.
Nov. 12.—Acting Ensign H. F. Moffat, to Acting Master.
Nov. 14.—Acting Ensign Julius F. Beyer, to Acting Master.
Nov. 19.—Acting Ensign Samuel H. Mead, to Acting Master.
Nov. 21.—Acting Master Frederick D. Stuart, to Acting Volunteer Lieutenant. Acting Ensigns Joseph McCart, Robert C. McKenzie, and Ezra L. Robbins, to Acting Masters.
Nov. 25.—Acting Volunteer Lieutenant J. B. Breck, to be Acting Volunteer Lieutenant-Commander.
Nov. 26.—Acting Volunteer Lieutenant T. B. Du Bois, to be Acting Volunteer Lieutenant-Commander.
Nov. 29.—Acting Master Henry J. Cook, to be Acting Volunteer Lieutenant.
Nov. 30.—Acting Volunteer Lieutenant W. H. West, to be Acting Volunteer Lieutenant-Commander. Acting Ensign Henry A. Green, to be Acting Master.

Resigned.

Nov. 3.—Acting Third Assistant Engineer William H. White.
Nov. 4.—Acting Assistant Paymaster George F. Barker.
Nov. 5.—Acting Master Robert Spavin; Acting Assistant Surgeon Franklin Nickerson.
Nov. 8.—Acting Ensign James S. Benjamin.
Nov. 9.—Acting Assistant Paymasters William A. Purse, Isaac G. Worden, and C. M. Dunham.
Nov. 11.—Acting Assistant Surgeon S. Chester Smith; Acting Assistant Paymaster E. K. Winship.
Nov. 12.—Acting Assistant Paymaster W. R. Sherwood; Acting Assistant Pay-

master F. W. Gardner; Acting Assistant Surgeon J. E. Warner; Acting Third Assistant Engineer Zalmon T. Williams; Acting Ensign William F. Rayuolds, Jr.

Nov. 14.—Acting Third Assistant Engineer John H. Penn; Acting Assistant Paymaster J. Henry Sellman.

Nov. 15.—Acting Master Samuel B. Gregory.

Nov. 16.—Acting Third Assistant Engineer James B. German.

Nov. 17.—Acting Third Assistant Engineer R. H. Alexander.

Nov. 18.—Acting Assistant Paymaster E. H. Brink.

Nov. 21.—Acting Assistant Surgeon Thomas J. Reed; Acting Master Henry Oakley.

Nov. 23.—Acting Master Charles H. Corsen; Acting Ensign Colin C. Starr; Acting Third Assistant Engineers W. L. McKay and John Thompson, Jr.; Acting Assistant Surgeon Charles A. Manson.

Nov. 26.—Acting Ensign Joshua Simmonds.

Nov. 28.—Acting Assistant Surgeon Francis H. Atkins; Acting Assistant Paymaster Lynford Lardner; Acting Master's Mate G. W. Barnes.

Nov. 30.—Acting Ensign Harrison Banks; Acting Third Assistant Engineer Charles E. Black.

Nov. 4.—Acting Master's Mate Joseph R. Delan.

Nov. 8.—Acting Master's Mate James Cummins.

Nov. 9.—Acting Master's Mate Wallace W. Reed.

Nov. 16.—Acting Master's Mate Robert F. Gray; Acting Master's Mate H. B. Eddy.

Revoked.

Nov. 7.—Acting Master John A. Phillips.

Nov. 8.—Acting Ensign A. W. Starbuck; Acting Third Assistant Engineer Thomas G. Farrouts; Acting Third Assistant Engineer E. H. Grover; Acting Third Assistant Engineer Daniel Gorman.

Nov. 11.—Acting Assistant Paymaster Henry Stuyvesant.

Nov. 16.—Acting Master Charles H. Saulisbury.

Nov. 17.—Acting Ensign Edward Balch.

Nov. 19.—Acting Master's Mate Albert R. Arey.

Nov. 21.—Acting Masters Courtland P. Williams and William Richardson (that they might be appointed Acting Masters and Pilots); Acting Master William H. Harrison; Acting Third Assistant Engineer F. C. Taylor.

Nov. 22.—Acting Master Oliver B. Warren.

Nov. 25.—Acting Third Assistant Engineer Charles J. Morgan.

Nov. 26.—Acting First Assistant Engineer Rodney Nichols; Acting First Assistant Engineer Jacob Tucker.

Nov. 30.—Acting Master W. B. Stoddard: Acting Gunner William Mortimer.

Nov. 7.—Acting Master's Mate John Rigg; Acting Master's Mate Charles W. Payne.

Nov. 8.—Acting Master's Mate Ezra C. Colvin.

Nov. 9.—Acting Master's Mate Warren S. Cammett.

Dismissed.

Nov. 5.—Acting Second Assistant Engineer George S. Hall (by sentence of Court-Martial). Acting Second Assistant Engineer J. W. Anderson.

Nov. 7.—Acting Ensign Andrew Stockholm.

Nov. 12.—Acting First Assistant Engineer Francis Henderson; Acting First Assistant Engineer Benjamin F. Morey; Acting Gunner William Lordau.

Nov. 15.—Acting Third Assistant Engineer George Street.

Nov. 16.—Acting First Assistant Engineer Dennison A. Lockwood.

Nov. 17.—Acting Master Newell Graham; Acting Third Assistant Engineer Edward Merritt.

Nov. 21.—Acting Ensign Charles Thomas; Acting Third Assistant Engineer John H. Hopkins.

Nov. 25.—Acting Master Franklin Hopkins, Jr.

Nov. 28.—Acting Ensign William Henderson.

Nov. 11.—Acting Master's Mate D. C. Harrington.

Nov. 18.—Acting Master's Mate, Henry Crosby.

Miscellaneous.

Nov. 12.—Acting Second Assistant Engineer James H. Plunkett, sentence of Court-Martial reducing him one grade, not approved, and he is directed to await orders. Acting Third Assistant Engineer George C. Brown, sentence of Court-Martial dismissing him, not approved, and he is relieved from arrest with a reprimand from the Department.

Nov. 15.—Acting Third Assistant Engineer William Gaul, reduced to First Class Fireman for the term of two years, and to forfeit three months' pay as First Class Fireman, by sentence of Court-Martial.

Mississippi Squadron.

Nov. 21.—Acting Volunteer Lieutenant A. R. Langthorne, detached from the Mississippi Squadron, and ordered to the North Atlantic Squadron.

Nov. 22.—Acting Ensign F. W. Grafton, detached from the Mississippi Squadron, and ordered to the North Atlantic Squadron.

Appointed Acting Master.

Nov. 7.—Thomas McElroy.

Nov. 25.—Acting Masters W. E. H. Fentress and Thomas McElroy, ordered to the Mississippi Squadron. (Returned prisoners.) Acting Ensign Simon Strunk, ordered to Mississippi Squadron. (Returned prisoner.)

Appointed Acting Ensigns.

Nov. 4.—Persifer Frazer, Jr.
Nov. 7.—W. R. Cooper and Charles C. Cushing (for special duty on Acting Rear-Admiral Lee's Staff); Zachariah T. Tibbatts.
Nov. 8.—John B. Pratt, Charles L. McClung, C. B. Plattenburg.
Nov. 10.—J. J. Irwin.
Nov. 11.—Isaac Wiltse.

Appointed Acting Master's Mates.

Nov. 4.—David B. Balthis.
Nov. 5.—C. W. Botten.
Nov. 15.—Harlan P. Bosworth.
Nov. 23.—Henry Clifton.
Nov. 25.—A. H. Ahrens.
Nov 26.—Robert W. Rogers.
Nov. 28.—E. C. Kraley.
Nov. 29.—F. B. Chase.

Appointed Acting First Assistant Engineers.

Nov. 10.—Charles F. Yeager.
Nov. 26.—Josephus Blake.

Appointed Acting Second Assistant Engineers.

Nov. 21.—William H. Collins.
Nov. 23.—John W. Street; L. S. Everson.

Appointed Acting Third Assistant Engineer.

Nov. 10.—Silas H. Lancaster.
Nov. 22.—George W. Postlethwait.

Appointed Acting Gunner.

Nov. 23.—Thomas Dunlop.

Promoted.

Nov. 8.—Acting Master Peter O'Kell, to Acting Volunteer Lieutenant.
Nov. 10.—Acting Volunteer Lieutenant William R. Hoel, to Acting Volunteer Lieutenant-Commander.

Resigned.

Nov. 7.—Acting Master's Mate J. L. Cilley.
Nov. 8.—Acting Master's Mate R. M. Hawkins; Acting Carpenter J. O. Baker.
Nov. 15.—Acting First Assistant Engineer John C. Houston.
Nov. 17.—Acting Ensigns Joseph Beauchamp and J. W. Litherbury.

Nov. 23.—Acting Master's Mate Joseph B. Morton; Acting Second Assistant Engineer Michael Norton.
Nov. 25.—Acting Master's Mate J. K. Lull, Jr.
Nov. 29.—Acting Ensign Frank D. Campbell.

Revoked.

Nov. 8.—Acting Master's Mate J. W. Wickwire.
Nov. 9.—Acting Second Assistant Engineer W. L. Tolle.

Dismissed.

Nov. 10.—Acting Second Assistant Engineer Eugene Callagher, to date from the 29th September, 1864.
Nov. 12.—Acting Master E. C. Brennan.
Nov. 15.—Acting Ensign George W. Platt.
Nov. 16.—Acting Ensign Henry S. O'Grady.
Nov. 28.—Acting Master's Mate Edward T. Lincoln.

JUSTICE TO OUR OFFICERS.

[WE give special prominence to the following communication on a most vital subject. Strong as it is, we wish the disgrace which rests upon our Government in this matter were even more emphatically characterized, so that our loyal Congressmen should redeem us at once from its stigma, by neglecting all other business until they had made some show of compensating our gallant and self-sacrificing defenders. While they live, in God's name, supply their necessities—if nothing more; and when they die, let not their wives and families be sacrificed, like the Indian widow, on the same death-pile. We shall harp upon this topic until the tardy justice is done.—ED.]

WE sincerely trust the present Congress will not adjourn without passing at least two vitally important measures of bare justice to the brave officers of our Army and Navy. First and foremost, they must have an

INCREASE OF PAY.

It is no longer a question whether they are to live like gentlemen, but whether they are to live at all. We have not now to consider how on earth the married ones shall support their families, but how the single ones are to support themselves. The public at large, ruffling their feathers pleasantly at the idea of "fat offices" and unctuous "pickings," and remembering a few quartermasters and others who have been "on the make" and "made a good thing out of it—"with what not other slang thoughts—forget that the *Army is no custom-house*. Neither is the Navy a post-office. Congress knows better. Congress knows that the pay of officers of the Army and Navy is fixed by law, and that they cannot receive one cent more than their lawful allowances, in any event whatever, except, in the Navy, for prize-money, the good fortune of a very, very few lucky ones. Setting aside this rare exception, the pay now actually received by officers in active service is as follows:

ARMY.	Per month.	NAVY.	Per year.
Lieutenant-General	$720.00	Rear-Admiral	$5,000.00
Major-General	445.00	Commodore	4,000.00
Brigadier-General	299.50	Captain	3,500.00
Colonel of Infantry	194.00	Commander	2,800.00
Lieutenant-Colonel	170.00	Lieutenant-Commander	2,343.00
Major	151.00	Lieutenant	1,875.00
Captain	118.50	Master	1,500.00
First Lieutenant	108.50	Ensign	1,200.00
Second Lieutenant	103.50	Midshipman	500.00

With the single exception of twenty dollars per month added to the pay of each, in 1857, the pay of the Army was, in 1860, substantially what it was made in 1808! And since 1860 *it has been reduced*. The forage allowance, amounting to from sixteen to fifty dollars a month, according to rank, has been cut off, and the rate of commutation for servants' pay has been reduced from thirteen to eleven dollars a month. The Navy pay has been changed since the war, to conform to that of the Army.

In the meanwhile, two things have happened:

1st. Prices of all necessaries of life have doubled, except those that have trebled.

2d. The pay of the private soldier has been increased from eight to sixteen dollars a month.

In thousands of cases privates have received bounties, varying from five hundred to twelve hundred dollars, for one year's service, thus making their compensation in money, with all expenses paid beside, equal or greater than that of a lieutenant, who has to find himself in every thing! No wonder that the enlisted men lay up money, while their officers must often go in debt to keep their backs covered.

The Government allows an officer of the Army thirty cents for each ration. He cannot draw his rations in kind. In nine cases out of ten he is obliged to buy them from the Government; and so he pays back to the Government over fifty cents for what the Government allows him thirty.

An officer is allowed for his servant the pay and allowances of a private soldier— as it is? No; as it was in 1857! He gets eleven dollars a month to pay a servant, when he cannot hire a small boy for less than fifteen dollars with stealages, or a decent man for twenty dollars; is allowed thirty cents a day for feeding his servant, who would think himself starved on double that sum; and receives two dollars and fifty cents a month to clothe him. How many suits of clothes will thirty dollars a year buy?

From all these items, making up the exact totals we have stated, the paymaster deducts five per cent. on the excess over six hundred a year, and the collector of internal revenue calls for five per cent. on the amount paid last year. That means ten per cent. on this year's pay, for last year's was spent long ago. Civilians are allowed to deduct the house-rent of themselves and families from the amount liable to tax. Officers are denied even this privilege.

Our present worthy Chief Magistrate, in one of his apt little speeches, is said to have told a delegation of "neutral Kentuckians," some two years ago, that the time had come when, as the mackerel fisherman said to his passengers, they must do one of three things: Fish, cut bait, or go ashore.

Gentlemen of the Thirty-eighth Congress, let us in like manner assure you that the time has now come when we must do one of three things: 1st. Lose valuable officers;

2d. Put gold *to par*; 3d. Increase the pay of the officers of the Army, at the very least, fifty per cent. for the lower grades, and in graduated proportion for the higher.

We speak more in detail of the Army, because the pay of that service is minced up into small fractions. But the same arguments apply equally to the case of the Navy.

We urge this as simple justice to our brave defenders. While they risk their lives for us, let us at least enable them to live decently!

If every officer who has an influential friend will set him to work; if every influential citizen who has a friend in shoulder-straps will put his shoulder to the wheel in earnest; if every editor who cares for any thing beyond party will spare a few lines of type; if every member of Congress, who knows the facts, will use his knowledge and his influence in the direction of his judgment, it will be done. But whatever is to be done, must be done quickly.

ORGANIZATION OF THE STAFF.

We gave our views on this subject so fully in our last February number, and the views therein expressed were so generally adopted by the Military Committees of the two Houses—though nothing came of it—that we have nothing to add in this place, except that we do hope another session will not be allowed to pass without the adoption of the much-needed measures recommended not only by us and by most of the commanding generals, but by universal experience.   R. B. I.

THE UNITED STATES SERVICE MAGAZINE.

VOL. III.—FEBRUARY, 1865.—NO. II.

THE VICTORY AT NASHVILLE.

BY CAPTAIN JAMES F. RUSLING, A. Q. M.

WE have glanced over most of the newspapers of the day, and have read some well written accounts of the battles here, but so far have met with none that elucidate the facts, as they actually occurred. With a view to this, and as a humble contribution to current history, in order to put fairly on record the great events that have just transpired here, we propose to give *in extenso*, but as briefly as possible, such an account of the same as to an eye-witness here—" part of which I was, and all of which I saw"—seems true and logical.

It will be remembered, that on or about the 20th day of November, Hood crossed the Tennessee, and with his whole army pushed straight for Pulaski. Our cavalry, which was then too feeble for more than observation, fell back covering our infantry, and both retired without much fighting to the vicinity of Columbia. Here, posted behind Duck River, some show of fighting was made, but only a show. Our forces were pressed so closely, that we had only time to destroy the Railroad bridge, and, hastily setting fire to the pontoon bridge, abandoned it to the enemy. Thence to Franklin, but eighteen miles from Nashville, it was a scrub race, to see which army should first cross Harpeth River. If Hood crossed first, Scho-

field was cut off, and Nashville, with its vast stores,—a most tempting prize to the starved and ragged rebels,—was likely to fall. But if Schofield crossed first, his trains were safe, and a stand at Franklin would enable Thomas at Nashville to collect well the forces already hastening to his relief. It will be recollected that Thomas was in chief command, but remaining in Nashville, because the natural brain of our movement here, while Schofield was in command of the forces in the field actually before Hood. Fortunately for the country, the race to Franklin was won by Schofield, and once across the Harpeth he gathered up all his forces and planted them like a rock in the path of the advancing enemy. His infantry was outnumbered, and his cavalry in effect nowhere; but he had nevertheless to fight Hood now, both to give Thomas needed time, and to enable his own trains to get safely off. Hood, confident of success, lost no time in attacking, and though terribly bruised, as his own official report well discloses, was nevertheless yielded possession of the battle-field, and our own forces, under cover of the night, withdrew in good order to the defences of Nashville.*
But the time thus gained by us was every thing, more precious to Thomas "than gold, yea than much fine gold." Our wagon trains, though sorely beset by Forrest, in the main had been got off safely to Nashville, and meanwhile the last of A. J. Smith's command had arrived from Missouri, and at the last moment Steedman, just in the nick of time "to save his bacon," got in from Chattanooga. In truth, he did not *save* it entirely, as a few of his last cars, loaded with troops, were attacked and captured by Forrest, almost within sight of Nashville. Hood, apparently nothing abashed by his punishment at Franklin, followed close on our heels, as we withdrew to Nashville, and the next day completed his investment of the city, from the river round to the river again. Any tolerable map will now show the situation here very clearly. At Nashville, the Cumberland makes a sharp bend North, and within the bend, on the south side of the river, lies the city. Hood at once stretched his forces across the bend, along the crests of a series of hills, some four or five miles or so from the city, his flanks covered by cavalry, and thus boldly confronted our own works, on a somewhat similar but better series of hills, nearer of course to Nashville. He thus sat down seriously before our works, cutting our communications with Johnsonville, Decatur, and Chat-

---

* Hood, in his official report, acknowledging "the loss of many gallant officers and men," amongst them enumerates Major-General Cleburne, and Brigadier-Generals Williams, Adams, Gist, Strophel, and Granberg killed, and Major-General Brown, and Brigadier-Generals Carter, Monigel, Quarles, Cockerill, and Scott, wounded; and Brigadier-General Gordon a prisoner. Thirteen General officers lost in a preliminary fight, would be a suspicious "victory" to any but a *Confederate* General.

tanooga, and immediately began to feel our lines, as if meaning to attack. Next he planted batteries on the Cumberland, and thus closed that artery for supplies to all but armored gunboats. Our only line of communication thus left open was the Louisville and Nashville Railroad, already overwhelmed with Government rolling stock, withdrawn from Nashville and below, and a slender precarious line, at best, nearly two hundred miles in length, liable to be cut by guerrillas at any moment, and which Forrest was only waiting for the Cumberland to fall, to cross and smash at his leisure. We were thus pretty thoroughly cooped up and penned in for a time, and timid people at a distance, who knew nothing about our strength or the state of our supplies here, or at Chattanooga, naturally enough grew nervous. There was, however, no real cause for alarm at any time, especially after Hood let his first forty-eight hours here slip by without assaulting. Had he attacked at once on arriving here, and massed heavily on our right, the weakest point in our line at that time, though since made one of the strongest, he might have given us some trouble—though he could scarcely have succeeded in his enterprise. In fact, our last re-enforcements, Smith and Steedman, gave Thomas such a happy preponderance of infantry and artillery, that from the hour they were both safely in, nobody here who knew much of affairs ever seriously doubted our ability to hold Nashville at all hazards, and against all contingencies. With Smith, or about that time, came also eight navy gunboats, including the iron-clad Monitor Neosho—a mere chunk of iron, absolutely invulnerable to all ordinary shot, and whose monster guns could readily upset any river batteries the enemy could bring against her. In ample time, too, citizens were impressed and sent to the fortifications, with pick and shovel. The military forces of the Quartermaster's Department, some five thousand strong, were also early under arms, and at work on the intrenchments. Two goodly lines of works, exterior and interior, were thus hastily constructed, encircling the town at a distance varying from a mile to two miles, frowning with forts and redoubts, and bristling with rifle-pits, and crowning our whole outlying hills from the Cumberland around to the Cumberland again. We were thus ready to receive Hood, our forces all thoroughly on hand, and prepared at all points to meet his attack. So long ago as December 5th or 6th, Thomas waited, but Hood did not come. He tempted him with reconnoissances, but he would not follow. He peppered him with round shot, but he would not respond. He complimented him with shell, but he would not answer. Hood evidently had the strange idea, that Thomas would either evacuate, without fighting, or would be starved into a surrender, by the destruction of his communications, and, therefore, that all *he* had to do was to make good his investment, and strike, as he was able, at the Louisville Railroad à la Sherman at Jonesboro, when aiming for Atlanta. He most singularly mistook his man. He forgot he was dealing with the Rock of Chickamauga. A novice in war might have known Thomas better. His forces all in hand, and his works well completed, with fair supplies of all kinds on hand, and abundance of most, Thomas's once anxious brow had long since cleared thoroughly up; his usually quiet eyes began now to gleam with the "fierce light" of battle; and it was soon apparent to all, who happened much at Head-Quarters, that "Old Pap George," as his soldiers persist in calling him, prudent General as he is, would very speedily be "spoiling for a fight!"

Our subsequent battle here would have been delivered now, instead of later, for General Thomas was fully ready, was confident of his troops, and knew his troops to be confident of him; but one thing more was yet needed, to make his anticipated victory doubly sure, and that was cavalry. "A horse! A horse! A kingdom for a horse!" might well have been the burden of his cry now, as of Richard the Third's, four centuries ago, as reported by Shakspeare. He had plenty of men, and tolerably good men, too, but little more than half enough horses, and the equine quadrupeds were not to be had anywhere, in the regular way, within the required time. In this juncture, the Secretary of War came to his rescue, and telegraphed Wilson, his Chief of Cavalry, to impress and seize all serviceable horses anywhere within the military division of the Mississippi, whether in Tennessee or Kentucky, and so to remount his men quickly, at all hazards, in any way. The order was rigorously carried out; a week's time or so sufficed to secure the required mounts, and finally, December 11th or 12th, Thomas at last felt himself fully prepared "to move upon" Hood's "works."

Jack Frost, however, now set in, and soon all the hills about Nashville were aglare with ice. Neither man nor beast could now keep his feet, and so Thomas for some days yet was still further compelled to "nurse his wrath to keep it warm." But now at last the hour had struck, and the time had come. On Wednesday, December 14th, there came a thaw, with evidence at sundown of a general break-up, and Thomas at once issued his orders for attack on Thursday at early dawn. His plan of battle was simple, yet well matured, and will well bear consideration. The future historian, judging it by its rich results, will pronounce it superb. As we have said, the right of his line rested on the Cumberland, covered by gunboats, and extended thence in order as follows: Sixteenth Army Corps, Brevet Major-General A. J. Smith commanding; Fourth Army Corps, Brigadier-General Wood commanding; Twenty-Third Army Corps, Major-General Schofield commanding; and a Provisional organization of white and colored troops, Major-General Steedman commanding, thus round to the Cumberland again, his left also covered by gunboats. His plan was to demonstrate boldly on the left, where the enemy was strongest, while he in reality massed every thing compactly on the right, where the enemy were actually weakest, and thus with the gunboats covering to overwhelm Hood's left, mash in his line, and roll it back on the centre, and, having thus got well upon his flank and rear, to crush his centre, too, if possible, as the result of the first day's work. This having been done, the job assigned for the second day was to smash Hood's right, and then either to envelope him with our wings, or at all events to bruise and hammer him so roundly, that he would be glad to pull up stakes and push straight for the Tennessee. In pursuance of this plan, then, A. J. Smith was ordered to advance at daylight, December 15th, his right covered by Wilson's Cavalry, the gunboats also co-operating, if necessary. Wood was ordered to leave only a heavy curtain of skirmishers in front of his works, to mass every thing else compactly on Smith's left, and thus to hold himself in readiness to support Smith's attack, at a moment's notice. Schofield received similar orders, but to mass instead on Wood's left, and to hold himself rather in reserve. Steedman, in addition to holding the extreme left, was also placed in charge of the inner line of works, with a force composed of the garrison proper of Nashville, Brigadier-General Miller commanding; a Provisional Division of white and colored troops, Brigadier-General Cruft commanding; and the *quasi* Military Organization of the Quartermaster's Department, Brevet Brigadier-General J. L. Donaldson, Chief Quartermaster, Department of the Cumberland, commanding. In accordance with his orders, before dawn Steedman on the left deployed a heavy line of skirmishers, consisting principally of excellent colored troops, and soon after daylight he pushed his line up to and across the Murfreesboro Pike. The enemy's pickets resisted stoutly, but presently fell back, and Steedman pursued, until he came plump up against a battery, planted beyond a deep rocky cut of the Chattanooga Railroad, too long for his line to flank and impossible for it to cross. Not knowing this at first, his men eagerly charged the battery, and would probably have carried it handsomely, had not the deep cut aforesaid prevented them from reaching it. As it was, they fell back with considerable loss; but their attack had been so eager and vehement, that Hood was doubtless misled to believe, that the whole army was there in force. A fatal mistake for him, as he subsequently learned to his grievous cost; for, almost immediately, Thomas opened in full blast on our right; A. J. Smith supported by Wood and covered by the Cavalry, swept forward like an avalanche on Hood's feeble left; and, almost before the enemy knew we were advancing, we were upon him, and over him, were crushing his line, storming his batteries, and flanking his positions, and in a trice, so to speak, his whole left wing was hopelessly doubled up and gone forever. This let the Cavalry loose, and now Wilson swept round and past our right like a thunderbolt. One Division, under Brigadier-General Johnson, he dispatched down the Cumberland to look after Chalmers, and a battery reported there, which was afterwards taken; with the other two, Croxton's and Hatch's, he covered Smith's right, and hung like an avenging cloud on the flank and rear of the Rebels, as they fell sullenly back on their centre.

Hood now saw his mistake of the early morning, and, from the heights about Nashville, could be distinctly seen in the distance his long lines of infantry and artillery, hurrying frantically over from his right to support his imperilled centre. His position was yet a very strong one, stretching along the wooded sides and crests of a series of high hills, covered with skilful breastworks, fringed with rifle pits and abattis, and bristling with cannon, that swept all the sides and gorges, and Hood now evidently bent all his energies to hold it to the last. A. J. Smith, though brave as a lion, was too good a General to butt his brains out against such a position, and so he halted to reconnoitre and report. As the result of his observations, Wood was brought well up on Smith's left, and Schofield, who had hitherto been chafing in reserve, was moved out, and swung round on Smith's right, while Wilson was pushed out still farther round to the right, so as to outflank and gain the rear of Hood's new position, if he found it practicable. Hood's line was now thoroughly felt, by both artillery and infantry, from point to point, and though there were some successes here and there, yet the enemy held his ground so stubbornly, that little was effected until just at nightfall, when Wood charged a battery that had been shelling his line most of the afternoon, and carried it with a rush in the handsomest style. This substantially closed the operations of the first day, and our army bivouacked on the field thus so manfully won. Sixteen pieces of artillery, and over 2,000 prisoners were the fruit of the day's work, and Thomas rode home to his head-quarters at dark, to telegraph to Washington the results of his beginning.

As he left the position he had occupied chiefly through the day, he remarked to an officer, "So far, I think we have succeeded pretty well. Unless Hood decamps to-night, to-morrow Steedman will double up his right, Wood will hold his centre, and Smith and Schofield again strike his left while the Cavalry work away at his rear." His words had almost the prescience of prophecy; for nearly this exact movement took place next day. Under cover of the night, Hood drew back his right centre and right, so as to straighten the new line he had been forced to assume, and in the morning was found in position along the Overton Hills, some two miles or so to the rear of his original line.

It will be seen that Hood had thus shortened his line, by drawing in and concentrating his forces, and had planted himself squarely across the Granny White and Franklin Pikes to cover his trains, that were already, no doubt, fast hurrying to the rear. All his strong lines of works nearer the city, upon which it was afterwards found he had bestowed a vast deal of labor and care, were thus wholly abandoned, because obviously untenable after the thorough smashing and turning of his left as on Thursday, and it was soon evident to all that his present stand was now only in desperation. Indeed everybody now felt, that Hood was in fact already well whipped, and that, if let alone, he would of his own accord, soon depart whence he came. But Thomas, sturdy old soul, had not the least idea of letting him alone. He had given "Old Pap" too much trouble, to stop yet awhile. And so, with the break of day, our skirmishers were up to, and over, and through his old works. Thence our lines swept easily and steadily forward, on the centre and left, until a thick curtain of Rebel skirmishers, and the opening of their artillery warned us to halt and consider. Hood's new position, on examination, as already indicated, proved to be one of great strength, and, as was afterwards found, had been selected and carefully fortified by him days before, in wary anticipation, doubtless, of all possible contingencies. His line on Thursday had been originally over six miles long, until his left was doubled up, or rather battered in, when it was reduced to about four. But here on Friday he occupied a line scarcely three miles in length, running along the wooded crests of closely connecting hills, and which even a better General than Hood might well have regarded with complacent satisfaction. The two keys to his position were directly on and covering the Granny White and Franklin Pikes, leading to Franklin, Columbia, Pulaski, and so down the country to the Tennessee. Both of these, it will be freely admitted, were admirably adapted for defence, as well by nature, as by the work of Hood's industrious axes and shovels, and here now the enemy grimly stood prepared to deliver a final battle, that was undoubtedly to decide for this war at least the fate of Tennessee and perhaps, also of Kentucky. If successful here, Hood could retire at his leisure, his trains intact, sweeping the country as he marched; or for that matter, if he chose, could return to the front of Nashville, and try another bout with "the chuckleheaded Thomas," as the Rebel General Cheatham is reported to have dubbed him, because of his obstinate fighting at Chickamauga. If unsuccessful, his trains were menaced, his army endangered, Tennessee in effect lost, the *morale* of his troops gone, and a rapid flight down the country, and across the Tennessee at Florence, with Thomas hacking and thundering at his heels, his only alternative. A more prudent Commander would have thought twice and hesitated long, before accepting such perilous chances. But Hood never was a prudent Commander, and Thomas now was only too glad to grapple with such an audacious blunderer. According, as indicated the night before, Thomas now at once pushed forward his left, and as Steedman advanced he found the Murfreesboro and Nolensville Pikes, as had been expected, comparatively free of the enemy. A few cavalrymen disputed his advance here and there, but their resistance was feeble, and practically amounted to nothing. As he came up to the Overton Hills, however, and stretched across to connect with Wood, the enemy opened on him with an advanced battery, and in pursuance of his previous instructions Steedman halted now and awaited orders. Wood meanwhile had come up early on the Franklin Pike, and was now engaged in briskly shelling the enemy's lines on Overton Knob, though only meaning to hold him in position there. Both he and Steedman, as yet, were acting only as foils, and they were both directed now to await the further development of movements off, on the right. There, massed on or about the Granny White Pike, and extending well to the right of it, were A. J. Smith and Schofield, with the Sixteenth and Twenty-Third Corps, with Croxton and Hatch of Wilson's Cavalry eagerly co-operating, feeling briskly but most intently all points of the enemy's position there, but unable as yet with all their assiduity to find the vulnerable point now desired.

The day thus wore on apace. Noon came, with but little valuable result, as yet. Smith and Schofield were both chafing, and eager to assault, and both felt confident of their ability to carry the opposing lines; but Thomas, as yet, refused them his consent. He was not yet fully ready; he had sent the cavalry well around to the right, to gain Hood's flank, and menace his rear, and he was still waiting to hear the result, before he launched at Hood's head these twin thunderbolts of war.*

Now, however, well on to four o'clock, P. M., news from the cavalry suddenly came, in a prolonged fire of rifles and carbines, that swept round the Rebel flank, and crept up along Hood's rear, and then the hour had struck, and the time had come. "Now tell Generals Schofield and Smith to advance," was Thomas's quiet order. Away sped his aides, spurring like the wind; but before the order could reach either Smith or Scho-

---

* The query, "*Where* was Forrest all this time?" will, doubtless, occur to the reader. The answer is, that Hood had previously scattered his cavalry, a part being sent off "on the rampage," down the Cumberland after our transports, and the balance on a wild goose chase, around Murfreesboro, where they got thoroughly drubbed, about the time Hood was being pummelled on Thursday. Thomas, it is reported, knew of Forrest's being thus away, before ordering his attack.

field, they had both already caught the meaning of the fierce fire along the Rebel flank and rear, and, without waiting to hear from their imperturbable old chief, they both at once ordered a general assault; and, simultaneously, with levelled bayonets and ringing cheers, their lines swept superbly forward, up to, and over, and around the Rebel works, while Wood and Steedman on their left, catching up the inspiration, pressed gallantly forward, and almost in a twinkling, our general movement carried all before it. For a moment, there was hot work. The whole rebel line, from end to end, was ablaze with musketry and a roar with cannon. The hills shook, the earth trembled, and the whole field was like "the sulphurous and gaping mouth of hell." But in thirty minutes or so, the conflict was mainly over, and what were left of the Rebels were in full retreat —almost pell-mell—down the Granny White and Franklin Pikes, and so away for Dixie. Some few stood their ground bravely, and fought most desperately to the last. But many abandoned their muskets, where they rested between the logs of the breastworks, and others threw muskets, knapsacks, blankets, every thing aside, that would impede their locomotion, as they fled wildly and panic-stricken, apparently, away from the battle-field. Said a captured Rebel Brigadier-General to the writer afterwards, in speaking of this charge and rout,

"Why, sir, it was the most wonderful thing I ever witnessed. I saw your men coming, and held my fire—a full brigade, too —until they were in close range, could almost see the 'whites of their eyes,' and then poured my volley right into their faces. I supposed, of course, that, when the smoke lifted, your line would be broken, and your men gone. But, it is surprising, sir, it never even staggered them. Why, they did not even come forward on the run. But, right along, as cool as fate, your line swung up the hill, and your men walked right up to, and over my works, and around my brigade, before we knew they were upon us. It was astonishing, sir, such fighting. If I must say it, it was perfectly splendid." Our reply was, "Yes, it was pretty good. Our men have learned to fight now. The first year of the war you gave us Big Bethel and Bull Run, and they were instructive lessons. But now we are paying you back, with Chattanooga and Atlanta, Nashville and Savannah."

"What," said he, very eagerly, "has Sherman got Savannah?"

"No, not yet! But he is well on the way there, and he will have it very soon. And then, for Charleston and Richmond! After that, you will 'cave in' all round, and then Maximilian might as well 'get up and git,' and Canada will have to behave herself."

"Ah," said he, apparently very sorrowfully, "I fear we shall never come together again."

"Oh yes, we shall, General," I replied. "Never you fear for that. 'Blood is thicker than water;' and when we *do* come together again, if they care to fight us, we'll whip the world in arms!"

The General laughed, took a proffered drink of whiskey and a cigar, and so we parted—*he* for the Provost-Marshal's, and *I* for my "confiscated" Nashville quarters.

Pardon this digression. As we have indicated, General Hood's whole army, once so exultant, was, now and here, thus thoroughly routed. Over five thousand prisoners, including one whole Division, one major-general, three brigadier-generals, and over two hundred commissioned officers, here threw down their arms, in addition to the killed and wounded; and the afternoon's work produced, besides, some forty pieces of artillery, many flags, and an almost innumerable quantity of small arms. The total results of both battles, as near as can be ascertained here, at this writing, foot up about as follows: nearly eight thousand prisoners, including five general officers, fifty-six pieces of cannon, one head-quarters' wagon train, many flags, and small arms, almost by the field full. If this was not a good pounding, a pretty thorough thrashing, not to say smashing, of one of Jeff. Davis's armies, we would like King Jeff. to tell us what it was. History will declare, that no other victory of this war has been more thorough and complete, not even excepting Bull Run. Hood's campaign, and not Sherman's, thus proved to be "Moscow over again!" Night alone closed the conflict, and our troops again bivouacked on the battle-field, wearied with the pursuit, and surfeited with prisoners. Had Thomas now had a fresh Division of reliable cavalry, to hurl remorselessly on Hood's shattered and fleeing columns, he would have "gobbled up" the most of his trains, and the balance of his artillery, and not five thousand Rebs would have recrossed the Tennessee, in all probability. As it was, he resumed pursuit early in the morning, and at this writing is still driving and harrying Hood, as he hurries into Dixie. It is not germain to this paper to trace his progress further, as our only object in writing at all, is merely to elucidate events that occurred just here.

In conclusion, however, we may add a word of general eulogy—not much, however, nor should we particularize; for where all did so well, and behaved so heroically, it would be invidious to select for praise, or to omit from honor, any command or anybody. Besides, none need either here. Their great and splendid achievements are now the nation's wild pride and exultant joy, and so they will remain forever. Heroes all, from Thomas to his lowest soldier, the nation will extend to each and to all its profoundest thanks, and embalm the names of their fallen comrades in its memory forever. Conquerors with Sherman at Atlanta, they are now again fit conquerors at Nashville, while yet his victorious legions are marching through Georgia, or thundering, perchance, at the gates of Savannah. In view of these great triple triumphs, for Freedom and the Union, made by the same common army, in one campaign, let the nation reverently resolve once more to "thank God, and take courage" for the future.

"In the name of our God, we have set up our banners, and through Him we shall yet do valiantly!"

NASHVILLE, TENN., December 20th, 1864.

SEEKING THE BUBBLE.

> * * * * "Then a soldier,
> Full of strange oaths, and bearded like the bard;
> Jealous in honor, sudden and quick in quarrel;
> Seeking the bubble reputation
> Even in the cannon's mouth." * * * *
> As You Like It.—Act II., Scene VII.

BEDLAM IN BLUE: A NIGHTMARE.

"Is this the adjutant's office?" I asked of a slouchy sentinel got up in a pants-in-your-boots style, who, like young Lochinvar, had obviously come out of the West. No salute to my new shoulder-straps. "Yep," gaped private L. curtly, without rising from the wagon bucket whereon he was seated nursing his musket and his right boot like twins.

"G'win, g' right in," he continued, seeing that I hesitated, and was about to go through the, to him, incomprehensible pantomime of knocking against the tent pole.

Lifting the curtain, this tableau discovered itself. Two hospital tents thrown into one. Both full of men in uniform. The front tent a confused group of statues of officers folding papers and waiting for something; seventeen of these. A short, square-built, lean, but not thin, muscular, but not stout, officer standing in the back-ground, almost against the pole that divides the two tents, reading a paper and biting his under lip slowly. Forehead drawn to a focus. Clear gray eyes, a little reddened as by over-strained nerves, intent upon the paper. Dark-brown hair, with a short half-curly warp, needs brushing a very, very little. Ditto the neatly fitting coat. The eighteenth statue is resting his hands alternately on the table that divides him from the last named figure, and talking monotonously while the gray eyes read. From the back tent a dozen clerks produce a scratching notice, occasionally broken by a low whisper, by the planing noise of the lively eraser furtively correcting a mistake, or by the *p'too* of the tobacco spitter.

Entering the tent, I too take a paper from my breast pocket

and become a statue. The flap drops heavily and shuts out the day. An awful feeling creeps over me, my brain begins to revolve slowly, the tent and all in it fade out in a whirling mist, my knees sink beneath me, and seat me on a hard bench. Whether it is the shock of meeting tangible matter thus abruptly, I know not, but the figure and all the statues come upon me again like so many locomotive lights rushing through the night mist; a shiver runs up my spine, my forehead cools suddenly, and the glamor is past. How ridiculous! Why, here I am alive and sound, seated on a hard bench in the adjutant-general's office at our department head-quarters, with my detail in my hand, waiting my turn after eighteen others. And the figure? Thought everybody knew him! Why that is Colonel Cromwell, Lieutenant-Colonel Oliver Cromwell, our assistant adjutant-general as the laws call h*i*m, our adjutant-general as we call him, our adjutant as the "Lochinvars" call him. Ha, ha!

Who laughed? oh, horror! I did! The clerks stop scratching, the gray eyes look me through, the statues focus upon me such a stare as was never before stared except in Havana by beady eyes set in lemon color. Did you ever laugh out *ha, ha!* in a high domed church just as the great organ suddenly stopped *staccato?* Then you felt as I did.

Nonsense! There are no goblins to-day. This is real; of course it is. Why there's old Major Chittick talking now; the eighteenth statue, standing up before the colonel, talking in a measured monotone, with a corn husk in his voice.

"You see, Colonel," he drones, "our ridgment when they enlisted, our boys's told 'ts gon to be a cav'ly ridgment, and they c' min, good many of 'em to my certin knowledge, 'th that un-'stannin, tho' t'wan't put down in wri*tin*. Well, fust the Guv-'nor he said he'd see 'twe get our hos*sis*, 'n we wai*tid* fust one week 'n then 'nother 'n month in 'n out till 't come time 't the ridgment was full, and still we didn't seem to git our hos*sis* somehow, though the Guv'nor alwez said they's com*in*, 'n then, le'ss see, 'pears to me 'twas about the fust or second week of Sep-tember; yes, twas the fust; no, 'twant neither; 'ts second; what am I thinkin about? 'ts eleventh o' Sep-tember for cer*tin*, there was a young officer come down, I 'xpect you know him don't you, Colonel? he's a poot' nice look'n officer, black hair, 'n smooth face; I forget his name, Aikin, Aikin—no, Paine! no, that wan't it; well, it's all one, he belonged to the artillery, rig'lar 'till'ry, mebbe you can call his name, Matthews, Abbott, Webster, Hib— no I forget it; well as I was a sayin——"

"Excuse me, major," says the gray eyed, with a look and tone keen and polished as Dr. Peacack's favorite steel instruments, "but has this young officer applied for leave?"

"Well, no," says the major, not at all jostled from his self-composed monotone, I think he's on 'cruitin service now, you'd know his name in a minute if I could remember it, Polhemus, Pol— Andrews, no I can't get it, 'ts on the tip of my tongue now, how provokin, 'tis 'stonishin' how a little thing like that will work through a man's head. Colonel, supposo you call over a few of the names of the reg'lar *ar*-tillery officers, you know 'em poot' much all of 'em I guess."

Is there any thing but bone in that skull? Cartilage, perhaps, or bone in a veal state! Surely that flash from the gray eyes would have fired any thing in the shape of nerve tissue and set it quivering like jelly in the supper room during the *galop* below.

"Major," says the Colonel with a Damascus edge on every word, "my time is not my own, or I should be only too happy to hear your little story and to look over the army register with you, or the New York Directory if you like, for that important name. Let me speak, please. You want to go home on recruiting service?"

"Well, you see, our ridgment when it enlisted"—

"Your application is disapproved. There are seven officers away from your regiment now on recruiting service, including both the Colonel and Lieutenant-Colonel. Captain Rolles, write disapproved and respectfully returned on that. We'll send it back through the regular channels."

"Häow?"

"Through the regular channels, corps, division and brigade commanders. Good morning, Major." "What is your business, sir," turning to a shabby statue in a black suit with gilt buttons turned green, cast-brass captain's shoulder straps, and a miner's black hat surrounded by a general officer's gold cord.

"Well, but Colonel," persists Major Chittick, irrepressibly, "half a minute, please, if you'd just let me explain, you see, our ridgment"—

"Can't be granted, sir."

"Our ridgment——"

"Good morning, Major."

The drone, after making a half dozen more attempts to speak, like the little revolving figures on a hand-organ, gives up the attempt to finish his autobiography then and there and disappears, slouchingly.

"Well," says Colonel Cromwell, snapping his fingers. "Your business, please? My time is not my own, remember."

The Chaplain—it is seedy Chaplain Bender, getting up some shirk or other, I'll warrant you—evidently thinks it is *his*, by the precious minutes he consumes in fumbling in his pockets. A good chance to get a fair look at the Colonel while there is no untransparent Chittick in the way and the Chaplain is fumbling for the greasy papers he will presently fish up.

Scrupulously neat, but requires a little brushing; would be

almost finikin if he had the time. Uniform strictly according to regulations. Features large but very regular. Eyes large, deep set, but not in caves; lit up so sometimes that they seem prominent. Roman nose indicating firmness; an accurate Roman, neither too large nor too broken; rare to be seen. Set mouth, large but not too large. Chin rather less than full, but decided. Head squareish, but inclined to length, and giving you the impression of a well-crystallized mind, polarizing toward decision. Cheeks a little wasted, and that parchment complexion so familiar in the visages of American public men; discolored by the smoke of the brain-fire burning away too rapidly, flaring in the wind, fanned night and day. About five feet seven in height, but standing straight as an arrow, looks half a head taller. As he stands now his left hand resting on the table before, leaning forward a little, intent, with pen just raised, he reminds you strikingly of his namesake the Protector. The name? No, it is more than the name that makes that resemblance so startling. But there is a *fineness*, almost delicacy, about this man, in strong contrast with the sturdiness of the great Oliver.

Old Tickley Bender, as they irreverently call him in our regiment, has by this time extricated the inevitable greasy paper from the recesses of somewhere, and, holding it out, doubtfully, toward the Colonel, clears his throat for the exordium.

"Hem,—could I—ah—(a pause, draws back)—I see you're busy. I—ah—won't—"

"Not at all, sir," says the Colonel. "I have just time to hear you, if you will say what you want as briefly as possible, and hand me your application, without wasting time in apologies."

The Chaplain (standing on one leg). Well—ah—I ask your pardon (waves his hand). I see you're busy. I—ah—

The Colonel (quietly). Your business, if you please.

The Chaplain (standing on the other). I can wait—

The Colonel (crisply). I cannot!

The Chaplain. Well, you—ah—see our Colonel, that is Colonel Heavysterne, thought if I—I presume you are acquainted with our Colonel—but I see you're busy—perhaps—

The Colonel. Go on, sir.

The Chaplain (very softly). But, perhaps, some of these other gentlemen—if so, I will not intrude—I can wait.

The Colonel (sotto voce). Damnation!

The Chaplain. Häow?

The Colonel (wearily, decidedly). You can either go on or stop; not both. If you go on I will attend to you, if you stop I'll attend to some one else; but I must insist on your coming to the point, without any more rigmarole.

The Chaplain (meekly). I beg pardon, sir. I'm sure I really intended no offence. I know how very busy you gentlemen are. I remember saying to our Adjutant, the other day, "Adjutant," says I, "you have very hard work. It must require pe-cu-liar gifts,"—those were my very words, Colonel, I assure you, as our Adjutant could tell you, and, doubtless, would be pleased to do were he here, as, unfortunately, he is not, being confined to his tent by a severe attack of chronic——

The Colonel (left fist, knuckles down on the table sharply; left arm rigid as iron, as in the pictures of the Protector). One word, sir, what is your business?

Chaplain. I was just about to state, sir; but I see you are busy (making as if to withdraw), I can call again——

Colonel (quickly). No, you can't! Once for all, your business.

Chaplain. I see you are—

Colonel. Yes, yes. Your business!

Chaplain reluctantly hands greasy paper to Colonel Cromwell, who runs his keen eyes over it, stroking his tawny cavalry-moustache the while.

"Can't be done," he says, presently.

"Häow?"

"Disapproved by brigade commander. Not forwarded through corps and division commanders. Necessarily disapproved. Besides, a chaplain's not a proper person to arrest deserters."

"We are not in any corps, I understand."

"You are in the 26th Corps."

"I was not aware of the fact. Could I make a few remarks? I see you're busy, but perhaps a few words."

"I shall be happy to hear from you in writing. Respectfully returned, disapproved, Mr. Rolles,—Captain Rolles will send it back through the proper channels, sir."

"Do I understand you? I think you said——"

"Corps, division, and brigade commanders."

"My wife is very ill, not expected to live, at last accounts," sighs the chaplain. "It's a very hard case, Colonel. But I see you are busy. I will not interrupt you further. When we left home, you see, gentlemen, we expected the war would be over in three months at the very outside, and I started off, as we all did, leaving the affairs of my flock in a very unsettled—Well, I see you're busy, I will call again. (Goodm——"

But Colonel Cromwell does not hear him. He has turned to a short, thick-set man, with fishy eyes and oily countenance, in a slop-shop uniform, turned greenish, who is sputtering away a terrible mixture of bad German and worse English, with a general effect quite as soothing to the attuned ear as the rumble of a Broadway stage. His accents grow more Teutonic and his gesticulations more fierce and erratic as he proceeds. The Colonel is vainly and very softly endeavoring to persuade him that the Prussian Army Regulations, though admirable in themselves, are usually expected to yield to those published at Washington, where there is any conflict between the two. Dutchy palpably thinks the service done for, if that's the case. Presently it turns out that he wants the United States to pay for his uniform. Some General Blenker has promised him that it shall be so. On the smiling announcement, by Colonel Cromwell, that officers are expected to buy their own uniforms, five other statues, all of a size and pattern with the first Teuton, jump forward, and dash headlong into the conversation. Conversation? Babel. Every man talks at once, gesticulating with his whole body, a terribly guttural mixture. Who is talking German, and who broken English? Presently there is a lull on the German ocean of gabble, and the Colonel tells the first officer to put his application in writing. Some minutes more of din arise before this novel idea soaks in; but it does so finally, and acts as a gentle anodyne, for the Teutons give the spasm-salute of their kind, bow simultaneously with great respect, and withdraw, jabbering peacefully, every man for himself, in his native tongue.

Seven statues gone. No, only six, for here is Chaplain Bender again!

"Ad-ju-tant," he drawls, sleepily, smilingly, "could I speak a word with you? I think I could explain—"

Colonel Cromwell gazes at him curiously, but speaks no word; such a glance as the Gorgons might have cast in their sternest moments. Unexpectedly up rises a brawny, long-armed officer, the same who has been twice addressed as Captain Rolles, and, without removing his cigar, jets out in a deep bass, a monosyllable—"*Leave.*"

His long forefinger punctuates the remark, "Played out. Leave!"

Mr. Bender reddens to brickness, and takes the hint. The big youth laughs a quiet laugh, his eyes undergo a temporary eclipse, and he subsides into tranquillity at his side-table.

"Captain, you shouldn't have done that," begins Colonel Cromwell, sternly, ending by resting his hand, affectionately, on the big youth's head, who looks up at him, with his great blue eyes, the look of a worshipper.

"Do you intend to keep me waiting all the morning?" says, in a loud tone of voice, the eighth statue, who has already made several attempts on the Colonel's attention.

"No, sir," replies Colonel Cromwell, simply.

"Because if you do, sir," continues the loud man, irascibly, "I want you to know, sir, that I come direct from the people, and that you are the servants of the people, not their masters, and that even by you, men dressed in a little brief authority, sir, we expect, sir, to be treated with civility, sir; yes, sir, I repeat it, with civility."

"And so," remarks the Colonel, placidly, "you always treat others with the same civility you expect, eh?"

"There is some mistake, sir," roars the loud man; "you evidently don't know who I am, sir. There is my card, sir;" producing a dirty bit of pasteboard, whereon was printed in common newspaper type, "Hon. Isaac Slushmyer, M. C., XXXVI. Dist., N. Y., Shurk's 4 Corners, Wyoga Co., N. Y."

"Weren't you in the service once?" and the gray eyes look him through, opaque though he seems.

"Yes, sir. I was, sir. While this war was prosecuted for a constitutional object, sir, I had the honor of commanding a brigade, under the beloved and chosen leader of our armies of citizen soldiers; but I cannot lend my sword, or my name to an infamous crusade for the subjugation of a noble race, and the extinction of the old constitutional landmarks."

"Tigar!" cries Captain Rolles unexpectedly, simulating that postscript to "three cheers."

"Rolles! be silent," says Colonel Cromwell; this time very sternly, but the big youth looking very sad, he smiles in spite of himself in a favorable moment.

The loud man glares venom at the big youth, who puffs back sweet innocence in return.

"I remember," says the Colonel, in a curious, deliberate, tone. "I saw your name in a General Order, I think." As if suddenly recollecting, "ah, yes! I remember perfectly."

In more than one General Order had he seen it; the quondam Brigadier-General having been thrice dismissed for swindling, drunkenness, cowardice, or some such trifles, and twice reinstated, on the ground that he was "earnest," or had "raised a brigade," or what not.

The de-starred does not seem to relish this last pointed allusion, and proceeds more moderately, "Then you are aware, sir, of the relentless persecution by which I was hunted down in consequence of my views and of the triumphant manner in which the free people of old Wyoga have vindicated my course in opposition to the imbecility, the extravagance, the crimes, of an imbecile and corrupt administration, trampling under foot——"

"I beg pardon, sir, but have you any business with me?"

"Ah, of course an office-holder must not listen to the truth about his master. I apologize. I understand your pitiful condition, sir."

Captain Rolles gets up suddenly, in a state of fist, but apparently thinks better of it, for he puts on his cap and stalks out to cool, merely glaring at the Congressman, in passing.

Cromwell's left arm is down on the table again, rigid. "Sir," he says, with a corner on every word, " if you have any business with me, mention it. If you say a single word that does not pertain to your business, I will put you out of the office. If you choose to insult me, you may do so with impunity; my hide is too thick to be hurt by your slime. But if you say a word disrespectful to my superiors or the Government, I shall put you in the guard-house and have you tied up by the thumbs till you learn that even a member of Congress can be made to behave like a decent human being."

The Congressman livid. The Colonel doesn't move a muscle or turn a hair. The ball in his cheek works a little, perhaps: that is all. Great powers! Can the man be used to such scenes and yet alive and not insane?

Presently the Congressman, cooling down to the normal temperature of the shyster, and cocking his hat defiantly on one side, after the manner of the disciples of Faro, " I want to know where the Ammerrrikin Gahrds 's camped?"

"What regiment?" asks the Colonel, as politely as any dancing-master, in tones of silver, strangely contrasting with the clear steel accent a moment ago.

"The Ammerrrikin Gahrds," but no combination of letters whereof I am master can do justice to the Fulton Market pronunciation and inflection.

"What is the number of that regiment?"

"Sixth Regiment, Cahsmapahlitan Brigade."

"State number?"

"We don't recognize any State numbers. I raised the regiment myself in the Sixth Ward, and the Governor has nothing to do with it?"

"Know the Colonel's name?"

"Terence O'Flaherty."

"Ah, yes. Second Brigade, Third Division, Twenty-sixth Corps. Orderly!" ringing a sharp spring bell, "Orderly, show this gentleman"—no emphasis on that word—"the way to the Twenty-sixth Corps."

The Congressman bows and retires up, following the Orderly. Presently a heavy fall against the tent ropes, a stolid " beg pardon," and an unmistakable volley of Five Points, excites the Colonel's bell and a sharp inquiry as to the cause of this unseemly row. Enter Captain Rolles to explain, his big lips twitching curiously, shading his eyes from the gray ones by looking at me or any one rather than at his Chief. Says the Congressman ran in to him and got spilled in the mud; not his, the big youth's, fault; apologized for it; can't be helped. Colonel Cromwell evidently suspects something wrong, but takes pattern from the Irishman's parrot and remains silent, although evidently keeping up a devil of a thinking.

One of the clerks comes in with what seems to me a couple

of reams of paper, which he says are "orders to be signed;" all on half sheets, too.

"Can I see General Bulger?" says the next statue.

"He's engaged," replies the Colonel, beginning to sign rapidly, but talking at the same time. "What is your business?"

"My name is Chickweed, Colonel Chickweed, of Chickweed's Light Horse, 68th Pennsylvania Cavalry."

"What is your business, Colonel?"

"Private."

"Ah, very well. Then suppose you see the General's private Secretary. Orderly! show this officer to Mr. Swelman."

"No, sir!" barks the Colonel of Light Horse angrily. "I will not see any of your understrappers. I will see the General or nobody, sir, by G—!"

"Or nobody? Then see me. I'm nobody!"

"Dash your impudence, sir, what the dash and dashnation do you mean?" he roars, filling the dashes after the style usual among the armies in Flanders and elsewhere.

"You'll find swearing room outside," says Colonel Cromwell quietly, signing away like a good fellow.

"I shall stay, sir, until I see General Bulger. You can't shove me to the wall, sir, with any of your West Point insolence!"

"No, your Five Point manners save you! Hadn't you better let me make you up a bed in the back office? Or perhaps you'd better send for your mess kit and a change of linen. Make yourself at home! (a pause, during which the signing continues and the Chickweed glares redly). Seriously, sir. You can't see General Bulger, because he is very much engaged and refuses to be seen except by the Corps Commanders. But I shall be very happy to attend to your business, if you will only tell me what it is."

A pause, during which several clerks enter and whisper several questions which Colonel Cromwell answers off-hand, never ceasing the work of signing, "O. Cromwell," "O. Cromwell," as fast as can be. The Chickweed smooths his feathers a little, and consents to ask, gulping his wrath,

"What has been done with my resignation?"

"Hasn't come."

Then ensues another spat, Chickweed hotly insisting that his resignation came in weeks ago and has been lost; Cromwell mildly, monotonously, asserting that it never came. Enter an orderly with a huge pile of yellow envelopes. Huge? It melts away rapidly enough under Colonel Cromwell's eyes. See him read the letters and assort them into half a dozen smaller piles, as fast as big Captain Rolles, with his fingers and thumbs, can open them. Yes, and during the process, see how he skilfully picks out three or four of the statues and sends them off rejoicing; the sutler who wants a pass to bring in a couple of dozen pipes of whiskey for an officer's mess, as he says; Chaplain Bledsoe who wants to go on the next flag of truce or some one of the many errands of comfort that his brother Chaplain Bender is pleased to shirk; the two privates, cripples at that, whom a stupid Provost-Marshal somewhere has sent fifteen hundred miles out of their way, because their regiments were in this army months ago, and he cannot bother himself to keep the run of changes; many such statues he singles out, calls up by a look of the gray eyes, brings to the point at once, and satisfies with a word. No hesitation, no doubt, not a hitch; and all the time he goes on reading and sorting the letters as exactly and regularly as a steam engine.

"Look at that," he says quietly, tossing one of the letters to Colonel Chickweed; "that's the paper you insisted came in weeks ago and was lost here."

"Well, I declare—"

"What's the date? Twelfth. *Yesterday*. Now, Colonel, let me ask you, as a favor, to remember this. You've been often in my office, have always made trouble in the same way, and it has always turned out the same way. If you will return to your camp, your resignation will be accepted, and the order sent to you this evening, or early to-morrow morning, through the proper channels."

"How?"

Then the same story over again. Nobody cares to remember what the proper channels are. Every one thinks himself an exception to the regulations. A gorgeous orderly, obviously of Teutonic extraction, interrupts the present explanation, by entering grandly, saluting majestically, and exclaiming in a wonderful dialect: "De Dchjene*ral* sendiss gomblmends, and vish to see de Atchi*dant*-Dchjene*ral*." Another majestic salute, right about face, and exit.

More statues come in with more papers, and confront him importunately as he moves rapidly off, disregarding them and the old statues too, who put up mad appeals for just a second. But he can't spare a second. General Bulger has sent for him.

And I am left alone with a tent full of clerks and personal applicants. Heavens! If they should know I am detailed to assist Colonel Cromwell, and forthwith set upon me! Can they read my detail through the yellow envelope? Have they heard it? Do they guess it? I perspire. What *shall* I do? Take a place as night editor on a New York daily paper? Apprentice myself in a rolling-mill,—a whirring, clanking, pounding, thundering, red-hot rolling-mill? File saws? Listen to a concert of hand-organs? Enlist in a German regiment? Run for Congress? Walk slowly down Broadway? Go to sea in a Vanderbilt steamer? Any thing rather than this horrible office! Where there is opening letters and signing papers, correcting clerks' mistakes, answering questions, being browbeaten, being insulted, being sent for by generals, and harassed by a thousand demons, who jump on your chest and twist crochet needles into your finest nerves—never, never, never coming to the point; from morning till night, "a chivying and a chivying" endlessly. Horror! I am found out! They rush at me! Help, help! Wildly I dart out into the cold air; unheeding my detail; unheeding the sentinel; unheeding Major Chittick talking amicably to the sentinel about "our ridgment;" unheeding any thing save escape from my pursuers. Flying before them like the wind, I stumble over a pile of papers and fall down, down, down, down, down a precipice of special orders into a lake of ink below, bristling with steel pens and peopled,—merciful Heaven!—peopled with finny personal applicants—eels, eels. They are round my neck. I'm choking! Help! Help! Gog, gog, gl——

What's the matter?

"Time to take your beef-tea, dear." And there is my own sweet little wife standing by the bedside with a cup of that essence of life ready for my lips, daintily adding the teaspoonful of sherry the doctor likes to prescribe. I stretch forth my right arm to take it. I forgot—I haven't any. How funny not to have any right arm.

"His fever is broken," says the dear old doctor, creaking up softly from behind the bed.

So it was all the fever, after all. All a nightmare. Thank Heaven!

A WORD FOR THE QUARTERMASTER'S DEPARTMENT.

II.

WITH this hasty *résumé* of operations in the East, let us now turn to operations in the West. As Richmond was the objective point in the East, so Vicksburg and Chattanooga were the objective points in the West. The one was vital, as controlling the commerce of the Mississippi; the other highly important, as the centre and heart, so to speak, of a great system of railroads. The natural bases of course were St. Louis and Louisville, or rather Cincinnati, as Louisville, in the beginning, was in so-called neutral but practically hostile territory. Operations began first at St. Louis, and there for a time all interest centred. The young and buxom Northwest felt that the Mississippi of right belonged to her; that it had been so intended by the Creator from the beginning, as her natural outlet to the ocean; and that, moreover, it had been fairly bought and paid for out of the National Treasury, to come with her as her special dowry when she gave her hand to the Union. She, therefore, felt in honor bound to reopen this pathway to the Gulf, and at the first call of the President for troops, her hardy sons sprang eagerly to arms. They rapidly assembled at St. Louis and Cairo, armed and equipped with but little more than their fowling-pieces, and their home-spun, but with a fierce determination burning in their hearts to clear the Mississippi of all obstructions, at whatever hazard and whatever cost. General Frémont was early assigned to the command, in the hope that his name would serve as a talisman to gather about him many that would otherwise be reluctant to quit their homes, and the event no doubt answered the expectation. For a time he was entirely successful, and the comprehensive policy and plans he inaugurated, most of which have since been adopted and carried out by his successors, though "modified" at the time for reasons of State, will insure him full justice in the future, however much he may suffer now at the hands of his contemporaries. Of his subsequent removal, and of the causes that led thereto, it is not pertinent to this paper to speak. How far the failure of his Quartermaster's Department contributed to his troubles is fairly a matter of consideration, though we do not propose here to discuss the right or wrong of General McKinstry's trial and dismissal. McKinstry's successor at St. Louis was an old and experienced officer of the Quartermaster's Department, and a man of signal abilities in a variety of ways. With characteristic pluck and energy he went rapidly to work, and dismal as was the out-look at first, he soon succeeded in concentrating in the hands of the Government the whole available resources of the West. Its clothing, camp, and garrison equipage came mainly from the East; but subsistence and forage lay all around on the fruitful prairies, and all the Government had to do was to reach forth its hands and grasp them. So, also, the bulk of its animals, and means of transportation generally, were close at hand. With these resources, the Quartermaster's Department faithfully followed up and supplied the troops in the minor movements in Missouri, during the fall of 1861, and subsequently in the spring of '62, when Halleck decided to send Grant against Forts Henry and Donelson, it placed the whole commercial marine of the Ohio and upper Mississippi at his disposal. The Tennessee and the Cumberland very speedily were covered with steamers and barges, conveying troops, animals, and supplies of all descriptions, and wherever Grant and his lieutenants found it necessary to move, the Quartermaster's Department promptly appeared, close upon their heels. Nashville was soon occupied by Buell, and then came the movement down the Cumberland and up the Tennessee to Pittsburg Landing. Meanwhile our forces were slowly but surely descending the Mississippi, and with the spring of

'63, began the siege of Vicksburg. The enemy had here undoubtedly a strong hand, and with characteristic recklessness staked his all on the turning of the cards; but the audacious strategy of Grant, in making the detour by Grand Gulf, and so to the rear of Vicksburg—unequalled save by Napoleon's passage of the Splugen—disconcerted all his arrangements, and in the end gave into our hands his boasted and the now world-renowned Gibraltar of the West. To the vast operations of the Quartermaster's Department here, we have space merely to allude. It will be remembered, that the rebels had concentrated at Vicksburg the resources of the Southwest, and besides had drawn from Bragg all that could be spared without leaving him wholly at the mercy of Rosecrans. A lieutenant-general commanded the stronghold, so important was it considered, and a movable column under Joe Johnston, a very prudent and able general as time has since disclosed, was left free to operate in the rear according to circumstances. To complete the situation, Jeff Davis himself made a pilgrimage from Richmond to address and encourage the garrison, and when the drama at last began fairly to develop, the eyes of all Rebeldom and its sympathizers everywhere were fixed intently upon its scenes. To oppose these, and to conduct vigorously the required siege, Grant weakened all other points, as far as they would bear it, and concentrated every thing at Vicksburg as the one strong point, vital for us to win if we lost all others, because sure to involve the rest when itself should fall. His total force at Vicksburg and about there must certainly have averaged throughout nearly, if not quite, one hundred thousand men, with their usual complement of animals, wagons, equipments, etc., besides the additional *impedimenta* of intrenching-tools and siege-trains. The immense work thus entailed upon the Quartermaster's Department—to embark and disembark an army almost at will, to keep its own supplies well up, and see that the supplies furnished by other departments came promptly forward, and to bring all of every kind, clothing, subsistence, forage, ammunition, etc., a thousand miles down a long and dangerous river, proverbially beset with snags and sawyers, currents and quicksands, the reader may possibly imagine, but we surely shall not attempt to describe. The sagacious forethought, and the capacious plan, as well as patient attention to detail, and iron nerve that the job required, were well found in the Chief Quartermaster at St. Louis, and for months the Mississippi, from Cairo to Vicksburg, literally swarmed with crafts of all descriptions. Of course Vicksburg fell, for Grant was before it, inexorable as fate, backed by a Quartermaster that knew "no such word as *fail*," and with its fall our flag floated undisputed on the Mississippi from its sources to the Gulf.

Meanwhile, Rosecrans had fought at Murfreesboro, and now

after long, and, to some, unaccountable delay, was moving on Tullahoma and Stevenson. From Stevenson he set out to flank Chattanooga, but was brought to bay at Chickamauga by Bragg's superior numbers, and was forced back on Chattanooga with the loss of prestige, though not of honor, thanks to that sturdy soldier, George H. Thomas. It was not the first time we had reached the Hawk's-Nest, though it was the *first* that we had occupied it. Buell a year before had threatened it from Huntsville and Stevenson, and a portion of his column had even appeared before it across the Tennessee. But Bragg's bold march north, not surpassed in daring by any thing in this war, compelled him to retrace his steps to the Ohio, and the ground thus lost was now again but barely recovered. Flushed with his success at Chickamauga, the enemy followed close upon our heels as we withdrew to Chattanooga, and when it was found that we had decided to hold the town, accepting the risks, Bragg deliberately hemmed it in on all sides, save the river to the rear of it, and evidently calculated with confidence on its surrender in the end. The situation was certainly critical, one full of hazard to the army, and not without cause for dismay to the country. A better man than either Rosecrans or Grant might well have quailed before its gloom. The troops, broken in spirit, barefoot, ragged, and soon on half rations, cowered in their meagre intrenchments, while an exultant and insolent foe, nearly if not twice their numbers, taunted them daily with their weakness from the surrounding eminences, from which our slightest movements were at all times to be seen. The river to Bridgeport was sealed against supplies that way by rebel batteries and sharpshooters, bristling on its bluffs or lining its banks. The surrounding country, never very prolific, had already been stripped bare by the retreat of one army and the advance of another. The fall weather was fast setting in with unwonted severity, and yet the only line of supplies for full fifty thousand men, and say thirty thousand animals, was by that terrible wagon-road over Waldron Ridge or by Raccoon Mountain—and so sixty-five miles away to Stevenson, of itself certain destruction to the transportation of the army and liable at any hour to be interrupted by a foray of rebel cavalry. Nay, even at Stevenson itself, whence the railroad ran to Nashville, and so to the Ohio, there was a wretched deficiency of supplies of all kinds, the average run of cars daily, even so late as November 1st, being less than half the number actually required to supply the army. The country has not yet forgotten, nor will it ever forget, the sad accounts we then had, of how at Chattanooga, brave men lived on a cracker a day, gleaning the refuse of the camps for something additional, and how horses and mules, in the wretchedness of their hunger, gnawed trees, rails, boards, wagons, harness, any thing they could find, until they fell dead in their tracks by thousands from pure starvation. When the entire situation is thus taken in, with winter soon approaching; when the only line for supplies still open would cease to be practicable for any thing but pack-trains; a ragged and hungry, not to say starving army on hand, with no prospect of improvement in the future, but rather of even worse —we may well believe, as was reported at the time, that even brave spirits then at Chattanooga contemplated capitulation as among the ultimate possibilities, and evacuation and disastrous retreat to Nashville as among the immediate necessities of the hour. Whatever failures or shortcomings the Government may have been guilty of elsewhere in this war (and it must needs have been guilty of some, because a human government), let the nation not fail to remember that in this great crisis of affairs, so big with the destinies of us all, it acted with the utmost and most commendable promptness and energy. Nay, the people at Washington, from the President down, could not have done more than they did to strengthen and support and encourage, in every proper way, the then struggling army of the Cumberland. They seized the gallant Hooker, and hurried him West, with two corps from the Army of the Potomac, to open and protect new lines of supplies. They dispatched the Quartermaster-General direct to Chattanooga, with plenary powers to reform and reorganize, and do generally about as he pleased, provided he supplied the army. They summoned the hero of Vicksburg, though scarcely yet recovered from a fit of sickness so as to sit his saddle, and authorized him to assume charge of everybody and every thing West of the Alleghanies down to the Gulf, with the one sole charge to hold stoutly on to Chattanooga to the last, as with the unyielding grip of death, no matter what the hazard or what the cost. Then the Secretary of War himself left Washington and repaired to Louisville, and told Grant in person to go ahead as he pleased, and he would sustain him, provided he "filled the bill." Our Lieutenant-General, then, however, only Major-General, did go ahead, as directed, and with characteristic energy and earnestness. Forthwith he telegraphed to Thomas (Rosecrans was already relieved), "Hold on to Chattanooga at all hazards! You must not evacuate! Will be with you myself in three days, or as soon as I can get there." This meant work, and Thomas's answer, bull-dog and plucky all through, must have secured him a warm place in Grant's heart forever after. "Have no fears. Will hold the town till we starve!" Next, Burnside was directed to hold Knoxville, at whatever risk, demonstrating toward Chattanooga as he was able, and Sherman was ordered up from Memphis, to march overland to Bridgeport with all haste.

These preliminaries once settled, the next thing was to find an officer to take chief charge at Nashville, the primary base, to accumulate supplies there as rapidly as possible by rail and river, from the North; to reform and repair (and reconstruct from Stevenson) the Nashville and Chattanooga Railroad; to open up new lines of supplies both to the front and rear, and to address himself generally to the work of relieving the army already at Chattanooga, as well as to provide for the additional force now hastening to concentrate in that important region. Fortunately, the Quartermaster-General was not without the man. He was already on hand at Baltimore, in charge of the Middle Department, and Meigs summoned him by telegraph from the West to repair to Nashville and assume chief charge there, as Senior and Supervising Quartermaster of the Department of the Cumberland. As we have already intimated, there was evidently a heavy job of work on hand, and it remained to be seen whether the new comer was equal to the occasion. A vast department, its ramifications extending through a great army, and over hundreds of miles of territory, was to be reformed and reorganized. Railroads were to be reopened and re-equipped. The Cumberland and the Tennessee were to be navigated and patrolled. Animals, *matériel*, and supplies of all kinds, not only for present use at Chattanooga and Knoxville, but in anticipation of the great spring campaign on Atlanta, should Chattanooga be held, were to be accumulated and stored. It were idle to expect all this of one man. The brain of a Carnot even would have sunk beneath the task. The problem was simply too vast and grand for any single intellect to grasp and solve. Meigs was clear-headed enough soon to see this, and it was not long before he relieved the officer at Nashville of the immediate care of the troops at the front, and assigned another to take charge there as Chief Quartermaster of the army in the field. These were both old officers of the Quartermaster's Department, quiet in manner, but of distinguished ability, not afraid of hard work, and plenty of it, and they both buckled to the work of educing order out of chaos with a grim earnestness that promised well for the future. About the same time Meigs ordered General Allen from St. Louis to Louisville, and Colonel Swords, then at Louisville, to Cincinnati. With Swords thus at Cincinnati, Allen at Louisville, controlling also St. Louis and Cairo; Donaldson at Nashville, supervising also all beyond, and Easton well hold of the army—a regular quartermaster's four-horse team—the Quartermaster-General no doubt at last felt sure of his work, if any team of officers could do it. At all events he had selected the best men to be had, and all were soon working in thorough harmony, with a common system, for the same great end. The good results, of course, were not long in showing themselves. Supplies soon commenced to pour rapidly and steadily in and forward, and January had not set fairly in before the army was up again to full rations, and thus the question was settled as to whether the army could be sustained at Chattanooga, provided it could hold its own against the enemy. The defeat of Bragg at Lookout Mountain, and his subsequent overthrow on Missionary Ridge—perhaps the most disastrous defeat of the war—settled the problem at Chattanooga in all its aspects, and from that time on, the only remaining question was, as to whether the Quartermaster's Department would be equal to the requirements of the great proposed campaign of the spring against Atlanta. As to this the Quartermaster-General himself at first, so at least it was reported before the campaign opened, was not without his fears; but his own work West at least was done, and so he returned to Washington, assured that the officers he had installed would accomplish all possible things and attempt even the seemingly impossible, if they were at all achievable.* Now began the great work of the winter of 1864. The railroad was opened from Chattanooga to Knoxville and beyond, one hundred and ten miles. The Memphis and Charleston Road from Stevenson, through Huntsville, to Decatur, eighty-four miles, and the Tennessee and Alabama, from Decatur to Nashville, one hundred and twenty-two miles, were reconstructed—thus giving a double line from the front to the rear. Then came the completion of the Nashville and Northwestern Railroad, from Nashville seventy-eight miles, to the Tennessee River at Reynoldsburg or Johnsonville—and the Edgefield and Kentucky Railroad, from Nashville sixty-five miles, to the Cumberland River at Clarksville. These two last were to reach navigable waters, in even the dry season, when the Cumberland at Nashville was impracticable for boats, and together with the Louisville and Nashville Road, it was thought, as it subsequently proved, would be sufficient to keep up supplies pretty well for the summer, even when no other lines for supplies were practicable. Meanwhile the Chief Quartermaster at Louisville, with omnivorous hands, ransacked the Northwest, and all winter long, while the high water lasted, a perfect stream of transports, loaded with material and supplies of all descriptions, came pouring down the Ohio and the Mississippi, and thronging up the Cumberland to Nashville. Nashville became a great *entrepôt*, a vast granary and storehouse, filled to repletion in all its parts, and even then, though a hundred cars per day went regularly to the front, and storehouses were built everywhere by the acre, great quantities of army stores were piled up almost mountain high out of doors, or with only such poor pro-

---

* General Sherman, in his official report, in speaking of his supplies, says, "I know that more solicitude was felt by the Lieutenant-General commanding, and by the military world at large, on this, than on any other one problem involved in the success of the campaign."

tection from the weather as paulins or wagon-covers could give them. When the spring rise was over, Louisville reported that the Northwest was empty; that all its available resources had been placed at Nashville; and that if General Sherman had not now enough there, he could at least get no more until the new crops were grown and harvested. Nashville reported abundance to commence on, and sufficient to last, as was thought, if matters progressed well. So at least thought Sherman, when in May he started from Nashville to open the campaign from Chattanooga, though he was resolved to march any how when Grant crossed the Rapidan. "Sir," said he to the Quartermaster at Nashville, just before leaving for the front, at least it is so reported of him, "I shall move from Chattanooga when the Lieutenant-General orders me; ready or not ready. And if you don't have my army supplied, and keep it supplied, we'll eat your mules up, sir! eat your mules up!" And William Tecumseh no doubt thoroughly meant it. For that's the style of the great Chieftain of the West. Nevertheless his army, huge as it was, though composed of the three great armies of the Ohio, the Cumberland, and the Tennessee, all consolidated into one, did *not* have to eat mules. On the contrary, from the hour he left Chattanooga, until our flag floated in triumph over the battlements of Atlanta, neither his men nor his animals, multitudinous as they were, ever wanted an hour for any thing of the great essentials. Clothing, subsistence, medicines, forage, ammunition, all were pushed rapidly and steadily forward, to meet the troops as they required them, whether at Dalton or Marietta, the Etowah or the Chattahoochie, and the concurrent testimony of the army, as repeatedly telegraphed to the Secretary at the time by Sherman himself, was, "No army was ever better supplied, all things considered, since war began."* Burned bridges were rebuilt, and the railroad reconstructed behind him as he advanced, and the work was continually prosecuted, with such marvellous energy, that the troops were hardly ever in camp, for the night, before in the distance could be heard the welcome whistle of the coming locomotive.† Of course a large portion of the work here spoken of was performed by officers of the Railroad Department; and to Colonel D. C. McCallum, General Manager United States Military Railroads, great praise is especially due;

---

* Says Sherman in his official report:—" From that day to this (May 1st to September 15th), stores have been brought forward in wonderful abundance, with a surplus that has enabled me to feed the army well, during the whole period of time, although the enemy has succeeded more than once in breaking our road for many miles at different points."

† Says General Sherman in his official report, not published until after the above was written, "Bridges have been built with surprising rapidity, and the locomotive whistle was heard in our advanced camps almost before the echo of the skirmish-fire had ceased."

but then, it will be remembered, that the Railroad Department is only a branch of the Quartermaster's Department, merely one of its many auxiliaries, because all railroad men are hired materials provided, and expenses paid by the Quartermaster's Department.

When it is remembered that Sherman, according to his official report, already widely published, moved out from Chattanooga in May last with just less than a hundred thousand (100,000) effective men and a hundred guns, which means by the usual computation, say one hundred and fifty thousand souls and sixty thousand animals to provide for; that he was then one hundred and fifty-one miles from Nashville, his primary base, and fully two hundred more from his true bases at Louisville and St. Louis; that he afterwards steadily advanced, without a single retreat, one hundred and thirty-eight miles more, through a hostile country, fighting his way across the Etowah and the Chattahoochie, up and into his objective point Atlanta; that throughout this whole period, over a single slender line of railroad, amounting in all to just less than three hundred miles, his enormous supplies yet reached him regularly, day by day, right along; we say when all these things are considered, with their necessary adjuncts, we then may form some slight estimate of the vast and prodigious work performed by the Quartermaster's Department at Nashville and beyond, during the great campaign of Sherman so gloriously closed by the capture of Atlanta. To itemize just a little: November 1st, 1863, the Quartermaster's Department employed at Nashville about five thousand men all told, of all classes of operatives; September 1st, 1864, it was working a force of over fifteen thousand, and then reported itself short. November 1st, 1863, it found some four thousand men at work upon United States military roads; September 1st, 1864, it had over ten thousand. November 1st, 1863, it found one hundred and twenty-three miles of railroad in feeble operation, averaging only forty cars per day, for even that distance; September 1st, 1864, it had nine hundred and fifty-six miles in full blast, averaging one hundred and fifty cars per day to all points where stores were needed, whether at Huntsville or Chattanooga, Knoxville or Atlanta. During the same period it transported by railroad troops and freight to the front and rear, whose figures run up into the hundreds of thousands, and the figures as to animals, forage, subsistence, clothing, &c., would be quite bewildering, had we space or were it proper to recount them here. Of course, in accomplishing these prodigious results, the Quartermaster at Nashville owed much to his brother officers at Louisville, Cincinnati, and in charge of the armies in the field, as well as his own immediate subordinate officers, for their earnest and faithful co-operation. Without their cordial and magnificent backing, no-doubt he would have failed, or at the best have succeeded but indifferently. Nevertheless, the chief responsibility and immediate work fell mainly on his shoulders; and to him, therefore, for high qualities, both of organization and administration, history will award the lasting honors. Had he not "filled the bill," Sherman would have had his head off in a whistle. As it was, he was forthwith brevetted Brigadier-General U. S. A., "for meritorious and distinguished services in the campaign terminating with the capture of Atlanta." This, though tardy justice, was yet eminently right and fitting in all respects, and the country and the Army alike will rejoice at such full recognition, at last, of so faithful and able a public servant. As the first great step toward recognizing the worth and dignity of bureau work as well as of mere field services, as a public writer we say sincerely, hail! and on the part of the Quartermaster's Department especially, present to the Government our unfeigned thanks. Now that the precedent is thus fairly set, let the War Office go ahead and reward other proper bureau officers in the same way, according as they deserve, and it will have achieved the lasting gratitude of the Army and the country. For why should not brains have its just and fitting reward as well as mere bravery? Both are alike essential to the success of our armies, and the one is always divine and rarest, while the other is often merely—so to speak—a bull-dog quality, mostly common to all Americans, whether officer or private.

We would not close this article without calling attention to the brevet brigadiership conferred also on the Chief Quartermaster of General Sherman's army in the field. He, too, has won his "stars" fairly, and we doubt not, will wear them well and worthily. To him and the Chief Quartermaster at Nashville above all others, belongs the credit of having sustained by railroad, at an enormous distance from its base, for the first time in history, one of the largest armies of modern times. The feat thus accomplished is unprecedented in the history of warfare, and has put at fault all the calculations of modern logistics. Meade, in the East, halts at Culpeper, not seventy-five miles from his base at Alexandria and Washington, the resources of his railroad quite exhausted. Sherman, in the West, moves and fights as he wills at Atlanta, full five hundred miles from Louisville and St. Louis.

We have thus sketched, very imperfectly, we know, some of the operations of the Quartermaster's Department as connected with the chief operations of the war. As will be noticed, we have grouped our remarks, apart from what pertains *ex necessitate* to the Quartermaster-General, around six (6) officers chiefly, because those officers, of all other quartermasters in this war, and the armies they have been connected with, stand out to-day most prominently before the country. In doing this, we must not be understood as reflecting upon other quartermasters or other movements, or as detracting in the least from their respective merits. On the contrary, we have several others in our mind now, as we write, who are indeed of very great and eminent ability. But in a paper like this, meant for a mere sketch, it is only possible to speak of what seems greatest and most conspicuous. The various expeditions along the Southern coast and to the Gulf, the side campaigns in West Virginia, Missouri, Kansas, and Arkansas, and the recent brilliant operations of Sheridan in the Valley of the Shenandoah, all of which involved heavy labor and responsibility on the part of various quartermasters, we must pass over entirely, as our paper has already swelled beyond the dimensions of one magazine article into two. Other matters, however, relating to real defects in the Quartermaster's Department, and some needed reforms, and especially the new organization at dépôts of quartermaster's employés into a military force, and a better reorganization of the department generally, we must not wholly omit, though they must all be reserved for a subsequent paper. We feel that our task is here wholly completed, if we have indicated somewhat the prodigious work, and consequent real, not to say rare, ability required of the Quartermaster's Department, and so led the reader to a better and kinder appreciation of its much abused officers.

ANA OF THE WAR.

PICKINGS AND PICKETINGS.

II.

In the early days of the war, the rebels had not learned the art of civilized warfare. At that time, to leave barrels of poisoned whiskey and torpedoes in places which were to be surrendered or evacuated was considered a master-stroke of ingenuity by officers high in command, and to kill prisoners in a cruel and unusual manner was far commoner even than now —as, for instance, when, after Ball's Bluff, Federal prisoners were tied neck to neck and rolled over a precipice in the very wantonness of wickedness. On the breaking out of the war in 1861, the December number of Debow's Review—the leading magazine of the South—contained an article by George Fitzhugh, which was warmly endorsed by the Southern press, as setting forth the social, military, and political programme of the Confederate States Army, and in which the writer advocated the shooting of pickets and the murder of the enemy in every manner, whether recognized by the ordinary code of war or not. This he claimed would be perfectly fair in the South, though not in the North, owing to disparity of numbers and the superior strength of the Federal Government. It ran thus:

> "As a matter of necessity, we would encourage the shooting of pickets. We of the South are accustomed to the use of arms, are individually brave and self-reliant, can creep upon their pickets *and shoot them in the night*, and thus carry out in detail our defensive policy of exhausting in detail the superior numbers of the invading North. . . . In a new country like ours, where pickets can be approached furtively, and where all the country-people are first-rate marksmen, there is no better means of harassing and exhausting an invading army *than by cutting off its outposts in detail.*"

In accordance with this programme, the murder of Federal pickets was, in the beginning of the war, extensively undertaken by the "Secesh," and not generally discontinued until the latter discovered, to their great amazement, that they themselves lost by it quite as many as the enemy, it being "a game at which two could play." An amusing anecdote records the fact that one morning a Federal and Southern soldier fired at each other in the following fashion:

> "The Northern man, stepping boldly out from cover and exposing his entire person, folded his arms, and coolly called upon the astonished rebel to fire and be sure of his aim. This invitation puzzled him, and he hesitated at first, probably being afraid of some Yankee trick in which he would be outwitted; but at last diminishing his fears, he levelled his piece and fired. *Vit* went the minnie over the Yankee's head.
>
> "Stand up now and give me a show," said the live target, stretching his arm out and grasping his rifle. The rebel doubtingly placed himself in position, and away sped the bullet, striking—the edge of the rebel's coat sleeve and burying itself in a tree in the rear.
>
> "Both parties were puzzled, and remained silent a few moments; but the Yankee was much chagrined, and proposed another trial. The rebel assented, and the second trial was as bloodless as the first. So was the third, fourth, and fifth. At the last discharge, the Yankee's wonder knew no bounds when he discovered the result, and he immediately yelled out: "*Damn it! WE CAN'T SHOOT!*" "I believe you," was the reply, and they approached each other, laughing heartily at the ludicrous turn their duel had taken, and protesting that they had made good shots before, if they didn't just then. After a merry chat of a few minutes, they bade each other good-bye, hoping to meet again after the war should be over, and returned to tell their comrades of their adventure, which both agreed was too good to keep."

"One day," said a correspondent from the Army of the Southwest, "the Federal pickets hailed their adversaries with, 'Let's stop firing and have a talk.' 'Agreed,' said 'Secesh;' so they held a conversation of about five minutes, something after this style:

> "*Federal:* 'Why do you want to break up the Government?'
> "*Secesh:* 'Because you Yankees want to destroy our institutions, and put niggers on a level with white men.'
> "*Federal:* 'We aint Yankees—we're Western men, and don't want to injure you or your institutions, but to protect all loyal citizens in all their legal rights.'
> "*Secesh*: 'Well—this is a d——d bad war, anyhow. Good-bye!'
> "*Another Secesh:* 'Hallo—don't shoot yet! I'll sing Dixie, and Bob will dance.'
> "*Federal:* 'Well—go ahead!'
> "(Secesh mounts the fence and sings. Bob comes out of the bush into plain

sight, and dances himself into a state of frantic excitement. Federal cries '*Time!*' when Bob and his friend rush into their hiding-places—'*All right!*—go ahead!'—and the firing begins again.)"

The following picket anecdote was narrated by an officer of the regular United States cavalry to a friend of the writer. The narrator was near the spot at the time and knew the deserter—a fact which I mention since it has already appeared in print, but in a form not so true to life. One morning when our army was wasting in vain in the Chickahominy swamps, some of our "picketers," while getting up a bit of breakfast by the road-side, were startled with—

"How are yees, *by's?*"

The *Feds* looked—and lo, over the bushes was staring with what was meant to be a peculiarly conciliating grin, one of the most grotesque of Irish faces, appended to one of the worst clad of Irish bodies.

"And what are yees afther doing, gintlemin?" he inquired.

"Making coffee. Have some?" was the laconic answer.

"Yees won't be afther shootin' or captivatin' me?" was the cautious answer.

"Devil a bit of it. Come down!"

"By me sowl—and its very temptin' ye are—and its iligant manners that ye've got intirely—an' its mesilf that likes the company of gintlemin as can affoord to have their bite and sup of the *caw-fy*, ivery day. Sure an' its beautiful that yees make it. A cup is nothing when it's so good."

"Well, take another."

"An' I just will. Sure and that's splindid *caw-fy*. The ribbles—bad cess to them!" (sinking his voice to a confidential whisper) " don't give us the divil av a tasthe av the stuff."

"Well—take another cup!"

"Yees won't call it bad manners av I do—sure an ye're so pilite. Sure ye seem to be comfortable intirely,—and ye have iligant clothes an the hoigth av good livin'!"

"That's so."

"Well *by's*—(with an insinuating Irish smile, intended to be extremely enticing), *I belave I'll stay by the caw-fy, and* quit the ribbles intirely."

And Pat was as good as his word. He remained with the coffee and the Union.

On one occasion when General Milroy's division was in the Shenandoah Valley two of our pickets were captured by rebel guerrillas, who after tying them each to a tree, left them to starve to death. One, however, after many hours of weary labor, during which he often despaired, lest weakness and death might intervene, contrived to loosen or sever his bonds, and then untied his comrade. It is worth noting that this atrocious system of guerrilla warfare was first introduced by the Confederates, and that not informally or in a manner admitting of defence, but by their government issuing commissions to guerrillas and irregular troops under the very name! The thief and murderer Morgan who has made himself even more infamous than Albert Pike of Indian notoriety, served under one of these disgraceful commissions.

Soldiers on picket duty have at times odd encounters with civilians. It is said that on one occasion, a well known quondam type-setter from Chicago when picketing in the service of Colonel Ellsworth in Virginia, had occasion to stop a very haughty specimen of the chivalry, who came riding along driven by his servant.

Zoo-zoo stepped into the road, holding his bayonet in such a way as to threaten horse, negro and white man all at one charge, and roared out, "tickets!"

With indescribable contempt the Virginian handed his pass to the negro, and bade him get out and show it to the Zouave. This was done.

"All right!" said the latter, glancing at it—"move on!" With this he gave the black man a jerk which sent him spinning several paces down the road, and turning to the Virginian inquired sharply; "well—what do you want?"

"Want? I want to go on, of course. That was my pass."

"Can't help it," was the reply, "it says 'pass the bearer,' and the bearer of it has already passed. You can't get two men through *this* picket on one man's pass."

The Virginian reflected a moment, glanced at the bayonet in front of him, and then called out to his black man to 'come back!' Sambo approached cautiously, but fell back in confusion when the 'shooting stick' was poked at his own breast.

"Where's your pass, darkey?" inquired the picket.

"Here, massa!" said the slave, presenting the same he had received from the gentleman in the carriage.

"Won't do," replied the holder of the bayonet. "That passes you *to* Fairfax, but I can't let any one come *from* Fairfax on *that* ticket. Move on!" An impulse from his foot sent Sambo down the road at a hard gallop. Turning to the Virginian he cried:

"Now sir, if you stay here any longer, I shall take you under arrest to head-quarters."

The gentleman caught up his reins, wheeled around—and off at the best trot his horse could manage, over the sacred soil—possibly reflecting that it might have been worth his while to be civil to "the infernal Yankee." Whether Sambo ever returned to his master and to the blessings of "the institution" is not recorded.

It is said that a member of the regimental staff of the 8th Alabama regiment lying at Richmond, lost himself one morning in the woods. Coming upon the Union pickets, the secesh officer was brought to a stand, and mistaking the character of the men, inquired for his regiment. The picket directed him to the Federal Colonel's tent for information. He went there and was told to consider himself as a prisoner. He shrugged his shoulders and merely replied: " A d—d funny mistake of our pickets to send me the wrong way."

Mistakes like this sometimes occur in the best regulated military families. There is a legend current that during "the emergency" of 1862 a certain company in Pennsylvania once surrendered without striking a blow to another company of the same regiment—believing them to be secesh. Their captors deprived them of their colors. Of the same class is the following anecdote from the St. Louis, Mo., "Democrat" of September 29, 1864.

"GENERAL ROSECRANS CAPTURES THE MILITIA CAMP.—General Rosecrans is determined not to be caught napping in the present excitement. He visits all the camps and outposts, to see that the soldiers under him are on the alert. On Tuesday night, the General, accompanied by Major Bond, mounted his horse and galloped out to Camp Sheridan, the stamping ground of General Pike's Enrolled Militia. It was midnight when the two officers arrived at the camp, and not being hailed, they dashed into the centre of the camp, and dismounted. A soldier came forward from some place of concealment and hailed the officers—

"'Who goes there?'"

"'Friends,' answered the General.

"'Friends, heh? Well, what next?'

"'Nothing next; but you are all prisoners.'

The militiaman got his eyes open by this time, and seeing the stars of a Major-General before him, supposed the veritable old Pap Price was before him. He dropped his gun by his side, folded his arms and appeared resigned to his fate. A German soldier now came up and asked what was going on. He was told that the camp had been captured, and he had to surrender.

"'We will see about that,' said the German, tightening his belt, and preparing for a fight. The two soldiers then escorted the General and his Aid to head-quarters, and when they discovered that it was 'Old Rosy,' and not 'Old Pap,' who had captured their camp, they felt greatly relieved, and made up their minds not to be caught napping again."

Civilians, however, as well as soldiers, sometimes make mistakes by getting within the lines—witness an anecdote dating from December, 1863.

"IN THE LINES; OR, HOW THE COTTON SPECULATORS GOT TAKEN DOWN.—A good story is going the rounds in regard to a citizen of New Orleans, one of those neutral individuals who are on the fence ready to jump on either side policy dictates to be for their interest. He left New Orleans about two months since, bound for the Confederate lines, with the intention of investing what money he had in cotton. The friend who related the incident to me said that just before starting he met him in the street, and, after exchanging the usual commonplace remarks, inquired:

"'What are you up to now, Brown?'

"'Oh, I've just made a good thing; been into the Confederacy and brought out thirty bales of Cotton. Bound up again to-morrow, and if nothing happens I'll bring back four times that quantity.'

"'Be careful, Brown, or you'll get gobbled up. They'll have you in the rebel army.'

"'Oh, no fear of that. They all know me to be a good Confederate. Besides, I've got British papers.'

"A month later the two friends met, Brown looking decidedly downcast and seedy. Wallace accosted him with:

"'Well, Brown, how about that cotton?'

"'Don't talk to me about cotton. Lost every thing.'

"'How's that?'

"'Well, you see, I got up to Bayou Sara the same night the rebels made their raid into the place. I had plenty of time to escape, same as good many others did, but I thought I was all right, and so, with a friend, sat down to a game of poker, just to show that we didn't feel at all alarmed. Presently in came some 'rebs' and began to search us. On my partner they found a lot of Confederate money, and they wanted to know what right he had in the Federal lines with Confederate money. So they just took it. Of course I was convinced now that I was all right —my money was all greenbacks. 'What are you doing in the Confederacy with Federal money?' they asked. So they took mine too.'

"'That was rough. Is that all they did to you?'

"'All! No, sir. They stripped me of every thing; and one big fellow gave me such a kick as to take me off my feet, with the remark that if they ever caught me in the Confederacy again with so little money they'd hang me.'"

In September, 1864, the rebels succeeded in driving from the army of the Potomac all its fresh beef—or 2,500 head of cattle. The next day a Confederate picket cried out to a Yankee in the same duty.

"Hallo, Yank—we've got some fresh beef; what'll you take for some coffee!"

"Take!" was the reply—"why we'll take Atlanta!"

Nothing more was said on the subject of international exchanges by the representative of the Cottonocracy.

The following picket incidents, near the Chattahooche, are from the letter of one who was "on the spot, or near the spots:"

"The other day one of the Johnnies swam the river, and came into our lines. One of our boys asked him where he was going?

"'Well,' said Johnnie, 'General Hardee made a speech a day or two ago, and told us to strike for our altars and our fires, and as my fire is in Tennessee, I'm going to strike for it across lots.'

"Another reb called out to one of our men across the river:

"'Yank; oh, Yank, who is your commander?'

"'General Sherman,' says Yank; 'what do you want to know for?'

"'Oh, nothing,' says Johnnie; 'only I think he must command us, too; for whenever you get marching orders we get them, too; with the difference that we go in advance.'

"Two corps crossed the river a few days ago. The rebs found it out, and called to our pickets:

"'Oh, Yank! We're coming over, to give you'ns h—l to-morrow. We've got 40.000 re-enforcements.'

"'The h—l you have! Where did you get them?'

"'Oh, they're some old Sherman has sent us.'

"'Oh, yes; I think I see it.'

"I asked a rebel Major when he thought the war would end?

"'Well,' says he, 'I think it will end this fall.'

"'Why do you think so?'

"'Well, you won't have any one to fight by that time, if you keep on as you have done since May.'

"The rebel pickets asked one of our boys how long he thought the war would last?

"'Oh, about twelve years,' answered Yank.

"'Good God! ain't Vallandigham, and them Copperheads up there, going to help us any?'"

In the army of the Southwest, as well as of the Potomac, frequent interviews with hostile pickets have resulted in establishing a somewhat extensive personal acquaintance, between both officers and men, on either side. The following incident, narrated to me by an eyewitness, somewhat oddly illustrates this phase of mixed society—a phase, by the way, which originated with the *elite* of the Philadelphia "Peace Democracy," in 1863, and was by them applied to circles, which they affected to regard as less exclusively aristocratic than their own.

A Federal Colonel, wearing as a cloak a handsome long blue cape of fine broadcloth, happened to encounter, during a scout, a rebel of the same rank, with whom he held a few minutes truce. The Confed was much pleased with the cape, and offered in exchange a new Federal overcoat, in his possession. Colonel A. (the Federal) was well satisfied with the trade, and went his way rejoicing. The next day, during a skirmish, the rebel in his cape was taken prisoner by a handful of our men. Knowing that the showy garment which he wore must, of course, be immediately recognized, and that he would be supposed to have killed the owner, the prisoner was terribly alarmed, entreating his captors not to shoot him until he had seen the officer in command.

"Well—there he is!" exclaimed a high private, pointing to the dignitary in question, who was advancing at a distance of a hundred and fifty yards.

Without waiting for a nearer approach, the rebel began to roar at the top of his voice: "A. ain't dead yet! A.'s alive!— Colonel A. *is* alive. I left him last night at the Corner—*and I got this cape in a fair trade from him.*"

A roar of laughter greeted these last words, and Reb was forgiven. It being more convenient to let him go than keep him, a parole was soon effected, and he was allowed to retain his cherished cape, on the express condition that he would return it "after the war"—which he earnestly promised to do.

Trusting that these anecdotes, illustrating soldier-life, have been of interest to the reader, I would urge him, if gifted with the slightest talent in the art of writing, to neglect no opportunity to jot down such illustrations of army life, and of the stirring times in which we live. The time is coming when they will be of real value, as reflecting the *inner life* of the people, and their habits and feelings during the great War of the Emancipation—as it will evidently be eventually called. During our Revolution there were but few incidents of the kind recorded, and those which were, have been assiduously reproduced, until every schoolboy knows them. It is, perhaps, no exaggeration to state, that every American, whose eyes shall have perused this page, during the present year, has heard, not one, but several narratives, or anecdotes from friends in the army, all of which would be well worth recording. Trusting that many will do so, and suggesting that the UNITED STATES SERVICE MAGAZINE would be the best medium for their publication, I conclude my chapter.

MILITARY ESPIONAGE.

MILITARY espionage has been from time immemorial, in all countries and among all nations, regarded as a military offence of great criminality. Its penalty is death by hanging. This is the common law of war. Some nations have, by orders, decrees, or municipal laws, defined what constitutes this offence, and provided for the trial and punishment of the offender. It should be observed, however, that espionage being an offence at the common law of war, punishable by death in a particular mode, a spy may be executed without any municipal law on the subject, and that municipal laws in regard to espionage are binding only on the State which makes them. They form no part of the international code.

As there is much looseness and ambiguity in the use of the word *spy* by unprofessional writers, it may be well at the outset to ascertain its exact technical meaning. In the "Instructions for the Government of the Armies of the United States in the Field," prepared by Dr. Lieber and General Hitchcock, and published in General Orders, No. 100, series of 1863, paragraph 88, we find the following definition: "A spy is a person who secretly, in disguise or under false pretence, seeks information with the intention of communicating it to the enemy. The spy is punishable with death by hanging by the neck, whether or not he succeed in obtaining the information or in conveying it to the enemy." If it is meant by this that any person who *secretly* " seeks information with the intention of communicating it to the enemy," is necessarily a *spy*, the definition is incorrect. A citizen may *secretly* seek such information with the same intention without being a spy. The act is treasonable, whether done secretly or openly, but a traitor is not necessarily a spy. A prisoner of war may, with the same intention, secretly seek information, but by doing so he does not become a spy. Again, an enemy who comes within our lines without disguise or false pretence and seeks information, no matter how secretly, is no spy. If captured he must be treated as a prisoner of war; he may be confined with rigor as a dangerous person, and his exchange refused; but he cannot be hung as a spy. The terms "in disguise or under false pretence" are the essential requisites of the offence of military espionage; secrecy has nothing to do with it.

General Halleck, in his work on "International Law and Laws of War," chap. xvi., § 26, says: "*Spies* are persons who, *in disguise* or *under false pretences*, insinuate themselves among the enemy, in order to discover the state of his affairs, to pry into his designs, and then communicate to their employer the information thus obtained. The employment of spies is considered a kind of clandestine practice, a deceit in war, allowable by its rules."

The next question which we propose to discuss is, can any one be compelled to act the part of a spy, and is it justifiable to employ spies? On this subject Vattel says: "Spies are generally condemned to capital punishment, and not unjustly; there being scarcely any other way of preventing the mischief which they may do. For this reason, a man of honor, who would not expose himself to die by the hand of a common executioner, ever declines serving as a spy. He considers it beneath him, as it seldom can be done without some kind of treachery. The sovereign, therefore, cannot lawfully require such a service of subjects, except, perhaps, in some singular case, and that of the last importance. It remains for him to hold out the temptation of a reward, as an inducement for mercenary souls to engage in the business. If those whom he employs make a voluntary tender of their services, or if they be neither subject to nor in anywise connected with, the enemy, he may unquestionably take advantage of their exertions, without any violation of justice or honor."—*Droit des gens*, liv. 3, ch. 10, § 179. Halleck says: "No authority can require of a subordinate a treacherous or criminal act in any case, nor can the subordinate be justified in its performance by any orders of his superior. Hence the odium and punishment of the crime must fall upon the spy himself, although it may be doubted whether the employer is entirely free from the moral responsibility of holding out *inducements* to treachery and crime. That a general may profit by the information of a spy, the same as he may accept the offers of a traitor, there can be no question; but to seduce the one to betray his country, or to induce the other, by promises of reward, to commit an act of treachery, is a very different matter. The term *spy* is frequently applied to persons sent to reconnoitre an enemy's position, his forces, defences, &c., but not in disguise, or under false pretences. Such, however, are not *spies* in the sense in which that term is used in military and international law, nor are persons so employed liable to any more rigorous treatment than ordinary prisoners of war. It is the *disguise*, or *false pretence*, which constitutes the perfidy, and forms the essential elements of the crime, which, by the laws of war, is punishable with an ignominious death."—*Int. Law*, ch. xvi., § 26.

We fully concur with these writers. We are aware that it is

said by many good men that the strict rules of morality are not applicable to war, and that a general in the field may do many things not sanctioned by the principles of pure ethics which apply to the ordinary transactions of life. We are not of that opinion. We believe that war in many cases is perfectly justifiable; nay more—that it is the duty of a nation and of its rulers to prosecute a justifiable war with all the means which God has placed at their disposal. At the same time we believe that such a war can and ought to be conducted according to the rules of the strictest morality; that is, that the party waging a just war should always do what is *right*, and should never do what is *wrong*.

But, it is said, Washington, and Wellington, and other good men employed spies, and offered inducements to others to become spies. We can only answer that "Washington, and Wellington, and other good men" did many things which in their day were deemed perfectly justifiable and proper, but which in our day, and with the light we have, cannot be justified. It may be said that the principles of morality are always the same, and that what is right or wrong at one time must be right or wrong at all times. And this may be true as an abstract proposition. But it must be remembered that there has been a progress in ethical science as in all other sciences, and that what was deemed right in former times is now considered as unquestionably wrong. We must, therefore, judge of men and their acts according to the age in which they lived and the light of religion and morality which was given them as guides. The acts of a general of the present day are not to be measured by the same standard of morality as those of Alexander, Cæsar, Frederick, and Washington, any more than the effect of the artillery used in the Army of the Potomac or before Charleston is to be measured by that used by Turenne and Vauban.

The employment of spies is no offence against the laws of war, and it gives to the enemy no cause of complaint. The matter is therefore narrowed down to simply a question of right between the general and the spy he employs. That the former may purchase and use the information so obtained we think there can be no doubt. Nor do we believe there is any wrong in his accepting the proffered services of a spy, provided the latter is made fully acquainted with the nature of his offence against the enemy, and the ignominious punishment which must follow his capture. But we do not think a general is justifiable in seducing by promises of reward a fellow being to commit towards an enemy an act of treachery which makes him a felon at law, and may subject him to a felon's death.

The next point we propose to consider is that of the duration of the offence of military espionage, or rather the limitation of the time of its punishment.

There is a law of limitation which applies to the punishment of military offences, resembling in a measure that which applies to offences at the civil law. The criminality of some military offences ceases with the completion of the act and the return of the perpetrator to the jurisdiction of the opposing belligerent, while others are punishable at any and all times, at least so long as the war continues. To the latter class belong those offences which are assimilated to capital crimes at the civil law, such as military murders and assassinations, poisonings, inhuman treatment of prisoners, acts of military perfidy. For example, the taking of life by guerrilla bands or other unauthorized belligerents, is a military murder, which is as subversive of civilized society as a murder in time of peace. Hence the crime is considered to adhere to the actor, and the penalty continues to attach. On the other hand, the act of spying is an offence only under the laws and usages of war; it is no crime against society in time of peace. Hence a successful spy, safely returned to his own army, and afterwards captured as an enemy, is not subject to punishment for his acts as a spy; he is entitled to be treated as a prisoner of war, but he may be subjected to restraint and held in close custody as a person individually dangerous. On this subject Saalfeld remarks: "The spy himself, except a subject who serves as a spy against his own sovereign, is not guilty of any *crime* in the sense that term is used in the law of nations, and although military usages (*Raison de guerre*) universally permit the execution of a spy, nevertheless their procedure is not to be considered as a punishment, but simply as a means of prevention (or of deterring persons from the commission of the act of spying); this also serves as a reason why he who has ceased to be a spy cannot be executed. The severe treatment of the spy is permitted by the international law only against him *who is caught in the act;* but if the spy has committed, at the same time, a crime at international law, he may at any time be punished for this particular crime." Other authors and local statutes, although less definite and positive in their language, speak of the punishment of a spy when "caught," or "apprehended" as a spy, that is, in the commission of the act of spying. The statute of the United States of April 10th, 1806, says, "when *found* lurking as spies," &c. We know of no authority for considering this as a *crime* at penal law which adheres to the perpetrator after he has escaped within the lines of his own army, that is, beyond the military jurisdiction of the offended belligerent, and beyond his power of punishment. There are numerous instances in modern history confirmatory of this view of the laws of war, that is, cases of spies who have escaped when committing the act, and on being afterward captured, have been treated, by the offended and capturing belligerent, as ordinary prisoners of war. In this, as in many other cases, usage has established principles which have not heretofore been formally announced by writers on public law.—Saalfeld, "Manual of the Positive Law of Nations," Ed. 1833, p. 206; "Regulations of the Armies of the United States, in the Field," § 104; Napier, "Peninsular War," Brussels ed., 1839, vol ii., p. 628.

The case of Spencer Kellogg, who was executed by the rebel authorities of Richmond, is one in point. He was charged with having been a spy within the rebel lines in the winter of 1861 and 1862. This was not denied. But he escaped to our service without detection, and a year or two afterwards was captured in battle as a prisoner of war. He was nevertheless tried and condemned for his previous act as a spy. Our government demanded that he should receive the treatment of a prisoner of war, as he could not then be lawfully punished as a spy. He was nevertheless executed, and the enemy afterwards alleged that he was also tried and condemned as a deserter. Whether he was so tried and found guilty is not known. It is believed, however, that he was entirely innocent of the latter charge, and if he was executed as a deserter it was an act of murder on the part of the enemy.

The case of Major André has excited more interest and elicited more discussion than any other in the history of military espionage, and an examination of these discussions will afford much information on many questions connected with this branch of military jurisprudence. The facts and circumstances of the case are fully stated in Sargeant's "Life of André."

After a long correspondence with Arnold, under the direction of General Clinton, the names of both parties being assumed, Major André agreed upon a meeting with the former for the purpose of arranging terms for the surrender of West Point and its dependencies, and the sum which was to be paid to Arnold for his treason; and on the 20th of September he repaired on board the British vessel, the Vulture, then lying in the Hudson river below Haverstraw. On the night of the 21st of September a boat came to the Vulture with the following passes:

"HEAD-QUARTERS, ROBINSON HOUSE, September 20, 1780.
"Permission is given to Joshua Smith, Esquire, a gentleman, Mr. John Anderson, who is with him, and his two servants, to pass and repass the guards near King's Ferry at all times. B. ARNOLD, *M. Gen'l.*"

"HEAD-QUARTERS, ROBINSON HOUSE, September 21, 1780.
"Permission is given to Joshua Smith, Esq., to go to Dobb's Ferry with three Men and a Boy with a Flag to carry some Letters of a private Nature for Gentlemen in New York and to return immediately. B. ARNOLD, *M. Gen'l.*"

"N. B. He has permission to go at such hours and times as the tide and his business suits. B. A."

John Anderson was the name under which André had carried on his correspondence with Arnold, and under which he now acted and was introduced to Smith. He still, however, wore his uniform of a British officer, but on entering the boat to go ashore he put on a large blue surtout or watch-coat, which concealed his uniform, and in this disguise he met Arnold and passed our line of sentinels. After passing within our lines he, at the suggestion of Arnold, exchanged his uniform for the dress of a citizen. Having arranged with Arnold the details of the surrender of his post and command, and the sum to be paid for his treason, André started on his return to the British lines, under his assumed name, and disguised in his citizen's dress, with the following pass in his hands, and the treasonable papers which he had procured from Arnold concealed in his stockings:

"HEAD-QUARTERS, ROBINSON HOUSE, Sep'r 22d, 1780.
"Permit Mr. John Anderson to pass the guards to the White Plains, or below, if he chuses. He being on Public Business by my Direction.
"B. ARNOLD, *M. Gen'l.*"

But before reaching the enemy's lines he was arrested by our militia pickets, and after trial and condemnation was, on the 5th of October, by the order of General Washington, executed as a spy.

These are the main points of the case in its legal bearing; but the popularity of André, and the sympathy on both sides for the accomplished victim of Arnold's selfishness and treason, raised many other questions which will be considered in this discussion.

In the first place André was arrested as a *spy*, and his case was referred by Washington to a Military Commission or Board of Officers for their opinion. There was no dispute about the facts. The documentary evidence and André's own statements agreed in every essential particular. André denied nothing; and orally, in his letter to Washington, and in his written statement to the court, confessed every thing.

The following is Washington's letter to the Board:

"HEAD-QUARTERS, TAPPAN, Sept. 29th, 1780.
"GENTLEMEN: Major André, Adjutant-General to the British army, will be brought before you for your examination. He came within our lines in the night on an interview with Major-General Arnold, and in an assumed character; and was taken within our lines, in a disguised habit, with a pass under a feigned name, and with the enclosed papers concealed upon him. After a careful examination, you will be pleased, as speedily as possible, to report a precise state of his case, together with your opinion of the light in which he ought to be considered, and the punishment that ought to be inflicted. The Judge-Advocate will attend to assist in the examination, who has sundry other papers, relative to this matter, which he will lay before the Board. I have the honor to be, Gentlemen, your most obedient and humble servant,
G. WASHINGTON."

On the same evening, the Board submitted all the documents in the case with the following report:

"The Board having considered the letter from his Excellency, General Washington, respecting Major André, Adjutant General to the British army, the confession of Major André, and the papers produced to them, REPORT to His Excellency the Commander-in-Chief, the following facts, which appear to them concerning Major André.

"*First*, That he came on shore from the Vulture sloop-of-war, in the *night* of the 21st of September, inst., on an interview with General Arnold, *in a private and secret manner.*

"*Secondly*, That *he changed his dress within our lines, and under a feigned name, and in a disguised habit, passed our works at Stoney and Verplank's Points*, the evening of the 22d of September, inst., and was taken the morning of the 23d of September, inst., at *Tarry Town, in a disguised habit*, being then on his way to New York, and, *when taken*, he had in his possession several papers which contained *intelligence for the enemy.*

"The Board having maturely considered these facts, DO ALSO REPORT to His Excellency General Washington, that Major André, Adjutant General to the British Army, ought to be considered as a Spy from the enemy; and that, agreeable to the law and usage of nations, it is their opinion he ought to suffer death."

The next day Washington approved the Report, as follows:

"HEAD-QUARTERS, September 30th, 1780.
"The Commander-in-Chief approves of the opinion of the Board of General Officers, respecting Major André, and orders that the execution of Major André take place to-morrow at five o'clock, P. M."

And the proceedings and sentence were announced in the morning General Orders of October 1st. In "after General Orders," it was announced that "the execution of Major André is postponed till to-morrow." And in "Evening Orders," of same date, it was announced, "Major Andre is to be executed to-morrow at twelve o'clock precisely. A battalion of eighty files from each wing to attend the execution."

On the 1st of October, André wrote to Washington, requesting a change in the mode of execution, and that he might not die on a gibbet. It was decided, on consultation, that the request could not be granted, but through motives of compassion no reply was sent, and André supposed, until he approached the place of execution, that he was to be shot.

We will now consider the legal points raised in this case.

The main, if not only point urged by André in his letter to Washington, and in his statement to the Board, was that the imposture was unintentional, as he had Sir Henry Clinton's orders not to go within an enemy's post, or to quit his own dress. The facts are, that finding it too late to finish his business and return to the Vulture that night, he put a surtout coat over his uniform, and rode with Arnold to Smith's house, passing our picket line on the way. On being challenged, he at first hesitated, but afterwards proceeded with Arnold to the place of concealment, where he replaced his uniform with a citizen's dress. Whatever may have been his previous *intentions*, and there can be no doubt of the sincerity and truth of his statements, it cannot be disputed that he entered our lines *under an assumed name, his uniform concealed by an overcoat, and afterwards changed for a citizen's dress*, and that the object of his visit and disguise was *to obtain and convey intelligence to the enemy*. These facts made him a *military spy*.

Superficial writers are sometimes disposed to attach undue importance to a change of dress, forgetting that *disguise* does not consist in dress alone, and that any *false pretence*, coupled with other circumstances, may make a man a spy. It mattered not whether André entered our lines in his uniform or with his uniform concealed by his overcoat, or when or where he changed his uniform; the question is, was he within our lines in disguise, either as to name or dress, or under a *false pretence* as to character or business, and was he captured before he had escaped to his own lines, and within the protection of his own government?

Suppose André had entered our lines under a flag of truce, and in the full uniform of a British officer, with the insignia of his rank displayed, under the pretence of negotiating a cartel, or some other legitimate object of recognized *commercia belli*; but the evidence proved that this *pretence* was *false*, and that his real object, as shown by his acts, was to bribe our officers to treason, or by clandestine and unlawful means, obtain plans of our fortifications, returns of our garrisons, etc., no one can deny that " he would have been guilty of the offence of military espionage, because he was guilty of the very thing which constitutes the criminality of the offence—*military treachery*.

If there was any doubt in regard to the common law of war on this subject at the time, and we think there could have been none whatever, the statute laws of his own country were perfectly decisive of the question. Without referring to other laws, we will merely quote the Act of Parliament of 1749, which provides for "the trial of all spies, and of all persons whatsoever, who shall come and be found in the nature of spies, to bring or deliver any seducing letters or messages from any enemy or rebel, or endeavor to corrupt any captain, officer, or other in the fleet to betray his trust," &c.

It must be presumed, that André was acquainted with this and similar laws of England, and with the practice of his government on this subject, as had been exemplified in the case of Captain Hale and others in that war. Hence, when Colonel Tallmadge, in answer to André's question as to his probable fate, referred him to Hale's case, he manifested the utmost uneasiness, denying the similarity of the cases, but failing to point out any essential dissimilarity.

Again, Sir Henry Clinton and other friends of André attempted to exculpate him on the ground that he acted on the suggestion, or under the direction of Arnold, and was protected by his pass, issued while still in office, and exercising his command. It does not appear that André himself attached much if any importance to this point of defence; but it has since been urged with much pretence of plausibility and force. Those who have used this argument, seem to have entirely overlooked the legal maxims, that no man can take advantage of his own wrong, and that fraud taints the acts of each and every *particeps criminis*. If André had been no party to the fraud and treason of Arnold, and had acted under his advice and direction, ignorant of the criminal object in view, the case might have borne a very different aspect. On the contrary, he was fully advised, and perfectly understood the criminal character of the negotiations, and the object of the meeting. He was one of the principals in the fraud and treason, and fully understood the peril to which he exposed his life. It is true, that he did not originally intend to run this risk, but when he unexpectedly encountered it, he voluntarily, after a moment's hesitation, incurred it, for the sake of the advantages which he expected his government to derive from it.

On this point we think there can be no doubt or dispute among those who will fully examine the question, and we conclude this subject by quoting the remarks of General Halleck, in his International Laws and Laws of War: "Notwithstanding the criminal character of a spy, it has not unfrequently happened that men of high and honorable feelings have been induced to undertake the office; and, although this fact has somewhat lessened, in popular opinion, the odium of the act, it has failed to diminish the severity of its punishment. Two of the most notable instances of this kind to be found in military history, occurred during the war of the American Revolution. After the retreat of Washington from Long Island, Captain Nathan Hale recrossed to that island, entered the British lines, *in disguise*, and obtained the best possible intelligence of the enemy's forces, and their intended operations; but, in his attempt to return, he was apprehended, and brought before Sir William Howe, who gave immediate orders for his execution *as a spy*. And these orders were carried into execution the very next morning, under circumstances of unnecessary rigor, the prisoner not being allowed to see a clergyman, nor even the use of a Bible, although he respectfully asked for both. Every one remembers the story of Major André,—how he ascended the Hudson river, within the American lines, where he bargained with Arnold for the surrender of West Point and its defences; how he was captured in his attempt to return to New York *in disguise*, and with the documentary evidence of his bribery of Arnold concealed upon his person; and how, after a full examination, and due deliberation, he was condemned, and ordered by Washington to be executed *as a spy*. These two officers—Hale and André,—were nearly of equal rank and age; both had talents and accomplishments, which gave promise of future greatness, and which had already endeared them to large circles of admiring friends. They both committed the same military offence, and both suffered the same punishment, but, with this difference, that while the British did every thing in their power to add to the ignominy of Hale's execution, the Americans spared no exertions to lighten the hours of André's captivity, and to show their regret that the stern exigencies of the war required his death. Again, while the Americans unanimously condemned the barbarous treatment which Hale received before his execution, they, with equal unanimity, acknowledged the justice of his sentence. Many of the English, on the contrary, while acknowledging the kind treatment of André by the American officers, and their expressions of sympathy for his fate, not only complained, at the time, that his sentence was unjust, and his execution a "blot" upon the reputation of Washington, but these charges have since been repeated by some of their ablest writers, and especially by Lord Mahon in his "History of England," and by Phillimore in his "Commentaries of International Law." It is not denied that André was within the American lines, *in disguise*, for the purpose of gaining information of the disposition of our forces, and of closing negotiations with Arnold for their surrender; but, it is contended, that being there with the authority of Arnold, and under a passport from him, he was not legally *a spy*. André, himself, never attempted so flimsy a defence; he scorned all prevarication, and was condemned on his own confessions. His defenders seem to forget that the passport of a traitor, given for treasonable purposes, could afford no protection. It had no more legal force than Arnold's agreement to surrender the American defences; if Washington was bound to recognize this passport, he was equally bound to carry out the entire agreement, by surrendering to the enemy West Point and its garrison !"

The opinions of ordinary historians, journalists, annalists and writers for magazines, are usually of very little value on disputed points in science, ethics, or jurisprudence. What is called professional or technical knowledge is necessary for the solution of such questions. Nevertheless, it may be of interest to refer to the opinions which have been expressed by various persons on the question of André's condemnation and execution as a *spy*.

American writers, with, we believe, a single exception, and that a lady (Mrs. Childs), actuated by feeling rather than judgment, and a full understanding of the case, have approved the report of the Board and the action of Washington. Among English writers there has been, as might well be expected, a diversity of opinion. As was very natural, under the first misrepresentations of the true facts of the case, some very warmly and earnestly condemned the conduct of Washington; and a few recent authors, either from ignorance of the facts, or, what is more probable, actuated by national prejudice, have denied the legality of the sentence, and charged Washington with injustice and cruelty in its execution.

Winterbotham, Hinton, Coke, Romilly, Mackinnon and Locker, some of them very competent judges of military jurisprudence, have admitted that André was lawfully executed. Even the attorney-general of the colony, it is said, expressed to Sir Henry Clinton, before the execution of André, that he was legally a spy. On the contrary, Sir Henry himself always contended that the execution was illegal; but he based it on a misstatement of facts and an erroneous theory of the law. He said that André was under the protection of a flag of truce, that he was compelled by Arnold to enter our lines, and also to change his dress, all of which was untrue. Again, that Arnold's pass and orders were a legal protection, which is opposed to the common law of war and even to British statute law then in force. The Marquis Cornwallis charged that the court was composed of foreigners ignorant of the English language, and several of the coarsest and most illiterate of the American Generals; and Simcoe asserted very positively that Washington ordered the execution for the purpose of conciliating the French auxiliaries. There seems to have been a very general error in regard to the composition of this court, several writers stating that it was composed of only three members, and even Lieutenant-Colonel Whiting, in his publication of the "Revolutionary orders of Washington," states in a note that it consisted of Greene, La Fayette, and Steuben. The court in fact consisted of fourteen general officers, viz.:—Greene, Stirling, St. Clair, La Fayette, Howe, Steuben, Parsons, Clinton, Knox, Glover, Patterson, Hand, Huntington, and Starke. The Judge Advocate General was Colonel John Lawrence. Few if any military courts were ever composed of men more distinguished for their character, talents and services. Five of these, viz.: St. Clair, Stirling, Clinton, Howe, and Starke, had held commissions in the British service before the revolution, and Steuben and La Fayette were familiar with the laws and usages of military service in Europe. We have the authority of the latter that notwithstanding the strong sympathy felt by all the members for André, the Board were unanimous that he was legally a spy, and ought to suffer death.

We have already alluded to the opinions of Lord Mahon and Mr. Phillimore. The national prejudices of these men, as manifested in their works, render their opinions of no weight whatever. The only other British writer of any note who has expressed the opinion that André was not legally executed, is Sir Edward Cust, a lieutenant-general in the British army, and author of a voluminous but not very reliable work, called "Annals of the Wars of the Eighteenth and Nineteenth Centuries." His statements and assertions are too gross, absurd, and destitute of truth to have any historical weight. He says that the Board proceeded "by a series of interrogations to extract from their unfortunate prisoner something like an acknowledgment" of his guilt as a spy; and that "upon this enforced confession they convicted him of being a spy;" that he had entered "into the American lines under the sanction of a flag of truce, with none of the intentions of a spy;" and that "his change of dress was adduced as fatal to the character of a mere military messenger, although it was only a great-coat over his half-uniform." Again, he says: "The treachery of General Arnold did not make Major André a spy, and it was pitiful in the meanest degree to wreak vengeance upon an humble agent because he could not reach the principal belligerent. But granting that this is an erroneous view of the offence, and that military law must consider Major André as a spy, how despicable was the petty exercise of power that could insultingly erect in the view of the unfortunate officer the gallows on which he was to be hung, several days before the execution."

It is hardly necessary to remark that these assertions are disproved by contemporaneous history. The last one is newly manufactured, as all accounts represent that André expected to be shot, till, at the moment he was approaching the place of execution, he first discovered the gallows. On the trial André was especially cautioned to make no disclosures that he did not wish to make.

It is not our object, however, to pursue this historical discussion; we have taken André's case simply to illustrate points in the law of military espionage.

It will be noticed in his case that André was not dealt with under any statute law, but under the common law and usages of war. He was not tried by a court-martial, nor with the formal proceedings of such a court. It was simply a Board which gave an *opinion*, but passed no *sentence*. Washington took upon himself the responsibility of pronouncing sentence, and of designating the mode of its execution.

It is proverbial that the information obtained from professional spies is unreliable. Moreover, they almost invariably act a *double* part, selling information, true or false, to both sides.

THE AMAZONS.

ANCIENT historians tell us that there once existed a race of warlike women, who formed a community without the aid of the stronger sex, founded cities, conquered powerful nations, and were for a long period invincible in warfare, until Hercules, amongst his other exploits, brought off the belt of Hippolita with its owner, and her subjects dwindled away like the bees when their queen is withdrawn from the hive. This Scythian tribe, they say, sprang from a daughter of the Earth, who was a virgin to the waist, and a viper in the rest of her person. They went up to assist King Priam when his capital was in danger from the Greeks. One of their queens visited Alexander, as the Queen of Sheba did Solomon, but not content like her with simply admiring his glory, sought from his embraces a son, that might combine the virtues of the greatest man and the greatest woman then living in the world.

Others speak of a Libyan tribe, that inhabited Hespera, an island rich in all manner of precious stones, with which doubtless they adorned their persons, and under their Queen Myrina, with her army of thirty thousand infantry and two thousand horse, protected by corselets of snake skins, and armed with a long sword, a spear, and a bow, which they used in the Parthian fashion, penetrated as far as Thrace, and after many victories returned again to Africa.

Raleigh believes in the existence of such a once powerful nation in ancient times, and he, as well as the Spanish historians, relates the same story of such a people on the banks of the Amazon.

Sir John Mandeville vouches for their existence in his day in the island of Amazonia, somewhere near Suez; and Lopez, in his description of Congo, mentions such a nation near Monomotapa, which, like their prototypes of old, burned off the right breast, to handle their bows more conveniently and shoot the better; and he adds, "that these women were the strongest guards of this Emperor, all the Eastern Portugals do know."

How much of reality there may have been in such fables, credited by respectable historians, and referred to by many poets as true, or whether the whole is not sheer fiction, who can tell? Strong-minded women, even now-a-days, venture to pass the bounds prescribed to their sex—push forward into professions appropriated to men—and, as they sometimes wear the garment peculiarly masculine, who can say but in days of yore a nation of them may have been clad in armor, may have lived without husbands, or, if they had any, have unfitted them for manly exercises, usurped their employments, and kept them as cotqueans and spinsters?*

It is quite odd, however, that at this very day, according to a late traveller in Africa,† that pleasant king of Dahomey, who has every morning at his palace-gate a fresh pile of human heads, actually entertains a considerable force of such Penthesileas and Thalestrises, who never marry, are his principal soldiers, and are armed according to their several services, with blunderbusses, muskets, knives, and bows with poisoned arrows, and, like the old Amazons, without precisely the same beauty we see in their representation on ancient gems and bas-reliefs, which negro features and negro shapes do not yet quite approach, are scantily clad, dance constantly to the sound of tom-toms and kettledrums until they are too fat for such Terpsichores,—doubtless the Pyrrhic dance—as they fight courageously and successfully.

We now and then see persons of the softer sex in the fierce garb of the soldier, usually the gay uniform of the Zouaves, more convenient perhaps to them and more attractive from its bright colors, though from their figures one would think that they were better suited to the heavy cavalry. Some even have been noted for their exploits, and their sex has been discovered only when in need of a surgeon.

Crowds of females of no enviable reputation in various capacities usually attend an army—but these Daughters of the Regiment are amiable only in the opera. Our natural repugnance to such unfeminine audacity may be a prejudice; but still we hardly sympathize, as we ought, perhaps, even when Venus is wounded by Diomedes, or Clorinda is slain by Tancred.

Anacreon long ago told women (I take Moore's prose translation), that "Nature hath given horns to bulls, and hoofs to horses, swiftness of foot to hares, to lions a gaping of teeth, to fishes the faculty of swimming, to birds to fly, to men magnanimity. What then does she give *them*? BEAUTY: instead of all shields, instead of all spears; for she who is beautiful subdues both iron and fire."

---

* "Viros ad texturam muliebriaque deputavit exercitia."—*Diod. Sic.* 2, 11. (Latiné.)

† "A Mission to Gabele, King of Dahomey, with Notices of the so-called Amazons," etc. By Richard F. Burton. Lond., 1864.

SHERMAN'S WINTER CAMPAIGN THROUGH GEORGIA.

The campaign of the great military strategist, SHERMAN, which has just terminated with the fall of Savannah in the South, and the defeat and almost utter annihilation of one of the two chief Confederate armies as a result of it, is destined to furnish *material* for the profound study of military minds of the present and future ages; hence a brief and careful *résumé* of the campaign itself, as well as of the causes that led to it, will be read with more than usual interest.

To the thorough understanding of the subject, it is necessary that we should briefly review the situation anterior to the first Georgia campaign, that terminated with the fall of Atlanta.

In May last, we find Johnston at Dalton and Tunnel Hill, heavily fortified in the mountain-ranges with forty thousand men, his flanks well protected, and his position so admirably chosen, that he covered Atlanta and its approaches, except by a long and difficult march upon his flanks. Sherman, with about eighty thousand men, was in his front, with an army well disciplined and equipped, and eager for battle and victory, but harassed constantly by raids upon their long lines of communication, over which their subsistence was drawn. It is the firm opinion of many well-informed military men, that Sherman was opposed to a farther advance from his base towards the interior, and would have chosen the East Tennessee route had it been practicable. But, with Johnston in force in his front, he had no alternative but an advance upon him.

The country is familiar with his brilliant summer campaign, and it has passed into history as one of the most successful of the war, filled with hard battles, brilliant victories, noble valor, and remarkable strategy. It gave us Atlanta with its barren fruits, opened to us the railways centring there, repossessed us of one hundred and forty miles of territory, but left us one hundred and forty miles farther from our base. Still, Hood's army was powerful for harm, and the enemy still possessed railway communication from Virginia to the Mississippi, *viâ* Macon, Fort Valley, Montgomery, and Mobile. The importance of this to the enemy, who derived the greater portion of his subsistence from the Southwest, Sherman was quick to see, and he at once decided upon his plans for the winter campaign, if he had not done so before. A few days of careful study of all the details—the strength of the enemy at Wilmington, Charleston, and other points between Hood and Lee, the fortifications likely to be encountered, the nature of the country, the probability of subsisting his army on the country—convinced him of the practicability of cutting his way to the coast. His plans were in due time submitted to the War Department and General Grant, by whom they were indorsed, and Sherman at once turned his attention to Hood.

The rashness and ambition of the rebel leaders were well known, and Sherman, uncovering his right flank at Atlanta, like the spider in the fable, invited him to walk into the parlor. Hood was not slow to see the advantages of assuming the offensive, and, by emulating Sherman's mode of warfare, strike his communications in the rear, beat him at his own game of flank, compel the evacuation of Atlanta and northern Georgia, and make the name of J. B. Hood, General, the glory of the Confederacy.

On the morning of the 20th of September, Hood's cavalry quietly moved round and occupied a position across the Montgomery and Atlanta Railway, intending to deceive Sherman into the belief that it was merely a precaution to cover any attempt of the latter to advance in that direction. It must be confessed that Hood concealed his intentions well, and covered his movements with mystery to those not familiar with his characteristics; yet the keen eye of Sherman was upon him; and when, on the 2d of October, he boldly crossed the Chattahoochie at Campbellton, and threw forward his columns upon Sherman's rear, instead of Sherman having been taken by surprise, he manifested not the slightest concern. On the contrary, he continued the work of collecting supplies at Atlanta, and arranging its details for his contemplated invasion. The people of the North, and the army, opened their eyes in astonishment at the apparent procrastination of Sherman in defending his communications; and this astonishment was not at all lessened, when he did change front in pursuit of the wily Hood, to find that his efforts to intercept the rebel leader were slow, and destitute of his usual energy. It is true that at Allatoona Corse did give Hood an energetic resistance—immortalized himself and his command; but, beyond this, Hood's movements were without opposition of any serious kind. While slowly pursuing the enemy to the Alabama line, supplies of clothing, ammunition, and other necessary stores, were collected at Chattanooga, the railway repaired to Atlanta, and the stores, &c., shipped forward. Meanwhile, Thomas had been sent back to Nashville, secretly to organize and equip the recruits and convalescents, and to organize a new wing with these and the corps commanded by Schofield and Stanley. So successful was the hero of Chickamauga, that by the time Hood had crossed the Tennessee, Thomas was ready to meet him with an army as large as the invading one.

Again changing front to the south, Sherman rapidly countermarched to Atlanta in one day, rested his troops, laid in six teen days' rations of bread, an extra supply of salt, an abundance of ammunition, and in one day after his arrival was ready to move; having taken the precaution to destroy the railway track to Chattanooga, and burn the city, so that it could not be reoccupied by the military.

On the evening of the 15th, Regimental Adjutant read an order to the troops, in which Sherman informed them that he had cut loose from his base, and would lead them by a long and difficult march to a new one. Then it was that the army, for the first time, solved the mystery with which Sherman had surrounded his movements.

The army saw the wisdom of their beloved leader. Hood was no longer in their front; Lee had sufficient work in hand to employ every man; no troops could be spared from Charleston, Savannah, Wilmington, Mobile, or the Trans-Mississippi Department; the route was now open to Milledgeville, Macon, Augusta; the railway feeders of the South at our mercy, and Savannah ready to open its gates to the knock of Federal bayonets; and, as a consequence, the confidence of the men in their chieftain was materially strengthened.

During the interval that elapsed between the time that Sherman gave up the pursuit of Hood, and his arrival at Atlanta, the latter had penetrated to Franklin, Tennessee, where he found Thomas confronting him. Confident of his ability to dislodge Thomas, and satisfied in his own mind that Sherman had been forced to fall back, and would ere many days assail his rear, he saw the necessity of immediate action. To attack and defeat Thomas, move upon and occupy Nashville, would immortalize him, and wipe out the stain upon his reputation that followed his insane attack at Atlanta.

Then followed the battle of Franklin, adding new laurels to Thomas's brow, and covering Hood with additional dishonor. His course was desperate; he saw, for the first time, his error; that Sherman was so far on his way that he could not hope to throw himself between him and the coast. Some desperate stake must be made. Nashville, with its granaries and storehouses, foundries, and plunder, was before him; a barren and impoverished country in his rear. It took him but a moment to decide. Nashville once in his possession, he could recruit and refit his army, and inaugurate an offensive war of invasion, such as that of Lee and Early in Maryland and Pennsylvania. Upon the results of the battle at Nashville we need not here dwell. Hood's defeat was the natural result of Sherman's well-laid plans and Thomas's superior manœuvres; and in that victory, as well as in that of Savannah, the troops of both armies alike deserve to share the honors, and inscribe upon their banners "Nashville" and "Savannah."

But let us return to Sherman. Having arranged every

thing, divided his army into two wings,—the right composed of Blair's (17th) Corps, and Osterhaus's (15th) Corps, under Major-General Howard; and the left composed of Williams's (20th) Corps, and Davis's (14th) Corps, under Major-General Slocum; with the 20th and 15th on either flank, and Kilpatrick's fine division of Cavalry, reporting direct to the commanding General,—Sherman cut loose from Atlanta on the morning of the 16th of November, Slocum moving out on the Georgia Railway, which he destroyed to Social Circle, a distance of sixty miles, while Howard and Kilpatrick made a feint upon Macon, drawing all the forces away from Milledgeville and other points. Kilpatrick was expected to demonstrate within five miles of the city, but drove the enemy into his hastily-erected works, which he charged, capturing eight guns, which he could not bring off without considerable loss. Withdrawing his force, he left Macon on the southwest, and moved upon Howard's flank.

Meanwhile, on the 20th, Slocum's column occupied Milledgeville, the capital, stampeding the Governor, State officers, Legislature, and the entire male population.

Slocum thus far had met no enemy. Howard, however, at Griswoldville encountered three brigades of infantry militia, whose commander, Brigadier-General Young, offered battle. Howard promptly accepted the challenge, and sent in General Walcott's brigade of the Fifteenth Corps, who quickly routed them, capturing General Young and many of his command. In the engagement, Walcott received a severe flesh-wound.

Howard and Kilpatrick effectually destroyed the railway between Gordon and Milledgeville, thereby severing the last link that connected the government at Richmond with their Trans-Mississippi Department.

The advance into the interior had spread terror and dismay among the inhabitants, many of whom deserted their homes to the mercies of their negroes and the invading hosts, who appropriated all that the plantations afforded. The teams had all been replenished by fresh mules, mounted men remounted impressed horses, and the commissary wagons filled with an abundance of provisions. Protecting the citizens from unnecessary annoyance, and private property, and the State House, and Executive Mansion, from injury, one day's halt was made, when the column crossed the Oconee River, burning all the bridges in their rear.

One column followed the line of the Central Railway, and most effectually destroyed it to Millen. Another column moved upon Louisville, in Jefferson County, from which point Baird's Division of Davis's Corps, and Kilpatrick's cavalry, moved upon Waynesboro', with the two-fold object of cutting the Savannah and Augusta Railway and making a *feint* upon the latter city, for the purpose of drawing the attention of General Bragg, who had collected about ten thousand men at Wilmington, to that point. Kilpatrick found Wheeler strongly posted at Waynesboro', attacked and drove him from his position, and, with the assistance of Baird, tore up several miles of the railway.

While Kilpatrick and Baird were demonstrating upon Augusta, Slocum and Howard occupied Millen and all the other important towns, destroying all the foundries, shops, cotton, &c., &c.

Throwing himself between the Ogeechee and Savannah Rivers, the better to protect his flanks, Sherman at once moved upon Savannah. In this last stage of the campaign he encountered considerable annoyance from the cavalry in his rear, and the felling of timber upon the roads in his front. Nevertheless, the marches averaged thirteen miles per day. Slocum, on the 10th of December, struck the Savannah and Charleston Railway ten miles from the city, cutting it off from all railway communication with the outer world.

With his usual promptness, Sherman at once invested the city, from the Savannah to the Ogeechee, the nearest point being three miles from the city. Hardee, who commanded, was strongly posted, with thirteen thousand men, in a line of works which, with the aid of the swamps, furnished an excellent line of defence. A charge upon the line would have cost many valuable lives, and might possibly have ended in defeat. With no siege-guns, his army located in the swamps and on the barren and unhealthy rice plantations where no supplies could be obtained, his troops on one cracker per day, there were some who felt concerned for the safety of the command. Sherman, however, had prepared for the contingency. By his direction, Howard, under cover of darkness, bridged the Ogeechee, threw Hazen's Division across to the island, and invested Fort McAllister—the only obstruction to the passage of vessels from the ocean to the right of the line at King's Bridge.

The investment having been effected on the 13th, the fort was carried by Hazen with nine regiments, who captured the entire garrison, with its siege-guns and ammunition.

This was the crowning victory of the campaign. The possession of the fort gave us a free water-course to the army, as well as siege-guns with which to shell the city.

Hardee had now no alternative but to stand a siege or evacuate. He chose the latter course, and gave us the city, with its guns, ammunition, foundries, shops, thirty-three thousand bales of cotton, &c., &c.

The importance of this brilliant campaign, that perhaps has no parallel in history, cannot be over-estimated. So carefully had Sherman arranged the details of his movement, selected his route of march, and proportioned the work to his different commanders, that he has emerged from the enemy's country after a winter's march across half the continent, in twenty-seven days, with an army in finer physical condition than on setting out, the possessors of better transportation than ever before, all the railways running through Georgia torn up, and the iron so effectually destroyed that they cannot be rebuilt, forty-two of the finest counties foraged over, over two hundred towns and villages occupied, all the cotton destroyed, the country rendered unfit for reoccupation by Hood, a new and short base of supplies obtained, Savannah once more led back to the Union, and all this accomplished by the great military genius of one man, and the endurance and valor of his command. Well may the loyal masses of the North shout pæans of praise to Sherman and Thomas, and the immortal men who have followed the starry banner from the Ohio to the ocean!

Looking back upon the situation previous to Sherman's march, Hood, Hardee, and Bragg can now see how grandly Sherman has outgeneralled them, and how wofully they were in error when they supposed that an assault upon his rear would compel his retreat. Had Hood been satisfied to follow the example of Johnston and continue on the defensive, Sherman to-day would not be on the coast, and Hood's army reduced to a mere mob of fifteen thousand or twenty thousand men. Hood committed many errors in his military career, but this last error should consign him to oblivion, while it places at the head of the list of military leaders the names of GRANT and SHERMAN.

[The following thoughtful and well-written verses were not inserted, as was intended, in the January number. They are still instructive and appropriate at the beginning of this eventful year.—ED.]

ON THE THRESHOLD.

The Moon-Queen mounts the car of Night, and from her Amazonian seat
Reviews the legionary stars whose spear-crests sparkle round her feet;
Her face a shadowy sharpness wears—a spectral pallor, cold and clear,
And solemnly athwart the sky she moves beside the Parting Year.

Into the hollow Past, like ghosts, the dark Hours, one by one, have gone;
Only the Last, still trembling, halts upon the threshold of the Dawn.
Halt on its threshold still, gray Ghost, and make me of thy wisdom wise,
Ere the Sun's pencil write "To-Day" upon the tablet of the skies!

What do thy mates and thou bear back into the measureless abyss
That sepulchres the Year yet warm? What burdens leave ye unto this—
This Child—for whom the Sovereign Sun a Father's gentle office fills,
And, from his amber couch new-risen, leads slowly up the Eastern hills?

"The Year's dark hours that—all save one—have passed beyond the verge of Night,
Bear many a memory of Wrong still dimly countervailing Right;—
Bear many a tardy-budded Joy, and many a Sorrow scantly healed;—
Hatreds unquenched, and sated Loves; Lies blazoned; Truths still unrevealed:

"Bear many a crimson stain of Strife, with radiant gem-spots interspun
Of Souls crushed out by warring hosts—fresh Martyrs in a Cause begun,
And then to later Souls resigned its perfect triumph-arch to rear;
Too vast to be englobed within the circle of the parted Year!

"Bear these; and with them, echoing far through all the cycling rings of space,
Grand pæans from the lifted hearts of a regenerating race;
Thanksgiving tones, like mighty peals from myriad minster-bells at morn,
Whose deep vibrations air shall keep to thrill the ages yet unborn!

"The lusty Child-Year creeping now, Sun-guided, toward the upper light,
Shall catch the unwoven threads of Time dropped by the other in his flight;
Shall seize them in his agile hands, and, deftly blending tint and tone,
Shall weave, along his halcyon course, a gleaming tapestry of his own!

"In this the buds of Joy shall bloom; the sated Loves renew their youth;
The blazoned Lies be overwrought by symbols of eternal Truth;
Through all the woof, in glittering lines, the glories of the Right increase,
And the empurpled stains of Strife glow golden in the light of Peace!"

Dark Hour that tremblest still upon the pregnant threshold of the Dawn,
I give thee to the hollow Past, and hail the Promise-bearing Morn!
For lo! the Sovereign Sun leads forth, to full-orbed Day, the Infant Year!—
God grant—lost Hour—the rosy Child may in his mission prove thee Seer!

1864–5.   O. D. G.

LITERARY INTELLIGENCE
AND
NOTES ON NEW BOOKS.

PERHAPS no American book of recent publication has received or has deserved a more general perusal than the "Memoirs of Lieutenant-General Scott," written by himself" (2 vols., Sheldon & Co., New York. $4.00). On this account we shall make no extended review of it. If those who have not read it, do not, they cannot know its real value from a magazine article. Not designed as a complete history, it is a noble aid to the history of the principal momentous events which have transpired in this century, witten by one who can, without a spice of arrogance declare, "*Quorum magna pars fui.*" It is the life of a great soldier, general, diplomatist, and gentleman. As a soldier, his career is illustrated by his rapid rise in his profession, his eager service, his magnanimous self-sacrifices, and valiant self-exposures in the great northern battle-fields of our last war with England. As a general of the highest order, he is manifested in his judicious organization and control of the Army in time of peace, his marvellous Mexican campaign (the rationale of which is here presented in a clearer and truer light than ever before), and his reception of the new rank of Lieutenant-General, till then unprecedented, except in the case of Washington. As a diplomatist, he shines in the humane character of a peace-maker, in nullifying South Carolina nullification; on the northeastern boundary, on the Canadian frontier, and on the Pacific coast. And as a gentleman, whose life, in the words of Mr. Thackeray, "may be read in young ladies' schools with propriety, and taught with advantage in the seminaries of young gentlemen," he has no superior among the public men of America. Pure, devout, patriotic, refined, and elegant; true to his friends, magnanimous to his enemies, generous to all; cultivated in polite learning, a purist in language, he challenges the admiration of all. We mean this for no random eulogy on General Scott: all this, and more, is to be found in his book—for the actions of his life here recorded are his best eulogy. Unlike most history of contemporary events, these memoirs are true and unbiased; and this, notwithstanding that he has had to discuss some nice points of public controversy,—as, for example, the courts-martial before which he has been obliged to appear; the treatment of his political enemies; and his famous quarrel with General Jackson.

He gives an excellent chapter on the political causes of the war, in speaking of a time before the war seemed imminent: but he wisely abstains from a detailed view of the present struggle. Let us hope that he has prepared copious notes on this subject for posthumous publication. We like trite quotations when they are particularly apposite, and to General Scott, of colossal form and colossal eminence, may be most fitly applied the well-known verses:—

"Like some tall cliff, that lifts its awful form,
Shoots from the vale, and midway cleaves the storm,
Though round its breast the rolling clouds are spread,
Eternal sunshine settles on its head."

"The American Boys' Book of Sports and Games: A Repository of In-and-Out-Door Amusements for Boys and Youth;" published by Dick and Fitzgerald, New York, is a book that will delight the young people. It is a complete cyclopædia of sports, games, and amusements of all imaginable kinds—is attractive in its outward appearance, and is profusely illustrated with well-made and instructive wood-cuts—numbering more than six hundred. The publishers state that, while they have laid other nations under contribution in preparing their work, the details of all games have been conformed to our American method of playing; and they have certainly succeeded in producing by far the handsomest and most complete work of the kind that has yet been issued. We know of no present that will give a boy more lasting and varied pleasure. 600 pages, $3.50.

MORRIS'S MODIFIED TACTICS. 2 vols. 18mo. D. Van Nostrand, Publisher.

When our armies were first organized, at the commencement of the war, regiments were required to learn a large number of movements, with all their arbitrary and precise details, which served no other purpose than to make pleasing show-drills. When these same regiments were sent to the field, they very soon discovered that a very small portion only of their laboriously learned tactics was of any practicable use, and even that portion required to be simplified.

Commanding officers, desirous of saving their men from all unnecessary fatigue, and learning from experience the simplest and quickest methods of putting their troops in the formations desired, naturally adopted such changes as were in accordance with common sense. Finding that subdivisions could not be marched through woods by their front, they marched them by their *flank*. Finding simultaneous movements were fatiguing to the men, and consumed valuable time, besides often causing the advancing column to halt, while some preparatory or intermediate movement was executed; of course, successive movements were preferred. The result has been what might have been expected; as the movements do not conform to the tactics, the tactics must conform to the movements.

It will, therefore, be readily understood, how important it was that a system should be prepared which should reject all obsolete explanations and evolutions, and teach the movements which have resulted from experience, and are constantly employed in the field.

The system by General MORRIS supplies this want fully. He has retained nothing which has not been found useful. Two small volumes contain all the tactics required for infantry. He has omitted all superfluous commands and parts of commands, and has made simple general rules, thus saving tedious repetitions of explanations.

The color-guard is placed on the right of the left wing, in order to have the color leading when a line marches "by the right of companies." The ranks are one pace apart, which affords greater ease in the march by the front, and facilitates the doubling of files, when facing by the flank. Files *always* dress and touch towards the guide, and the difficult and useless "fixed pivot" is abolished. Many of the movements are made from a column of fours on the march, to save time and useless manœuvring. The manual of arms has been revised to suit the rifled musket. The manual for the short rifle is placed by itself. All deployments are made by the *flank*, and by the shortest paths. The close column by division is formed by filing the divisions successively behind or before each other. The line of battalions in mass is formed from a column of fours on the march, by conducting each battalion over the shortest line to its position and then forming the close column.

A tabular form is used to separate the commands of the general and the colonel, which shows their relative order, and is a valuable aid to the memory.

In short, the work cannot be better described than by calling it a *simplified system of flank movements.* $2.00 per set.

"Following the Flag," by "Carlton" (with Illustrations; 1 vol. 16mo, $1.50; Ticknor and Fields), is an admirable narrative—simple enough for the comprehension of boys, and yet worthy the study of larger people—of the Campaigns of the Army of the Potomac, up to November, 1862. The illustrations are good, and the map diagrams very clear.

"A Manual for the Medical Officers of the United States Army. By Charles R. Greenleaf, M. D., Assistant Surgeon U. S. A. Philadelphia: J. B. Lippincott & Co., 1864" (pp. 199).—It is truthfully said in this little work, "The Medical Officer has really less opportunity than any other for becoming acquainted with his duties: he has no guide, and must rely either on his own common sense or whatever instruction he can gain from those around him." Those of the least experience know that the regulations to which a newly appointed medical officer naturally turns for information afford only the most meagre outlines—outlines that are to be filled up by verbal instruction—of the military requirements in time of peace, with the explanation that they "apply, as far as practicable, to the medical service in the field." Not one-tenth of what he is held to is contained in the Blue Book. Scattered through innumerable orders, circulars, and letters of instruction, are the real rules that are to guide him; and more bewildering than a prairie snow-storm is the confusion of amendments, additions, revocations, and alterations that have been showered from the official sky. Hitherto each has had to find a trail for himself, and to learn experimentally which routes lead to sloughs, and which were cut-offs. We have here a condensation of fact and elimination of error that almost open a royal road.

The compiler has arranged, with patient care, the prominent duties of medical officers, and, in each instance, has added the official reason why. The great feature is the confidence it inspires, by naming the number and source of every order as the authority for its various statements. Nor is it made tiresome by quoting more than the gist of the matter. Without bearing any official character, or making pretence to have the stamp of infallibility, it carries upon its face the mark of its own merit, and shows, so that those who run may read, its correctness. To October, 1864, it fairly replaces the entire mass of orders.

There are two or three topics that are not treated of, such as the requirements from Hospital Stewards and the constitution of Veteran Reserve Corps, which make it not literally perfect; but the daily duties of a medical officer are well laid down, and, in almost every particular, are implicitly to be followed.

EDITOR'S SPECIAL DEPARTMENT.

The dark days are surely passing away: the sunlight is scattering into thin mist the clouds of doubt, despondency, and danger: the storm which, typhoon-like, burst upon us with unanticipated fury, is rumbling off to the fabulous caves. The hoped-for but long uncertain success at Atlanta, is forgotten in the greater glory of Savannah. And while that still dazzles us with a full-orbed blaze, new light breaks in the West. The bold march of Hood, threatening Nashville and the North, is suddenly transformed into a defeat, which closes in a wild, disorderly retreat. Amid the general rejoicing, there was but one drop of regret, which gave secessionists, North and South, a gleam of hope, and now that is gone. The fiasco at Fort Fisher was the spot in our sun; when lo! in a moment, almost unexpected, the news comes that Fort Fisher has fallen, and the entire sweep of the horizon glows with an unclouded blaze. More thunder there will be, but it will be "out of a clear sky,"—the thunder of our guns as we finally push the rebels and the rebellion to the wall.

The value of Wilmington, as a port of entry to the rebels, is well understood. It was, so to speak, their only open port. From it cotton and emissaries went out to bolster the rebellion abroad; into it came arms, ammunition, iron, clothing, supplies of all kinds, to uphold the Confederacy a little longer at home. Let us look for a moment at this noted locality. Situated on the northeast branch of the Cape Fear River, and separated from the Brunswick River by Eagle's Island, it is eighteen miles from New Inlet, the land extending from the city to the Inlet in a long narrow tongue, which ends at Federal Point. New Inlet is the principal entrance, and the forts at Federal Point being in our possession, we entirely control the river channel. These fortifications consist of *Mound Battery*, at the very extremity; numerous detached batteries and intrenchments on both the river and ocean fronts; Fort Fisher, a very powerful bastioned work, commanding in every direction; and some other works, soon abandoned by the rebels, just north of Fort Fisher. Upon the strength of Fort Fisher the rebels placed their entire dependence: Beauregard and Whiting declared it impregnable; and to capture that was the design of General Grant in sending an expeditionary force, under Generals Butler and Weitzel, to co-operate with a naval squadron under Rear-Admiral D. D. Porter. On the 25th of December the troops landed, but, after skirmishing and a reconnoissance, it was decided to withdraw without attacking. The same night and the next morning, Butler withdrew, and set sail for Fortress Monroe. Upon this first movement "forward and back," we do not design to dwell. It is not a pleasing task to dissect failures, and is rendered doubly unpalatable by the immediate demonstration that they were totally unnecessary failures.

Whatever may be thought of the opinions of Generals Butler and Weitzel, there were two men who were stung to the very heart by this result,—Grant and Porter. They both acted with a vigor and energy which insured success. Porter went to Beaufort to reorganize his divisions, to take in coal, ammunition, and supplies, and determined to take the work, unaided, if need be. Grant removed Butler and sent him to Lowell; picked out a good man, with his usual sagacity,—General A. H. Terry,—remanded the *same troops* which Butler had brought back, with some slight additions in numbers, to Beaufort, to join Porter; and *delenda est* was the motto for the redoubtable Fort Fisher. The rebels had laughed at our failure and had bragged greatly—we mean no pun—about the fort and its defenders, Whiting and Lamb—but the laughter was soon turned into mourning.

The vast fleet of navy ships and transports once more breast the tongue of land and its forts. Whiting and Lamb have another chance to show their breeding. Colonel Comstock, the Engineer-in-Chief, a brave and able officer, reconnoitres the work. The troops land, under cover of the gunboats, above the fort, and occupy the deserted earthworks. For three days the navy bombard, and the army rest and organize. The fire of the ships is terrific; the Ironsides and monitors stand close in and draw the fire, thus giving the fleet a knowledge of the number, calibre, and position of the guns. Embrasures are blown open, traverses disappear, guns are dismounted. The fleet engages in three divisions: the first led by the Brooklyn, and numbering 116 guns; the second by the Minnesota, 176 guns; and the third composed of the flotilla of gunboats, 123 guns. The storm of fire was so terrific that soon the fort ceased to reply, but its sheltered garrison was waiting our attack. At length, on the third day, Sunday, January 15th, the columns moved forward. The army column consisted of four brigades, commanded by Curtis, Pennybacker, Bell, and Abbot—that is, Paine's entire division and Abbot's Brigade, all under the orders of Major-General Ames. On the sea-front, a storming party was formed of about fifteen hundred sailors and marines. On all points the navy fire was concentrated. The attack of the land troops was at once successful; Curtis's Brigade reached the parapet and gained a foothold, the vessels throwing their shells always directly in front of them as they advanced; by ten o'clock at night the entire fort was in our possession. Thus driven out, the rebels ran southward, to the cover of works nearer the Inlet, and were all captured: five hundred dead were found in the fort; General Whiting and Colonel Lamb were wounded and captured; two thousand prisoners were taken, and guns, variously estimated at from fifty to one hundred, were the trophies of the victory. Our losses are named at nine hundred. Curtis, Pennybacker, and Bell were wounded; and Lieutenants Preston and Porter of the Navy were killed, in the unsuccessful attack of the sailors and marines.

Regretting that we must leave to our gigantic brethren, the dailies, the details of intelligence, we pause to look at what should be the results of this victory.

1. Blockade-running is at an end; and the resources of the rebels have received thereby a terrible check. To what extent this will cripple them, let us present the following statistics:—" The special report of the Secretary of the Rebel Treasury in relation to the matter shows that there have been imported into the Confederacy at the ports of Wilmington and Charleston, since October 26, 1864, 8,632,000 pounds of meat, 1,507,000 pounds of lead, 1,933,000 pounds saltpetre, 546,000 pairs of shoes, 316,000 pairs of blankets, 520,000 pounds of coffee, 69,000 rifles, 97 packages of revolvers, 2,639 packages of medicine, 43 cannon, with a large quantity of other articles of which we need make no mention. Besides these, many valuable stores and supplies are brought by way of the Northern lines into Florida, by the port of Galveston and through Mexico across the Rio Grande. The shipments of cotton made on Government account since March 1, 1864, amount to $5,296,000 in specie. Of this, cotton to the value of $1,500,000 has been shipped since the 1st of July and up to the 1st of December. It is a matter of absolute impossibility for the Federals to stop our blockade-running at the port of Wilmington. If the wind blows off the coast, the blockading fleet is driven off. If the

wind blows landward, they are compelled to haul off to a great distance to escape the terrible sea which dashes on a rocky coast, without a harbor within three days' sail. The shoals on the North Carolina coast are from five to twenty miles wide, and they are, moreover, composed of the most treacherous and bottomless quicksands. The whole coast is scarcely equalled in the world for danger and fearful appearance, particularly when a strong easterly wind meets the ebb-tide. It is an easy matter for a good pilot to run a vessel directly out to sea or into port; but, in the stormy months, from October to April, no blockading vessel can lie at anchor in safety off the Carolina coast. Therefore supplies will be brought in despite the keenest vigilance." All this is at an end.

2. Wilmington should at once be attacked, for to our judgment it is now untenable, notwithstanding its strong works. Removing the obstructions in the Cape Fear River which lie just opposite Fort Fisher, our vessels can run up to Eagle Island just opposite the town—if there is no delay. A land-force co-operating on the long spit of land, will have its flanks thoroughly protected on the river and the sea, while our boats can drive all rebel resistance from its front; and Fort French, just south of the city, iron-clad though it be with T-iron, must fall. We repeat, that we cannot see how it is possible for Wilmington to hold out against an *immediate* movement upon it.

3. Wilmington is a "back door," not only to Richmond, but to Charleston. From it runs northward the famous Weldon Road to Richmond; and, crossing the Brunswick River, the roads to Charlotte, and to Columbia, Augusta, and Charleston. Once more is the Confederacy "cut in two," or rather in three; and its vitality, hydra though it be, seriously endangered. The control of the Mississippi is one clear cut; Sherman's wide swarth through Georgia, another; and the movement from captured Wilmington will isolate Richmond and Charleston.

If these judgments are just, we cannot too highly estimate the last success at Wilmington, nor too greatly regret the mistaken judgment which abandoned the original project. Nor can we withhold our unstinted praise from General Grant, who projected the movement of the land troops, and who repaired at once the error of Butler; and from Admiral Porter, the admirable naval organizer and commander, whose ardor was proof against the cold water of the first withdrawal.

The co-operation of Porter and Terry was hearty and generous, and, in the opinion of the former, contributed largely to the success. General Terry deserves the highest praise for his dispositions; while his subordinates who stormed the work will ever rank among the bravest men in the history of forlorn hopes.

When we last went to press we left Sherman, on the 9th of December, skirmishing with the retreating enemy, fifteen miles from Savannah. On the 11th, Slocum, with the Fourteenth and Twentieth Corps, began the investment, and Howard soon swung his corps into line to complete it, about three miles and a half from the city, and extending from the Savannah River to the Ogeechee. Captain Duncan of the Scouts boldly and successfully ran down the river to communicate with the fleet. On the 12th, Howard detached Hazen, with the Second Division of the Fifteenth Corps, to assault Fort McAllister, which commanded the approach by the Ogeechee. The assault was brilliant and successful. Hazen carried the fort while Sherman and Howard were spectators from the roof of Cherve's rice-mill. The excitement was intense, for, when that was taken, Savannah must fall. Notwithstanding the vigorous resistance of the garrison, Hazen's impetuosity was rewarded, and an hour afterwards Sherman and Howard were in a small boat, on their way to the fleet. The meeting of these commanders with Foster and Dahlgren was a joyous one, and Sherman at once wrote to say that Savannah would soon be ours. The cordon of investment was drawn closer, the troops rested and reorganized, great guns put into position, and the city summoned. Although Hardee declined to surrender, he determined to fly, and while one road of egress was still open, he crossed the river on the Union causeway, and left the terrified city to the hero of Atlanta. Savannah was literally surprised; many had flocked there as to a city of refuge; there were not ten days' provisions in the place, and there was no time to destroy the five hundred bushels of rice and thirty-three thousand bales of cotton which fell into our hands. Thus ended Sherman's "grand march," which turned into the most magnificent "quick step" ever contributed to the "Music of the Union."

We have thus epitomized the great event, because we have a thing or two to say upon this hint. A meeting of the citizens gave utterance to sentiments of loyalty unlike any before heard in rebeldom. Charmed with deliverance from despotism intermixed with anarchy; pleased with the treatment of Sherman and his Lieutenant, Geary, who was appointed military governor; glad to get food to eat, and feeling once more, after years of estrangement, the old home sentiment under the conquering but protecting standard of the Union, they bow to the decrees of Government, and even suggest to the State to call a convention, which shall have in view the ending of the strife between "the two sections of the country."

Never did tidings give more joy to our sanctum than did these. Georgia never went out of the Union, even by a *soi-disant* legitimate method. The people were never consulted. The whirlwind swept over it, and it was prostrated. Many who have since become bitter upholders of the war never recognized either the right or the necessity of original secession: and now, should Georgia come back, those of her sons who, loving her well, have kept their first love for their whole country, have happy proof that she regards them as just and true men. The noblest of the Southern States, the richest in resources, the most manifest in destiny, the Empire State of the South, God send an early day when she shall shake the dust of treason from her skirts, and lead the van in a regenerated as well as reconstructed republic!

The effects of this conquest in a military point of view are marvellous and manifold; the Confederacy again bisected; a great commercial port open; a loyal prosperity assured; its supremacy to Charleston established *in æternum;* and a magnificent base secured for future operations in the South, upon which Sherman is now engaged.

The moral effects are greater. The power and skill of the Union arms manifested and vindicated; the rebel boasts and lies exposed; the Confederacy shorn of its brightest stolen jewel; the work of reconstruction grandly begun, and the Richmond oligarchy shaking to its foundations. Europe believes that we can manage our own affairs. One word more: we have no sympathy with those coldhearted men at the North who begrudge supplies, or urge unrelenting punishment. Now is the time for kindness, generosity, amnesty, and these the people upon whom they may most properly be conferred.

Not enough has transpired of General Sherman's present movements to enable us to predicate any thing with certainty. A small force was sent to the Southwest; another to Hardeeville, probably to cloak our movements. Sherman went to New Orleans to look after other portions of his department, but if Charleston is not trembling, it is because her fear has passed that, and become paralysis. A late dispatch from Secretary Stanton says:—

"General Sherman renewed the movement of his forces from Savannah last week. The Fifteenth and Seventeenth Corps went in transports to Beaufort on Saturday, the 14th. The Seventeenth Corps, under Major-General Blair, crossed Port Royal Ferry, and, with a portion of General Foster's command, moved on Pocotaligo. General Howard, commanding that wing of the Army, reported on Sunday that the enemy abandoned his strong works in our front during Saturday night. General Blair's Corps now occupies a strong position across the railroad, covering all approaches eastward to Pocotaligo."

Hood has made good his escape, but with such enormous losses and destruction of *morale* that he must act strictly on a weak defensive. His fifty thousand men and ninety guns with which he encircled and threatened Nashville have dwindled down to twenty-five thousand, including his forced conscripts, and not guns enough to fire a grand salute. In spite of our best efforts, rain and mud impeded our attempts to cut him off, and so he crosses the Tennessee, and takes a long breath, after many short and gasping ones. The admirable paper which we present on the victory at Nashville makes further editorial comment unnecessary.

General Grierson started from Memphis on the 21st of December, on a raid to cut the Mobile and Ohio Railroad. The destruction was complete from the neighborhood of Corinth to Oholona. Bridges, trestles, arms, wagons, and cars were destroyed in great numbers.

We cannot fail to mention with praise and satisfaction the important movements in Western Virginia, which resulted in the destruction of the very valuable and important salt-works at Saltville.

Stoneman left Knoxville with three cavalry brigades, sixteen hundred men, under Burbridge and Gillem, on the 13th of December. The enemy's force, against which they moved, was about fifteen hundred strong—three brigades under Vaughan, Duke, and Morgan, the whole commanded by Breckenridge. Gillem, who is a most dashing officer, cleared Vaughan's cavalry out of Jonesboro, beat Morgan in the vicinity of Kingsport, was joined by a brigade of Burbridge, and made a rapid march to Bristol. This cut the enemy's force in two. On the 15th they were at Abingdon, but were followed by Vaughan. Gillem turned and beat Vaughan, and destroyed the buildings and machinery at the lead-mines fifteen miles east of Wytheville. He then joined Burbridge, just as Breckenridge was pressing him very hotly, turned the scale, and while Breckenridge was in retreat, the command moved on Saltville. Here the great salt-works were ruined, railroad-iron, shells, and shot dropped into the tubed wells, the kettles destroyed, foundries, mills, and bridges burned, five thousand bushels a day of salt, and two millions of dollars (real money) lost to the Confederacy. Well done, all who took part in this splendid march of four hundred and sixty-four miles in eighteen days of battle; but particular plaudits to Gillem!

From the Potomac and the James we get nothing but vague reports of changes in the position of troops, and occasional shelling, to keep the armies awake. We shall get much more before long. The war must have its crowning battle at Richmond, or Lee must evacuate, and when he does the war ends.

FOREIGN AND INTERNATIONAL.

It is an instructive and very amusing study of human nature to watch the Anglo-rebel press, as it comments, criticises, dogmatizes, and prophesies upon the American war. It stultifies itself once a week at least; but with honest Dogberry as an English model, it is more than content, it is anxious, to "write itself down an ass." Sherman and Thomas lie terribly, of course, until the news is confirmed by rebel confession, and then what they said they would do, and did, suddenly becomes, to the Toots of the Times, of no kind of importance. They shout with merry laughter at the foolish attempt of Porter and Butler to take the impregnable Fort Fisher, but when Porter and Terry take it, they only stop shouting: it is nothing to brag about.

Spain, at last, finding the grapes of St. Domingo very sour, abandons the leaf, by a vote of the Cabinet War Junta. England quickens the abandonment by acknowledging the independence of St. Domingo. Will Spain turn all her energies against Peru? She had better not.

Mexico, after all, is not pacified. The southern part swarms with republicans, who only need organization to give the Imperialists an overthrow. Porfirio Dias has soundly thrashed General Courtois d'Herbal, at Etla, near Oajaca; and the great Mars of the Franco-Austrian power, General Bazaine, has taken the field against the victor. Let Mexico fight on—help will not be forever withheld. She can be free; God gives her a noble chance. We have still the ghost of a hope that she will use it.

CORRESPONDENCE.

BEFORE PETERSBURG, January 11, 1864.

THERE is no particular news on our front; the very heavy rains have washed the works a good deal, but they are quickly repaired; volunteer officers and men soon acquire practical field engineering. Our batteries on the right, near the Appomattox, watch the Richmond and Petersburg Railroad track, and a steam workshop near the Petersburg Dépôt, to which they pay their respects almost daily, calling spiteful but harmless replies, for the most part, from the rebel Chesterfield and Goose-Neck batteries. Frequently the batteries on Cemetery Hill take up the quarrel, and pour down on Fort Steadman, and we all find ourselves in a general uproar.

The most interesting detail of the hour is in the uniform accounts given by rebel deserters of the general disgust and hatred felt towards Jeff. Davis by soldiers and citizens of Dixie, and of the almost universal desire of all but those in authority to have peace and restoration to the Union. You will be surprised to learn that these accounts come from old soldiers, and from Virginia and the Cotton States. Within the last week, I have conversed with deserters from the following corps, who tell the same tale:—41st Alabama, 46th Virginia, 26th South Carolina, 60th Alabama, Ambulance Corps, Archer's Reserve, Macon's Artillery.

Thus, you see, we are receiving not only deserters from the enemy's pickets, but they come from non-combatant and *élite* corps in rear. They are appalled at the strength, vigor, and perseverance of the Union Government, and I have no doubt that all parties are pretty much in despair. But the controlling men are desperate, and will resort to desperate extremities. Time is important; we should strike harder and heavier blows than ever, before they recover from the general alarm, and organize the black legion.

If you send us the right sort of men in the coming three hundred thousand, we can finish the work by June; but if you send us bounty-jumpers and substitutes, we shall have more than a year's work before us, and you more taxes, political intrigues, foreign entanglements, domestic demoralization, &c., &c.

A DAY'S MARCH.

GALESVILLE, ALA.

READER,—By the above you will see that I am no longer in the "State of Georgy." We are "into Alabamy" about seven miles; and after about three weeks' hard marching hither and thither, as the rebels see fit to lead, we have at length halted. For how long, I know not.

Feeling somewhat in a mood for writing, however, let our halt be long or short, I will endeavor to improve the time, in part at least, by holding intercourse with the civilized world, through the medium of my pen. But of what shall I write? A thousand subjects crowd upon the mind with claims of interest; but which would be most interesting is difficult to decide. There is Southern Scenery, Southern Fertility, Southern Agriculture, Southern Climate, Southern Treason, Southern Suffering, Southern—a great many things that might afford themes for interesting letters. And then there is the Evening Camp Scene, that no painter can portray; the "Thousand and One" "Grape-vines," too, that we hear passing through camp daily, when we get cut loose from the outer world, as we have been for the last three weeks.

The "March of a Day," too, might afford sufficient inspiration for one letter. The "March of a Day!" What a conglomeration of ideas is contained in that short phrase! True, most folks, except those who are actively engaged in it, associate nothing more with the phrase than the simple change of location by the army, or a part of the army, for a distance of perhaps eight or ten miles. But what a faint idea does this present of the reality! Perhaps after dark, the evening before, an orderly rides rapidly up to regimental head-quarters, with a paper in a large yellow envelope. He hands it in to the colonel in his tent. Orders to move! The adjutant is ordered to notify company commanders to be ready to move by daylight to-morrow morning. Company commanders notify their men. This requires the men in the regiment and the cooks to be up at least two hours before daylight.

So at about three A. M., all over the camp, men are chopping and splitting up rails with which to make fires. Then you can hear the men pounding their coffee in their tin cups with the butts of their bayonets. All over the camp, too, is a continual gabble: talking, shouting, singing, swearing—a perfect Babel! Who can sleep in such a place? There is no use trying. Before I get accustomed to the noise and confusion now in camp sufficiently to enable me to sleep, Green, the colored cook, thrusts his black face and curly head in at the tent door, and announces: "Breckfas' ready, gemmen. De sun looks mos' bu'ful cumin' up ova dat ar' mounting." So we have to practise upon one part of "Poor Richard's" maxim, "Early to rise," willing or unwilling. We roll over, yawn, slowly rise; wash, dress, comb hastily; gather round half a dozen tin cups, tin plates, knives, forks, and spoons, spread out upon an oil-cloth, which is spread out upon the ground. For breakfast we have *coffee, crackers*, and *salt pork*.

Breakfast is scarcely over when the bugle at brigade head-quarters sounds "*Strike tents.*" In a moment all the regimental bugles catch up "the joyful sound," and all blow, "Strike tents!" "Strike tents!" "Strike tents!" too. A regular shout now rises from the men, and in a moment you can see acres of tents melt away like April snow. Soon all these tents and blankets are seen only in little bundles, tied up ready, at the proper signal, to be shouldered by the men. The field that a moment ago was covered white with tents, is now seen covered with armed men, standing among their smoking camp-fires, and the little poles and forks upon which their tents were lately stretched.

After an hour, or perhaps two, spent waiting on somebody, the proper signal is given by the bugle (for every movement is made in obedience to the sound of the bugle); cartridge-boxes, haversacks, canteens, knapsacks, shelter-tents, and blankets are put on, and arms are shouldered. At the proper signal, also, every man takes his proper place, and, with arms at "right shoulder," all move off. But we don't move far. We get out to the road, perhaps, to find that somebody else occupies it, or that somebody that precedes us in the march is not yet ready to occupy it. "Halt" is blown by the bugler. Arms are stacked. We lie round for an hour or more, perhaps. Again the bugle sounds, "Attention." The men all gather up to their guns and "take arms." "Forward" is blown, and off we go again. We move, perhaps, only a mile or two when we run against somebody's wagon-train, blocking up the road. Again we stop; stack arms; lounge round perhaps for an hour or two. We move again. Soon, however, we again overtake the blockading train; a team of mules are down in the mud—mules, mud, harness, chains, all in one promiscuous mass! Drivers are whipping and cursing; wagon-masters and guards are, some with rails prying, and others grunting and going through the motions of pushing at the wheels; and all cursing and swearing at the drivers and the mules. But "it is no go!" It is useless to wait here. So we take through the fields and bushes on either side of the train, and push forward.

It is now past noon, and we have made but two or three miles of the twenty to be travelled to-day. Lost time must now be redeemed, if possible. There is no time now to stop for dinner; so on we move with rapid steps. We have but few "halts" for rest. We are now sweeping up through a level fertile valley; now straggling through the brushy woods; now passing through the deep and winding mountain pass; now climbing the steep and rugged mountain side; now wandering along its rocky ridge; and again we descend the other slope into the neighboring valley. Thus we go "marching along," while many a witty remark is made, and many a laughable scene is witnessed. Shoes frequently give out, and leave the soldier to make his march in his bare feet. As I made the march to-day with the rest, I noticed a soldier with but one shoe on, and with his other foot tied up in a piece of cloth. Supposing that there was something the matter with his foot that he could not wear his shoe on it, I inquired. "Oh, there is nothing the matter with the foot," said he; "the matter is all with the shoe. It gave out, and I threw it away."

Passing by a large frame-house, or rather what had been a large frame-house, now stripped of the weather-boarding and every thing except the roof standing upon the bare studding, I noticed that some soldiers had placed a large board over where the door had been, with "ADMITTANCE NIX," written in large letters with chalk. On another board, on the studding where the hall had been, was written, "ROOMS TO LET HERE."

At another time we were passing a large, deserted plantation, and in the gateway that opened into the yard, in front of a little old negro-cabin, some soldier had placed the bed of an old buggy, and had set on it a little wood stove, in which he had kindled a fire; and on a board stuck up on the gate-post was written with chalk, in large letters, "HOT COFFEE HERE AT ALL HOURS." On the side of the old cabin was written, in like manner: "PIG'S FEET," "FRESH OYSTERS," "HOT COFFEE," "WARM MEALS AT ALL HOURS," "HAM AND EGGS," "FRESH SAUSAGE," "TURTLE SOUP," &c., &c. The novelty, or rather the ridiculousness, of these things, here, where the like had not been seen perhaps since the war commenced, or perhaps never called forth from the soldiers, as they went trudging by, one continued stream of witty remarks. One would, perhaps, cry out, "And how are *you*, restaurant?" Another, "Bully for the restaurant!" Another, "And how are *you*, cooking-stove?" Another, "Bully for the cooking-stove!" Another, "Cooking-stoves are played out!" Says another, as he comes waddling along, almost "played out" himself, "I'll take the ham and eggs, just now." Another, "I'll take a dish of oysters, waiter." The next calls out, "Waiter, bring me a cup of hot coffee!" Another, "I'll take some chicken, waiter; fetch along enough for the chaplain, too." Another, "Fetch on your pig's feet, waiter." Thus it went while the whole column was passing. Thus these Union soldiers passed the time in jollity and mirth, scarcely seeming to realize the fatigue and labor of the march.

General Sherman has broken loose from his base of supplies, and, it is said, has given liberty to live off the country. At least that is the understanding with the men; and they are not slow in understanding such permission to mean, "Go for it, boys! Don't starve in a plentiful country! Forage liberally; for what *we* don't take, *Hood's men* will get."

Hence towards evening there are about as many chickens, turkeys, pigs, and geese in the regiment as there are men. And, oh, what loads of fresh pork, mutton, veal, and sweet potatoes some men can carry in addition to their warlike equipments! In the rear of each brigade what a caravan of poor mules and old worn-out horses! Some with bridles on, some with only ropes round their necks. All are, however, loaded with immense bundles of all kinds of "*traps:*" camp-kettles, large and small; coffee-pots and frying-pans, of all sorts and sizes. On the top of all these, some have bags of sweet potatoes, chickens, turkeys, geese, parts of sheep, hogs, calves, &c., &c.

Well is it for the man whose mule or old horse does not "*get down*" under his load. When such is the case, it requires a large amount of labor and swearing to get the "traps" off, and the mule up, and the "traps" all on again, and then get up again to his proper place in the grand cavalcade. And happier still is the mule-driver, or rather mule-*leader*, whose mule is able, when he gets down, to get up again when the "traps" are removed from his back. A good-natured, honest Dutchman had got an old horse and an old buggy, and put his "traps" into it, and was getting along swimmingly, till we came to one of those places, often found in this Southern world, where the surface of the earth lies upon a foundation that very obligingly yields to downward pressure, and when a wagon-wheel gets through the surface into it, the longer it stays in one position, the deeper it sinks into the mire. Here the Dutchman's horse sank, floundered, fell, stuck fast in the mud. The buggy, too, sinks in the mud, sticks fast, and is likely there to stick. In a cavalcade like this there are more Priests and Levites than good Samaritans, and each feeling that to help the Dutchman in distress was none of his business, and that he had enough to do to get along himself, all pass by on the other side of the Dutchman in his calamity. It is now dark, and I happen to come along that way; so he comes running to me, calling out, "Shaplein! Shaplein! mine horse ish entire gone up,—complete pugged out!" And sure enough there the old horse was, but I thought, from the fix he was in, he looked more like being "entire" gone *down*, or *under*, than "gone up"—completely swamped in the mire, and the buggy up to the axles in the mud. There is no use in trying to get this "rig" along any farther. It must be accounted for now as "expended," or "lost in the service." So I take a bundle of hay out of the buggy and lay it by the old horse's head, helped Shake to get his "traps" along, and we leave the poor old horse to his fate.

As evening approaches, we find here and there men sitting or lying by the roadside, waiting for the ambulances. They have given out on the march. On we move, but the camp, though anxiously looked for by all, is not yet reached. The shades of evening close in round us. It is now dark, and still we trudge along. We meet a man on horseback. "How far to camp?" "How far to camp?" rings out all along the line, as he passes. "Two miles and a half," "Two miles and a half," he answers as fast as he can utter it, to keep up with the inquiries put to him. So on we move to overcome the "two miles and a half." But, oh, how long they seem to-night! Every hill we ascend, and every bend in the road we pass, we anxiously look to see the camp-fires. But we are often disappointed. At length we descry the glimmer of the distant camp-fires. The sight calls forth a shout from the men all along the line. After sundry and patience-trying stops we finally reach camp. And, oh, what a camp! Upon a steep hill-side, while there is plenty of level land in the neighborhood: rocky, too, and a perfect thicket, while there is plenty of clear, smooth land all around. Who made such a selection of a camp as this? No difference. It has been made by the proper authority, and our duty is simply to submit. We march by faith. We fight by faith. We crawl up this hill-side, and in among these rocks and bushes, in the dark, to camp for the night, by faith. We have not faith, however, to believe that the officer who selected such a place in which for us to camp, camps to-night himself in just such a place. There are more curses than prayers among the men in the bushes just now. We have had no dinner to-day. We have made a march of over twenty miles. We cannot do without supper also. But what a place this is in which to get supper! No wonder the cooks grumble, and some of them even swear. The brush is rid off sufficient space on which to build fires. Fires are kindled—a little coffee is made —a little meat is fried. With salt pork, coffee, and crackers we make our supper. We spread down our blankets among the bushes, retire to rest, and are soon oblivious to the toils, and trials, and dangers of "this cruel war."

Such is a brief sketch of "The March of a Day"—a long and toilsome day. But it, with all its toils, and labors, and dangers, is gone—gone forever! All its thoughts, and words, and deeds are recorded in God's book of remembrance, to stand in uneffaceable record till the day of final accounts. Ah, and are all these foolish and wicked oaths I have heard uttered this day, by both officers and men, recorded there, to be remembered on that great day, for which all other days were made, against those who uttered them? Uttered perhaps in anger, perhaps in jest, perhaps in simple thoughtlessness. But there they are, and all other thoughts, and words, and deeds, whether good or bad; and with this record against us, we are one day nigher eternity,—one day nigher death, the resurrection, and final judgment. Oh, that we could all improve by the past; and that our noble soldiers, while they each day make "A Day's March" in the discharge of their duty in our country's cause, may make also "The March of a Day" towards that better country where wars, and fightings, and wearisome marchings are unknown, is the earnest wish of him who writes. RANDAL ROSS,

Chaplain 15th Regt, O. V. V. I.

PERSONAL ITEMS.

Major-General George H. Thomas has been appointed major-general in the regular Army, to date from December 15th, the day of his recent great victory over Hood, and to fill the vacancy occasioned by the resignation of General John C. Frémont.

Major-General A. S. Webb has been appointed Chief of Staff to Major-General Meade, commanding Army of the Potomac.

Brevet Major-General A. H. Terry has been appointed a full major-general of volunteers, and brigadier-general in the regular Army, for distinguished services in the capture of Fort Fisher.

Brigadier-General Edward Ferrero has been brevetted major-general, for gallant conduct and meritorious service before Richmond and Petersburg.

Brigadier-General E. B. Brown has been assigned to the command of the district of Rolla, Missouri.

The President has nominated Brigadier-General Ames brevet major-general, and Colonels Pennypacker, Curtis, and Bell brevet brigadier-generals, for gallantry at the capture of Fort Fisher.

The following-named officers have been promoted by the President to be brevet brigadier-generals in the regular Army, for meritorious and faithful service:—Brevet Colonel R. S. Satterlee, Colonel A. E. Shiras, Major L. Easton, Colonel E. D. Townsend, Colonel William Hoffman, Brevet Colonel D. H. Vinton, Brevet Colonel Stewart Van Vliet, Brevet Colonel Rufus Ingalls, Colonel Edmund Schriver, Brevet Colonel B. W. Brice, Colonel George Wright.

Brigadier-General Robert B. Potter (Second Division, Ninth Corps) has been brevetted major-general, to date from August 1st, for distinguished and gallant conduct in the several actions since crossing the Rapidan.

Brigadier-General O. B. Willcox, commanding the First Division of the Ninth Army Corps, has been brevetted major-general, to date from the 1st of last August.

Brigadier-General Joseph D. Cox has been promoted to be a major-general of volunteers, for distinguished services.

Brigadier-General Frank Wheaton (Major 2d U. S. Cavalry) has been brevetted major-general, for conspicuous gallantry at the battles of Winchester, Fisher's Hill, and Cedar Creek.

Colonel Cyrus Hamlin, eldest son of the Vice-President, has been promoted to the rank of brigadier-general, for distinguished services.

Colonel Henry G. Thomas (19th U. S. Colored Troops, and Captain 11th U. S. Infantry) has been appointed brigadier-general, for conspicuous gallantry before Petersburg.

Colonel Wm. R. Brewster (73d New York Vols.) has been brevetted brigadier-general, for distinguished services and gallant conduct in the present campaign before Richmond.

Colonel Andrew W. Denison has been brevetted brigadier-general, for meritorious services in the field.

Colonel Joseph B. Hamblin (65th New York) and Colonel Wm. H. Penrose (4th New Jersey) have been brevetted brigadier-generals, for conspicuous gallantry at the battles of Winchester, Fisher's Hill, and Cedar Creek.

Colonel Henry L. Abbot (1st Connecticut Artillery) has been brevetted brigadier-general, to date from August 1st, for distinguished and gallant services before Richmond.

Colonel E. L. Molineux (159th New York Vols.) has been brevetted brigadier-general, for distinguished services in the field.

Colonel E. J. Davis (1st Texas Cavalry) has been brevetted brigadier-general, for distinguished services in the field.

Colonel Joseph Bailey (4th Wisconsin Cavalry) has been brevetted brigadier-general, for distinguished services in the field, and appointed to the command of the District of Baton Rouge.

Colonel Thomas J. Lucas (16th Indiana Mounted Infantry) has been brevetted brigadier-general, for distinguished services in the field.

Colonel Wm. Myers, Chief Quartermaster of the Department of Missouri, has been brevetted brigadier-general.

Colonel N. B. M'Laughlin (57th Massachusetts Veteran Volunteers) has, for distinguished and gallant services at Poplar Grove Church, Va., September 30, 1864, been appointed a brigadier-general of volunteers, to rank from that date.

Colonel R. B. Hayes (23d Ohio Vols.) has been appointed brigadier-general, for gallant and meritorious services in the Shenandoah Valley.

Colonel George D. Wells (34th Massachusetts Volunteers) has been nominated by the President for promotion, for distinguished services at the battle of Cedar Creek, Virginia.

Colonel William Cogswell, of the 2d Massachusetts Infantry, has been made brevet brigadier-general, since the arrival of Sherman's army at Savannah.

Colonel James R. Slack (47th Indiana Volunteers) has been appointed brigadier-general, for distinguished services.

Lieutenant-Colonel William T. Clark, Chief of Staff and Assistant Adjutant-General of the Department and Army of the Tennessee, has recently been promoted by the President to be a brigadier-general of volunteers.

The meeting of the adjutant-generals of the United States, which assembled recently at Columbus, Ohio, adjourned to meet at Boston on the 10th of July proximo.

Commodore James S. Palmer assumed command of the Western Gulf Blockading Squadron November 30th, upon Admiral Farragut's sailing for the North.

The President has remitted the court-martial sentence of Admiral Wilkes to a period of one year from its date (May 3, 1864), at which time the Admiral is to be restored to active duty.

Among the promotions in the Medical Department sent to the Senate by the President are the following:—Medical Inspector-General Joseph K. Barnes, to be surgeon-general, with the rank of brigadier-general, August 22d, 1864, *vice* Hammond, dismissed. Surgeon Madison Mills, to be medical inspector-general, with the rank of colonel, December 1, 1864, *vice* Barnes, appointed surgeon-general.

Surgeon George Suckley has been appointed Medical Director of the Department of Virginia and North Carolina.

OFFICIAL INTELLIGENCE.

The Army.

Appointments Confirmed by the Senate.

Brigadier-General William T. Sherman, United States Army, Major-General of Volunteers, to be Major-General, August 12, 1864, vice Wool, retired.

Brigadier-General George H. Thomas, United States Army, Major-General of Volunteers, to be Major-General, December 15, 1864, vice Frémont, resigned.

Brigadier-General Philip H. Sheridan, United States Army, Major-General of Volunteers, to be Major-General, November 8. 1864, vice McClellan, resigned.

Major Winfield S. Hancock, Quartermaster United States Army, and Major-General of Volunteers, to be Brigadier-General, August 12, 1864, vice McPherson, deceased.

Captain Philip H. Sheridan, Thirteenth United States Infantry, Major-General of Volunteers, to be Brigadier-General, September 20, 1864, vice Sherman, appointed Major-General.

Passed Assistant Surgeon Somerset Robinson, to be Surgeon.

Captain John L. Broome, to be Major in the Marine Corps.

First Lieutenant William H. Parker, to be Captain in the Marine Corps.

Second Lieutenant Lewis E. Fagan, to be First Lieutenant in the Marine Corps.

Francis N. Harrington, of the District of Columbia, to be Second Lieutenant in the Marine Corps.

First Lieutenant John A. Burroughs, to be Captain in the Marine Corps.

Second Lieutenants Frederick T. Peet and Edward P. Meeker, to be First Lieutenants.

Acting Volunteer Lieutenant William P. Hall, to be Acting Volunteer Lieutenant-Commander.

Acting Masters J. S. Warner, James C. Gibson, George W. Rogers, John Rogers, Henry S. Wetmore, John W. Atkinson, and Peter O'Kell, to be Acting Volunteer Lieutenants for duty on the Mississippi Squadron.

Field-Officers' Courts.

The following opinion of the Judge-Advocate General of the Army, upon the proceedings under Section 7, Act of Congress approved July 17, 1862, is published for the information of the Army:—

> WAR DEPARTMENT,
> BUREAU OF MILITARY JUSTICE,
> December 7, 1864.

To the Adjutant-General:

The following is respectfully submitted, in reply to the questions suggested by the communication of Major Stickney, 24th Veteran Reserve Corps, and the records accompanying it:

The Field-Officers' Court, under the Act of Congress of July 17, 1862, supersedes the Regimental Court in all cases when there is a field officer with the regiment. If there are two such officers present, the order should be issued by the regimental commander; otherwise, by the brigade or next superior commander.

The act was intended to provide a means for summary punishment of the lighter grades of offences previously triable by Regimental Courts, and it has not been held to be necessary to make up the records with the formality required in cases tried by court-martial. Though it is preferable to have the record of each case made up separately, it is not considered a fatal irregularity to unite the proceedings in a number of cases, without repeating the order detailing the trying officer in each.

The record should show the charge upon which each prisoner was tried, and the plea, finding, and sentence in the case.

It is not necessary to spread the evidence upon the record, and therefore it need not be set forth that the prisoner had an opportunity to offer evidence and make a statement.

The jurisdiction is confined to cases which were triable before a Regimental Court. The 66th Article of War limits the jurisdiction of Regimental Courts to the trial of offences not capital. The second charge against Private John Reilly is an offence within the 9th Article of War, and should not, therefore, have been the subject of investigation in this proceeding. As, however, the other charge on which the party was tried is one of which the officer clearly had jurisdiction, and as his finding on this will support the sentence, which does not seem at all disproportionate to the offence, it is not recommended that it be disturbed.

J. HOLT,
Judge-Advocate General.

Dismissals,

For the Week ending December 3, 1864.

Lieutenant-Colonel R. S. Donaldson, 50th United States Colored Troops, to date November 26, 1864, for (while in command of a recruiting rendezvous, at Vicksburg, Mississippi) having accepted money from a State Recruiting Agent, by way of gratification, and in consideration of certain certified copies of muster-in rolls, to be furnished said State Agent, such acceptance of money being in violation of the Sixteenth Article of War.

Captain Frank T. D. Ketcham, 16th United States Colored Infantry, to date November 25, 1864, for having tendered his resignation, on account of incompetency, while under charges (disobedience of orders, insubordination, appropriating the company funds for his own use and benefit, stealing a horse and equipments, and offering the same for sale, lying, and drunkenness on duty).

The following officers, to date October 31, 1864, for the causes mentioned; having been published officially, and failed to appear before the Commission:

Disobedience of orders and absence without leave.

Captain Theodore Conkey, 3d Wisconsin Cavalry.

Absence without leave.

Captain Martin H. McChesney, 2d New York Mounted Rifles.
First Lieutenant William F. McNamara, 69th Pennsylvania Volunteers.
First Lieutenant John E. Gharrett, 1st United States Colored Artillery (heavy), to date November 26, 1864, having tendered his resignation, assigning as a reason therefor a lack of confidence in Colored Troops, and consequent unfitness for holding an appointment in that branch of the service.
First Lieutenant Matthew H. Ward, Quartermaster 9th Michigan Cavalry, to date November 30, 1864, for absence without leave.

The following officers, to date November 25, 1864, for absenting themselves from their commands in the engagement of October 19, 1864:—
Second Lieutenant J. C. Burbridge, 10th West Virginia Volunteers.
Second Lieutenant William G. W. Price, 15th West Virginia Volunteers.

Second Lieutenant Albert Weber, 7th Regiment Veteran Reserve Corps, to date November 25, 1864, with loss of all pay and allowances, for fraudulently drawing two months' pay while absent without leave.

Second Lieutenant Obed Enson, 3d Colorado Cavalry, to date November 26, 1864, for disobedience of orders, drunkenness, dishonesty, and utter worthlessness as an officer.

Second Lieutenant J. P. Robertson, 8th Missouri State Militia Cavalry, to date November 26, 1864.

Second Lieutenant John C. Taggert, 69th Pennsylvania Volunteers, to date April 19, 1864, for absence without leave.

For the Week ending December 10, 1864.

Lieutenant-Colonel Napoleon B. Knight, 1st Delaware Cavalry, to date December 2, 1864, for disobedience of orders, neglect of duty, and incompetency.

Captain F. L. Taylor, 34th New Jersey Volunteers, to date December 2, 1864, for having tendered his resignation on a frivolous pretext.

Captain Henry G. Beschioff, 41st Missouri Volunteers, to date December 8, 1864, for gross neglect of duty, in allowing certain prisoners of war, under his charge, to escape.

Assistant Surgeon William Crouse, 38th United States Colored Troops, to date September 21, 1864, for drunkenness and neglect of duty.

First Lieutenant R. F. Chesebro, Quartermaster 38th Indiana Volunteers, to date August 21, 1864, for absence without leave.

First Lieutenant George P. Sanford, 13th United States Infantry, to date December 7, 1864.

Second Lieutenant Edward F. Nixon, 7th Pennsylvania Cavalry, to date December 7, 1864, for his disgraceful conduct in surrendering the block-houses under his charge to the rebel forces under Forrest, October 1, 1864.

For the Week ending December 17, 1864.

Captain August Gudath, 178th New York Volunteers, to date December 15, 1864, for absence without leave, and worthlessness.

First Lieutenant Edgar M. Blanche, 5th Massachusetts Colored Cavalry, to date December 15, 1864, for absence without leave.

First Lieutenant Samuel Fessenden, Quartermaster 7th Rhode Island Volunteers, to date December 13, 1864, for having on five several occasions been so drunk as to render him unfit for duty, conduct unbecoming an officer and gentleman, disrespect to his superior officers, and repeated disobedience of orders.

First Lieutenant John Beadle, 108th New York Volunteers, to date November 21, 1864, for absence without leave, having been published officially, and failed to appear before the Commission.

Lieutenant Homer L. Wells, 2d Mississippi Colored Infantry Volunteers, to date August 22, 1864.

Second Lieutenant Hoyt Palmer, 10th Regiment Veteran Reserve Corps, to date December 14, 1864, for drunkenness.

Second Lieutenant N. M. Rust, 4th United States Colored Troops, to date November 23, 1864, having been reported for cowardly desertion of his command, in the face of the enemy.

The following officers, to date November 14, 1864, for the causes mentioned, having been published officially, and failed to appear before the Commission:—

Chaplain David Hodson, 89th Indiana Volunteers, for absence without leave, and offering a bribe to the Surgeon in charge of Officers' Hospital, Memphis, Tennessee, to procure him a leave of absence.

First Lieutenant Thomas Oliver, 51st New York Volunteers, for absence without leave and disobedience of orders.

For the Week ending December 24, 1864.

Lieutenant-Colonel John Bowles, 1st Kansas Colored Volunteers, to date December 17, 1864, for neglect of duty, in not rendering the reports required by paragraph 468, of the Army Regulations; absence without leave, and repeated disobedience of War Department orders, directing him to join his regiment.

Captain W. Angelo Powell, Company A, 1st West Virginia Veteran Cavalry, to date December 17, 1864, for absence without leave, disobedience of orders, and wanton neglect of Government property.

Captain John A. P. Fleming, 54th Illinois Volunteers, to date December 22, 1864, for inefficiency, worthlessness, and neglect of duty.

Captain H. F. Crossman, 2d Battalion Veteran Reserve Corps, to date December 21, 1864.

First Lieutenant Robert Sims, Battery B, 1st New Jersey Artillery, to date November 28, 1864, for absence without leave, having been published officially, and failed to appear before the Commission.

The following officers, to date November 28, 1864, for the causes mentioned, having been published officially, and failed to appear before the Commission:—

Absence without leave.

Captain John McMenamin, 13th New York Cavalry.
First Lieutenant J. W. McComas, 5th Maryland Volunteers.
First Lieutenant Thomas Allen, 5th Rhode Island Artillery.
Captain Oscar O. Bowen, 47th New York Volunteers.
Second Lieutenant George H. Bartram, 183d Pennsylvania Volunteers.

Disobedience of orders and absence without leave.

First Lieutenant Allen E. Ellsworth, 118th Illinois Volunteers.
First Lieutenant Charles Green, 1st Missouri Light Artillery, to date December 22, 1864, for worthlessness, and habitual neglect of duty.
Lieutenant Clarence R. Smith, 1st Arkansas Volunteers, to date December 22, 1864, for conduct unbecoming an officer and gentleman, habitual drunkenness, and maliciously circulating false reports derogatory to the character of the officers of his regiment, and the enlisted men belonging to his company, and for inefficiency and incompetency in the performance of his official duties.

For the Week ending December 31, 1864.

Major Lymon W. Brown, 11th Missouri Cavalry, to date December 24, 1864, for falsely certifying that a quantity of salt, which he drew from the Subsistence Department, was for his own use, whereas the same was intended for sale, and was so sold, to persons "outside of the lines," in violation of General Orders and trade regulations; and for preferring false charges against the commanding officer of his regiment, and for inefficiency as an officer.
Captain H. Bowen, Jr., 151st New York Volunteers, to date September 19, 1864, for absence without leave; having been published officially, and failed to make satisfactory defence before the Commission.

The following officers, to date December 5, 1864, for the causes mentioned, having been published officially, and failed to appear before the Commission:—

Absence without leave.

Captain Andreas Seelig, 46th New York Volunteers.
First Lieutenant Charles S. Hazen, 3d New Hampshire Volunteers.
Assistant Surgeon Peter E. Sichler, 10th New York Cavalry.

Disobedience of orders.

Captain Eli F. Scott, 83d Indiana Volunteers.
Captain John Logan, 6th Iowa Cavalry, to date December 28, 1864, for allowing the men under his command to pillage, for drunkenness, and for inefficiency as an officer.
Captain John Gregson, Assistant Quartermaster United States Volunteers, to date December 29, 1864, for conduct unbecoming an officer, neglect of duty, and absence without leave.
Captain Dudley C. Wyman, 11th Wisconsin Volunteers, to date December 29, 1864, for pillaging and allowing the men under his command to pillage, while in command of an expedition which left Brashear City on the 22d of October, 1864.
Chaplain A. J. Lyon, 11th West Virginia Volunteers, to date December 24, 1864, for absence without leave and worthlessness.
First Lieutenant Stanley Mourton, 3d United States Infantry, to date December 24, 1864, for desertion, disobedience of orders, and not accounting for public funds and property in his possession.
Lieutenant W. H. Creighton, 25th New York Cavalry, to date December 23, 1864, for absence without leave, and failure to answer satisfactorily to infamous charges preferred against him.
Lieutenant Emil Newberger, Quartermaster 13th Illinois Cavalry, to date December 28, 1864, for fraudulently disposing of a horse, the property of the United States.
Second Lieutenant E. Knapp, 17th Illinois Cavalry, to date December 27, 1864, for absence without leave, conduct unbecoming an officer and gentleman, and prejudicial to good order and military discipline.

Second Lieutenant Samuel Major, 9th Illinois Cavalry, to date December 28, 1864, for disobedience of orders, and allowing his men to straggle and pillage, thereby losing four men, captured by the enemy.

Dishonorably Discharged.

For the Week ending December 24, 1864.

Captain Erasmus D. Witt, 205th Pennsylvania Volunteers, from date of muster in, for having tendered his resignation on account of physical disability, resulting from his own imprudence.

Second Lieutenant Philo J. Tuttle, 39th New York Volunteers, from date of muster in, for having tendered his resignation on the ground of incompetency.

For the Week ending December 31, 1864.

Second Lieutenant Lewis Thomas, 80th New York Volunteers (20th New York State Militia), from date of muster in, for having tendered his resignation on the ground of incompetency.

Exempt from Dismissal.

WAR DEPARTMENT,
ADJUTANT-GENERAL'S OFFICE,
WASHINGTON, Dec. 13, 1864.

The following-named officers, charged with offences, and heretofore published, are exempt from being dismissed the service of the United States, the Military Commission instituted by Special Orders, No. 53, series of 1863, from the War Department, having reported that satisfactory defence has been made in their respective cases, viz.:—

Captain J. C. Battersby, 1st New York Cavalry.
First Lieutenant Charles S. Edmonds, 69th Pennsylvania Volunteers.
Captain George F. McKnight, 12th New York Battery.

December 22, 1864.

Captain William P. Jordon, 29th Maine Veteran Volunteers.
First Lieutenant Edward Freeman, 19th Pennsylvania Cavalry.
First Lieutenant Joel M. Straight, 38th Wisconsin Volunteers.

Jan. 2, 1865.

The following-named officers, charged with offences, and heretofore published, are exempt from being dismissed the service of the United States, the Military Commission instituted by Special Orders, No. 53, series of 1863, from the War Department, having reported that they are exempt, for the causes set opposite their respective names:—

First Lieutenant Frank Kimball, 75th United States Colored Troops, he having been previously honorably discharged, on account of physical disability, by Special Orders, No. 409, November 21, 1864, from this office.

Second Lieutenant H. O. Grossman, 138th Pennsylvania Volunteers, he having made satisfactory defence before a Board of Officers convened in the field.

First Lieutenant William Dunham, 1st Vermont Heavy Artillery, he having made satisfactory defence before the Military Commission.

E. D. TOWNSEND,
Assistant Adjutant-General.

Dismissals Revoked.

The orders of dismissal heretofore issued in the following cases, have been revoked:—

First Lieutenant John T. Hasson, 75th United States Colored Infantry, and he is discharged for absence without leave, to date August 1, 1864.

Second Lieutenant John D. Paddock, 75th United States Colored Infantry, and he is honorably discharged, upon the report of a Board, to date December 6, 1864, on account of physical disability.

For the Week ending December 31, 1864.

Major Albert A. Pitcher, 18th New York Cavalry, and he is honorably discharged, to date November 27, 1864.

Captain Simson Hamburger, 91st New York Volunteers, and he is honorably discharged, to date November 17, 1864.

Lieutenant J. J. Medlicott, 2d West Virginia Cavalry, and he is honorably discharged, to date October 8, 1864.

Restored to Commission.

The following officers, heretofore dismissed, have been restored with pay, from the date at which they rejoin their regiments for duty, provided the vacancies have not been filled by the Governors of their respective States:—

First Lieutenant Hiram F. Winchester, 1st Regiment Potomac Home Brigade, Maryland Volunteer Cavalry, and Second Lieutenant Henry P. Field, 16th New York Cavalry.

Captain J. R. Locke, 64th United States Colored Infantry.
Lieutenant-Colonel W. W. S. Snoddy, 207th Pennsylvania Volunteers.
Lieutenant-Colonel William Blakely, 14th Pennsylvania Cavalry.
First Lieutenant George Pidge, 9th New York Heavy Artillery.
First Lieutenant Asa Farnam, 95th Illinois Volunteers.

Exonerated.

WAR DEPARTMENT,
ADJUTANT-GENERAL'S OFFICE,
WASHINGTON, Dec. 7, 1864.

Captain William R. Howe, Assistant Adjutant-General of Volunteers, heretofore published as absent without leave, is exonerated from such charge, he having had proper authority for his absence.

E. D. TOWNSEND,
Assistant Adjutant-General.

Regular Navy.

Appointed Vice-Admiral.

Dec. 22.—Rear-Admiral David G. Farragut, appointed Vice-Admiral of the Navy of the United States.

Dec. 14.—Rear-Admiral David G. Farragut, detached from command of the West Gulf Squadron, and granted three months' leave.

Orders, &c.

Dec. 20.—Commodore William Smith, detached from command of the Navy Yard, Pensacola, Fla., and granted three months' leave.

Dec. 14.—Captain Percival Drayton, detached from command of the Hartford, and granted leave.

Dec. 21.—Captain Thornton A. Jenkins, detached from command of the Richmond, on the reporting of his relief, and ordered North. Captain Theodore P. Greene, ordered to command the Richmond.

Dec. 28.—Captain John B. Marchand, ordered to the Naval Station, Baltimore, Md.

Dec. 30.—Captain J. B. Marchand, orders of the 28th instant revoked, and he is ordered to duty with Rear-Admiral Gregory.

Dec. 3.—Commander Benjamin M. Dove, detached from duty at Beaufort, N. C., on the reporting of his relief, and ordered to duty in charge of stores at Cairo, Ill.
Commander John J. Young, ordered to command Naval Rendezvous at Brooklyn, N. Y.

Dec. 5.—Commander John Downs, ordered to report to Rear-Admiral Gregory, for such duty as he may assign.

Dec. 12.—Commander William Ronckendorff, ordered to duty as member of a Board at New York.

Dec. 13.—Commander Samuel Lockwood, ordered to report to the Secretary of the Treasury as Light-House Inspector of the First Light-House District.

Dec. 14.—Commander Peirce Crosby, detached from command of the Muscoota, and ordered to command the Metacomet. Commander George M. Ransom, detached from command of the Grand Gulf, and ordered to command the Muscoota. Commander N. C. Bryant, ordered to duty at Naval Station, Mound City, Ill.

Dec. 16.—Commander E. R. Calhoun, detached from command of the Saugus, on the reporting of his relief, and waiting orders.

Dec. 17.—Commander Samuel Lockwood, orders as Light-House Inspector suspended for the present.

Dec. 28.—Commander J. W. A. Nicholson, placed on waiting orders.

Dec. 30.—George M. Colvocoresses, detached from command of the Dacotah, and ordered to command the Wachusett. Commander Napoleon Collins, detached from command of the Wachusett.

Dec. 3.—Lieutenant Commander Oscar F. Stanton, ordered to temporary ordnance duty at New York. Lieutenant-Commander W. C. West, detached from ordnance duty at Philadelphia, and ordered to duty at Beaufort, N. C.

Dec. 8.—Lieutenant-Commanders Charles A. Babcock and Robert Boyd, Jr., ordered to the Mississippi Squadron. Lieutenant-Commander James A. Greer, detached from the Mississippi Squadron, on the reporting of his relief, and waiting orders. Lieutenant-Commander James W. Shirk, detached from the Mississippi Squadron. Lieutenant-Commander Samuel Magaw, detached from command of the Florida, and ordered to command the Lenapee.

Dec. 9.—Lieutenant-Commander S. P. Quackenbush, ordered to the South Atlantic Squadron. Lieutenant-Commander John Madigan, detached from the South Atlantic Squadron, and ordered to report to Commodore Engle, at Philadelphia.

Dec. 14.—Lieutenant-Commander Lewis A. Kimberly, detached from the Hartford, and granted leave. Lieutenant-Commander James E. Jouett, detached from command of the Metacomet, on the reporting of his relief, and ordered North. Lieutenant-Commander W. E. Fitzhugh, detached from command of the Sebago, on the reporting of his relief, and ordered North, as a witness before a Board in session at Philadelphia. Lieutenant-Commander D. B. Harmany, detached from the Naval Rendezvous at New York, on the reporting of his relief, and ordered to command the Sebago.

Dec. 16.—Lieutenant-Commander Thomas S. Phelps, detached from the U. S. Coast Survey, and ordered to command the Saugus.

Dec. 20.—Lieutenant-Commander Greenleaf Cilley, detached from the North Atlantic Squadron, and placed on leave.

Dec. 21.—Lieutenant-Commander Charles J. McDougal, detached from the East Gulf Squadron, and ordered to command the Camanche, San Francisco, California. Lieutenant-Commander Edward Terry, detached from the Richmond, and ordered North. Lieutenant-Commander George S. Norton, detached from the Lackawanna on the reporting of his relief, and ordered to the Richmond.

Dec. 27.—Lieutenant-Commander William M. Gamble, detached from the Rendezvous at Brooklyn, New York, on the reporting of his relief, and waiting orders.

Dec. 2.—Lieutenant Samuel W. Preston, ordered to the North Atlantic Squadron.

Dec. 5.—Lieutenant A. R. Yates, ordered to examination, for promotion in West Gulf Squadron. Lieutenant Clark Merchant, ordered to physical examination, for promotion at Philadelphia.

Dec. 9.—Lieutenant Nathaniel W. Thomas, ordered to temporary ordnance duty, at Boston Navy-Yard.

Dec. 14.—Lieutenant Herbert B. Tyson, La Rue P. Adams, and John C. Watson, detached from the Hartford, and granted leave.

Dec. 15.—Lieutenant Thomas S. Spencer, ordered to the Muscoota.
Dec. 21.—Lieutenant William H. Barton, ordered to the Lackawanna.
Dec. 21.—Lieutenant Hayden T. French, detached from the Dictator, and ordered to the Juniata.

Dec. 9.—Ensign Benjamin H. Porter, ordered to the North Atlantic Squadron.
Dec. 12.—Acting Ensign G. M. McClure, ordered to special duty at Erie, Penn.
Dec. 13.—Ensign Philip W. Lowry, detached from the Sacramento, and granted sick leave.
Dec. 14.—Acting Ensigns George D. B. Gliddens and William H. Whiting, detached from the Hartford, and granted leave.
Dec. 22.—Acting Ensign Charles J. Barclay, detached from the Wachusett, and granted leave.
Dec. 31.—Ensign John C. Pegram, ordered to the Dictator.

Dec. 1.—Assistant Surgeon E. C. Ver Meulen, ordered to the Naval Rendezvous at Portsmouth, N. H.
Dec. 9.—Assistant Surgeon D. McMurtrie, ordered to the Muscoota.
Dec. 14.—Surgeon Philip Lansdale, detached from the Hartford, and granted leave. Assistant Surgeon William Commons, detached from the Hartford, and granted leave. Surgeon J. W. Shively, ordered to temporary duty on board the Vermont. Passed Assistant Surgeon J. H. Macomber, detached from the Galena, and ordered to the St. Louis. Surgeon J. M. Brown, ordered to temporary duty at Navy Yard, New York. Surgeon J. S. Dungan, ordered to the Naval Asylum. Surgeon A. L. Gihon, detached from the St. Louis, on the reporting of his relief, and ordered North.
Dec. 27.—Assistant Surgeon Edward R. Dodge, detached from the West Gulf Squadron, on the reporting of his relief, and ordered North. Assistant Surgeon Edward D. Payne, detached from the West Gulf Squadron, on the reporting of his relief, and ordered North. Assistant Surgeon E. R. Hutchins, detached from the Massachusetts, on the reporting of his relief, and waiting orders.
Dec. 28.—Passed Assistant Surgeon A. Hudson, detached from the Onondaga, and ordered to the Sabine. Passed Assistant Surgeon H. M. Wells, detached from the Sabine, and ordered to the Onondaga.
Dec. 31.—Surgeon George Clymer, ordered to special duty in Washington, D. C.

Dec. 1.—Paymaster J. S. Post, detached from the St. Louis, on the reporting of his relief, and ordered to settle his accounts.
Dec. 2.—Assistant Paymaster George W. Beaman, ordered to duty as Assistant to the Purchasing Paymaster of the Mississippi Squadron.
Dec. 5.—Paymaster Henry R. Day, detached from duty as Inspector of Stores at Baltimore, on the reporting of his relief, but will remain Paymaster of the Station. Assistant Paymaster W. N. Watmough, detached from the Nereus, on the reporting of his relief, and ordered to settle his accounts.
Dec. 7.—Assistant Paymaster Arthur Burtis, Jr., ordered to the Muscoota.
Dec. 10.—Paymaster A. E. Watson, detached from the Naval Station at Mound City, Ill., on the reporting of his relief, and waiting orders. Paymaster W. W. Williams, ordered to Mound City, Ill., as Inspector in charge of Provisions and Clothing.
Dec. 14.—Paymaster William T. Meredith, detached from the Hartford, and ordered to settle his accounts.
Dec. 16.—Paymaster Edward Foster, ordered to the Lancaster. Fleet Paymaster J. B. Rittenhouse, detached from duty as paymaster of the Lancaster, on the reporting of his relief, but will continue his duties as Fleet Paymaster.
Dec. 19.—Paymaster John S. Gulick, detached from duty as Paymaster of the Receiving-Ship Princeton, and of the Naval Asylum at Philadelphia, but will continue his duties as Paymaster of the Station. Paymaster James D. Murray, ordered to duty as Paymaster of the Receiving-Ship Princeton and of the Naval Asylum at Philadelphia.
Dec. 23.—Assistant Paymaster G. F. D. Barton, ordered to the St. Louis.
Dec. 24.—Paymaster James Hoy, Jr., detached from duty under Rear-Admiral Gregory, on the reporting of his relief. Paymaster F. M. Taylor, ordered to duty under Rear-Admiral Gregory.

Dec. 28.—Paymaster T. H. Looker, detached from special duty at Baltimore, Md.
Dec. 29.—Paymaster Frank C. Crosby, ordered to duty at Naval Station, Baltimore, Md.

Dec. 14.—Chaplain Chester Newell, ordered to the Practice Ship Sabine.
Dec. 23.—Chaplain George Jones, ordered to the Navy Yard, Washington, D. C.

Dec. 14.—Chief Engineer Thomas Williamson, detached from the Hartford, and granted leave. Chief Engineer James W. King, ordered to report to Rear-Admiral Gregory, at New York.
Dec. 21.—Chief Engineer George R. Johnson, ordered to duty at Chester, Pennsylvania.

Dec. 9.—First Assistant Engineer Horace McMurtrie, ordered to duty at East Boston, with Chief Engineer Hoyt.
Dec. 14.—First Assistant Engineers F. A. Wilson and E. B. Latch, detached from the Hartford, and granted leave.
Dec. 30.—First Assistant Engineer William D. Pendleton, ordered to special duty at New York.

Dec. 1.—Second Assistant Engineer Henry Holmes, detached from the Sagamore, and waiting orders.
Dec. 2.—Second Assistant Engineer George W. Melville, detached from the Wachusett, and ordered to duty in Torpedo-boats, under Rear-Admiral Porter. Second Assistant Engineer George R. Holt, ordered to the Tahoma.
Dec. 7.—Second Assistant Engineer James H. Chasmar, detached from the Mohongo, and ordered to the Muscoota.
Dec. 14.—Second Assistant Engineers Hugh L. Pilkington and Isaac De Graff, detached from the Hartford, and granted leave.
Dec. 19.—Second Assistant Engineer Alfred S. Brower, detached from the Dictator, and granted sick leave.
Dec. 20.—Second Assistant Engineer Joseph Hooks, detached from the Passaic, on the reporting of his relief, and ordered North. Second Assistant Engineer Richard M. Hodgson, detached from the West Gulf Squadron, and granted sick leave.
Dec. 22.—Second Assistant Engineer Philip Miller, ordered to the Dictator.
Dec. 24.—Second Assistant Engineer William J. Montgomery, detached from the Onondaga, and granted sick leave.
Dec. 27.—Second Assistant Engineer Albert Jackson, ordered to the Spirea.
Dec. 28.—Second Assistant Engineer Edward Gay, detached from the Tacony, and granted sick leave.
Dec. 31.—Second Assistant Engineer John McIntyre, ordered to the Wachusett.

Dec. 1.—Third Assistant Engineers Lemuel Bernard, William E. Sibley, and Frank M. Ashton, detached from the Sagamore, and waiting orders. Third Assistant Engineer J. F. Knowlton, detached from the Conemaugh, and waiting orders.
Dec. 7.—Third Assistant Engineer J. Henry Lewars, ordered to the Wachusett. Third Assistant Engineer Robert S. Stedman, detached from the Wachusett, on the reporting of his relief, and waiting orders.
Dec. 14.—Third Assistant Engineer James E. Speights, detached from the Hartford, and granted leave.
Dec. 31.—Third Assistant Engineer H. D. McEwen, detached from the Wachusett, on the reporting of his relief, and ordered to examination. Third Assistant Engineer Jefferson Brown, ordered to the Wachusett. Third Assistant Engineer J. H. Harmany, ordered to the Agawam.

Promoted.

Dec. 8.—Second Assistant Engineers Henry Brown, Henry C. McIlvaine, and Robert S. Talbot, to be First Assistant Engineers. Third Assistant Engineers Robert N. Ellis, Robert L. Webb, John C. Cross, James E. Fallon, Charles M. Van Tine, William H. Crawford, and William A. H. Allen, to be Second Assistant Engineers.
Dec. 12.—Second Assistant Engineers Thomas H. Bordley and Peter Rearick, to be First Assistant Engineers. Third Assistant Engineers Luther R. Harvey and James W. Patterson, to be Second Assistant Engineers.

Resigned.

Dec. 5.—Midshipmen F. William Rawdon and George E. Hubbell.
Dec. 6.—Assistant Paymaster Charles Fairchild.
Dec. 10—Midshipman Gustavus J. Guild.
Dec. 15.—Midshipman George S. B. Sullivan.
Dec. 16.—Midshipman Harold S. Peck.
Dec. 19.—Midshipman James S. Tomkins. Midshipman F. P. Abercrombie.
Dec. 24.—Gunner H. W. Fitzosborn, on the reporting of his relief.
Dec. 29.—Midshipman Borradial Brown. Surgeon Alexander M. Vedder.
Dec. 30.—Midshipman Walter H. Fox.

Dropped from the List.

Dec. 19—Midshipman Charles C. Hoyt.

Miscellaneous.

Dec. 30.—The President remits two years of the sentence of suspension in the case of Commodore Charles H. Wilkes.

Volunteer Navy.

Orders, &c.

Dec. 3.—Acting Volunteer Lieutenant Henry J. Cook, detached from the Roanoke, and ordered to the Potomac Flotilla. Acting Volunteer Lieutenant C. De Bevoise, detached from the Potomac Flotilla, and ordered to the Roanoke. Acting Volunteer Lieutenant C. P. Clark, ordered to the Mississippi Squadron.
Dec. 8.—Acting Volunteer Lieutenant William G. Saltonstall, detached from temporary ordnance duty at Boston, and ordered to the Mississippi Squadron. Acting Volunteer Lieutenant Pierre Giraud, detached from command of the Mobile, and waiting orders.
Dec. 12.—Acting Volunteer Lieutenant C. F. W. Behm, detached from the Cornubia, and granted sick leave.
Dec. 14.—Acting Volunteer Lieutenant George D. Upham, detached from the Hartford, and waiting orders. Acting Volunteer Lieutenant C. F. W. Behm, ordered to command Naval Rendezvous, New York.
Dec. 15.—Acting Volunteer Lieutenant T. F. Wade, ordered to temporary duty on board the Receiving-Ship Vandalia.
Dec. 16.—Acting Volunteer Lieutenant C. W. Wilson, ordered to command the Napa.
Dec. 17.—Acting Volunteer Lieutenant L. N. Stodder, detached from the Adela, and waiting orders.
Dec. 22.—Acting Volunteer Lieutenant B. C. Dean, ordered to command the Gertrude.
Dec. 23.—Acting Volunteer Lieutenant Thomas F. Wade, orders to the Vandalia, revoked.
Dec. 24.—Acting Volunteer Lieutenant William McGloin, detached from the Grand Gulf, and ordered to the West Gulf Squadron.
Dec. 27.—Acting Volunteer Lieutenant G. E. Nelson, ordered to command the Spirea.
Dec. 30.—Acting Volunteer Lieutenant B. W. Loring, detached from the Wave, and waiting orders.

Appointed Acting Masters.

Dec. 15.—Edmund A. Roderick, U. S. S. Don.
Dec. 19.—Thomas Andrews, and ordered to the West Gulf Squadron.

Appointed Acting Masters and Pilots.

Dec. 5.—E. A. Decker, North Atlantic Squadron.
Dec. 7.—William Tilby and John G. Hudson, North Atlantic Squadron.
Dec. 15.—Jacob Lindee, North Atlantic Squadron.
Dec. 16.—John Robinson, William Stewart, W. H. Wroten, Bernard Crone, Frank Rane, John H. Collins, Christopher Lawrence, John W. Grivet, Benjamin Lancashire, James Maycock, John Nicholson, Henry Rehder, James Redding, and Richard Riggs, and ordered to the West Gulf Squadron.

Dec. 1.—Acting Masters James F. Alcorn and J. W. Stapleford, detached from the Conemaugh, and waiting orders.
Dec. 2.—Acting Master George P. Durand, placed on waiting orders.
Dec. 7.—Acting Masters George R. Durand and H. S. Borden, ordered to the Muscoota.
Dec. 8.—Acting Master L. W. Hill, detached from the Vandalia, and ordered to the National Guard. Acting Master G. H. Pendleton, ordered to the Lenapee. Acting Master Charles Potter, ordered to command the National Guard. Acting Master William B. Newman, ordered to the Wachusett. Acting Master C. M. Marchant, detached from the Ohio, on the reporting of his relief, and ordered to the National Guard.
Dec. 9.—Acting Masters William H. Hobbs and J. S. Williams, detached from the Adela, and waiting orders.
Dec. 12.—Acting Master and Pilot Henry North, detached from the Stepping-Stones, and granted leave.
Dec. 14.—Acting Master D. C. Kells, detached from the Galena, and ordered to the Cambridge.
Dec. 15.—Acting Master John White, ordered to the South Atlantic Squadron.
Dec. 16.—Acting Master Foster Willis, ordered to the Napa.
Dec. 20.—Acting Master C. M. Marchant's orders to the National Guard revoked, and ordered back to the Ohio.
Dec. 22.—Acting Master L. W. Hill, detached from the National Guard, and ordered to the East Gulf Squadron. Acting Master Charles Potter, detached from command of the National Guard, and ordered to the West Gulf Squadron. Acting Master H. Clay Wade, detached from command of the Gertrude, on the reporting of his relief, and ordered North.
Dec. 27.—Acting Master J. S. Williams, ordered to the Spirea.
Dec. 29.—Acting Master J. W. Stapleford, ordered to the Conemaugh.
Dec. 31.—Acting Master Samuel C. Cruse, granted sick leave.

Appointed Acting Ensigns.

Dec. 2.—W. B. Browne, East Gulf Squadron; Thomas H. Wheeler, U. S. S. Shenandoah; Charles H. Gaylor, U. S. S. Proteus.
Dec. 6.—William L. Gilley, Potomac Flotilla; Joseph A. Scarlett, U. S. S. North Carolina.
Dec. 9.—Charles R. Haskins, U. S. S. Wachusett.
Dec. 10.—George A. Johnson, U. S. S. Sangamon; Denny M. Hayes, Potomac Flotilla; Richard L. Hartford, Potomac Flotilla.
Dec. 12.—James Courtney, U. S. S. Grand Gulf.
Dec. 13.—L. N. Rollins and John Davis, Potomac Flotilla; Calvin S. Wilcox, U. S. S. Alabama; F. H. Lathrop, U. S. S. Agawam.
Dec. 15.—Charles H. Sawyer, U. S. S. Meteor; W. A. De Witt, U. S. S. Selma.
Dec. 16.—Theodore A. Comstock, U. S. S. Iosco.
Dec. 23.—John P. Thompson, U. S. S. Laburnum.
Dec. 28.—A. J. Kendall and Henry Richdale, East Gulf Squadron.
Dec. 29.—J. E. N. Graham, U. S. S. Circassian.
Dec. 30.—William C. King, U. S. S. Eutaw.
Dec. 31.—William H. Fogg, U. S. S. Muscoota; Paul Boyden, N. A. B. Squadron.

Appointed Acting Ensigns, and ordered to the School-Ship Savannah.
Dec. 2.—Oliver B. Holden, George E. Wise, and D. H. Howes.
Dec. 3.—Maurice M. Gorman and Adolphus Landergren.

Dec. 5.—Andrew R. Hazard, John A. Partridge, J. W. Goodrich, George H. Book, and Clement H. Perchard.
Dec. 6.—Bartholomew G. Allen and James R. Harding.
Dec. 7.—William F. Killgore and William W. Beck.
Dec. 8.—Albert B. Hall.
Dec. 9.—John A. Kelly.
Dec. 10.—John A. Bennett, Charles S. Thurston, and Martin Vollosher.
Dec. 13.—George G. Randall, Benj. C. Townsend, and August Sebelin.
Dec. 15.—James L. Wilson.
Dec. 16.—J. W. Goodrich, John B. Lawrence, and George A. Thompson.
Dec. 19.—Mandeville P. Powers.
Dec. 20.—Henry J. Dunn.
Dec. 23.—Charles J. Goodwin.
Dec. 27.—Charles C. Dunbar.
Dec. 28.—John D. Thomas.
Dec. 29.—Alfred F. McIntyre.
Dec. 30.—George V. Cassedy.
Dec. 31.—Albert A. Davis and C. M. Jones.

Appointed Acting Ensigns and Pilots.

Dec. 12.—John E. Lewis, North Atlantic Squadron.
Dec. 13.—William Montague, North Atlantic Squadron.
Dec. 16.—A. Bellandi, West Gulf Squadron.

Dec. 1.—Acting Ensigns J. D. Hademan and William A. Byrne, detached from the Conemaugh, and waiting orders. Acting Ensigns Norman McLeod, C. Carven, and Charles Hicks, detached from the Sagamore, and waiting orders.
Dec. 3.—Acting Ensign William Young, detached from the Mercedita, and ordered to the Morse. Acting Ensign H. F. Dorton, detached from the Sophronia, and ordered to the Morse. Acting Ensign Adolphus Dennett, detached from the Morse, and ordered to the Sophronia.
Dec. 6.—Acting Ensign Joseph W. Munro, ordered to the Savannah for instruction. Acting Ensign H. E. Tinkham, ordered to the Kensington.
Dec. 7.—Acting Ensigns R. M. Clark and N. Larsen, ordered to the Muscoota.
Dec. 8.—Acting Ensigns T. B. Stokes and R. M. Wagstaff, ordered to the National Guard. Acting Ensign M. W. Tillson, ordered to the Lenapee. Acting Ensign J. Hadfield, ordered to the Gemsbok. Acting Ensign F. W. Sanborn, detached from the Gemsbok, and ordered to the Lenapee. Acting Ensign Samuel Carpenter, detached from the Navy Yard, Boston, and ordered to the National Guard. Acting Ensign W. A. Abbott, detached from the Ohio, and ordered to the National Guard. Acting Ensign George Anderson, ordered to the Nereus. Acting Ensign Henry Taylor, ordered to the Lenapee.
Dec. 9.—Acting Ensign F. A. Stranberg, detached from the Adela, and waiting orders. Acting Ensign William M. Swasey, ordered to the East Gulf Squadron. Acting Ensign Harvey L. Ransom, detached from the Aroostook, and granted sick leave. Acting Ensign Henry Curwen, detached from the West Gulf Squadron, and ordered to instruction on board the Savannah.
Dec. 10.—Acting Ensign J. M. Cowan, detached from the Calypso, and ordered to the St. Louis. Acting Ensign Hazard Marsh, detached from the St. Louis, on the reporting of his relief, and ordered North. Acting Ensign J. W. Goodwin, detached from the Sangamon, on the reporting of his relief, and ordered North. Acting Ensign E. W. Seaman, ordered to the National Guard.
Dec. 12.—Acting Ensign Henry G. Macey, detached from the Mercedita, and ordered to command the Periwinkle. Acting Ensign G. B. Mitchell, ordered to return to duty in the Potomac Flotilla. Acting Ensign John Daley, ordered to the Periwinkle. Acting Ensign C. H. Danforth, ordered to the Circassian.
Dec. 13.—Acting Ensign W. B. Rankin, detached from the Restless, on the reporting of his relief, and ordered North. Acting Ensign John W. Almy, detached from the Wissahickon, on the reporting of his relief, and ordered North. Acting Ensign H. E. Tinkham, orders to the Kensington revoked, and ordered to the Restless. Acting Ensign H. F. Dorton, detached from the Morse, and ordered to the Wissahickon. Acting Ensign John Lourie, ordered to the Morse.

Dec. 15.—Acting Ensign G. W. Baker, ordered to temporary duty on board the Vandalia.

Dec. 16.—Acting Ensign Henry C. Whitmore, detached from the Nantucket, and ordered North. Acting Ensign E. N. Seaman, detached from the National Guard, and waiting orders. Acting Ensign Norman McLeod, ordered to the Napa. Acting Ensign Alfred Hornsby, ordered to the National Guard. Acting Ensign W. J. Herring, detached from the Calypso, and ordered to the Napa. Acting Ensign William B. Arrants, ordered to the Suwanee.

Dec. 22.—Acting Ensign William A. Beattie, detached from the Sunflower, on the reporting of his relief, and ordered North.

Dec. 23.—Acting Ensign H. E. Tinkham, orders to the Restless revoked, and ordered to the Bat.

Dec. 24.—Acting Ensign James Courtney, detached from the Grand Gulf, and ordered to the Muscoota. Acting Ensign N. Larsen, detached from the Muscoota, and ordered to the Grand Gulf.

Dec. 27.—Acting Ensigns W. A. Byrnes and Ezra Bartlett, ordered to the Spirea.

Dec. 28.—Acting Ensign Peter Howard, placed on waiting orders.

Dec. 30.—Acting Ensign W. B. Trufant, detached from the Mississippi Squadron, and ordered to the Shawmut. Acting Ensign George Smith, detached from the Supply, and ordered to the Bat. Acting Ensign F. A. Strandberg, ordered to the State of Georgia.

Dec. 31.—Acting Ensign R. R. Barclay, detached from the Augusta, and ordered to the Dictator. Acting Ensign Theodore Nickerson, detached from the Augusta, and ordered to the Bermuda. Acting Ensign George Y. Miller, detached from the Dictator, and ordered to report to Rear-Admiral Porter for duty.

Appointed Acting Master's Mates.

Dec. 6.—James Hawkins, U. S. S. Acacia.
Dec. 8.—Oscar F. Balston, U. S. S. Agawam.
Dec. 10.—Mason C. Easterbrook, East Gulf Squadron.
Dec. 12.—W. J. McFadden, U. S. S. Acacia.
Dec. 13.—F. A. Dran, U. S. S. Alabama.
Dec. 15.—William D. McMichael, U. S. S. Portsmouth; Henry M. Guilford, U. S. S. Dumbarton; Robert Burns, U. S. S. Shenandoah; Edward Nash and Joseph Recketson, U. S. S. Roanoke; John Neil and James Patterson, U. S. S. Roanoke; George B. Foster, U. S. S. Genesee; Otis G. Spear, U. S. S. Bienville; Harvey White, U. S. S. Althea; William Brown, U. S. S. Ft. Gaines.
Dec. 16.—Frederick Fietz, U. S. S. George Mangham; Richard Williams, U. S. S. Philadelphia; Edward K. Greene, North Atlantic Squadron.
Dec. 17.—Edward H. Grier, Potomac Flotilla.
Dec. 19.—Thomas G. Cartwright and John E. Johnston, Navy Yard, Washington, D. C.
Dec. 22.—Andrew B. Langworthy, North Atlantic Squadron.
Dec. 23.—Oliver O'Brien, U. S. S. Canandaigua; Alfred C. Smith, Potomac Flotilla; Peter M. Beam, Jr., Potomac Flotilla.
Dec. 24.—George W. Frear, East Gulf Squadron.
Dec. 27.—H. D. Jones, U. S. S. Suwanee.

Appointed Acting Master's Mates, and ordered to the School-Ship Savannah.

Dec. 2.—Frederic C. Bailey.
Dec. 9.—Ezra C. Colvin.
Dec. 12.—D. W. Burroughs.
Dec. 13.—Henry M. Wadsworth.
Dec. 23.—Henry S. Bolles.
Dec. 27.—George Dennis.
Dec. 29.—William Thompson.
Dec. 30.—Allen W. Snow.

Dec. 1.—Acting Master's Mate H. D. Baldwin, detached from the Conemaugh, and waiting orders.

Dec. 3.—Acting Master's Mate John McCormick, ordered to the Nereus. Acting

Master's Mate E. M. Reed, detached from the Unadilla, and ordered to the Sabine. Acting Master's Mate G. W. Pratt, ordered to the Rachel Seaman.

Dec. 6.—Acting Master's Mate J. H. Lovejoy, detached from the Tallapoosa, and granted sick leave. Acting Master's Mate C. C. Chamberlain, detached from the Suwanee, and ordered to the Neptune. Acting Master's Mate E. W. Walton, detached from the Sagamore, and waiting orders.

Dec. 7.—Acting Master's Mates C. A. Stewart and W. H. Fogg, ordered to the Muscoota. Acting Master's Mate C. S. McCarty, ordered to the Muscoota. Acting Master's Mate Thomas Brown, ordered to instruction on board the Savannah. Acting Master's Mate W. E. Bridges, ordered to the Roanoke. Acting Master's Mate Daniel Ward, ordered to the Suwanee. Acting Master's Mate W. Rushmore, ordered to instruction on board the Savannah.

Dec. 8.—Acting Master's Mate John McCormick, orders to the Nereus revoked, and granted sick leave. Acting Master's Mate J. F. Bickford, ordered to the Lenapee.

Dec. 14.—Acting Master's Mates W. H. Hathorne, Charles Brown, and James Morgan, detached from the Hartford, and ordered to instruction on board the Savannah.

Dec. 24.—Acting Master's Mate H. D. Baldwin, ordered to the Periwinkle.

Dec. 31.—Acting Master's Mate J. S. Reynolds, detached from the Tulip, and granted sick leave.

Appointed Acting Assistant Surgeons.

Dec. 5.—Edward W. Seymour, and ordered to the Receiving-Ship North Carolina.
Dec. 16.—Alfred W. Minor, and ordered to the South Atlantic Squadron.
Dec. 17.—Joseph G. Ayres, and ordered to the Receiving-Ship Ohio.
Dec. 19.—J. H. Wright, and ordered to the Mississippi Flotilla.
Dec. 27.—Michael H. Coe, and ordered to the John Adams.
Dec. 31.—Stephen C. Bartlett, and ordered to the Receiving-Ship North Carolina.

Dec. 1.—Acting Assistant Surgeon E. R. Hutchins, detached from the Conemaugh, and waiting orders. Acting Assistant Surgeon P. C. Whiddon, detached from the Sagamore, and waiting orders.

Dec. 3.—Acting Assistant Surgeon J. K. Walsh, detached from the Mercedita, and waiting orders.

Dec. 6.—Acting Assistant Surgeon P. C. Whiddon, ordered to the Wando.

Dec. 7.—Acting Assistant Surgeon J. K. Walsh, ordered to the Nereus.

Dec. 9.—Acting Assistant Surgeon D. T. Whyborn, detached from the Adela, and waiting orders.

Dec. 10.—Acting Assistant Surgeon G. H. Butler, ordered to the Mahaska.

Dec. 14.—Acting Assistant Surgeon John H. Blodgett, detached from the Commodore Read, and ordered to the Morse.

Dec. 17.—Acting Assistant Surgeon A. R. Rice, detached from the Calypso, and ordered to the Tallapoosa. Acting Assistant Surgeon D. T. Whyborn, ordered to the Albatross.

Dec. 27.—Acting Assistant Surgeon William Clendaniel, detached from the Louisiana, and ordered to the Nipsic. Acting Assistant Surgeon Howard M. Rundlett, detached from the John Adams, on the reporting of his relief, and ordered North. Acting Assistant Surgeon Joseph G. Ayres, detached from the Ohio, and ordered to the West Gulf Squadron. Acting Assistant Surgeon Edward W. Seymour, detached from the North Carolina, and ordered to the West Gulf Squadron. Acting Assistant Surgeon E. R. Hutchins, ordered to the Massachusetts.

Dec. 28.—Acting Assistant Surgeon W. H. Holmes, ordered to the Hibiscus. Acting Assistant Surgeon George M. Hatch, ordered to the Spirea.

Dec. 30.—Acting Assistant Surgeon M. C. Drennan, detached from the St. Lawrence, and waiting orders.

Appointed Acting Assistant Paymasters.

Dec. 1.—Charles C. Ward, and waiting orders.
Dec. 2.—Warren E. Rice, and waiting orders.
Dec. 5.—Thomas A. Swords, and waiting orders.

Dec. 10.—Charles C. Brinckerhoff, and waiting orders.

Dec. 12.—Thomas F. Houghton, and waiting orders. James S. Giraud, and waiting orders.

Dec. 14.—Benj. Abrahams, and waiting orders. Grenville Bacon, and waiting orders. John E. Frock, and waiting orders. George W. McLane, and waiting orders.

Dec. 16.—Austin T. Hubbard, and waiting orders.

Dec. 27.—Charles O. Hodgdon and Rufus McConnell, and waiting orders.

Dec. 29.—Charles W. Crary, and waiting orders.

Dec. 1.—Acting Assistant Paymaster J. F. Wood, detached from the Sagamore, and ordered to settle his accounts. Acting Assistant Paymaster E. M. Hart, ordered to the Gov. Buckingham. Acting Assistant Paymaster John Macmahon, ordered to instruction at New York. Acting Assistant Paymaster Edgar K. Sellew, ordered to instruction at New York. Acting Assistant Paymaster George A. Farro, ordered to instruction at New York. Acting Assistant Paymaster Charles W. Seeley, ordered to instruction at New York.

Dec. 2.—Acting Assistant Paymaster L. C. Tripp, ordered to the St. Louis. Acting Assistant Paymaster G. C. Boardman, ordered to the Galena. Acting Assistant Paymaster C. W. Seeley, ordered to the Crusader.

Dec. 5.—Acting Assistant Paymaster George R. Watkins, ordered to duty at Baltimore, as Inspector in Charge of Stores. Acting Assistant Paymaster Henry Russell, detached from the Morse, and ordered to settle his accounts. Acting Assistant Paymaster George A. Ferre, ordered to the Morse. Acting Assistant Paymaster Benj. F. Munroe, ordered to the Nereus.

Dec. 6.—Acting Assistant Paymaster John Macmahon, ordered to the Kensington. Acting Assistant Paymaster Edgar K. Sellew, ordered to the Gemsbok.

Dec. 7.—Acting Assistant Paymaster Samuel Thomas, Jr., detached from the Victoria on the transfer of stores and accounts, and waiting orders. Acting Assistant Paymaster L. C. Tripp's orders to the St. Louis revoked, and he will remain attached to the Otsego.

Dec. 8.—Acting Assistant Paymaster G. W. Burkitt, ordered to the Vicksburg.

Dec. 9.—Acting Assistant Paymaster B. J. Donahue, detached from the Mississippi Squadron, and waiting orders. Acting Assistant Paymaster A. J. Greeley, ordered to the Jacob Bell. Acting Assistant Paymaster Thomas L. Tullock, detached from the Adela, on completion of transfer, and ordered to settle his accounts.

Dec. 10.—Acting Assistant Paymaster Edwin Boss, ordered to the National Guard. Acting Assistant Paymaster E. L. Turner, ordered to the Lenapee.

Dec. 12.—Acting Assistant Paymaster O. F. Browning, detached from the Mercedita, on completion of transfer, and ordered to settle his accounts. Acting Assistant Paymaster Frank H. Arms, detached from special duty at Port Royal, S. C., and ordered North. Acting Assistant Paymaster H. C. Machette, detached from the Mississippi Squadron, and ordered to Washington, D. C., to settle his accounts. Acting Assistant Paymaster H. J. Bullay, ordered to the Lenapee.

Dec. 13.—Acting Assistant Paymaster W. E. Foster, detached from the Memphis, on the reporting of his relief, and ordered to settle his accounts. Acting Assistant Paymaster Frank H. Arms, orders of the 12th inst. revoked, and ordered to the Memphis.

Dec. 14.—Acting Assistant Paymaster Warren E. Rice, ordered to the Lenapee.

Dec. 21.—Acting Assistant Paymaster G. N. Simpson, Jr., detached from the Louisiana, on the completion of transfer, and ordered to settle accounts. Acting Assistant Paymaster J. M. Altaffer, ordered to the West Gulf Squadron. Acting Assistant Paymaster C. C. Brinckerhoff, ordered to the West Gulf Squadron. Acting Assistant Paymaster John Macmahon, orders to the Kensington revoked, and ordered to the Napa. Acting Assistant Paymaster E. M. Hart, orders to the Gov. Buckingham revoked, and waiting orders.

Dec. 23.—Acting Assistant Paymaster Thomas F. Houghten, ordered to the Aroostook. Acting Assistant Paymaster D. W. Van Houton, ordered to the Mississippi Squadron. Acting Assistant Paymaster L. C. Tripp, detached from the (late) Otsego, and ordered to the Gov. Buckingham. Acting Assistant Paymaster E. St. Clair Clarke, detached from the Aroostook, on the reporting of his relief, and ordered North to settle his accounts.

Dec. 24.—Acting Assistant Paymaster Thomas F. Houghton, orders to the Aroostook revoked, and ordered to the Sophronia. Acting Assistant Paymaster Charles D. Mansfield, ordered to the Aroostook. Acting Assistant Paymaster F. F. Hastings, ordered to the State of Georgia.

Dec. 27.—Acting Assistant Paymaster W. W. Bassett, ordered to the Patapsco. Acting Assistant Paymaster W. S. Creevey, detached from the Patapsco, on the reporting of his relief, and ordered North to settle his accounts.

Dec. 28.—Acting Assistant Paymaster John E. Frock, ordered to the Spirea.

Dec. 29.—Acting Assistant Paymaster G. R. Watkins, detached from the Allegany and from the Naval Station at Baltimore, on the reporting of his relief, and waiting orders.

Dec. 30.—Acting Assistant Paymaster C. H. Boardman, ordered to instruction at New York. Acting Assistant Paymaster C. M. Burns, Jr., detached from the Stettin, on the reporting of his relief, and ordered to settle his accounts. Acting Assistant Paymaster Jonathan C. Chapman, detached from the Commodore Hull, on the reporting of his relief, and ordered to settle his accounts.

Dec. 21.—Acting Chief Engineer Alexander McCausland, detached from the Connecticut, and granted sick leave.

Appointed Acting First Assistant Engineers.

Dec. 2.—Philander S. Young, U. S. S. Mahaska.
Dec. 13.—W. S. Ternbohm, U. S. S. Camanche.
Dec. 27.—William Braidwood, U. S. S. Chimo.
Dec. 29—Benjamin C. Bourne, U. S. S. Iuka.

Dec. 3.—Acting First Assistant Engineer Isaac B. Hewitt, detached from the Calypso, and ordered to the Lady Sterling.

Dec. 8.—Acting First Assistant Engineer David Frazer, detached from the Mobile, and waiting orders.

Dec. 30.—Acting First Assistant Engineer Charles O. Morgan, detached from the Grand Gulf, and ordered to the South Atlantic Squadron.

Appointed Acting Second Assistant Engineers.

Dec. 2.—Charles C. Howe, U. S. S. Crusader; John Deturbe, U. S. S. Tahoma.
Dec. 3.—Patrick J. McMahon, U. S. S. Mahaska.
Dec. 5.—Samuel D. Edwards, U. S. S. Cambridge; Emile L. Golsten, U. S. S. King Philip; James J. Sullivan, U. S. S. Wando.
Dec. 9.—William H. Crawford, U. S. S. Eutaw; William Welcker, U. S. S. Lenapee.
Dec. 10.—Curtis Stanton, U. S. S. Onondaga; James H. Finn, U. S. S. Cohasset.
Dec. 13.—Daniel R. McElroy, U. S. S. Mendota; Henry M. Noyes, U. S. S. Ticonderoga.
Dec. 15.—Othello D. Hughes, U. S. S. Chocura; Charles W. O'Neill, U. S. S. Poppy; Marcellus Villazon, Picket-Boat No. 6.
Dec. 16.—Michael F. Rogers, West Gulf Squadron.
Dec. 20.—Daniel Berry, U. S. S. Passaic.
Dec. 22.—William Sloat, U. S. S. Peoria; Charles L. Williams, U. S. S. Winooski.
Dec. 27.—Aaron H. Showerman, U. S. S. Spirea.

Dec. 1.—Acting Second Assistant Engineer Robert Whitehill, detached from the Conemaugh, and waiting orders. Acting Second Assistant Engineer P. H. Kendrickson, detached from the Conemaugh, and waiting orders. Acting Second Assistant Engineer Henry B. Green, ordered to the Tahoma. Acting Second Assistant Engineer James Fagan, detached from the Muscoota, and ordered to the Tallapoosa.

Dec. 2.—Acting Second Assistant Engineer William Campbell, detached from the Pontoosuc, on the reporting of his relief, and ordered to the Grand Gulf.

Dec. 3.—Acting Second Assistant Engineer George A. Hall, detached from the Grand Gulf, and ordered to the Juniper. Acting Second Assistant Engineer James Sullivan, detached from the Juniper, on the reporting of his relief, and ordered to the Grand Gulf.

Dec. 7.—Acting Second Assistant Engineer James H. Pelton, ordered to the Nauset. Acting Second Assistant Engineer Archibald E. McConnell, ordered to the Squando.

Dec. 10.—Acting Second Assistant Engineer John W. Reed, ordered to the North Atlantic Squadron.

Dec. 12.—Acting Second Assistant Engineer William Lanman, detached from the Mercedita, and waiting orders.

Dec. 16.—Acting Second Assistant Engineer Thomas McIntosh, ordered to the Freeborn. Acting Second Assistant Engineer William P. Magaw, detached from the Freeborn, on the reporting of his relief, and ordered to the Florida.

Dec. 20.—Acting Second Assistant Engineer William A. Leavitt, detached from the Wyoming, and ordered to the Napa.

Dec. 22.—Acting Second Assistant Engineer Robert Whitehall, Jr., ordered to the Winooski. Acting Second Assistant Engineer Thomas Fitzgerald, ordered to the Winooski.

Dec. 23.—Acting Second Assistant Engineer Isaac Johnson, ordered to the Cambridge.

Dec. 24.—Acting Second Assistant Engineer James F. Powers, ordered to the West Gulf Squadron.

Dec. 28.—Acting Second Assistant Engineer William T. Goff, ordered to the Merrimack. Acting Second Assistant Engineer John B. Dick, ordered to the Calypso.

Dec. 30.—Acting Second Assistant Engineer Thomas W. Hineline, detached from the Victoria, and granted sick leave.

Appointed Acting Third Assistant Engineers.

Dec. 1.—John M. Lord, U. S. S. Hibiscus; George Westinghouse, Jr., U. S. S. Muscoota; Joseph T. Vinall, U. S. S. Tallapoosa.

Dec. 2.—Michael J. Carroll, U. S. S. Tahoma; Charles W. Forbes, U. S. S. Connecticut; William Holland, U. S. S. Connecticut; John Allen, U. S. S. Connecticut.

Dec. 3.—Richard Law, U. S. S. Poppy.

Dec. 10.—William H. Fisher, U. S. S. Dai Ching; John Agnew, South Atlantic Squadron; John Corsen, South Atlantic Squadron; William H. Missimer, South Atlantic Squadron; David Holtz, U. S. S. Saugus.

Dec. 12.—John H. McDonald, U. S. S. Santiago de Cuba; Joseph Hunt, U. S. S. Periwinkle.

Dec. 13.—Lemuel M. Poole, U. S. S. Mendota.

Dec. 15.—W. L. Lewis, U. S. S. Narcissus.

Dec. 16.—George Anderson, U. S. S. Arkansas; John Lewis, U. S. S. Arizona.

Dec. 17.—Thomas Holt, U. S. S. Napa; William H. Demming, U. S. S. Napa; Stephen Rand, U. S. S. Merrimack.

Dec. 24.—Burt Hamilton and Frederic L. Hearson, U. S. S. Fah-Kee.

Dec. 27.—Walter A. Webster, Edward G. Park, Robert B. Lincoln, Jr., Alonzo D. Parsons, and John M. Yound, West Gulf Squadron.

Dec. 28.—William N. Gilbert, U. S. S. Calypso; Michael T. Harrigan, U. S. S. Circassian.

Dec. 29.—Humphrey Ginglen, U. S. S. Fort Morgan; Charles Parker, North Atlantic Squadron.

Dec. 30.—Charles H. Pennington, U. S. S. Republic; Charles S. Cobb, Francis M. Kennedy, Joseph W. Goff, Isaac S. Evans, Charles D. Wrightington, and Corey C. Freeman, ordered to report to the Commandant of the Norfolk Navy Yard for duty on such vessels as he may assign.

Dec. 1.—Acting Third Assistant Engineer Thomas Clark, detached from the Calypso, and ordered to the Tallapoosa.

Dec. 2.—Acting Third Assistant Engineer Jeremiah Barringer, detached from Picket-Boat No. 6, and ordered to the Winooski.

Dec. 9.—Acting Third Assistant Engineers T. Gavaghan, George A. Slight, Thomas Lorby, and Clark Hartt, detached from the Adela, and waiting orders.

Dec. 10.—Acting Third Assistant Engineer John C. Batchelder, detached from the Dai Ching, and ordered North.

Dec. 12.—Acting Third Assistant Engineers William Ellis, William McComb, John H. Hopkins, and David J. Lanahan, detached from the Mercedita, and waiting orders. Acting Third Assistant Engineer Chester R. Merrill, detached from the Santiago de Cuba, on the reporting of his relief, and ordered to the Potomac Flotilla. Acting Third Assistant Engineer John A. Strieby, ordered to the Periwinkle.

Dec. 13.—Acting Third Assistant Engineer B. Frank Teal, detached from the Tulip, and granted sick leave.

Dec. 14.—Acting Third Assistant Engineer William T. Longee, detached from the Lenapee, on the reporting of his relief, and ordered to the Fort Morgan. Acting Third Assistant Engineer James W. Kent, detached from the Calypso, and ordered to the Periwinkle. Acting Third Assistant Engineer George R. Dunkley, detached from the Calypso, and ordered to the Hibiscus. Acting Third Assistant Engineer Isaac A. Conover, ordered to the Lenapee. Acting Third Assistant Engineer James Lockwood, ordered to the Tahoma.

Dec. 15.—Acting Third Assistant Engineer William McCombe, ordered to the Morse.

Dec. 17.—Acting Third Assistant Engineers G. W. Kiersted and George A. Dean, ordered to the Napa.

Dec. 21.—Acting Third Assistant Engineer George O. Rogers, detached from the North Atlantic Squadron, and granted sick leave.

Dec. 22.—Acting Third Assistant Engineer Lucius Harlow, ordered to the Peoria. Acting Third Assistant Engineer Thomas Campbell, ordered to the Peoria.

Dec. 23.—Acting Third Assistant Engineer Jarvis B. Edson, detached from the Fah-Kee, and ordered to the Cambridge. Acting Third Assistant Engineer Christopher McCormick, ordered to the Cambridge.

Dec. 27.—Acting Third Assistant Engineer James Hollingsworth, ordered to the Spirea. Acting Third Assistant Engineer John Mee and Henry J. Johnson, ordered to the Spirea.

Dec. 28.—Acting Third Assistant Engineer William Hopkins, ordered to the Merrimack. Acting Third Assistant Engineer George M. Smith, ordered to the Calypso. Acting Third Assistant Engineer George Bertram.

Dec. 31.—Acting Third Assistant Engineer James H. Blessing, detached from the Newbern, and granted sick leave. Acting Third Assistant Engineer George A. Dean, granted sick leave. Acting Third Assistant Engineer Samuel H. Linn, detached from the Aries, and ordered to report to Commodore Dornin for duty.

Promoted.

Dec. 2.—Acting Master W. L. Martine, to Acting Volunteer Lieutenant.

Dec. 6.—Acting Ensigns C. F. Taylor and F. G. Osborne, to Acting Masters.

Dec. 8.—Acting Ensign R. Sommers, to Acting Master. Acting Volunteer Lieutenant Edward Conroy, to Acting Volunteer Lieutenant-Commander.

Dec. 9.—Acting Volunteer Lieutenant Pierre Giraud, to Acting Volunteer Lieutenant-Commander.

Dec. 10.—Acting Master B. C. Dean, to Acting Volunteer Lieutenant.

Dec. 12.—Acting Volunteer Lieutenant Wm. B. Eaton, to Acting Volunteer Lieutenant-Commander.

Dec. 15.—Acting Ensigns John White, Joseph A. Bullard, and John J. Butler, to Acting Masters.

Dec. 16.—Acting Ensign Henry G. Macy, to be Acting Master.

Dec. 22.—Acting Volunteer Lieutenant C. F. W. Behm, to be Acting Volunteer Lieutenant-Commander. Acting Master George E. Nelson, to be Acting Volunteer Lieutenant. Acting Ensign David Organ, to be Acting Master.

Dec. 24.—Acting Master William McGloin, to be Acting Volunteer Lieutenant.

Dec. 29.—Acting Ensign Henry Taylor, to be Acting Master.

Dec. 31.—Acting Ensign John K. Barker, to be Acting Master.

Resigned.

Dec. 2.—Acting Assistant Paymaster Theodore Kitchen. Acting Ensign C. L. Weeden.

Dec. 5.—Acting Assistant Surgeon Joseph Stevens. Acting First Assistant Engineer Charles H. Harrington.

Dec. 6.—Acting Second Assistant Engineer W. W. Tunis.
Dec. 8.—Acting Assistant Paymaster Theodore E. Smith.
Dec. 12.—Acting Assistant Paymaster F. C. Hills.
Dec. 14.—Acting Volunteer Lieutenant Frank Smith. Acting Assistant Paymaster H. J. Bullay.
Dec. 15.—Acting Master J. P. Randall.
Dec. 17.—Acting Masters George Williams and W. O. Lundt. Acting Assistant Paymaster George W. Burkett.
Dec. 19.—Acting First Assistant Engineer F. A. Bremon.
Dec. 20.—Acting Assistant Paymaster Stephen T. Brown. Acting Ensign George Kendall.
Dec. 23.—Acting Assistant Paymaster William B. Crosby, Jr.
Dec. 28.—Acting Assistant Paymaster Charles H. West. Acting Third Assistant Engineer George A. Slight. Acting Master John Dillingham.
Dec. 30.—Acting Second Assistant Engineer Isaac Johnson.
Dec. 31.—Acting Ensign John M. Richards.

Dec. 2.—Acting Master's Mates Charles C. Jones and James H. Gordon.
Dec. 3.—Acting Master's Mate Richard Wilcox.
Dec. 5.—Acting Master's Mate Robert Anderson.
Dec. 6.—Acting Master's Mate William Cook, Jr.
Dec. 7.—Acting Master's Mate William W. Brandt.
Dec. 15.—Acting Master's Mate George R. Avery.
Dec. 19.—Acting Master's Mate John Williams.
Dec. 22.—Acting Master's Mate Joseph J. Tinelli. Acting Master's Mate Daniel McCool.
Dec. 30.—Acting Master's Mates William H. Hathorne, Charles S. McCarty, and John C. Constant.

Revoked.

Dec. 1.—Acting Third Assistant Engineer David Girty.
Dec. 2.—Acting Second Assistant Engineer T. O. Reynolds.
Dec. 3.—Acting Third Assistant Engineer J. Snowden Bell.
Dec. 9.—Acting Second Assistant Engineer R. D. Faron.
Dec. 12.—Acting Second Assistant Engineer R. A. Copeland. Acting Ensign and Pilot C. B. Parry.
Dec. 13.—Acting Ensign V. J. Young. Acting Ensign Daniel Lester.
Dec. 15.—Acting Ensign William Bourne.
Dec. 17.—Acting Ensign William B. Marchant. Acting Second Assistant Engineer Charles L. Fowler.
Dec. 19.—Acting Ensign G. B. Mitchell. Acting Second Assistant Engineer H. S. Walcott.
Dec. 22.—Acting Ensign Thomas Tierney.
Dec. 28.—Acting Third Assistant Engineer James H. Eppes.

Dec. 1.—Acting Master's Mate Christopher H. Foster.
Dec. 24.—Acting Master's Mate E. W. Walton.

Dismissed.

Dec. 5.—Acting Third Assistant Engineer Peter Innis.
Dec. 6.—Acting Assistant Paymaster Augustus Esenwein. Acting Assistant Paymaster H. D. Kimberly. Acting Ensign William H. Dumont.
Dec. 12.—Acting Ensign Joseph L. Penfield.
Dec. 14.—Acting Third Assistant Engineer Edward Missett.
Dec. 17.—Acting Ensign Milton Griffith.
Dec. 23.—Acting Ensign A. A. Robinson.
Dec. 27.—Acting Assistant Surgeon William J. Gilfillan.
Dec. 28.—Acting Gunner William Finnigan.
Dec. 29.—Acting Master and Pilot William Jones. Acting Ensign John N. Yeaton.
Dec. 30.—Acting Ensign W. H. Thomas.
Dec. 29.—Acting Master's Mate V. B. Gates.

Miscellaneous.

Dec. 9.—Sentence of Court-Martial, cashiering Acting Master J. W. Caswell, mitigated to suspension from duty for three months without pay.

Dec. 10.—Sentence of Court-Martial, dismissing Acting Third Assistant Engineer Robert J. Ewing, mitigated to suspension from duty for two months on half pay. Sentence of Court-Martial approved, sentencing Acting Third Assistant Engineer C. H. Bartram to confinement for six months.

Dec. 12.—Order dismissing Acting Ensign and Pilot G. M. Lawrence revoked, and his resignation accepted, to date from August 2d, 1864.

Dec. 21.—Acting Third Assistant Engineer Robert T. Ewing, suspended from duty for two months on half pay.

Dec. 9.—Sentence of Court-Martial, dismissing Acting Master's Mate W. J. Lewis, mitigated to "suspension on half pay for two months," and confinement to the limits of such vessel as Rear-Admiral Porter may direct for the same length of time. Sentence of Court-Martial approved, that Acting Master's Mate James H. McClure, be "reduced to the rate of Ordinary Seaman for fifteen months, and at the expiration of that time to be dishonorably discharged from the Naval Service of the U. S."

Dec. 10.—Sentence of Court-Martial, dismissing Acting Master's Mate John McGovern, mitigated to "suspension from duty for three months without pay."

Died.

Acting Ensign Edward Winnemere, of the U. S. S. Yantic, on the 24th December, 1864, of wounds received in action.

Mississippi Squadron.

Dec. 15.—Acting Volunteer Lieutenant George W. Brown, detached from the Mississippi Squadron, and ordered to the South Atlantic Squadron.

Dec. 23.—Acting Volunteer Lieutenant Henry S. Wetmore, detached from the Atlantic Squadron, and granted sick leave.

(Mr. Wetmore belongs to the Miss. Squadron, but was detached for duty in the North Atlantic Squadron at the request of Admiral Porter.)

Dec. 20.—Acting Master Michael Hickey, ordered to report to Acting Rear-Admiral Lee, for duty. (Exchanged prisoner.)

Appointed Acting Master's Mates.

Dec. 1.— W. H. Roberts.
Dec. 6.—Charles E. Pelton.
Dec. 20.—Acting Master's Mate E. N. Wild, ordered to report to Acting Rear-Admiral Lee, for duty.

Appointed Acting Gunner.

Dec. 12.—David Damon.

Resigned.

Dec. 1.—Acting Chief Engineer Edward Merriman.
Dec. 7.—Acting Assistant Surgeon H. Beauchamp.
Dec. 31.—Acting Master's Mate Herman Alms.

Revoked.

Dec. 1.—Acting Master's Mate E. D. O'Bryon.
Dec. 3.—Acting Second Assistant Engineer E. L. Morse.
Dec. 22.—Acting Master's Mate John A. Leaman.
Dec. 23.—Acting Master's Mate Charles Jordan.
Dec. 24.—Acting Master's Mate E. A. Turpin.

Dismissed.

Dec. 2.—Acting Third Assistant Engineer Richard Nugent.
Dec. 3.—Acting First Assistant Engineer John Connelly.
Dec. 29.—Acting Master's Mate John Thompson.

JUSTICE TO OUR GALLANT DEFENDERS.

[We have received several communications from officers of high rank, on the subject of pay. Among them is the following, which needs no editorial comment, but that of our heartiest sanction and earnest hope for the justice so imperatively demanded by the necessities of men who deserve a thousand-fold what we can ever pay them.—ED.]

THE PAY OF THE ARMY.

THE present pay of the Army was established in peaceful times, when gold was at par, and all the necessaries of life much cheaper than they are in these warlike times, when the price of gold ranges from two dollars twenty-five to two dollars fifty cents. A captain of infantry, who, before the war, received and lived comfortably on, with his family, one hundred and eighteen dollars fifty cents, in gold, per month, which, at the present rate (say two dollars twenty-five cents), would now be worth to him two hundred and sixty-six dollars sixty two cents. So that now he gets less than one-half the pay he did in peaceful times, whilst his expenses are more than doubled, and the risk of life infinitely greater.

Before the war, our officers, stationed mostly in places where they could have their families with them, were seldom obliged to maintain two separate establishments, as they are now, when so completely separated from their families. Thousands upon thousands of our volunteers, who rushed to the protection of our national flag, when first assailed, left comfortable homes and a lucrative business to peril their lives in the cause of the country. What a sad record it would be could the number be stated of those who never saw those homes again, or returned only to find their inmates in want, and their business ruined, with the prospect of commencing life anew, weighed down possibly by wounds which but illy fitted them for the additional struggle required. There are thousands now in the service who have this sad prospect before them; many who, actuated by the highest patriotism, still remain in the field, although there is a continued tug at their heart-strings to go home to provide for the dear ones there.

Surely Government should try to compensate as adequately as possible those who so freely make these sacrifices for it. The pains and penalties attaching to a state of war are many, and although the war be prosecuted for the good of all, they are not equally shared by all. Those who risk their lives and limbs in the field, should be well paid by those who remain at home and risk neither.

It is a fact worthy of the highest credit to our people, that their money has been as freely poured out in this struggle, as has the blood of our brave soldiers in the field; but more of it should go towards paying our soldiers, and less into the pockets of those who do not do the fighting.

The pay of army officers is subject to a tax by Government, which amounts to five per cent. on the excess over fifty dollars per month, so that a captain's is reduced from one hundred and eighteen dollars fifty cents, to one hundred and fifteen dollars eight cents, or forty-one dollars ten cents per year; and correspondingly for every other rank. It certainly would be a very proper measure to exempt the pay of officers from this tax altogether, and the pay should be *doubled* for all officers and soldiers with the exception of the general officers, who do not need so large an increase.

Instead of the pay being made to depend upon the commutation value of so many rations, servants, &c., each officer should receive a certain fixed salary. This has often been proposed and recommended by our authorities, but has never become a law, although it is difficult to find a single well-founded objection to it.

The distinction made in the Navy, between the pay of officers when on sea and on other duty, is an admirable one, and should be introduced into the Army, making the pay of the officer doing duty in the field higher than that of one out of the field, and the pay of an officer on leave of absence, or waiting orders, less than either. By the present arrangement, the officer exposing his life every day in the field, separated from his family and comfortable home, gets less pay than one who is in quiet enjoyment of both; for the latter draws commutation of fuel and quarters, which is not allowed to the former. This is placing a premium upon an avoidance of duty in the field, which, to say the least of it, is very bad policy.

Every argument which can be made use of in favor of increasing the officers' pay, applies with double force to the pay of the *enlisted* men, those who are, after all, the real patriots of this war.

Congress being now in session again, this important matter of the pay of those on whose shoulders the whole welfare of our country depends, should occupy its earliest and most serious attention. Strengthen the hearts, and consequently the arms, of our brave soldiers in the field, by providing for them in such a way that they may always feel amidst the storm of battle, no matter what happens to them, the dear ones at home have bread to eat and a home to cover them. No one, except one who has felt the *want* of such a feeling, can know how that reflection *does* strengthen the arm and brave the heart in time of peril!

Protect your defenders, and they will protect you.

[We are very glad to see that Mr. Wilson has introduced into the Senate a bill to increase the compensation of certain officers of the Army in the field. The first section provides that the commutation price of rations, to all officers below and including brevet brigadier-generals, shall be fifty cents after the 1st of March, instead of thirty cents, as at present; but this shall not apply to officers who are entitled to commutation for quarters, or to officers of the Veteran Reserve Corps.

The second section relieves all officers of the Army and Navy from the payment of income tax. The third section provides that every officer who remains in the service, except those in the Veteran Reserve Corps, and those on detached duty, who get commutation for quarters, shall at the close of the war be entitled to three months' pay, on being honorably mustered out of the service. This applies to volunteer officers only. The above was referred to the Committee on Military Affairs.

This is a movement in the right direction, but is only, we hope, a first step.—ED.]

WASHINGTON, D. C., January 19, 1865.

To the Editor of the "United States Service Magazine."

SIR:—In the January number of your Magazine there is an article headed "A Word for the Quartermaster's Department," wherein a statement is made which I wish to correct.

The writer relates a story, which he says "was rife at the time," in relation to a remark said to have been made by me to some quartermaster who presented a requisition to me for one hundred teams "to go to Warrenton or Culpepper, or somewhere about there," for the use of General Pope's army.

This story, if "rife at the time," is, like many others told around the camp-fires, *without any foundation in fact.*

The language attributed to me is not such as I am in the habit of using, and I have not the slightest recollection of having made any such remark.

The writer was evidently misinformed, and unintentionally does me injustice when he attributes it to me.

By publishing this correction in the next number of your Magazine, you will greatly oblige, Yours, truly, F. H. RUCKER,
Brigadier-General and Chief Quartermaster,
Dépôt of Washington.

THE UNITED STATES SERVICE MAGAZINE.

VOL. III.—MARCH, 1865.—NO. III.

REORGANIZATION OF THE ARMY.*

A PRESIDENTIAL election has just terminated, and the war, so our enemies say, is to continue four years longer. This being the idea, it becomes every one interested in the struggle to gird up his loins, buckle on his armor, and prepare for the strife in the coming spring, which, if it takes place at all, will throw into the shade any which has yet taken place.

Our army needs reorganizing, and every one is, or should be, clamorous for it. Our system is defective, *more so* than that of the rebels, and we should take advantage of the coming winter to remedy its defects.

We commenced this war on a small scale. It has been growing, growing, until now it is colossal, and far exceeds the proportions assigned it in anticipation by our greatest military minds. Perhaps in nothing have the civil powers of the Government made a greater mistake than in disregarding the councils of our military men. General Scott's assertion in regard to thirty thousand men and a Hoche to lead them, at the beginning was received with incredulity, and the *now* celebrated, and pre-eminently sane Sherman was declared insane for stating that two hundred thousand men were required to carry on operations in

---

* This article, by a distinguished general now in the field, should command universal attention. It is well-reasoned and practical.—ED.

Entered according to Act of Congress, in the year 1865, by C. B. RICHARDSON, in the Clerk's Office of the District Court for the Southern District of New York.

the Mississippi Valley. That the advice of such men should have been disregarded at first was, perhaps, considering all things, but natural. But now that our eyes have been opened to the magnitude of the task before us, to discard such advice is not only unnatural; it is criminal. When we are suffering a slight indisposition we are willing to try the simple pill of some good-natured quack as a remedy, but when our complaint assumes the form of a dangerous illness, we eagerly seek the advice of the most experienced and talented medical man we can find. Our "sick man," as they called Turkey some years ago, is dangerously ill. We have called in for consultation a large number of Doctors, some of whom are capable, but many are mere quacks, whose advice, if we do not discharge them, may outweigh in the end the opinions of the capable ones and kill our sick man.

It used to be a jest in the Mexican war that the Mexicans had almost as many generals as privates in their army, and we seem fast approaching that point in our organization. Take up an army register (if a recent one had been published the effect would be more startling), and look over our list of general officers. It is astonishing how many there are, and still more astonishing how many have been tried, found wanting, and laid away on the shelf to make political speeches or command posts which might be better commanded by captains, at a much less expense to the Government. One hundred and fifty brigadier and seventy major-generals is an ample allowance for half a million of men. We have something like three hundred of the former and one hundred of the latter, whilst many of the brigadier-generals have major-generals' commands in the field, and our brigades are commanded by colonels, lieutenant-colonels, and majors. Many of the general officers now in service are notoriously incompetent, others are unwilling to perform the duties assigned them in active service, and have influence enough to obtain comfortable easy places out of the field, which could be quite as well filled, perhaps in many cases better, by officers of inferior rank who have been disabled doing their duty in front of the enemy. These surplus generals should be mustered out of the service, not only to rid the service of unworthy members, but to enable the authorities to reward those who have shown themselves capable and willing to perform the duties of *soldiers* in the field.

The number of general officers will thus be considerably reduced; the expenses of the war lessened, and the Government be enabled to reward many meritorious officers who are now necessarily neglected and are performing the duty without either the pay or the rank. To determine those who should be mustered out, a board of competent general officers should be convened in each army, whose duty it should be to examine and report upon the services, claims, and capabilities of all generals serving with or formerly on duty in such army, with the recommendation in each case. These reports should be submitted to a general board with orders to continue the investigation, and report to the Secretary of War such as should be mustered out.

A law of Congress authorizes the President to confer upon volunteer officers rank by *Brevet*. But by a singular provision the brevet officer cannot draw the pay of his brevet grade. This is a most unjust and impolitic law, and is as much as saying that whilst the Government wants and will accept the services of officers of a certain grade, it is unwilling to remunerate them with a corresponding pay. Surely this is not offering much inducement to officers to strive for promotion, and no capable military force can be created unless such inducement is shown, more especially now that the reduced value of our currency is such that very many officers of inferior rank could more easily earn a comfortable subsistence for themselves and families by returning to those pursuits in civil life which they left to fight the battles of their country. By the regulations a brevet officer cannot exercise his brevet rank in command unless specially assigned by the President. If an officer is worthy of brevet, he is fitted to exercise a corresponding command without its being made necessary for him to use political or other influences to get himself assigned by the President. Congress therefore, instead of making the brevet an empty title, should confer upon brevet officers not only the absolute right to command according to rank, but the right to draw the corresponding pay.

But there is another law of Congress which acts with still greater injustice upon officers, more especially those of the lower grades. It is that in reference to *servants*. Each officer of the army is by law entitled to commutation for a certain number of servants varying from one to four. This commutation is made up as follows:

The pay of a private soldier	$11 00
The clothing allowance of a private soldier	2 50
One ration per day commuted at thirty cents	9 00
Total monthly allowance for servant	$22 50

An officer is frequently so situated that it is impossible for him to obtain a servant from civil life, and by the old laws and regulations he was allowed to use a private soldier as such by having him so mustered, deducting from his pay account the pay and clothing to which the soldier was entitled (thirteen dollars and fifty cents), and dropping the soldier's ration from the company return. Thus the officer, instead of the Government, bore the expenses of a private soldier, whose services the Government could claim at any time it wanted them.

The first amendment made to this law by Congress was to declare that the increased pay (two dollars) allowed private soldiers should not apply to officers' servants, so that the commutation value on the officer's pay account remained eleven dollars instead of being increased to thirteen dollars, and by a subsequent Act to sixteen dollars per month. (Section 4, Act approved 17th July, 1862.)

The next act affecting this subject is that passed by Congress and approved June 15th, 1864. In section 1 of this Act, it is *Provided*, That if any officer in the regular or volunteer forces shall employ a soldier as a servant, such officer shall not be entitled to any pay or allowances for a servant or servants, but shall be subject to the deduction from his pay required by the third section of the Act entitled "An Act to define the pay and emoluments of certain officers of the Army, and for other purposes," approved July 17th, 1862. This latter law reads: "That whenever an officer of the Army shall employ a soldier as his servant, he shall, for each and every month during which said soldier shall be so employed, deduct from his own monthly pay the full amount paid to or expended by the Government per month on account of said soldier."

It results from these laws that a lieutenant or captain who employs a soldier as a servant loses not only the commutation for his servant as stated above (twenty-two dollars and fifty cents), but also all the cost to the Government of such soldier, viz.:—

Commutation for servant	$22 50
Monthly pay	16 00
Monthly clothing	2 50
Monthly rations	9 00
Total deduction from officer's pay	$50 00

A colonel, lieutenant-colonel, or major, entitled to two servants, each loses seventy-two dollars and fifty cents; a brigadier-general, entitled to three servants, loses ninety-five dollars; and a major-general, entitled to four servants, loses one hundred and seventeen dollars and fifty cents per month of his pay for employing *one* soldier as servant. This surely could not have been the intent of the law. If so, it is not only unjust but very unreasonable, for the Government is not only remunerated for the loss of the soldier's services, but is paid by the officer for the privilege of using him, whilst the officer has to pay, in addition to pay of the soldier, his wages as servant.

Now it generally happens in the field that it is out of the question for officers to obtain private servants, more especially line officers, all the negroes who come into our lines being offered superior inducements by the Government. To employ a soldier then is the only resource of an officer to do those thousand and one things which he cannot do and at the same time attend to his military duty. These laws are both unjust and unreasonable, and should be at once amended, for they are creating very great dissatisfaction amongst a class of men who are absolutely necessary to us in carrying on the present struggle.

There are several of the laws already passed by Congress which need overhauling and amendment. Now, in regard to those new laws which Congress should pass to increase the efficiency of our army.

The *first* one should be a law making the regiments of volunteers, after once being mustered into the service of the United States, United States forces in every respect, all promotions and appointments in which shall be made by the General Government.

At the commencement of the war, in 1861, volunteers in regiments, companies, and batteries, flocked to the service, officered, in many cases, by incompetent officers, and having in the ranks many men capable of making good officers in time, numbers of whom have since risen to the highest rank. Gradually, as the difficulties and hardships of the military profession developed themselves, a portion of the most indifferent of the officers were weeded out, and better men, although not in all cases the best, were substituted in their places. But, unfortunately, no well organized system, founded upon military merit as it developed itself, could be instituted, from the fact that each State appointed its own officers; and as there was no means by which the Governors could be informed of those best fitted, in a military point of view, to fill the positions, they were frequently governed more by political and personal considerations than any thing else in making the appointments. This has given rise to much discontent and heartburning amongst those who, having a real aptitude and liking for the profession, have, by their distinguished services in the field, gained the approbation and warm recommendation of their military superiors. Nothing is so disheartening to one with the true feelings of a soldier as to have his just claims to promotion overlooked, and to have one he knows in every way unfitted for the position appointed in his place.

Of course where there are so many appointing powers, the rules governing the appointments will be various; and whilst some governors, fortunately for the reputation of the troops from their States, will not make an appointment unless backed by military recommendation, others, and we are sorry to say the majority, seem actuated by exactly the opposite feeling, and to regard with special jealousy any military interference with their prerogative of the appointing power. It results from this state of things that in some regiments young, active, enterprising, soldierly men rise to the highest rank, and not unfrequently are taken up by the General Government and made General officers, whilst in other regiments, serving probably in the same brigade, men equally meritorious are entirely overlooked, and become disgusted with the service. Hence it is that we have no uniform system of promotion and appointments under which any one who distinguishes himself may be certain of receiving reward. The best way to prevent crime is to render the punishment of it certain and speedy: so the best way to promote merit, in the military as well as in all other professions or pursuits, is to render the recognition of it sure and systematic.

We hazard nothing in saying that we have in our service the finest material for an army that the world can produce, but in order to make the most of it we must profit by the experience of other nations, and follow some military rule in organizing it. We might just as well expect our projectiles to violate Newton's laws and describe special curves for our benefit, as to expect to form an *army* out of our material without going the right way about it. Men and officers of every grade should be taught to look to those above them as the source of all promotion, and to strive to please them, not by a cringing subserviency, but by the exhibition of a high and noble desire to obey orders, enforce discipline and regularity, and by coolness and bravery in time of danger. In this way *only* can soldiers be made.

But it will be objected to this that military men are as liable to make mistakes as any others, and as liable as any to be governed by prejudices and partialities. Those who make this objection understand but little of the military profession, and a short experience in the field and going through two or three battles would serve to demonstrate the fallacy of it. If military men fail in making proper selections, is it likely that non-military ones are going to be any more successful? The military profession is like all others in one respect at least. All who belong to it have one great object in view—success. And no officer fit for his position will allow prejudice or partiality to force him to select an incompetent assistant, because, if he does his experience on the field will have taught him that his assistant will fail him at a critical period and jeopardize what he is striving for—military success. What merchant of any standing would select his own brother if he were not a competent sailor, to command one of his vessels about to make a dangerous voyage with a valuable cargo? And is it to be supposed that in making a selection for the most difficult operation in the world—the handling of men in battle—one would be less careful than in protecting mere property? No, military men are bound by every consideration to select those best capable of assisting them in the operations before them, and in nine cases out of ten they will do it. If *they* fail nobody else can succeed.

In any other country in the world it would appear frivolous and absurd to urge this view of the case with so much argument, but we are writing in America and for the American public, which heretofore has had little necessity for or opportunity of learning what is requisite to create and maintain a large army.

All our three years' regiments are now very much reduced, and in many cases two and three of the remnants are consolidated into one Regiment or Battalion, in consequence of which the name and record of some of these regiments become obliterated. Instead of providing new regiments, in which all, both men and officers are incompetent from want of experience, these old regiments should be filled up to the maximum standard, so that full use may be made of the old material in them. The best way to do this will be after the French system, to organize each regiment into three battalions of four companies. One of these battalions should be kept at home to organize, drill, and equip the new recruits, and when one of the field battalions becomes reduced and in want of reorganizing, it should be ordered home, and the home battalion take its place in the field. By this means the regiments will be kept full and in an organized and efficient condition.

The advantage of such a system will be apparent to any one if he will but reflect that these home battalions can be thrown into the field at short notice and at a critical period of a campaign, as just so many well organized re-enforcements. Let any one consider the effect upon the campaign last summer in Virginia could each one of our tired, worn-out regiments have been reinvigorated in the midst of the struggle with a battalion of four hundred fresh well disciplined men; or the effect of such a force thrown into Washington or Baltimore during Early's operations in Maryland. During the whole of this war, we have entered upon every campaign without any reserves to fall back upon in case of need; a thing no military man in any other country would think of for a moment. It is true, we have had the whole country to draw on as a reserve; but a *reserve*, properly so called, is a well organized force to throw into a breach at a critical period, not a disorganized mass such as our new regiments form when first sent into the field. A reserve of forty thousand men organized in Pennsylvania last winter would have enabled us to hurl Early across the Potomac without drawing a single man from our other armies. Heretofore our want of experience has been our excuse, but this will serve us no longer, and by a timely foresight we should provide against the repetition of the border scenes of last summer.

Ever since this war commenced it has been dinged into our ears by politicians, newspaper correspondents, and other high authorities, that the rebellion was to be put down in thirty, sixty, ninety days, &c., when military men serving in the field have been well aware from the signs before them that there was no truth in the cry. This cry is now stronger than ever, and we are every day told of the exhaustion of the enemy, the discontent of his men, their numerous desertions, and their want of food. It is true that they cannot get as many men as they want, and that some of them desert; but those who remain fight with just as much determination as ever, and there is no want of food among them, and not likely to be with such a large extent of agricultural country under their control, and the will of a despot to supply his army with provisions even if the rest of the population has to starve. To prove this it is only necessary to refer to the number of armies which the valley of the Shenandoah has supported for the past three years, and the large amount of provisions which General Sheridan has recently destroyed there; and the present bold move of the talented Sherman adds force to the argument.

Our people have been so accustomed to hear about "gobbling up" an army of seventy or eighty thousand men after it is once defeated, that they really begin to think such things ought to be of every day occurrence, notwithstanding the yearly demonstration of the fallacy of such an idea. There has scarcely been a great battle during the war in which our army has been successful, but what our people have cried out "the backbone of the Rebellion is broken," "the enemy has met with a defeat which he can never recover," "his army is totally broken up," &c., as prominent examples of which we may cite, Antietam, Gettysburg, Cedar Creek, and Atlanta. On the other hand, whenever our army is worsted the people on the other side (we are all of one stock) cry out "the federal army totally defeated," "the independence of the Confederacy insured," "the enemy has received a blow which must convince him we are not to be conquered," &c., for examples of which we refer to the seven days' fight, Pope's Bull Run, Cane River, &c.; and yet, notwithstanding all this, large armies continue to traverse the country in all directions, the rebellion is not yet put down, nor is the independence of the Confederacy established.

The former result can be obtained *in time*, provided we make proper use of the material we have on hand; but in order to arrive at that end in the shortest time, not a week nor a day should be lost in preparing our material.

Although not of a desponding nature, we are not among those who consider the rebellion at its *last* gasp; and are in favor of so providing against contingencies that the war cannot last twelve months longer, except under the most extraordinary circumstances. If all our armies are in good serviceable condition in the spring, and we have thirty or forty thousand well disciplined reserves to use at any point where most needed, we see great hopes of attaining the end towards which the eyes of the whole nation, indeed of the whole world, are now anxiously turned, during the coming year. If, which God grant, we do not have to make use of this large force in the spring, we shall at least have the satisfaction of knowing that for the first time in the war we have been fully prepared for all contingencies, and of reflecting that we are better off than if, in consequence of a lack of preparation, we had been defeated, or the struggle prolonged. Besides which, the money and time spent in organizing this large force are not likely to be thrown away, since there are a good many clouds of war rising all over the world; we have several accounts to settle *after* this war is over; and there is no telling when we may be called upon to meet some of the well disciplined legions of Europe in arms.

To prove we do not stand alone in our idea in regard to the duration of the war, and the necessity for further efforts, we need only cite the answer given by the Commander-in-chief a few days ago in New York in reply to a question as to whether he did not believe that *ninety days* would bring the end. He significantly answered, "I am not a 'ninety days' man; but we shall see what will happen in *six months.*" If, in the opinion of the highest military authority in the land, it is even possible that the war will continue for six months longer, are we justified in disregarding such an opinion and delaying for a single day the preparations which can alone insure its successful termination?

IN THE FIELD, January 1, 1865.

NAPOLEON I.—A BIBLIOGRAPHICAL SKETCH.

EXTRACT FROM A LETTER TO THE EDITOR.

DEAR SIR:— * * * My query had more especial reference to those lives (*Mémoires pour servir*) which do not deal with the external and public acts of the man alone, but give you insight into his motives, his essential and distinctive qualities.

Whatever I once had of faith in the correctness of "History," has been rudely shocked by what I have seen in this war of how "History" is made. "Facts" I am skeptical of. Character I believe in. And I want to get such knowledge as I can of Napoleon's self. * * *   I am very respectfully yours,
R. D. M.

IN answer to our correspondent's question, a question which many a military reader is doubtless ready to put, it might be sufficient to point out the Memoirs of Bourrienne; those of the Duchess of Abrantes; the records of Napoleon's conversations at St. Helena conveniently collected in Abbott's "Napoleon at St. Helena" (New York, 1855); and the "Correspondance de Napoléon I.," now publishing by order of Napoleon III. But no one or two books are sufficient to give a complete view of such an extraordinary man, and we have thought that a glance at the whole field of Napoleonic literature, pointing out what has already been done towards throwing light on the character and career of the greatest personage of modern times, if not "the foremost man of all this world," might not be unacceptable to our correspondent and to our readers in general; the more so as such a sketch does not seem to have been undertaken before.

The age of Napoleon is one, of the delineation of which history and biography will never be weary. Such is the variety of incidents which it exhibits—the splendid and heart-stirring events which it presents—the immortal characters who played their part on its stage—and the important consequences which have resulted from their deeds, that the interest in its delineation, so far from diminishing, seems rather to increase with the lapse of time, and will continue through all succeeding ages, like the eras of Themistocles, Cæsar, and the Crusades, to form the noblest and most favorite subjects of historical description. Already more than ten thousand works, including pamphlets, have been written on Napoleon or on the events of his reign, forty of which are devoted to the campaign of 1815. Amid such an immense mass of material, it will only be possible here to enumerate a few of the more important sources of information.

During the Emperor's tenure of power, his iron despotism kept the French press in shackles, while a state of war made his private life as much a sealed book to the outer world as that of Jefferson Davis is now.

Beginning, therefore, with French writers, and following the order of publication, we note first Fabry's three works, "La Régence à Blois," "Itinéraire de Buonaparte depuis son départ de Doulevant," and "Itinéraire de l'île d'Elbe à l'île Sainte Hélène" (Paris, 1814, 1815, 1816). These narratives are not favorable to Napoleon, but they contain some curious details.

In 1823 was published "Mémoires pour servir à l'histoire de France sur Napoléon," written at St. Helena by Generals Gourgand and Montholon, and published from manuscripts corrected throughout by the Ex-Emperor's own hand. The later volumes contain Napoleon's notes on the various works of Jomini, Dumas, De Pradt, Pillet, Rogniat, Chabouillon, and others. The whole present, if not facts and motives, at least what Bonaparte desired to go forth to the world as such. Gourgand's character suffered in 1827 from the revelations made by Sir Walter Scott, who found among the documents at the Colonial Office, some which showed General Gourgand as either betraying his master to Sir Hudson Lowe, and afterwards to the British Government in London, or else as guilty of falsehood. The sharp paper controversy which ensued was expected by Scott to lead to a duel, which he made preparations to meet, writing to Clerk, "*I will not balk him, Jackie.*" Montholon, subsequently, while sharing Louis Napoleon's imprisonment at Ham, wrote "Histoire de la Captivité de Ste. Hélène" (Paris, 1846), which was translated and published in England and this country. General Montholon, the companion in exile of Napoleon, was also his executor, and thereby came into possession of all his papers. The Emperor, before his death, specially charged him not to publish any memoir or document concerning him for the space of twenty-five years. Hence the delay in issuing this book. Its details of the petty and absurd controversies with the Governor of St. Helena must be read in connection with Forsyth's "History of the captivity of Napoleon at St. Helena, from the letters and journals of the late Lieutenant-General Sir Hudson Lowe, and official documents not before made public" (3 vols., London, 1853).

Ségur's famous work, "Histoire de Napoléon et de la grande armée pendant l'année 1812" (Paris, 1824), which appears to be written with fairness, nevertheless gave rise to numerous hostile criticisms, particularly that of General Gourgand, which led to a duel between them in 1825. As a work for the military student it is recommended by Marmont (a very high authority), along with the Archduke Charles's "Principles of Strategy" and the Memoirs of St. Cyr.

"Histoire de l'ambassade dans le grand-duché de Varsovie en 1812," by M. de Pradt (Paris, 1815). The author of this damaging work, almoner to the Emperor, and Bishop of Poitiers, was appointed in 1812 Minister to the Grand Duchy of Warsaw; but having failed to fulfil the intentions of the Emperor, he was disgraced. De Pradt represents Napoleon as saying that but for him he would have made the conquest of the world. His book is written with great bitterness, but the details are trustworthy. Napoleon never denied them. He said at St. Helena that this work and the "Narrative of Napoleon Buonaparte's journey from Fontainbleau to Frejus in April, 1814, by Count Trouchses Waldburg" (London, 1815), were the two publications which had injured him most in public opinion.

One of the best books which can be consulted on the character of Napoleon, notwithstanding the clamor which it raised, is Mad. de Staël's posthumous work, "Considerations sur les principaux événements de la Révolution Française," published in 1818. Mad. de Staël has there judged Bonaparte with all the penetration and sagacity for which she is famous. She pronounces Egotism to be the clue to his character. The following details, furnished by her, are curious: "The marshals of France, amidst the fatigues of war, at the moment of the crisis of a battle, used to enter the tent of the Emperor to ask his orders, without being allowed to sit down. His family did not suffer less than strangers from his despotism and his pride. Lucien preferred living a prisoner in England, to reigning under the orders of his brother. Louis Buonaparte, whose character is greatly esteemed, was constrained by his probity to renounce the throne of Holland; and, can it be believed, that when conversing with his brother during two hours by themselves, and that brother obliged by indisposition to lean painfully against the wall, Napoleon never offered him a chair: he used to continue standing himself from the fear that any one should think of using the familiarity with him of sitting in his presence."

The "Mémorial de Saint-Hélène" by Las Casas, has passed through various editions, the texts of which present notable variations. On its first appearance in 1824, its accuracy was suspected on various points, and it gave occasion to numerous criticisms; whereupon the author modified some passages. As a supplement and corrective, the "Suite au Mémorial de Sainte-Hélène," by Grille and Musset-Pathay should be consulted.

Many very curious details of the private life of the Emperor may be found in the interesting works of his private Secretary, Baron Fain, entitled respectively "Manuscrit de 1812," "Manuscrit de 1813," and "Manuscrit de 1814" (Paris, 1823 to 1827).

The "Histoire de France depuis le 18th Brumaire jusqu'à la paix de Tilsit" (Paris, 1829), by M. Bignon, who was appointed in the will of Napoleon to edit the work, is a mere apology for the Emperor and nearly worthless to the student of his character.

Perhaps the most useful single work for our correspondent's

purpose, despite its occasional misstatements, is the celebrated "Mémoires sur Napoléon" of his fellow-student at Brienne, afterwards his private Secretary, Bourrienne (Paris, 1829). The latter was appointed on the staff of General Bonaparte at the close of his campaign in Italy in 1797, and from the moment of his arrival at head-quarters, then at Gratz, he was set to work to write at the dictation of the General. He became his private secretary and the confidant of all his thoughts. After the treaty of Campo-Formio, he followed his master to Rastadt, to Paris, and thence to Egypt; he returned with him from that adventurous expedition to be at once the witness and one of the actors in the memorable and not less hazardous enterprise of the 18th Brumaire. He accompanied the First Consul in the rapid campaign of Marengo, returned with him to the capital, and received the title of Councillor of State. Installed at the Tuileries in the same apartment, and almost occupying the same chamber with the Emperor, it was his duty at all hours of the day and night to answer the call of the most sleeplessly active man of his age. His subsequent banishment to Hamburg is ascribed to his having made an improper use of state secrets in some money speculations. Probably like some one else that we read of, he told his broker to act as though he had heard good news.

The passionate admirers of Napoleon never could pardon Bourrienne for his revelations of certain weaknesses in their idol, and they accused him loudly of ingratitude. Divers attempted refutations were published, the most important being an anonymous work entitled "Bourrienne et ses erreurs voluntaires et involuntaires" (Paris, 1830). On the whole, however, when he is not speaking of himself, and when he has no reason to prevaricate or to be silent for his own credit, the many and curious details which he alone has preserved, make his book an invaluable repository of facts. Those who are old enough to remember the first appearance of Bourrienne's Memoirs, will recall the sensation it produced even in this country, where the English translation was at once republished. What Coleridge thought of it may be gathered from a passage in his "Table-talk," under the date of July 8, 1830:—

"Bourrienne is admirable. He is the French Pepys—a man with right feelings, but always wishing to participate in what is going on, be it what it may. He has one remark, when comparing Bonaparte with Charlemagne, the substance of which I have attempted to express in "The Friend," but which Bourrienne has condensed into a sentence worthy of Tacitus, or Machiavel, or Bacon. It is this: that Charlemagne was above his age, while Bonaparte was only above his competitors, but under his age! Bourrienne has done more than any one else to show Bonaparte to the world as he really was—always contemptible except when acting a part, and that part not his own."

We now come to the fascinating memoirs of the Duchess d'Abrantes (Paris, 1831–1835), in which Napoleon appears in a more amiable light, and his motives seem to be of a higher kind than in preceding accounts. Unfortunately a part of the charm of the original is lost in the present English translation.

The Duchess d'Abrantes undertook the work of memoirs of her own times with singular and almost peculiar advantages. Her mother, Madame Permon, a Corsican lady of high rank, was extremely intimate with the family of the Buonapartes. She rocked the future emperor on her knee from the day of his birth; and the intimacy of the families continued till he was removed to the command of the army of Italy, in April, 1796. The authoress herself, though then a child, recounts with admirable spirit, and all the air of truth, a number of early anecdotes of Napoleon. After his return from Egypt, she was married to Junot, then Governor of Paris, and subsequently admitted as an habitual guest in the court circle of the Emperor. In her memoirs we have thus a picture of the private and domestic life of Napoleon from his cradle almost to his grave; we trace him through all the gradations of the *Ecole militaire*, the artillery service, the campaigns of Italy, the return from Egypt, the Consulate and the Empire, and live with those who have filled the world with their renown as we would do with our most intimate acquaintances and friends.

"Mémoires tirés des papiers d'un homme d'état," 13 vols. (Paris, 1831-1838). This work, known as one of the best historical collections of this century, is valuable as throwing light on the policy and diplomatic intrigues of the reign of Napoleon.

"Sentiment de Napoléon sur le Christianisme," by the Chevalier de Beauterne (Paris, 1843). This work contains the religious conversations of Napoleon at St. Helena. It is charitable to infer from this, and also from Montholon's work, that he who in active life and when in good health appeared to be a fatalist and an infidel, nevertheless died as good a Catholic as could be expected. Here also will be found some extremely curious details of the last moments of Napoleon, which bear evidence of authenticity. On this subject, see also "Mémoires du Docteur F. Antomarchie, ou derniers moments de Napoléon" (Paris, 1825).

The works of Dumas, "Precis des événements militaires" (19 vols., Paris, 1817), and Jomini, "Guerres de la Révolution" (Bruxelles, 1842), and "Vie de Napoléon" (Paris, 1827), are purely military. In that point of view it is impossible to exaggerate the importance of the last named, which Halleck's translation has first made accessible to the English reader. The translator's notes add to the value of the original work, and despite some blunders, the translation is, on the whole, a good one.

What shall be said of Thiers's works—"La Révolution Française" and the "Consulât et l'Empire?" Written at first to flatter a people and to promote his own political advancement, the long series of volumes, begun about 1824, has now come to a close; and, with the additional motive of the flattery of a dynasty, his frequent perversion of the truth culminates in a description of the battle of Waterloo, which is as much a romance as that contained in "Les Misérables." But although no one need go to Thiers for accuracy of facts, it is doubtful whether the literature of any country affords a historical work surpassing this in the splendor of the painting, the clearness of the story, or the depth and shrewdness of thought with which it is interspersed. The pervading principle, or want of principle, with Thiers, is expediency. His policy, like that of his hero, is Machiavellian. For example, the mere circumstance of England being in possession of an Indian Empire, is gravely put forward as a reason, in sound policy and justice, for the wanton invasion of Egypt.

His summing up of the character of Napoleon at the close of the last volume of the "Consulate" is, however, discriminating and impartial. Despite his admiration for Napoleon, he admits that "when his power became supreme, he restrained himself no longer, and of the qualities of a political genius he retained only the smaller portion—intelligence—whilst *the moral qualities had altogether disappeared.*"

One of the most useful books for the student of military science is the "Mémoires du Maréchal Marmont, Duc de Raguse" (9 vols., Paris, 1837). Nor is it without anecdotes of the Emperor which are significant of character. For example, Marmont tells (without much comment) how Bonaparte—who went to bed at five or six, and rose at midnight—sent for *him*—who was just then ready, after all his fatiguing duties, to go to bed—and kept him talking on unimportant matters (*standing*, too, of course) all the rest of the night; although he knew that poor Marmont was to fight all the next day, at least. Those who have seen service will realize what such an incident implies.

Passing by the vast crowd of *mémoires*, anecdotes, and poetry, which relate more or less to Napoleon—some of which, like *Les Cent Jours* of Chaboullon, the Memoirs of the Duc de Rovigo (Savary), and those of St. Cyr and Rapp, are valuable, but of which it is impossible here even to give a list—we conclude the enumeration of French publications by calling attention to the all-important " Correspondance de Napoléon I." now publishing by order of the Emperor Napoleon III. Leaving out only his family and domestic letters, most of which were published in 1833, under the title of " Lettres de Napoléon à Josephine," or, in 1854, in the " Mémoires et correspondance du roi Joseph," this invaluable collection may be said to embrace every thing from the hand of the Emperor, or dictated by him, which has come down to our day. The fifteen volumes already published bring the work down only to August, 1807, from which some little idea of the immense activity of the Emperor may be gained, as well as of the mine of wealth which is here for the first time offered to exploration. The archives of the Empire contributed to the collection not less than forty thousand separate pieces; the War Department more than twenty thousand, and so on. By the express command of the present Emperor, no alteration, abridgment, or modification of the text has been permitted, and the Commissioners have not even done what Colonel Crocket requested a friend to do for his manuscript speech, *put the grammar into it.* It would not have been amiss if the letters of Washington and Franklin had been reproduced with the same fidelity. With the materials which this work furnishes, it is now possible to write a good life of Napoleon the First; but the man is perhaps not yet born who will do it.

In these letters, dispatches, orders, and memoranda, many of them secret and confidential, Napoleon has laid bare the sentiments and motives which influenced his actions during the busy years over which they extend, and, like the Commentaries of Cæsar, they form a monument more imperishable than brass—more durable than that which now covers his ashes. They display his unrivalled judgment, sagacity, foresight, and discrimination—his indefatigable perseverance, activity, industry, and that attention to the minutest circumstances, without which the success of the most ably combined plans may be endangered. But the monument, like a medal, has its reverse. There we discover the recklessness of the means employed for accomplishing ends—the duplicity, fraud, hypocrisy, perfidy, rapacity, cruelty, which cast a shade over those higher qualities that would excite unmixed admiration but for the purposes to which they were applied.

We can easily conceive the anxiety which the career of the great conqueror inspired among the English; a fearful looking for of judgment to come, which betrays itself in all their literature of the period; an apprehension which made Hannah More say that nothing calmed her terrors but reading the xlvi. Psalm.

The alarm rose to its height on the threatened invasion of Great Britain, and, among other consequences, gave occasion to what Pitt pronounced the most eloquent sermon he had ever read, that of Robert Hall, on the fast-day appointed to be kept October 19, 1803. The sermon is well known, but it illustrates the feeling of the times so well, that a short extract may be pardoned. Speaking of Napoleon, the preacher exclaims:—

"Recollect for a moment his invasion of Egypt, a country which had never given him the slightest provocation; a country so remote from the scene of his crimes that it probably did not know there was such a man in existence (happy ignorance, could it have lasted!); but while he was looking around him, like a vulture perched on an eminence, for objects on which he might gratify his insatiable thirst for rapine, he no sooner beheld the defenceless condition of that unhappy country, than he alighted upon it in a moment. In vain did it struggle, flap its wings, and rend the air with its shrieks: the cruel enemy, deaf to its cries, had infixed his talons, and was busy in sucking its blood, when the interference of a superior power forced him to relinquish his prey, and betake himself to flight. Will that vulture, think you, ever forget his disappointment on that occasion, or the numerous wounds, blows, and concussions he received in a ten years' struggle? It is impossible. It were folly to expect it. He meditates, no doubt, the deepest revenge. He who saw nothing in the simple manners and blood-bought liberties of the Swiss to engage his forbearance; nothing in proclaiming himself a Mahometan to revolt his conscience; nothing in the condition of defenceless prisoners to excite his pity; nor in that of the companions of his warfare, sick and wounded in a foreign land, to prevent him from dispatching them by poison, will treat in a manner worthy of the impiety and inhumanity of his character, a nation which he naturally dislikes as being free, dreads as the rivals of his power, and abhors as the authors of his disgrace."

The lies with which the British public were entertained during the contest with France, are among the most amusing reading now which can be found, the most foul-mouthed and improbable libels against Bonaparte, as it was the fashion to call him, being greedily swallowed by all classes. Women hushed their babies by threats that "Bony" was coming, and men quaked in their shoes lest the Monster should in very truth gobble them up. Some idea of the style in which the Emperor's character was handled by English writers, when he was at the height of his power, may be found in Goldsmith's "Secret History of the Cabinet of Bonaparte:"* London, 1810.

---

* "Vain of his person, he is fond of showing himself in public; but, conscious of his crimes, he takes care to be always well guarded. It is impossible for language to convey an adequate idea of his fears and apprehensions of assassination. Facts, however, may throw some light upon the subject. He met, not long since, in the corridor of the Tuileries, Madame Despaux, milliner to the Empress, who resides in the Rue Grammont. This woman had been sent for about midnight, with orders to bring with her some masquerade dresses, &c., for her Imperial Majesty and her Majesty of Holland. It was dark in the corridor, and the woman mistook her way; unfortunately for her she was met by Bonaparte; he had not a clear view of her; he was so much alarmed that he called out for lights, guards, &c. *He fainted*, and in his rage he ordered the woman to be sent to prison for six months, saying, "*j'en suis quitte pour la peur.*" This anecdote is known to all Paris. * * *

"This nefarious hypocrite, of whom it may be said. *Cujus ibct rei simulator atque dissimulator*, wishes very much to affect Frederic the Great; he stoops and takes snuff like him, very frequently out of his waistcoat pocket. He waddles like the Bourbon family, and has learned to dance, because he heard that Louis the XIVth danced. * * * * * * *

"He has two inconsistent propensities, which are seldom found united in the same man; he has much immoral intercourse with women, but he has shown himself addicted to that vice with which Socrates is accused, perhaps falsely, with respect to Alcibiades. In this vice he is very ably seconded by his Prince, Arch Chancellor Cambacérès! * * * * *

"All friends of mankind will hear with pleasure that this curse of the world is epileptic. He has also scrofulous eruptions on his breast, proceeding, as the French physicians say, from the itch badly cured, *la Galle rentrée*, which he had to a very great degree when he lived in his garret, previous to the 13th Vendemaire.

The British had recovered their equanimity when in 1822 appeared the valuable work of O'Meara, entitled "A Voice from St. Helena," containing notes of the Emperor's conversations in that island, which the worthy Doctor succeeded in carrying off in spite of the inquisitorial searches of Sir Hudson Lowe. Dr. O'Meara was an Irishman who happened to be acting as surgeon in the *Bellerophon* (pronounced by the sailors the *Billy Ruffian*) on the 7th August, 1815, when the Emperor came on board that ship to surrender himself into the hands of the British government; and his professional skill as well as his knowledge of the Italian language attracted the notice of the ex-emperor, who, when he was about to be conveyed to the *Northumberland*, requested O'Meara to go with him in the capacity of medical attendant to St. Helena, whither his own physician had refused to accompany him. In this difficult situation he acted to the entire satisfaction of Sir George Cockburn, who then had charge of Bonaparte, and of his successor, Sir Pulteney Malcolm, and he also received the thanks of Lord Melville; but not harmonizing so well with the measures of Sir Hudson Lowe, which he deemed arbitrary and cruel, a rupture took place, and he returned to England, where he preferred to the Admiralty accusations against Sir Hudson Lowe for tyrannical conduct towards his prisoner, and was rewarded for his pains by having his name erased from the list of naval surgeons. If, as in the other writings on St. Helena, we remark in O'Meara's book certain contradictions and misstatements, we must not accuse the Doctor, who was really a truthful and conscientious man. Like the other chroniclers of St. Helena, he was sometimes duped by the habitual lying of the great man, and besides, he was not sufficiently acquainted with French history to appreciate all that he heard. "The Quarterly Review" did not fail to pounce down upon the weak points of his book, but it will always remain an interesting and valuable record.

Down to the time when Scott's "Life of Napoleon Buonaparte" was published (1827), there did not exist a tolerable account of his remarkable career in the English tongue. Scott wrote for readers thoroughly ignorant of the subject, and readers the whole of whose prepossessions were on his side. His work is feeble, hastily written, without research, and composed entirely from a high Tory point of view. Nevertheless he had access to some good materials; no serious or important error has ever been pointed out in his narrative, and some parts, such as the admirable description of Bonaparte's first Italian campaign, are, in point of style, worthy of the author of "Ivanhoe." A chival-

---

"Never was there in one human being such a combination of cruelty, tyranny, petulance, lewdness, luxury and avarice, as there is in Napoleon Bonaparte. Human nature had not before produced such a frightful being!"

rous gentleman in feeling, Scott scorned to treat the fallen enemy of his country and his party with indignity, and despite his violent prejudices, his remarks on the personal character of Bonaparte are conceived in the spirit of a lofty impartiality. He says, for example, that before we judge Napoleon by the temptations to which he yielded, we ought to remember how much he may have resisted. In truth, Scott was sometimes too generous; as, for example, when he rejected with scorn all idea of Napoleon's having been at all *profligate*. Scott was too pure a man to believe that Bonaparte was quite as licentious as he could find leisure to be. To the admirers of the great novelist, melancholy associations add interest to this, almost his last literary labor. Written for the highly honorable purpose of paying the debts, for which he had unfortunately become liable, the publication of the "Life of Buonaparte" realized the startling sum of £18,000; but the enormous labor of writing nine volumes in a twelvemonth, in the midst of pain, sorrow, and ruin, was too much for that great heart, and Scott's health failed before he had freed himself from all his encumbrances.

Scott's "Life" suited the prejudices of the English better than that of Hazlitt, which came out in the following year. Hazlitt was as thorough a Radical as Scott was a Tory, and he appeared as the champion of an historical character which he conceived to be unjustly and wantonly attacked by his countrymen. He occupied much more time than Scott in his researches, and, not satisfied with books and written documents, Hazlitt saw and conversed with the persons most likely to afford him information. His work, in consequence, contains anecdotes and facts which throw a new light on many subjects.

Alison's "History of Europe from the Commencement of the French Revolution to the Restoration of the Bourbons" (London, 1832–1842), is by far the most popular historical work of this century. The ninth edition was published in 1853; it was reprinted in Paris, Brussels, and the United States; and has been translated into French, German, Hindostanee, and Arabic. Despite the author's gross political prejudices, and a fondness for exaggerated and frothy declamation, he has aimed to be truthful and impartial, and he is generally successful in the attempt. He seems to have been aware of the bias in his own mind, and he therefore goes honestly to work to counteract it, and to afford the reader, at every step, the means of verifying his statements and testing his conclusions.

Alison's estimate of the character of Napoleon, though marked with some traces of the exasperated feelings with which the English conducted the war against him is, in the main, candid and just. He bears the following tribute to the gigantic intellect of the Emperor:—

"Never were talents of the highest genius of the most exalted kind, more profusely bestowed upon a human being. The true scene of Napoleon's glory, and the most characteristic of the ruling passion of his mind, was his cabinet. Those who are struck with astonishment at the immense information and just discrimination which he displayed at the council-board, and the varied and important public improvements which he set on foot in every part of his dominions, will form a most inadequate conception of his mind, unless they are at the same time familiar with the luminous and profound views which he threw out on the philosophy of politics in the solitude of St. Helena. Never was evinced a clearer proof of the truth, which a practical acquaintance with men must probably have impressed upon every observer, that talent of the highest order is susceptible of any application, and that accident or supreme direction alone determines whether their possessor is to become a Homer, a Bacon, or a Napoleon. It would require the observation of a Thucydides, directing the pencil of a Tacitus, to portray. by a few touches, such a character; and modern idiom, even in their hands, would probably have proved inadequate to the task. Equal to Alexander in military achievement, superior to Justinian in legal information, sometimes second only to Bacon in political sagacity, he possessed, at the same time, the inexhaustible resources of Hannibal, and the administrative powers of Cæsar."

Life is short, and Alison's History of Europe is long; but he who has not read it has in reserve a book as entertaining from the author's paradoxical views, as it is from its readable style. The continuation (1815–1851) is more superficial, though useful as almost the only history of our own times.

The prejudices which influence European authors, and which make most of the lives of Napoleon either a panegyric or a libel, have naturally influenced American writers, and the few who have treated the subject have added little to our materials for forming a judgment of Napoleon's character.

Joel Barlow's last poem was a withering expression of his sentiment towards Napoleon. It was dictated at Wilna by the American Minister in December, 1812, while lying on his bed, to his Secretary, Thomas Barlow, only a night or two before the van of the French Army, which had been defeated by the burning of Moscow, entered Wilna on their retreat, the same month in which he died. It was copied in diplomatic characters, and sent to Mrs. Barlow, in Paris. It is entitled "Advice to a Raven in Russia," and closes thus:—

> "Go back and winter in the wilds of Spain;
> Feast there awhile, and in the next campaign
> Rejoin your master, for you'll find him then,
> With his new millions of the race of men,
> Clothed in his thunders, all his flags unfurled,
> Raging and storming o'er a prostrate world!
> War after war his hungry soul requires;
> State after state shall sink beneath his fires.
> Yet other Spains in victim smoke shall rise,
> And other Moscows suffocate the skies.
> Each land lie reeking with its people slain,
> And not a stream run bloodless to the main,
> Till men resume their souls, and dare to shed
> Earth's total vengeance on the monster's head."

Channing has judged the Emperor with perhaps too great severity, hardly giving him credit even for his great public works. "The boasted internal improvements of Napoleon scarcely deserve to be named, if we compare their influence with the operation of his public measures." He admits that

> "There is, however, one great work, which gives Bonaparte a fair claim on the gratitude of posterity, and entitles him to an honorable renown. We refer to the new code of laws, which was given to France under his auspices. His participation in this work has indeed been unwarrantably and ridiculously magnified. Because he attended the meetings of the Commissioners to whom it was assigned, and made some useful and sagacious suggestions, he has been praised, as if he had struck out, by the miraculous force of his genius, a new code of laws. The truth is, that he employed for this work, as he should have done, the most eminent civilians of the Empire; and it is also true that these learned men have little claim to originality; for, as an author [Scott] observes, the code 'has few peculiarities making a difference between its principles and those of the Roman law.'
>
> "It was, however, the misery of Bonaparte, a curse brought on him by his crimes, that he could touch nothing without leaving on it the polluting mark of despotism. His usurpation took from him the power of legislating with magnanimity, where his own interest was concerned. He could provide for the administration of justice between man and man, but not between the citizen and the ruler. Political offences, the very class which ought to be submitted to a jury, were denied that mode of trial. Juries might decide on other criminal questions; but they were not permitted to interpose between the despot and the ill-fated subjects who might fall under his suspicion. These were arraigned before 'special tribunals invested with a half military character,' the ready ministers of nefarious prosecutions, and only intended to cloak, by legal forms, the murderous purposes of the tyrant."

Channing very justly observes in the article from which we quote (Christian Examiner, 1827), that a just estimate of the late Emperor of France is important. "That extraordinary man, having operated on the world with unprecedented power during his life, is now influencing it by his character. That character, we apprehend, is not viewed as it should be. The kind of admiration which it inspires, even in free countries, is a bad omen. The greatest crime against society, that of spoiling it of its rights, and loading it with chains, still fails to move that deep abhorrence which is its due; and which, if really felt, would fix on the usurper a brand of indelible infamy. Regarding freedom as the chief interest of human nature, as essential to its intellectual, moral and religious progress, we look on men who have signalized themselves by their hostility to it, with an indignation at once stern and sorrowful, which no glare of successful war, and no admiration of the crowd, can induce us to suppress."

There are few more scathing passages in English literature than the following, which we quote as well because it is one of the most eloquent which Channing ever wrote, as because it applies a wholesome corrective to the idolatry of power of which America, no less than France, furnishes too many instances. Channing's whole soul was inspired with the love of freedom, which he says is but another name for justice, honor, and benevolence, and he had no sympathy with that feminine and Celtic type of character which loves a master.

"We close our view of Bonaparte's character, by saying that his original propensities, released from restraint, and pampered by indulgence to a degree seldom allowed to mortals, grew up into a spirit of despotism as stern and absolute as ever usurped the human heart. The love of power and supremacy absorbed, consumed him. No other passion, no domestic attachment, no private friendship, no love of pleasure, no relish for letters or the arts, no human sympathy, no human weakness, divided his mind with the passion for dominion, and for dazzling manifestations of his power. Before this, duty, honor, love, humanity, fell prostrate. Josephine, we are told, was dear to him, but the devoted wife, who had stood firm and faithful in the day of his doubtful fortunes, was cast off in his prosperity, to make room for a stranger, who might be more subservient to his power. He was affectionate, we are told, to his brothers and mother; but his brothers, the moment they ceased to be his tools, were disgraced; and his mother, it is said, was not allowed to sit in the presence of her imperial son. He was sometimes softened, we are told, by the sight of the field of battle strewn with the wounded and dead. But if the Moloch of his ambition claimed new heaps of slain to-morrow, it was never denied. With all his sensibility, he gave millions to the sword, with as little compunction as he would have brushed away so many insects, which had infested his march. To him all human will, desire, power, were to bend. His superiority, none might question. He insulted the fallen, who had contracted the guilt of opposing his progress; and not even woman's loveliness, and the dignity of a queen, could give shelter from his contumely. His allies were his vassals, nor was their vassalage concealed. Too lofty to use the arts of conciliation, preferring command to persuasion, overbearing and all-grasping, he spread distrust, exasperation, fear and revenge through Europe; and, when the day of retribution came, the old antipathies and mutual jealousies of nations were swallowed up in one burning purpose to prostrate the common tyrant, the universal foe."

Headley's "Napoleon and his Marshals" (New York, 1846), need not detain us long. Griswold, a judicious critic, thus characterizes it:—"The author has taken up the subject with ardor, but with little previous preparation; the work, therefore, indicates imperfect information, immature views of character, and many hasty and unconsidered opinions. The style has the same melodramatic exaggeration, which the whole design of the work exhibits."

In quite a different spirit is written the following admirable passage, from "Scenes and Thoughts in Europe," (New York, 1852), by one of our best living writers, George Henry Calvert. It marches straight to the point, like the charge of a column of infantry. Calvert adopts and explains Bourrienne's and Coleridge's weighty aphorism:

"Bonaparte was behind his age; he was a man of the past. The value of the great modern instruments, and the modern heart and growth, he did not discern. He went groping in the mediæval times to find the lustreless sceptre of Charlemagne, and he saw not the paramount potency there now is in that of Faust. He was a great cannoneer, not a great builder. In the centre of Europe, from amidst the most advanced, scientific nation on earth, after eighteen centuries of Christianity, not to perceive that lead in the form of type, is far more puissant than in the form of bullets; not to feel that for the head of the French nation to desire an imperial crown was as unmanly as it was disloyal; that a rivalry of rotten Austria and barbaric Russia, was a despicable vanity; not to have yet learned how much stronger ideas are than blows, principles than edicts—to be blind to all this, was to want vision, insight, wisdom. Bonaparte was not the original genius he has been vaunted; he was a vulgar copyist, and Alexander of Macedon, and Frederick of Prussia, were his models. Force was his means, despotism his aim, war was his occupation, pomp his relaxation. For him the world was divided into two—his will and those who opposed it. He acknowledged no duty, he respected no right, he flouted at integrity, he despised truth. He had no belief in man, no trust in God. In his wants he was ignoble, in his methods ignorant. He was possessed by the lust of isolated, irresponsible, boundless, heartless power, and he believed that he could found it with the sword, and bind it with lies; and so, ere he began to grow old, what he had founded had already toppled, and what he had bound was loosed. He fell, and as if history would register his disgrace with a more instructive emphasis, he fell twice, and exhausted France, beleaguered by a million of armed foes, had to accept the restored imbecile Bourbons."

We have not left space to make the extracts we should like to make from Emerson's excellent paper on "Napoleon; or, the Man of the World," in "Representative Men." The leading thought, however, is that Napoleon is the representative of the middle class of society. "Bonaparte is the idol of common men, because he had in transcendent degree the qualities of common men. . . . When you have penetrated through all the circles of power and splendor, you were not dealing with a gentleman, at last, but with an impostor and a rogue: and he fully deserves the epithet of Jupiter Scapin, or a sort of scamp Jupiter."

Not such is the judgment of John S. C. Abbott, who prefaces his "History of Napoleon Bonaparte" (N. York, 1855) by the following indiscriminate eulogy:—"The history of Napoleon has often been written by his enemies. This narrative is from the pen of one who reveres and loves the Emperor. The writer admires Napoleon because he abhorred war, and did every thing in his power to avert that dire calamity; because he merited the sovereignty to which the suffrages of a grateful nation elevated him, because he consecrated the most extraordinary energies ever conferred upon a mortal, to promote the prosperity of his country; because he was regardless of luxury, and cheerfully endured all toil, and all hardships, that he might elevate and bless the masses of mankind; because he had a high sense of honor, revered religion, respected the rights of conscience, and nobly advocated equality of privileges, and the universal brotherhood of man." This view, while doubtless possessing the merit of originality, is open to the objection of being throughout in point-blank contradiction to the facts. Its audacity illustrates the saying attributed to the author's hero, that there is but one step from the sublime to the ridiculous.

In truth, however, so varied and singular is the combination of qualities which Napoleon's character exhibits, and so much at variance with what we usually observe in human nature, that there is no man can say he has a clear perception of what it actually was. Brave, without being chivalrous; sometimes humane, seldom generous; insatiable in ambition; inexhaustible in resources; without a thirst for blood, but totally indifferent to it when his interests were concerned; without any fixed ideas on religion, but with a strong perception of its necessity, as a part of the mechanism of government; a great general with a small army, a mighty conqueror with a large one; gifted with extraordinary power of perception, and the clearest insight into every subject connected with mankind; without exclusive information derived from study; but with the rarest aptitude for making himself master of every subject from actual observation; ardently devoted to glory, and yet incapable of the self-sacrifice which constitutes its highest honors; he exhibited a mixture of great and selfish qualities, such as, perhaps, never were before combined in any single individual. His greatest defect was the total and systematic disregard of truth, which pervaded all his thoughts. He was totally without the straightforwardness or honesty which forms the best and most dignified feature in the Gothic or German character. His intellect was the perfection of the Celt or Greek, without a shadow of the magnanimity and rectitude which has ever characterized the Roman and Gothic races of mankind. As for Americans, they will never cease to prefer duty to glory, patriotism to self-seeking, Washington to Napoleon.

THE WIND AND THE WEATHERCOCK.

Said the rude Wind once to the veering Vane,
"What a fidgety thing you are!
You turn and you turn and you turn again,
And people look up and stare."

The modest Weathercock replied:
"I fain would be quiet and still,
But 'tis you that shift from side to side:
I only obey your will."

MORAL.

Often the fault which in *others* we find
Is but *our own*, to which we are blind.

NEW YORK STATE MILITIA.

II.

SERVICES IN 1861.

The stirring events of the past three years, have crowded upon each other with such rapidity, and the war drama being enacted upon our continent has assumed such vast proportions, that through the mass of military operations finished and progressing, the mind with difficulty wades back to the commencement of the struggle, and notes its early incidents and battles. And yet it is doubtful, whether at any time in the course of this unfortunate contest, the public heart was ever wrought up to that pitch of excitement and anxiety, which the opening of hostilities first produced. The firing upon the national flag at Fort Sumter, had taken away all hope of a peaceable solution of our difficulties, and the dread reality of civil war, with its approaching trials, its cruel sacrifices, and its bitter hates, broke with fearful force upon the Northern people. They were unprepared, so soon, to look upon their former brethren as enemies, and still the expulsion of Anderson and his command from a United States fortress, placed them in that attitude.

Solemn as were the consequences, rather than consent to a dismemberment of the republic, they accepted the alternative of war.

Before full preparation could be made for the prosecution of this war, considerable time necessarily elapsed. The wants of the General Government, however, were urgent, the national capital was in danger of being entered at any moment by armed men from the seceding States, and the smallness of our Army rendering it wholly inadequate for efficient service, an immediate call was made upon the loyal States for seventy-five thousand (75,000) militia. New York was able, through her organized regiments, to respond promptly to this call to the amount of a little over half her quota, and eleven regiments of her "National Guards" left for Washington, in the following order:—

		1861.	Strength.
5th.	Colonel C. Schwarzwalder	April 29th,	600
6th.	Colonel Joseph C. Pinckney	" 21st,	650
7th.	Colonel Marshall Lefferts	" 19th,	1,050
8th.	Colonel George Lyons	" 23d,	900
12th.	Colonel Daniel Butterfield	" 21st,	950
13th.	Colonel Abel Smith	" 23d,	1,086
20th.	Colonel George W. Pratt	May 7th,	785
25th.	Colonel Michael K. Bryan	April 23d,	500
28th.	Colonel Michael Bennett	" 30th,	563
69th.	Colonel Michael Corcoran	" 23d,	1,050
71st.	Colonel Abram S. Vosburgh	" 21st,	950
	Total		7,934

Of the above, the 5th, 6th, 7th, 8th, 12th, 69th, and 71st were from the city of New York; the 13th and 28th from Brooklyn; the 20th from the County of Ulster, and the 25th from the city of Albany.

The sensation which attended the departure of these regiments was most deep. The friends of the soldiers, fathers and brothers, and in many instances mothers, wives, and sisters, thronged the avenues of the different regimental armories, waiting to say farewell to those dear to them, who were about, for the first time, to essay the perils and hardships of war. The citizens came out by thousands to witness their leaving, and bid them "God-speed!" and many a wet eye and throbbing heart, testified to the intense anxiety with which all regarded the character of the work upon which they were entering. And it was not without reason that such anxiety was entertained. Maryland was then in a state of violent agitation, and threatening to follow the course of the seceding States;—a large portion of her population being greatly disaffected towards the Union. Washington, too, was supposed to be a prize coveted by the rebel government, and it was thought more than probable that a struggle would speedily ensue for its capture. The troops, therefore, first sent forward, left under circumstances of peculiar danger, from the fact that they were obliged to traverse the State of Maryland, and, in many instances, to pass through the city of Baltimore, before reaching the national capital.

But the New York Militia regiments never hesitated to obey the orders of their Commander-in-Chief. Promptly, upon the call of the Governor, they assembled at their respective headquarters, and within forty-eight hours most of them were ready to march to the relief of Washington. And certainly, through the entire history of this war, no scene was attended with the exhibition of such noble and pure patriotism as that incident to their departure. The cities of New York, Albany, and Brooklyn, poured forth their populations into the streets to rend the air with cheers. From every flag-staff floated the national colors, and balconies and windows were crowded with fair occupants, waving banners and handkerchiefs in enthusiastic approbation of the valor of the citizen soldiers; while these soldiers, drinking in from the beaming faces of their friends fresh draughts of patriotic fervor, went to their different points of embarkation, with loud huzzas mingling with the strains of martial music.

The first to leave the city of New York was the 7th Regiment, Colonel Marshall Lefferts commanding, on the 19th of April, numbering ten hundred and fifty (1,050) men. This organization, as is well known, had long been the pride of New York, and was looked upon as the "crack" regiment on the island. Composed of young men in the bloom of manhood, and connected with all the active business pursuits of the great metropolis, their departure was the cause of the most intense excitement through a large class of its citizens, and the scenes attending it are thus described in one of the city daily journals:—

"The regiment formed in Lafayette Place, about four o'clock P. M., in the presence of an immense crowd, each window of each building being filled with such fair applauders, as might cheer the heart of the forlornest bachelor, if there were any such among those noble soldiers. Once in line, they proceeded through Fourth street to Broadway, down that great thoroughfare to Courtlandt street, and across the ferry, in boats provided for the purpose, to Jersey City. The line of march was a perfect ovation. Thousands upon thousands lined the sidewalks. It will be remembered as long as any of those who witnessed it live to talk of it, and beyond that it will pass into the recorded history of this fearful struggle. 'The regiment' marched, not as on festival days, not as on the reception of the Prince of Wales, but nobly and sternly, as men who were going to the war. Hurried was their step, —not so regular as on less important occasions. We saw women, we saw men shed tears as they passed. Amidst the deafening cheers that rose, we heard cries of 'God bless them!' And so along Broadway, and through Courtlandt street, under its almost countless flags, the 'gallant 7th Regiment' left the city."

News of the fight in Baltimore, in which the Massachusetts soldiers were killed, had been received before the regiment left New York, which, of course, added greatly to the excitement attending its departure, and forty-eight rounds of ball-cartridge were served out to its members.

This noble regiment crossed the Potomac with the first troops that entered Virginia, when Alexandria and Arlington Heights were occupied, and labored with the New Jersey Brigade in the construction of "Fort Runyon."

Following the 7th Regiment, were the 6th, 12th, and 71st Regiments, which left New York on Sunday, the twenty-first of April. Similar demonstrations of popular enthusiasm and plaudits of approbation, accompanied them through their entire line of march.

"Cheers from ten thousand voices swelling in prolonged chorus, the waving of handkerchiefs by fair hands, the display of flags and streamers, made the scene one of the most animated and exciting ever witnessed in the city."

On the 23d of April the 8th and 69th Regiments, from the city of New York, the 13th from Brooklyn, and the 25th from Albany, left the State. The departure of the 69th, composed entirely of Irish citizens, was made the occasion of a most patriotic demonstration on the part of their immediate friends and admirers. In order to go into the field with full ranks, Colonel Corcoran opened the rolls of his regiment to recruits. He left with ten hundred and fifty (1,050) men, but the number who had enrolled their names as willing to march and serve under him, amounted, the evening before the embarkation of the regiment to six thousand five hundred (6,500).

Besides the crowds of eager spectators who lined Broadway

upon the march of the 69th to the steamer Adger, about two thousand (2,000) Irishmen, members of civic societies, escorted them with music and banners. Colonel Corcoran, who had been suffering from bad health, arose from a bed of sickness to accompany his regiment, and the carriage which conveyed him to the steamer was so pressed upon by the admiring multitude, that it was with difficulty the police restrained them from bearing him bodily in their arms.

The 8th Regiment, Colonel Lyons, embarked in the ship Montgomery with nine hundred (900) members. The line of their march was the scene of wild enthusiasm, their friends gathering in balconies and windows, and cheering and inspiriting the soldiers with their smiles and warm approvals. The 13th upon leaving Brooklyn, and the 25th on leaving Albany, received also from their respective cities like manifestations of the popular approbation.

On the 29th of April, the 5th Regiment, six hundred (600) strong, under Colonel Schwarzwalder, composed entirely of German citizens, left New York on board the steam transport Kedar, for Annapolis. On the 30th of April, the 28th Regiment, Colonel Michael Bennett, of Brooklyn, embarked in the Star of the South, and on the 7th of May, 1861, the 20th Regiment, from Ulster County, under the command of Colonel George W. Pratt, closed the noble column of New York Militia moving to the relief of the capital.

The regiments enumerated were mustered into the United States service, and performed duty through terms varying from thirty days to three months; most of them, however, for the latter period.

The 5th, served three months at Baltimore and in North-Eastern Virginia, crossed the Potomac at Williamsport, July 9, 1861, and at the time of the battle of Bull Run was serving under General Patterson. They returned to New York on the 2d of August. A good portion of their service was rendered at and in the vicinity of the Relay House, near Baltimore—they being employed upon guard, picket, and scout duty. "Their vigilance frequently prevented serious results to the body of troops stationed at that post. The railroad was also an object of the special vigilance of the 5th, and the prevention of attempts to place obstacles on the tracks, was one way in which their services were valuable."

The 6th Regiment left New York by water for Washington. Its destination however was subsequently changed to Annapolis, where it remained during most of its three months' term, engaged in guard and garrison duty, and on small expeditions. The first month one half of the regiment was stationed at Camp Misery, between Annapolis and Baltimore; four companies at Camp Butler; one company at Fort Madison; the head-quarters being at Annapolis. The remaining two months, one half the regiment was at Annapolis Junction, the rest being at Annapolis. A detachment of one hundred men under command of Major Stafford, while returning from Washington in a propeller on the Potomac, was attacked at Mathias Point by about one thousand rebels; but two howitzers were brought to bear upon the enemy, and they were soon dispersed.

The 7th served thirty days at Washington upon guard duty and returned to New York on the 31st of May. The following is an extract from a complimentary order of the War Department, issued the day previous to the regiment's leaving Washington: "It is the desire of the War Department in relinquishing the services of this gallant regiment, to make known the satisfaction that is felt at the prompt and patriotic manner in which it responded to the call for men to defend the capital when it was believed to be in peril, and to acknowledge the important service which it rendered by appearing here in an hour of dark and trying necessity. The time for which it had engaged has now expired. The service which it was expected to perform has been handsomely accomplished, and its members may return to their native city, with the assurance that its services are gratefully appreciated by all good and loyal citizens, whilst the Government is equally confident, that when the country again calls upon them, the appeal will not be made in vain to the young men of New York."

The 8th Regiment went by water to Annapolis, and subsequently served at the battle of Bull Run in the First Brigade (Colonel Andrew Porter's), Second Division (Colonel Hunter's), and honorable mention is made of its services in the report of Colonel Porter. The regiment returned to New York July 27th.

The 12th Regiment, commanded by Colonel Butterfield, left New York on the steam-ship Baltic, for Fortress Monroe, whence they were sent to Annapolis. From thence they went to Washington, and were, by constant drilling, brought to an admirable condition. Thence on the 7th of May they were ordered, *via* Baltimore and Harrisburg, to Hagerstown, and joined General Patterson at Martinsburg. Taking part in that campaign, they tendered their services until August 2d. They arrived in New York on the 1st of August.

The 13th went per steamer Marion to Annapolis, where they remained under command of General Butler until the 19th of June, quartered in the buildings of the United States Naval Academy. During that time detachments from the regiment were employed in searching for the light-ships which had been removed by the rebels. Two were found, recaptured, and brought to Annapolis. Expeditions were also sent to the "eastern shore" of Maryland, which were successful in finding many hundred stand of arms there concealed. On the 19th of June the regiment was ordered to Baltimore, where the balance of their term of service was passed—they voluntarily remaining ten days longer than the term of their enlistment, at the request of General Dix.

The 20th went by railroad to Perryville, and thence by steamer to Annapolis, spent its term of service in guarding the railroad, on picket duty, and on guard duty at Baltimore.

The 25th went to Washington and spent part of its time in building fortifications at Arlington. The 28th served its term at and near Washington, and was encamped below Arlington Heights.

The 69th, Colonel Corcoran, served at Bull Run, in the Third Brigade (Sherman's), First Division (Tyler's). Its loss is thus stated in Colonel Sherman's report: Killed, thirty-eight; wounded, fifty-nine; missing, ninety-five: total, one hundred and ninety-two. Among the captured was Colonel Corcoran. The 69th and 79th New York Militia, the 13th New York Volunteers and the 2d Wisconsin, with a company of artillery, under Captain Ayres, made up the Third Brigade. They were in the hottest part of the fight, and all suffered severely. Colonel Sherman's Brigade before going into action, made a junction with Hunter's Division and formed in the rear of Colonel Porter's Brigade. It was just before making this junction, that Lieutenant-Colonel Haggerty, of the 69th, in attempting to intercept the retreat of a party of the enemy was shot, and fell dead from his horse. The fight which followed was near the Stone Bridge, crossing Bull Run, at which the brigade first took its position. It crossed the stream, with the exception of Ayres' Battery, at a ford which had been indicated to Colonel Sherman, by observing early in the day, a horseman of the enemy cross at the same point. The crossing was made in obedience to orders from the Division Commander, that the brigade should go to the assistance of Colonel Hunter, then engaged with the enemy. Immediately after crossing, the brigade ascended the steep bluff opposite, with its infantry meeting with no opposition. Shortly after ascending the bluff, Colonel Sherman received orders from General McDowell to join in the pursuit of the enemy who were falling back to the left of the road, by which the army had approached from Sudley Springs. Colonel Sherman says: "Placing Colonel Quimby's Regiment of Rifles (13th New York Volunteers) in front, in column by division, I directed the other regiments to follow in line of battle, in the order of the Wisconsin 2d, New York 79th, and New York 69th." These regiments attacked the enemy successively, the 69th being the last engaged. The part it took in the fight is thus described in the official report. After the Wisconsin Regiment had been repulsed a second time, the account proceeds: "By this time the New York 69th had closed up, and in like manner it was ordered to cross the brow of the hill and drive the enemy from cover. It was impossible to get a good view of the ground. In it there was one battery of artillery, which poured an incessant fire upon an advancing column, and the ground was irregular, with small clusters of pines, affording shelter, of which the enemy took good advantage. The fire of rifles and musketry was very severe. The 79th headed by its colonel (Cameron) charged across the hill, and for a short time the contest was severe. They rallied several times under fire, but finally broke and gained the cover of the hill. This left the field open to the New York 69th, Colonel Corcoran, who, in his turn, led his regiment over the crest, and had in full open view the ground so severely contested. The firing was very severe, and the roar of cannon, musketry, and rifles incessant. It was manifest the enemy were here in great force, far superior to us at that point. The 69th held the ground for some time, but finally fell back in disorder."

Colonel Corcoran was captured after the fight, and during the retreat. The manner of his capture is thus described by Colonel Sherman, in his account of the retreat: "On the ridge to the west, we succeeded in partially re-forming the regiments, but it was manifest they would not stand, and I directed Colonel Corcoran to move along the ridge to the rear, near the position where we had first formed the brigade. General McDowell was there in person, and used all possible efforts to reassure the men. By the active exertions of Colonel Corcoran, we formed an irregular square against the cavalry, which was then seen to issue from the position from which we had been driven, and we began our retreat towards that ford of Bull Run by which we had approached the field of battle. There was no positive order to retreat, although for an hour it had been going on by the operations of the men themselves. The ranks were thin and irregular, and we found a stream of people stirring from the hospital across Bull Run, and far towards Centreville."

Colonel Corcoran was missing immediately after the cavalry charge, near the building used as a hospital. Colonel Cameron was mortally wounded during the charge in the early part of the battle, while leading his regiment. The 69th returned to New York the 27th of July.

The 71st Regiment served in front of Washington, and at Bull Run was in the Second Brigade (Burnside's), of the Second Division (Hunter's). This brigade, besides the 71st Regiment, New York, was composed of the 1st and 2d Rhode Island Infantry, the 2d Rhode Island Battery, and 2d New Hampshire Volunteers. The 71st was engaged in some severe fighting, and behaved with gallantry. Colonel Burnside thus speaks of the services of the regiment, in his supplementary report: "I beg to again mention the bravery and steadiness manifested by Colonel Martin, and his entire regiment (71st), both in the field and during the retreat." The numbers engaged did not exceed five hundred, as a number were on the Potomac Flotilla, and a large guard was left at the Navy Yard. The published losses were twenty killed, forty-three wounded, and many prisoners. The 71st returned to New York on the 26th of July.

In addition to the New York Militia regiments, which served for three months, four regiments,—the 2d, 9th, 14th, and 79th, organized for three years.

The 2d, Colonel Tompkins, was in the battle of Bull Run, in the Second Brigade (Schenck's), of the First Division (Tyler's). Its loss, as reported a week after the battle, was twenty-four killed, and twenty-seven wounded.

The 9th, Colonel Stiles, upon entering the United States service, went to Washington, and thence to Harper's Ferry, and was at that place under General Patterson, at the time of the battle of Bull Run.

The 14th Regiment, Colonel Wood, from Brooklyn, left for Washington on the 20th of May, was in the battle of Bull Run, in the First Brigade, Second Division. Its loss, as reported a week afterwards, was twenty-five killed, and fifty-eight wounded, besides prisoners;—Colonel Wood among the captured. Colonel Porter, commanding the brigade, mentions, in terms of praise, the conduct of the officers of the 14th: "In the last attack, Colonel A. M. Wood, of the 14th New York State Militia, was wounded, together with Captains R. B. Jourdan and C. F. Baldwin, and Lieutenants J. A. Jones, J. R. Salter, R. A. Goodenough, and C. Scholes, and Adjutant Laidlaw. The officers of the 14th, especially Major James Jourdan, were distinguished by their display of spirit and efficiency throughout the action."

The 79th Regiment departed from New York, for the seat of war, on the 2d of June, eight hundred strong, exclusive of band and drum corps. They were escorted to the cars by the Caledonian Club, nearly half of whose members were in the ranks of the regiment. In the battle of Bull Run, as heretofore stated, they formed a portion of Sherman's Brigade. Their loss, as given in Colonel Sherman's report, was thirty-two killed, fifty-one wounded, and one hundred and fifteen missing;—subsequent accounts placed the killed at thirty-three, and wounded at sixty-six. Among the killed was Colonel Cameron, the commanding officer. He is mentioned in Colonel Sherman's report as having been mortally wounded, in the charge made by the 79th, and followed by the 69th Regiment, and subsequently the report says: "Colonel Cameron had been mortally wounded, carried to an ambulance, and reported dying." His body fell into the hands of the enemy. With the battle of Bull Run, closed the active service of the militia regiments during 1861, the first year of the war; the positions occupied by the different regiments, upon guard or garrison duty, being supplied by the volunteer organizations then rapidly concentrating at Washington. Mortifying as was the disaster, which befell the Union arms, at the battle of Bull Run, the New York Militia regiments did as good fighting, certainly, as was done on that occasion. Though, like all the troops engaged, they were for the first time brought to encounter the realities of a battle-field, still their former experience in military manœuvres, and their habit of associating together, rendered them much more effective in service than the early volunteer organizations, which, in many instances, lacked both on the part of officers and men, the requisite military knowledge to enable them to act thoroughly in concert, and with a proper regard to discipline. The volunteers did not want in courage, but were wholly incapable of exercising that cool determination, which long military drill almost invariably imparts to the soldier. In this respect, the militia were superior to them, and possessed, moreover, a certain regimental and State pride, which incited them to deeds of bravery, and prevented their wavering, except when sorely pressed or in extreme danger of capture.

The fighting of the 69th and 79th New York State Militia was, at the time, highly commended, not only by the officers in command upon the day of the battle, but by different civilians, correspondents of the press, who witnessed the fight. Even several of the rebel papers praised the gallantry of these regiments. Had the entire force been composed of as good material, and been led by as brave officers, though we might not have won the battle, it would have been, upon our part, a desperately contested fight, and would never have ended in the disgraceful rout, so galling at the time to the Northern heart.

But, independent of the service rendered by the New York Militia regiments in the field, the promptness with which they first moved to the defence of Washington, probably insured its safety. Had that city been lost at the commencement of the war, though it might have been recaptured, the effect at the time of its falling into the hands of the secessionists, would have proved disastrous to our interests with foreign powers. The moving of the militia regiments from New York, at the moment it was feared the national capital was in danger, and the uprising of the masses to cheer them onwards upon their patriotic mission, gave to the Government the assurance that the popular sentiment was strongly aroused, and in its character thoroughly Union. Political, or partisan bias, was, for the time, overwhelmed in the universal feeling, that the integrity of the nation must be preserved at all hazards, and that a disruption of the States would never be tamely submitted to by the Northern people.

The alacrity with which the militia responded to the call which summoned them for the first time to the fortress and the battle-field, to protect that flag which it had been their pride to carry upon all festival occasions, the flag of their native or adopted country, and to them the emblem of civil and religious liberty; the alacrity, we say, with which they marched, was, to the Government, the strongest indication that the great resources of the loyal States were entirely at their command, to suppress the rebellion and secure the Union of the States.

The heart of the whole Irish population was bound up in the success of the 69th, and the death of Lieutenant-Colonel Haggerty and the capture and long confinement of Colonel Corcoran, brought thousands of recruits into the Union armies. The Scotchmen too, vying with the bravery of the 79th, in whose ranks many of their countrymen and companions met their death (among them the brave Colonel Cameron), contributed their full quota towards swelling the legions of the republic. The gallant "7th," by its promptness in moving to Washington, when the peril was supposed to be imminent, aroused, among the young men of New York, a military spirit, which led them by hundreds to seek commissions in the volunteer service, and failing to become officers, to join the ranks of the early organizations. Indeed, all the militia regiments which first left the State, exerted an influence by their cheerfully rendered service, upon the citizens of their immediate neighborhood, which threw into the ranks of the volunteers, thousands of young and stalwart men, anxious to prove their devotion to their country and its flag.

That we do not misstate the feeling which actuated the New York Militia, when we say their service was "cheerfully rendered," we have but to look back at the activity and energy which characterized both officers and men in their preparations to leave for the scene of danger.

The little delays and disappointments which at times occurred in furnishing them with proper equipments for the field, were borne with uneasiness and frequently with irritation. All were anxious to be off to Baltimore and Washington, and those regiments were regarded most fortunate which received the earliest transportation.

An incident is related in connection with the departure of the 20th (Colonel George W. Pratt's) Ulster County Regiment, which shows the temper that pervaded the different organizations. The regiment arrived in New York city from Ulster County on the 28th of April, 1861, with the intention of proceeding by steamer to Washington. On their arrival in the city, they found that no transportation had been provided for them, and they went into the Park Barracks, where they remained until the afternoon of Sunday the 5th of May. They then received orders to return to their homes, as advices had arrived from Washington calling only for volunteers to serve for two years—and for this reason it was alleged, no more militia regiments could be accepted. This order caused great consternation among the rank and file. They had enlisted in the hope of being engaged in the impending conflict, and expected to see actual service. Many of them had given up lucrative positions, left homes and families, for the purpose of manifesting their patriotism and sustaining the honor and integrity of the American flag. On the following evening (May 6), a special order was received from Washington, ordering them to proceed at once to the capital. When this news was imparted to the troops, a scene of genuine enthusiasm ensued; cheer upon cheer rang upon the air; the President, the Governor, General Scott, Colonel Pratt, and in fact every name the troops could think of, was wildly cheered. Colonel Pratt was deeply affected at the enthusiasm manifested by his men, and took no measures to check their outbursts of joy. After order had been restored, he made a few remarks, thanking his regiment for the manner in which they had borne the many disappointments to which they had been subjected, and congratulating them upon the prospect of a speedy entry upon active service. He said "they would come back covered with glory." Alas! how true was this prophecy, how literally has it been fulfilled. He who uttered it, sleeps with the honored dead, " covered with glory." His regiment entering the general service for three months, at the expiration of its term reenlisted for the war,—and upon nearly every battle-field in Virginia and Maryland has the 20th New York Militia been distinguished for its bravery. Its commander received his mortal wound at the second battle of Manassas. After his death, the county from which it was recruited (the County of Ulster), filled up its ranks, at repeated intervals, until it has sent of its sons into this organization alone, some twelve or fourteen hundred men. As we are considering in the present article, the services of the militia in 1861, it would be out of place to enter into any extended account of the services of the 20th through the war. We can however say with truth, that the regiment has " covered itself with glory," and the battle-fields of the Peninsula, of Manassas, Antietam, South Mountain, Fredericksburg, and Gettysburg, bear most eloquent witness to its devotion and bravery. In the winter of 1864, the New York 20th returned home upon a furlough, and the small band of men (only some two hundred) who brought back their tattered colors, covered with marks of honorable service, their thinned ranks made up of scarred and wounded heroes, proved how faithfully they had verified the predictions made of their gallantry, when first leaving for the seat of war.

To appreciate properly the services of the New York Militia regiments at the commencement of the rebellion, we must go back, in imagination, to the period when Washington was feverish with excitement, and when the arrival of the New York 7th, was hailed with joy both by citizens and officials. We must note the successive arrival of other regiments, each, in its turn, adding to the sense of security beginning to be felt by the inhabitants. We must watch the alacrity with which the members of the different organizations went to work in strengthening the fortifications of the capital; we must see them laboring from morning till night, digging trenches and throwing up embankments; going out upon picket duty; making incursions into the neighboring country and clearing it of dangerous or suspicious characters; guarding railroads, and entering with spirit upon all the varied duties of a soldier's life; we must follow them to the first battle-field where bravely they enter upon the fight with troops familiar with every surrounding location, and prepared, by a long expectation of this very struggle, to meet them with desperate resistance; we must watch one, and another, and another, of these militia soldiers fall in the dread conflict, until their dead and wounded are counted by hundreds, and then we can realize how thoroughly in earnest were the New York Militia regiments, when they formed the vanguard of the Union Army, in its earliest encounter with rebellion. Though their efforts were not crowned with victory, still their patriotism in offering themselves among the first to save their government and country from destruction, will ever be held in remembrance by the nation and their native State. Their dead alone will keep their record sacred; and, in years to come, when peace once more shall shed its blessings over our land, and the memory alone of our dead heroes shall be left us, certain it is, that the recollection of none will be cherished more fervently, than that of the citizen soldiers, who fell the first victims in the strife.

"There is a tear for all that die,
   A mourner o'er the humblest grave,
But nations swell the funeral cry,
   And Triumph weeps above the brave.

"A tomb is theirs on every page,
   An epitaph on every tongue:
The present hours, the future age,
   For them bewail, to them belong."

NOTES ON THE MAY CAMPAIGN ON THE JAMES RIVER.

II.

THE ADVANCE TOWARDS RICHMOND AND BATTLE OF DRURY'S BLUFF.

AT three o'clock, in the morning of the 12th, the army was again in motion, and this time it was confidently believed that something was to be effected commensurate with the force we had, and the extensive preparations for this expedition. Turner's and Terry's Divisions of the Tenth Corps advanced towards Richmond on nearly parallel roads, Turner on the right and Terry on the left; while Ames' Division of the same corps marched out to the vicinity of the railroad at Chester Station, and took up a strong position facing towards Petersburg. About noon the column on the right, debouched into a beautiful valley, perhaps six miles from Fort Darling. Terry, on the left, struck the turnpike and extended his line of skirmishers to the railroad, so that the line reached thence to James River. Opposite the centre of the line was an elevated plateau, on which are found houses and belts of woods. Here the rebel skirmishers were met. Our line was very carefully advanced; indeed, there appeared to be an excess of caution in advancing the skirmishers of Alford's Brigade; and after some time the rebels were driven from the belt of woods where they had taken position, and retreated precipitately across an open field to another thick wood, bordering Proctor's Creek.

Though there were but a hundred or two of them, it had taken three or four hours to accomplish this! At this latter position, skirmishing was continued till dark, when the enemy retired across the creek to the high land beyond. A road leading from the plateau from which they had been driven at this point, was their only means of egress from the valley, as a few yards to the right the ravine through which the creek runs in its course to the river is well-nigh impassable. The creek too, here, is quite deep and very rapid. On the morning of the 13th, Weitzel's Division of the Eighteenth Corps pushed across this creek, their right in the road by which the enemy had retreated, and up the slopes, driving the Rebel skirmishers before them; and the whole Eighteenth Corps advanced and took position on the right of the line, which it held till the battle of the 16th; from the turnpike towards the river, Turner's Division advanced along the turnpike, and took position to the left of it. Terry was still farther to the left, his line extending across the railroad. His left was thrown forward, in a very dashing style, and captured a redoubt and several guns.

During the 14th, the whole line was advanced, and the enemy were driven from a strong line of defences, after a very feeble resistance. The feebleness of the resistance offered can only be accounted for by supposing that their numbers were insufficient to hold so extended a line. There could not have been at that time more than three brigades in front of our two corps. Rebel prisoners state that, previous to the night of the 15th, there were but two brigades, but that during that night fourteen thousand men from Richmond re-enforced them. There is little doubt that a vigorous attack on the 14th, or perhaps in the early morning of the 15th, would have crushed the rebel force. The position of the forces after the rebels abandoned their first line of works was this: our army occupied a position along those works, our right extending to within a mile of the river, and uncovered; our left across the railroad, and so advanced that the line made an acute angle with the river. Our first line—a line in one rank—was advanced three or four hundred yards beyond the deserted works, and covered by a low breastwork, made against fences, and some portions of it facing into woods.

There were, in front of our main line, three strong redoubts, so arranged that the guns from one face of each swept the field across which our troops moved to the advanced line. Nothing was done towards making the works we had captured defensive; though a few hours' labor would have made a vast difference in the resistance we were enabled to offer when attacked. It is said, with how much truth I know not, that Generals Smith and Weitzel strongly urged the withdrawal of the forces on the evening of the 14th, and if this were not done, we should attack on the morning of the 15th. We did neither, remaining quiet during the forenoon of the 15th; and about noon the enemy came out and attacked Heckman's Brigade, on the extreme right of our line, furiously; the firing extended all along the line, and lasted till four o'clock P. M. The evening after that was very quiet, and a most lovely Sunday evening. It had been cloudy and rainy for several days, but about noon the clouds had dispersed, and the atmosphere had become clear.

> "'Twas one of those ambrosial eves
> A day of storm so often leaves
> At its calm setting, when the West
> Opens her golden flowers of rest,
> And a moist radiance from the skies
> Shoots trembling down."

We laid down to rest after that gorgeous sunset, hoping that the same hour on the morrow would behold our banner proudly floating in victory; for we knew that orders had been issued, and dispositions made, for an advance of our whole line at five o'clock in the morning; and we could move onward but a few hundred yards before meeting our foe.

The baggage of the army had been ordered up the day before, and every thing belonging to one division had arrived—tents, officers' baggage, and all—showing conclusively that no backward movement was intended.

At about four o'clock, in the morning of the 16th, the enemy began the attack: they opened a furious artillery fire against the right, left, and centre, and, under cover of the fog, which was exceedingly dense, passed around our right flank and attacked Heckman's Brigade in the rear. A few sentinels of negro cavalry posted from the right of this brigade to the river—too few to offer any serious resistance—were the only protection of that flank. Heckman's Brigade was soon forced back with heavy loss, and Heckman himself made prisoner. In a few minutes after the first attack, the battle raged along the whole line. Beauregard massed his men and hurled them in columns successively against different portions of our attenuated line, breaking off battalion after battalion, until the whole were finally forced to retire,

I have spoken above of an "advanced line" and a "main line," but in reality there was but *one* line, stretched out in one rank, and with gaps in some portions of it at that. There was no continuous second line, but a few regiments were placed, at intervals, a few hundred yards in rear of the first line.

Notwithstanding this weak formation, a most determined resistance was offered by our men. Several regiments of the Tenth Corps were sent to the support of the Eighteenth; but the enemy steadily gained ground, so that, at nine o'clock, the mansion occupied by General Butler as his head-quarters was in their possession. If brave deeds performed by subalterns and privates could have availed any thing that morning, the Eighteenth Corps would have beaten back the enemy; but no amount of heroism could overcome the difficulties of their position. The fog was one of the difficulties. And what a fog! It hung like a thick pall over every thing. To venture a rod away from the lines, was to lose one's self. Heckman's capture, and doubtless the capture of many on both sides, was owing to the fog. There were many ludicrous incidents, and hair-breadth escapes arising from the same cause. General Weitzel was riding along outside of the lines, when he came upon a soldier who had been captured by a rebel. The man threw his arms around his captor, and called out to the General, "Don't come here, General—I'm a prisoner." The General very coolly drew a revolver, and said, "We'll change hands, I think," and the rebel turned over his arms to his quondam prisoner, and with him marched into our lines. The Lieutenant-Colonel of the Nineteenth Wisconsin was lost in the fog, and captured by two rebels, and they were soon lost too; he proffered to guide them, and managed to conduct them to his own regiment.

The rebel General Bushrod Johnson's Adjutant rode through a group of Union soldiers, and inquired the way to Johnson's head-quarters. The men paid little attention to what he said, and he passed along, and came to another group, near which a captain was standing, and again inquired; receiving no satisfactory answer, he was moving off, when a private noticed him, and said to the captain, " That's a reb." The captain immediately halted him and said, " I can't tell you where Johnson's head-quarters are, but I will conduct you to General Smith's head-quarters.

At nine o'clock, when the Eighteenth Corps was forced back beyond Butler's head-quarters—a distance of a mile or more—the Tenth Corps still held its position. The enemy had not attacked the left of this corps as vigorously as he had its right, and the Eighteenth. Indeed, General Whiting, who commanded the rebel right wing, was relieved of his command the same evening, because he had not pressed our left with greater vigor; and D. H. Hill was put in his place. Turner's Division had the right of the Tenth, and received fierce attacks during the whole morning; finally, a portion of the line was lost, and it became necessary for the safety of the whole army that it should be retaken and held for a short time.

Two regiments of Alford's Brigade, which had been lying in the woods near the works deserted by the enemy on the 14th, were ordered forward, and they moved in splendid style across an open field, swept by the enemy's fire, and occupied the slight intrenchments from which our men had been driven.

There were not wanting evidences of the desperate character of the contest at this point. All along in front of the low breastworks, and within two or three yards of many of them, the rebel dead and wounded were lying in great numbers. And the woods in front were full of the sufferers, judging from the groans and cries. Their loss in killed and wounded was very heavy; the victory was dearly bought.

In a few minutes after these regiments advanced, the left regiments of the Eighteenth Corps retired; and soon a column of the enemy was on their right flank, and moving around to the rear, enveloping them.

In a little time the red battle-flag was floating on an angle of the intrenchments, three or four hundred yards in their rear.

Still they flinched not. The rebel sharpshooters were annoying them continually by a fire from front and flank and rear— a fire doubly annoying, because they could not return it. For an hour or more, they occupied this exposed position. At last, every thing on the left had retired, and our troops were in full retreat, when the order was given to these regiments to withdraw. The left regiment retired first: when the right regiment rose and faced about, and began to move to the rear, the rebels opened a most terrific fire of both artillery and small-arms. They moved at double-quick, somewhat accelerated by the storm that was beating upon them; but of this regiment alone, over seventy men fell in traversing a space of three or four hundred yards. The intrenchments reached, there was for a few minutes a scene of indescribable confusion. But order was soon brought out of what appeared a chaos. The broken brigades and battalions were rallied under a galling fire from the enemy, who occupied a portion of the line of intrenchments, and then deliberately drawn off. So the battle ended. There was some skirmishing in covering the retreat, and the enemy captured some of our wounded in ambulances near the railroad. Nearly all the baggage of one division was lost; and most of it, with a quantity of ammunition, fell into the hands of the enemy.

Little use was made that day of artillery in the Tenth Corps. Its principal function appeared to be to get out of danger. Several pieces were lost by the Eighteenth Corps, among them two or three twenty-pounder Parrotts. What were they doing there, if we did not intend attacking Fort Darling?

At nine o'clock our tired troops reached their camps, with nearly four thousand fewer effective men than when they marched out four days before. The enemy followed cautiously, and established their line along our front, at a distance of from one and a half to two miles from the intrenchments.

This fine army was then, to all intents and purposes, bottled up, and the cork put in, duly sealed.

TWENTY-FOUR HOURS OF OUTPOST DUTY.

Outpost duty as described in the books, and outpost duty as we have it in our Virginia campaigning, are very different matters. The outposts of the two armies are at times very close together. Usually heavy skirmish-lines are advanced beyond the main fortifications, and the men cover themselves from the fire of the enemy, by slight intrenchments which they acquire a wonderful facility in extemporizing. At night, both sides throw forward videttes, and not unfrequently they advance to within three or four yards of each other. A tree is shown in our front, on one side of which, it is said, a Union vidette was posted one night, and on the other a rebel; the Union sentinel had advanced first in the dark, after which the other came out in search of his proper post, and both reached the same tree, and neither would give way; so there they remained until relieved.

In the instructions commonly given for outpost duty, the idea of falling back is very prominent; indeed, judging by their conduct, some appeared to receive the impression that the principal duty of outposts is to retire when attacked. In the operations here, the idea of falling back at all has not been admitted; outposts have been expected not merely to fight, but to fight brigades and divisions moving against them *en masse;* and the idea of *supporting* a line of outposts, is for the supports to remain in the rear, until the advanced line is driven in upon them; and then there is much glory to be gained in retaking the line.

For the few days succeeding the battle of the 16th, Beauregard was not disposed to allow our forces to be idle, but pressed up in front of the Tenth Corps with menacing demonstrations.

At sundown, on the evening of the 19th, the outposts were relieved in front of Terry's and Ames' Divisions. The right of the line was held by Terry, and two regiments from Turner's Division (the Eighty-ninth and One Hundred and Forty-second N. Y.) had reported to him for duty. These were posted near Ware Bottom Church; the Eighty-ninth on the right, and the One Hundred and Forty-second next it, and two regiments of Ames' Division to the left of the latter regiment.

The right regiment was well protected by deep ravine, and thick, almost impassable wood in front of it. There is a grove of stately pines surrounding Ware Bottom Church, and the line runs from that church nearly south, through a pine wood, and crosses an open field several hundred yards wide, then enters and is continued through a slash of timber. From the right towards the centre, several roads pass through the line perpendicularly. The line of outposts consisted of one rank deployed at an average distance of about three paces, and protected in some portions by slight breastworks, and the pine trees. No man or officer was to be allowed to sleep; every one to be ready for action at a word. Hardly had the men got their position, when the enemy marched up silently at two or three points, to within a few yards of the line, and began an attack. A single shot was fired; then in a moment the woods were all ablaze with the flashes of guns, and the air was alive with bullets. For a few minutes the firing was terrific. Then the stillness which succeeded was only broken by an occasional shot from a rebel sharpshooter. It was a clear moonlight evening—so clear that sharpshooters in several instances fired at officers standing behind trees, scarcely missing them.

The attack was repeated twice during the night, but they were quickly repulsed.

The lines were so near together that the commands of their officers could be distinctly heard in moving their troops. We could hear their artillery as they moved it from left to right, and from every indication expected hot work in the morning. nor were our expectations disappointed. In the morning of the 20th all was quiet until about seven o'clock, when the rebels opened fire with artillery, enfilading our line, or a portion of it, from both flanks.

The battery which was firing upon our right was located near the Howlett House, but it did not continue long. The rebels charged in line of battle on the regiments in Ames' front, and forced them back with little difficulty to within a hundred or hundred and fifty rods of the intrenchments. Still continuing a furious fire on the left of the regiments in Terry's front, they advanced to drive them from their position, as they had driven the others. But they were met by men with steady nerves and cool determination, and who were eager to avenge the loss of their comrades on the 16th, they having been compelled on that day to receive, without returning, the rebel fire.

These stood their ground with unflinching tenacity, sending destruction into the ranks of the assailants at each advance.

The struggle in Ames' front during the day was to regain the ground which had been lost. A single regiment—the veteran Thirteenth Indiana—numbering between two and three hundred men, was sent to retake a line from which a thousand men had been driven. The open field over which they passed was swept by the fire of the rebel artillery. They failing, the Ninety-seventh Pennsylvania, having about three hundred men, was sent to their assistance. Here occurred one of those fearful butcheries which have been not unfrequent in the progress of this war. The regiment was advanced over ground so exposed, and under so murderous a fire, that it seemed impossible that any thing should be left.

There was obviously some blundering. It is claimed that Major Pennypacker, in command of the regiment, misunderstood the order of General Ames, or rather of Colonel Dobbs, and that when it was perceived where he was going, a staff-officer was dispatched to prevent his moving in that direction, but could not reach him in time. On the other hand, it is affirmed that Major Pennypacker obeyed the orders which he received, with strictness and fidelity. The regiment advanced in magnificent style, closing up without the least appearance of wavering, as the shot and shell ploughed through, making great gaps in its ranks.

The field was in full view from the intrenchments, and the admiration of the multitude of lookers-on was excited by the dauntless courage displayed by this noble regiment. But it was all in vain. It was not in human valor to breast the storm which met them, and overcome the odds against them.

They were finally broken, and fled in confusion, one hundred and seventy-five of their number sacrificed.

In the early part of the day it became obvious to the officers in command of Terry's front that the enemy was present in heavy force, and that they were determined to push us from our position, and information accordingly was sent to headquarters. Again and again did they assault the position of the line held by the One Hundred and Forty-second New York, and were as often hurled back. The lines here were very close together, the rebels hidden by a slight ridge in the ground, and their skirmishers were covered by bushes and irregularities in the surface.

From morning till noon the rebel fire from both artillery and small-arms was incessant. It was answered with the utmost coolness and deliberation, our men only firing when the enemy showed themselves in plain sight. The pieces of the men became exceedingly foul; and finally, about half of the Eighty-fifth Pennsylvania advanced to the line occupied by the left companies of the One Hundred and Forty-second New York. There was a lull in the firing, and two of these companies retired a few yards to clean their guns; while they were doing this, the rebels charged upon the line they had just left. The Eighty-fifth retired in haste. The men of the One Hundred and Forty-second, some of them with the water still in their guns, sprang forward, and in a moment the rebels were flying back to the cover of their rifle-pits. But the rebel commanders were too determined to be foiled thus. The firing ceased for about half an hour. Every one knew that a storm was brewing. Still no supports arrived. Those men who had in fact been engaged, at short intervals, for over twenty hours, and whose arms had become almost useless, were left to breast the storm alone.

There are three roads running perpendicularly through the line. With breathless attention they awaited the attack. "Here they come!" ran along the line in a low murmur, as the heads of the rebels appeared above the crest of the ridge in front, a heavy column on each road. As they rose into full view, a volley went crashing through their ranks, staggering the whole column. They answered with a shout, to which our men responded, and on they came with the most perfect steadiness, though every shot from our rifles seemed to tell. They are within a few yards of the line—resistance is useless—the order is given to retire—a regiment can no longer hold three brigades at bay.

A little distance in the rear was a small reserve, which had not been brought up. While the broken regiment was rallying at this point, a brigade of Terry's Division arrived, marching in by the flank. For a few minutes after their arrival there was a scene of indescribable confusion. No one seemed to know what was to be done. At last some of the regimental commanders, apparently on their own motion, succeeded in forming line of battle, and moved forward to repossess the position from which our troops had been driven.

One regiment (at least, and I think two) of Howell's brigade, before they were in sight of the enemy, and while but a few pattering shots were striking among the trees, broke and fled. The gallant Thirty-ninth Illinois, and equally gallant Sixty-seventh Ohio, joining with the One Hundred and Forty-second New York—which had rallied in a very brief space of time—advanced and drove the enemy from the line, and with a wild hurrah rushed forward, nearly into their rifle-pits. But Beauregard was not yet inclined to yield the point. Again the tokens of preparation for attack were heard. All was quiet, save a shot now and then from a sharpshooter.

Here occurred one of those little incidents which often turn the tide of events. There were but four regiments that would have stood up against a heavy attack; the ammunition of one of these regiments was nearly exhausted, and their guns well-nigh useless; another regiment had very little ammunition.

The heavy columns, which the rebels were preparing to throw upon them, could hardly have failed to crush them. It was a pause of the most intense anxiety to every one who had the slightest appreciation of the circumstances. Only the *drunk* or *insane* could fail to perceive the imminent peril of the whole force. There they stood, with bated breath, waiting for the bursting of the storm. Suddenly an officer in gray uniform dashed up, emerging from the cover of the woods at a point where a road runs obliquely into the line, approaching to within twenty or thirty yards before he was uncovered. He at once saw his mistake, and quick as a flash called out: "Hold your line, boys; I'll bring up re-enforcements," and wheeled his horse; but the ruse failed. In a moment he was on the ground, badly wounded, his horse having fallen dead upon him.

This was Brigadier-General Walker, of the Confederate Army. He had, with his large brigade, arrived from Petersburg at about two o'clock in the morning, and during the day had been in front of the left companies of the One Hundred and Forty-second New York.

He had ridden in to make a personal reconnoissance of the position, preparatory to the attack which they were about to deliver, having left Beauregard's head-quarters but a few minutes before. The apparently trifling incident of his capture prevented the attack, and saved three or four regiments from annihilation.

An amusing incident occurred just after the capture of General Walker.

Colonel Howell, who was in command of the troops, seeing his condition, very politely asked the General what he could do for him, intimating his wish to serve him in any way possible.

Walker, as was natural, was in a state of considerable excitement, and, strange to say, was unprepared for kind treatment; for, ridiculous as it may appear, he had been led to believe that we had adopted a harsh policy in relation to prisoners, and so he responded to Howell's proffer of attention rather gruffly, saying: "My advice to you is to move out of this as quickly as possible." "Why, sir?" said Colonel Howell. "Because, sir," replied the General, "we have three or four divisions just out there, who will drive you out in a few minutes." Colonel Howell replied, in his inimitably polite manner—and probably without the slightest intention of perpetrating a witticism—"We shall be highly delighted to meet them, sir. We shall be highly delighted to meet them, sir."

It was, no doubt, true that they had "three or four divisions," in fact, Beauregard's entire force, in the immediate vicinity. D. H. Hill, Bushrod Johnson, Howe, Ransom, Colquitt, Haygood, and I think. Pickett, in addition to Walker and Beauregard himself, were in our immediate front. These officers, except Walker, were present at Drury's Bluff on the 16th.

The capture of Walker ended the fight for the day. It was about four o'clock, and at sunset the outposts were relieved. Thus terminated "Twenty-four Hours of Outpost Duty," the line in Terry's front being the same as the preceding evening, and the enemy holding the position from which they had driven Ames in the morning.

The Petersburg papers of the next day acknowledged a loss of six hundred men in this affair of the outposts.

During the night of the 21st, the rebels made a serious demonstration, advancing in force across the open field, in front of the portion of the works occupied by Ames' Division. Then occurred one of those magnificent displays which are occasionally seen in war.

The whole heavens were lit up by the blaze of artillery, and the bursting of shells. A shot from one of our batteries caused a grand explosion in the rebel lines. This attempt of the enemy to press up to our intrenchments was repulsed, and they retired, having suffered severely. On the 27th and 28th a large portion of the force was withdrawn, and, under command of Major-General W. F. Smith, embarked for White House.

A WORD FOR THE QUARTERMASTER'S DEPARTMENT.

III.

In opening this third paper on the Quartermaster's Department, in which we propose to glance at some of its alleged defects, and to consider some proposed reforms, we do not know how better to commence than to take up the subject of wagon transportation. It was the custom in the first years of the war, after each one of the Potomac failures, to charge the blame thereof to the unwieldiness of General McClellan's wagon trains. This was apparently a tolerably good excuse, though in reality a very bad one, as the transportation of the Army of the Potomac has never yet exceeded, nor even equalled, that of the most of our Western armies. In the campaign of the past summer, the Army of the Potomac, as near as we can arrive at the figures, appears to have numbered ordinarily about one hundred and twenty-five thousand (125,000) effective fighting men. Its transportation is reported to have consisted of about four thousand two hundred (4,200) wagons, eight hundred (800) ambulances, thirty thousand (30,000) artillery, cavalry, ambulance, and draught horses, four thousand five hundred (4,500) private horses, and twenty-two thousand (22,000) mules, making an aggregate in all of some fifty-six thousand (56,000) animals. This is just about one-third ($\frac{1}{3}$) animals to the men, about the same ratio as obtained during its Peninsular campaign and ever since; whereas the ratio among Western armies, during the same time, and always, has been usually one-half ($\frac{1}{2}$), and generally very nearly two-thirds ($\frac{2}{3}$) animals to the men. The figures in General Sherman's combined army, during the Atlanta campaign, footed up generally about as follows: One hundred and twenty thousand (120,000) effective fighting men, six thousand three hundred (6,300) wagons, nine hundred (900) ambulances, thirty-two thousand (32,000) artillery, cavalry, ambulance, and draught horses, four thousand five hundred (4,500) private horses, and thirty-six thousand (36,000) mules, making an aggregate in all of some seventy-two thousand (72,000) animals.

These figures are simply enormous, and will give the reader some slight conception of what an army really is, if he will but consider them for a moment. For example, an army of one hundred and twenty-five thousand (125,000) men, marching in column four (4) abreast, and the intervals but six (6) feet apart, which is less than the usual interval of troops on the march, would extend over a distance of thirty-five (35) miles, without making any allowance for the usual intervals between regiments, brigades, divisions, and army corps. So with the wagons. On good roads where trains are kept well closed up, it is calculated that each six-mule team will occupy on an average about sixty (60) lineal feet; this would give about ninety (90) teams to the mile, a large average on most marches, so that six thousand three hundred (6,300) teams would ordinarily require about seventy (70) miles. If the weather or roads are bad, of course they will straggle along indefinitely, and thus require much more. An ambulance on the march usually occupies about forty (40) feet, so that nine hundred (900) ambulances would occupy a distance of about seven (7) miles. So, with the artillery, an army of one hundred and twenty-five thousand (125,000) men will usually have at least two guns to the thousand men, which would make two hundred and fifty guns, or say forty batteries of six pieces each. Now, a battery on the march, as a general thing, will occupy fully three hundred (300) yards, so that forty batteries alone would take about seven (7) miles. These figures, thus roughly taken, foot up one hundred and nineteen (119) miles, as the free and easy marching distance of an army of the size of the two great ones that we have had operating East and West during the past campaign, and this too without counting in accurately our Bedouin Arabs, the cavalry, that always swarm along for miles together, besides, in apparently almost interminable columns. Of course no General with a moderate stock of brains would ever think of marching his troops thus in one continuous line, and hence the necessity of parallel roads in moving an army, to keep your troops massed and well in hand.

From these calculations, thus roughly made, we think there are two conclusions fairly deducible. First, that the movements of large bodies of troops, under the best of circumstances, are *ex necessitate rei* slow and tedious; and second, that it is impossible for them to move at all without an adequate and well sustained Quartermaster's Department. How the Confederates have managed to get on these four years, the condition of Dixie generally considered, is one of the unexplained mysteries of Jeffdom so far, and fairly a prodigy of modern logistics. We commend the above calculations to our parlor soldiers, our carpet knights, and fireside critics generally, and shrewdly suspect that these valiant stay-at-home Jominis would be a little more lenient in their fierce and learned military criticisms, were they to familiarize themselves just a little with the multiplicity and magnitude of the details here involved, before sharpening again their "gray *goose* quills." Wagons, ambulances, horses, mules, harness, forage, subsistence, clothing, tentage, ammunition, all to be provided by one Department or another, and all to be transported in sufficient quantities, go where the army may, and in whatever weather, be it fair or foul. In fact, as we have already said in our January article, an army is simply "a vast community on legs, with all its appointments and appurtenances complete, here one day, and the next day gone, bearing within itself all the elements of life and motion," and, when fairly considered in all its aspects, is in truth a most prodigious and wonderful machine. If well organized and thoroughly in hand, with the right men in the right places, and a controlling brain at the top, its Quartermaster's Department can be run as readily as a crack locomotive on the Hudson River Railroad; but without such a Department, the finest army ever on the planet, no matter who commanded it, could never move materially from its base, and it would, in truth, soon go to pieces of its own weight, from the very nature and necessity of things. Bearing this well in mind, it is certainly at least creditable to our Quartermaster's Department that, with the exception perhaps of the Red River campaign, our armies in this war have never anywhere been unduly hampered or embarrassed by our wagon trains, huge and unwieldy as they necessarily appear. For nearly two years and a half in this war, before coming to post duty, it was the fortune of the writer to march with them day after day, in summer and winter, over the vilest of secesh roads, from Yorktown to the front of Richmond and back again, through Burnside's memorable campaign, and to Chancellorsville and back again, through Meade's movement from Culpepper to Centreville and back again; in fact, pretty much all about "the sacred soil of Virginia," where, after a half an hour's rain any day the bottom drops out, and your mules seem more likely to pay a visit to Pekin than to go ahead; and yet, he cannot now recollect an instance where the trains were ever unduly behind on a march, or, so to speak, badly in the way on a retreat. That they ever seriously impeded our armies in the East, on the Peninsula or elsewhere, so as to bring to naught well conceived military movements, "the time has come" for the country to know, has always seemed to those familiar with affairs a small excuse for great failures.

Thus much for wagon transportation, which, after much observation, mostly in the field, we are persuaded can scarcely be improved. The common army wagon might possibly be made a little lighter, in some respects, without impairing its strength or decreasing its durability; and it would, perhaps, be somewhat benefited for most purposes by an efficient lock, within the immediate reach and control of the driver, instead of the primitive lock-chains now in use, that compel him to stop and dismount whenever his wheels require to be locked or unlocked. Yet, take it all in all, with its six mule team well in hand, driven with one line by a detailed Yankee or a live contraband, seated securely on the rear tongue-mule, and brandishing his blacksnake as the sceptre of his power, it is by far the best and cheapest species of land locomotion that was ever put into the hands of a modern army. So, too, with our ambulances. In the first year of the war we had all sorts and descriptions of ambulances, except the right sort; from the lumbering four-horse coach style to the funny, teetering, tottering, "one-horse shay" style. But the common two-horse or two-mule ambulance carriage, as now in use in all of our armies, strong and compact, without being unduly heavy, has long since superseded all others, and will no doubt long maintain its place, as a legitimate cousin of the army wagon.

In the matter of water transportation, however, we surmise there is probably room for considerable reform. The war has now continued so long, and the transport service of the army generally has been so extensive, that it is time the whole subject of sea-going vessels was at least tolerably reduced to order and system. The same remark will apply substantially to river transportation, though in a more limited sense, because the difference of depths in our rivers requires a greater variety in the vessels used. The expeditions to Hatteras, to Port Royal, to New Orleans, to Texas, and now more recently to Wilmington, as well as the continuous work that resulted after most of these, together with our heavy operations on the James, the Cumberland, the Tennessee, and the Mississippi, have all given us a wide and rich experience, from which many profitable lessons ought now to be drawn. The first and most obvious one, it seems to us, is that the time for make-shifts and expedients as to transport vessels is past, and the time for some uniformity as to character and equipment, some adaptation to the end desired, and much real comfort and security, as well as economy, has now come. Had the probable magnitude and extent of our marine service been rightly comprehended in the beginning of the war, and the Quartermaster's Department been directed to govern itself accordingly, the Government might have had ere now a magnificent fleet of National transports, built or at least adapted to their special service, lightly armed for whatever emergency might occur, and with officers and crews regularly commissioned and enlisted for the peculiar duty required of them.

It requires no extraordinary knowledge, we suppose, for any one to perceive that an army transport, to be thoroughly effective, needs special adaptation to the end had in view. Transports merely for subsistence, forage, &c., of course, need not vary materially from ordinary sea-going vessels. But transports intended for troops and animals, it is obvious at a glance, require certain marked and peculiar features, without which it is simply impossible to secure the best and largest service in the shortest possible time. They must be, first, staunch and strong, without being clumsy, roomy and of moderate draft, but need not be swift, except in special instances; and, secondly, they should be so constructed and equipped, with bunks, gun-racks, water-tanks, fire-apparatus, &c., for troops, and stalls, feeding-troughs, water, &c., for animals, that the largest possible carrying capacity, compatible with comfort and security, may be always obtained from the smallest possible space afloat. Then again all Government transports, for whatever duty, it seems to us, should be of a peculiar build or finish, so as to be readily recognizable as public vessels, the same as our Navy, the country, and the ocean over. So, too, to our mind, each one should go equipped with a light armament of handy guns, ready for defence, or offence either, for that matter, on a moderate scale, should occasion require. One thing more is necessary to secure safe and thorough handling of such vessels, and that is, *well selected and well disciplined officers and crews.* These are only obtainable by a well digested system of commissions and enlistments, having in view the special service required of them, and "to this complexion," we predict, will our marine service "come at last," and thus rid itself of the nondescript, hybrid seamen,—neither sailor, soldier, nor yet civilian,—that so much embarrass and, in too many instances, half paralyze it now. Some such plan (we care not for details), if adopted in time, would have been far cheaper to the nation in the long run, because by regulating every thing, it would have prevented, to a great extent, the ruinous prices we have often had to pay, and would have substantially abolished the wide discrepancies between charter parties, wages, &c., now frequently found existing among equal steamers, belonging at least to adjacent, if not the same, ports. Such a plan, surely, it is obvious to every one, would have met, much more fully, the peculiar wants and necessities of the service, than our present slip-shod, incongruous, get-along-somehow, make-shift system, that gives the Government, at best, it is notorious, only hulks and tubs, instead of trim and serviceable transports, and, as is proven by the experience of Great Britain, in her East Indiamen and otherwise, is entirely feasible, if only taken vigorously in hand. We repeat, we doubt not that this will ultimately be "the conclusion of the whole matter" in our own case, as it has already been, we believe, with most European nations; and then the Quartermaster's Department will prove itself as free and independent on the river and the sea, as it now is confessedly able and strong upon the land.

[To be continued.]

CAPTURES AND PRIZE MONEY.

In reading General Sherman's report of the capture, in Savannah, of thirty odd thousand bales of cotton and other property, to the value of many millions of dollars, the questions were asked: "If Admiral Dahlgren had captured this property on the ocean or in Savannah River, would not the proceeds have been distributed as prize money? And if so, why are not General Sherman and his army entitled to the same reward?" These inquiries caused us to examine the laws of capture and prize, and we submit to our readers some of the results of this investigation.

CAPTURES.

As a general rule of war, all property of an enemy, and all property of a neutral which has become hostile by its position or use, or the acts of its owner, is subject to capture. That which is captured afloat on the ocean, in ports or rivers, is called *prize*, and that which is captured by land forces or on land is usually called *booty*, although included in the general term *prize*. The title to all booty is deemed to pass to the captor as soon as he gains a firm possession; but that to maritime prizes is not considered complete till the captured property is formally condemned by a prize court.

The general rule which subjects all enemy's property on land to capture has been somewhat modified by modern usage, although the principle is recognized in all legal divisions. This modification is only in regard to private property. All movable property belonging to the hostile State is subject to be seized and appropriated to the use of the captor. The rule extends to the property of municipal and other public corporations, and includes not only implements and munitions of war, but also provisions, and whatever else may be useful to either of the belligerents in prolonging the war.

In regard to private property on land, writers on international law give three cases where it is unquestionably liable to seizure and confiscation: First, by way of penalty for military offences; second, by way of contributions for the support of an invading army, and as an indemnity for expenses incurred in reducing and governing the territory conquered or occupied; and, third, private property taken on the field of battle, or in a captured fortress or town. We copy the remarks of General Halleck under these three heads:

"In the *first* place, we may seize upon private property, by way of penalty for the illegal acts of individuals, or of the community to which they belong. Thus, if an individual be guilty of conduct in violation of the laws of war, we may seize and confiscate the private property of the offender. So, also, if the offence attach itself to a particular community or town, all the individuals of that community or town are liable to punishment, and we may either seize upon their property, or levy upon them a retaliatory contribution, by way of penalty. Where, however, we can discover and secure the individuals so offending, it is more just to inflict the punishment upon them only; but it is a general law of war that communities are accountable for the acts of their individual members. This makes it the interest of all to discover the guilty persons, and to deliver them up to justice. But if these individuals are not given up, or cannot be discovered, it is usual to impose a contribution upon the civil authorities of the place where the offence is committed, and these authorities raise the amount of the contribution by a tax levied upon their constituents.

"In the *second* place, we have a right to make the enemy's country contribute to the expenses of the war. Troops in the enemy's country may be subsisted either by regular magazines, by forced requisitions, or by authorized pillage. It is not always politic, or even possible, to provide regular magazines for the entire supplies of an army during the active operations of a campaign. Where this cannot be done, the general is obliged to resort to military requisitions, or to entrust their subsistence to the troops themselves. The inevitable consequences of the latter system are universal pillage, and a total relaxation of discipline; the loss of private property and the violation of individual rights are usually followed by the massacre of straggling parties, and the ordinary peaceful and non-combatant inhabitants are converted into bitter and implacable enemies. The system is, therefore, regarded as both impolitic and unjust, and is coming into general disuse among the most civilized nations—at least for the support of the main army. In case of small detachments, where great rapidity of motion is requisite, it sometimes becomes necessary for the troops to procure their subsistence wherever they can. In such a case the seizure of private property becomes a necessary consequence of the military operations, and is, therefore, unavoidable. Other cases of similar character might be mentioned. But even in most of these special and extreme cases, provisions might be made for subsequently compensating the owners for the loss of their property.

"In the *third* place, private property taken from the enemy on the field of battle, in the operations of a siege, or in the storming of a place which refuses to capitulate, is usually regarded as legitimate spoils of war. The *right* to private property, taken in such cases, must be distinguished from the *right* to permit the unrestricted sacking of private houses, the promiscuous pillage of private property, and the murder of unresisting inhabitants, incident to the authorized or permitted sacking of a town taken by storm, as described in the preceding chapter. In other words, we must distinguish between the *title* to property acquired by the laws of war and the *accidental circumstances* accompanying the acquisition. Thus the right of prize in maritime captures, and of land in conquests, may be good and valid titles, although such acquisitions are sometimes attended with cruelty and outrage on the part of the captors and conquerors. So with respect to the right of booty acquired in battle or assault; the acquisition may be valid by the laws of war, although other laws of the same code may have been violated by the general or his soldiers in the operations of the campaign or siege."—*International Law*, Chap. XIX.

There are two other cases where private property is undoubtedly liable to capture and confiscation, or rather two cases which involve the same principle, and which might be considered as only one, viz.: where the mass of the people take up arms, and the entire population engage in hostilities. This may result from choice on their part, or from compulsion. Sometimes the people of a country, or particular district, devote themselves and property to belligerent purposes; and sometimes their own government, by conscriptions and forced contributions, bring all private persons within the list of combatants, and make all private property virtually government property, and therefore hostile. Unquestionably all private property so used, or liable to be so used, for hostile purposes, is subject to capture and confiscation.

The same principle applies to cases of civil war or rebellion, where a class or portion of the people take up arms against the legal authority of their government. Such wars are usually confined to a particular section of country, the entire population of which is in insurrection or rebellion. And where a whole community become combatants, the private property of its individual members becomes hostile, and is liable to capture and confiscation. The reason for the exemption of private property on land from confiscation in ordinary international wars is, that most of the individual members of the belligerent states take no active part in the war, and are therefore enemies only in the legal sense of that word. Where the reason for the exemption does not exist, the exemption itself cannot be claimed.

All enemy's property on the high seas, and in bays and navigable rivers, whether public or private, is liable to capture and condemnation as prize of war. So also of all property of our own citizens and of neutrals, engaged in illegal trade with the enemy, or otherwise rendered hostile by the acts of its owners, or of the vessels in which it is carried. It therefore usually happens that in wars between commercial nations, the value of maritime prizes very greatly exceeds that of booty captured on land.

PRIZE MONEY.

It is an elementary principle of the laws of war, as well as international law, that all captures in war, whether made on sea or land, and whether of public or private property, inure to the benefit of the government of the capturing party, and that the government is responsible for all such captures illegally made. If the captured property, or any part of its proceeds, is distributed among the captors, it must be authorized by local law, and without such local law the capturing party can claim no pecuniary interest in the captures he makes. But it is the practice of almost all civilized governments to give to the captors a certain specified portion of all captured property, not only to prevent its waste and destruction, but also as "a reward for bravery and a stimulus to exertion."

By the early Jewish laws a distinction was made in booty between animate and inanimate things, the latter being given to the individuals who captured them, while the former were distributed, proportionally, to those who engaged in the battle and those who guarded the baggage. Afterwards all booty was distributed alike, to the whole army proportionally. Among the Greeks booty was sometimes distributed by lot, and sometimes sold at auction, and the money proportionally divided.

Among the Romans in early times, each one retained the plunder which he captured; but afterwards the soldiers were obliged to bring all booty into the common, which was sold by the general, and of the proceeds a part was consigned to the public treasury, and a part distributed *pro rata* to the army. In this distribution the centurion received double the prize money of a soldier, the horseman triple, and a tribune quadruple. The rule, however, varied at different times.

In the middle ages pillage was the general practice, but the evils were so great that the system of distribution was substituted, and in some countries strenuous measures were adopted to prevent soldiers from leaving their ranks for the purpose of plunder. The States-General of Holland passed ordinances or decrees that the heirs of those killed in battle or siege should receive a double share of prize money, and that those who should pillage or plunder before the enemy was entirely beaten should suffer death, and that the pillage so gotten by them should be forfeited to the use of the sick and wounded.

The distribution of booty or prize money resulting from its sale is now generally adopted among modern nations, the distribution being sometimes regulated by special decrees after the capture; but not unfrequently the whole matter has been left to the discretion of the commander.

In France prize ordinances fully provide for the distribution of maritime prizes, but less positively for land captures or booty, and it has been complained that the matter is left too much to the discretion of the authorities making the distribution. In some countries this distribution is made by permanent courts or commissions under fixed rules or laws, and in others by officers specially appointed, and under rules formed for the particular occasion.

As the legislation and practice in Great Britain in regard to prize and booty form the basis of our laws on these matters, we will briefly notice their history and present condition.

From very early times the Admiral's Court in England has had jurisdiction of all maritime questions, and subsequently, by special warrant, of all cases of prize, and questions in regard to prize money. As the English have been engaged in maritime wars so much more frequently than in hostilities on land, and as captures of pirates, slavers, and smugglers were often made in times of peace, there was a standing proclamation for granting and distributing prize money to the navy. This permanent system of jurisdiction and action in regard to prizes and prize money has given great uniformity to the decisions of the courts on these matters.

While the Admiral's Court in early times determined all questions of maritime prize, all causes respecting booty were decided in the Court of Chivalry, before the constable and marshal. This court took jurisdiction of booty, prisoners of war, ransom, and all captures of goods beyond the seas. After the abolition of the office of Constable of England, the jurisdiction of the Earl Marshal was disputed, and the court finally ceased to act as such. The last case tried by it was in 1737. But its jurisdiction did not in general pass either to the admiralty or common law courts; but was exercised by military officers under the authority of the crown. For a time booty was distributed to the soldiers on the spot, and if there were any disputes they were decided by the commander-in-chief. But this often led to great abuses, relaxing discipline and causing the plunder, waste, and useless destruction of public and private property. It was therefore directed that all such captures should be reserved by the commanding general for the government, and an exact account be kept, in order that the money value might be equitably divided among the captors. The act of 2 William IV., c. 53, enumerates, as legitimate subjects of booty, all arms, ammunition, stores of war, goods, merchandise and treasure belonging to the State or any public trading company of the enemy, and found in any of the fortresses or possessions, and all ships and vessels in any road, river, haven, or creek belonging to any such fortress or possession. But no statute passed in regard to determining the legality of any such captures, or their distribution. This power, it was held, remained vested in the Crown, and was exercised through the Lords of the Treasury, under a royal sign-manual warrant, appointing a board of trustees and establishing a scheme of distribution. The Lords of the Treasury hear counsel upon points as to what shall or shall not be considered legal booty. By the statute of 1840, the Crown, on the advice of the Privy Council, may refer questions of booty of war to the Court of Admiralty.

After the war in the Spanish Peninsula Wellington presented to the ministry of war a claim, for himself and army, of prize money to the amount of about five millions of dollars, for arms, military stores, provisions, forage, baggage, vessels, specie, &c., captured in Spain and France, on battle-fields, and in towns, forts, &c. The claim was allowed and paid. In speaking of this claim, Dupin, in his "Military Force of Great Britain," says: "The Government awards the soldiers, in the same manner as the navy, the property of all captures made by their services during the course of the war."

The value of the booty captured at Tarragona in 1813, and at Genoa in 1814, was distributed by royal warrants, *pro rata*, to the military and naval forces employed in these captures. By royal warrant in 1845, the Scinde booty, amounting to several millions of rupees, was distributed to the army in India. In these distributions the amount awarded to the commander, or commanders-in-chief, was one-eighth part of the whole.

In the foregoing cases the warrant of distribution was made some time after the captures; but in the Russian war of 1854, the royal proclamation preceded the captures, and directed that the net proceeds of all prizes and booty, taken by naval or land forces, should be distributed alike to the captors as soon as the prizes were finally adjudged, and the value of the booty ascertained. The allowance of the commander-in-chief, by this proclamation, was one-quarter of one-tenth, and to the other general officers, three-quarters of one-tenth of the net proceeds; one-eight of the remainder to the field officers, and seven-eighths to the company officers, non-commissioned officers, and soldiers, according to classes. And in the event of any difficulty arising in regard to the class in which any one was entitled to share, the question was to be determined by the commander-in-chief.

In the campaign of 1860, against Pekin, most of the booty found in the imperial summer palace fell into the hands of the French, who were the first occupants, and it was distributed among their troops. That which fell to the share of the English was collected together by prize agents, sold at public auction, and the proceeds immediately distributed as prize money. Whether any previous authority for this had been given is not stated; but Lieut.-Colonel Wolseley, in his narrative, remarks: " If Sir Hope Grant had contented himself with promising that the question of prize money should be referred to the Home Government, after their recent Indian experience, our men would have been very dissatisfied, seeing every French soldier going about with his pockets filled with dollars and Sycee silver."

It has thus happened that while the English law of maritime prize has been so admirably developed and settled by the learned and able decisions of the British courts of admiralty, so little advance has been made in the laws of war in regard to booty; while the English prize decisions have been published and circulated throughout the world, decisions relating to booty have never been published, and probably no permanent records have been kept. This resulted from the want of a permanent tribunal, or authority, by which such questions could be discussed and determined.

Our own laws respecting maritime prizes, and the distribution of their proceeds as prize money to the captors, are modelled after those of Great Britain, and the decisions of our prize courts have been as able as those of the British admiralty. The most recent law in regard to prize money directs, that where the enemy's force is equal or superior to that of the captors, the entire prize money goes to the latter; but if inferior, one-half goes to the navy pension fund, and the other half to the captors. The share of distribution to the commanding officer of the fleet, or squadron, is one-twentieth; to the commander of a single ship, three-twentieths, if acting independently, and one-tenth of what goes to his ship, if under the immediate command of a superior officer; to the remaining officers and men doing duty on board, and borne upon the books, all the residue, according to their respective rates of pay in the service.

The fifty-eighth article for the government of the armies of the United States, provides that "all public stores taken in the enemy's camps, towns, forts, or magazines, whether of artillery, ammunition, clothing, forage, or provisions, shall be secured for the service of the United States." This article is borrowed from a corresponding British article, which directs that such stores shall be secured for *the king's service;* but the effect of the two are entirely different, the king having power, not given by statute, but derived from immemorial usage, to award to the captors the value of such captures as prize money, while the President of the United States can make no such distribution of public money without the authority of Congress. It has thus happened that, by almost literally copying British laws on this subject, we have given to our navy and privateers the full benefit of prize money, while our land forces have been debarred of all benefit whatever from captures made from the enemy in war. Undoubtedly this distinction was not originally intended, but resulted from closely copying English laws, without fully considering the difference in the constitutional powers of the king and the President. And this distinction between the two services can be removed only by an act of Congress. Would it be wise and proper to do this? We think so, and offer the following as some of the reasons which might be adduced in favor of such legislation.

In the first place, the absence of a law for the equal division of booty, or rather of its value, seriously affects the discipline and efficiency of an army, by encouraging *marauding* or *pillage*. It is impossible to extirpate from the human heart the desire of pecuniary gain, and if soldiers are deprived of all interest in the property which they capture and account for, they will straggle from their ranks for the purpose of private plunder; no matter what penalties may be prescribed by law or the orders of a commanding general, it has been found impossible in our service to prevent such marauding, and the practice, with its attending horrors, seems to be on the increase. The pillage of private property is necessarily attended by numerous murders, both of the soldiers who plunder, and of the people who are plundered. It is the opinion of experienced officers that these great evils would be mostly avoided by a legal division of booty among all the officers and soldiers. All good soldiers would then have a pecuniary interest in preventing any private pillaging by their greedy and cowardly companions, and all captures would be brought to the common stock. Such a law would also tend to prevent illegal captures, for as no one could profit by them, they would seldom be made.

In the second place, such a law would prevent the useless destruction of captured property. So long as officers and soldiers have no interest in such captures, they take very little pains to preserve them. It may be said that existing laws and military regulations *require* them to take care of captured property, and that they should be punished for neglect of duty. This is all very well in theory; but, until human nature changes, men will take more care of that in which they have a personal interest, than of that which belongs exclusively to the government. This is manifest in every department of life, and soldiers and sailors are not different from other men. The rebel pirates burn the ships and cargoes which they capture, because they cannot have them condemned as prize. If there were any possibility of getting them into port and receiving prize money out of them, not one would be destroyed. Our sailors are very careful to bring every vessel, every bale of cotton, and every yard of cloth that they capture, because it is for their pecuniary interest to do so. Give the same interest to our land forces, and, on the capture of a fort, town, or dépôt, we shall no longer hear of wholesale burning and destruction of the captured property.

In speaking of the injurious consequences of depriving soldiers of prize money, or of unreasonably delaying its distribution, Lieutenant-Colonel Wolseley remarks: "Let it be more clearly understood that all valuables taken will be sold for the benefit of the prize fund, which will be appropriated to whatever purposes her Majesty may decide upon, as soon as the campaign is over, and the discipline of our army will always be maintained. The temptation to enrich one's self at our enemy's expense is very great. Try and stop by forbidding it in orders, and punishing those caught *flagrante delicto*, and the consequence is, that as the good men only obey, remaining poor, whilst they see their disobedient comrades becoming rich, discontent follows as a natural consequence. Any who have ever been present at the assault of a town will, I am sure, agree with me in thinking that no price is too high which we can pay for the prevention of those dreadful scenes of riot and consequent insubordination which have upon several occasions followed such an event. Discipline once relaxed, as it must be when plunder is permitted, its entire fabric of regulations break down in one moment, which it takes many months of subsequent reorganization to reassert."

Again: "When *looting* (an Eastern word for military pillage) is once commenced by an army, it is no easy matter to stop it. At such times human nature breaks down the ordinary trammels which discipline imposes, and the consequences are most demoralizing to the very best constituted army. Soldiers are nothing more than grown-up school-boys. The wild moments of enjoyment passed in the pillage of a place live long in a soldier's memory. Although, perhaps, they did not gain sixpence by it, still they talk of such for years afterwards with pleasure. Such a time forms so marked a contrast with the ordinary routine of existence passed under the tight hand of discipline, that it becomes a remarkable event in life, and is remembered accordingly. I have often watched soldiers, after the capture of a place, wandering in parties of threes or fours through old ranges of buildings, in which the most sanguine even could scarcely hope to find any thing worth having; yet every one of them bore about them that air of enjoyment which is unmistakeable. Watch them approach a closed door; it is too much trouble to try the latch or handle, so Jack kicks it open. They enter; some one turns over a table, out of which tumbles, perhaps, some curious manuscripts. To the soldier they are simply waste paper, as he lights his pipe with them. Another happens to look round and sees his face represented in a mirror, which he at once resents as an insult by shying a footstool at it; whilst Bill, fancying that the 'old gentleman' in the fine picture-frame upon the wall is making faces at him, rips up the canvas with his bayonet. Some fine statue of Venus is at once adorned with a mustache, and then used as an 'Aunt Sally.' Cock-shots are taken at all remarkable objects, which, whilst occupying their intended positions, seem somehow or another to offend the veteran's eye, which dislikes the *in statu quo* of life, and studies the picturesque somewhat after the manner that Colonel Jebb recommends to all country gentlemen who are desirous of converting their mansions into defensible posts. The love of destruction is certainly inherent in man, and the more strictly men are prevented from indulging in it, so much the more do they appear to relish it when an opportunity occurs. Such an explanation will alone satisfactorily account for the ruin and destruction of property, which follow so quickly after the capture of any place. Tables and chairs hurled from the windows, clocks smashed upon the pavement, and every thing not breakable so injured as to be valueless henceforth."

In the third place, such a law is desirable in order to remove the present invidious distinction between the navy and the land service. All partial, and invidious legislation does harm, by creating jealousy and ill feeling. It is, therefore, always desirable to harmonize the two arms of service by equalizing, so far as possible, their rights, duties, emoluments, and rewards. Any departure from this basis is in its effects injurious.

We presume no one in the army envies the good fortune of Farragut, Dupont, Porter, and Lee, in receiving hundreds of thousands of dollars of prize money during this war; but they can see no good reason why Grant, Sherman, Thomas, Sheridan, and Meade, should not be equally rewarded; nor can they understand why soldiers who have waded the pestilential swamps of Arkansas, Mississippi, Alabama, Georgia, and South Carolina, to meet and defeat the rebel armies, are not as much entitled to receive prize money from their captures, as sailors who have served in vessels and boats on the same rivers and coasts. They regard the present distinction as unreasonable, invidious, and unjust. It cannot be said that the navy is not as well paid as the army, nor that their duties are more severe or dangerous, nor that their services are more valuable. And it certainly would be unjust to say that sailors require " a stimulus to exertion," while soldiers need no such incentive.

We will state a few examples of the unjust operations of our present law as to prize money. In the War of 1812, one of our military officers seeing a crippled English merchantman on the coast, took his garrison in some hired boats and captured the vessel, with a most valuable cargo. He not only received no prize money, but was not even reimbursed the expenses of the capture. Again, during the present war, a military officer planned an expedition to cut out a most valuable prize. The naval forces which acted under his guidance, with his assistance, got in prize money the full value of the capture; neither he nor his men could receive a cent of it. An armed transport with troops between New York and Charleston captured a blockade runner with a cargo of cotton, and took her into port, where she was condemned as prize of war; but the captors could receive no part of the prize money. Had they known this at the time, they would very probably have burned her at sea, as the rebel pirates do their captures.

But it has been said, that, however just may be the claim, to allow prize money to the army would cause too heavy an expense to the country at the present time. We answer, if so, why is it allowed to the navy? There certainly is no more reason for giving it in one case than the other. But we do not think that such a law, if it contains proper guards and limitations, would cause any additional expense to the country. On the contrary, we believe that by the prevention of the destruction of public and private property, and of straggling, pillaging, and marauding, it would save to the country and to the nation much more money than would be distributed by the way of prize. Let the amount of prize money which can be distributed to any person of either service, in any one year, be limited to a specified sum, according to rank and command—the surplus to be turned into the public treasury or given to the naval and military pension funds; let the law provide that the value of all captured property which may be pillaged, or unnecessarily destroyed by the captors, shall be deducted from any prize money to which the destroyers or pillagers may be entitled. We are confident that a law could be formed with such provisions and safeguards as to cause an actual saving to the public treasury, while it would prevent the horrors of pillaging and marauding.

WOMEN IN THE WAR.

I.

MANY and strange are the tales told of the heroism shown by women during the great War of Emancipation. As I write, a young lady in full regimentals is lecturing on her experience of field and frays through the country; and I might say with truth that no editor can turn over a morning's "exchange papers" without encountering authentic anecdotes of some fair and fast Polly or Lucy who, led by the spirit of patriotism, love, or fun, has donned the blue breeches and follows the drum, as well as the example of Boadicea and the Amazon, until discovered by some unlucky accident.

> "At, certamina accidente
> Inter fortes pugnavit,
> Bomba vestem sed pandente
> Candidas mammas monstravit."

And indeed, when we reflect on what thousands upon thousands of women who have lost every means of support through the ravages of the enemy, who have seen their lovers and perhaps every male relative enter the army, or who have been fired by a burning zeal to serve their country, and encouraged by the narratives of those of their own sex who have succeeded in wild and patriotic adventures, it does not seem wonderful that occasionally a vigorous and healthy damsel should have ventured to don the uniform and shoulder a musket. Those who generalize on the impropriety and unladylikeness of such conduct, are unquestionably in the right, according to the practical parlor standard of life; but they know very little of the vast variety of phases which humanity assumes, or of the strange and wonderful moulds into which it is forced by Nature and circumstances.

Our Women in the War may be divided into two classes: firstly, the regular soldiers in uniform, most of whom conceal their sex and pass for men; and secondly, that very useful body, the spies and scouts who dress and act according to circumstances, appearing perhaps as a stylish dame surrounded by admirers in the morning, and then walking over the same ground after midnight as a ragged and dissipated youth, dropping into billiard-rooms and the divers haunts of secesh, and detecting their plots against the Union cause. "The Proteus of 1864 is a woman."

One of the many strange incidents of the war during 1863, is told in the following paragraph from the *Memphis Argus*:

"DEATH OF A CAVALRY SOLDIER WHO PROVES TO BE A WOMAN.

"A short time since a soldier, belonging to a Missouri cavalry regiment, was entered at the Overton Hospital for treatment for fever contracted in camp. Two or three days ago the soldier died, but not before it had been revealed that the supposed young man was a woman. It seems that she entered the army early in the war, and served her time faithfully as a soldier, until mustered out. During all this time she was enabled to retain the secret of her sex. A short time after leaving the service she re-entered it again as a veteran, and had been with the regiment to which she was attached a month or two when sent to the hospital in this city. Her real name, we learn, could not be ascertained, but her experience, as related by herself, was the old story over again. She had followed her lover into the army, and to be near him had willingly braved the dangers of the battle-field and borne the hardships and exposures of campaign life. Her years could not have been more than twenty; though who can estimate those in bitter experience which had been her lot? Poor girl!"

Yet be it remembered, that however it was done, that "poor girl" died serving the great cause of God and Union; and that, whatever the motive may have been which led her to the war, her deeds were purer and nobler and her life better than any of those of the millions of sympathizers with the Rebellion, who crawl around and spit their venom on all that is philanthropic and brave.

The correspondent of the Cincinnati *Times*, writing in 1863 from Camp Dick Robinson, thus describes a young lady who "tarried among the tents" of the East Tennesseans:

"One of the features of the First Tennessee Regiment is the person of a brave and accomplished young lady of but eighteen summers, and of prepossessing appearance, named Sarah Taylor, of East Tennessee, who is the stepdaughter of Captain Dowden. Miss Taylor is an exile from her home, having joined the fortunes of her stepfather and her wandering companions, accompanying them in their perilous and dreary flight from their homes and estates. Having determined to share with her male friends and relatives the dangers and fatigues of a military campaign, Miss Taylor has donned a neat blue chapeau, beneath which her long hair is compactly yet gracefully arranged, and bears at her side a highly finished regulation sword, with silver mounted pistols in her belt, all of which gives her a very neat appearance.

"She is quite the idol of the Tennessee boys, who look upon her as a second Joan of Arc. And Miss Taylor is indeed full of courage and skilled in many manly accomplishments. Having become an adept in the sword exercise and a sure shot with the pistol, she is determined to aid in the great cause of restoring to their homes her exiled and oppressed countrymen, or, failing in that, to offer her own life in the sacrifice."

"A gentleman," continues the editor of the *Times*, "who was on the ground on Saturday night the 19th, when the order was issued to the Tennesseans to march to re-enforce Colonel Gerrart, informs us that the wildest excitement prevailed in the whole camp, and that the young lady above alluded to, mounted her horse, and, cap in hand, galloped along the line, like a spirit of flame, cheering on the men. She wore a blue blouse, and was armed with pistols, sword, and rifle. Our informant, who has been at the camp the whole time since the arrival of the Tennesseans, says that Miss Taylor is regarded by the whole corps as a guardian angel who is to lead them to victory. These persecuted men looked upon the darling girl who followed their fortunes through sunshine and shadow with the tenderest feeling of veneration, and each would freely offer his life in her defence.

"There was but little sleep in the camp on Saturday night, so great was the joy of the men at the prospect of meeting the foe; and at a very early hour in the morning they filed away jubilantly, with their Joan of Arc in the van."

A very brave girl was Miss Mary Wise, who served truly for the love of her country, against whose good name there was never a shadow of reproach, and whose final disappearance from the stage of war is thus recorded in the Washington *Chronicle*, October, 1864:—

THE "BRAVE SOLDIER-GIRL."

To the Editor of the Chronicle:

I beg leave to furnish THE CHRONICLE a further incident in the history of the soldier-girl who received her pay by the order of the President.

Miss Mary Wise found a good friend in, and a home with, Mrs. Captain E. B. Gates, at Lincoln Hospital, where she soon made the acquaintance of Sergeant Forehand, of the Veteran Reserve Corps. This friendship soon ripened into affection, and the result was a marriage scene last evening at the above-named hospital, in which the soldier-girl and the sergeant were the principal actors. In other words, Miss Mary Ellen Wise (formerly James Wise, private of Company I, Thirty-fourth Regiment Indiana Volunteers), and Segreant F. Forehand, of the Veteran Reserve Corps, were made man and wife—Uncle Sam thereby losing a brave soldier, and the sergeant finding a good wife. The ceremonies were performed by the chaplain of Lincoln Hospital, and were witnessed by quite a number of their soldier-friends.

Miss Mary has made many friends by her gentle and unassuming manners. They start for the New Hampshire home of the bridegroom to-morrow. May the now happy pair live to tell their grandchildren of the many hard-fought battles through which both have passed, and tell over the many amusing camp incidents so familiar to the sergeant and his companion, is the heart-felt wish of their friends. W. H. M.

The first female recruits in the service of the United States, were, I believe, Miss Mary Hancock and her three friends. Whether any of this party actually went to the war I am not informed, but should be pleased to learn. The circumstances of their enlistment were thus described in the Easton *Express*, June 22d, 1861:—

JOAN OF ARC IN THE WEST.

"At a flag-raising at North Plato, Kane County, Illinois, after the stars and stripes had been duly hoisted, the assembly adjourned to the village church, where some speeches were made by patriotic gentlemen, and an opportunity was offered for young men to come forward and enlist, the company at Plato not being quite full. Not a man went up! This aroused the patriotism as well as anger of the village schoolmistress, who, with many other ladies, was present, and she walked boldly forward to the secretary's desk, and headed the muster-roll with a name rendered illustrious as having been affixed to the Declaration of Independence, with the prenomen Mary. She was followed by another lady, and lo and behold, the Plato company was not long in filling its ranks! The muster-roll, bearing the names of the spirited young vivandiers (*sic!*), has been sent to headquarters, and the company accepted by the 'powers that be.' Since that day four flag-raisings have come off in that portion of Kane County, and Mary and May—the soldier-girls—in uniforms of white, red, and blue, have attended all of them, at the request of the officers, marching as pioneers at the head of their company. The captain says he could not get along without them, and after the flag has been sent up he allows them to fire three guns in honor of the Union, the Stars and the Stripes. Whether he will deprive the place of the valuable services of a good teacher, and a lover of a pretty sweetheart, by carrying his Joan of Arc to the wars with him, remains to be seen. Much of the success of the recruiting service, and of the patriotic fire burning now in old Kane, is attributed to the gallant conduct and bright eyes of these young ladies."

The following story of one who became a soldier "all for love" was thus narrated by the *Chicago Post*, in May, 1863, at which time the heroine in question arrived in that city from Louisville, Ky.:—

"She gave her name as Annie Lillybridge, of Detroit, and stated that her parents reside in Hamilton, Canada West. Last Spring (1862) she was employed in a dry goods store in Detroit, where she became acquainted with a Lieutenant W., of one of the Michigan regiments, and an intimacy immediately sprang up between them. They corresponded for some time, and became warmly attached. During the ensuing Summer, Lieutenant W. was appointed to a position in the Twenty-first Michigan Infantry, then rendezvousing in Iona county.

"The thought of parting from her lover nearly maddened the girl, and she resolved to share his dangers and be near him. No sooner had she determined on this course than she proceeded to act, and, purchasing male attire, she visited Iona, and enlisted in Captain Kavanagh's company of the Twenty-first Regiment. While in camp she managed to keep her secret from all; not even the object of her attachment, who met her every day, being aware of her presence.

"Annie left with her regiment for Kentucky, passed through all the dangers and trials of camp life, endured long marches, and slept on the ground without a murmur. At last, before the battle of Pea Ridge, in which her regiment took part, her sex was discovered by a member of her company, upon whom she enjoined secrecy after relating her previous history.

"On the following day she was under fire, and from a letter in her possession it appears she behaved with marked gallantry, and shot with her own hand a rebel captain who was in the act of firing upon her friend, Lieutenant W. But the fear of being discovered continually haunted her.

"After the battle she was sent, among others, to bury the dead, and among the first corpses found by her was that of the soldier who had discovered her sex. Days and weeks passed by, and she became a universal favorite with the regiment; so much so, that her Colonel (Stephens) frequently detailed her as regimental clerk—a position that brought her in close contact with her lover, who at this time was major or adjutant of the regiment.

"A few weeks subsequently, when out on picket duty, she received a shot in the arm that disabled her, and, notwithstanding the efforts of the surgeon, her wound continually grew worse. She was sent to the hospital at Louisville, where she remained several months, when she was discharged by the post-surgeon, as her arm was stiffened, and rendered useless.

"She implored to be permitted to return to her regiment, but the surgeon was unyielding, and discharged her. Annie immediately hurried homeward. At Cincinnati she told her secret to a benevolent lady, and was supplied with female attire.

"She declares she will enlist in her old regiment again, if there is a recruiting officer for the Twenty-first in Michigan. She still clings to the lieutenant, and says she must be near him if he falls, or is sick, and that where he goes she will go."

Since I began to make inquiries relative to women-soldiers in our Federal army, I have been amazed at finding their number so much greater than I should ever have supposed. In fact, within a few hours of the time at which I write, on October

25th, 1864, I have heard of several perfectly authenticated instances of the kind, which I do not, however, consider myself authorized to publish; and I have read, through the courtesy of a young lady, who has herself served *en militaire*, and been promoted, a letter from a young girl to this lady, and detailing her own adventures in the Army of the Potomac. Having contrived to evade the usual examination, she enlisted in a company in which her brother was already serving, and by persuasion induced him not to betray her secret. She fought in five or six "first-class battles," ending with that of Gettysburg, maintaining a reputation for bravery, and never betraying her sex. Her brother, however, who had behaved with great generosity, sharing with her his bounty money, and inducing her to hoard her own, finally informed their colonel of her sex, on which occasion that officer paid a high compliment to her shrewdness and courage. The letter from which I glean these facts is well written, and indicates not only an intense desire to return to soldier life, but also much natural eloquence, and an education.

The concluding paragraph of an article which appeared in the Louisville *Journal*, in the Spring of 1863, confirms what I have said in reference to the number of women warriors in our service:—

"A few weeks since, a captain, accompanied by a young soldier, apparently about seventeen years of age, arrived in this city, having in charge some rebel prisoners.

"During their stay in the city, the young soldier alluded to had occasion to visit headquarters, and at once attracted the attention of Colonel Mundy, as being exceedingly sprightly, and possessed of more than ordinary intelligence. Being in need of such a young man at Barracks No. 1, the Colonel detailed him for service in that institution.

"A few days later, however, and the startling fact was disclosed that the supposed young man was a young lady, and the fact was established beyond doubt by a soldier who was 'raised' in the same town with her, and knew her parents. She acknowledged the fact, and begged to be retained in the position to which she had been assigned, since, having been in the service ten months, she wished to complete her term of enlistment. Her wish was granted, and she is still at her post.

"On learning the facts above stated, we took occasion to visit the barracks, and having been introduced to Frank Martin, (her assumed name) gleaned the following incidents connected with her extraordinary career during the past ten months:

"'Frank' was born near Bristol, Pa., and her parents reside in Alleghany city, where she was brought up. They are highly respectable people, and in good circumstances. She was sent to the convent in Wheeling, Virginia, at twelve years of age, where she remained until the breaking out of the war, having acquired an excellent education and many accomplishments.

"She visited home after leaving the convent, and after taking leave of her parents proceeded to this city in July last (1862), with the design of enlisting in the Second East Tennessee Cavalry, which she accomplished, and accompanied the Army of the Cumberland to Nashville. She was in the thickest of the fight at Murfreesboro, and was severely wounded in the shoulder, but fought gallantly, and waded Stone River into Murfreesboro, on the memorable Sunday on which our forces were driven back. She had her wound dressed, and here her sex was disclosed, and General Rosecrans made acquainted with the fact.

"She was accordingly mustered out of the service, notwithstanding her earnest entreaty to be allowed to serve the cause she loved so well. The General was very favorably impressed with her daring bravery, and superintended the arrangements for her safe transmission to her parents. She left the Army of the Cumberland resolved to enlist again in the first regiment she met. When she arrived at Bowling Green she found the Eighth Michigan there, and enlisted, since which time she has been and is now connected with it.

"She is said to be an excellent horsewoman, and has been honored with the position of bugler to the regiment. She h·s seen and endured all the privations and hardships incident to the life of the soldier, and gained a high reputation as scout, having made several remarkable expeditions, which were attended with signal success.

"'Frank' is only eighteen years of age, and is quite small, but has a beautiful figure. She has auburn hair, which she wears quite short, and her large blue eyes beam with intelligence. Her complexion is naturally very fair, though it is slightly bronzed at present from exposure. Her conversation denotes more than ordinary accomplishments, and, what is stranger than all, she appears to be refined in her manners, giving no evidence whatever of the rudeness which might naturally be expected from her late associations.

"'Frank' informs us that she has discovered many females in the army, and is now intimately acquainted with a young lady who is a lieutenant in the army. She has assisted in burying three female soldiers, at different times, whose sex was unknown to any but herself."

Such is the history of Frank Martin, as given in the *Louisville Journal*. Were it not for the difference of the family name, I should suppose the soldier-lassie in question to be identical with the well-known Frank *Morgan*, whose adventures, as told me by one who had frequently seen her, coincided in several particulars with those of Miss Martin. *La Belle* Morgan, as I am informed, enlisted in a Michigan regiment, served nine months as a private, was wounded, and entered the Invalid Corps, where her sex was at last discovered. When known to be a girl she was, however, employed by General Boyle as clerk in the Provost-Marshal's office, and became quite a celebrity.

[To be continued.]

THE ARMY OF THE DEAD.

BY MRS. LUCY H. HOOPER.

We kneel before the altar,
  With hearts not wholly steeled;
We pray, "God bless our heroes,
  Afar on flood and field!"
While for our living soldiers
  Our fervent prayers are said,
Oh, let us, too, remember
  The Army of the Dead!

Oh, army past all counting,
  Heroic, true, and brave!
Fame often claims our noblest,
  But oftener the grave.
The lips that knew no falsehood,
  The hearts that knew no fear,
Death read them from his roll-call—
  They answered, "We are here!"

The grave has reft them from us,
  To silence and to gloom;
The names we so have honored,
  Are written on a tomb.
Alas! so oft with mourning
  Our praising we must blend;
The list began with Ellsworth—
  O Lord, where will it end?

And let us, too, remember
  The nameless who are gone,
For them we wreathe no laurel,
  For them we grave no stone.
War wraps them in a shrouding
  Of mystery and gloom;
Full many a household darling
  Lies in a nameless tomb.

They lie 'neath Southern waters,
  They sleep 'neath Southern sod,
Unknown, save by their loved ones,
  Unnoted, save by God.
There's not a Northern churchyard
  But holds a soldier's grave;
O Christ! they learned Thy lesson,
  To die that they might save.

Hereafter, oh, hereafter!
  When this fell war is o'er,
When the old flag triumphant
  Waves o'er the South once more,
When for a land united
  Our thanks to God are said,
Then, *then* shall we remember
  The Army of the Dead!

LITERARY INTELLIGENCE
AND
NOTES ON NEW BOOKS.

"A NARRATIVE OF THE CAMPAIGN IN THE VALLEY OF THE SHENANDOAH, IN 1861. By Robert Patterson, late Major-General of Volunteers." 8vo, 128 pp. 1865. At the very outset of the rebellion, when we knew nothing of large armies, nothing of the resources and intentions of the South, but little of strategy, and far less of the tactical manœuvres of large bodies of men, the disaster at Bull Run occurred; a shameful panic, due not to want of numbers, nor of individual valor, but to want of discipline, drill, and even elementary military knowledge. Divisions as well as brigades were commanded by colonels; unknown personally, or by insignia, to the officers and men. The troops were raw, difficult to handle, about as much at home in a battle-field as a young bear at an opera. There were the existing elements of defeat, when that glittering host left Washington.

A distinct column, not to be on that field, had been sent to Harper's Ferry and the Valley of Virginia, under command of Major-General Robert Patterson, an old soldier, who on more occasions than one had exhibited rare sagacity in Mexico, as second in command to General Scott. Among these occasions we place his countermand of General Twiggs's orders just before the battle of Cerro Gordo; we should otherwise have been defeated there.

General Patterson's command was principally composed of three months' men; he had very few regulars, few guns, and but little cavalry.

What regulars he had were taken from him, and he was expected with his force, less than twenty thousand strong, so to amuse, threaten, or attack, Joe Johnston at Winchester, as to keep him in his front—and away from Bull Run—until after a certain specified time. This he did; but the specified time was not the right time.

The calamity of Bull Run set the investigators, unmilitary *quid nuncs*, to work to find, and invent causes; and here they seemed to have a chance: it was charged upon Patterson that he failed to do his work; that he did not keep Johnston long enough, and that he did not immediately follow him, bearing to the left, and come as a new, and neutralizing element upon that field when Johnston did.

With soldierly instinct, General Patterson at once asked for a court of inquiry. Upon the quibble that he was now out of service—honorably discharged—this was denied him. Carped at, because supposed to be without redress, by Congressmen and committees, he has borne all these charges in silence, until, in a fitting moment, not too late for his reputation; he brings out a narrative of that campaign. It is sensible, clear, armored by documents, reports, and letters; and it is conclusive.

How any one for a moment supposed, that when he was at Martinsburg or Bunker Hill, and Johnston at Winchester, he could keep Johnston from going up the valley when he chose, we do not see.

How he was expected to attack Johnston's intrenchments at Winchester, with an inferior and raw force, and with scarcely any artillery, we cannot imagine; and yet he asked specifically for orders to attack, if it was deemed necessary for the general good, even to sacrifice his army.

Why he did not follow Johnston is the only grave question, and this is abundantly met. The term of service of his troops was expiring, and he could not keep them; and *besides*, he had been informed that the eventful battle had been fought and won, five days before he turned—of necessity—homeward. We have abstained from statistics for want of space. The great facts are as above stated, and however much we could desire that Patterson's force had whipped Johnston, driven him up the valley, arrived at Bull Run, and turned a sad defeat into a *crowning* victory (albeit the first), these were impossible things, and General Patterson must stand acquitted of blame for not accomplishing them.

We have received from Messrs. D. Appleton & Co., of New York, the "History of the Romans under the Empire, by Charles Merivale, B. D.," vols. 5 and 6. Well suited by its admirable typography for a gentleman's library, no lately-written history better deserves such a place. It increases in interest as it describes the cruelties of Nero, and the crazy fickleness of Caligula; but the intense sensation culminates in the siege and capture of Jerusalem under Vespasian and Titus. The author is learned, without stiffness or pedantry; just, without political bias; of excellent judgment and skill in sifting and arranging the vast and heterogeneous materials from which his work is written. When completed, it will be an immortal work. Cloth, $2.00 per vol.

From Messrs. Roberts Brothers, of Boston, we have received one of the most delightful books we have read for many a day, "The Seer; or Common-places Refreshed: by Leigh Hunt," in 2 vols. (12mo, each vol. about 334 pp.) The word Seer he uses in its ordinary meaning, of one who sees, and not one gifted with second sight. The numerous essays which make up the volume, are on common subjects, "Windows," "Pebbles," and the like. They are slender texts upon which he writes lay-discourses, full of tenderness, wit, fine fancy, and varied scholarship. As a critic of delicate taste, he has no equal. Keats's poem of "St. Agnes' Eve," is the subject of one paper, and his comments upon this most charming work are perfectly charming. Among the others we would call especial attention to is his exquisite paper on Anacreon, designed for the uneducated. These volumes will do more to give the American people a just estimate of Leigh Hunt than any of his larger works; and when we add, that to their other excellences they add that of entire purity, freedom from thought, innuendo, or implication of licentiousness, we mean to express our unqualified admiration and commendation of Leigh Hunt, as presented in these charming essays. His "Common-places" are not only refreshed, but healthfully refreshing. Cloth, $3.00

The "Diary of Mrs. Kitty Trevylyan," is a story of the times of Whitefield and the Wesleys, by the authoress of "Chronicles of the Schönberg-Cotta Family." The story of the life and death of Luther, was extremely well told, and almost universally read. While we cannot say that this work equals it in interest, it is certainly due to the authoress, that we should express our admiration of her historical accuracy, and her use of the English literary language of one hundred and fifty years ago. Of the religious tendency, we have nothing to say, but it does not need the heart of a Methodist to believe that these were holy men, whose eloquent lips were touched with "hallowed fire," and that they endeavored in all honesty to destroy a formalism which should not, but sometimes does, encrust our holiest liturgies. New York: M. W. Dodd. 12mo, 436 pp. $1.75.

From Messrs. J. B. Lippincott & Co., of Philadelphia, we have received the sixth volume of that most excellent work "Chambers's Encyclopædia; a Dictionary of Universal Knowledge." (Royal 8vo, 827 pp. Cloth, $4.50.) Carefully compiled, handsomely illustrated, full as to its lexicon, it brings all subjects of which it treats, up to the present time; it may be consulted with confidence by those seeking information, and will be found useful as a book of reference to those who would refresh their memories. The old arrangement of a two-book library was, the Bible and Shakspeare. To these add Chambers's Encyclopædia, and there would be no dearth of reading, and that of the best kind.

Messrs. Ticknor & Fields have sent us "A Tribute to Thomas Starr King, by Richard Frothingham. (1 vol. 16mo, $1.50.) Mr. King was a man of many characters, most of them conducive to great public usefulness. He was a very *smart* man, quick in perception of the exact relations in which he stood to the world around him; a good writer; a self-made scholar; a wonderful orator; a self-sacrificing patriot. As for his liberal Christianity, it was a thought too liberal for us, in its doctrines, at least. The book is not a dispassionate review of his life, but a most enthusiastic eulogy.

"Shakspeare's Sonnets." (1 vol. 4to., $1.50. Ticknor & Fields.) Beautiful shadows; apparitions of human passion; amorous, without sensuality; read by few, understood by fewer, and yet eminently Shakspearian.

Messrs. Ticknor & Fields send us "Poems by David Gray, with Memoirs of his Life." A gifted youth, in the same category with Kirke White and Keats—hopes of immortality dashed by early death. The book is beautifully printed. 12mo, 250 pp.

"Lyra Anglicana" (12mo, 288 pp.), and "Lyra Americana" (12mo., 295 pp.), are collections of sacred poetry, by English and American authors respectively; collected and arranged by Rev. George T. Rider, M. A. The editor has done his work well, and has, from the vast treasures at his disposal, carefully selected beautiful things, "new and old,"—memories of saintly devotion, as incentives to our own piety. Published by D. Appleton & Co., New York. $2.00 per vol.

A charming little volume, for all its sadness, is "Cousin Alice: a Memoir of Mrs. Alice B. Haven." (12 mo, 392 pp. New York: D. Appleton & Co. $1.50.)

JEAN INGELOW is a poetess, and a good one. Her ballad—"The High Tide," makes modern eyes moist as the readers think of "my son's wife, Elizabeth." Is she also a good story-teller, a *raconteuse?* Even so. Her "Studies for Stories" are natural, pleasing, and in style as excellent, vigorous, simple English as we have ever read. At the opposite extreme from the sensational, they give moral instruction of the best kind in the simplest manner. A good book for young people. Boston: Ticknor & Fields.

The Report of the Chief of the Bureau of Ordnance (Navy Department, November, 1864) is clear, instructive, and admirably rendered. We especially note the topics—"Composition of Batteries" on ships-of-war; "Gunpowder and Nitre," and the strong recommendation for a "Gunnery Ship," for special training of officers and men in gunnery and all its details. This Bureau is handsomely and effectively managed by Captain Henry A. Wise, its present Chief.

General McCall has published a short sequel to his report of the Pennsylvania Reserves in the Peninsula, at the close of which he states, as a summary:—

"1st. That my division was attacked at three o'clock P. M., June 30th (battle of Nelson's Farm, or New Market Cross-Roads), not at five o'clock, as stated by General McClellan.

"2d. That it did not give way in less than an hour, as stated by General McClellan, but fought till nightfall (about four hours), with what result let the country judge.

"3d. That the New Jersey Brigade was not sent to occupy a portion of my deserted position, as stated by General McClellan, but was sent to the relief of General Kearney, who had called for aid.

"4th. That General McClellan's report to President Lincoln, that 'he had lost but twenty-five guns on the field of battle, twenty-one of which were lost by McCall's Division giving way under the onset of superior numbers,' *is not in accordance with facts.*"

OTHER BOOKS RECEIVED.

"Lion-Hearted." By Mrs. Grey. Philadelphia: T. B. Peterson & Brothers.

"Uncle Nat; or, the Good Time which George and Frank had, Trapping, Fishing, Camping Out, etc." By Alfred Oldfellow. With Illustrations. New York: D. Appleton & Co. 12mo, 224 pp.

"Autumn Holidays of a Country Parson." Boston: Ticknor & Fields. 12mo, 352 pp.

"The Correlation and Conservation of Forces." A Series of Expositions by Professors Grove and Helmholtz, Drs. Mayer and Faraday, Prof. Liebig and Dr. Carpenter, with an Introduction by Edward L. Youmans, M. D. New York: D. Appleton & Co. Small 8vo, 438 pp.

"The Lost Love." By the author of "John Drayton." Philadelphia: T. B. Peterson & Brothers.

"Following the Drum." By Mrs. Brigadier-General Egbert L. Viele. Paper, 12mo, 262 pp.

"Uncle John's Library" (First Book, Second, Third, Fourth, Fifth, and Sixth Books). 6 vols., sq. 16mo. Illustrated. New York: D. Appleton & Co. 60 cents per vol.

"Our Young Folks: an Illustrated Magazine for Boys and Girls, January, 1865." Small 8vo, 80 pp. Illustrated. Boston: Ticknor & Fields. Per year, $2; per No., 20 cents. [The best attempt of its kind we have ever seen.—ED.]

"House and Home Papers." By Harriet Beecher Stowe. 1 vol. 16mo. $1.50.

"The Boy Slaves; or, Life in the Desert." By Captain Mayne Reid. 1 vol. 12mo. Illustrated. $1.50.

"The Military System of Switzerland; or, How to Raise an Efficient Army without Offering Bounty, or Resorting to Draft." Pamphlet, 15 pp. Frank Taylor, Washington.

"The Experience of a French Detective." By "Waters," author of "The Autobiography of a London Detective." New York: Dick & Fitzgerald. 8vo, 224 pp. 75 cents.

EDITOR'S SPECIAL DEPARTMENT.

THE ADVANCE OF SHERMAN.—This invincible soldier has not let the grass grow under his feet. With wonderful energy he has arranged for the government and comfort of captured Savannah, asked for and received proper re-enforcements, gained the intelligent co-operation of the navy, and while the rebels are wondering what he will do next, he moves, nothing daunted by freshets and mud, in two grand columns, upon Charleston and Branchville. Howard advances along the Charleston and Savannah Railroad, while Slocum ascending the Savannah River to Sister's Ferry and Robertville, about thirty miles above Savannah, branches off northward to the great railroad which connects Charleston and Augusta, on which the principal strategic point is Branchville. We have no space for the details, which will hereafter be given in a separate article, and which are at present somewhat confused, coming as they chiefly do from unwilling rebel sources, but the general philosophy of the movement may be presented in few words. Leaving Major-General Grover as military governor of Savannah, his advance of Howard's wing, the Seventeenth Corps leading, first swept the rebels under McLaws away from Pocotaligo Bridge, having crossed the Coosawatchie, and thus secured a strong temporary base and dépôt at the head of Broad River, into which the Pocotaligo empties. The next point on the railroad contested by the rebels was Salkehatchie on the Combahee, which was flanked and taken. Still onward, he took Ashepoo Bridge, where the railroad crosses the Ashepoo River, and found himself, as he expected, confronted by the principal forces covering Charleston, at Jacksonboro, on the Edisto. While these movements were going on, a considerable Union force, we learn from rebel sources, landed at Grimball's, on Stono River, two miles southwest of Charleston, across the Ashley River.

Meanwhile Slocum, commanding the left wing, after encountering serious obstacles in moving up the Savannah, principally in the matter of transportation, moved his supplies by the right bank, pontooned the river at or near Sister's Ferry, and set out for the railroad between Augusta and Branchville. He crossed the Coosawatchie, the left branch of the Combahee, Whippy Swamp, the Big Salkehatchie; then was heard from on the Upper Edisto; and at length, amid the confusion of reports, we find Branchville and Orangeburg taken, the railroad communications destroyed, and Columbia threatened. To complement the grand movement, Kilpatrick moved with speed towards Augusta with his famous cavalry, keeping the flank of the great army free from danger.

The rebel papers allowed that if Branchville was taken, Charleston must fall, and they were right. Branchville is a very strong point, flanked on the south and west by the Edisto, and on the north and west by the head-waters of the Santee; it is the terminus of the Columbia Railroad, and has been the chief source of supplies to Charleston. From it the Charleston and Wilmington Railroad is within easy striking distance, and that struck, all supplies are cut off from the doomed city. The day for which Charleston has been long laying up wrath is at hand. Will the Charlestonians burn their city? Let that be as they please; it will injure no one. To aid the advance of Howard, which in itself gives Slocum the best chance to effect his purpose, our gunboats line the coast, and can run up all the streams mentioned, making Howard's right flank a double tower of strength.

The movement is yet incomplete, but the promise is most brilliant, and we argue confidently from what Sherman has done to what he will do. His actions exceed even the eager hopes and expectations of our people.

In fine, to appreciate General Sherman's magnificent new march, and to gain some idea of the colossal plan now instituted for a final onset from all quarters upon the contracted and quaking rebellion, let us look at the strategic points, particularly marked as such, by railroad junctions and termini. Southward from Richmond, the only thoroughfare open to the rebels is that known as the Danville Road, which passes through Greensboro and Salisbury to Columbia, South Carolina. This cut, anywhere, straitens the supplies of Lee, and renders Richmond, sooner or later, untenable. Now, to look at the other extremity, Sherman is, while we write, in and beyond Columbia, and as he moves northward on that road, he effects more and more completely this very purpose.

Then the column which moves on Florence (the junction of the Wilmington and Columbia and the Raleigh and Charleston Roads) completely isolates both Charleston and Wilmington, making their fall only a question of time, and of no distant time. We are not therefore surprised to hear that Charleston is being evacuated.

Further, an advance from Florence upon Raleigh, the most important strategic point in North Carolina, is aided by an expedition now moving from Newbern, with twenty thousand men and forty or fifty miles of railroad iron for putting the road in running order as they go. Add to this that Stoneman and Burbridge are said also to be moving from East Tennessee towards Raleigh, and the new and final bisection of the Confederacy seems certain. The plan is really stupendous; the execution, thus far even, a marvel in military history. Sherman and Grant are now, for the first time, fairly on the interior line; the coast cities are doomed beyond a peradventure; and Lee, now entirely entangled in this consummate network, must fight, fly, starve, or surrender. If he fights, he must come out and fight at a great disadvantage in position and numbers. Whither can he fly? All avenues are cut off. Starvation is destruction, and surrender is the end. We do not say that there will be no checks or delays in this plan; but such are the Federal designs, such the fair, immediate probabilities. The final result seems now certain.

As soon as the season opens we shall hear, too, of a movement in the Valley of Virginia. Sheridan's force is anxiously awaiting the *laisses allez* of the great herald, and Richmond will have an additional menace from the north.

General Gillmore, an excellent officer, with the prestige of captured Pulaski and battered Sumter, has again been appointed to the command of the Department of the South, and will be of aid to Sherman. Foster, a good general, retires for a while, incapacitated by his old wound.

Since writing the above, the news has been received of the evacuation of Charleston and Wilmington, to which special reference will be made in the next issue.

RICHMOND.—The Gordian strategic knot of the rebellion, which so many have striven in vain to untie by strategic processes, is at Richmond, and must be cut by Grant's sword. The exact manner in which this is to be done, does not yet transpire; but, judging from the past, it seems evident that the most feasible way is to force Lee to evacuate and fight in the field. To do this, his communications must be cut, and these are at present the Southside and the Danville Railroads; the cutting of the first would indeed only occasion the evacuation of Petersburg, but it would be a long step towards cutting the other.

During the winter, and pending the movements of Sherman and Thomas, we cannot think that General Grant has designed to make a serious attempt to do this. We believe he has limited the movements of the forces immediately around Richmond to keeping up a good circulation, and threatening the rebel right, thus causing them to feel that they were in such danger that they could make no large detachments, unless they should incline to detach their whole army, and move southwestward. Whether the recent movement upon and around the works on Hatcher's Run was meant for any thing more, remains to be seen, for, while we write, it is still incomplete. That Lee will evacuate Richmond we do not believe, because with that evacuation the rebel cause is lost not only in our eyes, but on foreign exchanges, and, still worse, in the eyes of their own people. So far they have successfully defied the "On to Richmond" boast of many "consular armies," and with each success they have more completely identified the fate of Richmond with that of the rebellion.

As far as we are informed of the latest movement it was thus: On Tuesday, January 31, the orders were issued and preparations begun, all the corps were ready to move, the sick and baggage were sent to City Point, and the batteries all along the line cracked their throats, apparently to confuse the enemy, but to our mind—as the stratagem has been so often tried—really to put him on the look-out.

Once more Gregg puts his three brigades of cavalry in motion before daylight on Sunday, the 4th, upon the Jerusalem Plank-Road, drives away the enemy from Rowanty Creek, which he crosses on bridges of his own construction, and then sends his scouts out towards Dinwiddie Court-House, while he moves upon the Boydton Plank-Road. The country is extremely difficult to handle troops in, being intersected by many confusing cross-roads, and thickly interspersed with forests, swamps, and thickets.

At 5 A. M. of the same day, Warren moved by the Halifax Road with the Fifth Corps, and, a little after, Humphreys moved with two divisions of the Second Corps.

The plan was, in its general points, similar to the former one. Humphreys was to attack the works in front, while Warren, himself flanked by Gregg, was to pounce upon their right flank.

If the movement should succeed, the rebel right was to be rolled back, we were to gain their rear, and then strike the Southside Railroad. The crossing, after continued skirmishing, was fully effected. Humphreys' line was formed and slightly intrenched; and there was then a delay, not accounted for, but supposed to be to let the Fifth Corps come up on Humphreys' left.

While affairs were in this condition, our line was vigorously attacked three times, and three times rolled back the enemy's force, under the energetic command of General Humphreys and the valor of his divisions.

During the night of Monday, the line was re-formed, Humphreys on the right, Warren on the left, flanked by Gregg, and the Sixth and Ninth Corps in easy support. Warren sent out Crawford about mid-day to seize Dabney's Mill, a strong position in front, and he was successful at first, but the rebels massed Pegram and Gordon's Divisions of Early's Corps, and Mahone's of Hill's, and succeeded in driving back Crawford and the supports sent him, and in throwing a portion of our left and centre into confusion. The retreat was not very far, and we hold the new line from the Squirrel Level Road, across the run, with our advance towards Dabney's Mill; something gained, a new point of departure for the next move.

The peace diplomacy has culminated, but it will rise again. Jacques and Gillmore, Blair and Singleton, were forerunners, not, however, prophetically appointed. And at length a conference took place for four hours, on a vessel in Hampton Roads, between Messrs. Stephens, Hunter, and Campbell, on the part of the Richmond authorities, and President Lincoln and Secretary Seward, for the Government; a conference conducted with consummate skill on the part of our authorities.

That both parties desire peace, this meeting is a direct additional proof; but there was also much indirection about it. On the rebel part it had three indirect purposes. First, in order at least, they wanted that informal recognition which the reception of their commissioners *at Washington* would give. Secondly, they wish to temporize, to have a cessation of hostilities, in which, released for a time from their terrible straits, they might look about them for new expedients, by which to save their lives and salve their pride. Thirdly, and failing in the other two, they wish to raise a new blast, by which to "re-fire the rebel heart," and give a new start to the war. We have stood firm; not an iota have they gained, and "firing the rebel heart" will be like blowing embers where there is no fuel; they burn brightly for a moment, and then vanish into cinders.

But we feel fully satisfied that this is not the end of peace negotiations. A step has been taken. Even a year ago they scorned a conference. Now they have had one; and at some early day in the future, when they are in greater straits, this peace conference will be the new point of departure, and different terms will be readily discussed.

In spite of Lee's appointment as generalissimo (which gives him really no new powers), in spite of mass meetings in the African church, those greater straits will soon come; and if to avert them they arm the slaves, let the reader judge what would be the effect of pitting against each other a corps of colored soldiers armed for freedom, and a corps armed to perpetuate their own slavery. There would not be much fighting; *verbum sat.*

We need not spend many words in recording the abortive effort of the rebel iron-clads to pass down the James River, remove the obstructions, run the batteries, and play havoc with our transports at City Point. It came near succeeding, but did not.

On the 24th of January, the iron-clads Virginia, Fredericksburg, and Richmond, and the wooden war-vessels Drewry, Nansemond, and Hampton, with a flotilla of torpedo-boats, left their anchorage at Howlett's, ran past Fort Brady, removed some of the obstructions, encountered no opposition from the north bank, but were fortunately checked by shoals and the batteries on the south bank. The Richmond, Virginia, and Drewry, got aground, and a lucky shell from Fort Parsons blew up the Drewry, whereupon the scheme was abandoned. Our floating defences were inadequate, as Admiral Porter had taken away most of the gunboats; and the double-ender Onondaga, for reasons unexplained, retired at once down the river, without attempting to check the rebel fleet.

MAJOR-GENERAL A. E. BURNSIDE.

In the January number, an article on the Quartermaster's Department contains an implied charge upon General Burnside, for the delay in the pontoons at Fredericksburg, and for the want of success at the explosion of the mine at Petersburg. The article is a valuable one, contains many important facts, and is written by a responsible officer; but we wish, editorially, to withdraw these assertions with regard to General Burnside. Such judgments should only be based upon substantial evidence; and the recent investigation of the mine disaster certainly does not charge upon, but rather exonerates, the distinguished officer referred to. His former valuable service, and his constant readiness to do all in his power for his country and her great cause, entitle him to our respect and to this explanation.

MAJOR-GENERAL O. B. WILLCOX.

As we have seen numerous errors of statement, with regard to the career of this distinguished officer, we desire to place him correctly upon the record. As a colonel, he was the real captor of Alexandria, at the time that Ellsworth fell. This he accomplished with his own regiment (1st Michigan), a section of Sherman's Battery, and Stoneman's Company of Cavalry. Ball's Company of Virginia Cavalry (probably the first capture of rebels in the war) there fell into his hands. Three days before the battle of Bull Run he took (it is believed) the first colors captured in the war, from an Alabama regiment at Fairfax Station. At Bull Run he commanded a brigade of Heintzelman's Division, recaptured Rickett's guns, and fell wounded into the hands of the rebels, three hundred yards in advance of that battery. After thirteen months' imprisonment, he succeeded Stevens in the command of the First Division, Ninth Corps, which he handled skilfully at South Mountain and Antietam. When Burnside succeeded McClellan, Willcox commanded the Ninth Corps in the battle of Fredericksburg. At Knoxville he commanded the left wing, and made a masterly retreat from Bull's Gap to Cumberland Gap, in presence of a superior force, without losing a man or a wagon.

In the organization for the campaign of 1864, General Willcox was assigned to the Third Division of the Ninth Corps. The number of this division was changed to the First, in September last. For "distinguished and gallant services in the several actions since crossing the Rapidan," he has been brevetted a major-general.

CORRESPONDENCE.

BEFORE PETERSBURG, February 16, 1865.

Editor " U. S. Service Magazine:"

SIR:—I take occasion to inform you, as a correction to the newspaper reports of our last movement, that there are the following errors in the newspaper correspondents' statements that I know of:—

1st. The Sixth Corps did not, nor any part of it, fire into the Fifth.

2d. There were no ammunition-wagons destroyed or abandoned.

3d. The movement did not at all contemplate, as far as I know, a lodgment west of Hatcher's Run, or on the Southside Railroad, but merely to capture any wagon-trains the cavalry could reach.

4th. There was no panic; the troops engaged were pressed back by superior numbers, but held the enemy before reaching the intrenchments.

FIFTH CORPS.

MILITARY NOTES AND QUERIES.

S. L. H., Vicksburg.—"Through what interval does the rear-rank man aim in firing to the left oblique?" *Answer.*—Over the left shoulder of the man in front of him.

E. R. H., Sacramento, Cal.—"In loading a piece of artillery, when does No. 3 leave the vent, after sponging the piece, or after the cartridge is rammed home?" *Answer.*—After sponging.

OBITUARY.

BRIGADIER-GENERAL JAMES ST. CLAIR MORTON.

JAMES ST. CLAIR MORTON, son of the distinguished physician and naturalist, Dr. Samuel George Morton, was born in Philadelphia, in the year 1829. The rare qualities of mind which he exhibited at a very early age were nurtured and fostered by his father, and the habits of industry and study thus acquired in his youth eminently qualified him for the severe tasks and brilliant career of his later life. Entered as a Cadet at West Point, he graduated in June, 1851, second in a class of forty-two members, and was commissioned second-lieutenant of engineers. From August 18th, 1851, to May, 1852, he was on duty as assistant to the officer in charge of the military defences in Charleston Harbor. From May, 1852, to September, 1855, he was assistant to the officer in charge of construction of Fort Delaware. From September, 1855, to June, 1857, he was stationed at West Point, N. Y., as acting-assistant professor of civil and military engineering at the Academy. From June, 1857, to March, 1858, he was assistant engineer in construction of fortifications at Sandy Hook, entrance to the harbor of New York. From March, 1858, to July, 1859, he was on duty under the Treasury Department, as engineer Third Light-House District, extending from Gooseberry Point, Massachusetts, to Squam Inlet, New Jersey. From July, 1859, to July, 1860, he was in charge of the Potomac Water-Works, after which he was assigned to duty under the Navy Department, as engineer of the "Chiriqui Expedition," which was undertaken in August, 1860, and concluded in November, of the same year; following this he was engineer in charge of the construction of the Washington Aqueduct. From April, 1861, to March, 1862, engineer in charge of the construction of Fort Jefferson, Tortugas, Florida. Recovering from a fever contracted while in Central America, he was assigned to the engineering operations at Fort Mifflin. Reporting capable for field duty, he was ordered to report in person, in May, 1862, to Major-General Halleck, and by him ordered to report to General Buell, commanding the Army of the Ohio, and appointed engineer-in-chief of that army. At about this time General Buell commenced his retreat, for the purpose of intercepting Bragg in his advance towards Louisville. The necessity of abandoning Nashville becoming a question of vital importance, Captain Morton was called upon for his opinion, as chief-engineer, which he gave to the effect that with the aid of the fortifications he had already constructed and those he could construct before attack could be made, the place might be held by a comparatively small force. The result proved the correctness of this opinion, for, an attack having been made, the works were found by the enemy so formidable in their character as to preclude all possibility of success, and they were forced to retire with some loss, without even an attempt to storm. By this time five forts were completed, and a line of intrenchments, extending around the city; the minor points being defended by cotton-bales.

Soon after the arrival of General Rosecrans at Nashville, Captain Morton was charged with the organization of the "Pioneer Brigade," a body composed of details of twenty men from each regiment of the Army of the Cumberland, which, in three days after reporting for duty, were ordered to march on Murfreesboro. Their services at the battle of Stone River, called forth the following eulogium from the Commanding General in his official report:—

"Among the lesser commands which deserve special mention for distinguished service in the battle is the Pioneer Corps, a body of seventeen hundred (1,700) men, composed of details from the companies of each infantry regiment, organized and instructed by Captain James St. Clair Morton, Corps of Engineers, Chief Engineer of this army, which marched as an infantry brigade with the left wing, making bridges at Stewart's Creek, prepared and guarded the fort at Stone River, on the nights of the 29th and 30th, supported Stoke's battery, and fought with valor and determination on the 31st, holding its position until relieved; on the morning of the 2d advancing with the greatest promptitude and gallantry to support Van Cleve's Division against the attack on our left; on the evening of the same day, constructing a bridge and batteries between that time and Saturday evening. The efficiency and *esprit de corps* suddenly developed in this command, its gallant behavior in action, the eminent service it is continually rendering the army, entitle both officers and men to special public notice and thanks, while they reflect the highest credit on the distinguished ability and capacity of Captain Morton, who will do honor to his promotion to brigadier-general, which the President has promised him."

Immediately following the battle, Captain Morton was appointed brigadier-general of volunteers, and afterwards confirmed by the Senate. During the six months that the army remained at Murfreesboro, General Morton was engaged in the construction of the immense and impregnable fortifications of that place, known as Fortress Rosecrans, consisting of a series of lunettes, some three miles in circuit, interiorly commanded by strong redoubts containing block-houses, mounted with heavy guns.

General Morton accompanied the army in its advance from Murfreesboro to Chattanooga, continually employed in the construction and repair of roads and bridges, destroyed by the enemy in his retreat. Upon the capture of Chattanooga, he immediately commenced the construction of the fortifications of that city, which proved so efficient in sheltering our army upon its retreat after the battle of Chickamauga, where he was wounded.

When General Rosecrans was relieved, General Morton was ordered to report for duty at the Engineer Bureau, as major of engineers. His subsequent movements and death are detailed by Major General Parke, commanding Ninth Corps, as follows:—

"HEAD-QUARTERS, NINTH ARMY CORPS,
"October 31st, 1864.

"Lieutenant-Colonel ADAM BADEAU,
"*Military Secretary, Head-Quarters, Armies of the United States.*

"COLONEL:—In reply to your communication of the 28th inst., asking the particulars of the death of Major James St. Clair Morton, Engineer Corps, I have the honor to inform you that that officer reported to Major-General Burnside, then commanding the Ninth Corps, for duty as engineer, on the 18th of May, 1864, while the army was at Spottsylvania. From that date, to the 17th June, he performed the arduous and dangerous duties of his position, with an activity, zeal, and ability, which often called forth the praise of his Commanding General. He was noted in the corps for his personal gallantry, and in the attack made by General Ledlie's Brigade, First Division, at the North Anna, he took a conspicuous part, narrowly escaping death, as a bullet tore through his hat. On the morning of the 17th June, he received orders from General Burnside to place the troops making the assault in their proper position, and to direct at what point they should strike the enemy's works. When this had been accomplished, feeling deeply interested in the success of the movement, he went forward with General Hartranft, commanding the attacking brigade. When it was evident the attack had failed, he was retiring with the troops when he was struck in the breast by a rifle-ball and mortally wounded. Captain Shadley, Acting Aide to General Hartranft, immediately went to him, but I believe he expired without a word.

"In his death this corps and his country lost a valuable officer, and his memory will long be cherished among those who were fortunate enough to have known him. "I have the honor to be, very respectfully,

"Your obedient servant,
"JOHN G. PARKE,
"*Major-General Commanding.*"

Thus he fell, closing an eventful and brilliant career, in the thirty-fifth year of his age.

In person he was tall, graceful, and commanding; in disposition confiding and generous, ever winning the respect, confidence, and admiration of those with whom he chanced to be thrown.

He contributed to military science the following works:—"Memoir on Sea-Coast Defences," "American Fortification," "Dangers and Defences of New York City."

THE PAY OF OFFICERS.

A CORRESPONDENT of high rank in the Army sends us the following proposed schedule for officers' yearly salaries, in lieu of the present arrangement of distinct pay, rations, &c., &c.:—

	IN THE FIELD.	ON OTHER DUTY.	ON LEAVE.
Major-General	$6,500	$5,000	$3,000
Brigadier-General	4,800	8,000	1,800
Colonel	8,800	2,800	1,500
Lieutenant-Colonel	8,500	2,500	1,800
Major	8,200	2,200	1,100
Captain	2,900	1,900	1,000
First Lieutenant	2,600	1,600	900
Second Lieutenant	2,400	1,400	800
Brevet Second Lieutenant	2,200	1,200	700

To this he adds—"Double the pay of the *enlisted men.*"

OFFICIAL INTELLIGENCE.

The Army.

Appointments Confirmed by the Senate.

TO BE MAJOR-GENERALS OF VOLUNTEERS.

Brigadier and Brevet Major-General Alfred H. Terry, January 15, 1865.
Brigadier-General Peter J. Osterhaus, July 23, 1864.
Brigadier-General Joseph A. Mower, August 12, 1864.
Brigadier and Brevet Major-General George Crook, October 21, 1864.
Brigadier and Brevet Major-General Godfrey Weitzel, November 17, 1864.
Brigadier-General Jacob D. Cox, December 7, 1864.
Brigadier-General Thomas J. Wood, *vice* Crittenden, resigned.

TO BE MAJOR-GENERALS OF VOLUNTEERS BY BREVET.

Brigadier-Generals Charles R. Woods and John M. Corse, U. S. Vols., October 5, 1864.
Brigadier-General Giles A. Smith, U. S. Vols., September 1, 1864.
Brigadier-Generals M. D. Leggett, John W. Geary, and John E. Smith, U. S. Vols., January 12, 1865.
Brigadier-Generals A. S. Williams, Judson Kilpatrick, and Absalom Baird, U. S. Vols., January 12, 1865.
Brigadier-General William F. Barry, U. S. Vols., September 1, 1864.
Brigadier-General Rufus Saxton, U. S. Vols., January 12, 1865.
Brigadier-General Adelbert Ames, U. S. Vols., January 15, 1865.
Brigadier-General John M. Brannan, U. S. Vols., January 23, 1865.
Brigadier-General Robert O. Tyler, U. S. Vols., August 1, 1864.
Brigadier-General Benjamin H. Grierson, U. S. Vols., February 10, 1865.
Brigadier-General John C. Robinson, U. S. Vols., June 27, 1864.
Brigadier-General Henry J. Hunt, U. S. Vols., July 6, 1864.
Brigadier-General William H. Emory, U. S. Vols., July 23, 1864.
Brigadier-General Orlando B. Willcox, U. S. Vols., August 1, 1864.
Brigadier-General S. W. Crawford, U. S. Vols., August 1, 1864.
Brigadier-General Charles Griffin, U. S. Vols., August 1, 1864.
Brigadier-General Francis C. Barlow, U. S. Vols., August 1, 1864.
Brigadier-General Romeyn B. Ayres, U. S. Vols., August 1, 1864.
Brigadier-General D. McM. Gregg, U. S. Vols., August 1, 1864.
Brigadier-General Robert B. Potter, U. S. Vols., August 1, 1864.
Brigadier-General Alexander S. Webb, U. S. Vols., August 1, 1864.
Brigadier-General L. Cutler, U. S. Vols., August 19, 1864.
Brigadier-General Nelson A. Miles, U. S. Vols., August 25, 1864.
Brigadier-General T. E. G. Ransom, September 1, 1864.
Brigadier-General Gersham Mott, August 1, 1864.
Brigadier-General Alfred T. A. Torbert, U. S. Vols., August 1, 1864.
Brigadier-General James H. Wilson, U. S. Vols., October 5, 1864.
Brigadier-General James B. Ricketts, U. S. Vols., August 1, 1864.
Brigadier-General Cuvier Grover, U. S. Vols., October 19, 1864.
Brigadier-General George W. Getty, U. S. Vols., August 1, 1864.
Brigadier-General Frank Wheaton, U. S. Vols., October 19, 1864.
Brigadier-General Wesley Merritt, U. S. Vols., October 19, 1864.
Brigadier-General George A. Custer, U. S. Vols., October 19, 1864.
Brigadier-General Emory Upton, U. S. Vols., October 19, 1864.

Brigadier-General Thomas W. Egan, U. S. Vols., October 27, 1864.
Brigadier-General George J. Stannard, U. S. Vols., October 28, 1864.
Brigadier-General August V. Kautz, U. S. Vols., October 28, 1864.
Brigadier-General Edward Ferrero, U. S. Vols., December 2, 1864.
Brigadier-General Joseph J. J. Bartlett, U. S. Vols., August 1, 1864.
Brigadier-General Lewis A. Grant, U. S. Vols., October 19, 1864.

TO BE BRIGADIER-GENERALS OF VOLUNTEERS.

Colonel John D. Stevenson, of Missouri, from November 29, 1863.
Colonel Gustavus A. D. Russy, of Virginia, May 23, 1862.
Colonel William D. Whipple, of New York, July 17, 1863.
Colonel Alvin C. Gillem, of Tennessee, August 17, 1863.
Colonel James H. Wilson, October 30, 1863.
Colonel John B. McIntosh, 3d Pennsylvania Cavalry, July 21, 1864.
Colonel George H. Chapman, 3d Indiana Cavalry, July 21, 1864.
Colonel William Grose, 36th Indiana, July 30, 1864.
Colonel Joseph A. Cooper, 6th Tennessee, July 30, 1864.
Colonel John T. Crofton, 4th Kentucky, July 30, 1864.
Colonel Charles C. Wolcot, 46th Ohio, July 30, 1864.
Colonel John W. Sprague, 63d Ohio, July 30, 1864.
Colonel James W. Reilly, 104th Ohio, July 30, 1864.
Colonel Luther P. Bradley, 51st Illinois, July 30, 1864.
Colonel Charles R. Lowell, 2d Massachusetts Cavalry, and Captain in the 6th U. S. Cavalry, October 19, 1864 (since died of wounds received in battle).
Colonel William H. Powell, 2d Virginia Cavalry, October 19, 1864.
Colonel Thomas C. Devin, 6th New York Cavalry, October 19, 1864.
Colonel Alfred Gibbs, 1st New York Dragoons, and Captain in the 3d United States Cavalry, October 19, 1864.
Colonel Ronalds McKenzie, 2d Connecticut Artillery, and Captain in the United States Corps of Engineers, October 19, 1864.
Colonel R. B. Hays, 23d Ohio, October 19, 1864.
Colonel James R. Stack, 47th Indiana, November 10, 1864.
Lieutenant-Colonel Joseph A. Haskins, Major in the 3d United States Artillery, August 5, 1864.
Colonel James D. Fessenden, August 8, 1864.
Colonel Daniel D. Bidwell, 49th New York, August 11, 1864 (since killed in battle).
Colonel Eli Long, 4th Ohio Cavalry, Captain 4th U. S. Cavalry, August 18, 1864.
Colonel Isaac H. Duval, 9th West Virginia, September 24, 1864.
Colonel Thomas A. Smyth, 1st Delaware, October 1, 1864.
Colonel Ferdinand Vanderveer, 35th Ohio, October 4, 1864.
Colonel Thomas J. Lucas, 16th Indiana Mounted Infantry, November 10, 1864.
Colonel E. J. Davis, 1st Texas Cavalry, November 10, 1864.
Colonel Patrick H. Jones, 154th New York.
Colonel Joshua B. Howell, 85th Pennsylvania, September 12, 1864 (since died).
Colonel Charles C. Doolittle, 18th Michigan.
Lieutenant-Colonel William Hartstuff, Assistant Inspector-General Twenty-third Army Corps.
Colonel James Gilbert, 27th Iowa, February 9, 1865.
Colonel R. K. Scott, 68th Ohio, January 12, 1865.
Colonel James J. Gilbert, 27th Iowa Vols., February 9, 1865, vice D. McM. Gregg, resigned.

TO BE BRIGADIER-GENERALS OF VOLUNTEERS BY BREVET.

Colonel H. C. Hobart, 21st Wisconsin Volunteers, January 12, 1865.
Colonel S. H. Roberts, 139th New York Volunteers, October 28, 1864.
Colonel Wager Swayne, 43d Ohio Vols., February 5, 1865.
Colonel Clark R. Weaver, 17th Iowa Vet. Volunteer Infantry, February 9, 1865.
Colonel David Shunk, 8th Indiana Volunteer Infantry, February 9, 1865.
Colonel William R. Brewster, 73d New York Volunteers, December 2, 1864.
Colonel William H. Madill, 141st Pennsylvania Volunteers, December 2, 1864.
Colonel John Ramsey, 8th New Jersey Volunteers, December 2, 1864.

Colonel George W. West, 17th Maine Volunteers, December 2, 1864.
Brevet Colonel C. H. Morgan, United States Volunteers, December 2, 1864.
Brevet Colonel G. H. McKibbin, United States Volunteers, December 2, 1864.
Colonel William B. Woods, 67th Ohio, January 12, 1865.
Colonel A. Pardee, Jr., 147th Pennsylvania, January 12, 1865.
Colonel Henry A. Barnum, 149th New York, January 12, 1865.
Colonel George P. Buell, 58th Indiana, January 12, 1865.
Colonel B. F. Fearing, 92d Ohio, December, 1864.
Colonel Amos Beckwith, January 12, 1865.
Colonel Smith D. Atkins, 92d Illinois Mounted Infantry, January 12, 1865.
Colonel G. A. Pennybacker, 97th Pennsylvania, January 15, 1865.
Colonel J. C. Abbott, 7th New Hampshire, January 15, 1865.
Brevet Colonel Cyrus B. Comstock, United States Volunteers, January 15, 1865.
Colonel A. S. Hartwell, 55th Massachusetts Volunteers, December 30, 1864.
Colonel Morgan H. Chrysler, 2d New York Veteran Cavalry, January 23, 1865.
Colonel Benjamin Harrison, 17th Indiana Volunteers, January 23, 1865.
Colonel William T. Clark, United States Volunteers.
Colonel R. K. Scott, 68th Ohio Volunteers.
Colonel Jack L. Casement, 103d Ohio Volunteers.
Colonel George W. Schofield, United States Volunteers.
Colonel Nathan A. M. Dudley, 30th Massachusetts Veterans.
Colonel George S. Dodge, Chief Quartermaster Army of the James, for valuable services at Fort Fisher, January 15, 1865.
Colonel E. D. Osband, 3d Colored Infantry, October 5, 1864.
Colonel Edwin L. Hays, 100th Ohio, January 12, 1865.
Colonel Emerson Opdyke, 125th Ohio, February 7, 1865.
Colonel John H. Ketcham, 150th New York Volunteers.
Colonel W. P. Richardson, 25th Ohio Volunteers.
Colonel A. C. Voris, 67th Ohio Volunteers.
Colonel A. F. Stevens, 13th New Hampshire Volunteers.
Colonel Oliver Edwards, 39th Massachusetts Volunteers, October 19, 1864.
Colonel J. S. Robinson, 82d Ohio Volunteers.
Colonel James H. Ford, 2d Colored Cavalry.
Colonel James S. Brisbin, United States Colored Troops, and Captain in the 6th United States Cavalry.
Colonel Henry D. Washburn, 18th Indiana Volunteers.
Colonel William Coggswell, 2d Massachusetts Volunteers.
Colonel Thomas H. Benton, 29th Iowa Volunteers.
Colonel J. Howard Kitching, 6th New York Artillery, August 1, 1864.
Colonel James A. Williamson, 4th Iowa Volunteers.
Colonel S. L. Glasgow, 23d Iowa Volunteers.
Colonel J. P. C. Shanks, 7th Indiana Cavalry.
Colonel E. F. Winslow, 4th Iowa Cavalry.
Colonel G. H. Sharp, 120th New York Volunteers.
Colonel Benjamin F. Sweet, 8th Veteran Reserve Corps.
Colonel William Gamble, 8th Illinois Cavalry.
Colonel Isaac C. Bassett, 82d Pennsylvania Volunteers.
Colonel William H. Ball, 122d Ohio Volunteers, October 19, 1864.
Colonel John W. Horn, 6th Maryland Volunteers, October 19, 1864.
Colonel Charles H. Tompkins, 1st Rhode Island Light Artillery, October 19, 1864.
Colonel John F. Ballier, 98th Pennsylvania Volunteers, July 13, 1864.
Colonel W. L. McMillen, 95th Ohio Volunteers, December 16, 1864.
Colonel L. F. Hubbard, 5th Minnesota Volunteers, December 16, 1864.
Colonel S. G. Hill, 35th Iowa Volunteers, December 15, 1864 (since dead).
Colonel Daniel C. McCallum, additional aide-de-camp, September 24, 1864.
Colonel Edgar M. Gregory, 91st Pennsylvania Volunteers, September 30, 1864.
Colonel Napoleon B. McLaughlin, 57th Mass. Volunteers, September 30, 1864.
Colonel James Gwin, 118th Pennsylvania Volunteers, September 30, 1864.
Colonel A. L. Pearson, 155th Pennsylvania Volunteers, September 30, 1864.
Colonel George D. Welles, 34th Massachusetts Volunteers, October 12, 1864.
Colonel John I. Curtin, 45th Pennsylvania Volunteers, October 12, 1864.
Colonel T. M. Harris, 10th West Virginia Volunteers, October 19, 1864.
Colonel J. Warren Keifer, 110th Ohio Volunteers, October 19, 1864.

Colonel E. L. Mollineux, 159th New York Volunteers, October 19, 1864.
Colonel William H. Penrose, 15th New Jersey Volunteers, October 19, 1864.
Colonel E. P. Davis, 153d New York Volunteers, October 19, 1864.
Colonel J. E. Hamlin, 65th New York Volunteers, October 19, 1864.
Colonel James W. Forsyth, October 19, 1864.
Colonel William B. Tibbitts, 21st New York Volunteers, October 21, 1864.
Colonel H. G. Sickles, 198th Pennsylvania Volunteers, October 21, 1864.
Colonel Robert McAllister, 11th New Jersey Volunteers, October 27, 1864.
Colonel A. M. Blackman, 27th United States Colored Troops, October 27, 1864.
Colonel H. T. Collis, 114th Pennsylvania Volunteers, October 28, 1864.
Colonel James Jourdan, 158th New York Volunteers, October 28, 1864.
Colonel N. Martin Curtis, 142d New York Volunteers, October 28, 1864.
Colonel Alonzo G. Draper, United States Colored Troops, October 28, 1864.
Colonel Samuel A. Duncan, United States Colored Troops, October 28, 1864.
Colonel Guy V. Henry, 40th Massachusetts Volunteers, October 28, 1864.
Colonel Benjamin C. Ludlow, United States Colored Troops, October 28, 1864.
Colonel Milton S. Littlefield, 21st U. S. Colored Troops, November 26, 1864.

FOR PROMOTION, BY BREVET, IN THE ARMY OF THE UNITED STATES.

Brigadier-General Montgomery C. Meigs, Quartermaster-General, to be major-general by brevet.
Colonel Charles Thomas, Assistant Quartermaster-General, to be brigadier-general by brevet.
Brevet Colonel James L. Donaldson, to be brigadier-general by brevet.
Medical Inspector Joseph R. Barnes, to be surgeon-general, with the rank of brigadier-general.

Dismissals,

For the Week ending January 7, 1865.

Captain Albert F. Ransom, Commissary of Subsistence, United States Volunteers, to date December 30, 1864, for conduct unbecoming an officer and gentleman.
Captain Gilbert H. Barger, 122d Ohio Volunteers, to date October 23, 1864, for shamefully deserting his company and regiment while engaged with the enemy in the battle of Cedar Creek, Virginia, October 19, 1864.

The following officers, to date December 13, 1864, for the causes mentioned, having been published officially, and failed to appear before the Commission:—
For neglect of duty in losing certain important papers necessary for the trial of Captain R. B. Hoover, 200th Pennsylvania Volunteers, charged with defrauding the Government, Captain J. M. Opdyke, 53d Pennsylvania Volunteers.

Disobedience of orders, and absence without leave.

Captain Charles J. Quinn, 63d New York Volunteers.

Absence without leave.

Captain Charles A. Osborne, 11th Michigan Cavalry.
First Lieutenant James A. Russell, 140th Pennsylvania Volunteers.
Lieutenant William Geoffry, 182d New York Volunteers.
Lieutenant E. T. Lewis, 1st New York Mounted Rifles.
First Lieutenant Felix Vanderbury, 178th New York Volunteers.
First Lieutenant Louis Menzel, 119th New York Volunteers.
Second Lieutenant Ferd. Maggi, 39th New York Volunteers.
Captain Francis J. Matther, 86th Indiana Volunteers.
Captain Henry McIntire, 35th United States Colored Troops, to date November 20, 1864.
Assistant Surgeon Lafayette Avery, 3d Missouri Cavalry, to date December 30, 1864, for habitual drunkenness and neglect of duty.

First Lieutenant Edward McCaffrey, 79th Pennsylvania Volunteers, to date January 5, 1865, for absence without leave.

First Lieutenant Thomas H. Y. Bickham, 19th United States Infantry, to date January 5, 1865, for disobedience of orders, absence without leave, and not accounting for public money in his possession.

For the Week ending January 14, 1865.

Major Henry Plessner, 9th Ohio Cavalry, to date January 11, 1865, for conduct unbecoming an officer and gentleman, incompetency, cowardice, and utter worthlessness as an officer.

Major Napoleon B. Brown, 101st Illinois Volunteers, to date January 12, 1865, for incompetency and worthlessness.

Captain E. M. Ives, 42d United States Colored Troops, to date January 7, 1865, for having tendered his resignation while under charges (conduct unbecoming an officer and a gentleman, and appropriating to his own use rations issued to his company).

Captain James D. Austin, 53d United States Colored Infantry, to date January 9, 1865, for having tendered his resignation "for the good of the service."

The following officers, as of the dates set opposite their respective names, for the causes mentioned, having been published officially, and failed to appear before the Commission:—

Desertion.

Captain James Connor, 124th Indiana Volunteers, to date October 4, 1864.

Absence without leave, and disobedience of orders.

Captain Thomas M. Gibson, 33d Missouri Volunteers, to date December 22, 1864.

Absence without leave.

Captain J. W. Day, 1st Indiana Heavy Artillery, to date December 22, 1864.

First Lieutenant Augustus W. Hoff, 3d Maryland Volunteers, to date December 22, 1864.

Second Lieutenant John Boker, 15th New York Artillery, to date December 22, 1864.

Captain Gasper Wolfe, 15th New York Artillery, to date December 22, 1864.

First Lieutenant William S. Mead, 69th Ohio Veteran Volunteers, to date January 7, 1865, for absence without leave.

First Lieutenant Clinton Beach, Regimental Quartermaster 16th United States Colored Troops, to date January 7, 1865, with a forfeiture of all pay and allowances now due, or that may become due, for having tendered his resignation on the ground of incompetency, and having acknowledged over his own signature to the selling of two barrels of United States coffee to a trader, the same having been drawn by him for issue to his regiment.

First Lieutenant Albert St. Clair, 10th Tennessee Volunteers, to date January 10, 1865, for drunkenness and desertion.

First Lieutenant William H. Castle, 105th Ohio Volunteers, to date January 10, 1865, for desertion.

First Lieutenant James C. Weems, 8th Tennessee Volunteers, to date October 27, 1864, "for having tendered his resignation for the good of the service, while his command was in the face of the enemy."

The following officers of the 16th Kansas Cavalry, to date January 10, 1865, for withdrawing from the lines, without proper leave, in the presence of the enemy:—

First Lieutenant Henry T. Stith.
Second Lieutenant Silas Dexter.

Second Lieutenant Peter Gordon, 16th United States Colored Troops, to date January 7, 1865, for having tendered his resignation on the ground of dissatisfaction with the branch of the service with which he was connected.

For the Week ending January 21, 1865.

Colonel John F. Tyler, 1st Infantry, Missouri State Militia, to date January 13, 1865, for fraudulent conduct in connection with transportation passes, trading in substitutes, and sanctioning the same in employés under his control, he being at the time on duty as Assistant Provost-Marshal.

Colonel John E. Wynkoop, 20th Pennsylvania Cavalry, to date January 18, 1865.

First Lieutenant William McIlwrath, 9th Cavalry, Missouri State Militia, to date January 18, 1865, for causing a communication to be published in which his superior officers are treated with contempt and disrespect.

For the Week ending January 28, 1865.

The following-named officers, to date January 2, 1865, for the causes mentioned, having been published officially and failed to appear before the Commission:—

For defrauding men enlisted by him of their local bounty.

Captain Timothy Pearson, 15th Massachusetts Battery.

Absence without leave.

First Lieutenant F. D. Martin, 52d New York Volunteers.
Captain Hugh F. Ozone, 170th New York Volunteers.
Captain Martin Laughlin, 16th New York Artillery.
First Lieutenant Michael McIntire 3d Michigan Cavalry.
First Lieutenant David K. Mitchell, 119th Pennsylvania Volunteers.
Captain Charles Hilbert, 17th New York Volunteers, to date January 23, 1865, for absence without leave, and the good of the service.
Captain John W. Fenton, 132d New York Volunteers, to date January 23, 1865, for conduct unbecoming an officer, in entering an eating-saloon at Newbern, North Carolina, kept by a colored man, creating a disturbance therein, and assaulting the said proprietor. This while he, the said Fenton, was in company with an improper female character.
Captain Henry McCabe, 8th Cavalry, Missouri State Militia, to date January 23, 1865, for habitual drunkenness, and neglect of duty.
First Lieutenant E. H. Johnson, 1st Maryland Potomac Home Brigade Cavalry, to date January 25, 1865, for incompetency, utter worthlessness, and neglect of duty.
Second Lieutenant Wallace Keller, 16th New York Cavalry, to date January 23, 1865, for absence without leave.

Dishonorably Discharged.

Captain Augustus Hani, 204th Pennsylvania Volunteers (5th Pennsylvania Heavy Artillery), to date January 3, 1865, for having tendered his resignation on the ground of incompetency.

Dishonorably Mustered Out.

The following officers of the 35th Kentucky Volunteers, from date of muster-in, for violation of paragraph 89, Mustering Regulations, in transferring men from company to company, thereby fraudulently swelling the ranks to secure improper musters into the service of the United States:—

Colonel Edmund A. Starling.
Lieutenant-Colonel Edward R. Weir, Jr.

Dropped from the Rolls of the Army.

The order heretofore issued dropping Captain James S. Hall, Signal Corps United States Army, from the rolls, has been revoked.

Dismissal Amended.

The order of dismissal heretofore issued in the case of Captain Francis J. Matther, 86th Indiana Volunteers, has been amended to read Captain Francis J. Mattler.

Dismissals Revoked.

The orders of dismissal heretofore issued in the following cases have been revoked:—

Colonel Edward Bacon, 6th Michigan Heavy Artillery, and he is honorably discharged, to date October 31, 1864.

Surgeon William H. Tanner, 178th New York Volunteers, and he is honorably discharged, to date November 22, 1864.

Second Lieutenant Jerome McBride, Veteran Reserve Corps.

Second Lieutenant P. J. Champion, Veteran Reserve Corps.

Captain Michael Gleason, 23d Illinois Volunteers.

Captain R. W. Houghton, 3d New Hampshire Volunteers, and he is honorably discharged, to date November 19, 1864.

Lieutenant W. H. Bicker, 3d Pennsylvania Cavalry, and he is honorably discharged, as of the date at which he reached a loyal State after his release by the rebels.

The order heretofore issued cashiering First Lieutenant Francis A. Young, 20th Regiment Veteran Reserve Corps, has been revoked.

Exempt from Dismissal.

WAR DEPARTMENT,
ADJUTANT-GENERAL'S OFFICE,
WASHINGTON, Jan. 23, 1865.

The following-named officers, charged with offences, and heretofore published, are exempt from being dismissed the service of the United States, the Military Commission instituted by Special Orders No. 53, series of 1863, from the War Department, having reported that satisfactory defence has been made in their respective cases:—

Colonel William T. Lynch, 58th Illinois Volunteers.

Chaplain Samuel Day, 8th Illinois Volunteers.

Surgeon Charles E. Cady, 138th Pennsylvania Volunteers, charged with offences, and heretofore published, is exempt from being dismissed the service of the United States, he having made satisfactory defence before a Board of Officers, convened by General Orders No. 33, November 16, 1864, from Head-quarters 6th Army Corps.

WASHINGTON, Jan. 30, 1865.

Captain J. W. Day, 1st Indiana Heavy Artillery, charged with offences, and heretofore published, is exempt from being dismissed the service of the United States, he having made satisfactory defence to the charge of absence without leave before a Military Commission convened in the field.

E. D. TOWNSEND,
Assistant Adjutant-General.

Restored to Commission.

The following officers, heretofore dismissed, have been restored, with pay from the date at which they rejoin their regiments for duty:—

Chaplain Asa S. Fiske, 4th Minnesota Volunteers, provided the vacancy has not been filled, evidence of which must be obtained from the regimental commander.

Second Lieutenant Justus E. Bell, 6th Minnesota Volunteers, provided the vacancy has not been filled, evidence of which must be obtained from the Governor of his State.

Lieutenant-Colonel R. S. Donaldson, 50th United States Colored Troops.

Captain James H. Greene, 8th Wisconsin Volunteers, provided the vacancy has not been filled by the Governor of his State.

Additional Paymaster William W. White, United States Volunteers.

Captain Theodore Conkey, 3d Wisconsin Cavalry, provided the vacancy has not been filled, evidence of which must be obtained from the Governor of his State.

Second Lieutenant George A. Tappan, 82d United States Colored Infantry, provided the vacancy has not been filled, evidence of which must be obtained from the Commanding General Department of the Gulf.

Captain Charles E. Robinson, Commissary of Subsistence, United States Volunteers, heretofore dismissed, has been restored to his position and rank in the service.

E. D. TOWNSEND,
Assistant Adjutant-General.

Regular Navy.
Orders, &c.

Jan. 24.—Commodore H. K. Thatcher, detached from command of the Colorado, and appointed to command the West Gulf Squadron. Commodore James S. Palmer, relieved from the command of the West Gulf Squadron, on the arrival of Commodore Thatcher, and granted permission to either return North or remain on duty in the Squadron. Commodore William Radford, ordered to command the James River Division of the North Atlantic Squadron.

Jan. 16.—Captain A. K. Long, detached from Court at Boston, on the reporting of his relief.

Jan. 18.—Captain William Rodgers Taylor, detached from command of the Juniata, and granted sick leave.

Jan. 19.—Captain H. S. Stellwagen, detached from the command of the Constellation, and waiting orders.

Jan. 28.—Captain Charles S. Boggs, detached from special duty at New York, and ordered to command the Connecticut.

Jan. 30.—Captain James M. Alden, detached from command of the Brooklyn, and waiting orders.

Jan. 12.—Commander John J. Almy, detached from special duty at New York, and ordered to command the Juniata.

Jan. 18.—Commander E. W. Carpenter, detached from duty on Court-Martial at Boston, and also from duty as Prize Commissioner at Key West, Fla. Commander M. C. Marin, detached from Ordnance duty at Boston, and ordered to duty on Court-Martial.

Jan. 20.—Commander Edward Donaldson, detached from Ordnance duty at Baltimore, and ordered to command the Receiving-Ship Constellation at Norfolk, Va.

Jan. 23.—Commander John Guest, detached from command of the Iosco on the reporting of his relief, and ordered North. Commander Edward Donaldson's orders to command the Receiving-Ship Constellation revoked.

Jan. 24.—Commander A. S. Baldwin, detached from Inspector's duty at New York Yard, and ordered to command the Receiving-Ship Constellation. Commander William A. Parker, detached from command of James River Division of the North Atlantic Squadron, and ordered to report to the Department.

Jan. 30.—Commander A. S. Baldwin's orders to the command of the Constellation suspended, and he will resume his duties at New York.

Jan. 2.—Lieutenant-Commander E. P. Williams, ordered to temporary Ordnance duty at Boston Navy Yard.

Jan. 4.—Lieutenant-Commander Nathaniel Green, detached from the Naval Academy, and ordered to the West Gulf Squadron. Lieutenant-Commander James A. Greer, ordered to the Naval Academy, on the completion of the duty assigned him by Acting Rear-Admiral Lee. Lieutenant-Commander William M. Gamble, ordered to the West Gulf Squadron.

Jan. 9.—Lieutenant-Commander George U. Morris, detached from the command of the Shawmut, on the reporting of his relief, and ordered to command the Chenango. Lieutenant-Commander John G. Walker, detached from the command of the Saco, and ordered to command the Shawmut. Lieutenant-Commander H. N. T. Arnold, detached from the command of the Otsego, and waiting orders.

Jan. 11.—Lieutenant-Commander Charles H. Greene, detached from the Vincennes, and ordered to report to Commodore James S. Palmer for duty in the West Gulf Squadron.

Jan. 12.—Lieutenant-Commander James W. Shirk, ordered to special service at Philadelphia.

Jan. 14.—Lieutenant-Commander James S. Thornton, ordered to report to Rear-Admiral Paulding for duty.

Jan. 20.—Lieutenant-Commander John Madigan, ordered to temporary Ordnance duty at Boston.

Jan. 23.—Lieutenant-Commander Edward Simpson, ordered to duty under Rear-Admiral Gregory. Lieutenant-Commander James S. Thornton, ordered to command the Iosco.

Jan. 25.—Lieutenant-Commander Weld N. Allen, detached from the Tuscarora, and granted sick leave. (Wounded in the attack on Fort Fisher.) Lieutenant-Commander James Parker, detached from the Minnesota, and ordered to command the Maumee. Lieutenant-Commander Ralph Chandler, detached from command of the Maumee, and ordered to report to Rear-Admiral Porter for such duty as he may assign.

Jan. 26.—Lieutenant-Commander J. N. Miller, detached from the Monadnock, on the reporting of his relief, and ordered to the Naval Academy.

Jan. 27.—Lieutenant-Commander John Madigan, ordered to special duty under Commodore T. A. Hunt.

Jan. 30.—Lieutenant-Commander Lester A. Beardslee, detached from the Wachusett on the reporting of his relief, and ordered to the Connecticut.

Jan. 11.—Lieutenant H. T. French, orders to the Juniata revoked, and granted sick leave.

Jan. 13.—Lieutenant John McFarland, detached from the East Gulf Squadron, and granted sick leave.

Jan. 18.—Lieutenant G. K. Haswell, ordered to temporary duty at Naval Rendezvous, Brooklyn, N. Y.

Jan. 19.—Lieutenant Sylvanus Bachus, detached from the Constellation, and waiting orders.

Jan. 24.—Lieutenant William F. Stewart, detached from the St. Louis, on the reporting of his relief, and ordered North. Lieutenant Edwin M. Shepard, ordered to the St. Louis.

Jan. 25.—Lieutenant Herbert B. Tyson, ordered to the Connecticut.

Jan. 26.—Lieutenant Larue P. Adams, ordered to the Monadnock.

Jan. 30.—Lieutenant John W. Philip, ordered to the Wachusett. Lieutenant Thomas L. Swan, detached from the Brooklyn, and ordered to the Naval Academy.

Jan. 2.—Ensign John C. Pegram, orders to the Dictator revoked, and ordered to the Wachusett. Acting Ensign Nicoll Ludlow, detached from the Wachusett, and ordered to the Dictator.

Jan. 10.—Ensign R. P. Huntington, detached from the Mohican, and granted sick leave.

Jan. 23.—Ensign Ira Harris, Jr., detached from the Powhatan, and granted sick leave. (Wounded in the attack on Fort Fisher.)

Jan. 30.—Acting Ensigns D. R. Cassell, C. D. Sigsbee, and C. H. Pendleton, detached from the Brooklyn, and waiting orders.

Appointed Surgeon.

Jan. 24.—Passed Assistant Surgeon Somerset Robinosn (commission dated January 13th, 1865).

Jan. 3.—Surgeon Lewis B. Hunter, detached from the Naval Rendezvous, Philadelphia, and ordered to the North Atlantic Squadron, as Fleet Surgeon. Surgeon Philip Lansdale, ordered to the Naval Rendezvous, Philadelphia, Penn.

Jan. 7.—Assistant Surgeon William Commons, ordered to the Patapsco. Assistant Surgeon S. H. Petty, detached from the Patapsco, on the reporting of his relief, and ordered North. Assistant Surgeon David Mack, Jr., detached from the Naval Hospital, Chelsea, Mass., and ordered to the Suwanee. Assistant Surgeon William K. Van Reypen, ordered to the Naval Hospital, Chelsea, Mass.

Jan. 12. Passed Assistant Surgeon A. Matthewson, detached from the Saco, and ordered to the Shawmut. Assistant Surgeon C. H. Page, detached from the Eutaw, on the reporting of his relief, and waiting orders.

Jan. 14.—Assistant Surgeon Thomas N. Penrose, ordered to the Princeton.

Jan. 19.—Surgeon John R. Messersmith and Assistant Surgeon Stephen J. Clark, detached from the Constellation, and waiting orders.

Jan. 24.—Assistant Surgeon William P. Baird, detached from the Passaic, on the reporting of his relief, and ordered North. Assistant Surgeon William Commons, orders of the 7th instant modified, and he will report for duty on board the Passaic.

Jan. 27.—Passed Assistant Surgeon M. Bradley, detached from his present duties in the Mississippi Squadron, and ordered to special duty with the Fleet Surgeon of the same squadron.

Jan. 30.—Surgeon George Maulsby and Assistant Surgeon H. S. Pitkin, detached from the Brooklyn, and waiting orders.

Appointed Assistant Paymaster.

Jan. 11.—Charles F. Guild, and to remain on duty with Rear-Admiral Porter.

Jan. 4.—Paymaster Casper Schenck, detached from the Juniata, on the reporting of his relief, and waiting orders.

Jan. 19.—Paymaster H. H. Pangborn, detached from the Constellation, on the completion of transfer, and ordered to settle his accounts.

Jan. 26.—Paymaster John S. Cunningham, detached from the Washington Navy Yard, on the reporting of his relief, and waiting orders. Paymaster James Fulton, ordered to the Navy Yard, Washington, D. C.

Jan. 30.—Paymaster G. E. Thornton, detached from the Brooklyn, on completion of transfer, and ordered to settle his accounts.

Jan. 31.—Paymaster A. H. Gilman, detached from Naval Station, Mound City, Illinois, on the reporting of his relief, and waiting orders. Paymaster R. C. Spalding, ordered to Mound City, Illinois. Paymaster William A. Ingersoll, detached from the Colorado on completion of transfer, and ordered to settle his accounts.

Jan. 3.—Chief Engineer Montgomery Fletcher, detached from the Saranac, and ordered North, on the reporting of his relief. Chief Engineer James F. Lamdin, ordered to the Saranac.

Jan. 4.—Chief Engineer W. H. Rutherford, detached from the Wachusett, on the reporting of his relief, and waiting orders.

Jan. 13.—Chief Engineer Thomas Williamson, ordered to duty under Rear-Admiral Gregory.

Jan. 30.—Chief Engineer Mortimor Kellogg, detached from the Brooklyn, and waiting orders. Chief Engineer William H. Rutherford, ordered to duty connected with the machinery of the Tonawanda.

Reinstated.

Jan. 5.—Frank W. Perkins, as a midshipman, and ordered to the Naval Academy.

Placed on the Retired List.

Jan. 27.—Lieutenant-Commander Richmond Aulick.

Resigned.

Jan. 14.—Assistant Surgeon J. H. Austin.
Jan. 16.—Assistant Surgeon William Longshaw, Jr.
Jan. 20.—Midshipman Charles C. Eames; Ensign R. P. Huntington.
Jan. 25.—Midshipman E. M. Taylor.
Jan. 27.—Midshipman W. C. Jameson.
Jan. 28.—Midshipman William H. Cole.

Revoked.

Jan. 20.—Midshipman Zachary T. Cole.

Volunteer Navy.

Orders, &c.

Jan. 17.—Acting Volunteer Lieutenant-Commander Pierre Giraud, ordered to report to Rear-Admiral Gregory for command of the Huntsville.

Jan. 25.—Acting Volunteer Lieutenant-Commander William Budd, detached from temporary duty at the Navy Yard, Portsmouth, N. H., and ordered to command the Florida.

Jan. 26.—Acting Volunteer Lieutenant-Commander Thomas P. Ives, detached from the Washington Navy Yard, and granted six (6) months' leave.

Jan. 3.—Acting Volunteer Lieutenant George D. Upham, ordered to command the Donegal.

Jan. 16.—Acting Volunteer Lieutenants E. H. Faucon, T. A. Harris, and Francis S. Wells, detached from the North Atlantic Squadron, and ordered to the Mississippi Squadron.

Jan. 20.—Acting Volunteer Lieutenant Benjamin W. Loring, ordered to the North Carolina.

Jan. 26.—Acting Volunteer Lieutenant W. H. Garfield, detached from the command of the Banshee, and ordered to the command of the Calypso. Acting Volunteer Lieutenant Frederick D. Stuart, detached from the command of the Calypso, on the reporting of his relief, and ordered to command the Emma Henry.

Jan. 31.—Acting Volunteer Lieutenant Frederick F. Baury, detached from the Colorado, and waiting orders.

Appointed Acting Masters and Pilots.

Jan. 4.—Jesse L. Forlaw and James W. Taylor, North Atlantic Squadron.
Jan. 10.—John Sayres, North Atlantic Squadron.
Jan. 11.—Forrest B. Owens, North Atlantic Squadron.
Jan. 17.—John A. Wilson, North Atlantic Squadron.
Jan. 23.—Levi Jump, North Atlantic Squadron.
Jan. 31.—Charles Tooker and Samuel O. Scranton, North Atlantic Squadron.

Jan. 3.—Acting Master F. W. Partridge, ordered to the Donegal.

Jan. 4.—Acting Master G. B. Thompson, detached from the Hetzel, on the reporting of his relief, and ordered North. Acting Master William Rogers, ordered to the Hetzel.

Jan. 6.—Acting Master N. B. Heath, detached from the Augusta, and ordered to the West Gulf Squadron.

Jan. 9.—Acting Master N. B. Heath, orders of the 6th instant revoked, and he will remain attached to the Augusta. Acting Master Charles Potter, orders to the West Gulf Squadron revoked, and he is granted sick leave.

Jan. 11.—Acting Master J. F. Alcorn, ordered to the Isonomia.

Jan. 13.—Acting Master H. L. Sturges, detached from special duty with the Army, and ordered to report to Rear-Admiral Porter. Acting Master E. M. Stoddard, ordered to the Naval Rendezvous, State street, New York. Acting Master C. H. Baxter, ordered to the North Carolina.

Jan. 19.—Acting Masters Abram Allen, A. W. Kempton, and E. B. Mallett, detached from the Constellation, and waiting orders.

Jan. 20.—Acting Master W. F. Hunt, detached from the Saco, and ordered to the Annie. Acting Master J. R. Wheeler, ordered to the command of the Annie. Acting Master William F. North, ordered to the Constellation.

Jan. 23.—Acting Master Joseph Marthon, ordered to the Chenango. Acting Master Charles F. Langley, detached from duty under Rear-Admiral Gregory, and ordered to the Chenango.

Jan. 24.—Acting Master C. W. Buck, ordered to the Coast Survey Steamer Vixen.

Jan. 25.—Acting Master W. H. Hubbs, ordered to the Connecticut.

Jan. 27.—Acting Master George F. Wilkins, detached from the Union, and ordered to the command of the W. G. Anderson.

Jan. 30.—Acting Master C. W. Lamson, ordered to the Florida. Acting Master Robert Barstow, detached from the Brooklyn, and waiting orders. Acting Master Edmund Kemble, detached from command of the Niphon, and ordered to the West Gulf Squadron.

Jan. 31.—Acting Masters Edwin Coffin and L. B. King, detached from the Colorado, and waiting orders.

Appointed Acting Ensigns and Pilots.

Jan. 4.—Charles Tengwall, U. S. S. Commodore Perry; J. J. Kelleher, U. S. S. Samuel Rotan; William J. Lewis, U. S. S. Lackawanna; H. D. Packard, U. S. S. Pink; F. R. Jaschke, U. S. S. Tritonia.

Jan. 5.—George A. Thompson, Picket-Boat No. 3; George Thomas, Potomac Flotilla.

Jan. 11.—F. W. Worstel, U. S. S. Tacony; William H. Brown, U. S. S. Wyalusing.

Jan. 17.—G. L. Sands, U. S. S. Powhatan; Thomas Brown, U. S. S. Pontoosuc; G. H. Dexter, U. S. S. Clyde.

Jan. 23.—B. F. Fries, U. S. S. Supply.

Jan. 25.—Thomas E. Ashmead, waiting orders.

Jan. 31.—J. B. Tew, U. S. S. Quaker City; Charles H. Smitten, U. S. S. Union.

Appointed Acting Ensigns, and ordered to the School-Ship Savannah.

Jan. 3.—John E. Smith. *Jan.* 4.—Edward J. Maitland.
Jan. 9.—Alfred H. Martine. *Jan.* 10.—Charles B. Pyne.
Jan. 17.—Charles W. Richardson. *Jan.* 19.—John R. P. Atkins.
Jan. 20.—Allen W. Snow and L. Granville Sampson.
Jan. 21.—G. H. Barry and George W. Beverley.
Jan. 23.—Allen W. Cobb and William S. W. Cragin.
Jan. 24.—Franklin Young and Charles A Gallishan.
Jan. 26.—Thomas C. Kelley. *Jan.* 28.—Leonard Denton.
Jan. 31.—Noah D. Joyce and Otis L. Haskell.

Appointed Acting Ensigns.

Jan. 3.—James Hobbs and William F. Gragg, North Atlantic Squadron.

Jan. 17.—Samuel Weskett and John Brown, North Atlantic Squadron.

Jan. 3.—Acting Ensign P. N. Luce, detached from the Augusta, and ordered to the Donegal. Acting Ensign F. P. Bibles, detached from the Cornubia, and ordered to the Donegal. Acting Ensign E. B. J. Singleton, detached from the Vermont, on the reporting of his relief, and ordered to the Niphon. Acting Ensign C. F. Dunderdale, detached from the Savannah, on the reporting of his relief, and ordered to the Calypso. Acting Ensign A. D. Stover, ordered to the Savannah. Acting Ensign Peter Howard, ordered to the Vermont. Acting Ensign Christopher Carven, ordered to the Niphon. Acting Ensign J. D. Hademan, ordered to the Niphon.

Jan. 5.—Acting Ensign William Brown, detached from the Constellation, and ordered to the Cambridge.

Jan. 7.—Acting Ensign Charles E. Beck, detached from the Cambridge, and granted sick leave.

Jan. 10.—Acting Ensign Richard Bates, detached from the North Atlantic Squadron, and ordered to the Mississippi Squadron for special duty. Acting Ensign E. N. Semon, ordered to the Naval Rendezvous, State.

Jan. 11.—Acting Ensign Oliver P. Knowles, detached from the Stepping-Stones, and waiting orders. Acting Ensign Thomas J. Rollins, detached from the Saco, and waiting orders.

Jan. 12.—Acting Ensign Charles Ekman, detached from the Somerset, on the reporting of his relief, and ordered North. Acting Ensign Orlando S. Roberts, detached from the Stars and Stripes, on the reporting of his relief, and ordered North. Acting Ensign W. A. Abbott, detached from the National Guard, and ordered to the Stars and Stripes.

Jan. 13.—Acting Ensign James T. Bowling, detached from the Magnolia, on the reporting of his relief, and ordered North. Acting Ensign Arnold Harris, detached from special duty with the Army, and ordered to report to Rear-Admiral Porter. Acting Ensign C. F. Dunderdale, detached from the Calypso, and ordered to the North Carolina. Acting Ensign William Symonds, ordered to the North Carolina. Acting Ensign E. T. Strong, ordered to the Naval Rendezvous, Brooklyn, N. Y.

Jan. 17.—Acting Ensign Edward Ryan, detached from the Para, on the reporting of his relief, and ordered North.

Jan. 18.—Acting Ensign J. W. Almy, ordered to the Chimo. Acting Ensign Henry D. Whittemore, detached from the Savannah, and ordered to the Calypso.

Jan. 19.—Acting Ensign O. P. Knowles, ordered to the National Guard. Acting Ensigns William H. McLean and H. D. Foster, detached from the (late) Otsego, and ordered to the Constellation. Acting Ensigns E. H. Miller and George H. Drew, detached from the Constellation, and waiting orders.

Jan. 20.—Acting Ensign Chas. E. Rich, detached from the Eutaw, and ordered to the Constellation. Acting Ensign A. D. Stover, detached from the Savannah, and ordered to the Annie. Acting Ensign O. F. Wixon, detached from the Saco, and ordered to the Mohican. Acting Ensign A. H. Ostrander, detached from the Saco, and ordered to the Potomac Flotilla. Acting Ensign Wm. H. Platt, detached from the Saco, and ordered to the Potomac Flotilla.

Jan. 23.—Acting Ensign A. A. Franzen, detached from the John Adams, on the reporting of his relief, and ordered North. Acting Ensign A. R. Hazard, detached from the Suwanee, and granted sick leave.

Jan. 25.—Acting Ensigns James Bertwistle and Fred. A. O'Connor.

Jan. 26.—Acting Ensigns J. D. Hademan, E. B. J. Singleton, C. Carven, and C. J. Goodwin, detached from the Niphon, and ordered to the Connecticut.

Jan. 27.—Acting Ensign William Churchill, ordered to the South Atlantic Squadron. Acting Ensign Robt. H. Carey, detached from command of the W. G. Anderson, and ordered to the Union.

Jan. 28.—Acting Ensign George M. Prindle, detached from the Banshee, and ordered to the Receiving-Ship North Carolina.

Jan. 30.—Acting Ensigns C. E. Beck, T. J. Rollins, and Thomas E. Ashmead, ordered to the Florida. Acting Ensigns C. H. Littlefield and H. H. Arthur, detached from the Brooklyn, and waiting orders.

Jan. 31.—Acting Ensign Franklin C. Ford, detached from the Keystone State, and granted sick leave. Acting Ensigns J. L. Vennard and Willis G. Perry, detached from the Colorado. Acting Ensign Charles H. Smitten, detached from the Union, on her arrival at Key West, and ordered to report to Acting Rear-Admiral Stribling for duty in the East Gulf Squadron. Acting Ensign James E. Hurlburt, detached from the Massachusetts, and ordered to the South Atlantic Squadron.

Appointed Acting Master's Mates.

Jan. 4.—George H. Russell, U. S. S. Cornubia; Thomas S. Flood, U. S. S. Portsmouth; Charles Heath, U. S. S. Glide; Charles Harcourt, U. S. S. Metacomet; William R. Campbell, U. S. S. Eolus.

Jan. 7.—Charles R. Patterson, U. S. S. Don.

Jan. 9.—George Emerson, U. S. S. Iosco; A. J. Holtzman, Potomac Flotilla.

Jan. 10.—Harry Setly, Potomac Flotilla; George H. Fletcher, U. S. S. Constellation.

Jan. 11.—John C. Howard, U. S. S. Shamrock.

Jan. 17.—G. T. Hohn, U. S. bark Restless.

Jan. 31.—Thomas J. Kelley, U. S. S. Ohio.

Appointed Acting Master's Mates, and ordered to the School-Ship Savannah.

Jan. 9.—Frank W. Turner.

Jan. 14.—William C. Davie and Henry M. Page.

Jan. 16.—E. F. Crawford.

Jan. 19.—Anthony T. Jennings.

Jan. 23.—Gideon V. Brownell.

Jan. 27.—James Moran and Gilbert H. Prindle.

Jan. 4.—Acting Master's Mate John R. P. Atkins, detached from the Fort Morgan, and granted permission to report for hospital treatment at New York.

Jan. 5.—Acting Master's Mates E. D. Conover and George W. Marchant, detached from the Augusta, and ordered to the Cambridge. Acting Master's Mate E.

L. Estabrook, detached from the Augusta, and ordered to the Massachusetts. Acting Master's Mate A. Vanderbilt, ordered to the Malvern.

Jan. 6.—Acting Master's Mate James West, detached from the Richmond, and ordered to instruction on board the Savannah. Acting Master's Mate Nelson Richmond, ordered to instruction on board the Savannah.

Jan. 7.—Acting Master's Mate William H. Ketching, Jr., ordered to instruction on board the Savannah. Acting Master's Mate David Fader, ordered to instruction on board the Savannah.

Jan. 19.—Acting Master's Mates Stephen Jones, P. M. Ryder, George H. Fletcher, and M. H. Wilson, detached from the Constellation, and waiting orders. Acting Master's Mates Charles P. Weston and W. C. Howard, ordered to the Sea-Foam.

Jan. 23.—Acting Master's Mate William Smith, ordered to the Chenango.

Jan. 25.—Acting Master's Mate Thomas Dalton, detached from the Saratoga, and granted sick leave.

Jan. 27.—Acting Master's Mate John McCormick, ordered to the Princeton.

Jan. 30.—Acting Master's Mates James W. De Camp, Thomas Stanfield, R. C. Tyler, Charles Cameron, ordered to the Florida.

Jan. 31.—Acting Master's Mates Arthur B. Arey, Edward A. Gould, A. F. Tucker, Martin V. Thomas, and J. W. Wallace, detached from the Colorado, and granted leave.

Appointed Acting Assistant Surgeons.

Jan. 13.—James C. Bassett, and ordered to the Ohio.
Jan. 14.—William S. Bowen, and ordered to the Ohio.
Jan. 18.—Charles A. Manson, and ordered to the Ohio.
Jan. 19.—George F. Brickett, and ordered to the Ohio.
Jan. 20.—Granville Le Compte, and ordered to the Kanawha.
Jan. 24.—John N. Coonan, and ordered to the Wissahickon.
Jan. 28.—Augustus H. Abernethy, and ordered to the Dai Ching.

Jan. 4.—Acting Assistant Surgeon Charles S. Eastwood, detached from the State of Georgia, and ordered to the Lenapee.

Jan. 6.—Acting Assistant Surgeon H. C. Van Gieson, ordered to the Nipsic. Acting Assistant Surgeon Louis Michael, detached from the Augusta, and waiting orders.

Jan. 7.—Acting Assistant Surgeon Stephen C. Bartlett, detached from the North Carolina, and ordered to the State of Georgia.

Jan. 11.—Acting Assistant Surgeon C. S. Eastwood, orders to the Lenapee revoked, and he will remain attached to the State of Georgia. Acting Assistant Surgeon Stephen C. Bartlett, orders to the State of Georgia revoked, and ordered to the Lenapee.

Jan. 12.—Acting Assistant Surgeon John D. Malone, detached from the Shawmut, on the reporting of his relief, and ordered to the Eutaw.

Jan. 16.—Acting Assistant Surgeon George C. Reynolds, detached from the (late) Otsego, and waiting orders. Acting Assistant Surgeon George W. Hatch, detached from the Spirea, and waiting orders.

Jan. 19.—Acting Assistant Surgeon Louis Michael, ordered to the Neptune.

Jan. 20.—Acting Assistant Surgeon Wm. S. Bowan, detached from the Ohio, and ordered to the J. L. Davis.

Jan. 24.—Acting Assistant Surgeon C. H. Manson, detached from the Ohio, and ordered to the James Adger. Acting Assistant Surgeon Samuel C. Johnson, detached from the Wissahickon, on the reporting of his relief, and ordered North. Acting Assistant Surgeon W. W. Myers, detached from the James Adger, on the reporting of his relief, and ordered North. Acting Assistant Surgeon A. S. Bassett, detached from the Ohio, and ordered to the Hibiscus.

Appointed Acting Assistant Paymasters.

Jan. 3.—J. F. Reeves, and waiting orders.
Jan. 5.—B. H. Lawson, and waiting orders.
Jan. 9.—Alvin H. Humphreys, and waiting orders.
Jan. 10.—R. A. Vilas, and waiting orders.
Jan. 13.—Martin B. Patterson, and waiting orders.

Jan. 14.—William A. Carpenter, Charles N. Case, Jr., and George H. Read, and waiting orders.
Jan. 16.—J. Bayard Redfield, and waiting orders.
Jan. 17.—James W. Hanson and Thaddeus Bell, and waiting orders.
Jan. 19.—Charles P. Thompson, L. G. Morrow, and Charles A. McDaniel, and waiting orders.
Jan. 20.—H. Trumbull Stancliff and Lewis F. Whitin, and waiting orders.
Jan. 21.—Matthew T. Trumpbour and E. P. Sheldon, and waiting orders.
Jan. 28.—Theophilus Fravel, and waiting orders.

Jan. 4.—Acting Assistant Paymaster G. W. Morton, ordered to the Juniata. Acting Assistant Paymaster C. H. Boardman, ordered to the Fah-Kee. Acting Assistant Paymaster Thomas A. Swords, ordered to the Niphon.
Jan. 5.—Acting Assistant Paymaster J. H. Bulkley, ordered to the Vicksburg.
Jan. 6.—Acting Assistant Paymaster Martin Duane, detached from the Augusta, on completion of transfer, and ordered to settle his accounts.
Jan. 10.—Acting Assistant Paymaster George W. McLane, ordered to the Magnolia. Acting Assistant Paymaster L. G. Billings, ordered to the A. D. Vance.
Jan. 11.—Acting Assistant Paymaster Franklin Miller, ordered to the A. D. Vance. Acting Assistant Paymaster L. G. Billings, orders to the A. D. Vance revoked, and ordered to settle his accounts.
Jan. 14.—Acting Assistant Paymaster Charles O. Hodgdon, ordered to the Mississippi Squadron. Acting Assistant Paymaster J. S. Giraud, ordered to instruction at New York. Acting Assistant Paymaster H. D. Kimberly, order dismissing him revoked, and he will return to duty.
Jan. 16.—Acting Assistant Paymaster T. Baker, ordered to the Maratanza.
Jan. 19.—Acting Assistant Paymaster John McMahon, detached from the Napa, on the reporting of his relief, and waiting orders. Acting Assistant Paymaster E. M. Hart, ordered to the St. Mary's. Acting Assistant Paymaster H. T. B. Harris, orders to the Naubuc revoked, and ordered to the Napa.
Jan. 20.—Acting Assistant Paymaster C. P. Thompson, ordered to report to the Department for special duty. Acting Assistant Paymaster Charles H. Hill, detached from the Saco, and ordered to settle his accounts.
Jan. 21.—Acting Assistant Paymaster Charles C. Ward, ordered to the Flambeau. Acting Assistant Paymaster J. W. Holmes, detached from the Dumbarton, on the reporting of his relief, and ordered to settle his accounts. Acting Assistant Paymaster F. V. D. Horton, detached from the Flambeau, on the reporting of his relief, and ordered to settle his accounts. Acting Assistant Paymaster Rufus McConnell, ordered to instruction at New York. Acting Assistant Paymaster C. M. Case, Jr., ordered to the Casco. Acting Assistant Paymaster Charles W. Crary, ordered to the Dumbarton.
Jan. 23.—Acting Assistant Paymaster James F. Reeves, ordered to the Mississippi Squadron.
Jan. 24.—Acting Assistant Paymaster S. Thomas, Jr., ordered to the Harvest Moon. Acting Assistant Paymaster R. B. Rodney, detached from the Massachusetts, on the reporting of his relief, and ordered to settle his accounts. Acting Assistant Paymaster Lawson E. Rice, detached from the Harvest Moon, on the reporting of his relief, and ordered to the Massachusetts. Acting Assistant Paymaster A. H. Humphrey, ordered to the Annie. Acting Assistant Paymaster J. S. Giraud, ordered to the Gettysburg.
Jan. 28.—Acting Assistant Paymaster George H. Read, ordered to the Thomas Freeborn. Acting Assistant Paymaster Thaddeus Bell, ordered to the Naubuc. Acting Assistant Paymaster A. D. Bache, ordered to the Chenango. Acting Assistant Paymaster Levi F. Whitin, ordered to instruction at New York. Acting Assistant Paymaster J. B. Redfield, ordered to the Kenwood. Acting Assistant Paymaster H. B. Wetherill, detached from the Kenwood, and ordered to settle his accounts.

Promoted for Good Conduct, &c.

Jan. 1.—Acting Ensigns Thomas Stothard and Henry Welton, to Acting Masters.
Jan. 6.—Acting Ensign George W. Wood, to Acting Master.

Jan. 9.—Acting Ensigns D. Rodney Brown and Henry Pease, Jr., to Acting Masters. Acting Ensign James M. Alden, to Acting Master (for duty on the staff of Rear-Admiral Porter).
Jan. 14.—Acting Ensign George W. Adams, Jr., to be Acting Master.
Jan. 16.—Acting Ensign Abraham Rich, to be Acting Master.
Jan. 17.—Acting Ensign F. A. Miller, to be Acting Master.
Jan. 30.—Acting Ensign John F. Otis, to be Acting Master.
Jan. 31.—Acting Ensign F. P. B. Sands, to be Acting Master.

Resigned.

Jan. 3.—Acting Assistant Surgeon William Clendaniel; Acting Third Assistant Engineer Joseph P. Phillips.
Jan. 4.—Acting Volunteer Lieutenant Quincy A. Hooper; Acting Third Assistant Engineers Michael Doyle and Frank McCartley; Acting Ensign Marcus Baird.
Jan. 5.—Acting Assistant Paymaster T. E. Smith (on the reporting of his relief).
Jan. 6.—Acting Master David H. Sumner.
Jan. 10.—Acting Master R. M. Cornell; Acting Assistant Paymaster W. J. Coit (on the reporting of his relief).
Jan. 11.—Acting Ensign G. W. Hammond. Acting Third Assistant Engineer Edward W. Maples.
Jan. 13.—Acting Assistant Paymaster S. T. Savage (on the transfer of his accounts to his successor).
Jan. 14.—Acting Assistant Paymaster W. W. Bassett.
Jan. 17.—Acting Master and Pilot William Reed; Acting Ensign Thomas S. Russell; Acting Assistant Paymaster Charles H. Noyes.
Jan. 18.—Acting Assistant Surgeon William H. Taggert.
Jan. 19.—Acting Assistant Paymaster James Garnett (to take effect on the reporting of his relief).
Jan. 20.—Acting Ensign William Symonds; Acting Assistant Surgeon J. F. A. Adams; Acting Assistant Surgeon Franklin W. Brigham.
Jan. 23.—Acting Ensign John D. Barclay.
Jan. 28.—Acting Assistant Paymaster D. A. Dickinson (to take effect on the reporting of his relief); Acting Assistant Surgeon John R. Richardson.
Jan. 30.—Acting Assistant Paymaster H. T. Mansfield.

Jan. 4.—Acting Master's Mate Thomas Topliffe.
Jan. 11.—Acting Master's Mate J. G. Bache.
Jan. 12.—Acting Master's Mate A. J. Emery.
Jan. 20.—Acting Master's Mate E. D. W. Parsons.
Jan. 25.—Acting Master's Mate Charles Seymour.
Jan. 31.—Acting Master's Mate Edward Thompson.

Revoked.

Jan. 10.—Acting Ensign Milton Griffiths.
Jan. 14.—Acting Ensign Horace T. Draper.
Jan. 16.—Acting Ensign George Gairy.
Jan. 19.—Acting Ensign Benjamin F. Macintire.
Jan. 25.—Acting Ensigns Harrison B. Cleaves and Frank Watson.
Jan. 31.—Acting Ensign and Pilot Benjamin F. Ricketson.

Jan. 4.—Acting Master's Mate Henry E. Holbrook.

Dismissed.

Jan. 7.—Acting Ensign James R. Smith.
Jan. 17.—Acting Assistant Paymaster A. B. Thornton.
Jan. 18.—Acting Master Enos O. Adams.

Jan. 6.—Acting Master's Mate Dennis Carroll.
Jan. 28.—Acting Master's Mate Thomas H. Lawrence.

SHERMAN'S ATLANTA CAMPAIGN.

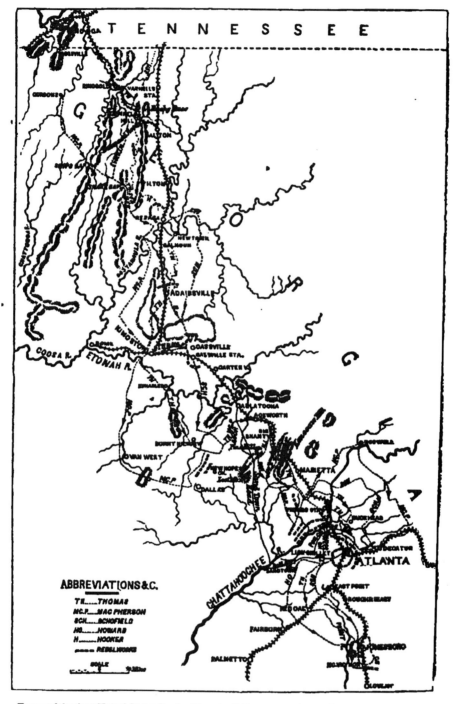

Engraved for the "United States Service Magazine," from a complete and accurate map just prepared by the U. S. Coast Survey, and kindly furnished for the purpose.

THE UNITED STATES SERVICE MAGAZINE.

VOL. III.—APRIL, 1865.—NO. IV.

SHERMAN'S ATLANTA CAMPAIGN.

BY COLONEL S. M. BOWMAN.

THE military situation of the United States on the opening of spring, 1864, indicated preparation for campaigns and operations heretofore unexampled during the progress of the war. For weeks previous to the month of May, all the railways and water-courses in the loyal States were crowded with soldiers returning to their respective regiments, and with new recruits hastening to the front, to bear a hand in the impending conflict. Transports laden with enormous quantities of ordnance stores and supplies, for a while literally monopolized all the thoroughfares of trade and travel, and evidently the then coming military operations were designed to test the power and resources of the Confederacy to the utmost extent.

Grant had been made lieutenant-general, and put in command of all the armies of the United States. Never before in America had a general been put in command of armies so large, and operating over territory of such vast extent. His armies dotted the continent from the Potomac to the Rio Grande, and thence around and along the sea-coast, and back to the Chesapeake. His lines might have been traced by the smoke of camp-fires along the rivers, through the valleys, on the hill-tops, over the mountains, across the plains, and around the coast, throughout a zigzag journey of five thousand miles.

Entered according to Act of Congress, in the year 1865, by C. B. RICHARDSON, in the Clerk's Office of the District Court for the Southern District of New York.

Nor had the Navy Department been idle. Small and almost powerless at the beginning of the war, our Navy had now become a powerful co-operating force, and could already point with just pride to achievements scarcely less valuable and glorious than the work done by the Army. And at the time Grant and Sherman were ready to start on their great parallel campaigns— May 1, 1864—not less than six hundred vessels of war hung like an electric cloud, and flashed their signal-lights along twenty-five hundred miles of rebel coast; four thousand heavy guns were in readiness to thunder at rebel defences; and while, throughout the vast circuit of the Army of the United States, *reveillé* and roll-call vexed the sun in his morning walk across the continent, fifty thousand seamen, on ship-board, answered " ay," and ready for duty.

By the 1st of May the plans of the Lieutenant-general began to develop. Grant, himself, proposed to strike at Richmond, the head of the Confederacy, and at Lee's army, the visor that had so effectually protected it, while Sherman was to pierce its heart and destroy its vitals. It was left to the Navy to paralyze its Briarean arms and break its ribs.

The two great campaigns were parallel and concurrent, but not strictly co-operative. Grant's *point d'appui* was on the Rapidan, while Sherman's was at Chattanooga in Tennessee. The Alleghany Mountains separated them, and a thousand miles of distance intervened, so that after the start, frequent communication was impossible. Sherman could only reach Atlanta, his objective point, by a single line of railway, across a wild and mountainous country, and each day's march would only put him so much farther into the wilderness. Grant could change his base at pleasure as he advanced, and according to circumstances, with water communication, and transports within hailing distance, and no danger from lack of subsistence or munitions of war. Sherman would have to drive the enemy back, recover and repair the railroad, and then protect it or perish. Sherman's troops were composed of men chiefly from the Northwest,—men who had spent their youth in subduing the forest, inured to hardship and toil; active, intelligent, brave, and withal happy in the recollection of victories won in previous campaigns. Grant had what was left of that brave old Army of the Potomac that had fought under McClellan, McDowell, Pope, Burnside, Hooker, and Meade, against the best troops of the South, and against the best generals of the Confederacy—an army worthy of everlasting remembrance for its sufferings, patience, courage and perseverance, not less than for victories won at Antietam and Gettysburg. The balance of his command was composed, chiefly, of new recruits and colored troops.

Sherman had estimated the force required to reach and capture Atlanta at one hundred thousand men and two hundred and fifty pieces of artillery; he started with ninety-eight thousand seven hundred and ninety-seven men and two hundred and fifty-four guns. This force was divided as follows:—Army of the Cumberland, Major-General Thomas, sixty thousand seven hundred and seventy-three men, one hundred and thirty guns; Army of the Tennessee, Major-General McPherson, twenty-four thousand four hundred and sixty-five men, ninety-six guns; Army of the Ohio, Major-General Schofield, thirteen thousand five hundred and fifty-nine men, twenty-eight guns. Sherman's intention was to make these proportions fifty thousand, thirty-five thousand, and fifteen thousand, but that wretched *fiasco* known as the Red River Expedition kept back some of McPherson's troops, and, besides ruining itself, did as much as possible towards impeding Sherman. However, it will be seen he was promptly furnished within twelve hundred of the number he asked for.

By the 1st of May, Sherman had made all things ready. Few persons except his admiring army, and the careful student of military history, will ever appreciate the remarkable skill which Sherman had exhibited in selecting and mobilizing his forces; in providing his transportation; in guarding by many devices his lines of communication; in disposing and strengthening his outposts and garrisons over that immense stretch of country which lay far to the rear under his care, and the successful invasion of which would not only have brought inconceivable loss and chagrin to our cause, but might, perhaps, have checked and ruined his campaign. As in the East it was needful to so dispose of the troops that no flank attack on Maryland could be made, and no offensive return by Lee, as he was forced slowly back to Richmond, so it was Sherman's task to guard his flanks and rear from Forrest's Cavalry, the strongest and best body of that arm in the Confederate service, and led by a most daring and indefatigable officer. But the Richmond campaign had the simplest possible task in this respect—the mere sealing of one single defile between mountain ridges, the closing of the Shenandoah Valley by a respectable army of occupation. Sherman had hundreds of miles over which to stretch his scanty chain of outposts, and to depend on skill in disposition to make up for the wide stretch of country in which he played his gigantic game. In the actual result, while Early raided once through the length and breadth of Maryland, defeating and driving our troops back into the very breastworks of Baltimore and Washington; while a second time he marched into the heart of Pennsylvania, burning our towns and exacting forced contributions; while yet a third time he crossed the Potomac with his cavalry, and pillaged and preyed again on Maryland—Sherman kept his vast tract of country in his own control, and every attempt on the part of the enemy to destroy his communications resulted in his own disaster.

On the 6th of May, Thomas lay at Ringgold, McPherson at Gordon's Mill, on the Chickamauga, and Schofield at Red Clay, on the Georgia line. The Confederate General Johnston was in and about Dalton, sixty thousand strong—fifty thousand infantry in the three corps of Hardee, Hood, and Polk, all able men, and ten thousand cavalry under Wheeler. The latter force exceeded ours.

Whoever is familiar with the country in Northern Georgia, knows that to have driven an army like Johnston's directly back from Dalton to Atlanta, by an attack in front on his positions, would have been a sheer impossibility. But Sherman ascertained that fact very soon, and did not resort to doubtful experiment to prove it to others. He had arranged at the outset a series of movements which, being successful, gave him the title of the "great flanker."

McPherson's army was at once moved from Gordon's Mill, by a rapid and circuitous march of thirty to forty miles, through Snake Creek Gap, to Resaca, a point eighteen miles below Dalton, on the Western and Atlanta Railroad, and, of course, on the enemy's left flank and rear. Meanwhile, on the 7th of May, Thomas marched directly from Ringgold, seized the strong position at Tunnel Hill, driving the enemy's cavalry before him, and confronted his position at Dalton. This latter point was covered by the Great Rocky Face Ridge, cloven by the narrow Buzzard Roost Gap, through which the railroad runs. This gap was well stocked with *abattis*, was artificially flooded by the waters of a creek, and swept from end to end by batteries posted on the spurs on either side, and from a commanding ridge at the farther end. Of course, it was out of the question to carry it. But Thomas made a strong feint against the gap, while Schofield moved down on Dalton from Cleveland, about thirty miles northeast from Chattanooga. On the 9th, Thomas renewed his attack so vigorously, that Veicht's Division of Howard's (Fourth) Corps, in the language of Sherman's official report (for of this we must now begin to make use), "carried the ridge, and turning south towards Dalton, found the crest too narrow, and too well protected by rock epaulements, to enable him to reach the gorge, or pass." Geary's Division of Hooker's Twentieth Corps, also, remarkably distinguished itself by its bold push for the rocky summit. In a word, so well was the whole demonstration carried out, that McPherson was able to reach within a mile of Resaca, finding only a picket force to oppose him. On the 8th, he reached Snake Creek Gap, completely surprising a brigade of cavalry which was coming to watch and hold it. Sherman's instructions to him had been, to either carry Resaca or to break up the railroad at some point below Dalton, by a bold attack, and then to fall back to a strong defensive point near Snake

Creek, and stand ready to fall upon the enemy's flank when he retreated, " as" (says Sherman) " I judged he would."

But McPherson found that the wily enemy had taken care to make Resaca too strong for his assault, and there was no cross-road leading rapidly to the railroad. He, therefore, fell back on Snake Creek Gap.

On the 10th, therefore, Sherman sent Hooker's Corps of Thomas's army over to McPherson's support; followed it by Palmer's (Fourteenth), and then by all of Schofield's army. Howard's Corps alone was left to amuse Johnston in front, all the rest of the army being in motion, next day, on Snake Creek Gap and Resaca. McPherson had already led off once more against this latter point, preceded by Kilpatrick's Cavalry, which drove the enemy from a cross-road two miles this side of Resaca, after a sharp skirmish. Thanks to the dense forests, and the inconceivably rough and impracticable nature of the intervening country, which made the forced march of our gallant troops painful and slow; and thanks to the prudence and skill of Johnston, in preparing good roads for himself from Dalton to Resaca, in anticipation of emergency, the enemy was able to reach Resaca before us, in spite of all our efforts. But Sherman's bold and handsome movement brought the enemy down from his stronghold at Dalton, and Howard entered that town and pressed his rear. In this way, eighteen miles of the railroad line, to be carried, were already gained. Our losses at Rocky Face Ridge were rather less than one thousand killed and wounded, chiefly sustained by the Divisions of Geary, Wood, and Newton. The enemy's loss was less than our own.

On the 12th and 13th of May, our army, as has been said, deployed through Snake Creek Gap, Kilpatrick's advance skirmishing with the enemy, as did also the Fifteenth and Sixteenth Corps of Infantry at Resaca, on the 14th. Sherman found his opponent admirably posted. Without an instant's delay, he pontooned the Oostanaula, which the railroad passes at this point, and dispatched Sweeney's Division of the Sixteenth Corps to cross and threaten Calhoun, and Garrard's Cavalry Division to break the railroad between Calhoun and Kingston. There was heavy fighting in front of Resaca on the same day; but on the next—the 15th—the whole army attacked in front, with McPherson on the right, Thomas in the centre, and Schofield on the left, Howard connecting on the extreme left. Johnston's veteran army was in position, with Hood on the right, Hardee in the centre, and Polk on the left. On the 14th, there was no advantage gained by us; our left centre and left were chiefly engaged, and at one time were so closely pressed that Hooker's Corps was sent across from the right centre, our troops then succeeded in checking the enemy's attack. But the right took advantage of this movement to secure some important heights in its front. On the 15th, the tables were turned. Hooker's Corps, with Butterfield's Division in front, supported by those of Geary and Williams, carried by assault one of the enemy's strongest positions in their front, capturing four fine guns and many prisoners. That night Johnston escaped across the Oostanaula to Calhoun, burning the railroad bridge behind him. Our loss in the series of engagements known as the battle of Resaca was about five thousand, not a few of which being only slightly wounded, afterwards returned to duty. McLean's Division of the Twenty-third Corps suffered severely on the 14th. The enemy lost probably half as many as we in killed and wounded, and left in our hands nearly a thousand prisoners, eight guns, and many stores.

After the victory at Resaca, the whole army pressed on in rapid pursuit—now directly, now by circuitous routes, now pontooning, now struggling over bad roads, and always moving as skilfully, and by as many different roads, as possible. Sherman, directing all with an eagle eye, already on the 17th, had thrown J. C. Davis's Division of the Fourteenth Corps out to Rome, which it occupied, securing its forts, eight or ten heavy guns, seven fine mills and foundries.

On the 17th, there was a sharp artillery engagement at Adairsville, just below Calhoun, by Newton's Division in our advance. But the enemy continued to retreat, and, on the 18th, after some heavy skirmishing by the Twentieth and Twenty-third Corps, Kingston fell into our hands; and here Sherman gave his gallant troops a few days of much-needed rest, busy himself, meanwhile, in hurrying forward supplies for the future, and in re-establishing railroad and telegraphic communication with Chattanooga, which he did with surprising dispatch.

On the 23d of May, Sherman, leaving garrisons at Rome and Kingston, started, with twenty days' rations in his wagons, for Dallas. His object was to flank Allatoona, which was too strong to be carried in front. His troops covered many different roads, and were pushed along with boldness, skill, and celerity, although the country was very rugged, mountainous, and densely wooded, with few and obscure roads. Thomas's advance, on the 14th, had sharp skirmishing with the enemy's cavalry at Burnt Hickory, and, on the 25th, another skirmish at Pumpkin-Vine Creek, from which Hooker's Corps dislodged them. This latter skirmish at length led to a general engagement by Geary's Division of Hooker's Corps, and, finally, the whole of Hooker's Corps, who, near Dallas, came upon the enemy's line of battle. The main struggle, which was very severe, occurred near New-Hope Church, at the junction of the Ackworth, Marietta, and Dallas Roads. This junction Sherman ordered Hooker to seize, and the latter drove the enemy rapidly towards it, but a stormy and dark night fell before the conquest was achieved.

Three days were now employed in developing our line at this new position, which the enemy had handsomely intrenched in front of the Dallas and Marietta Roads. There was constant skirmishing, besides many reconnoissances, as leads to severe engagements. On the 28th, Johnston made a bold and daring assault on McPherson, just as the latter was closing on Thomas's army. But McPherson had thrown up good breastworks, and, after a long and gallant assault, the enemy was repulsed with most fearful slaughter—twenty-five hundred killed and wounded, besides three hundred other prisoners, were left in our hands, and the enemy's loss was over three thousand. McPherson's was certainly not one-third as great. During four days of heavy and constant fighting, Sherman had been extending his lines to the left, with the intention of enveloping the enemy's right, and occupying all the roads leading back to Allatoona and Ackworth. After the bloody battle at Dallas on the 28th, Sherman paused a few days to mislead the enemy as to his intentions, and then again pushed McPherson down on the left. This move was effected with ease and safety on the 1st of June, and meanwhile the cavalry seized and held Allatoona and Allatoona Pass. Johnston abandoned his stronghold at New-Hope Church, and, on the 4th, fell back to Kenesaw Mountain. Sherman at once in person examined carefully Allatoona Pass, and decided that it was the exact spot for his secondary base, for he had foreseen the necessity of such a base in this region. He at once gave detailed instructions for its defence and garrison; had the railroad built behind him; and, on the 9th, full and excellent supplies were discharged inside his camps by rail from Chattanooga.

Two divisions of Blair's Seventeenth Corps and Long's Cavalry now came up. On the 9th of June "forward" was again sounded from our bugles. Our army moved towards Kenesaw; and as at this point occurred the only repulse in Sherman's matchless campaign, and the only point in which criticism might expect matter for any thing but instruction and admiration, it is but fair to use the precise language of Sherman himself in its description. It will be seen that his report furnishes perfect and happy explanation of our solitary check at that point.

"On the 9th of June, our communications in the rear being secure and supplies ample, we moved forward to Big Shanty.

"Kenesaw, the bold and striking Twin Mountain, lay before us, with a high range of chestnut hills trending off to the northeast, terminating to our view in another peak called Brushy Mountain. To our right was the smaller hill, called Pine Mountain, and beyond it, in the distance, Lost Mountain. All these, though links in a continuous chain, present a sharp, conical appearance, prominent in the vast landscape that presents itself from any of the hills that abound in that region. Kenesaw, Pine Mountain, and Lost Mountain, form a triangle—Pine Mountain the apex, and Kenesaw and Lost Mountain the base, covering perfectly the town of Marietta and the railroad back to the Chattahoochie. On each of these peaks the enemy had his signal stations. The summits were covered with batteries, and the spurs were alive with men, busy in felling trees, digging pits, and preparing for the grand struggle impending.

"The scene was enchanting, too beautiful to be disturbed by the harsh clamors of war, but the Chattahoochie lay beyond, and I had to reach it. On approaching close to the enemy, I found him occupying a line full two miles long, more than he could hold with his force. General McPherson was ordered to move toward Marietta, his right on the railroad; General Thomas on Kenesaw and Pine Mountain, and General Schofield off toward Lost Mountain: General Garrard's cavalry on the left, General Stoneman's on the right; and General McCook looking to our rear and communications. Our dépôt was at Big Shanty.

"By the 11th of June our lines were close up, and we made dispositions to break the line between Kenesaw and Pine Mountains. General Hooker was on its right and front, General Howard on its left and front, and General Palmer between it and the railroad. During a sharp cannonading from General Howard's right or General Hooker's left, General Polk was killed on the 14th, and on the morning of the 15th Pine Mountain was found abandoned by the enemy. Generals Thomas and Schofield advanced, and found him again strongly intrenched along the line of rugged hills connecting Kenesaw and Lost Mountain. At the same time General McPherson advanced his line, gaining substantial advantage on the left. Pushing our operations on the centre as vigorously as the nature of the ground would permit, I had again ordered an assault on the centre, when, on the 17th, the enemy abandoned Lost Mountain, and the long line of admirable breastworks connecting it with Kenesaw. We continued to press at all points, skirmishing in dense forests of timber and across most difficult ravines, until we found him again strongly posted and intrenched, with Kenesaw as his salient, his right wing thrown back to cover Marietta, and his left behind Nose's Creek, covering his railroad back to the Chattahoochie. This enabled him to contract his lines, and strengthen them accordingly.

"From Kenesaw he could look down upon our camps, and observe every movement, and his batteries thundered away, but did us little harm, on account of the extreme height, the shot and shell passing harmlessly over our heads as we lay close up against his mountain town.

"During our operations about Kenesaw the weather was villanously bad, and the rain fell almost continuously for three weeks, rendering our narrow wooded roads mere mud gulleys, so that a general movement would have been impossible; but our men daily worked closer and closer to their intrenched foe, and kept up an incessant picket firing galling to him. Every opportunity was taken to advance our general lines closer and closer to the enemy.

"General McPherson watching the enemy on Kenesaw and working his left forward; General Thomas swinging, as it were, on a grand left wheel, his left on Kenesaw connecting with General McPherson; and General Schofield all the time working to the south and east, along the old Sandtown Road. On the twenty-second, General Hooker had advanced his line, with General Schofield on his right; the enemy—Hood's Corps, with detachments from the others—suddenly sallied and attacked. The blow fell mostly on General Williams's Division of General Hooker's Corps, and a brigade of General Hascal's Division of General Schofield's army.

"The ground was comparatively open, and the enemy drove in our skirmish lines; an advance regiment of General Schofield was sent out purposely to hold him in check until some preparations could be completed for his reception; and when he reached our line of battle he received a terrible repulse, leaving his dead, wounded, and many prisoners in our hands. [In his dispatch of the same evening, Sherman said the enemy's loss was 'not less than seven hundred or eight hundred men.' Two hundred killed were left on Whittaker's front.] This is known as the affair of the 'Kulp House.' Although inviting the enemy at all times to commit such mistakes, I could not hope for him to repeat them after the examples of Dallas and 'Kulp House,' and upon studying the ground I had no alternative in my turn but to assault his lines or turn his position. Either course had its difficulties and dangers; and I perceived that the enemy and our own officers had settled down into a conviction that I would not assault fortified lines.

"All looked to me to 'outflank.' An army, to be efficient, must not settle down to one single mode of offence, but must be prepared to execute any plan which promises success. I waited, therefore, for the moral effect to make a successful assault against the enemy behind his breastworks, and resolved to attempt it at that point where success would give the largest fruits of victory. The general point selected was the left centre; because, if I could thrust a strong head of column through at that point by pushing it boldly and rapidly two and one-half miles, it would reach the railroad below Marietta, cut off the enemy's right and centre from its line of retreat, and then, by turning on either part, it could be overwhelmed and destroyed. Therefore, on the 24th of June, I ordered that an assault should be made at two points south of Kenesaw on the 27th, giving three days' notice for preparation and reconnoissance: one to be made near Little Kenesaw by General McPherson's troops, and the other about a mile further south by General Thomas's troops. The hour was fixed, and all the details given in Field Orders, No. 28, of the 24th of June. On the 27th of June the two assaults were made, at the time and in the manner prescribed, and both failed, costing us many valuable lives, among them those of Generals Harker and McCook, Colonel Rice, and others badly wounded; our aggregate loss being near three thousand, while we inflicted comparatively little loss to the enemy, who lay behind his well-formed breastworks. Failure as it was, and for which I assume the entire responsibility, I yet claim it produced good fruits, as it demonstrated to General Johnston that I would assault, and that boldly; and we also gained and held ground so close to the enemy's parapets that he could not show a head above them."

Sherman instantly, on the failure of the Kenesaw assault, again resorted to skilful manœuvring. McPherson's whole army was thrown rapidly to the Chattahoochie on the 2d of July, "and the effect was instantaneous." The enemy fell back from his position, and Sherman in person entered Marietta next morning just as the enemy's cavalry were leaving it. He at once gathered up his columns to hurl them against Johnston's flank and rear, and to catch him in the confusion of crossing the Chattahoochie; but Johnston had foreseen and provided against all this, and had covered his movement well. "On the 4th and 5th still another movement forward and in flank, after lively skirmishing, drove the enemy across the Chattahoochie." On the 7th, Schofield effected a strong and commanding lodgment on the east bank of the river, surprising the guard, capturing a gun, and laying a good pontoon and a trestle-bridge. By the 9th, after a skilful handling of troops, three good points for passing the river, above the enemy's strong *tete-du-pont* had been secured, and there remained nothing for the latter but to abandon the last of his splendid defensive positions, and leave Sherman the undisputable master of the Chattahoochie. "This," says Sherman, "was one, if not the chief object of the campaign." Atlanta, however, lay but eight miles distant, and he resolved to capture it. First, however, he gave a little rest to his gallant troops. "But in anticipation of this contingency," says Sherman, "I had collected a well-appointed force of cavalry, about two thousand strong, at Decatur, Alabama, with orders on receiving notice by telegraph to push rapidly south," and break the railroad at Opelika,—a movement which would cut off all Johnston's supplies. The telegraphic notice was given, and Sherman's specific instructions were fulfilled to the very letter by Rousseau and his cavalry, who whipped

Clanton, and broke up thirty miles of road around Opelika, and thence reached Marietta with a loss of only thirty men, his raid occupying from the 10th to the 22d. On the 7th, it should be added, Garrard's Cavalry had occupied Roswell, and burnt the factories long used by the enemy for clothing his troops. Sherman, in describing this affair with his inimitable terseness and vigor, takes occasion, as usual in his writings, to condense a volume of martial law into one sentence. "Over one of the woollen factories the nominal owner displayed the French flag, which was not respected, of course. A neutral surely is no better than one of our own citizens, and we do not permit our own citizens to fabricate clothes for hostile uses."

On the 17th day of July, the grand army moved forward, and formed lines on the Peach-tree Road. On the 18th and 19th, McPherson and Schofield swung upon the Augusta Road at and near Decatur, and broke it up effectually, and Thomas crossed Peach Tree Creek in force by numerous bridges, directly in face of the enemy's intrenched lines. Heavy fighting occurred on all these days. But on the afternoon of the 20th, while our new lines were forming, the enemy made a fearful assault. It was an attempt to employ the tactics which so often, and with such extraordinary success, were played by Mahone and other officers in Lee's army during the present Virginia campaign—a sudden and desperate rush at a gap in our lines while forming Hooker's Corps. Newton's Division of Howard's Corps, and Johnson's of Palmer's, got the shock of Hood's whole army: for it was Hood who now commanded the enemy, Johnston being relieved during Sherman's pause at the river. Newton and Johnston very hastily intrenched; but Hooker's Corps was entirely uncovered. The gallant old corps stood its ground in its customary style, and after a terrible battle, drove the enemy back to his intrenchments. The enemy lost, as General Thomas officially reported, at least five thousand men, while our loss was only seventeen hundred and thirty-three, falling almost entirely upon Hooker's Corps. The enemy left on the field (besides three hundred dead bodies he carried away), five hundred and sixty-three dead bodies, buried by our troops; about one thousand severely wounded; seven stands of colors, and many prisoners. These are official counts. On the 22d, such was the effect of the tremendous affair of the 20th, Hood broke away from his entire admirable line of defence to his final, interior position of long finished redoubts, with water between them, and *chevaux de frise* thrown down everywhere in front.

It will be remembered that, while Thomas pushed forward in front, so to speak, against Atlanta, McPherson and Schofield were drawing their forces down the railroad from Decatur, and all were now converging towards the fated city.

On the 22d, Hood made one more desperate plunge to extricate himself from the toils of his terrible antagonist. Putting force enough over in his intrenchments to hold them, he massed all the rest of his army against our left, and threw his troops forward in a tremendous attack. At first a part of our lines gave way—for McPherson's lines were not wholly formed—and for a time the issue was doubtful. Six fearful assaults were made on the Fifteenth, Sixteenth, and Seventeenth Corps; but when night fell, after one of the bloodiest, hottest, and most skilfully conducted battles of the war, victory remained on our banners. The field of battle was ours, and many of the enemy's dead and wounded, and one thousand and seventeen unhurt prisoners, fell into our hands. General Logan officially computed the enemy's dead at three thousand two hundred and forty, of which number no less than two thousand two hundred, by actual count, were buried by our troops. It was generally admitted that the average number of wounded could not make the loss of the enemy less than twelve thousand. In characteristic style, Sherman computes it at "full eight thousand." Our own total loss, by official count, was seventeen hundred and twenty-two. In this battle we captured also eighteen stand of colors, and five thousand stand of arms.

It was here that Major-General James B. McPherson fell, an event that sent sorrow to the heart of the nation. He was not only a good officer but a good man; was not only greatly admired by his officers and men, but loved by all who knew him. Noble in all his impulses, pure in all his relations, true to the integrity of his country, able in council, and great as a military chieftain, his fall was a sad calamity to our cause and country. When the fact of his death was communicated to General Sherman he was affected to tears. No one knew him better or appreciated him more than he. His remains now repose in his native Ohio, and his memory lives in the hearts of his grateful countrymen; and here we pause at his new-made grave to repeat those beautiful lines of Collins, as a most fitting apostrophe to the memory of the noble soldier and Christian gentleman:—

> "How sleep the brave, who sink to rest
> By all their country's wishes blest!
> When Spring, with dewy fingers cold,
> Returns to deck their hallowed mould,
> She there shall dress a sweeter sod
> Than Fancy's feet have ever trod.
>
> "By fairy hands their knell is rung;
> By forms unseen their dirge is sung;
> There Honor comes, a pilgrim gray,
> To bless the turf that wraps their clay;
> And Freedom shall awhile repair,
> And dwell a weeping hermit there!"

The next day Garrard returned from his cavalry raid on the

Augusta Road. He had started on the 21st for Covington, forty-two miles east from Atlanta, and in that region had destroyed two bridges, several dépôts and storehouses, a train of cars, and two thousand bales of cotton, broken the railroad, and captured two hundred prisoners and many good horses, and lost but two men.

It now only remained to break the Macon Road. For this purpose Stoneman was sent with five thousand cavalry, and McCook with four thousand men, to meet on the railroad near Lovejoy's, and to tear it up, and also to attack and drive Wheeler; and, if all things proved favorable, to push on and recover our suffering prisoners, then not far beyond. But Stoneman did not go to Lovejoy's. He tore up much of the railroad, destroyed many bridges, cars, locomotives, and stores, and got down in front of Macon; but he did not perform the exact task required of him, and on his retreat was hemmed in by Iverson, and was himself captured, together with one thousand of his men, and two guns, besides losing many in killed and wounded. McCook, meanwhile, burned the dépôt at Lovejoy's, and also five hundred wagons, killed eight hundred mules, and tore up the road until surrounded by a heavy force of infantry and cavalry, when he handsomely cut his way out, losing about five hundred men as prisoners, and among them the able Colonel Harrison. Stoneman's failure to reach Lovejoy's was the cause of McCook's retreat. "On the whole," says Sherman, with his characteristic love of truth "the cavalry raid is not deemed a success;" and this terse remark tells the whole story. Sherman is not apt to praise in doubtful cases.

Simultaneously with his cavalry raids, Sherman undertook to extend his right flank, so as to get it upon the railroad at East Point. The army of the Tennessee, now under Howard, begun the movement on the night of July 26th. By the 28th, the line was well formed. About noon of that day, Hood threw his army once more against ours in the third and last of his series of terrific assaults. "The enemy," says Sherman, "had come out of Atlanta by the Bell's Ferry Road, and formed his masses in the open fields, behind a swell of ground, and after the artillery firing I have described, advanced in parallel lines directly against the Fifteenth Corps, expecting to catch that flank in air. His advance was magnificent, but founded on an error that cost him sadly; for our men coolly and deliberately cut down his men, and, spite of the efforts of the rebel officers, his ranks broke and fled. But they were rallied again and again, as often as six times at some points, and a few of the rebel officers and men reached our lines of rail-piles only to be killed or hauled over as prisoners. These assaults occurred from noon until about four P.M., when the enemy disappeared, leaving his dead and wounded in our hands."

In this affair the enemy's loss is estimated at six thousand,

and our own at five hundred and seventy-two; our excellent intrenchments, the skilful formation of our lines, and the handling of our troops accounting for the great disparity in losses, almost inconceivable. Had Davis's Division come up, as Sherman had planned, "what was simply a repulse would have been a disastrous rout to the enemy." But the tangled forests and want of roads prevented that arrival. Besides many wounded, one hundred and six well prisoners were captured, with five stands of colors and two thousand muskets.

After this terrible repulse, the enemy suffered Sherman to extend his right flank with facility and safety, and the latter soon closed in and began the siege of Atlanta. After some shelling, and a repulse, in which we lost about four hundred men, and after a careful examination of the topography of the country, Sherman had satisfied himself that to take Atlanta he must resort to new means, and concluded to plant his armies away below on the Macon Road, the enemy's main line of supply. The grand movement was assigned for the 18th of August, and the wagons loaded with fifteen days' rations. But, just then, news came that Wheeler was off with all his cavalry, raiding on Sherman's line of communications. "I could not have asked any thing better," said Sherman, "for I have provided well for such a contingency;" for this detachment left him superior to the enemy in cavalry. He now proposed to break the West Point Railroad at Fairborn, and the Macon Road at Jonesboro, and so force the evacuation of Atlanta by means of cavalry alone. Kilpatrick performed both operations, partially, bringing in a few prisoners and a gun, but losing three hundred men. This was not satisfactory; Kilpatrick had not done enough, and Sherman then resumed his original plan. He says:—

"All the army commanders were at once notified to send their surplus wagons, encumbrances of all kinds, and sick, back to our intrenched position at the bridge, and that the movement would begin during the night of the 25th. Accordingly, all things being ready, the Fourth Corps, General Stanley, drew out of its lines on our extreme left, and marched to a position below Proctor's Creek. The Twentieth Corps, General Williams, moved back to the Chattahoochie. This movement was made without loss, save a few things left in our camps by thoughtless officers or men. The night of the 26th the movement continued, the Army of the Tennessee drawing out and moving rapidly by a circuit well towards Sandtown and across Camp Creek; the Army of the Cumberland below Utoy Creek; General Schofield remaining in position. This was effected with the loss of but a single man in the Army of the Tennessee, wounded by a shell from the enemy. The third movement brought the Army of the Tennessee on the West Point Railroad, above Fairborn; the Army of the Cumberland about Red Oak, and General Schofield closed in near Digs and Mins. I then ordered one day's work to be expended in destroying that road, and it was done with a will. Twelve and one-half miles were destroyed, the ties burned, and the iron rails heated and tortured by the utmost ingenuity of old hands at the work. Several cuts were filled up with the trunks of trees, with logs, rock, and earth intermingled with loaded shells, prepared as torpedoes, to explode in case of any attempt to clear them out. Having personally inspected this work, and satisfied with its execution, I ordered the whole army to move the next day eastward by several roads: General Howard, on the right, towards Jonesboro: General Thomas, the centre, by Shoal Creek Church to Couch's on the Decatur and Fayetteville Road;

and General Schofield, on the left, about Morrow's mills. An inspection of the map will show the strategic advantages of this position. The railroad from Atlanta to Macon follows substantially the ridge or 'divide' between the waters of Flint and Ocmulgee Rivers, and from East Point to Jonesboro makes a wide bend to the east. Therefore the position I have described, which had been well studied on paper, was my first 'objective.' It gave me 'interior lines,' something our enemy had enjoyed too long, and I was anxious for once to get the inside track, and therefore my haste and desire to secure it."

On the 29th of August commenced a movement which will always remain unsurpassed in the history of our war for soldierly skill, both in conception and execution. Every thing worked to a charm. The various corps moved like mechanism over the appointed roads. On the 31st, Howard, on the right, had reached Jonesboro; Thomas, in the centre, was at Couch's; and Schofield, on the left, was near Rough and Ready.

Nothing was then left for the enemy but to come out and attack Thomas, and this he did most furiously and repeatedly with the corps of Lee and Hardee. But, after a desperate contest, the enemy fell back, repulsed, with a loss of fully three thousand men, four hundred being left dead on the field. Thomas and Schofield were already tearing up the railroad below Jonesboro; but all our columns were ordered to be at that point by noon of September 1st. Davis's Corps was ready, and, at four P. M., joined to Thomas's line, assaulted and carried the enemy's entire position, capturing nearly a whole brigade, with its general, and eight guns. The enemy's loss in this engagement was nearly five thousand, of which over two thousand were prisoners. It was Hood's final struggle; his communications were cut and his cause lost. The same night, he retreated from Atlanta, blowing up, according to Sherman, "vast magazines and stores," besides seven locomotives and eighty-one cars, the latter loaded with ammunition; nineteen heavy guns, three hundred muskets, and many stores, fell into our hands. Our losses in these engagements were about one thousand two hundred men. At daybreak, our army pursued Hood to Lovejoy's, thirty miles south of Atlanta, where he was strongly fortified; but the campaign was over, and our troops moved slowly back to Atlanta.

So was Atlanta won! When we reflect upon the enormous distance traversed,—upon its rugged and defensible character, it being nothing less than a penetration of the entire series of parallel Alleghany ranges,—upon the strong army and the able general of the enemy, contesting our advance, inch by inch, over ground entirely known to them and unknown to us, after years of preparation in roads and fortified places,—upon the fact that Sherman was obliged to rebuild bridges and railroads as he advanced, and protect his line of supplies all the way from Nashville to Atlanta, three hundred miles long,—upon the dazzling series of victories unbroken, save at Kenesaw, which crowned our banners,—upon the miraculous handling of troops, as if by mechanism, over the most wretched of roads, in the most impracticable of countries,—upon the skilful and extraordinary system of supplies, of food, forage, and ammunition,—upon the tremendous disparity of loss inflicted on the enemy, although he fought a defensive campaign,—upon the wonderful tactical genius of the great commander, whether on the march or in the battle,—this campaign must stand unsurpassed in the annals of history.

Napoleon's first Italy campaign was something like it. There Napoleon, marching from Southwestern France, threw his troops from the Maritime Alps, where he found them, along the coast, fighting his way among the neighboring mountains, like Sherman among the Alleghanies. He traversed all Northern Italy, but was forced to stay his troops on the mountains of the Styrian frontier, whence a faint glimpse could be had of far-distant Vienna, a city, he was destined never to reach. In the mountainous character of the campaign, in the length and boldness of the march, and in several other respects, the two campaigns are strikingly similar. But not as to success. Napoleon's lines of communication were frequently cut, and he was, at length, obliged to fall back, step by step, having failed to reach Vienna, his objective point; whereas, Sherman fought his way through, attained what he started for, and held on to it, and finally made it a point of departure for other operations equally valuable and glorious.

And now Sherman gave his victorious army a little rest. "Atlanta is ours," he wrote, "and fairly won. *Since the 5th of May we have been in one continued battle or skirmish, and need rest.*" But he himself was not idle. He had come to Atlanta to stay, and it was necessary to put his camp in order. The enemy had fled without making provision for his women and children. Sherman ordained that the city should be put in condition for defence at once, and all non-combatants be removed. He proposed to send all who desired it, together with their servants and effects, within Hood's lines, and asked his co-operation. Hood, while accepting the proposition, characterized the measure as "*unprecedented, studied and ungenerous cruelty.*" Sherman, in whose composition there is nothing of cruelty, but much of unaffected kindness, mingled with a high sense of justice, was deeply touched by this gratuitous imputation, whereupon he replied to General Hood in terms well calculated to end the wordy conflict, as follows:—

"GENERAL:—I have the honor to acknowledge the receipt of your letter of this date, at the hands of Messrs. Ball and Crew, consenting to the arrangements I had proposed to facilitate the removal south of the people of Atlanta who prefer to go in that direction. I enclose you a copy of my orders, which will, I am satisfied, accomplish my purpose perfectly. You style the measures proposed 'unprecedented,' and appeal to the dark history of war for a parallel as an act of 'studied and ungenerous cruelty.' It is not unprecedented, for General Johnston himself very wisely and properly removed the families all the way from Dalton down, and I see no reason why Atlanta should be excepted. Nor is it necessary to appeal to the dark history of war when recent and modern examples are so handy. You yourself burned dwelling-houses along your parapet, and I have seen to-day fifty houses that you have rendered uninhabitable because they stood in the way of your forts and men. You defended Atlanta on a line so close to the town that every cannon-shot and many musket-shots from our line of investments, that overshot their mark, went into the habitations of women and children. General Hardee did the same at Jonesboro, and General Johnston did the same last summer at Jackson, Mississippi. I have not accused you of heartless cruelty, but merely instance these cases of very recent occurrence, and could go on and enumerate hundreds of others, and challenge any fair man to judge which of us has the heart of pity for the families of a 'brave people.' I say it is a kindness to these families of Atlanta to remove them now at once from scenes that women and children should not be exposed to; and the brave people should scorn to commit their wives and children to the rude barbarians who thus, as you say, violate the laws of war, as illustrated in the pages of its dark history. In the name of common sense, I ask you not to appeal to a just God in such a sacrilegious manner,—you, who, in the midst of peace and prosperity, have plunged a nation into civil war, 'dark and cruel war,' who dared and badgered us to battle, insulted our flag, seized our arsenals and forts that were left in the honorable custody of a peaceful ordnance sergeant, seized and made prisoners of war the very garrisons sent to protect your people against negroes and Indians, long before any overt act was committed by the (to you) hateful Lincoln government, tried to force Kentucky and Missouri into the rebellion in spite of themselves, falsified the vote of Louisiana, turned loose your privateers to plunder unarmed ships, expelled Union families by the thousand, burned their houses, and declared by act of your Congress the confiscation of all debts due Northern men for goods sold and delivered. Talk thus to the marines, but not to me, who have seen these things, and who will this day make as much sacrifice for the peace and honor of the South as the best born Southerner among you. If we must be enemies, let us be men, and fight it out as we propose to-day, and not deal in such hypocritical appeals to God and humanity. God will judge us in due time, and He will pronounce whether it be more humane to fight with a town full of women and the families of a 'brave people' at our back, or to remove them in time to places of safety among their own friends and people."

Sherman is a "rude jouster" with the pen as well as with the sword, and Hood did not wisely to engage him thus. Hood had been so badly whipped by Sherman that he was in no mood to be civil or amiable; he was disappointed, angry, and proud; he had been so confident of his ability to hold Atlanta, and turn all Sherman's successes into a Moscow disaster, as Davis had vainly promised for him, in his celebrated Macon speech, that the matter of providing for the women and children of that famous city, was disagreeable to contemplate, and in making his ungenerous accusations against Sherman, he consulted his wounded pride rather than his judgment. It has its parallel in the incidents of the capture of Fort Donelson. When Grant had reduced that stronghold to the point of capture, Buckner sent a flag of truce, proposing an armistice and the appointment of commissioners to settle the terms of capitulation; to which Grant instantly replied, "No terms except immediate and unconditional surrender can be accepted," and added, "I propose to move immediately on your works." Buckner characterized Grant's course in the premises as both "ungenerous" and "ungracious;" but nevertheless Grant was right, and his soldierly bearing and manly words, on that occasion, commend him alike, as the gentleman and the soldier.

When Sherman first learned that Johnston had been relieved by Hood, he remarked to a friend, "I am perfectly willing to exchange Johnston for Hood. Jeff. Davis could not have done me a greater favor. I regard Joe Johnston as the best strategist in the Confederate army. Hood has more dash, but has only moderate ability. Be that as it may, however, we will soon have a chance to try him."

So heavy was the stress of war upon the abandoned women and children of Atlanta, that the mayor of that doomed city, with others, appealed to Sherman to revoke his orders in regard to their removal, and this gave him an opportunity of giving the reasons for the order, which he did in the following sensible and most exhaustive letter:—

"HEAD QUARTERS MILITARY DIVISION OF THE MISSISSIPPI,
IN THE FIELD,
ATLANTA, GA., Sept. 12, 1864.

"JAMES M. CALHOUN, Mayor; E. E. RAWSON and S. C. WELLS, representing City Council of Atlanta:—

"GENTLEMEN:—I have your letter of the 11th, in the nature of a petition to revoke my orders removing all the inhabitants from Atlanta. I have read it carefully, and give full credit to your statements of the distress that will be occasioned by it; and yet shall not revoke my order, simply because my orders are not designed to meet the humanities of the case, but to prepare for the future struggles, in which millions, yea, hundreds of millions of good people outside of Atlanta have a deep interest. We must have *Peace*, not only at Atlanta, but in all America. To secure this, we must stop the war that now desolates our once happy and favored country. To stop war, we must defeat the rebel armies that are arrayed against the laws and Constitution which all must respect and obey. To defeat these armies, we must prepare the way to reach them in their recesses, provided with the arms and instruments which enable us to accomplish our purpose.

"Now, I know the vindictive nature of our enemy, and that we may have many years of military operations from this quarter, and therefore deem it wise and prudent to prepare in time. The use of Atlanta for warlike purposes is inconsistent with its character as a home for families. There will be no manufactures, commerce, or agriculture here for the maintenance of families, and sooner or later want will compel the inhabitants to go. Why not go *now*, when all the arrangements are completed for the transfer, instead of waiting till the plunging shot of contending armies will renew the scene of the past month? Of course, I do not apprehend any such thing at this moment; but you do not suppose that this army will be here till the war is over. I cannot discuss this subject with you fairly, because I cannot impart to you what I propose to do; but I assert that my military plans make it necessary for the inhabitants to go away, and I can only renew my offer of services to make their exodus in any direction as easy and comfortable as possible. You cannot qualify war in harsher terms than I will. War is cruelty, and you cannot refine it; and those who brought war on our country deserve all the curses and maledictions a people can pour out. I know I had no hand in making this war, and I know I will make more sacrifices to-day than any of you to secure peace. But you cannot have peace and a division of our country. If the United States submits to a division now, it will not stop, but will go on till we reap the fate of Mexico, which is eternal war. The United States does and must assert its authority wherever it has power; if it relaxes one bit to pressure, it is gone, and I know that such is not the national feeling. This feeling assumes various shapes, but always comes back to that of *Union*. Once admit the Union, once more acknowledge the authority of the National Government, and instead of devoting your houses and streets and roads to the dread uses of war, I and this army become at once your protectors and supporters, shielding you from danger, let it come from what quarter it may. I know that a few individuals cannot resist a torrent of error and passion, such as has swept the South into rebellion; but you can point out, so that we may know those who desire a government, and those who insist upon war and its desolation.

"You might as well appeal against the thunder-storm as against these terrible hardships of war. They are inevitable; and the only way the people of Atlanta can hope once more to live in peace and quiet at home, is to stop this war,—which can alone be done by admitting that it began in error, and is perpetuated in pride. We don't want your negroes, or your horses, or your houses, or your land, or any thing you have; but we do want, and will have, a just obedience to the laws of the United States. That we will have; and if it involves the destruction of your improvements, we cannot help it. You have heretofore read public sentiment in your newspapers, that live by falsehood and excitement, and the quicker you seek for truth in other quarters, the better for you.

"I repeat, then, that, by the original compact of government, the United States had certain rights in Georgia, which have never been relinquished, and never will be; that the South began war by seizing forts, arsenals, mints, custom-houses, &c., &c., long before Mr. Lincoln was installed, and before the South had one jot or tittle of provocation. I myself have seen in Missouri, Kentucky, Tennessee, and part of Mississippi, hundreds and thousands of women and children fleeing from your armies and desperadoes, hungry and with bleeding feet. In Memphis, Vicksburg, and Mississippi, we fed thousands upon thousands of the families of rebel soldiers left on our hands, and whom we could not see starve. Now that war comes home to you, you feel very different; you deprecate its horrors, but did not feel them when you sent car-loads of soldiers and ammunition, and moulded shell and shot, to carry war into Kentucky and Tennessee, and desolate the homes of hundreds and thousands of good people, who only asked to live in peace at their old homes, and under the government of their inheritance. But these comparisons are idle. I want peace, and believe it can only be reached through Union and war, and I will ever conduct war purely with a view to perfect and early success.

"But, my dear sirs, when that peace does come, you may call on me for any thing. Then will I share with you the last cracker, and watch with you to shield your homes and families against danger from every quarter. Now, you must go, and take with you the old and feeble; feed and nurse them, and build for them in more quiet places proper habitations, to shield them against the weather, until the mad passions of men cool down, and allow the Union and peace once more to settle on your old homes at Atlanta. Yours, in haste,

"W. T. SHERMAN, *Major-General.*"

Wheeler had now been several weeks raiding in Sherman's rear, and was re-enforced by Forrest and Rhoddy, and these intrepid raiders had already done considerable damage. Sherman soon had Rosseau, Steedman, and Granger all after them, and forces from Memphis and Vicksburg co-operating. The railroad was immediately repaired, the telegraph restored, when Sherman made such combinations as to expel the enemy entirely from Tennessee. And thus ended this remarkable campaign which, according to the London *Star*, "was one of those victories which form the turning-point of great wars."

And what next? This will appear in our next chapter, under the title of "Sherman's Campaign through Georgia to the Sea." It will there be seen, how Sherman, in driving the rebel army down to, and out of Atlanta, according to the rebel press and the London *Times*, was "only being tolled on to his destruction."

CHLOROFORM.

BY DR. CHARLES C. BOURBAUGH.

> " There is
> No danger in what show of death it makes,
> More than the locking up the spirits a time,
> To be more fresh, reviving."—SHAKSPEARE, *Cymbeline.*

BURTON quaintly says in his "Anatomy of Melancholy:" "Though there were many giants of old in physic and philosophy, yet I say with Didacus Stella, 'A dwarf standing on the shoulders of a giant may see further than a giant himself.'"

What, then, is the likelihood, if the mounted individual happens to be another intellectual giant? One, for instance, of the calibre of James Y. Simpson, of Edinburgh? Will not the range of vision be proportionately increased? It would be idle and unprofitable to indulge in speculations as to the probable adoption of chloroform for purposes of anæsthesia if the way had not been paved for Dr. Simpson by the American discoveries of the anæsthetic properties of sulphuric ether, or, at least, of the practical application of those properties. Suffice it for us to know that he had that illustrious tripod, Morton, Wells, and Jackson, to stand upon, and that it was from an observatory built by their hands that he peered far into the dim and shadowy distance for some volatile agent, which, while it should wrap the sufferer in slumber more profound than that of

> "Poppy or mandragora,
> Or all the drowsy sirups of this world,"

should be more energetic in its action, more speedy in its effects, and more in harmony with physiological requirements, than the process of etherization.

Impressed with the conviction that some lethean anodyne less inconvenient, disagreeable, and otherwise objectionable than ether might be found in the broad domain of chemistry, this indefatigable man of science proceeded to experiment in his own person upon all volatile liquids or gases likely to produce insensibility to external impressions. Late one night, after a day of arduous labor, in company with two of his pupils, Dr. Simpson resumed his course of inhalations. The vapors of various substances were successively inhaled without any well-marked effect. A bottle of chloroform, till then more of a curiosity upon the laboratory shelves than an article of utility, was finally tried in its turn, "when immediately," says Professor Miller, "an unwonted hilarity seized the party; they became bright-eyed and very happy, and conversed with such intelligence as more than usually charmed the listeners who were not taking part in the proceedings. But suddenly there was a talk of sounds being heard like those of a cotton mill, louder and louder; a moment more, and all was quiet, and then—crash. On awaking, Dr. Simpson's first perception was mental. 'This is far stronger and better than ether,' he said to himself. His second was to note that he was prostrate on the floor, and that his friends were confused and alarmed. Hearing a noise, he turned around, and saw his assistant, Dr. Duncan, beneath a chair, his jaw dropped, his eyes staring, and his head half bent under him, quite unconscious, and snoring in an alarming manner. Then his eyes overtook Dr. Keith's feet and legs making valorous efforts to overturn the table, or more probably to annihilate every thing that was on it."

This discovery was made in 1847. Etherization was yet in its early infancy. Doubt had yet to be overcome; vulgar prejudice had yet to be removed. The fantastic clamor consequent upon its immediate action evoked smiles and laughter, but the heavy stupefaction that followed gave rise to distrust and painful apprehensions. Occasional fatal results increased the trepidation in regard to the use of anæsthetics in the professional as well as the popular mind. But pain is an object of such unconquerable dread, even among those who have fortitude enough to measurably stifle the natural expression of anguish, that the surgeon persevered in the use of his mysterious agency with the gradually increasing conviction that alarm was groundless.

Yet he was obliged to encounter at the outset an objection as unexpected as it was singular and ridiculous. He was told that pain has both its moral and physical uses, that it is a salutary and conservative manifestation of life force, that anæsthetics are unwarrantable luxuries, and that their employment is a wicked escape from the moral good that accrues from suffering, and is deliberately flying in the face of Providence. We are not aware that such a position is considered tenable at the present day. To err is human; if there be any erring in this case, it is on the side of humanity. Lord Bacon said, "I esteem it the office of a physician not only to restore health, but to mitigate pain and dolors."

Then came another puzzling question. "In other times," remarked Dr. Bigelow, of Harvard University, not long after the introduction of anæsthesia, "a fear of pain co-operated with a fear of death to resist an indiscriminate attack upon the stronghold of disease. In the annihilation of pain, let not an equal force be now brought to bear against vitality alone. The balance of surgical right has been shaken to its centre by the annihilation of an element whose preponderance may be truly said, in a majority of cases, to have turned the scale; and years must elapse before a standard of expediency can be adjusted." The present civil contest will go far toward elucidating and determining this as well as other *questiones vexatæ* which inevitably spring from a novelty involving so many serious considerations. Neither the Crimean nor the Italian campaigns, with all their valuable contributions to the statistical facts and records of anæsthesia, have definitively settled questions which had been in dispute before their outbreak. Guthrie, for instance, expresses grave doubts of the propriety of administering chloroform when a limb is badly lacerated near the body, and the resulting hemorrhage is profuse, and the nervous shock exhausting; while Dr. Snow, an acknowledged authority, says, "A state of great depression from injury or disease does not contra-indicate the use of chloroform. This agent acts as a stimulant in the first instance, increasing the strength of the pulse, and enabling the patient, in a state of exhaustion, to go through an operation much better than if he were conscious." When the war terminates, and its accumulating and ripening experiences are gathered into that treasure-house now in course of preparation under the direction of the Surgeon-General, the ground will have been so far preoccupied as to leave little or no occasion for dispute.

The question of the relative advantages of sulphuric ether and chloroform was satisfactorily determined in favor of the latter years ago. It is true that there are many excellent surgeons who still prefer the ether, believing that its administration is attended with greater safety. The adoption of chloroform in the army was based upon considerations which give it undoubted claim to preference. In all cases a far less quantity is required to produce the desired effect. It therefore presents the advantage of economy, and also of portability, which, on a march or during an engagement, is of no small moment. Its action is likewise more rapid and decisive, and its effect is more complete and persistent. Fewer inspirations suffice, and the preliminary stage of excitement is curtailed. The value of the time thus saved to the surgeon during and after a battle, when the wounded are crowding upon him, when the need of his active services is most pressing, when every moment is precious, and delay involves the life that is steadily ebbing away around him, is inestimable. In thousands of instances, as every army surgeon can testify, the sufferer has been narcotized, subjected to the amputation of a limb, the vessels tied, and the stump dressed within the time usually requisite for the full effect of ether. On the other hand, it is contended by the advocates of ether that the inhalation of chloroform is inherently more dangerous. The records of the war prove abundantly that their allegations are unfounded in fact. They show that the use of a preparation which is perfectly pure and uncontaminated by the presence of aldehyde, or any other of the poisonous principles to whose admixture an improperly prepared article is liable, is absolutely safe in all cases in which its use is clearly not contra-indicated, and that fears in reference to its undue activity are unfounded. In cases of mal-administration, when asphyxia results from criminally reckless or ignorant handling, or from the sudden and fatal aggravation of one of those diseased conditions of the cardiac or pulmonary systems which interdict recourse to anæsthetics, the unfortunate termination is, *cæteris paribus*, as certain, if not as rapid, from the abuse or injudicious use of the one as of the other.

These facts having been established, the importance of employing chloroform of undoubted quality cannot be over-estimated. Dr. C. T. Jackson, of Boston, has shown that the deaths originally resulting from this agent were attributable to the presence of some compound of amyle, the hypothetical radical of fusel oil, the poisonous oil of whiskey. Subsequent investigations proved that the methylic as well as the amylic combinations were concerned in the contamination, together with chloride of elaile and other chlorine compounds, alcohol and aldehyde. To obtain chloroform—which, as our chemical readers know, is a perchloride of formyle—free from impurity, it must be prepared from unquestionably pure rectified alcohol, to be diluted with water when used for distillation from chloride of lime. In testing a doubtful article, the appreciation of its density will not detect impurities unless they are present in considerable quantity. Berthé has suggested means for their detection which are equally simple and reliable. He tells us that if we add to chloroform which contains chloride of elaile a little potash, we transform the compound into chloride of acetyle, the presence of which is instantly detected by its nauseous odor. For the detection of the other impurities, especially the alcohols, which occur the oftenest, we need only bruise a little bichromate of potash in a small qantity of chloroform, adding a few drops of sulphuric acid. If the chloroform is pure, a reddish brown precipitate of chromic acid occurs; if not pure, the deposit, and frequently the fluid itself, assumes a green color, due to the presence of sesquioxide of chrome.

Fortunately for the honor of the service and the cause of humanity, the chloroform so far supplied to the medical officers of the army has been free from the taint of suspicion. The criminal avarice which risked the lives of our brave soldiers by the transmission to the camps and hospitals of adulterated and factitious medicines, stimulants, and nutrients, seems to have passed over, or, at least, lightly touched this matchless anodyne. The experience of the writer, as well as that of his fellow-associates in the service, with whom he has carefully compared notes, shows that among many thousand cases in field and hospital practice, they have not witnessed one case of fatal chloroformization. Undoubtedly cases of asphyxia have occurred under circumstances favoring an unfortunate issue, which will be reported through the proper channels, but as an item of personal observation and inquiry, cautiously conducted since the commencement of the war, the fact is deemed worthy of addition to the recorded summary of individual experience. Often in the heat and hurry of operations in time of battle, the anæsthetic was fairly crammed—if the expression be admissible—into the wounded sufferer in a manner that would be totally unwarrantable in other situations, and when the operation was concluded he would be hastily laid aside to recover his consciousness at his leisure, while another, in turn, was being plunged beneath the same oblivious condition. But they did recover invariably; and if in other hands, of which the writer has not become cognizant, the vital spirit quietly flitted away, if death ensued as the direct effect of the administration of chloroform, and not of hemorrhage or nervous shock, be this our answer to the doubting or the querulous: Thousands of useful lives have been saved to the country by submission to severe operations in a state of unconsciousness which otherwise could not have survived the shock upon the sensorium. Where chloroform has wrought, in a single instance, a transition to that dreamless repose from which there is no awaking this side the grave, it has prevented a thousand others. Every year numbers of passengers are killed by railway accidents, but millions are safely transported by the same conveyance. Many a shattered hulk of humanity which would have expired under the withering and consuming pain of an operation when susceptibility was exalted and sensibility intensified, have, with the aid of this sustaining staff, come back from the very verge of the death-shadowed valley. A fact so convincing is approved by reason and confirmed by experience.

One of the happiest uses to which chloroform has been applied during the war, is in the suppression of malingering. Cases of simulated disability almost daily attract the attention of the medical officers. So well feigned, sometimes, are these disqualifying defects or infirmities, and so pertinaciously adhered to, as to deceive old army surgeons accustomed to trickery. But through the involuntary revelations of this agency the exposure is complete. The mute have been betrayed into vociferous speech, and the deaf been made to hear. Anchylosed joints and binding cicatrices, which had stubbornly resisted flexion, have suddenly unfolded of their own accord. Rheumatism disappears as if by magic, and old adhesions break up before an exploration is made. Numerous cases of imposture thus detected have been restored to the service, which otherwise, by persistent continuance in deception, might have succeeded in obtaining a discharge.

The wise man tells us that there is nothing new under the sun. It is certainly remarkable that the great inventions and discoveries of modern times have been dimly foreshadowed, in one way or another, for centuries. Some of them, in fact, are but re-discoveries, or new applications of principles understood in remote periods. They have not been merely outlined or imperfectly realized in the reveries of genius or the vagaries of insanity, but many of them have had their prototypes vaguely shaped in the laboratories of those pioneers in scientific investigation who were destined to grope through darkness and doubt, and to struggle through hunger and poverty after an embodiment of their ideals, and finally to sink beneath the dark waters of oblivion before they had given their grotesque modellings "a local habitation and a name." The steam-engine, the magnetic telegraph, the stereoscope, the photograph, the aeronautics, auscultation, table turning, and spirit rapping have all had their antecedent presentments. It is doubtful whether even gas and lucifer matches have first *come to light* in our generation. But none of them have been more clearly foreshadowed than anæsthesia, and it seems almost incredible that its actual practical application for the annulment of physical suffering should so long have escaped attention. Herodotus tells us that the Scythians used the vapor of hemp-seed to induce stupefaction and counteract pain. Pliny the Elder, in describing the soporific power of the mandragora, says it was used " before cuttings and puncturings that they might not be felt (ante sectiones, punctionesque ne sentiantur)." Dioscorides, a physician of Cilicia, gives minute directions for its preparation when intended to be used "to cause insensibility—ποιειν αναισθησιαν, to produce anæsthesia—in those who are to be cut or cauterized." Both writers describe the stone Memphitis as an effective local anæsthetic when powdered and dissolved in vinegar. Apuleis, of Madaura, a century later, uses still more expressive language in favor of the stupefactive effect of mandragora. Even the Chinese, more than sixteen centuries ago, used cannabis to induce insensibility to the pain of surgical operations, as is proved by an ancient pharmacopœia preserved in the national library at Paris. Passing through the intervening period, we find numerous authorities whose suggestive observations are very striking, and as we approach nearer to our own day, we find this significant hint from Sir Humphrey Davy: "As *nitrous oxide*, in its extensive operation, appears capable of destroying physical pain, it may probably be used with advantage during surgical operations in which no great effusion of blood takes place." Even this pregnant suggestion was made half a century before the idea was carried into practical execution.

The artificial induction of sleep by medicated potions was also a favorite idea of the poets and story-tellers in the machinery of romance and the drama. Its ingenious application to the plot of Romeo and Juliet, and other plays of Shakspeare, indicates the prevalent notion of his day in regard to its practicability. Middleton, in his tragedy, "Women, Beware Women," published in 1657, pointedly alludes to the practice in ancient surgery. In Act IV., Scene 1, Hippolito says:—

> "I'll imitate the pities of old surgeons
> To this lost limb; who, ere they show their art,
> *Cast one asleep, then cut the diseased part.*"

Dr. Benjamin Rush, in 1803, literally anticipating the action of chloroform, expressed the hope "that a medium would be discovered that should suspend sensibility altogether, and leave irritability or the powers of motion unimpaired, and thereby destroy the pains of parturition." Ether inhalations were prescribed by eminent medical practitioners seventy years ago, in the treatment of catarrhal affections, spasmodic asthma, and hooping cough. But all these investigators stopped at the threshold, instead of crossing over; they rested under the shade of the tree, but neglected to pluck its fruit. The means had been provided; the instruments were within reach. Chance accomplished that which human sagacity failed to perceive. It was with anæsthesia as with nearly all the great facts and discoveries of natural science. They have been the result, not of logical deduction, but of a fortuitous chain of circumstances. Only eighteen years have elapsed since etherization startled the civilized world by the novelty of its claims. Its twin minister, more potent in the subdual of pain, loitered behind, that the public mind might be the better prepared for the comprehension and realization of its heaven-born mission. Who can measure the aggregate of suffering that has been averted within that brief period? And what an untold amount of human anguish might have been spared in the ages that have been entombed forever! It was not until 1831 that chloroform was simultaneously discovered by Guthrie, of Sackett's Harbor, and Soubeiran, of Paris; but the preparation and qualities of ether were described by Basil Valentine and others more than three centuries ago. Many of the narcotizing inhalations of the ancients were undoubtedly superior to nitrous oxide in anæsthetic power. The "spongia somnifera" of Theodoric is quite as worthy of a place in the pharmacopœia of 1860 as is much of the lumber with which it is encumbered. Yet they all "died, and left no sign."

Why so peerless and priceless a mode of assuaging pain was so long withheld, it is not within our province to inquire. It seems to be a part of that inscrutable economy whose ways are past finding out. If the boon is for the present and the future, it is for us and the myriads that are to follow to acknowledge its blessings reverently and humbly, and to experience that devout sense of gratitude which is due to the Good Giver for this sweet, oblivious antidote, this child of Night and Lethe, this φαρμακον νηπενθες.

GREAT BATTLES IN HISTORY.
No. IV.
ANTWERP, IVRY, STRALSUND, BREITENFELD.

The progress of the art of war in the sixteenth and seventeenth centuries was chiefly marked by the increasing value attached to the employment of artillery. All places of importance, as regards magnitude or situation, were carefully fortified; and even comparatively unimportant posts were provided with permanent means of defence. Instead of a series of battles in the open field, between numerous bodies of men, the results of which were to be decisive of the fate of nations, a campaign came often to determine little more than the possession of a town or two by one or the other of the hostile parties. From the necessity also, real or supposed, of placing garrisons in nearly every town or castle, the armies, when occasionally they did encounter each other, consisted often of numbers so small as to be of little avail but to exhibit the superior skill of the successful general, or the superior prowess of his followers. What has been stated will apply generally to the period extending from the commencement of the sixteenth century to the age of Gustavus Adolphus, or, we should perhaps rather say, down to that of Louis XIV., when improvements in the art of war began to be made more rapidly than before.

The present essay will illustrate these remarks, and prepare our readers for a more systematic and more interesting study of the essays which are to succeed it.

Siege of Antwerp, by the Spaniards under Alexander, Duke of Parma, from July 1st, 1584, to August 17th, 1585.

In the course of the contest which the Duke of Parma carried on against the people of the Netherlands, who had revolted against the tyranny of Philip II. of Spain, he resolved to gain possession of the city of Antwerp, on which that of the whole of Brabant may be said to have depended, supplied by it, as this province was, to a considerable extent, with corn imported from Zealand. Antwerp was, besides, the usual place of meeting of the provincial delegates,—the point, therefore, whither the inhabitants were accustomed to look for direction in their conduct.

In the month of July, 1584, the Duke of Parma concentrates, in the neighborhood of Antwerp, the forces at his disposal, amounting to not more than ten thousand infantry and seventeen hundred cavalry, but all of them veteran troops. The city

SIEGE OF ANTWERP.

Spaniards ■■ *Troops of the Low Countries* ■■

contained, at the period in question, a population of eighty-five thousand; and the hopes of the Spanish general to compel its surrender rest chiefly on the slow operations of famine. He encamps with a part of his army at (A A) near Beveren. With another part of it, Count Ernest von Mansfeld does the same at Stabroek (B B), on the opposite side of the Scheldt. Detachments of Spanish soldiers are stationed at intervals along the same side of the river to guard the dikes and accesses to it in that quarter. Forts Liefkenshoeck and Lillo are occupied by the Netherlanders.

By a sudden attack on the former of these forts, it falls into the hands of the Spaniards; and soon afterwards every other position is abandoned to them by the enemy on the Flemish side of the river.

Fort Lillo, on the contrary, is vigorously defended by a brave and experienced commander, Odet de Téligny. The Spanish officer, Mondragon, who had constructed it originally by the direction of the celebrated Duke of Alva, besieged it in vain during three weeks, when he retired from before it, after having suffered a loss of two thousand of his men.

Had the Duke of Parma succeeded in obtaining possession both of Forts Lillo and Liefkenshoeck (see their positions indicated on the plan), it would have been sufficiently easy for him to intercept the navigation between Antwerp and the lower part of the Scheldt. Now, however, he resolves to attain his object by the construction of a bridge over this river, where it bends and is narrowest, near Calloo, and he directs the forts or redoubts St. Mary and St. Philip to be erected (see plan) to protect the bridge while building.

During the execution of his orders the Duke attacks the forfied town of Dendermonde, situated between Ghent and Antwerp, and takes it with its citadel after a siege of only eleven days, on which the important city of Ghent also capitulates, together with Vilvorde, Herenthals, and Willebroek; and Antwerp is thus cut off from all communication with Brussels and Malines. By the capture of Ghent, the Spaniards acquire a rich provision of cannon, wagons, ships, or boats, and building materials for the projected bridge.

By these events Antwerp is restricted in looking for assistance to Zealand alone, and its hope of escape from the grasp of Spain rests entirely on the ability of the Zealanders to prevent the construction of the bridge, or their power to co-operate in destroying it after its completion.

The defences of the city are superintended by the burgomaster St. Aldegonde. Before the arrival of the Spaniards, he causes several additional redoubts to be raised around it, the older fortifications to be repaired, and the dikes, which prevent the waters of the Wester Schelde from flowing upon the territory of Waes, to be pierced, so as to inundate this whole region. But dissensions prevailing among the authorities, hinder the plans of St. Aldegonde from being fully carried into effect.

Whilst, in Antwerp, the throwing of a bridge over a stream more than two thousand feet wide and sixty feet deep, is regarded as impossible, and even an object of ridicule, the Duke of Parma has completed the greater part of his undertaking. As soon as Forts St. Mary and St. Philip have been constructed, they are furnished with cannon for the protection of the workmen engaged with the bridge. The masts of the largest vessels are then selected for framing, from the opposite sides of the river, a solid piece of carpentry, styled an *estacade*, and constituting a bridge wide enough for eight men to pass along it abreast. In this manner the width of the river has been reduced eleven hundred feet. But there still remains a distance of six hundred feet, which must be left open on account of the depth of the water, and which is intended to be occupied by a bridge of boats. In the mean time, a temporary platform, provided with artillery, is placed at each extremity of the *estacade*, to the fire of which every vessel ascending the river to the city, or descending from it, must necessarily be subjected.

The Duke of Parma profits by the inundation of the territory of Waes to have the vessels, of which he had obtained possession by the capture of Ghent, conveyed as far as Rupelmonde. There he causes the left dike of the Scheldt to be pierced through, and has them brought to Burcht, thence to the inundated grounds, and again in the direction of Calloo to the Scheldt. Odet de Téligny endeavors in vain to oppose this undertaking with the fleet of Antwerp. He arrives too late to accomplish his purpose, but takes a position on the dike to prevent the passage of the river by other vessels from Ghent.

A sufficient number of vessels has not yet been provided to enable the bridge to be completed. The Duke, therefore, orders a canal to be constructed from the moor near Stacken, by way of Beveren and Verebroek. By this canal the whole of the country on the west of the Scheldt is brought into communication with the Spanish camp, which is thus henceforth abundantly supplied with the boats and provisions that may be wanted. Notwithstanding the near approach of winter, the labors on the bridge are diligently pushed forward, and their completion early in the following spring secured.

About the 1st of December the Duke of Parma made a formal summons for the surrender to him of Antwerp. This was promptly rejected, chiefly, as we are told, on account of the hopes just then entertained of aid to be received from Queen Elizabeth, of England. Such aid, however, came not; and in the course of the winter the people of Antwerp encountered a severe loss in the capture by the enemy of the brave Odet de Téligny, on a mission with which he was intrusted to expedite the preparations of the Zealanders in their behalf.

The bridge of the Spaniards having been finished in March, 1585, as had been expected by them, fifteen hundred men and ninety-seven pieces of cannon were especially assigned for its defence, together with a fleet of forty armed vessels. In these circumstances, intelligence was received in Antwerp that the inhabitants of Brussels had submitted to the yoke of Spain, and it is not improbable that the Antwerpers would speedily have followed their example, had it not been at length announced to them that the naval armament from Zealand was coming up the Scheldt.

Count Justin, of Nassau, its commander, exhibited a degree of zeal and ability which was calculated to revive the spirits of the citizens. He lost no time in battering the walls of Fort Liefkenshoek, and then carrying it by storm.

It is now thought at Antwerp that the proper time had come for making an attempt to blow up the bridge, and then to procure, by means of the Zealand fleet, a renewed supply of provisions.

Two large fire-ships had been constructed at Antwerp by Frederick Gianibelli, an Italian, which it was intended should be preceded against the bridge by thirty-two smaller vessels, conveying only fireworks. These were to advance in four separate divisions, at intervals of half an hour, in order to create a succession of false alarms to occupy and fatigue the enemy's troops, and also to place them in a position most exposed to the action of the real fire-ships.

The night between the 4th and 5th of April was appointed for the execution of this project. Although it took place more rapidly than had been agreed upon, the second fire-ship attains successfully the bridge of boats, whence the Spaniards, encouraged by the presence of the Duke of Parma, make every exertion to thrust it by means of poles, but to no purpose. The Duke is forcibly conveyed by those who immediately surround him in the direction of Fort St. Mary, where he had no sooner arrived when a terrible explosion is heard to have taken place. He is thrown down with every one about him, and remains for several minutes insensible.

The injury caused by the explosion was very great. The waters of the river were violently disturbed down to their lowest depths. They were thrown beyond its banks and the neighboring dikes; and all the fortifications, situated on either side of it, were covered several feet deep with water. Almost all the timber-work of the left bank, to which the fire-ship had attached itself, as also a part of the bridge of boats, together with every thing that was upon it, was broken in pieces and thrown into the air. More than eight hundred men perished in various ways; and the Duke himself escaped, as it were, only by a miracle. Nothing seemed to hinder any longer the passage of the Zealand fleet from Liefkenshoek up the stream to Antwerp.

As soon as the explosion was heard in the city, St. Aldegonde sent several galleys to ascertain on the spot the condition of the bridge. They were instructed, if they should find that it had been destroyed, to communicate the fact by a signal, and then to sail to Lillo in order to set the Zealand fleet in motion, so that a combined attack may be made from the opposite quarters on the enemy's works. But the commanders of the vessels which had been dispatched were wanting in the courage required for approaching near enough to their object, and returned to Antwerp with the report that the bridge was yet uninjured.

The Duke of Parma was in the mean time exceedingly diligent in giving it the appearance, at least, of being so; and on the third day from the explosion, a small boat, coming from Lillo, passes under the bridge, and announces at Antwerp both the injury it had received, and its speedy reparation. In this manner, the Duke succeeds in gaining time for restoring fully the damage incurred, and supplying from the neighboring garrisons his loss of men.

Discouraged by some other fruitless attempts to reopen the

navigation of the Scheldt, the Zealanders resolve to give up entirely this design, and to direct their efforts instead to the destruction of the dikes between Stabroek and Antwerp, by which the country is protected from the waters of the Osterschelde, so as to be enabled to approach to Antwerp with flat-bottomed boats.

First of all, the Antwerpers judge it expedient to pierce through the Cauwenstein dike, extending from Fort La Croix, near the Scheldt, to the neighborhood of Stabroek. But the Duke of Parma, in order to repel every attack in this quarter, has been careful to have five redoubts constructed along this line. These redoubts are occupied by fresh troops, under the orders of experienced chiefs, and provided with cannon, and furnished, besides, with palisades, rendering access to them more difficult.

The Duke of Parma having intrusted the guarding of the bridge to Count Mansfeld, transfers himself to Stabroek to the east of the river.

In the mean time the Netherlanders have broken through the dike extending along that side of the stream, so as to inundate the whole of the country situated north of the dike of Cauenstein. A joint attack upon this is next concerted between the authorities in Antwerp and the Count of Hohenlohe, the admiral of the Zealand fleet. The latter fulfilled his part of the agreement. On perceiving the expected signals in the direction of the city, he approached the dike, and, disembarking the troops which he conveyed, made a general assault upon the redoubts, taking two of them. He was, however, eventually deprived of the advantages at first obtained, through the failure of the Antwerp flotilla to co-operate with him, as had been promised, and was obliged to retire.

A renewed attempt is appointed to be made, both against the dike and the bridge, on the 16th of May, 1585. Not fewer than two hundred vessels are to be employed against the former, and new machines, contrived by Gianibelli, are destined to blow up the latter, or at all events to hold in check the portion of the Spanish troops there posted for its protection.

While the fleets of the Netherlanders approach the dike on the opposite sides of it, their land forces from the north obtain possession of the part of it comprehended between the redoubts before captured by them. Here they intrench themselves, and a bloody contest ensues. And they succeed in conveying over the dike a transport vessel, after having lightened it of its load. Instead of prosecuting the advantages which he has obtained, Count Hohenlohe proceeds triumphantly to Antwerp, where he is received amidst the thunder of artillery and the ringing of bells.

Before long the Duke of Parma arrives at the dike with a re-enforcement of men and cannon. His presence revives the drooping spirits of the Spaniards. After five unsuccessful assaults on one of the redoubts which had been taken by the enemy, they regain possession of it.

The tide at length beginning to ebb, the hostile fleets are constrained to retreat, and the victory rests with the Duke. His loss in this quarter amounted to nearly eight hundred men; that of the Netherlanders to about two thousand. More than thirty vessels laden with provisions for Antwerp, and one hundred and fifty pieces of cannon, fall into the hands of the Spaniards.

The attempts which were, on the same day, made to destroy the bridge, were fruitless.

A general discouragement now pervades the minds of the besieged, aggravated by the want of provisions and by the information of the neighboring city of Mecheln having been taken by the enemy. The authorities are forced by the people to capitulate on the 17th of August, 1585.

During the lifetime of Henry III., the last king of France of the house of Valois, a formidable combination, denominated the League, had been organized in that country, at the head of which was, first, the Duke of Guise, and, subsequently, the Duke of Mayenne, and which had obliged the king to throw himself at last into the arms of the Huguenots, or French Protestants, to be enabled to maintain his authority. The king of Navarre, styled Henry IV., of the House of Bourbon, was the lawful heir to the throne. Mayenne, who was in possession of Paris and a great part of the kingdom, resisted his accession by all the means in his power, and only awaited the promised assistance of Spain to attack, and, as he confidently hoped, to destroy the Protestant and royal army. At length, Alexander Farnese, Duke of Parma, sent Count Egmont to him from the Netherlands with eighteen hundred cavalry; and he now determined to relieve the city of Dreux, twenty miles north of Chartres, then besieged by Henry IV.

Battle of IVRY, fought on the 14th of March, 1590, between Henry IV., of France and the troops of the League, commanded by the Duke of Mayenne.

Henry had raised the siege of Dreux immediately upon hearing of the approach of the Duke of Mayenne, and no time was lost by the hostile forces in coming in sight of each other at Ivry, between the rivers Eure and Iton. The royal army consisted of eight thousand infantry and twenty-five hundred cavalry, with six pieces of cannon; that of the League to thirteen thousand infantry and thirty-five hundred cavalry, with four pieces of cannon.

$a\,a$ and $b\,b$ on the plan represent positions successively occupied by the royal army on the 13th of March, and $d\,d$ is that of the opposite party on the same day.

BATTLE OF IVRY.

Royal Army
Army of the League

IVRY

On the following day, the order of battle of the former is (*d*) four hundred arquebusiers, (*e*) two hundred cavalry under the orders of the Marshal d'Aumont, (*f*) eight hundred arquebusiers in two divisions, (*g*) two hundred cavalry under the Duke of Montpensier, (*h*) two hundred cavalry under the Baron de Biron, (*i*) one thousand infantry in two divisions, (*k*) six hundred cavalry in five lines under the immediate command of the king, (*l*) thirty-two hundred infantry in eight divisions, (*m*) four hundred light cavalry in two divisions, under the Count d'Auvergne and the Chevalier Givry, and *n n* denote the six cannon; *o* denotes five hundred cavalry; *p*, twenty-four hundred Swiss; and *q*, three hundred cavalry, composing the reserve, under the Marshal Biron. A chain of light troops (*r r*) covers the front of the position.

The Duke of Mayenne's army is drawn up in a concave line as follows: *s*, is three thousand infantry in two divisions; *t*, three hundred German cavalry; *u*, eight hundred infantry; *v*, six hundred light cavalry in two divisions, before the right wing, under the orders of the Chevalier de Rosne; *w*, five hundred German cavalry; *x*, thirty-four hundred infantry; *y*, ten hundred Walloon lancers under Count Egmont; *z*, five hundred cavalry under the Duke of Mayenne in person; *a'*, four hundred Spanish arquebusiers on horseback; *b'*, forty-two hundred infantry, one half of them Swiss and the other French; *c'*, four hundred German cavalry; *d'*, sixteen hundred infantry in two divisions; and *e'* denotes the four cannon. A chain of light troops (*f' f'*) covers the front of the position.

VOL. III.—22

Before the battle began, Henry IV. is recorded as having ridden along the lines of his army, calling out to his soldiers, "When you fail to see any standards displayed, rally around the white crest of my helmet; you will always find it on the way of honor and glory." It commenced with the discharge of the artillery on both sides. The troops commanded by the Chevalier de Rosne suffer a considerable loss, whereupon he orders an attack to be made on the left wing of the royalists at A. Marshal d'Aumont encounters him at B, and obliges him to resume his position. The German cavalry, which had advanced from t to the support of De Rosne, are broken by a charge of the light cavalry of Givry and Auvergne from their position at m. These, then, carry disorder into the centre of the army of the League, but are at length driven back by Count Egmont to D, who is, in his turn, forced to fall back by the Baron de Biron and the Duke of Montpensier (g, h) to the post originally assigned to him.

For a considerable time occupied with restoring order in his centre, the Duke of Mayenne now only puts his squadrons in motion. And Henry IV., after another short address to his men, leads them forward himself.

The contest was a severe one, and Egmont and his troops especially distinguished themselves. The king deemed it necessary to order up to his assistance his entire reserve under the Marshal de Biron. At this crisis the result was still doubtful, when Count Egmont fell, shot by a pistol-ball. This might of itself have been sufficient to decide the day in favor of Henry. But about this moment his standard-bearer, severely wounded, was obliged to be conveyed from the field, and the soldiers were exceedingly discouraged by the fall of a young knight with a white crest, near the person of the king, and who was mistaken by them for the latter. In this emergency, Henry, taking off his helmet, exhibited his well-known countenance to his followers, and, with his bloody sword in his hand, excited them to the highest pitch of enthusiasm. Nothing could any longer resist their valor, and the victory was decided.

Some attempts were indeed still made by the Duke of Mayenne, after the defeat of his cavalry, to maintain the contest with infantry. The Swiss troops oppose to the enemy a vigorous resistance, but at length lay down their arms on perceiving themselves to be surrounded on every side, and a body of Germans, refusing to do the like, are for the most part cut down.

The army of the League takes to flight in two different directions—one portion of it on the route to Chartres, under the Duke of Nemours, and the other, under the Duke of Mayenne, upon Ivry, where it passes the River Eure, destroying the bridge behind it, and marching afterwards on Mantes. Barricades had been thrown up at Ivry, and were stormed by the Marshal de Biron upon his arrival.

All the baggage and artillery of the defeated troops are taken, and they lose also three-fourths of their original number, killed, wounded, or prisoners, or drowned in the Eure. The loss incurred by the royal army is estimated at five hundred men.

Other battles, fought and won in the same chivalrous spirit as that of Ivry, have conferred an undying renown on Henry of Navarre. But independently of the bravery and prowess repeatedly displayed by him, he ranks as a general with the most illustrious of his contemporaries,—with the Duke of Parma, with Coligni, with Condé, and with Maurice, of Nassau,—in introducing a higher degree of order and discipline among the soldiers of an army, and in preparing the way for the appearance of Gustavus Adolphus. And we may conclude our notice of the battle of Ivry by noticing the far greater importance then attached to cavalry than to infantry, in a serious and open contest with an enemy, an importance thenceforth destined gradually, for a time at least, to diminish.

Siege of STRALSUND, from the 13th of May to the 4th of August, 1628.

At the period in question, Stralsund was one of the Hanse

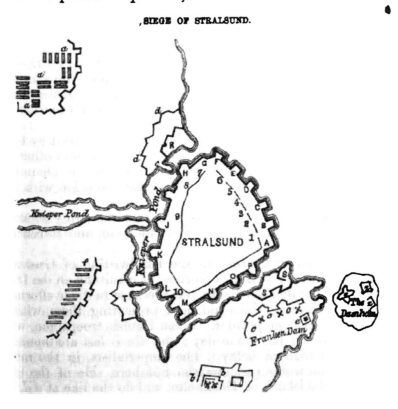

SIEGE OF STRALSUND.

towns, although acknowledging the feudal superiority of the Duke of Pomerania. The Emperor of Germany, Ferdinand II., deemed it to be expedient to place a garrison of his troops within its walls. An expedition, should one be thought desirable, might then be fitted out from its harbor against Sweden, which had furnished less or more of encouragement and aid to the German Protestants during the first ten years (of the so-called Thirty Years' War) of their struggle for religious liberty against the imperial authority.

To accomplish this design, General von Arnim was ordered to approach the city with a force of eight thousand men.

On the 13th of May, that general pitched his camp at $a\,a\,a$, and made the requisite demand to be admitted into the place. A negative reply having been promptly given, he next endeavors to attain his object by the stratagem of asking for a passage through the city of one thousand cuirassiers and five companies of foot soldiers, to be embarked thence for the island of Rugen. And this request being also refused him, he seizes possession of the small island of Daenholm, which was garrisoned by a small body of Danes that the magistrates of Stralsund had taken into their pay.

The latter, exceedingly irritated at this proceeding, having in vain required an immediate restoration of the island, lost no time in commencing hostilities against its captors, who were very soon reduced, by the want of provisions, to the necessity of embarking for the neighboring island of Rugen.

In the night between the 16th and 17th of May the Imperialists, by means of a surprise, obtain possession of the intrenchments of the city, at R and S, situated before the Knieper and the Franken gates. But they are expelled from them at six o'clock on the following morning, with loss.

The citizens of Stralsund are not a little encouraged by these events, as also by the arrival of munitions of war and other aid gratuitously bestowed upon them by the King of Denmark, and of several vessels from the south of Europe laden with provisions.

On the 17th of May a part of the Imperial army encamps near $b\,b$, in the vicinity of the Frankindamm, and intrenches itself.

A written communication, in the handwriting of Gustavus Adolphus, King of Sweden, is received at Stralsund on the 18th, encouraging the inhabitants to perseverance in their efforts at resistance, promising them aid, and presenting them with a vessel laden with gunpowder. Some Danish troops, too, with cannon, arrive on the same day; and these last are mounted on the walls without delay. The Imperialists, in the mean time, erect the works ($c\,c\,c$) on the Southern side of the city and against the island of Daenholm, and do the like at $d\,d$, on the western side. From these works a vigorous cannonade is maintained, and it is replied to with equal efficiency.

In the night between the 23d and 24th of May, the Imperialists make simultaneous attempts to storm the Franken, Knieper, and Hospital gates, at A, G, and H, but are repulsed, by the discharge of grape-shot, at all these points. They, however, obtain possession of the redoubt at S S, but are expelled from it by Captain Chemnitz on the early morning of the next day. The loss incurred in these contests by the Imperialists was so great as to induce General Arnim to ask for a suspension of hostilities in order to bury the dead.

On the 25th of May two companies of Scots and one of Germans, six hundred men in all, sent by the King of Denmark, arrive in Stralsund. Their commander, Colonel Holk, is intrusted with the chief command in the city. Hostilities are continued for some days without any marked successes on either side.

Four more companies of Scots arrive on the 29th, and the gate of the Hospital, so called, is vehemently bombarded by the Imperialists on the 30th and 31st of May, but without serious injury being done.

About this time there arrives a present from the king of Sweden, consisting of one hundred oxen, one hundred tons of powder, and six twenty-four-pounders.

The bombardment of the city continues. It receives a re-enforcement of two hundred Danish soldiers on the 4th of June, and another, three days afterwards, of two hundred Danish soldiers, together with fifty artillerists, six cannon and a mortar, and one hundred barrels of powder. The Imperialists prosecute their works of intrenchment, endeavoring to approach nearer and nearer to the ponds which surround the city; but they everywhere encounter obstacles to their progress from the sorties of the garrison.

On the 14th of June, the Imperialists construct the redoubt *e* on the dike (damm) of the Knieper, at the distance of a pistol-shot from the works of the besieged.

On the 25th, the Council of Stralsund concludes a formal alliance with the King of Sweden, who engages to maintain the rights and liberties of the city against all enemies; and on the same day six hundred Swedes enter the place, under Colonel Rosladin.

Two days after this, the Duke of Friedland (the celebrated Wallenstein) arrives with nine thousand men before Stralsund. A portion of them encamp at *ff*, and cannonade the redoubt at T.

In the morning of the 28th, three regiments of Imperialists make a fierce assault from the Frankendamm (*c c*) upon the redoubt at (S). The besieged are driven as far as the gate of the city, but, when re-enforced, they retake the redoubt. In this contest, which was the most sanguinary one during the siege, the loss of the Imperialists amounted to nearly one thousand men.

On the 29th, this redoubt, after another severe conflict, is again taken by the Imperialists, who remain in possession of it. Great consternation now pervades the city, and it is abandoned by a considerable portion of the female population who embark for Sweden.

Negotiations are entered upon by the two parties on the second day of July, which lead to no result. The bombardment is resumed on the following day, and endures twenty-four hours without interruption. On the 5th an armistice is concluded,— one, however, little respected by either party. On the 9th and 10th of July fresh re-enforcements arrive in the city from Denmark.

Stralsund being open on the sea side to supplies of men and provisions, Wallenstein at length only hopes to obtain possession of it by negotiation or stratagem. He quits the besieging army on the 15th of July, leaving the negotiations to be directed by General Arnim.

On the 18th of July, two thousand Swedish auxiliaries, under Colonel Leslie and Count Brahe, arrive in Stralsund; and on the 19th, a sortie is made from the city by the Franken gate (A), by means of which the redoubt at S is once more recovered from the enemy. In this contest the newly-arrived Swedish troops eminently distinguished themselves.

The Imperialists gradually withdrew their artillery from the works about the city, and retired from its vicinity on the 24th of July.

Their loss, from the commencement to the end of the siege, has been estimated to have amounted to ten thousand eight hundred infantry and twelve hundred cavalry.

At the period of the siege of Stralsund, Gustavus Adolphus was engaged in a contest against the Poles, which absorbed the greater portion of his attention. This was brought to a close in 1629, through the mediation of England and Holland; and he was then at liberty to direct the forces at his disposal against the overgrown power of the House of Austria, and at the same time to protect the Protestants of Germany from the oppressions of the Imperial government. He landed in the island of Rugen on the 24th of June, 1630, with an army of Swedes re-enforced by several regiments of Scots which he had taken into his service. His advance into Germany was for a time comparatively slow. The Protestant princes, having heretofore been unfortunate in their resistance to the emperor, hesitated to encounter the risks of another insurrection against him. But a treaty of alliance was at length concluded between Gustavus and the Elector of Saxony, the latter engaging not to come to any terms of accommodation with Austria, excepting with the consent of the King of Sweden. And the hostile armies then did not delay long in coming into conflict.

Battle of BREITENFELD (near Leipsick), on the 7th of September, 1631, between the Imperial general, Field-Marshal Tilly, and the combined Swedes and Saxons, under Gustavus Adolphus, King of Sweden.

Numerical force of the armies: Imperialists, twenty-one thousand infantry and eleven thousand cavalry; Swedes, eight thousand infantry and seven thousand cavalry, and Saxons eleven thousand infantry and four thousand cavalry.

Count Pappenheim, who had been sent forward with two thousand cavalry, by the Imperial commander-in-chief, to observe the enemy, transcended his orders, and attacked the Swedish advanced guard. He was on the point of being overwhelmed by superior numbers, when he was rescued by the arrival of two thousand additional cavalry, dispatched to his assistance by Tilly. In his mortification for the repulse which he had incurred, he set fire to the village of Podelwitz on his retreat.

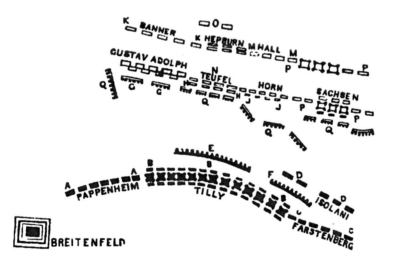

BATTLE OF BREITENFELD.

The allied order of battle is as follows: G (see plan) denotes the right wing of the Swedes, resting on Podelwitz, under the immediate command of Gustavus, and consisting of five regiments of cavalry, with infantry between them; K is four regiments of cavalry, also with intervening infantry in the second line, under General Banner; H denotes four brigades of infantry in the centre, under General Teufel; and L, three brigades behind them, in the second line, under General Hepburne; J is five regiments of cavalry, again intermingled with infantry, on the left wing, under General Horn, and M is three regiments of cavalry, under Colonel Hall, in the second line; at N, behind the centre and between the first and second lines, are ten squadrons of dragoons, constituting the first reserve; and at O, behind the centre of the second line, is a second reserve, composed of cavalry and infantry; and on the extreme left, at P, the Saxons are posted in two lines, the infantry in six brigades, and the cavalry to the right and left of it, under the orders of the Elector and of General Arnheim; one hundred pieces of cannon are distributed in front of the whole army (22), in fourteen batteries.

About noon the battle is begun by a heavy cannonade on both sides. Gustavus then, seeking to gain ground with his right wing, is vehemently attacked, in front and in flank, by Pappenheim, at the head of all his cavalry. This attack is again and again repeated without success, being in every instance repelled by the fire of the infantry intermingled with the cavalry of Gustavus. A forward and flanking movement of General Banner, from the second line, at length puts an end to its repetition.

Meanwhile, the Prince of Fürstenberg, on the right wing, had fallen upon the Saxons; the greater portion of whom, composed of recently-levied men, offered only a feeble resistance. Four of the older regiments, which stood their ground for a time, were at length obliged to yield to superior numbers, and to take refuge behind the Swedish left wing.

Tilly, now desiring to complete the victory, advanced with the infantry, moving at the same time towards his right against the Saxons and the left wing of the Swedes. By this movement, however, he was necessitated to stop the firing of his artillery, and a certain degree of disorder had spread among his men. In this state of things, General Horn, who commanded the Swedish left, had brought forward several batteries from the reserve, and had posted them in positions concealed from the enemy by cavalry. Their brisk and unexpected fire increased the confusion already prevailing among the latter; and all the attempts made by the Imperial cavalry to advance over the ditches in their way were frustrated by the miry state of the ground and the counter attacks of the Swedes.

Whilst Tilly was here engaged in vain, Pappenheim had been defeated, and driven entirely from the field by Baner. Gustavus now directed all the disposable troops of his right and centre towards his left; and with these he seized possession of the enemy's stationary batteries, which were then immediately turned against the latter. Although cannonaded both in front and in flank, Tilly made several unsuccessful efforts to retake his lost artillery. At length, first his infantry, and then his cavalry, broke their ranks and fled. He himself succeeded in reaching Halle with six hundred men, and there indicated Halberstadt as the rallying point of the fugitives from the field of battle.

We find the losses of the Imperialists estimated at twelve thousand killed and wounded, one hundred standards, twenty-six pieces of cannon, and the whole of their baggage. The Saxons lost two thousand, and the Swedes one thousand men.

The causes of the loss of the battle by the Imperialists were *first*, their failure to attack the Saxo-Swedish army in its passage of the defiles of the stream of the Loberbach, in order to assume the position which it actually held during the battle; *secondly*, the entire absence of a second line or reserve; *thirdly*, the unchangeable position of their artillery, which not merely became embarrassing to them in the attacks they made, but even positively injurious; *fourthly*, the unnecessary loss of time incurred after their defeat of the Saxons, enabling General Horn to make his dispositions for the defence of the Swedish left wing; and *lastly*, the want of unity in the attacks made by their generals, while, on the contrary, the Swedish generals acted throughout in the most entire harmony in all their movements.

SEEKING THE BUBBLE.

II.

* * Then a soldier,
Full of strange oaths and bearded like the pard;
Jealous in honor, sudden and quick in quarrel;
Seeking the bubble reputation,
Even in the cannon's mouth * * * *
As You Like It.—Act II., Scene VII.

IN NEW CLOTHES.

"What is an Adjutant?" she asked.

"An Adjutant? Why, an Adjutant is a-a-sort of an—don't you know what an Adjutant is? I thought everybody knew that?"

Please to remember, incredulous sir or madam, that this was in the first year—ay, in the first six months—of this present war, when you, too, probably, were as ignorant as Mary and I, and knew, perhaps, no more of the relative importance of officers than we did. For I, who had just been appointed adjutant of our regiment, though I hardly knew what my title meant, felt, I am sure, of vastly more consequence than does the worthy commander-in-chief in this year of grace, 1865.

"The Adjutant," I continued, "is,—err-a-a sort of assistant

to the Colonel, you know,—on the staff,—that sort of thing. Don't you know?"

"Oh, yes! How nice! Like General Thomas."

How could I explain that the very new Lieutenant William Jenkins, Adjutant of the Third District of Columbia Volunteers, was very little like the grizzled Adjutant-General of the Army whom she had mentioned? Women *won't* understand those things, you see.

While I was enjoying the luxuries of my first fever in the hospital, "our boys," as we used to call the regiment, had, for the most part, re-enlisted for three years, or during the war. The battle of Bull Run had just been fizzled—you can hardly say *fought*, of a battle into which a mob of green men bulge promiscuously under green commanders, and out of which, almost before they recover from the first terror of discharging their own muskets, they rush, jabbering and scared, away from an only less frightened enemy. The North had uprisen again. The last of the Southern sympathizers, now convinced that we could not subdue the South, resigned from the Army and Navy. General Blankhed had nearly stopped giving passes for ladies and children, and Jews and sutlers, and spies and Baltimoreans, to go through the lines to Richmond. Mrs. Greenhow was still in Washington, studying for the part of lioness by playing jackal, and wheedling facile senators with her best light-comedy attractions. The country still believed in Sigel. Strategy was beginning to be born. Washington was beginning to run to sheds. In short, it was the August of 1861, just after the first crisis of the national measles.

General McClellan, who had just fought some skirmishes in Western Virginia, and administered the oath of allegiance to the captives pursuant to instructions from the omniscient City of Washington, not having been defeated, was called to the command of the Army of the Potomac; and presently, as he showed himself, mounted on a handsome charger and followed by, I may say, a rather seedy staff—we thought them grand enough, however, and so, indeed, they soon became!—we all magnified him into a second Napoleon. All but Smallweed, our melancholy man, now promoted to be quartermaster. He and Colonel Heavysterne used to have high words on the subject. "Ah," the honest old Colonel would say, a genuine admiration beaming in his eye, "that's your sort! That's the man for me! We'll just go anywhere he says. Look at him, gentlemen! See how he rides!"

The Sceptic. Hur. Very pretty. Hoop-la! What's he ever done?

The Enthusiast. Why, he's licked the enemy, sir. That's what he's done, sir. His genius is equal to Napoleon's, sir. He's the man for my money!

The Chorus. { Yes, *sir!*
There's no discount on that!
That's so!
&c., &c.

The Sceptic. Going to make a Napoleon out of a man because he ain't been licked! Well, I'm d——d! Colonel, I thought you had more sense than that. There's the chaplain there; he's never been licked, either. Why don't you call him a second Duke of Wellington, and make a pair of 'em? No, *sir.* Show me a man that's done something, I say, and don't be clapping on all sail before the wind blows, in this sort of way.

The Enthusiast. What a man! Why, gentlemen, I b'lieve if th' Angel Gab'l was to come on earth, this Smallweed 'd say he was no great shakes, after all!

The Chorus. { Ah! Ha!
D——n such a man, anyhow!
&c., &c.

The Sceptic. (Puff. Puff.) Well! I don't run round after every oysterman that blows a tin horn, anyhow!

It was in this free way that we used to discuss our new general, and thus that we used to think of him. How far this spirit of unreasoning enthusiasm, that made us almost deify the young commander who hadn't been whipped, has since contributed to the downfall of this and other officers who have certainly had some merit, if not what we so hastily ascribed to them, and who might have been useful square pegs if we had not zealously shoved them into the round holes, let some recently-cradled Macaulay recite for our amusement and instruction when, deaf and toothless, we chump over the memories of these bloody years for the edification of our grandchildren, or somebody else's. I only recall facts.

The grand, the immortal Army of the Potomac was then a puling infant. Indeed, as it was found by its new leader, 'twas little more than a few scattered regiments cowering upon the banks of the Potomac, in hourly fear of the advance of the then invincible Beauregard, and busied principally in comparing notes as to who had behaved least badly at Bull Run. There were many shameless enough to use those two terrible epithets as a joke. The men who have since thought it funny to say "How are *you?*" then thought it exceedingly funny to jeer out "Bull Run!" or often, with even more exquisite wit, "Bully Run!" It was a merry jest. Being *apropos* of nothing, these funny dogs made it *apropos* of every thing. There had been nothing like it since "*Or any other man*" swept over this once happy land; but I think—yes, I think "How are *you?*" beat it.

Our regiment was rapidly recruited. Colonel Heavysterne was personally very popular, the number of three months' men from the district had been very large, and the scrofula of secession had about run its course among the men. One day, while fumbling among some blank passes, probably, it occurred to old General Blankhed that he might as well order us across the river. So as we had been quietly forgotten for a couple of weeks when there was hurry, and as there was now none, an aide dashed into our camp about one o'clock that night, with orders to the Colonel to break camp, and move over to Arlington Heights at daylight. As soon as the dear old fellow got the sleep partly out of his eyes, he ventured to ask the excited young aide where he was to get wagons. He didn't know. What was up? He didn't know. Was there any news? He didn't know. To whom were we to report when we got to Arlington Heights? He didn't know that either, but feebly suggested "commanding officer." "So the order says," said the Colonel; but who is he? Where shall I find him?" The The A. D. C. knew not. "Hur," said Smallweed, sadly,

> "A light blue eye, a soldier mean,
>   A feather of the blue,
>   A doublet of the Lincoln green,
>   No more than this you knew, old chap;"—

Etcetry.—Scott; and, when found, make a note on. Say, look here," addressing the retreating figure of the A. D. C., stumbling over the tent-cords in the vain attempt to find his horse, "they don't let you go about much alone; do they?"

Then there was a grand discussion as to wagons, Smallweed insisting that twenty-two wagons would do, and the Colonel, supported by Dr. Peacack, who had been awakened by the A. D. C. stumbling over his tent-cords, and afterwards backing his horse into his tent, contending for thirty as absolutely necessary.

Did you ever see a raw regiment move? We had *reveillé* at three, and an excited breakfast. Then there was a scramble for wagons in the dark, and cries of teamsters, and cursing of men who had jammed their fingers between hard corners, and whinnying of mules, and the crackling of fires lighted by the men out of irresistible wantonness, and hurrying to and fro of officers and sergeants, and the barking of the wagon-master's dog, and a confusion of tongues, advising, ordering, imploring, cursing, and everything done in a hurry and a scuffle, and as wrong as could be. Just about raw daylight, when everybody is standing about fagged and worried, remembering the last forgotten odds and ends, up dashes another aide with a long yellow envelope. The privates crowd round, peering over the Colonel's shoulder—remember, this is 1861, and a green regiment. "This is not addressed to any of you, gentlemen, I think," hints the Colonel, politely; whereupon all, save the more brassy, edge away, trying their best to look as if they hadn't been doing any thing wrong, and wouldn't at any price. The brassy brazen it out, and audibly suggest that some people give themselves airs all of a sudden. One of them is impudent enough to sing out an anxious inquiry respecting the price of cheese, in allusion to the honest Colonel's former business. The yellow envelope contains a countermand. We loaf around in the raw dawn, and in the early, feverish morning, awaiting further orders, ready to march at an instant's notice. Such are our new orders. Some of the men go to sleep; others become furtively and mysteriously intoxicated; others play cards; others, still, sing songs, in and out of tune. Those who cannot sing, sing the most, as usual. The mules kick and roll over, and make a terrible row generally. The teamsters straggle off, and come back drunk and insolent. No further orders come. The excitement of being ready to march at a moment's notice is wearing off. Only nine o'clock? It seems like five in the afternoon, we have been up and waiting so long. We begin to ache with waiting. Ten, eleven, twelve—all the hours up to six—pass, and no order. Most of the drunken men are sober, and some of them drunk again. Every nerve and muscle in the body of the poor adjutant quivers with fatigue. So, doubtless, with every one else. Smallweed volunteers to ride up to head-quarters, and see what's the matter. The Colonel hesitates, but finally consents. While he is gone, we dine on hard tack—that is, those of us who have not been making a steady lunch on hard tack ever since breakfast-time. It is dark when Smallweed trots back—I think no earthly consideration would induce him to ride at a canter, which he says is a pace only fit for doctors and chaplains—trots back with the news that old General Blankhed had forgotten all about us! Now, however, we are to march at once. So the regiment falls in; the train starts; off we march, down the dusty roads, by courtesy called streets; through the wilderness of dust they call "the avenue;" over the Long Bridge, to Arlington Heights. All Washington seems to turn out to look at us as we pass. Sutlers' wagons follow in our wake, selling pies to the stragglers. It is ten o'clock and pitch dark before we arrive at our destination. No one knows where we are to encamp. We arrive in a great camp of soldiers. We are to report "to the commanding officer," says our order. Who is he? Nobody knows. The colonels don't know; one thinks it's General Scott; a New York colonel, in full Zouave costume, thinks it is General Sandford. A wagon-master guides us to the tent of some second lieutenant, and points *him* out as the commanding officer. "Who do you report to?" our Colonel asks, scratching his head, perplexedly, of a venerable-looking Lieutenant-Colonel, who seems to have served in the revolutionary war. "Nobody," is the answer, gravely enough, and a staggerer it is. "But I think," says Grandfather Whitehead, kindly, "I think, if I were you, Colonel, I would just go into camp anywhere, and wait till they ordered me away! That's what I did, and I've been here nigh on to ten days!"

Well, we scramble into camp, somehow, and there, sure enough, we remain for three long days, unable to find "the Commanding Officer." No human ingenuity suffices to unravel the mystery. Presently, the Commanding Officer stumbles across us, in the shape of a middle-aged gentleman, in very undress uniform, and a singularly dirty shirt, who has come all the way from Arizona, where he commanded a company of at least twenty regulars, to command a division of volunteers in the grand Army of the Potomac. His mind is nicely arranged for a one-company post. He raps everybody over the knuckles because they don't know as much as he does, finds fault with everything, moves our camp to a place where there is wood and water, instructs the colonel in tactics, shows the men how to pitch tents, teaches the adjutant how to solve that mystery of mysteries, a "consolidated morning report," corrects the quartermaster's papers for him, inducts the commissary into the art of drawing rations, damns the surgeon for an old fool, insults the chaplain, and walks off, heartily cursing all volunteers, and intimating his decided belief that the army has gone to the dogs or worse. He leaves behind him every one astonished, many disgusted, but all, somehow, instructed in something. Smallweed took to him instantly, and stoutly defended him against the attacks of the many. Brave old Pike! The division learned to know and respect and follow you in spite of your roughness, and many an eye was damp when you were laid in your soldier's grave at Fair Oaks, to curse us no more. Brigadier-General Richard Pike, whilom a captain in the seventh cavalry, one of the "low down" graduates of West Point, was a true soldier, one of a type I have often met, who have done their work and passed from the scene; some, like him, into their grave, others crowded out and into quiet corners by the rising generation, better educated, with quicker brains, fitted for the occasion. They did their work, I say, and did it well. They taught us green volunteers everything we know of the thousand indispensable details of service; how to cook, how to eat, how to sleep, how to be soldiers. They worked hard and zealously. That they could not, ordinarily, rise superior to pipe-clay, came naturally of their education in the narrow sphere of a one-company post. The company fund and the orderly sergeant were greater in their eyes than all the strategy Jomini ever dreamed. Over them and through them, fed by their instruction and inspired by their example, those of us volunteers who are worth anything have become what we are. Let us own it, thankfully.

First, we were in Pike's Brigade; then, as the troops came pouring into Washington, the General got a division, with our brigade as a part of it, and Brigadier-General Isaac Slushmeyer, an enterprising New York young lawyer, from the vicinity of the Tombs, to command it. What a change! Mars turned shyster! Here is his first order from life:—

"HEAD-QUARTERS, SLUSHMEYER'S BRIGADE,
"PIKE'S DIVISION, ARLINGTON HEIGHTS, VA., Sept. 30, 1861.

"General Orders No. 1.
"I. In accordance with the requirements of Special Orders No. 28, of the 29th instant, from the head-quarters of said division, and of the unsought commission so flatteringly bestowed upon him by the worthy chief magistrate, the undersigned hereby assumes command of the above-named brigade.
"II. His staff will be as follows:—
"Captain Israel Salomans, Assistant Adjutant-General.
"Lieutenant A. J. Pidgeon, Aide-de-Camp.
"Lieutenant C. Muggins, Aide-de-Camp.
"Captain J. Sheppard Filch, Commissary of Subsistence.
"Captain Richard Terpin, Assistant Quarter-master.
"Surgeon G. Buster, Brigade Surgeon.
"III. Soldiers! In thus assuming control of one of the finest bodies of citizen-soldiery ever assembled for the vindication, disenthralment and maintenance of the best government ever framed by man—the government of Washington, of Kosciusko, of Lafayette, and of Buchanan—against the fratricidal assaults of the most wicked and unnatural rebellion ever inaugurated by foul treason, a decent respect for the opinions of mankind requires that your general should declare to you his fixed and unalterable purpose of leading you under the folds of our starry flag, emblem of the oppressed without regard to nationality, wherever the battle rages thickest, until the backbone of the rebellion being broken, there shall be no longer a rebel in arms opposed to us, and trembling Europe shall again witness the sublime spectacle of Columbia emerging from her fiery ordeal purified in the furnace of civil war, with one Constitution, one Flag, one People, one Destiny, again assuming our proud place among the tyrants of the earth, holding them, in the world-famed language of the Monroe doctrine, 'as we hold the rest of mankind, enemies in war, in peace friends!'
"Soldiers! Your General is a man, not of words, but of deeds. I am here, not to write, but to fight. Follow me, and victory is ours. Very truly, gentlemen, your friend and servant,
"By command of
"BRIGADIER-GENERAL SLUSHMEYER!
"ISRAEL SALOMANS, A. A. Gen."

"Hur," says Smallweed, reading it over the Adjutant's shoulder; "subject to the approval of a regular Democratic Convention."

"Well, now that's what I call poot nice," remarks the chaplain. "Le'ss hear 't again, 'gents."

The men looked blank when they heard it rattled off, in a stentorian voice, by the Adjutant, and in broken sentences, without regard to punctuation, after the most approved style which I had by this time managed to pick up. After parade, they tittered and joked about it in little knots. I heard the words "Gammon," and "Hail C'lumby," more than once as I passed the knots. Some people have an idea that common men like trashy writing. Well, I admit they like dime novels, if you please; but let me assure you that no one sees through the rigmarole and bluster of a political general quite so soon as the common soldier.

General Pike had drilled and drilled, and instructed and scolded us daily, with indefatigable zeal. Mounted upon a shaggy, square-headed, angular beast, innocent of the curry-comb and brush, branded with a scabby "U. S." on the shoulder, he would jolt along the picket-line with his arms and legs keeping loose time to the disjointed motions of Rosinante, looking, himself, for all the world, the very picture of a shabby orderly. I see him now, half unshaven; his tawny hair straggling into his eyes and ears; the vizor of his old-fashioned forage cap turned up in the manner adopted by our cavalry in Texas; his worn and faded flannel sack, held together by tarnished buttons in worn button-holes, over a dirty flannel shirt, just exposing a dirtier paper collar, secured about a brick-red neck, ornamented with stray, stubby hairs, by means of an old black kerchief tied in a hard knot; his sword-belt concealed by his coat; a rusty dragoon sabre of the heaviest pattern flying about his heels; his common dragoon trowsers unequally tucked into a pair of dirty dragoon boots, several sizes too large, and ornamented by *one* common very brass spur, originally valued at some thirteen cents, including the strap and buckle. I said he looked the very picture of a shabby orderly: surely, never was orderly, even from a western regiment, so shabby! And thus he would jolt along the picket-line, stirring up a sentinel here, reprimanding an officer there, praising one, and jeering at another; or would jog across the wet and slippery parade-ground, laboring to teach us, laboring harder to teach our commanding officers, the mysteries of the brigade drill; working, indeed, like a horse, and swearing always like the trooper he was. For the six weeks he commanded our brigade, I think he was never out of the camp. He was always at work, trying to straighten things out, as he said. Officers and men came to see the sterling stuff whereof he was made, and to admire his honest worth, while they could not resist laughing at his eccentricities, and at his shabbiness. Our new general changed all that. We heard of him occasionally in flatulent orders;—Smallweed used to declare they should have been dated, "*Head-quarters on the Stump.*" We saw him once at a review, swelling in a bran new uniform, in the midst of a gorgeous staff, looking for all the world like so many faro-dealers at a masquerade. Those of us who frequented Willard's, and enjoyed the squalid pleasures of Washington, met him oftener; the chaplain oftenest of all, I think. We heard of him, also, very often, through the veracious correspondents of the New York papers, as performing prodigies of labor and valor. Fast young officers, returning sickish and seedy from overstayed leaves, would sometimes bring extended passes, written in shaky characters by our new Brigadier, and would wink feebly when asked how and where they were obtained. Our melancholy quartermaster used to call these sprees of the youngsters *seeing stars*, and would laugh inwardly, as though that were the best of jokes; meaning to hint, I fear, that at least one wearer of these ornaments might have been a partaker in the rowse. Ah, well! Our first general was a soldier; this one proved a shyster, as many another since. How he was dismissed for drunkenness on duty—it was at the review just mentioned, almost the only occasion whereon he ever did any duty to be drunk on,—how he was reinstated, and presently dismissed again for corresponding with the enemy; how he was again reinstated, and again dismissed for cowardice *and* drunkenness (his horse being struck by a shell in some little skirmish into which General Pike forced him bodily, he suddenly disappeared, and was nowhere seen until some of our men, straggling for whiskey, on the return march, found him beastly drunk in a sutler's shop, miles in the rear, whereupon they half stripped him, and handsomely tattooing his body with the blackened tips of their ramrods, tied his coat round an empty whiskey barrel, and rolled him into the ditch to sober); how he went to New York, and became a prominent politician, fearless in his opposition to what he was pleased to term the present imbecile and corrupt administration; how he was finally elected to Congress, and dragged through the mire of immediate capitulation with a view to an ultimate surrender and a corruption of all the States, at the skirts of Benjamin and Fernando: what need to enlarge upon the oft-told tale? The days when we thought the Five Points would fight, and that shysters could command, went out with Fire Zouaves and their kind, with Slushmeyer and his kind. May they rot in peace!

All that long winter of 1861–'2, we lay in our tents on the south bank of the Potomac, drilling, reviewing, discharging, recruiting, getting sick, getting well, burying those who never got well, killing each other by accidental discharges of pistols or muskets, fattening the sutlers, feeding the hospitals, gambling, drinking, swearing, shirking, working, studying, or what not, according to our kind, but always expecting the great forward movement, and always getting disappointed. Examining Boards played havoc with officers who couldn't tell what five principal rivers flow into the Caspian sea, or how long a day's rations for y men would last z men, or the meaning of atramentarious or geoponic at first sight. Courts-Martial decimated the devotees of Willard's. One second lieutenant, aged fifty-seven, the father of our major, resigned for fear of the dreaded Examining Board. Young bloods resigned for fear of courts-martial. Old Surgeon Peacack was kept busy sending men to the hospitals, whence they seldom returned, and discharging others on certificate of disability. Dysentery and typhoid fever made their appearance; *nostalgia* raged fearfully. Do you know the disease better as *home-sickness* than by that doctor's Greek? Some went home on leave; others, favorites, rushed off on recruiting service, which in those days was better, because you could stay longer, had nothing to do, got your expenses paid, and could go on leave afterward! Every form of old-soldiering broke out sporadically, and had in turn to be learned, diagnosed, prognosed, and treated by that physician of the moral military diseases—the Adjutant. I had first to learn the Dying Mother fever: symptoms, laziness for some weeks, with occasional attacks of whiskey or cards—Willard's often makes its appearance. About the eighth day thereafter I usually observe a letter from sister Jane or cousin John, casually announcing, among other things, that "mother is very sick;"—shortly may be expected a telegram saying, "Come home immediately: mother is dying Lucy"—or John, perhaps. The treatment varies according to the case. Caustic is sometimes employed with success. Then there came the Ruined Business fever, in which the patient fancies he is to lose fabulous sums unless he starts for home within a quarter of an hour. Where these fevers are aborted by successful treatment, the Sick-Family-Dead-Parents-and-Absconding-Partner cholic frequently succeeds, and is often known to rage with great fury. Letters and telegrams may be expected in great numbers, but to the practised eye these symptoms need cause little alarm. If the treatment has been skilfully selected and firmly adhered to, the patient may be confidently expected, within a very few days, to show symptoms of convalescence, or else to enter upon the third stage of the fever, that of apyrexia, or resignation: he may now be discharged. Curious are the ways of the shirks!

We were beginning to show ourselves. Those officers who meant to make something were beginning to recover from the first bitter mortification of having their ignorance exposed by General Pike, and were studying with a will, tactics, regulations, books of instruction, military history, military biography, and a mort of weak translations from the French, beside. The backs of these began to straighten, even unto occasional stiffness, and the chests to widen. Their clothes fitted them better, and were more neatly brushed and cleaned than formerly. The regimental staff laid aside one morning the dark-blue shoulder-straps and gold cord, which their tailors had persuaded them were the appropriate ornaments for officers of their exalted rank. Card-playing with the men began to disappear, and the captains to occupy tents separate and distinct from those of the orderly sergeants. One day the non-commissioned staff left the Colonel's mess, and set up on their own account. "The boys" began to be "the men." "How are *you*, PETE," passed into

"H' y', cap.," and presently becoming "Good morning, captain," disappeared finally in a respectful military salute, awkwardly enough, but well meant, and rapidly improving with practice. These officers began to stay in camp, and look after their men, while the gay faction ranged off to town to drag the dissipations of Washington, fancying all the while they were men of spirit. One by one these fellows dropped off during the winter, through one of the approved channels by which effete officers are excreted.

To those of us who diligently tried to learn, it was truly astonishing then, though it is less so now, how much we had to learn. One thing seemed to open the way to a thousand others, before undreamed of. But you should have heard the talk at our mess-table about this time. All the regimental staff messed together. The old doctor, Surgeon Peacack, and Chaplain Bender, used to do the heavy talking, while Smallweed made it a point to controvert every thing advanced by either, the rest of us edging in a word or a sentence here and there, and the honest old Colonel Heavysterne listening intently, but never by any chance taking part, except now and then to keep peace in the family, when the dispute ran high, as it often did, over Waterloo and Fontenoy, Wellington and Napoleon, Hannibal and Washington, Sickles, Beauregard, cavalry and infantry, masked batteries, Bull Run, the regulations, and the relative merits of German and Irish soldiers. What plans were developed by the assistant surgeon for breaking the backbone of the rebellion by a new process; what grand schemes were ventilated by our scape-grace of a chaplain, of calling out a million cavalry to ride down the rebellion, or two million infantry to starve it out; how we decided what was to be done with Jeff Davis when we caught him, as we thought we should do in the course of a few weeks; how we concluded it would be wrong to hang any one below the grade of colonel; how our artillery was so immensely superior, that we must whip the rebels in three months; how the Confederacy was starving already and barefoot, and had no light to read by at night; how we were tired of "the nigger,"— though I doubt whether any of us knew what we meant by that ingenious phrase, fresh from the dictionary of secession; how General McClellan was greater than Napoleon, and equal to several Fredericks and no end of Wellingtons; how he wouldn't move till he got ready, but when he did, would sweep everything before him like an avalanche; how young Captain Petlam had been mittened by one secesh beauty near Alexandria, and Fippany was surely engaged to another; how Johnny Todd, now elevated to a lieutenancy, was giving a snake exhibition in his boots, and was like to die; how the caterer was a humbug, and didn't know his business; how the quartermaster was stingy; how the commissary was vile; how half the sickness in camp came from not drinking enough whiskey in the morning as an anti-fogmatic, and how the other half arose from the "doctor's stuff." Why enlarge upon what must have been the mess-table experience, during that memorable winter, of every one of us whose shoulder-straps were new?

Why, except that this is all the history of all that muddy winter of preparation.

Of preparation for the Peninsula!

Whereof, more anon, if it please you.

NAVAL STAFF RANK.

BY SURGEON RUSCHENBERGER, U. S. N.

JOHN A. ANDREW, LL. D., governor of Massachusetts, while addressing the graduating class of the medical school in the University at Cambridge, March 9, 1864, said: "There is never a surplus of competent and trustworthy men. They are always in request. Places are always waiting for them. But the men themselves do not always at the right time appear."

He limited this remark in some degree to the votaries of the medical and collateral sciences; but it is applicable to every vocation which needs instructed intellect for its efficient pursuit, and its truth has been continuously recognized from the earliest times. It applies to every peaceful art wrought at for the sake of livelihood or of wealth under the patronage of citizens. The skilful master of any art is sure of custom enough to secure him the means of enjoying life according to his own tastes independently of another's control or dictation.

But it is not easy to be a master in any thing. Natural talent, with patient and ever-active industry in its cultivation, are necessary to produce the skill which characterizes the master. Although men admit that labor is the sole means of acquiring skill, the hope of respectable ease or of wealth is not sufficient to induce them generally to endure the continuous toil which is almost always essential to the acquisition of exact knowledge in any profession. Hence it is that we encounter much more pretension than perfection in every vocation.

If it were easy to become a master, adepts would abound in every department: a Raffael or Murillo, a Mozart or Rossini, a Viart or Soyer, a Wellington or Napoleon, a Dieffenbach or Astley Cooper, a Daniel Webster or a Chatham, a Berzelius or Humphrey Davy, might be found in every village, and a Washington Irving, Walter Scott, or a Thackeray would be seen in every editorial chair, and a Benjamin Franklin would preside at every press. But, alas! it is not so, and probably never will be.

Deficiency of efficient master-men is observed throughout society. Even in those arts which are fostered by individual patronage almost exclusively, masters are not abundant. The great majority of men lack punctuality and rigid truthfulness as well as the master-hand in the execution of what may be intrusted to them. Perfection of execution, even in mechanic arts of the commonest necessity in our country, is comparatively so rare, that in each community a few men only are relied upon for all fine work. There are those whose judgment is much respected, who believe that wearing apparel of every sort is produced by the average workmen of London or Paris of better quality and finish than can be procured from the best workmen who ply their trades in Boston, Philadelphia, or New York. There are some articles of large consumption which are brought wholly or partly from foreign workshops, although all the materials of their structure abound in our land. Our opticians, for example, rely upon European manufacturers chiefly, if not entirely, for the glasses they mount and sell. Almost all nautical instruments used in navigating our ships are made in foreign workshops. Every one admits that the various fabrics of wool, silk, cotton, and flax, made in our country, are in quality and finish, and especially in the durability of their colors, inferior to the same articles produced in Europe and even in India. The reason for the deficiency of perfection in the mechanic arts and manufactures in the United States need not be considered here, or even alluded to.

In those vocations which require for their efficient exercise a higher degree of intellectuality and instruction, we are much better served. Amidst myriads of pretenders and charlatans, there are many learned physicians, and surgeons, and lawyers, and divines, and physicists, and engineers, who are unexceptionable practitioners, and among these, in each profession, there may be found here and there one qualified to be a leader anywhere. It may be said, nevertheless, that mediocrity generally characterizes almost all who are engaged in the practical application of the useful arts and sciences in our country; the exceptions are probably not much more than enough to prove the rule. Mediocrity prevails in all those arts which are sustained by private or individual patronage.

In time of war, like this, the nation needs the application of an art for which there is no private patronage. The military art must be taught and fostered at the cost of the government. Individual citizens have no occasion to employ armies or navies, or portions of either. Only nations are customers of those who trade in or practise the art and manipulate weapons of war.

A military academy was established at West Point, N. Y., under a law enacted March 16, 1802. A naval academy was begun at Annapolis, Md., October 10, 1845.

It was supposed that these two schools were sufficiently capacious to educate young men enough to supply the demand for officers of the line in both branches of the military establishment. But experience proves that much larger numbers are necessary than those institutions are capable of furnishing. The average quality of their graduates is above mediocrity. All are competent, and many are brilliantly excellent military men, that is, men taught to be amenable to military law, and trained to practise the military art.

In an article entitled "Naval Staff Rank" (United States Service Magazine, vol. i., p. 621, June, 1864), it was stated that a military establishment does not consist of a line alone. It cannot stand by itself. It requires the support of a staff which embraces a variety of vocations which are neither taught nor acquired in the military or naval academy. Those institutions only qualify their pupils to manipulate weapons and to perform those administrative duties of the military establishment which pertain to the line.

The navy is that part of the military establishment of a nation which is designed to combat its foes upon the sea, and is organized and equipped to serve on board of ships.

It consists of two primary classes, denominated the line and the staff.

The line is composed of a series of successively subordinate grades and rates. In the navy of the United States, as at present organized, they are as follows:—

GRADES AND RATES OF THE LINE OF THE NAVY OF THE UNITED STATES.

	Grades.		Rates.		Rates.
Commissioned Officers.	1. Vice-admiral.	Petty Officers.	14. Master's mate.	Privates.	27. Seaman.
	2. Rear-admiral.		15. Boatswain's mate.		28. Ordinary seaman.
	3. Commodore.		16. Gunner's mate.		29. Landsman.
	4. Captain.		17. Cox'n to R. Adm'l.		30. Musician, 1st class.
	5. Commander.		18. Capt. of forecastle.		31. Musician, 2d class.
	6. Lieut.-commander.		19. Quartermaster.		32. Boy, first class.
	7. Lieutenant.		20. Quarter-gunner.		33. Boy, second class.
	8. Master.		21. Capt. of maintop.		34. Boy, third class.
	9. Ensign.		22. Capt. of foretop.		
Warranted Officers.	10. Midshipman.		23. Capt. of hold.		
	11. Boatswain.		24. Capt. of mizzen-top.		
	12. Gunner.		25. Cockswain.		
	13. Master's mate.		26. Capt. of afterguard.		

Nine grades are commissioned, that is, appointed with the sanction of the Senate of the United States, and four grades are warranted, that is, simply appointed on executive authority. There is no limit to the duration of the appointments of commissioned and warrant officers.

There are thirteen rates of petty officers. They are appointed by the officer in command of the vessel on board of which they serve, and retain their rates during the period of enlistment if their conduct be satisfactory: if not, they may be reduced to the rate of seaman.

There are eight rates of privates. Both petty officers and privates enter the navy through the recruiting offices.

The staff of the navy is composed of those persons whose vocations are essential to enable those of the line to perform their duties. They are all military men, because, like those of the line, they are amenable to military law.

The staff consists of corps or departments, each embracing grades and rates. They are as follows:—

GRADES AND RATES OF THE STAFF OF THE NAVY OF THE UNITED STATES.

	Grades.	Rates.	Rates.
Commissioned Officers.	1. Surgeon.	Surgeon's steward.	Cooper.
	2. Assistant surgeon.		
	3. Paymaster.	Paymaster's steward.	Ship's cook.
	4. Assistant paymaster.	Fireman, 1st class.	Armorer's mate.
	5. Chaplain.	Fireman, 2d class.	Steward to admiral.
	6. Professor of mathematics.	Coal-heaver.	Cabin steward.
	7. Naval constructor.	Carpenter's mate.	Ward-room steward.
	8. Assistant naval constructor.	Sailmaker's mate.	Cook to admiral.
	9. Chief engineer.	Master-at-arms.	Cabin cook.
Warranted Officers.	10. First assistant engineer.	Yeoman.	Ward-room cook.
	11. Second assistant engineer.	Master of band.	Steerage cook.
	12. Third assistant engineer.	Ship's corporal.	Nurse.
	13. Carpenter.	Armorer.	
	14. Sailmaker.	Painter.	

Surgeon of the fleet is a temporary appointment, and does not constitute a permanent grade. Those assistant surgeons who on examination have been found qualified for promotion, are denominated passed assistant surgeons until promoted, but they are not appointed or commissioned as a distinct grade.

The precedence of the staff-corps is not definitely established.

The line of the navy is filled by the graduates of the Naval Academy. They are necessarily taught and prepared to exercise the profession of arms on the sea at the nation's expense. Men properly qualified to discharge the duties of naval line officers cannot be procured in any other manner.

But members of the staff-corps are obtained from the mass of the citizens. In view of the wide-spread pretension and mediocrity in educational and professional acquirements existing in all vocations in all parts of the country, the government has been forced to protect itself against the employment of incompetent persons in these departments by appropriate professional examinations. Since the year 1824, no person has been appointed an assistant surgeon in the navy who has not been previously examined and found qualified, nor has any assistant surgeon been promoted to be a surgeon until after he has been pronounced to be qualified in all respects by a competent board of examiners. And since the year 1845, engineers, prior to appointment as well as prior to promotion to any grade, are systematically examined by a board of competent officers.

Under this system, up to the year 1860, the small medical corps required has been filled with competent officers, but not always without difficulty. Vacancies created by resignation were always numerous in proportion to the limited numbers of the two grades, because, as a general rule, well-educated physicians or surgeons could find more agreeable and more profitable employment in private life.* Competent men, whose slender

---

* On the first of January, 1863, the total number of assistant surgeons in the navy was one hundred and seventeen. Of these, during the year, nine resigned,

patrimony made the naval service alluring, entered it, only to leave it as soon as more inviting prospects should open to their view. The compensation, considered in connection with the costliness of naval life, its vicissitudes and exposures, is not enough to attract and retain enterprising young men of skill in an organization in which they found their proper self-respect invaded in very many nameless ways, simply because, as is believed by almost all of them, a rank suitable to the respectability and usefulness of their profession has never been assigned them. The rank given by executive regulations, on paper, has not been practically recognized in the service. Those regulations have tended rather to found controversy and beget heart-burning and distaste for naval life than to secure them any palpable advantages or protection.

On entering the navy the assistant surgeon is a ward-room officer; and he may also find in the same mess, and accommodated no better than himself, a surgeon whose commission is more than thirty years old, who is nominally a captain in rank, and yet, in fact, has no more military consideration or respect than he had on the day of his promotion. Even this mere nominal rank is regarded to be offensive by gentlemen of the line. Many of them have manifested their disapproval by petitioning that it may be annulled. Yet few men are more appreciative of the value of surgical aid, or more reluctant to leave the shore without the company of a competent medical staff; probably none will testify more cheerfully to the efficiency of the medical officers of the navy than these same gentlemen—not only to their efficiency, but also to their moral and social worth.

The persistent opposition of line officers to the efforts of medical officers to obtain a rank or position relative to themselves, might be supposed to imply that there are some conclusive objections, growing out of the nature of military organization exclusively, and entirely independent of purely selfish or personal considerations. But it is not so. It has never been pretended that any degree of relative rank conferred upon a surgeon could possibly interfere in any manner whatever with the efficient performance of military duty, by the line, nor has it been suggested that relative military rank tends to lessen professional skill or intelligence. Indeed, if the fanciful assumption that augmentation of intellect and information inures to every grade progressively *pari passu* with promotion in lineal rank has any foundation, we might imagine that relative rank would bring an increment of skill to the staff officer for every step he is advanced in it. Under the ancient system of promotion by seniority, especially prior to the establishment of the Naval Academy, incompetent and slightly instructed men attained the

---

two were killed in battle, and two died of disease. The number of assistant surgeons is limited to one hundred and twenty by law.

highest grades in the line; and they often arrogantly acted as if they believed that high rank was equivalent to knowledge, and enabled them to direct in technical affairs of which they were totally ignorant. Such men were always opposed to giving the staff officers a definite position in the service, under a vague notion that every degree of rank conferred on the staff was necessarily deducted from the line.

While opinion, or rather prejudice of the kind prevails, the Government will encounter difficulty in supplying the demand for competent staff officers of every denomination. Adequate compensation and suitable relative position in the military organization are needed to attract and retain properly trained men in the staff corps. It is well known that the demand for medical officers is very much greater than the supply, and that, in spite of the facilities of admission offered by the Government, qualified candidates in sufficient numbers do not offer their services. Properly qualified engineers are also in demand.

John F. W. Ware, in an admirable little volume, entitled "Home Life," relates that "When the returning regiments—the wreck and remnant of that great Crimean struggle—marched in triumph through the streets of London, stepping to the martial strains of England's grand anthem, 'God save the Queen,' as the first rank wheeled beneath the gates of the Horse Guards—the great head-quarters of the army—the anthem died away, and slowly, sweetly, softly, and with an electric power that thrilled through every soldier's heart, and called, unbidden, warrior tears, arose the strains of '*Home, sweet, sweet Home!*' They were men who had faced death for months and years unmoved, and many of the quicker sensibilities had been blunted by familiarity with scenes of violence and blood, but there slumbered underneath, pure, strong and fervent, the love of home; and as those long and familiar notes fell on their ears, there amid old scenes and sympathetic faces, they were no longer war-worn veterans, proudly returning from hard-earned fields, but little children at the cottage door—the dear far-off long-left home! So it is with us, warriors on another field and in a sterner strife. Life's stirring duties and necessities, calling for the strong and stern in man, make us oblivious to, suspicious of, the finer sentiments, which proudly and foolishly we strive to crush. But in pauses of the fight, in scenes of peril and success, in moments of victory and triumph, some stray, secret influence of the long past comes surging over us—some well-remembered token of our own 'sweet home'—and we are children again in that far by-gone of better days!"

The idea of family and home is prominent in every cultivated mind. It ought not to be ignored in the policy of government, but its realization should be held up among the rewards attainable by those who enter its military service ashore or afloat.

> "Thou holy, sacred name of home!
> Prime bliss of earth! Behind us and before
> Our guiding star, our refuge. A father's eye,
> A mother's smile, a sister's gentle love,
> The table and the altar and the hearth,
> In reverend image, keep their early hold
> Upon the heart."*

Every man labors in youth and early manhood to acquire the means of livelihood and of the ultimate establishment of a home. His acquired knowledge, general and technical, he regards as his capital, through the use of which he may obtain distinction and competency, if not affluence. He does not toil simply to supply himself with food and raiment from day to day. He looks forward to something more. The idea of name, family, home and rest in his earthly world constitutes the motive force which urges his industry and cheers him in his hours of fatigue. His egoism is not solitary in its character, because it is ever connected with a hope of becoming the centre of social affections and approbation. Remove these from his prospect in the future, and he relaxes in his efforts, if he do not cease to labor in his vocation.

To allure men skilled in technical knowledge from home, from the common field in which their fellows toil, to engage permanently in military service, has not proved an easy task. Pecuniary compensation alone is not enough to induce men of fair professional prospects to abandon them for staff employments in the naval service. They demand at least that degree of social consideration in the military organization which is consistent with proper self-respect, and above the disparagement of any class with which they work in common. The skill of an engineer, naval architect or physician is the offspring of as much intellect and cultivation as the skill of the military seaman, and demands in its exercise manly qualities of not inferior character. It is not presumable that "competent and trustworthy men," master-men in vocations which are respectable and respected in all civil communities, will silently recognize a caste superiority, and yield universal and perennial precedence to any profession or class. Whatever men who are reared under the influence of established aristocracies may consent to, it is quite apparent that Americans cannot perceive that because they practice in any of the professions employed in the navy, they ought to acknowledge themselves to be forever the inferiors of every member of one class in it, composed of men in no respect better than themselves.

Professional men believe that they should occupy positions in military communities relatively equal in respectability to the positions of their professional brothers in civil life, and enjoy the attributes or advantages of those positions.

---

* My Dream of Life, by Henry Ware, Jr.

Proper official subordination, prompt and cheerful obedience to superiors in office, is never inconsistent with self-respect. No respectable staff officer ever finds the performance of his duty disagreeable because it is executed under the order of his superior in the line.

The difficulty of filling military staff offices with competent men is not confined to the United States.

The condition of the medical staff of the British Army has become a matter of grave national importance, says a respectable journal.* At present two hundred vacancies exist. The candidates, while few in number, have ceased to represent the intelligence or respectability of the medical schools. As a consequence the Director-General is seriously embarrassed, and the authorities are driven to expedients which, though relieving present pressure, are well calculated to perpetuate, if not materially increase, the existing unsatisfactory state of affairs. The plan has hitherto been pursued of promising much and performing little. The concessions of to-day are followed by the restrictions of to-morrow. The consequence of this system now stands proclaimed in a deficiency of medical officers so entirely unprecedented that the Government are at their wit's end to know what means to adopt for its remedy.

Medical men in England, where class distinctions in society are recognized, are not satisfied with the rank and precedence actually conceded to them in the army or in the navy. They believe themselves to be justly entitled to the position and its attributes which they have been nominally given within a few years past.

It is one of our habits to appeal to British military organization for precedents, and to find in them conclusive reasons for our own imitative course, without investigating either the principle or policy on which such British practices are based. An obsolete table of English naval precedence is brought forward triumphantly to show what should be the precedence of line and staff in the navy of the United States,† as if not a word can be reasonably uttered against such overwhelming authority, "which the experience of centuries has established in the naval service" of Great Britain.

Precedents serve as substitutes for reasoning in many instances. They are usually adduced to corroborate decisions, but they cannot alone be always received as conclusive evidence of what is right. Precedents are sometimes erroneously based. The scrutiny of progressive civilization has unsettled or overturned many notions which are sanctioned merely by antiquity, by showing that they are not founded in right or justice. Even

---

* Lancet, May 14, 1864.
† United States Service Magazine, vol. ii. p. 293.

the institution of slavery, from which the Jews escaped across the Red Sea under the lead of Moses to where there was no fugitive slave law to remand them back to their Egyptian master, has come to be regarded almost universally as a wrong, except only among barbarous and semi-civilized people.

It is wise to profit by the experience of others. But it is not wise to adopt without investigation the practices of foreign nations, and confess our inferiority and weakness by humbly imitating them. No thoughtful man who is acquainted with military organization in any considerable degree, can fail to recognize the propriety as well as the necessity of assigning to every member of such organization a definite position relatively to every other member of it. The relative positions of those of the line to each other are established and apparent; indeed, they settle themselves, because they constitute a line of individuals of whom no two are absolutely on the same level, though classed in various grades. Every one of the same grade is either superior or inferior in rank to the others. But the positions of those of the staff corps are necessarily to be made relative to those of the line, with whom they serve. The nations of Europe have each investigated this question, and determined a scale of rank for staff officers relatively to the line in their military establishments, but no two of them are precisely alike. The problem is not yet solved finally for the military establishment of the United States. In the navy it has been long discussed without any satisfactory decision. The systems of aristocratic and monarchical governments are referred to as authority to which, in the opinion of some, we ought to submit, while others of equal respectability believe that we should determine the question on principles and policy adapted to our own social and political condition.

Surgeon W. Whelan, Chief of the Bureau of Medicine and Surgery, Navy Department, in his annual report of October, 1863, states that:—

"Within a few years medical men have been elevated to the rank of rear-admiral in the British navy and major-general in the British army, while liberal pensions, the order of the Bath and Knighthood, are bestowed in cases of distinguished merit.

"Medical officers of the navy are at liberty to retire after a full-pay service of twenty-five years, upon most liberal allowances, when compared with line officers; and 'in case of distinguished service they receive a step of honorary rank.'

"The half-pay of a vice-admiral is five hundred and ninety-three pounds. The retired pay of a medical inspector-general varies from five hundred and forty-seven to six hundred and eighty-four pounds, the maximum being attained after thirty years' service.

"The half-pay of a rear-admiral is four hundred and fifty-six pounds; of a deputy inspector-general from three hundred and eighty-three to four hundred and sixty-five pounds, according to length of service; the maximum being attained after thirty years' service.

"The half-pay of the seventy senior captains is two hundred and sixty-four pounds; of the staff surgeons from three hundred and one to three hundred and thirty-seven pounds; the maximum being attained in twenty-five years.

"The half-pay of the next one hundred captains is two hundred and twenty-eight pounds; of surgeons from two hundred pounds on promotion to two hundred and forty-six pounds after ten years' service.

"Medical officers are entitled to the same allowance for wounds and injuries received in action as line officers of similar rank; and their families are entitled to like allowance in case of death.

"The humble position of medical officers of the British army previous to the royal warrant of October 1, 1858, awakened the earnest interest of the late Governor-General of India, Lord Dalhousie.

"In a minute of the reform of the medical service of India, his lordship observes:—

"'The surgeon and the assistant-surgeon rank invariably with the captain and lieutenant; but the rank is only nominal whenever medical officers, and others, are brought together on public duty. * * * It is impossible to conceive how such a system as this can have been maintained so long on the strength of no better argument than that it has been and therefore ought to have been.'

"It is impossible to imagine what serious justification can be offered for a system which in respect of external position postpones service to inexperience, age to youth; a system which gives a subaltern, who is hardly free from his drills, precedence over his elder, who perhaps has served through every campaign for thirty years; a system which treats a member of a learned profession, a man of ability, skill, and experience, as inferior in position to a cornet of cavalry just entering on the study of the pay and audit regulations; a system which thrusts down gray-headed veterans below beardless boys!

"In the French navy promotion extends to the rank of rear-admiral, and in the army to brigadier-general, and the Legion of Honor is as open, and advancement in it as certain, to medical as other officers.

"The medecin-en-chef, or fleet-surgeon, messes with the commanding officer of the squadron, but pays no mess-bill, the government making an allowance therefor of twenty francs per day.

"When the foundation of the Legion of Honor was under discussion in the Council of State, in May 1801, General Mathew Dumas proposed that the institution should be confined exclusively to military men, [those of the line]. The First Consul combatted such a narrow and invidious policy. 'Such ideas,' said he, 'might be more adapted to the feudal ages, when the chevaliers combatted man to man, and the bulk of the nation was in a state of slavery. * * * What is it now which constitutes a great general? It is not the mere strength of a man six feet high, but the coup de œil, the habit of foresight, the power of thought and calculation, in a word, civil qualities such as are found in a knowledge of human nature. The general who can now achieve great things is he who is possessed of shining civil qualities; it is the perception of the strength of his talents which makes the soldiers obey him. * * *

"'Not only does the general preserve his ascendency over his soldiers chiefly by civil qualities, but when his command ceases he becomes merely a private individual. * * *

"'The tendency of military men [those of the line] is to carry every thing by force; the enlightened civilian, on the other hand, elevates his views to a perception of the general good. The first would rule only by despotic authority: the last subject every thing to the test of discussion, truth, and reason. I have no hesitation, therefore, in saying that if preference were to be awarded to one or the other, it belongs to the civilian.'

"The council agreed that the proposed honor should not be confined to military service [in the line].

"In the Russian army, medical officers are progressively advanced from the rank of captain to that of general, and the same honors and pensions are bestowed with equal liberality. After the first six years' service medical officers receive increased pay, which continues after each succeeding five years.

"In the Belgian army promotion extends to the rank of major-general, and the relative military position determines the amount of retired and half-pay. In calculating the length of service for retirement, medical officers are permitted to count six years before they entered the service, as the time occupied in preparatory studies.

"In the Dutch army promotion extends to the rank of colonel.

"In the Prussian army advancement continues to the rank of colonel, and medical officers wear the same uniform as that of the corresponding military rank.

"In the Sardinian army the highest rank of the medical corps is that of major-general.

"In the Spanish army the advancement of medical officers extends to the rank of lieutenant-general. The medical inspector-general holds the same rank and enjoys the same privileges as the inspector-general of the different arms. Medical officers receive the same rates of retired pay as the corresponding military [line] ranks; they are permitted to count as seven years' service the time passed in preparatory studies.

"The director-general has the power to recommend medical officers for certain distinctions, as the 'Cross of Scientific Emulation,' the 'Cross of Isabella the Catholic,' the 'Cross of Charles III.,' and the 'Cross of St. Ferdinand.'

"In the Spanish navy the rank of medical officers is established upon the same liberal and satisfactory basis.

"In the Bavarian army medical officers attain the rank of colonel, and wear the same uniform as other officers of similar relative rank; when unfit for service from age or disease, the pension nearly equals their full pay.

"In the Austrian army the rank extends to major-general, and medical officers enjoy the same honors and privileges as corresponding military ranks [line grades]—wear the same uniform, and receive the same rates of retired pay.

"If a medical officer die of wounds or exposure on duty, the pension to his family is equal to two-thirds of his pay. If from other causes, to one-half of his pay.

"The director-general is *ex officio* a member of the Aulic council, and receives, as such, a liberal addition to his salary.

"In the army of Portugal medical rank extends to the grade of colonel.

"I refer to these facts merely to illustrate how unfounded is the idea that medical officers of the navy, in desiring a proper position in an artificial organization are striving for novel expedients or dangerous precedents. The experience of the civilized world seems to have acquiesced in the propriety of giving to every person in military life a position somewhat appropriate to the importance of his duties, and though long periods of peace had assured to the military branch an exclusive pre-eminence and power. Recent events most plainly demonstrate that it requires as much intellect, training, as high an order of moral qualities, to insure efficiency to the medical department as to any other branch of military service. It is now esteemed not less important to preserve life than to destroy it; and he who stands unmoved amid the unseen arrows of pestilence in the performance of his humane duties, surely evinces no lower order of courage than he who encounters the visible perils of war in another sphere.

"The health, and consequent efficiency of an army, or a fleet, in time of war, demands much care, solicitude, and watchfulness; and the State is mindful of its true interests when it encourages talent, zeal, and usefulness in so important a service.

"The rank of captain, recently conferred [March 13, 1863] on the senior surgeons, is not positively of as much value as their former rank of commander, at the time the second grade in the navy, while that of captain is now the third; so that promotion has reduced them one step in the military scale. In point of sea-service there are medical officers who surpass some of the admirals and commodores; and relatively to length of service, the sea-service of many medical officers is larger than that of the senior officer of the line.

"As preferment has been liberally bestowed upon line officers, four new grades having been created since the war, it is not, I hope, presumptuous to propose that those who have equally shared the perils of battle and dangers of climate, whose labors have been so great, and whose rewards have been so few, may at last receive a fitter recognition of their fidelity and usefulness.

"The war showed the absolute necessity of offering higher inducements in the shape of rank to medical officers of the army; and who will deny that the medical corps of the navy, so isolated and necessarily so self-reliant, should embody the best talent and the highest professional and social character the government can invite to its service? * * *

"I am so well aware of the feeling existing on this subject, that I should forbear to introduce it, did I not as fully know the worth and patriotism of those whose case I plead.

"I can safely refer to the records of the war for any instances of short-coming, or lack of zeal or interest, and yet while, as a corps, medical officers have proved so vigilant and efficient on every occasion of danger or duty, it is but seldom, indeed, that they receive a passing notice in official dispatches, as is so commonly the practice in the army.

"Perhaps some reorganization of the medical department might overcome the indisposition to enter the naval service now so generally manifested by young medical men. We have very considerable difficulty in keeping up the number of officers of the permanent service, while it requires all our exertions to provide, indifferently, for the temporary service.

"Many vessels are in commission without medical officers; for the simple reason that, after all sorts of publicity, we cannot procure them in sufficient numbers."

In the preceding extract from the report of the Chief of the Bureau of Medicine and Surgery of the Navy Department, may be seen precedents enough to show that there is no novelty in assigning a fixed position to staff officers in naval organizations. It shows, too, that employment in the navy of the United States is so little sought by competent members of the medical profession, that it is impossible to supply a sufficient number to fill the permanent medical corps. The facts suggest that a better position and better compensation are requisite to attract to and retain in the service men who are equal in professional qualifications to the existing standard; or the government must be content to trust the lives and health of officers and privates of the navy to an inferior class of practitioners. But an opinion has prevailed that the lives and health of men in the naval service are too valuable to be intrusted to incompetent hands; and yet, strange as it seems, those who are most nearly interested in securing when afloat the best skill the country affords, are advocating measures which are calculated to discourage from entering the navy those who are best qualified.

NOTE.—On the first day of 1865, the navy consisted of six hundred and seventy-one vessels of all rates. Each vessel in service requires one medical officer, and many of them two or three. Hospitals, recruiting offices, navy-yards, etc., employ seventy-seven; so that there are not less than seven hundred and eighty-four posts, each requiring at least one.

The existing laws authorize the appointment of two hundred medical men permanently, and an unlimited number temporarily, in the naval service. In the permanent navy there was a deficiency of twelve on the 1st of January, and since, three have died in battle. There are two hundred and forty-seven medical officers with temporary commissions, or an aggregate of four hundred and thirty-five, thus leaving three hundred and thirteen vessels without a surgeon of any kind.

During the year 1864, the casualties in the permanent medical corps were,—resignations, fifteen; deaths, thirteen;—total, twenty eight; and of the temporary appointments, the resignations were,—forty-seven; deaths, eight; dismissed, eight;—total, sixty-three; or an aggregate of ninety-one.

During the last four months of the year, no less than one hundred and three medical men, in different parts of the country, declined to accept the appointment of assistant-surgeon in the navy. Only ten were received into the medical staff during this period.

Now, as medical services on shore command fees, varying in the aggregate from two to ten, fifteen, and even twenty thousand dollars a year, competent men will not engage permanently in the navy for from twelve hundred and fifty to three thousand dollars per annum, with risks of climate and the sea, as well as the perils of battle, in addition to professional labors.

RELIEVED GUARD!

BY HENRY P. LELAND.

THERE at his post by oozy marsh that binds
    The borders of the bay,
Where moaned through rustling sedge the winter winds,
    The soldier silent lay.

Through the cold blue of heaven the evening star
    Set the first watch of night:
While 'thwart the west one lingering crimson bar,
    Crowned the dead day with light.

Slyly the gray fox peering, swiftly ran
    Along the dusky shore;
Stopping, perchance, with pricked up ears, to scan
    The wild fowl winging o'er.

The pulsing whir of wings that beat the air
    With a deep, trembling hum,
Unheeded pass the soldier there:
    Unseen the wild-fowl come.

Now o'er the line of marsh the new-born day
    Lifts up its rosy wings,
And through the frosty air, far down the bay,
    The "honk" of wild geese rings.

Unharmed the wild duck preens its plumage bright,
    Swimming the soldier near:
Gazing the while with eyes of liquid light,
    It sees no sign for fear.

Calmly at peace he lay, while the bright sun
    Tinged his pale cheek with red:—
Shot through the heart—his duty done—
    There lay the soldier, dead.

Whether 'neath sheltering roof or open sky
    We render the last breath,
God give us strength to calmly die
    With hope, for after death.

March 1, 1865.

OUR MORAL WEAKNESS.

A MOST curious feature of the unparalleled war power of the nation is the moral weakness of its representative men. It is still the more curious because revolutions are generally attended by too fanatical a conformity to the views and prejudices of the dominant party. In our own case we have reached that point of extreme gentleness which enables our enemies to inflict injuries and commit depredations with almost perfect impunity. Our grand operations are embarrassed by unrecognized bands, our soldiers are murdered in cold blood, citizens speak treason under the very ears of commanding officers, give information to the enemy, and perform other acts of the most culpable character, without experiencing severer punishment, as a rule, than a few days' confinement in a guard-house; or, with equal lack of justice, others are imprisoned for months without trial, and very probably upon mere suspicion.

We are not surprised, then, that the subjection of the spirit and strength of the rebellion has not been altogether commensurate with the gigantic triumphs and efforts of our armies. There are several reasons for this strange fact, all of which originate in a deficiency in moral strength. The first is, the mistaken conservatism, the retrospective tendency of the leading minds of our armies. The past is merely a lesson of experience, they consider it an unsolved problem. They are not up to the social ideas of the year. They still linger upon the threshold of the rebellion. They have fought and won great battles. For what? The principles of '61. They need to be advanced. The people are striving for the theories of a quarter of a century ahead. In the beginning, the war on the part of the Government was defensive. The South was the aggressor. The loyal people rallied to the defence of their flag, their nationality, their constitution, and their honor. The disloyal element, intent upon a separate national existence, endeavored to rend asunder the strong bonds that bind the Union into one of the great states of the world.

At first it was supposed the action of the South was the overfanaticism of a few misguided communities. A few months later demonstrated this opinion was a mistake. Unfortunately, at the end of more than three years of toil and danger, there are many men of our armies who have not yet discovered their error. They still labor in the dangerous belief that the South is to be induced to submit by courteous means. The war, consequently, drags along, and is gradually exhausting the powers of the nation.

There is not the least question, had the moral force of the commanders of our armies been as remarkable as their ability to cope with the enemy in the field, we would have had peace before this. To compel a people into submission by strength of arms may succeed in the beginning, but when backed by a weak, inefficient, and partial administration of law and order, the most that can be expected is but a semblance of obedience, a suppressed enmity, and an uprising the moment the actual presence of bayonets is removed. A powerful hand would have insured the reverse. There is no control which people so long remember, as that which emanates from the exercise of a rigid and just authority. Had this been the case in the local administrative department upon the occupation of territory, how different would have been the results of the victories, which have been thrown away by mismanagement and misgovernment.

Palpable injustice in some instances, and partial and dangerous forbearance in others, have done their natural work, and bitter enmity has resulted in one case, while contempt has followed in the other. There is no motive so uncompromising, when brought in antagonism to military force, as the spirit, the moral being of a people. Armies may conquer territories, devastate fields, burn cities, destroy commerce, but they can never extinguish that inner being, which burns in the breasts of men. Bayonets may destroy individuals, but they can never destroy a people. Military power may subject but it cannot conquer. Moral influence soothes the body and controls the mind. In men, the average of moral is greater than physical strength. The obduracy of the former controls all of the latter. Put men to the rack, their moral strength supports them in their suffering. The patriot woman by the side of her bleeding husband, by moral force rises into that sublime condition that weeps not over the sacrifice of being or companionship, but weeps that she has no other sacrifices to make. The moral strength of the Revolution triumphed over Great Britain. The moral force of the armies of 1865 will alone triumph over the revolution in the South.

We do not mean to convey the idea that the South is to be conquered by moral influence alone, nor even do we mean that moral tone and leniency, without justice, are synonymous. The difficulty has been in the fact that the war has been conducted merely in the light of the operations of armies. Campaigns against the enemy, when the people at home, our most dangerous enemy, have been entirely disregarded and overlooked. It is but natural to suppose that all the people of the South are hostile, and all should be treated in that light. Authority should be so exercised that those who are semi-hostile may reap the benefit of their obedience to the laws and Constitution of the United States in accordance with their repentance and disposition to become peaceable and reformed citizens of the United States. The transgression of orders, however, in their case, should be as severely punished as in the case of determined and known enemies. The opinion, that we have been more deceived by the rascality of Southern Union men than by real rebels, compromises the dignity of the national cause. Union men, like the majority of all men, will grasp at opportunities. Men are selfish. If a Union man does wrong, punish him. Punish all men who do wrong. In insurrectionary districts it is necessary to have a force with which to enforce obedience. This force should not be used to oppress and annoy the people and disturb order, but to free them and preserve peace.

Another, and perhaps the real reason for our continued failure in the war, is the absence of a defined, distinct, and determined governmental policy towards the South, prescribed by the Executive and enforced by the army.

The army has been left in a fog. This is no apology for the army, for had its commanders, as a rule, been bold men, they might have made a policy of their own, and worked an impression upon the mind of the South which would not soon be forgotten. Sherman has accomplished more through his iron determination, than by the steel weapons of his armies. The one merely cleared away the rubbish, the other built the superstructure.

In the outset the Government was too pacific; afterwards it was neither pacific nor specific. The authorities, to lay down a code of general principles, stern but equitable in spirit, and irrevocable in execution, would attain the results which alone will govern and subject the turbulent characters of the South. There are minds open to conviction, there are others who, beast-like, mistake their instincts for the dictates of reason. To define a policy, and require every Southern man to obey or suffer the penalty, would effect more than the innumerable petty annoyances to which they are now subjected without any distinct object. The secret is this—the war is generally misunderstood. It is construed as a crusade against the whole people of the South, when in reality it should be against the powers that control the revolution. Destroy the head of the rebellion, and you shatter its members. Too much personal spite and prejudice have been mixed up in the war, and no results corresponding with the magnitude of our efforts need be expected until this be changed.

By adopting, so to speak, a rational rule of action, and holding subordinates to a rigid accountability for its enforcement, would have the effect of at least uniformity of conduct towards the people of the South, and let them know what to expect. It is not supposed the Government at Washington can give the details of administration for each State or locality in the South, any more than it was able to plan in the cabinet the details of distant campaigns. The features of a policy could be prescribed, and each commanding officer should be responsible that the policy be carried out.

As matters now stand, upon the occupation of a certain district, an officer is appointed, with certain undefined administrative, legislative, and judicial powers. That officer is generally of little account in the field. He assumes his position and rules the people in as great a variety of ways as his feelings or prejudices may prompt. He is practically responsible to no higher authority than himself, except in case of open crime; and the people, instead of being impressed with the power of the United States, are most usually convinced of its weakness.

We must have the best men of our armies to govern conquered territory. Common sense, integrity, and strength of will are better than the highest scholastic abilities, or, as is more frequently the case, old age and its gentleness, or influence and its usual ignorance and arrogance. This point is sadly overlooked. Anybody is liable to be provost-marshal under the present ideas. It will be different when it is realized that to break up the rebel armies is not going to bring about peace, that the people must be influenced. This is to be accomplished only by consistent, equitable, and impartial measures. They must feel the effects of war, without engendering its animosities. They must feel its inexorable necessities, before they can realize the pleasures and amenities of peace. We want determined and unrelenting men, who can exercise their powers, with all the relentless rigors of justice. Our commanders are too democratic. They lose sight of the necessities of their situations. An army is a despotism. It can be nothing else, short of anarchy. The government of the people of the South will of necessity have to be a despotism; let it be a just one until the people are willing to restore themselves to the privileges of pure democracy. Our commanders have been as great in battle as in other respects they have been at fault. For instance: It is not magnanimous to sacrifice a thousand lives, conquer territory, and then support its inhabitants, let them do as they please; turn loose able-bodied men who take arms, turn guerrillas. We capture them and treat them as prisoners of war. Humanity was designed for peace, not for war. If we show mercy towards a legitimate enemy, it is magnanimity; if we execute a traitor, it is philanthropy. Humanity is a vulgar virtue; equitable mercy is the highest of human efficiencies. Boldness is a happy fault. The nation is being ruined because it is too subjective.

One of the very few officers in high command that has shown himself equal, so to speak, to the social, or, perhaps more correctly, the local influences of the South, is General Sherman. He seems to be a stern, imperturbable soldier, with more brain than heart, but sufficient of the latter to answer the demands of the times. He rose slowly and amid a singular category of accusations. In 1861 he was accused of insanity; time has convinced us of the reason for the assertion. Sherman, though right, was ahead of the times. All thinkers are crazy, because their ideas are too large for the comprehension of small intellects.

General Sherman has written several letters of instruction to his subordinate commanders upon the subject of the war, the treatment of the people of the South, and other matters more or less bearing upon national topics. The correct reasoning of these documents and the beneficial effects which they may have in directing the mind into profitable contemplation, have induced us to make some extracts from these letters, as not inappropriate in connection with the subject we have been considering. They contain valuable suggestions.

The war and its relation to the Government, subjects which in both cases have led to much speculation among politicians and writers, are discussed by the General from a military standpoint, which probably will prove the best and most successful in the end. He says:

"The war which prevails in our land is essentially a war of races. The Southern people entered into a clear compact of government, but still maintained a species of separate interests, history, and prejudices. These latter became stronger and stronger, till they have led to a war, which has developed fruits of the bitterest kind.

"We of the North are, beyond all question, right in our lawful cause, but we are not bound to ignore the fact that the South have prejudices which form part of their nature, and which they cannot throw off without an effort of reason or the slower process of natural change. Now the question arises, should we treat as absolute enemies all in the South who differ from us in opinion or prejudices—kill or disable them? Or, should we give them time to think, and gradually change their conduct so as to conform to the new order of things which is slowly and gradually creeping into their country?

"When men take arms to resist our rightful authority, we are compelled to use force, because all reason and argument cease when arms are resorted to. When the provisions, forage, horses, mules, wagons, etc., are used by our enemy, it is clearly our duty and right to take them, because otherwise they may be used against us.

"In like manner, all houses left vacant by an inimical people are clearly our right, or such as are needed as storehouses, hospitals, and quarters."

In another place:

"For my part, I believe that this war is the result of false political doctrine, for which we are all as a people responsible, viz.: that any and every people have a right to self-government; and I would give all chance to reflect, and when in error to recant.

"In this belief, while I assert for our Government the highest military prerogatives, I am willing to bear in patience that political nonsense of slave-rights, State rights, freedom of conscience, freedom of press, and such other trash, as have deluded the Southern people into war, anarchy, bloodshed, and the foulest crimes that have disgraced any time or any people.

"I know slave-owners, finding themselves in possession of a species of property in opposition to the growing sentiment of the whole civilized world, conceived their property in danger, and foolishly appealed to war; and by skilful political handling involved with them the whole South in the doctrine of error and prejudice. I believe that some of the rich and slaveholding are prejudiced to an extent that nothing but death and ruin will extinguish; but hope that as the poorer and industrial classes of the South realize their relative weakness, and their dependence upon the fruits of the earth, and the good-will of their fellow-men, they will not only discover the error of their ways, and repent of their hasty action, but bless those who persistently maintained a Constitutional Government, strong enough to sustain itself, protect its citizens, and promise peaceful homes to millions yet unborn."

His opinions in regard to the rights of the Government, and the inevitable consequences of a much longer continuance of the war, are still more apt, forcible, and logical. He writes:

"The Government of the United States has in North Alabama any and all rights which they choose to enforce in war—to take their lives, their homes, their every thing, because they cannot deny that war does exist there, and war is simply power unrestrained by constitution or compact. If they want eternal warfare, well and good; we will accept the issue and dispossess them, and put our friends in possession. I know thousands and millions of good people, who, at simple notice, would come to North Alabama and accept the elegant houses and plantations there.

"If the people of Huntsville think differently, let them persist in war three years longer, and then they will not be consulted. Three years ago, by a little reflection and prudence they could have had a hundred years of peace prosperity, but they preferred war. Very well; last year they could have saved their slaves, but now, it is too late—all the powers of earth cannot restore to them their slaves any more than their grandfathers. Next year their lands will be taken, for in war we can take them, and rightfully, too, and another year they may beg in vain for their lives. A people who will persevere in war beyond a certain limit ought to know the consequences. Many, many people, with less pertinacity than the South, have been wiped out of national existence."

On the question of guerrillas, perhaps the most difficult of all the problems of the war, the General has shown his soundness of policy. We recommend his views to the particular attention of all officers. In a letter written from Kenesaw Mountain, Georgia, to General Burbridge, commanding in Kentucky during the raid of Morgan in the summer of '64, the General spoke upon the subject of the raid freely, the substance of his letter being summed up by himself as follows:

"1st. You may order all your post and district commanders that guerrillas are not soldiers, but wild beasts, unknown to the usages of war. To be recognized as soldiers, they must be enlisted, enrolled, officered, uniformed, armed and equipped, by recognized belligerent power, and must, if detailed from a main army, be of sufficient strength, with written orders from some army commander, to do some military thing. Of course we have recognized the Confederate Government as a belligerent power, but deny their right to our lands, territories, rivers, coasts, and nationality —admitting the right to rebel and move to some other country, where laws and customs are more in accordance with their own ideas and prejudices.

"2d. The civil power being insufficient to protect life and property, *ex necessitate rei*, to prevent anarchy, 'which nature abhors,' the military steps in, and is rightful, constitutional, and lawful. Under this law everybody can be made to 'stay at home and mind his and her own business,' and if they won't do that, can be sent away where they must keep their honest neighbors in fear of danger, robbery, and insult.

"3d. Your military commanders, provost-marshals, and other agents, may arrest all males and females who have encouraged or harbored guerrillas and robbers, and you may cause them to be collected in Louisville, and when you have enough —say three or four hundred—I will cause them to be sent down the Mississippi, through their guerrilla gauntlet, and by a sailing-ship send them to a land where they may take their negroes and make a colony, with laws and a future of their own. If they won't live in peace in such a garden as Kentucky, why, we will send them to another, if not a better, land, and surely this would be a kindness to them. and a God's blessing to Kentucky."

One of the greatest embarrassments experienced by our armies arises out of the hostility of the non-combatants of the South. Upon this point the General also speaks. He says:

"But a question arises as to dwellings used by women, children, and non-combatants. So long as non-combatants remain in their houses, and keep to their accustomed business, their opinions and prejudices can in nowise influence the war, and, therefore, should not be noticed. But if any one comes out into the public streets, and creates disorder, he or she should be punished, restrained or banished, either to the front or rear, as the officer in command adjudges. If the people, or any of them, keep up a correspondence with the parties in hostility, they are spies, and can be punished with death or minor punishment.

"To those who submit to the rightful law and authority, all gentleness and forbearance; but to the petulant and persistent secessionist, why, death is mercy, and the quicker he or she is disposed of the better. Satan and the rebellious saints of heaven were allowed a continuance of existence in hell merely to swell their just punishment. To such as would rebel against a Government so mild and just as ours was in peace, a punishment equal would not be unjust."

Military necessity, an apology for numerous iniquities, is sometimes a legitimate reason for the exercise of extreme measures. The depopulation of Atlanta was one of those instances. Sherman had profited by the experiences and embarrassments of other commanders, and determined to rid his army and himself of the same difficulties. The whole population of Atlanta was ordered North or South. Atlanta was to become exclusively a military post. Instead of transporting supplies to the inhabitants of Central Georgia, he resolved only to feed his army. The wisdom of this policy is already beginning to show itself. Sherman is now working out great results. He has been enabled to do this because he has an army of soldiers, not of commissaries and clerks.

The determination to force the inhabitants of Atlanta led to several letters upon the subject. It would not be unprofitable to reproduce them entire. The bold spirit of these documents is not yet forgotten. We therefore trust to the memory of the reader to revive them. We cannot, however, refrain from the following eloquent putting of the question. It will be found in the reply to the Mayor of Atlanta, and dated September 12, 1864. After speaking somewhat in detail upon the subject of the depopulation, the General concludes:

"You might as well appeal against the thunder-storm as against these terrible hardships of war. They are inevitable, and the only way the people of Atlanta can hope once more to live in peace and quiet at home is to stop this war, which can alone be done by admitting that it began in error and is perpetuated in pride. We don't want your negroes, or your horses, or your houses, or your land, or anything you have; but we do want, and will have a just obedience to the laws of the United States. That we will have, and if it involves the destruction of your improvements we cannot help it. You have heretofore read public sentiment in your newspapers, that live by falsehood and excitement; and the quicker you seek for truth in other quarters the better for you.

"I repeat, then, that by the original compact of government, the United States had certain rights in Georgia which have never been relinquished, and never will be; that the South began war by seizing forts, arsenals, mints, custom-houses, &c., long before Mr. Lincoln was installed, and before the South had one jot or tittle of provocation. I myself have seen in Missouri, Kentucky, Tennessee, and Mississippi, hundreds and thousands of women and children fleeing from your armies and desperadoes, hungry and with bleeding feet. In Memphis, Vicksburg, and Mississippi we fed thousands upon thousands of the families of rebel soldiers left on our hands, and whom we could not see starve. Now that war comes home to you, you feel very different—you deprecate its horrors, but did not feel them when you sent carloads of soldiers and ammunition, and moulded shells and shot to carry war into Kentucky and Tennessee, and desolate the homes of hundreds and thousands of good people, who only asked to live in peace at their old homes, and under the government of their inheritance. But these comparisons are idle. I want peace, and believe it can only be reached through Union and war, and I will ever conduct war purely with a view to perfect and early success."

What we want, then, in our armies, and in the whole nation, is a greater exhibition of moral force. Let Sherman be repeated. There are other men who have the requisite decision and judgment. Let them be brought forward. We want them. The war will end when the moral strength of the North exceeds that of the South.

PERSONAL ITEMS.

Major-General J. M. Palmer arrived at Louisville, February 18th, to assume command of the new Department of Kentucky.

Major-General Curtis assumed command of the Department of the Northwest, February 13th; head-quarters at Milwaukee.

Major-General J. M. Schofield assumed command of the Department of North Carolina, February 9th. Head-quarters with the army in the field.

Brigadier-General J. A. Rawlins has been brevetted major-general, and has been confirmed by the Senate, to be chief of staff to Lieutenant-General Grant.

Brigadier-General J. R. Hawley has been appointed to the command of the Department of Wilmington, and Brevet Brigadier-General Abbott to that of the post of Wilmington.

Brigadier-General Saxton has been appointed Superintendent of the Recruiting Service, and Brevet Brigadier-General Littlefield, Mustering and Disbursing Officer in the Department of the South.

Brigadier-General George H. Gordon has been temporarily assigned to the command of the District of East Virginia, relieving General G. F. Shepley, who reports to Major-General Weitzel, Twenty-fifth Corps, for assignment to duty.

Brigadier-General L. A. Grant (Sixth Corps) has been brevetted major-general.

Colonel Forsythe, of Major-General Sheridan's staff, formerly of the 8th Illinois Cavalry, has been appointed to the vacant brigadier-generalship, made by the death of General Charles R. Lowell.

Colonel J. Wager Swayne, 43d Ohio Volunteer Infantry, has been brevetted brigadier-general for gallant services in the Georgia campaign.

Colonel George P. Foster, 4th Vermont Volunteers, has been brevetted brigadier-general, and appointed to the command of the Vermont Brigade in General Getty's Division in Sixth Corps.

Colonel R. D. Mussey has been appointed Superintendent of the Freedmen of East and Middle Tennessee.

Lieutenant-Colonel Stewart L. Woodford, 127th New York Volunteers, has been promoted to the rank of colonel, and temporarily assigned to the command of the city of Charleston.

Acting Rear-Admiral Thatcher arrived at New Orleans on the 28th of February, and assumed command of the West Gulf Squadron, vice Commodore Palmer. The latter officer will command the vessels left at New Orleans.

LITERARY INTELLIGENCE

AND

NOTES ON NEW BOOKS.

To Messrs. Little, Brown & Co., of Boston, we are indebted for the "History of New England, during the Stuart Dynasty, by John Gorham Palfrey, Vol. III.," (8vo, 648 pp.) Historians are usually self-appointed, and, in many cases, the idols of the den render them partial, unjust, and incomplete. But if New England had thoroughly scrutinized her list of gifted scholars for an historiographer—although their name is legion—she could have found no one fitter for the honorable position than the learned and accurate Palfrey. A life of literary culture and progress, with ardent study of general history, has made him eminently capable in the rhetorical structure and presentation of such a work; for many years a Unitarian divine, he is thoroughly versed in the theological discussions which have so much to do with New England history; a statesman, and (in the best sense) a politician, he understands the machinery of governments; an honest man, even in maintaining heterodox opinions, he states them as fairly as an opponent could desire; a careful and pains-taking editor, he has spared neither time, labor, nor trouble, in procuring, verifying, and collating his very varied and heterogeneous material. To all these qualifications Dr. Palfrey adds an intense love for New England, of which his labors, whatever their public success, would be, in his eyes, but a slight manifestation.

Had he, with more sense of self-interest, expended the same scholarship and research on some picturesque portion of general history, like those chosen by Prescott and Motley, he would have achieved greater reputation; but, unlike them, his aim was labor and not fame. Fame however he has also achieved. Dr. Palfrey's original design was to bring the history down to a later period, but the work grew upon his hands, and he is warned, by his increasing years and duties, to bring it to a close with the final expulsion of the direct line of Stuarts in 1688. The volume before us opens with the reign of Charles II., and a clear summary of affairs in England and France. The second chapter, containing an essay on the government and laws of Massachusetts, Connecticut, and Plymouth, is written with a full knowledge, principally obtained, we conceive, when, as Secretary of State of Massachusetts, he was, unlike most secretaries, the careful arranger and reader of the documents and papers of which he was *ex-officio* custodian. We remember to have penetrated with him into a certain iron room, ten or twelve years ago, and read, with some loss of personal identity, a few of those early records, of which he knew more than any man living. The third volume of his history is less preliminary, more varied, and, although not more valuable, far more interesting than the others, to the general reader. Among the topics of dramatic interest we notice King Philip's War in 1675; the visit of George Fox to Rhode Island, and the growth of Harvard College.

If, in a more extended review, we should find occasion to differ from Dr. Palfrey on some points, and to present our reasons for so doing, we prefer, in this short notice, to thank him for his noble work, to declare that New England owes him a debt of gratitude, and to hope that his noble example will be followed by some scholar who is worthy to bring the history down to the only proper limit of philosophical history—the faint memory of the oldest inhabitant.

When a poet, who has contributed to the language even one poem like *Marco Bozarris*, and few, among his few other pieces which are unworthy companions to it,—in his later life, as the autumn gives token of winter, presents to the world such a poem as "Young America," the duty of his friends—he has no enemies— is respectful silence. New York: D. Appleton & Co.

There are some wants long felt, and at length set aside, as not to be satisfied. One of these has been with us a copy of Gil Blas, of Santillane, in clear, generous type, white paper, the volumes not so large as to fatigue the hand—a book in short to be taken up in spare half-hours; to renew our acquaintance with Fabricio, Laura, Seraphina, the Archbishop, as representatives of human nature.

This want is at last met in the really beautiful edition of Gil Blas, translated by Smollett, and published by Little, Brown & Co., of Boston. It is in three volumes, 12mo, and is altogether the most satisfactory library edition we have seen. Those who are furnishing libraries, public and private, will of course have Gil Blas, and they will do well to see this edition before they buy.

As to the matter, we need only say that, having read Gil Blas many times, in French, Spanish and English, we seized upon this as soon as received, and devoured it again with more zest than any modern novel has excited by a first perusal.

Kindred with this in form, print, paper and binding, is an edition of Don Quixote, epic, satire, comedy, and gentle tragedy. The editor who should venture to recommend Don Quixote to his readers, would offer them an indignity, but we may and do recommend a reperusal in this elegant edition of Little & Brown. Four vols.

From Major John A. Bolles, Judge-Advocate of the Court, we have received a copy of the "Trial of John Y. Beall, as a Spy and Guerrillero," by military commission. The case is so universally known that we need not mention details. He who, in disguise, seized two steamboats carrying unarmed and peaceful travellers, and sunk one; who attempted to throw a train of cars off the track by placing obstructions, at night; and who, in various places, was a spy of the most undisguised character, could surely expect nothing but an ignominious death. The spirited speech—not argument—in his favor, by Mr. Brady, could, of course, do nothing for him, and the clear and exhaustive reply of Major Bolles was not needed to convict him. But that reply is valuable as a lucid exposition of the subject, to anticipate rebel cavils, to serve as precedent, and to mark this kind of offence for history in the manifold record of the war.

War has its great organic laws, which War punishes to vindicate the right, and as a terror to evil-doers.

Published by D. Appleton & Co., New York.

EDITOR'S SPECIAL DEPARTMENT.

The theatre of operations has become so contracted by the magnificent strategy of our leaders, that we may venture upon a statement of the plans and counter-plans with which this splendid battle-spring opens upon the military world. It is the climax of the colossal war.

1. The armies in front of Richmond are designed to hold Lee there; to prevent him from sending large re-enforcements southward; to beat him if he comes out to offer battle; to circumvent him if he flies, and to occupy Richmond, with which occupation the war will virtually close,—not because there are not other places where armies may concentrate, and strategic advantages be gained, but because the surrender of Richmond will display such weakness of resource, and such a trammelling in war room, that entire public opinion will do the work of defeat: the stubbornest European prejudices, already rudely shaken by the loss of Charleston, will irrevocably break down when Richmond falls.

2. Sherman and Schofield move up through North Carolina, driving the small rebel force, under the invincible—when retiring—Johnston, before them, to cut the southern communications with Richmond; to open the country now lukewarm in rebel sympathies to Federal influence, and to narrow the circle of the hunt until "chaos come again" in rebel precincts.

3. Sheridan, the most daring of riders, cuts the canals and railroads which supply Richmond from the west; threatens Lynchburg—a strong point, if they evacuate Richmond; causes the hurrying of troops, in wild confusion, to the north of the capital, and to Burkesville, and awakens new fears in the already quaking forces which still cling to the defences of Richmond and Petersburg. In fine, *our policy is to hem them in, and make them attack us at present, and only to cry,* "*Up, Guards,*" when we can move upon them at every point of an irresistible line.

Meanwhile, we are not idle elsewhere. Thomas is moving southward with a large body of mounted troops, and a large force threatens Mobile. Jets of volcanic flame answer everywhere to the great eruptions on the Eastern coast.

Such being a brief enumeration of our plans, let us look at the counter-plans of the Confederate General. Not in his councils, we can only guess at them, applying the proper tests of military science.

1. To hold Richmond to the last, because with Richmond falls the rebel cause. In case it must be abandoned, Malay-like to run *a muck*, and fall, sword in hand, either upon Grant's force, now strong, efficient, and ardent, which will be condign destruction; or, to try another short fatal battle-summer at the North, which, with Grant's army following and Sheridan's intercepting, would be rapid ruin. Indeed the havoc made by Sheridan with their communications and the lack of supplies, render this course extremely improbable.

2. To send troops to check Sherman, and throw him back upon the coast, thus restoring somewhat the *status in quo*, or rather the *status ante Sherman*, and thus diminishing the prestige of that general, whose name is a tower of strength, and a presage of destruction; but even here they fail, for they cannot find him where they want him, and he goes where they do not want him.

3. To evacuate Richmond, rally upon Lynchburg, there dig the *last ditch* in which

faute de mieux, the great secession treason will bury itself forever. Whatever be their policy, concentration is their only possibility, and concentration is ruin. Were the rebel armies well supplied, and in good spirits; had their later experiences of the war been even checkered by light and shade, and not one dead gloom of disaster; had the people still confidence in their leaders, when they rave out their promises of ruin to the republic, and certain success to the treason; did the soldiers still believe that the sacrifice of their lives would insure the success of their cause,—were one or even a few of these things in their favor, they might yet, closed in upon as they are by the Federal armies, make some mighty effort, and achieve some compensating victories; but they have no such hopes, no such trust. "On ne va pas à la guerre pour être tué," says Marshal Marmont. Men go to war to succeed, to win victories. Show the rebel soldiers, as every day's experience is showing them, that they have nothing further to hope, and they will desert in vast bodies, will feign to fight, and then retire, will seek to give themselves up as prisoners, will disintegrate the rebel armies, and make further resistance impossible.

Napoleon fought, in 1814, at La Rothière, at Laon and Craonne, but Arcis-sur-Aube demonstrated the folly of further resistance, and he was closeted in confusion at Fontainebleau, while the *débris* of his army was going through the motions of a battle at Paris. There is a striking moral parallelism; and if Napoleon could no longer make head against such stupid men as Blücher and Schwartzenburg, how can Lee, without skilful lieutenants, hope to win against Grant, Sherman, and Sheridan, aided by corps and division generals of the first order. We need say nothing about the great cause, nor quote Shakspeare to show what moral weapons are aimed at those "whose conscience with injustice is corrupted."

To illustrate these general remarks, we may refer to the principal events which have transpired, and movements which have been made, since our last issue. The rebel cause has received numerous "blessings in disguise." Charleston was evacuated, and in such haste that, although they burned most of the cotton, they left four hundred and fifty guns behind them. Of course the rebels are all the better off for evacuating Charleston. Fort Anderson fell, after a combined attack by the army and navy, and then Wilmington was given up on the 22d of February. Here again it is manifest—to them—that, whatever we have gained, they have lost nothing. Georgetown, on the Black River, above its junction with the Pedee, was taken by Admiral Dahlgren on the 28th—another knell for blockade-runners. On this expedition, the Admiral's temporary flag-ship, the Harvest-Moon, was blown up by a torpedo. The iron rim on the Atlantic is thick and all-excluding.

Johnston, who relieved Beauregard, at the request of the latter, it is said, now sets himself seriously to work to wreak vengeance on the insolent Sherman—the *Bête noir* or *Loup garou* of the Confederacy, who goes just where he wants to, and not where they want him; and while threatening Charlotte, and putting them on the *qui vive* there, turns aside to Cheraw, Laurel Hill, Fayetteville, and thus is within striking distance of Schofield. Schofield, a fighting general, accompanies the advance in his new department of North Carolina, and in the battle near Kinston, recovers a partial disaster, repulses the most desperate attacks of Hill and Hoke, and finally drives the enemy across the Neuse, while he occupies Kinston on the 13th. Bragg chronicles a great success, but finds it convenient to retire, with double loss. We do not enter into the details of Sherman's march, because of the vague knowledge we can have at present, and because we are promised full papers on his movements by a competent hand hereafter.

While we write, the rebel army is concentrated at Goldsboro, say thirty thousand strong, and Sherman and Schofield are in communication. With a good line of retreat, Goldsboro is strong, being the intersection of the North Carolina Railroad with the Wilmington and Weldon. But they cannot hold it, for Sherman will use his never-failing stratagem of marching around them without attacking, and tapping their rear; and so, like the wandering Jew, they must move on, or fight Sherman where he chooses to receive them, and where they must be beaten. Thus far the march of Sherman has met with but little opposition, and he has captured and destroyed immense amounts of valuable government property—at Columbia, forty-three pieces of artillery; at Cheraw, twenty-five pieces, and thirty-six hundred barrels of gunpowder; and at Fayetteville, twenty pieces, and large quantities of other war munitions. Later:—Schofield is at Goldsboro, and Sherman at Smithfield.

We copy from the *Herald* dispatch of Captain J. E. P. Doyle, the following, which will, by the aid of a map, present to our readers a clear view of Sherman's movements from Savannah and Beaufort to Fayetteville—

CHRONOLOGY OF THE CAROLINA CAMPAIGN.

JANUARY.

16th.—Right wing (Fifteenth and Seventeenth Corps) transferred from Savannah to Beaufort.
20th.—Left wing left Savannah, marching on either side of the Savannah River towards Augusta.
23d.—General Sherman transferred head-quarters from Savannah to Beaufort.
25th.—Left wing delayed by rains in camp, seven miles from Savannah.
26th.—Left wing at Springfield.
27th.—Advance of the left wing reached Sister's Ferry.
29th.—Right wing moved from Pocotaligo towards the Combahee River. Left wing in camp at Sister's Ferry delayed by rains and high water.
30th.—Right wing moving along Savannah and Charleston Railroad, and between the railroad and McPhersonville, encountering small parties of the rebel cavalry. Left wing still at Sister's Ferry.
31st.—Right wing at McPhersonville. Left wing at Sister's Ferry.

FEBRUARY.

1st.—Right wing moved from McPhersonville towards Hickory Hill. Left wing still water and mud bound at Sister's Ferry.
3d.—Right wing moved to Brighton's Bridge, over the Saltketcher, when enemy made resistance to the passage of the stream and burned the bridge.
4th.—Right wing effected passage of the Saltketcher. Left wing moved across the Savannah.
5th.—Right wing crossed Whippy Swamp. Left wing moved to Brighton, which had been burned by the rebel cavalry.
6th.—Advance of the right wing; fought Wheeler at Orange Church on the Little Saltketcher.
7th.—Right wing at Bambury, and midway on Charleston and Augusta Railroad. Left wing moved to Lawtonville, which was burned by the Twentieth Corps.
8th.—Right wing crossed the South Edisto River. Left wing in camp at Lawtonville.
9th.—Right wing at Grahamsville. Left wing reached Allendale.
10th.—Right wing crossed the North Edisto River. Left wing reached Fiddle Pond, near Barnwell.
11th.—Right wing captured Orangeburg. Left wing marched through Barnwell, which was left in ashes, and encamped three miles from White Pond Station.
12th.—Right wing made a rapid march from Orangeburg towards the Congaree and Columbia. The left wing tore up ten miles of the Charleston and Augusta Railroad.
13th.—Left wing crossed the South Edisto River.

14th.—Left wing crossed the North Edisto River.
15th.—Right wing effected the passage of the Congaree, and began shelling Columbia. General Carlin, in the advance of the left wing, skrimished with the rebels near Lexington, capturing and burning the town.
16th.—The right wing confronting Columbia. Left wing marched to Hart's Ferry, on the Saluda River, and crossed.
17th.—Right wing occupied Columbia. Same night Columbia was burned. Left wing reached the Broad River.
18th.—Right wing in camp at Columbia, and left wing in camp on Broad River.
19th.—Left wing crossed the Broad River, and destroyed Greenville and Columbia Railroad, camping near Alston.
20th.—Right wing left Columbia, destroying railroad to Winnsboro. Left wing moved to and crossed Little River.
21st.—The whole army was concentrated at Winnsboro, thus leading Johnston to suppose that it was Sherman's intention to push upon Charlotte.
22d.—Right wing engaged in passage of the Wateree River at Pay's Ferry, Left wing tore up the railroad above Winnsboro, and moved to Youngsville.
23d.—Right wing on Lynch Creek. Left wing reached Rocky Mount, Catawba River.
24th.—Part of the left wing crossed the Catawba (or Wateree) River.
25th.—Right wing captured Camden. Left wing passing Catawba River.
27th.—Left wing still engaged in difficult passage of the Catawba. General Carlin had a fight with Wheeler's Cavalry.
28th.—Right wing moved from Camden towards Cheraw, encamping on Lynch's Creek, and halting for three days, waiting for the left wing, delayed at the Catawba River, to get up.

MARCH.

1st.—Left wing moved to Hanging Rock.
2d.—Left wing marched to Horton's Ferry or Lynch's Creek.
3d.—The left wing being up, the whole army crossed Lynch's Creek.
4th.—Right wing captured Cheraw. Left wing crossed Thompson's Creek.
5th.—Right wing and part of the left crossed the Great Pedee River. Davis's Corps of the left wing moved up to Sneedsboro.
6th.—Davis crossed the Great Pedee, and the whole army was massed to move on Fayetteville.
7th.—Left wing moved to near Downing River.
8th.—Right wing at Laurel Hill.
9th.—The whole army marched on the several roads converging at Fayetteville to within twenty miles of the place.
10th.—Marched to within ten miles of Fayetteville in line of battle, anticipating an engagement with Hardee. Kilpatrick's Cavalry struck the rear of Hardee's retreating forces near Fayetteville, and engaged Hampton in one of the finest cavalry battles of the war.
11th.—The whole army entered Fayetteville, having been engaged in the campaign for fifty-four days, and having marched four hundred and forty-three miles.

From the environs of Richmond, for reasons already suggested, there is little to chronicle. There are rumors that the rebels have countermined one or more of our forts, but that the engineers cannot find the spot upon which a globe of compression would destroy the gallery: Doubtful. Reviews inspire and discipline the troops. General Grant receives his glorious due, in the shape of the gold medal voted by Congress. We watch the Southside Road, and the troops nearest the enemy lie upon their arms at the first scent of possible attack. Whether as a feint or not, Lee masses his troops in our front at Petersburg, and the great battle may begin at any moment.

In Richmond affairs are almost at their worst. The *Examiner* declared some time since that the evacuation of the capital would be the loss of all respect towards the Confederate government; and yet the Congress is deserted by its members, in spite of Lee's wail that "unless these abide in the ship" it must sink. Davis asks them to postpone their adjournment, and they give him, with the generosity of fear, one working day.

Admiral Semmes, they say, is planning a grand expedition down the James, by which he will break through our obstructions and do wonderful things. The transports, if he could get at them, he might sink, for his hand is in for that sort of thing, but the men-of-war may, like the unchivalrous Winslow, be mean enough to plate or chain their vessels, and then Semmes would have cold water thrown upon his plans, even as at Cherbourg. By the last accounts, the newspapers in Richmond were "temporarily" suspended. Only the *Dispatch* was left, and that found it a blessing to appear on half a sheet.

Sheridan's march deserves special mention. After the defeat of Early by Custer's Division near Staunton, he marched forward in rain and mud, inflicting immense damage upon the railroads and canal, and going very near Lynchburg and Richmond. We can present no better summary of his movements than will be found in the following dispatch:—

HEAD-QUARTERS, MIDDLE MILITARY DIVISION,
COLUMBIA, Va., March 10, 1865.

"Lieutenant-General U. S. GRANT, Commanding Armies United States:—

"GENERAL—In my last dispatch, dated Waynesboro, I gave you a brief account of the defeat of Early by Custer's Division.

"The same night this division was pushed across the Blue Ridge and entered Charlottesville at two P. M. the next day. The mayor of the city and the principal inhabitants came out, and delivered up the keys of the public buildings.

"I had to remain at Charlottesville two days. This time was consumed in bringover from Waynesboro our ammunition and pontoon trains.

"The weather was horrible beyond description and the rain incessant.

"The two divisions were during this time occupied in destroying the two large iron bridges—one over the Rivanna River, the other over Morse's Creek, near Charlottesville—and the railroad for a distance of eight miles in the direction of Lynchburg.

"On the 6th of March I sent the First Division, General Devin commanding, to Scottsville, on the James River, with directions to send out light parties through the country, and destroy all merchandise, mills, factories, bridges, &c., on the Rivanna River, the parties to join the division at Scottsville. The division then proceeded along the canal to Duguldsville, fifteen miles from Lynchburg, destroying every lock, and in many places the bank of the canal. At Duguldsville we hoped to secure the bridge to let us cross the river, as our pontoons were useless.

"On account of the high water, in this, however, we were foiled, as both this bridge and the bridge at Hardwicksville were burned by the enemy upon our approach. Merritt accompanied this division.

"The Third Division started at the same time from Charlottesville, and proceeded down the Lynchburg Railroad to Amherst Court-House, destroying every bridge on the road, and in many places miles of the road. The bridges on this road are numerous, and some of them five hundred feet in length. We have found great abundance in this country for our men and animals. In fact, the canal has been the great feeder of Richmond. At the Rockfish River the bank of the canal was cut, and at New Canton, where the dam is across the James, the guard-lock was destroyed and the James River let into the canal, carrying away the banks, and washing out the bottom of the canal.

"The dam across the James at this point was also partially destroyed.

"I have had no opposition. Everybody is bewildered by our movements. I have had no news of any kind since I left.

"The latest Richmond paper was of the 4th, but contained nothing.

"I omitted to mention that the bridges on the railroad from Swoop's Depot, on the other side of Staunton, to Charlottesville, were utterly destroyed; also all bridges for a distance of ten miles on the Gordonsville Railroad.

"The weather has been very bad indeed, raining hard every day, with the exception of four days, since we started. My wagons have, from the state of the roads, detained me.

"Up to the present time we have captured fourteen pieces of artillery—eleven at Waynesboro and three at Charlottesville.

"The party that I sent back from Waynesboro started with six pieces, but they were obliged to destroy two of the six for want of animals. The remaining eight pieces were thoroughly destroyed.

"We have captured, up to the present time, twelve canal-boats laden with supplies, ammunition, rations, medical stores, &c.

"I cannot speak in too high terms of Generals Merritt, Custer, and Devin, and the officers and men of their commands. They have waded through mud and water during this continuous rain, and are all in fine spirits and health.

"Commodore Hollins, of the rebel navy, was shot near Gordonsville, while attempting to make his escape from our advance in that direction.

"Very respectfully, your obedient servant,
"P. H. SHERIDAN,
Major-General Commanding."

FORT FISHER.

[The universal interest excited by the capture of the "impregnable" Fort Fisher prompts us to place on record, for future history, the following letter and sketch of the work, by General Comstock, the chief engineer of the expeditionary army.—ED.]

HEAD-QUARTERS UNITED STATES FORCES,
FORT FISHER, NORTH CAROLINA,
January 27, 1865.

SIR:—I have the honor to submit the following report of engineer operations in connection with the capture of Fort Fisher, together with a sketch of that work, and another of the country in its vicinity. Fort Fisher is situated on the peninsula between the Cape Fear River and the Atlantic Ocean, about a mile and a half northeast of Federal Point. For five miles north of Federal Point, this peninsula is sandy and low, not rising more than fifteen feet above high tide, the interior abounding in fresh-water swamps, often wooded and almost impassable, while much of the dry land, till one gets within half a mile of Fort Fisher, is covered with wood, or low undergrowth, except a strip about three hundred yards wide along the sea-shore. The landing of the troops composing the expedition was effected on the sea-beach, about five miles north of Fort Fisher, on January 12, and Paine's Division was at once pushed across the Cape Fear River, with instructions to take up a line to be held against any attack from the direction of Wilmington. This line, on the morning of January 13, was already defensible, and was further strengthened during the day; while, on the 14th, a second line was laid out, and begun under charge of Lieutenant J. H. Price in rear of its left. Pioneer companies were organized in Ames's and Paine's Divisions, and as during the 14th the fire of the rebel gunboat

PLAN AND SECTIONS OF FORT FISHER.

ABBREVIATIONS IN PLAN:

S. B.—Smooth-Bore. C.—Columbiad. B. L. R.—Blakely Rifle. P.—Parrott.
R.—Rifle. B.—Brooke. M.—Mortar.

Chickamauga killed and wounded a number of our men, Lieutenant O. Kuffe, with his company of the 15th Regiment New York Volunteer Engineers, was directed to build a battery for two 30-pounder Parrotts on the bank of the river, to keep her off.

On the afternoon of January 14th, a reconnoissance was pushed, under the direction of the Major-General Commanding, to within five hundred yards of Fort Fisher, a small advanced work being taken possession of. This was at once turned into a defensive line to be held against any attempt from Fort Fisher. The reconnoissance showed that the palisading in front of the work had been seriously injured by the navy fire; only nine guns could be seen on the land-front where sixteen had been counted on Christmas Day; the steady, though not rapid fire of the navy, prevented the enemy from using either artillery or musketry on the reconnoitering party; it seemed probable that troops could be got within two hundred yards of the work without serious loss, and it was a matter of great doubt whether the necessary ammunition could be supplied by the open beach if regular approaches were determined on. It was decided to assault, and the assault was made on the 15th, at half-past three P. M., after three hours of heavy navy fire, by three deployed brigades following one another at intervals of about three hundred yards, and each making its final rush for the west end of the land-face, from a rough rifle-pit, about three hundred yards from the work.

At the point attacked, the palisading was less injured than elsewhere, it being partially hidden, and it was necessary to use axes to cut, and timbers to batter it down, in order that the troops might pass readily through it. Powder-sacks for blowing these palisades down had been prepared, but were not used.

After seven hours' fighting, gaining traverse by traverse, the work was won.

Fort Fisher consists of two fronts—the first, or land-front, running across the peninsula at this point, seven hundred yards wide, is four hundred and eighty yards in length, while the second, or sea-front, runs from the right of the first parallel to the beach to the Mound Battery—a distance of thirteen hundred yards. The land-front is intended to resist any attack from the north; the sea-front to prevent any of our naval vessels from running through New Inlet, or landing troops on Federal Point.

1. *Land-Front.*—This front consists of a half bastion on the left, or Cape Fear River side, connected by a curtain with a bastion on the ocean side. The parapet is twenty-five feet thick, averages twenty feet in height, with traverses rising ten feet above it and running back on their tops, which were from eight to twelve feet in thickness, to a distance of from thirty to forty feet from the interior crest. The traverses on the left half bastion were about twenty-five feet in length on the top.

The earth for this heavy parapet, and the enormous traverses at their inner ends, more than thirty feet in height, was obtained partly from a shallow exterior ditch, but mainly from the interior of the work. Between each pair of traverses there was one or two guns. The traverses on the right of this front were only partially completed. A palisade, which is loopholed and has a banquette, runs in front of this face at a distance of about fifty feet in front of the foot of the exterior slope from the Cape Fear River to the ocean, with a position for a gun between the left of the front and the river, and another between the right of the front and the ocean. Through the middle traverse on the curtain was a bomb-proof postern, whose exterior opening was covered by a small redan for two field-pieces, to give flank fire along the curtain. The traverses were generally bomb-proofed for men or magazines. The slopes of the work appear to have been revetted with marsh sod, or covered with grass, and to have had an inclination of forty-five degrees, or a little less. On those slopes most exposed to navy fire the revetement or grassing has been entirely destroyed, and the inclination reduced to thirty degrees.

The ends of traverses as they rise above the parapet are very ragged. Still, all damage done to the earthwork can be readily repaired, its strength being about the same as before the bombardment. The damage done by the navy fire was, first to the palisades, which were so injured as in most places to be little obstacle to assaulting troops; second, to guns and carriages. There were originally on the front twenty-one guns and three mortars. Of these, three-fourths were rendered unserviceable by injuries to either gun or carriage. The gun in the right bastion, the field-pieces in front of the postern, and one or two mortars, were used against the assaulting troops.

There was a formidable system of torpedoes, two hundred yards in advance of this front, the torpedoes being about eighty feet apart, and each containing about one hundred pounds of powder. They were connected with the fort by three sets of wires; fortunately the sets leading directly to those over which the army and navy columns moved had been cut by shells, and no torpedo was exploded.

2. *Sea-Front.*—This front consists of a series of batteries, mounting in all twenty-four guns, the different batteries being connected by a strong infantry parapet, so as to form a continuous line. The same system of heavy traverses for the protection of the guns, is used as on the land-front, and these traverses are also generally bomb-proofed. Captain N. Adams, 4th New Hampshire Volunteers, and First Lieutenant J. H. Price, 4th United States Colored Troops, commanding pioneer companies of Ames's and Paine's Divisions, and First Lieutenant K. S. O. Kuffe, commanding company of 15th New York Volunteer Engineers, have, with their commands, been of great service in the construction of batteries and defensive works. First Lieutenant A. H. Knowlton, 4th New Hampshire Volunteers, has rendered valuable assistance in making sketches of Fort Fisher; as also private Schultze, 15th New York Volunteer Engineers.

Very respectfully, your obedient servant, C. B. COMSTOCK.
Lieut.-Col. and Brev. Brig.-Gen., Chief Engineer.

Major A. TERRY, A. A. G.

It may be added that in thirty bomb-proofs and magazines and their passages there were fourteen thousand five hundred feet of floor space, not including the main magazine, which was exploded, and whose demensions are unknown.

C. B. C.

OBITUARY.
BRIGADIER-GENERAL T. E. G. RANSOM.
BY A COMPANION-IN-ARMS.

" In war was never lion raged more fierce:
In peace was never gentle lamb more mild."—SHAKSPEARE.

AMONG the most prominent actors of the West, in what has been so well called "this fearfully glorious present,"—one of the most brilliant young captains in our army, and one who certainly had no superior of his years in the volunteer service, stood THOMAS EDWARD GREENFIELD RANSOM, who possessed, to a greater degree than ordinarily falls to the lot of man, the respect and love of all who knew him. Lieutenant-General Grant once said of him "he is my best fighting man." The fields and fortresses of eight States, in which he led the invincible legions of Illinois, who with

" Nerves of steel and hearts of oak,"

drove back the enemy; have witnessed his devotion, and his blood poured out on five battle-fields attests his valor. No story could be richer in deeds of daring and heroism than the story of the life of the young General, who died among the hills of Georgia of disease induced by the exposures of the service, as much "dead on the field," as if a rebel bullet had struck him to the heart.

Brigadier-General Ransom was born in Norwich, Vermont, on the 29th of November, 1834. In 1846 he entered the primary class of Norwich University—a Military College under the charge of his father, T. B. Ransom, then a Major-General of Militia of the State of Vermont. He was afterwards appointed Colonel 9th United States Infantry, displayed signal ability and bravery in the Mexican war, and fell at the storming of Chapultepec, Sept. 13th, 1847. The son inherited his father's sterling qualities, and has placed his name high on his country's roll of "brave men and worthy patriots, dear to God and famous to all ages." During the Mexican war young Ransom was taught engineering, under the tuition of his cousin, B. F. Marsh, on the Rutland and Burlington Railroad; but on his father's death he returned to the Norwich University, and continued there until the age of seventeen. In 1851 he entered upon the practice of his profession of an engineer, in Lasalle County, Illinois. Three years later he embarked in the real estate business at Peru, with his uncle, under the firm of Gilson and Ransom, and in December, 1855, removed to Chicago, to become a member of the firm of A. J. Galloway & Co., a house largely engaged in land operations. At a later period he removed to Fayette County, and while engaged in trade, acted as an agent for the Illinois Central Railroad Company. He was there when the war began, and immediately raised a company and reached Camp Yates, at Springfield, April 24th, 1861, where his company was organized into the 11th Illinois Volunteers, and on an election for field-officers being held, was elected major. The regiment was ordered to Villa Ridge, near Cairo, and there remained in Camp of Instruction until June, when they were ordered to Bird's Point, Mo. The regiment was mustered out of the three months' service, July 30th, and was reorganized and mustered in for three years, Ransom being elected lieutenant-colonel. On the night of the 19th of August, in a gallant charge under Colonel Dougherty, upon Charleston, Mo., Colonel Ransom received his first severe wound by a mounted foe, who pretended to surrender, but fired upon him as he approached to take his arms. After receiving the bullet in his right shoulder, he fired upon the rebel, instantly killing him. He was granted thirty days' leave, and reported for duty at the expiration of the seventh.

Accompanying General Grant up the Tennessee River, he participated in the capture of Fort Henry, on the 6th of February, 1862, and led his regiment in the assault upon Donelson, was again severely wounded, but would not leave the field until the battle was ended. His clothes were pierced with six bullet-holes, and a horse was killed under him. His wound, together with fatigue and prolonged exposure, did their work—a long sickness followed; but he would not leave his regiment, and moved with the 11th from place to place, being carried in an ambulance. For his skill and gallantry at Donelson, Ransom was promoted to the colonelcy—Wallace, who had been for some months commanding a brigade, receiving at the same time a commission as brigadier-general. At Shiloh, when General Wallace fell, Ransom led his regiment through the hottest part of the bloody battle, and, though wounded in the head early in the engagement, remained with his command through the day. In his official report, Major-General McClernand, in whose Division he was, spoke of Colonel Ransom at a "critical moment performing prodigies of valor, though reeling in his saddle, and streaming with blood from a serious wound." In June he was appointed as chief of General McClernand's staff, and served for a time on the staff of General Grant. Wherever there was hot work, the young colonel was to be found; leading the successful expedition against Clarksville, Tennessee; routing Woolward at Garrettsburg, Kentucky, and commanding a brigade in the van of the army when it moved into Mississippi. In January, 1863, Ransom was appointed a brigadier-general, his commission dating from Nov. 29, 1862. He next participated in the campaign against Vicksburg, commanding the First Brigade, Sixth Division, Seventeenth Army Corps. At Champion Hill, and during the siege operations, his gallantry was conspicuous. After the surrender, General Ransom's Brigade formed a part of General Logan's column of occupation. August 6th, he was appointed to the command of the post of Natchez, and captured, upon his arrival there, a large supply of ammunition, and five thousand head of cattle. He was next transferred to the Thirteenth Corps, and assigned to the command of a division. He accompanied the Texas Expedition under General Banks, in November, 1863, and led the troops detailed to capture the enemy's works on Mustang Island. He took part in the Red River Campaign, fully maintaining his high character as an efficient soldier. In the disastrous battle of Sabine Cross-Roads, April 8th, 1864, his Division of Infantry was ordered up to the support of Lee's Cavalry, by Major-General Franklin, then in command of the column. The writer was near him "amid sheeted fire and flame," while he rode hither and thither, vainly endeavoring to beat back the overwhelming numbers led against him by Generals Green and Mouton. No man ever behaved more gallantly. While directing the guns of the Chicago Mercantile Battery, his adjutant, Captain Dickey, was mortally wounded, and he himself severely hurt in the knee. The day following, four surgeons examined the wound at Pleasant Hill, and were divided in their opinion, two being in favor of amputation, while the others deemed it unnecessary. The General, who was an anxious listener to the conversation, raised himself on his couch, and said, "Well, gentlemen, as the House is equally divided on this subject, I will as chairman of the meeting decide the question. I shall retain the wounded leg, lead included." And so the matter was decided, and the gallant young captain ultimately recovered, although with a stiff knee, which was however, as he remarked, "better than no knee."

During the month of April, he was awarded a gold medal by the board of officers of the Seventeenth Corps for gallant conduct in the Vicksburg campaign. After recovering from his wound, Ransom was ordered to report to the Georgian Hero, General Sherman, and was assigned to the command of the Fourth Division, Sixteenth Army Corps, operating in the vicinity of Atlanta. He was soon promoted to the command of the left wing of the corps, consisting of Fuller's and Corse's Divisions, and was advanced in September, during the absence of General Blair, to the command of the Seventeenth Corps. From the date of the capitulation of Atlanta, the General suffered from a severe attack of dysentery, but would not, as his friends advised, give up command, or leave the post of duty. While his corps was in pursuit of Hood's Army, he continued to direct its movements, riding in an ambulance for several days, after he was unable from weakness to sit on his horse. Ere long he was utterly prostrated, and on the 29th of October, after giving the most minute orders in regard to his affairs, leaving messages of love for his widowed New England mother, and other dear friends, among the prairies of Illinois, and in the Union armies; and when his thirtieth birthday was waiting for him over in the month of November, he finished his glorious little week of life, and the spirit of T. E. G. Ransom, fit companion for Bayard and McPherson, Sedgwick and Wadsworth, and the hundred other heroes whose outpoured blood attests their love of freedom and right, passed away to that sunny land, where there is neither "battle nor murder, sedition, privy conspiracy, or rebellion." In accordance with his request, his remains were removed to Chicago, and were interred with distinguished honors by the Masonic fraternity—of which he was a member—aided by the military, and were followed to their last resting-place in the old cemetery by an immense concourse of citizens. The funeral-car, drawn by six horses, was appropriately draped; upon the coffin, and about it, were scattered floral wreaths and *immortelles*, while the sword of the young hero was placed across his breast. Over the coffin was thrown a historic flag. It was the regular garrison flag of Fort Brown, Brownsville, Texas, during the Mexican War. When Twiggs surrendered that fort to the enemy, an employé of the Government secured the flag and secreted it. It was subsequently presented by him to the 13th Maine Volunteers, and from their possession it passed into General Ransom's hands, over whose head-quarters in the field it was constantly displayed.

Thus closed the brief career of a man of fine genius, great military capacity, of unblemished personal character, of high promise, as well as noble performance. General Howard said of him: "He is a soldier of modesty, capacity, and bravery, equal to any in this army." What grander deeds of daring and heroism he might have achieved, what more glorious life he might have illustrated, no man can tell. How brief his little day; but, ah, how bright it was! What a record of marches and battles, with wounds and dangers and famous victories! always in the terrible front, ever present when history was to be made. It was not his destiny to fall, as he often expressed a wish to do, upon the field of battle, with the noise of conflict ringing in his ears, and shouts of "victory" from his companions, heralding his approach to "the land o' the leal." One of the earliest of the English poets has truthfully said,

> "Life is not lost, from which is bought
> Endless reunion."

Ransom's memory, and the memory of others like him, who have died that their country might live; who have, beyond all considerations of gain, rank, or station, seen only their country, and her well-being; will be cherished by all loyal dwellers therein; by their children, by their children's children, and to "the last syllable of recorded time." He is not dead, however; he is only gone before; for "they never die, who fall in a great cause;" and he most truly fell in a great cause—the struggle for the preservation of the Union—"this Holy War and Modern Crusade against Barbarism."

"Death," says Bacon, "openeth the gate to good fame." In this brief biography of my friend, it has not been my aim to make him too much a hero; to award him any, however slight, commendation to which he was not most justly entitled; and I cannot better leave him, than with the beautiful words applied to another, but which may be even more truthfully applied to Ransom: "Good friend! brave heart! gallant leader! true hero! hail, and farewell!"

OFFICIAL INTELLIGENCE.

The Army.

Military Prisons.

EXECUTIVE MANSION,
WASHINGTON CITY, D. C.,
February 15, 1865.

THE penitentiary at Albany, New York, the State prison at Clinton, New York, the penitentiary at Columbus, Ohio, the penitentiary at Jefferson City, Missouri, and such other prisons as the Secretary of War may designate for the confinement of prisoners under sentence of courts-martial, shall be deemed and taken to be military prisons.

ABRAHAM LINCOLN.

Dismissals.

For the Week ending February 4, 1865.

Colonel Jacob Van Zandt, 91st New York Volunteers, to date February 2, 1865, for interfering with the discipline of the 91st New York Volunteers, by ordering enlisted men thereof who were undergoing punishment to be released, and advising a non-commissioned officer not to obey the orders of the Lieutenant-Colonel commanding the regiment, pleading drunkenness as an excuse therefor. This while the said Van Zandt was not on duty, nor in command of his regiment.

Captain Nathan Willard, Commissary of Subsistence United States Volunteers, to date January 21, 1865, for not accounting for public funds in his possession, for drunkenness, and for conduct unbecoming an officer and a gentleman.

Captain Philip Bauer, 180th Ohio Volunteers, to date January 28, 1865, for drunkenness and absence without leave.

Captain G. W. Smith, of Smith's Independent Company Maryland Cavalry, to date January 28, 1865, for preferring frivolous charges against Lieutenant J. T. Fearing, of his command, by reason of personal animosity.

Captain Peter Litzel, 89th Indiana Volunteers, to date January 10, 1865, for absence without leave, having been published officially, and failed to appear before the commission.

First Lieutenant E. F. Jennings, 2d North Carolina Mounted Infantry, to date January 31st, 1865, for having tendered his resignation on the grounds of incompetency, and for the good of the service, while under serious charges.

For the Week ending February 11, 1865.

The following-named officers, as of the dates set opposite their respective names, for the causes mentioned, having been published officially, and failed to appear before the Commission:—

Desertion.

Second Lieutenant William P. Williams, 10th New Hampshire Volunteers, to date August 3, 1864.

Absence without leave.

Major Charles Burgess, 9th New York Artillery, to date January 16, 1865.

Second Lieutenant Robert Potts, 99th Pennsylvania Volunteers, to date January 16, 1865.

Major William Purcell, 16th Iowa Volunteers, to date February 4, 1865, for disobedience of orders and absence without leave.

Captain Uniacke C. Mackay, 10th United States Infantry, to date February 3, 1865, for absence without leave, and for fraudulent conduct.

Captain Adam Reissenger, 200th Pennsylvania Volunteers, to date February 3, 1865, for breach of arrest and desertion.

First Lieutenant George H. Rapp, 33d Missouri Volunteers, to date February 8, 1865, for absence without leave.

Second Lieutenant Seth Daniels, 68th United States Colored Troops, to date February 4, 1865, for worthlessness.

Second Lieutenant George Querner, 180th Ohio Volunteers, to date February 6, 1865, for drunkenness and absence without leave.

The following-named officers of the 27th Iowa Volunteers, to date February 8, 1865, for straggling beyond the lines alone, without arms, in violation of orders and good discipline, thereby subjecting themselves to be captured by the enemy:—

Captain Charles A. Slocum.
First Lieutenant Henry F. Tucker.

For the Week ending February 18, 1865.

Captain W. B. Dugger, 122d Illinois Infantry, to date February 16, 1865, for neglect of duty.

Captain Addison D. Sawyer, 22d Indiana Volunteers, to date February 16, 1865, for absence without leave and disobedience of orders.

Assistant Surgeon James P. Siddall, 22d Indiana Volunteers, to date February 16, 1865, for absence without leave and disobedience of orders.

Lieutenant John Weston, 12th Indiana Cavalry, to date February 10, 1865, for attempting to defraud the Government by certifying to false and fraudulent accounts.

First Lieutenant Heiskell Lofland, Quartermaster 35th Iowa Volunteers, to date February 15, 1865, for habitual drunkenness, neglect of duty, and general worthlessness.

First Lieutenant Erastus C. Root, 2d New York Heavy Artillery, to date January 23, 1865, for absence without leave, having been published officially, and failed to appear before the Commission.

First Lieutenant Charles S. Seep, 40th Missouri Volunteers, to date February 14, 1865, for gross intoxication, and conduct unbecoming an officer and gentleman.

The following officers, to date February 11, 1865, for the causes mentioned, having been published officially, and failed to appear before the Commission:—

Absence without leave.

First Lieutenant J. L. Stough, 12th United States Infantry.
First Lieutenant John Simons, 4th United States Infantry.

Second Lieutenant F. De L. Eakin, Company B, Battalion 90th New York Volunteers, to date Febuary 15, 1865, for neglect of duty in failing to have the rolls of his command made out and forwarded to the proper Commissary of Musters, thereby working prejudice to the interests of the enlisted men.

The following officers, to date January 23, 1865, for the causes mentioned, having been published officially, and failed to appear before the Commission:—

Absence without leave.

Second Lieutenant James E. C. Covel, 16th Iowa Volunteers.
Second Lieutenant Harry W. Lee, 16th Iowa Volunteers.
First Lieutenant James J. Bumpus, 21st Ohio Volunteers.
First Lieutenant Christopher T. Bybee, 6th Kentucky Cavalry.
Second Lieutenant Michael H. Kenneally, 63d New York Volunteers.
First Lieutenant Alexander Gray, 157th Pennsylvania Volunteers.
First Lieutenant Washington A. Huntly, 9th United States Colored Troops.
Second Lieutenant Samuel S. Simmons, 36th United States Colored Troops.

For the Week ending February 25, 1865.

Captain A. R. Ravenscroft, 22d Indiana Volunteers, to date February 20, 1865, for absence without leave.

Captain Edward Wertheimer, 54th New York Volunteers, to date February 21, 1865, for conduct unbecoming an officer and gentleman, conduct prejudicial to good order and military discipline, and for cowardice in the face of the enemy.

Captain Thomas T. Seal, Company I, 19th Pennsylvania Cavalry, to date February 22, 1865, for absence without leave, and gross neglect of duty.

Lieutenant Thomas Boyle, 18th New York Cavalry, to date February 21, 1865.

Second Lieutenant Lewis Gordon, 12th New York Cavalry, to date February 20, 1865, for absence without leave.

The following officers, to date January 30, 1865, for the causes mentioned, having been published officially, and failed to appear before the Commission:—

Absence without leave.

Captain G. B. Harrington, 2d Iowa Cavalry.
Second Lieutenant Joseph O'Neill, 7th New Jersey Volunteers.

Dismissals Revoked.

The orders of dismissal heretofore issued in the following cases have been revoked:—

Colonel G. Kammerling, 9th Ohio Volunteers, thus permitting him to stand out of the service of the United States on the muster-out as made on the rolls of his regiment.

Captain H. L. Smith, 5th New York Artillery, and he is honorably discharged, to date May 28, 1863.

Lieutenant Albert E. Kingsley, 29th Maine Volunteers, and he is honorably discharged, to date June 2, 1864.

The following-named officers of the 6th Michigan Heavy Artillery, and they are honorably discharged, to date October 16, 1864:—

Colonel Edward Bacon.
Captain Sylvester Cogswell.

Captain John C. Pepper, 84th Illinois Volunteers, and he is honorably discharged, to date July 9, 1863.

Captain Edwin M. Newcomb, 16th Iowa Volunteers, and he is honorably discharged, to date October 29, 1864.

Colonel A. Langworthy, 99th Ohio Volunteers, and he has been honorably discharged, to date September 4, 1862.

Captain Alexander Inness, 68th United States Colored Infantry, and he has been honorably discharged, to date October 27, 1864.

Captain Albert F. Ransom, Commissary of Subsistence, United States Volunteers, and he has been restored to his former rank and position in the service.

First Lieutenant Henry P. George, 2d Wisconsin Cavalry, and he has been honorably discharged, to date November 28, 1864.

Second Lieutenant R. H. Montgomery, 5th United States Cavalry, and he has been reinstated.

Captain J. F. McCreary, 138th Pennsylvania Volunteers, and he has been honorably discharged, as of the date of the order of dismissal.

Captain John W. Fenton, 132d New York Volunteers, and he has been discharged, as of the date of the order of dismissal.

First Lieutenant Jesse Johnson, 114th Ohio Volunteers, and he has been discharged, as of the date of muster-in.

Dishonorably Discharged.

Assistant Surgeon Charles E. Heath, 57th Massachusetts Volunteers, to date November 22, 1864, for having tendered his resignation on the grounds of physical disability, and it appearing from the remarks of his superior officers, that his design to leave the service arises "from cowardice only," and that he is "utterly worthless" as an officer.

Second Lieutenant D. R. S. Wells, 126th, Ohio Volunteers, to date February 20, 1865, on account of physical disability, resulting from his own imprudence, and for absence without leave.

Dishonorable Muster-out Revoked.

Colonel E. A. Starling, 35th Kentucky Volunteers, and he is mustered out and honorably discharged, to date December 29, 1864.

Lieutenant-Colonel Edward R. Weir, 35th Kentucky Volunteers, and he is mustered out and honorably discharged, to date December 29, 1864.

Restored to Commission.

The following officers, heretofore dismissed, have been restored with pay from the date at which they rejoin their regiments for duty, provided the vacancies have not been filled by the Governors of their respective States:—

Captain J. W. Day, 1st Indiana Heavy Artillery.
Captain William Osterhorn, 31st Missouri Volunteers.
Second Lieutenant Allen Ellsworth, 7th Iowa Cavalry.
Second Lieutenant William I. Laird, 17th Illinois Cavalry.
Captain Henry S. Burrage, 36th Massachusetts Volunteers.
Second Lieutenant Charles I. Carlin, 151st New York Volunteers.
Second Lieutenant A. C. Merritt, Signal Corps, heretofore dismissed, has been restored to his former rank and position in the service.
Captain G. W. P. Smith, of Smith's Independent Company Maryland Volunteers.
Captain Eli F. Scott, 83d Indiana Volunteers.
First Lieutenant Edward McCaffrey, 79th Pennsylvania Volunteers.

Exempt from Dismissal.

The following-named officers, charged with offences, and heretofore published, are exempt from being dismissed the service of the United States, the Military Commission instituted by Special Orders, No. 53, series of 1863, from the War Department, having reported that satisfactory defence has been made in their respective cases:—

February 20, 1865.

Surgeon D. B. Davendorf, 19th Wisconsin Volunteers.
Captain O. F Wisner, 22d New York Cavalry.
Captain William B. Snell, 13th Maine Volunteers.
First Lieutenant Alexander Annan, Quartermaster 103d, New York Volunteers.
Captain Albert M. Green, 6th Kentucky Cavalry.
Surgeon William Upjohn, 7th Michigan Cavalry.
First Lieutenant George W. McCormick, 7th, Michigan Cavalry.

February, 27, 1865.

Lieutenant-Colonel S. R. Mott, 57th Ohio Volunteers.
Lieutenant-Colonel George L. Montague, 37th Massachusetts Volunteers.

The following-named officers, charged with offences, and heretofore published, are exempt from being dismissed the service of the United States, they having been previously honorably discharged by the Special Orders set opposite their respective names:—

First Lieutenant Thomas B. Lamb, 21st Ohio Volunteers. Special Orders, No. 8, January 5, 1865, Head-quarters Department of the Cumberland.
Captain Carl Moritz, 37th Ohio Volunteers. Special Orders, No. 271, December 2, 1864, Head-quarters Department and Army of the Tennessee.

Dishonorable Discharge Revoked.

The orders heretofore issued, dishonorably discharging the following-named officers of the 9th Connecticut Volunteers, have been revoked:—

Colonel T. W. Cahill.
Captain William Wright.

Dropped from the Rolls.

Lieutenant William K. Hewitt, Adjutant 3d Wisconsin Cavalry, to date November 31, 1863, he having been reported absent without leave since that date, and his whereabouts unknown.

Regular Navy.

Orders, &c.

Feb. 14.—Commodore Joseph Lanman, detached from command of the Minnesota, and waiting orders.

Feb. 3.—Captain John A. Winslow, ordered to duty under Rear-Admiral Gregory.

Feb. 9.—Captain Melancthon Smith, detached from command of the Wabash, and waiting orders.

Feb. 15.—Captain Henry S. Stellwagen, ordered to command the Pawnee.

Feb. 21.—Captain John De Camp, ordered to command the Receiving-Ship Constellation.

Feb. 27.—Captain Edward Middleton, detached from the command of the St. Mary's, on the reporting of his relief, and ordered North.

Feb. 2.—Commander A. S. Baldwin, detached from duty as Inspector at New York, on the reporting of his relief, and waiting orders. Commander E. W. Carpenter, ordered to duty as Inspector at Navy Yard, New York.

Feb. 3.—Commander A. K. Hughes, detached from duty under Acting Rear-Admiral Lee, but will continue present duty under Commodore Livingston at Mound City, Illinois.

Feb. 7.—Commander E. W. Carpenter, orders to the New York Yard revoked.

Feb. 8.—Commander Thomas M. Brasher, ordered to command the Fredonia (Pacific Squadron). Commander A. S. Baldwin, ordered to resume his duties at the New York Yard.

Feb. 10.—Commander John P. Bankhead, detached from special duty at New York, and ordered to command the Wyoming. Commander John Downes, detached from special duty at Boston, and ordered to command the Grand Gulf.

Feb. 15.—Commander William Ronckendorff, ordered to command the Monadnock. Commander E. G. Parrott, detached from command of the Monadnock, on the reporting of his relief, and ordered to command the Miantonomah. Commander George B. Balch, detached from command of the Pawnee, on the reporting of his relief, and ordered North.

Feb. 17.—Commander George M. Colvocoresses, detached from command of the Wachusett, on the reporting of his relief, and waiting orders. Commander Robert Townsend, detached from command of the Mohongo, and ordered to command the Wachusett.

Feb. 21.—Commander John J. Young, detached from the command of the Rendezvous, Brooklyn, N. Y., on the reporting of his relief, and waiting orders. Commander James C. Williamson, detached from command of the Flag, and ordered to command the Rendezvous at Brooklyn, N. Y. Commander E. C. Bowers, detached from command of the Receiving-Ship Vandalia, on the reporting of his relief, and waiting orders. Commander M. C. Marin, ordered to command the Receiving-Ship Vandalia.

Feb. 23.—Commander N. C. Bryant, detached from the Naval Station, Mound City, Illinois, and ordered to Ordnance duty at that station. Commander A. K. Hughes, detached from Ordnance duty at Mound City, Illinois, and ordered to duty at the Naval Station at that place.

Feb. 24.—Commander A. D. Harrell, detached from command of the Chicopee, on the reporting of his relief, and ordered to report to Rear-Admiral Gregory for duty.

Feb 27.—Commander J. W. A. Nicholson, ordered to command the Mohongo. Commander M. C. Marin, orders to the Vandalia revoked. Commander George M. Colvocoresses, ordered to command the St. Mary's.

Feb. 3.- Lieutenant-Commander F. H. Blake, detached from command of the Vicksburg, and granted sick leave.

Feb. 6.—Lieutenant-Commander Edward P. Williams, detached from Ordnance duty at New York, and ordered to the South Atlantic Squadron. Lieutenant-Commander William P. McCann, ordered to command the Tahoma.

Feb. 8.—Lieutenant-Commander Edward Simpson, detached from duty at New York, and ordered to duty as Fleet-Captain of the West Gulf Squadron.

Feb. 9.—Lieutenant-Commander C. H. Cushman, detached from the Wabash, and waiting orders. Lieutenant-Commander William E. Fitzhugh, ordered to the Mississippi Squadron. Lieutenant-Commander Byron Wilson, detached from the Mississippi Squadron, on the reporting of his relief, and waiting orders.

Feb. 10.—Lieutenant-Commander T. S. Phelps, detached from the South Atlantic Squadron, and waiting orders.

Feb. 14.—Lieutenant-Commander S. P. Quackenbush, detached from the South Atlantic Squadron, and ordered North.

Feb. 23.—Lieutenant-Commander Thomas S. Phelps, ordered to command the Lenapee. Lieutenant-Commander Lewis A. Kimberly, ordered to the Colorado. Lieutenant-Commander Samuel Magaw, detached from command of the Lenapee and granted sick leave. Lieutenant-Commander Charles H. Cushman, ordered to temporary duty under Rear-Admiral Gregory.

Feb. 24.—Lieut-Commander Henry N. T. Arnold, ordered to command the Chicopee. Lieutenant-Commander William B. Cushing, detached from command of the Monticello, and waiting orders.

Feb. 8.—Lieutenant Governeur K. Haswell, detached from Naval Rendezvous in Brooklyn, and ordered to the Rendezvous in New York, under command of Captain Bullis. Lieutenant Joshua R. Bishop, detached from the Naval Academy, and ordered to the Wyoming.

Feb. 9.—Lieutenants E. C. V. Blake and Henry C. Tallman, detached from the Wabash, and waiting orders.

Feb. 14.—Lieutenant M. S. Stuyvesant, detached from the Minnesota, and ordered to the Naval Academy. Lieutenant William T. Sampson, detached from the South Atlantic Squadron, and ordered North. Lieutenant Edwin T. Woodward, detached from the Minnesota, and waiting orders.

Feb. 15.—Lieutenant John McFarland, ordered to the Galatea. Lieutenant Henry M. Blue, detached from the Naval Academy, and ordered to the Tuscarora.

Feb. 23.—Lieutenant George Dewey, detached from the Colorado, and waiting orders. Lieutenant George M. Bache, detached from the Powhatan, and waiting orders. Lieutenant C M. Schoonmaker, detached from the Augusta, and waiting orders.

Feb. 27.—Lieutenants George C. Remey and C. M. Schoonmaker, ordered to the De Soto.

Feb. 3.—Acting Ensign G. W. McClure, detached from special duty in New York, under Captain Bullis, and waiting orders.

Feb. 7.—Acting Ensign G. W. McClure, ordered to the Juniata.

Feb. 8.—Acting Ensigns Charles D. Sigsbee and George D. B. Glidden, ordered to the Wyoming.

Feb. 8.—Chaplain Charles R. Hale, detached from the Naval Academy, and ordered to the Colorado.

Feb. 9.—Chaplain Charles A. Davis, detached from the Wabash, and waiting orders.

Appointed Assistant Surgeon.

Feb. 14.—Howard M. Rundlett.

Feb. 3.—Surgeon James McClelland, detached from the Colorado, and waiting orders.

Feb. 7.—Surgeon John P. Quinn, detached from the Minnesota, and ordered to the Flag-Ship of the North Atlantic Squadron.

Feb. 9.—Surgeon H. F. McSherry, detached from the Wabash, and waiting orders.

Feb. 11.—Assistant Surgeon Charles S. Hubbard, detached from the Navy Yard, Boston, and ordered to the Connecticut.

Feb. 14.—Assistant Surgeon William S. Ford, detached from the Minnesota, and waiting orders.

Feb. 18.—Surgeon A. S. Gihon, ordered to the Navy Yard at Portsmouth, New Hampshire. Surgeon M. G. Delaney, detached from the Navy Yard, Portsmouth, New Hampshire, on the reporting of his relief, and waiting orders. Assistant Surgeon S. J. Clark, ordered to the Receiving-Ship Vandalia. Surgeon R. L. Weber, ordered to the Naval Rendezvous, Chicago, Illinois. Assistant Surgeon F. L. Du Bois, detached from the Naval Rendezvous, Chicago, Illinois, and waiting orders. Assistant Surgeon B. H. Kidder, detached from the Colorado, and ordered to the Naval Academy.

Feb. 24.—Surgeon Henry O. Mayo, detached from the Powhattan, and waiting orders.

Feb. 28.—Assistant Surgeon C. H. Page, ordered to the Navy Yard at Boston.

Feb. 3.—Paymaster C. C. Jackson, detached from duty under Acting Rear-Admiral Lee, but will continue present duty under Commodore Livingston, at Mound City, Illinois.

Feb. 6.—Paymaster J. A. Smith, ordered to the Receiving-Ship Constellation, at Norfolk, Virginia. Assistant Paymaster George W. Beaman, detached from duty as Purchasing Paymaster, at Cairo, Illinois, on the reporting of his relief, and waiting orders.

Feb. 9.—Paymaster George Cochran, detached from the Wabash, on the completion of transfer, and ordered to settle his accounts.

Feb. 13.—Assistant Paymaster G. W. Beaman, ordered to the Robb, and to take charge of the accounts of certain other vessels of the Mississippi Squadron. Paymaster George L. Davis, detached from all duty except that of Paymaster of the Receiving-Ship Great Western, at Mound City, Illinois. Assistant Paymaster H. N. Hanna (of the Agawam), to transfer accounts, &c., to his relief, and regard his resignation as accepted.

Feb. 14.—Paymaster Charles C. Upham, detached from the Minnesota, on completion of transfer, and ordered to settle his accounts.

Feb. 15.—Paymaster James Hoy, Jr., detached from special duty at New York, and ordered to the Fort Jackson.

Feb. 9.—Chief Engineer Alban C. Stimers, detached from the Wabash, and waiting orders.

Feb. 14.—Chief Engineer William H. Rutherford, detached from the Tonawanda, on the reporting of his relief, and waiting orders.

Feb. 24.—Chief Engineer George S. Bright, detached from the (late) San Jacinto, and waiting orders.

Resigned.

Feb. 13.—Assistant Paymaster H. M. Hanna.

Feb. 14.—Assistant Surgeon L. J. Draper (from the 2d inst.). Midshipman A. R. S. Foote.

Feb. 15.—Assistant Paymaster Henry A. Strong, on the reporting of his relief. Paymaster Clifton Hellen, on the reporting of his relief.

Feb. 28.—Assistant Surgeon S. J. Webber (to take effect on the 10th of April, 1865).

Dismissed.

Feb. 18.—Assistant Surgeon J. O. Burnett.

Volunteer Navy.

Orders, &c.

Feb. 6.—Acting Volunteer Lieutenant L. N. Stodder, ordered to command the Niphon.

Feb. 9.—Acting Volunteer Lieutenant Samuel Huse, detached from the North Atlantic Squadron, and ordered to the Navy Yard, Washington, D. C. Acting Volunteer Lieutenant L. G. Vassallo, detached from the Ticonderoga, and granted sick leave.

Feb. 13.—Acting Volunteer Lieutenant E. D. Bruner, detached from command of the Clematis, and ordered to command the Lillian.

Feb. 15.—Acting Volunteer Lieutenant William F. Shankland, ordered to command the Banshee. Acting Volunteer Lieutenant B. W. Loring, detached from the North Carolina, and ordered to the Naval Rendezvous, Washington, D. C.

Feb. 22.—Acting Volunteer Lieutenant W. H. Garfield, detached from command of the Calypso, on the reporting of his relief, and ordered to temporary duty at Boston. Acting Volunteer Lieutenant L. N. Stodder, detached from command of the Niphon, and ordered to command the Calypso.

Feb. 24.—Acting Volunteer Lieutenant William H. Latham, detached from the Flag, and waiting orders.

Appointed Acting Masters and Pilots.

Feb. 14.—Henry Buckless, North Atlantic Squadron.

Feb. 22.—J. B. Edwards, North Atlantic Squadron.

Feb. 2.—Acting Master H. L. Sturgis, ordered to the James Adger.

Feb. 3.—Acting Master A. H. Atkinson, ordered to the Sabine.

Feb. 6.—Acting Master J. N. Rowe, ordered to the Mercedita. Acting Master G. B. Thompson, ordered to the Sagamore. Acting Master C. C. Wells, ordered to command the Trefoil. Acting Master J. M. Smalley, detached from the North Carolina, and ordered to the Tahoma.

Feb. 7.—Acting Master Allen Hoxie, ordered to the Florida. Acting Master C. W. Lamson, orders to the Florida revoked, and granted sick leave.

Feb. 8.—Acting Masters Robert Barstow and E. B. Mallett, ordered to the Wyoming.

Feb. 9.—Acting Master A. H. Atkinson, orders to the Sabine revoked, and he is granted sick leave. Acting Master A. W. Kempton, ordered to the Sabine.

Feb. 10.—Acting Master A. Allen, ordered to the Tahoma. Acting Master George Cables, ordered to the Grand Gulf.

Feb. 15.—Acting Master J. C. Staples, detached from the Savannah, and ordered to the Florida.

Feb. 21.—Acting Master Samuel H. Field, detached from the Rendezvous at Cincinnati, and ordered to the Receiving-Ship Vermont. Acting Master Charles Potter, ordered to the Agawam.

Feb. 22.—Acting Master Edwin Coffin, ordered to command the Adela.

Feb. 23.—Acting Master W. F. Pratt, detached from the Commodore Perry, and granted sick leave. Acting Master George Ashbury, detached from the (late) San Jacinto, and ordered to the South Atlantic Squadron. Acting Master James L. Plunkett, ordered to the North Carolina.

Feb. 25.—Acting Master A. M. Newman, detached from the North Carolina, and ordered to the Galena. Acting Master Alfred Everson, to await orders.

Feb. 27.—Acting Master Alfred Everson, ordered to the De Soto.

Feb. 28.—Acting Master William Hedger, detached from the (late) Merrimack, and waiting orders. Acting Master G. H. Leinas, detached from the command of the Gem of the Sea, and waiting orders. Acting Master R. B. Arrants, detached from the Gem of the Sea, and waiting orders. Acting Master L. Wells, detached from the New London, and ordered North.

Appointed Acting Ensigns.

Feb. 1.—Aaron Vanderbilt, U. S. S. Malvern.

Feb. 2.—Robert Hunter, U. S. S. Wanderer.

Feb. 8.—William B. Marchant, and waiting orders.

Feb. 9.—W. R. Brown, U. S. S. Nansemond.

Feb. 11.—Roderick McMillen, and ordered to the Potomac Flotilla.

Feb. 13.—William T. Chatfield, U. S. S. Kittatinny; William C. Seymour, U. S. S. Sciota.

Feb. 14.—F. H. McDonald, U. S. S. Harvest Moon; Edward H. Sheer, U. S. S. Perry; Thomas J. Dill, U. S. S. Sweet-Briar; Stephen Jones, U. S. S. Sagamore; Charles C. Johnson, U. S. S. Chicopee.

Feb. 21. William H. Dumont, and waiting orders.

Feb. 22.—G. V. Demorest, U. S. S. Vicksburg; John Brann, U. S. S. O. P. Smith.

Feb. 23.—George H. Fletcher, U. S. S. Grand Gulf.

Feb. 24.—William L. Howarth, waiting orders.

Feb. 27.—John Walker, U. S. S. Gem of the Sea.

Appointed Acting Ensigns, and ordered to the School-Ship Savannah.

Feb. 2.—Joseph E. Armstrong.

Feb. 3.—Alexander Lewis and L. W. Savage.

Feb. 4.—Edward C. Remington and Isaac V. Braley.

Feb. 6.—Oliver A. Spear.

Feb. 14.—Joshua Cook, Jr., James W. Eaton, and P. R. Runnels.

Feb. 15.—William H. Reed.

Feb. 17.—Arthur W. Emerson.

Feb. 20.—P. C. Gooding and O. Darwin Owen.

Feb. 21.—Charles F. Barton and Carl E. Randrup.

Feb. 23.—J. W. A. Bennet.

Feb. 28.—John J. Wescott.

Feb. 2.—Acting Ensign Philo P. Hawkes, detached from the Fear Not, on the reporting of his relief, and ordered North.

Feb. 6.—Acting Ensign C. F. Dunderdale, detached from the North Carolina, and ordered to the Sagamore. Acting Ensign E. H. Miller, ordered to the Trefoil. Acting Ensigns J. W. Goodwin and J. H. Rogers, ordered to the Niphon. Acting Ensign Paul Borner, ordered to the Mercedita. Acting Ensign George H. Drew, ordered to the Tahoma. Acting Ensign C. A. Hodgdon, ordered to the Niphon. Acting Ensign William Mellen, ordered to the Tahoma. Acting Ensign Franklin J. Latham, ordered to the North Carolina.

Feb. 7.—Acting Ensign Peter W. Fagan, detached from the John Adams, and ordered North.

Feb. 9.—Acting Ensigns E. A. Small and Whitman Chase, detached from the Wabash, and waiting orders. Acting Ensign L. R. Chester, detached from the Pontoosuc, and granted sick leave.

Feb. 10.—Acting Ensign C. S. Lawrence, ordered to the Grand Gulf.

Feb. 13.—Acting Ensign A. H. Fuller, detached from the Hendrick Hudson, on the reporting of his relief, and ordered North.

Feb. 14.—Acting Ensign A. P. Bashford, detached from the South Atlantic Squadron, on the reporting of his relief, and ordered North. Acting Ensign William H. Jennings, detached from the Minnesota, and ordered to the Vandalia.

Feb. 15.—Acting Ensign H. B. Francis, detached from the Wissahickon, and ordered North. Acting Ensign Joseph Arant, detached from the Henry Brinker, and ordered to the Savannah.

Feb. 16.—Acting Ensign Logan Dyson, detached from the Roanoke, and ordered to the Potomac Flotilla. Acting Ensign George L. Sands, detached from the Powhatan, and ordered to the Potomac Flotilla. Acting Ensign William Chandler, detached from the St. Lawrence, and ordered to the Santiago de Cuba.

Feb. 17.—Acting Ensign Thomas E. Harvey, detached from the Canandaigua, on the reporting of his relief, and ordered North.

Feb. 18.—Acting Ensign James McVey, detached from the Proteus, and granted sick leave.

Feb. 20.—Acting Ensign Cleveland F. Dunderdale, detached from the Sagamore, and ordered to the Vanderbilt. Acting Ensign John Quevedo, detached from the Florida, and ordered to the Louisville. Acting Ensign William B. Marchant, ordered to the Sagamore. Acting Ensign John F. Merry, detached from the North Atlantic Squadron, and granted sick leave.

Feb. 22.—Acting Ensigns J. W. Goodwin and Albert A. Davis, detached from the Niphon, and ordered to the Adela. Acting Ensign William H. Dumont, ordered to the Adela.

Feb. 24.—Acting Ensign C. A. Hodgdon, orders to the Niphon revoked, and he is ordered to the Chimo. Acting Ensign Edwin B. Pratt, detached from the (late) San Jacinto, and waiting orders.

Feb. 25.—Acting Ensign Thomas S. Gay, detached from the North Atlantic Squadron, and waiting orders. Acting Ensign Charles R. Fleming, detached from the (late) San Jacinto, and waiting orders. Acting Ensign J. H. Rogers, detached from the Niphon, and granted sick leave. Acting Ensign H. L. R. Woods, detached from the Potomac Flotilla, and granted sick leave. Acting Ensigns J. L. Vennard and Willis G. Perry, ordered to the Galena.

Feb. 27.—Acting Ensign A. R. Hazard, ordered to the De Soto. Acting Ensign C. R. Fleming, ordered to the Trefoil.

Feb. 28.—Acting Ensigns William J. Kirby, Simpson Jenney, and Henry Hamre, detached from the (late) Merrimack, and waiting orders. Acting Ensigns B. P. Trask and Samuel T. Bliss, detached from the Gem of the Sea, and waiting orders.

Appointed Acting Assistant Surgeons.

Feb. 2.—George O. Burgess, and ordered to the Forest Rose.

Feb. 3.—James W. Wilson, and ordered to the North Carolina.

Feb. 8.—Robert J. Richards, and ordered to the South Atlantic Squadron.

Feb. 9.—Benjamin A. Sawyer, and ordered to the Ohio.

Feb. 10.—H. J. Babin, and ordered to the Ohio.

Feb. 11.—Prerley H. Johnson, and ordered to the North Carolina.

Feb. 13.—Lewis Darling, Jr., and ordered to the North Carolina.

Feb. 16.—Henry Shaw, and ordered to the Ohio.

Feb. 20.—Philip J. Gilbert, and ordered to the West Gulf Squadron; James D. Noble, and ordered to the Princeton.

Feb. 22.—John Gordon, and ordered to the Mississippi Squadron.

Feb. 23.—William H. Faxon, and ordered to the North Carolina.
Feb. 25.—Edward Macomb, and ordered to the North Carolina.
Feb. 27.—Nelson Ingraham, and ordered to the North Carolina; Henry C. Meredith, and ordered to the Princeton.

Feb. 4.—Acting Assistant Surgeon George C. Reynolds, ordered to the Chenango.

Feb. 8.—Acting Assistant Surgeon Israel Bushong, detached from the South Atlantic Squadron, on the reporting of his relief, and ordered North. Acting Assistant Surgeon A. H. Abernethy, orders to the Dai Ching revoked, and he is ordered to the North Carolina.

Feb. 9.—Acting Assistant Surgeon W. L. Campbell, detached from the Wabash, and waiting orders. Acting Assistant Surgeon J. W. Wilson, detached from the North Carolina, and ordered to the Preston.

Feb. 11.—Acting Assistant Surgeon A. H. Abernethy, ordered to the Donegal.

Feb. 13.—Acting Assistant Surgeon Edgar S. Smith, detached from the Potomac, and ordered to the Florida.

Feb. 16.—Acting Assistant Surgeon John E. Cobb, detached from the Newbern, and ordered to the Florida. Acting Assistant Surgeon Edgar S. Smith, detached from the Florida, and waiting orders.

Feb. 17.—Acting Assistant Surgeon George Doig, detached from the Emma, and ordered to the South Atlantic Squadron. Acting Assistant Surgeon M. C. Drennan, ordered to the Emma.

Feb. 22.—Acting Assistant Surgeon Henry Shaw, detached from the Ohio, and ordered to the Maratanza. Acting Assistant Surgeon John W. Hamilton, detached from the Maratanza, and granted sick leave.

Feb. 23.—Acting Assistant Surgeon James D. Noble, detached from the Princeton, and ordered to the Mississippi Squadron. Acting Assistant Surgeon Benjamin A. Sawyer, detached from the Ohio, and ordered to the Mississippi Squadron. Acting Assistant Surgeon P. H. Johnson, detached from the North Carolina, and ordered to the Hunchback.

Appointed Acting Assistant Paymasters.

Feb. 1.—G. H. Thompson, and waiting orders.
Feb. 6.—James D. Cassard, and waiting orders.
Feb. 7.—George E. Martin and J. C. Stoever, and waiting orders.
Feb. 8.—Seth E. Hartwell, and waiting orders.
Feb. 10.—George W. White, H. A. Thompson, and Myron M. Hovey, and waiting orders.

Feb. 1.—Acting Assistant Paymaster Henry S. Machette, ordered to the Donegal.

Feb. 3.—Acting Assistant Paymaster J. G. Orme, detached from the Whitehead, on the reporting of his relief, and ordered North to settle his accounts. Acting Assistant Paymaster George R. Watkins, ordered to the Whitehead. Acting Assistant Paymaster James W. Hanson, ordered to instruction at New York.

Feb. 4.—Acting Assistant Paymaster R. S. McConnell, ordered to the Nipsic. Acting Assistant Paymaster E. P. Sheldon, ordered to instruction at New York.

Feb. 6.—Acting Assistant Paymaster J. Bayard Redfield, orders to the Kenwood revoked, and he is ordered to duty as Purchasing Paymaster at Mound City, Illinois.

Feb. 7.—Acting Assistant Paymaster H. D. Kimberly, detached from the Kensington, and waiting orders. Acting Assistant Paymaster J. F. Wood, ordered to the Kensington.

Feb. 8.—Acting Assistant Paymaster E. T. Barker, ordered to the Mercedita. Acting Assistant Paymaster, John Macmahon, ordered to the Sagamore. Acting Assistant Paymaster Henry T. Stancliff, ordered to instruction at New York. Acting Assistant Paymaster James W. Hanson, ordered to the Trefoil. Acting Assistant Paymaster E. P Sheldon, ordered to the Tahoma.

Feb. 13.—Acting Assistant Paymaster O. F. Browning, ordered to the Ethan Allen. Acting Assistant Paymaster William R. Woodward, detached from the Ethan Allen, on the reporting of his relief, and ordered North. Acting Assistant Paymaster Lewis F. Whitin, ordered to the Tristam Shandy. Acting Assistant Paymaster H. T. Stancliff, ordered to the Agawam.

Feb. 15.—Acting Assistant Paymaster John Read, ordered to settle his accounts.

Feb. 16.—Acting Assistant Paymaster D. A. Smith, Jr., ordered to the Wyoming.

Feb. 17.—Acting Assistant Paymaster G. N. Simpson, ordered to the Sebago.

Feb. 18.—Acting Assistant Paymaster Seth E. Hartwell, ordered to instruction at New York. Acting Assistant Paymaster George E. Martin, ordered to instruction at New York.

Feb. 20.—Acting Assistant Paymaster H. B. Wetherill, detached from the Kenwood, on the reporting of his relief, and ordered to settle his accounts. Acting Assistant Paymaster L. G. Morrow, ordered to the Kenwood. Acting Assistant Paymaster H. K. Opp, ordered to special duty at the Philadelphia Navy Yard. Acting Assistant Paymaster William A. Carpenter, ordered to instruction at New York.

Feb. 21.—Acting Assistant Paymaster James F. Hamilton, detached from the Naval Station at Mound City, Illinois, and waiting orders. Acting Assistant Paymasters H. A. Thompson, Jr., G. W. White, and Theophilus Fravel, ordered to instruction at New York.

Feb. 24.—Acting Assistant Paymasters H. A. Thompson, Jr., George W. White, Theophilus Fravel, William Carpenter, and S. E. Hartwell, ordered to the Mississippi Squadron.

Feb. 28.—Acting Assistant Paymaster George E. Martin, ordered to the Adela.

Feb. 14.—Acting Chief Engineer A. K. Eddews, detached from the Minnesota, and ordered to the Tonawanda.

Promoted for Good Conduct, &c.

Feb. 7.—Acting Volunteer Lieutenants J. W. Smith, Edward Hooker, and E. F. Devins, to Acting Volunteer Lieutenant-Commanders. Acting Master James R. Wheeler, to Acting Volunteer Lieutenant.

Feb. 17.—Acting Ensign J. H. Cousens, to Acting Master.

Feb. 22.—Acting Ensign Edward A. Small, to Acting Master.

Feb. 25.—Acting Master's Mate Thomas S. Gay, to Acting Ensign, for gallant conduct in assisting to destroy the rebel ram Albemarle. Acting Ensign William L. Howarth, to Acting Master, for the same service as Mr. Gay.

Feb. 28.—Acting First Assistant Engineers J. W. Nystrom and George B. Whiting, to Acting Chief Engineers.

Resigned.

Feb. 1.—Acting Master C. B. Dahlgren.

Feb. 2.—Acting Ensign Thomas H. Marks.

Feb. 3.—Acting Master Norman Penfield; Acting Ensign William H. McLean.

Feb. 7.—Acting Master Charles H. Hamilton.

Feb. 9.—Acting Ensign Charles H. Pierce; Acting Assistant Surgeon Alfred E. Emery.

Feb. 10.—Acting Assistant Surgeon James R. Dran; Acting Master J. M. Smalley.

Feb. 13.—Acting Ensign F. Hopkins.

Feb. 15.—Acting Assistant Surgeon L. Michel; Acting Master Allen Hoxie.

Feb. 16.—Acting Ensign E. C. Bowers, Jr.

Feb. 18.—Acting Volunteer Lieutenant George Taylor; Acting Ensign Whitman Chase.

Feb. 20.—Acting Assistant Paymasters O. F. Browning and John R. Bowler.

Feb. 21.—Acting Masters Thomas Symmes and J. W. Stapleford.

Feb. 22.—Acting Assistant Surgeon Samuel H. Weil.

Feb. 24.—Acting Ensign Edward Ryan.

Feb. 25.—Acting Masters L. W. Hill and John J. Rogers; Acting Assistant Paymaster William E. Foster.

Feb. 28.—Acting Master George Ferris.

Revoked.

Feb. 9.—Acting Master and Pilot Charles M. Lane.

Feb. 14.—Acting Ensign Charles A. Stewart.

Feb. 15.—Acting Assistant Surgeon Daniel W. Jones.

Feb. 24.—Acting Assistant Surgeon F. W. Williams.

Feb. 25.—Acting Master C. W. Lamson.

Dismissed.

Feb. 13.—Acting Ensign W. G. Jones.

Feb. 18.—Acting Assistant Surgeon Joseph Welsh.

Feb. 21.—Acting Ensign Arnold Harris.

Feb. 24.—Acting Master George W. Frost.

C.B. Richardson, Publisher

THE UNITED STATES SERVICE MAGAZINE.

VOL. III.—MAY, 1865.—NO. V.

GRANT.

BY THE EDITOR.

UNDUE and premature praise of newly-appointed and untried generals was one of the principal faults of loyal men in the early days of the war. It was unjust to those bepraised, injurious to the cause, and, at last, very humiliating to the praisers. But we have learned a lesson. We are an educated people, on that point, at least. We no longer measure men by what they are "going to do," or for what we hope and wish they will do; but for what they *have done and are doing.* Sherman Poliorcetes is an historic character; we have the list of his cities captured; we have traced the route of his magnificent marches, and the fields on which his enemies have been beaten. Sheridan, the famous rider, is beloved of his countrymen because of his victory at Winchester; his famous *riposte* at Cedar Creek; his happy faculty of "settling new cavalry generals," and sending his enemies "whirling up the valley;" his terrible raid north of Richmond and Lynchburg, and his impetuous advance at the Five Forks and Burkesville. Thomas is the Rock of Chickamauga and the hero of Nashville. Meade has his enduring *arc de triomphe* at Gettysburg. And so it is with hundreds whom we cannot now mention, but whose worthy deeds are already recorded by History. But all will agree that there is no one among our great captains whose fame

---

Entered according to Act of Congress, in the year 1865, by C. B. RICHARDSON, in the Clerk's Office of the District Court for the Southern District of New York.

is more real and solid, whose highest office is based upon a firmer foundation, and who stands before the world as a more exalted hero, than the commander-in-chief, Lieutenant-General Grant.

We have often had occasion to present partial estimates of his character, as they have been elicited by particular actions: his bravery, his endurance, his good common sense, his freedom from affectation of greatness, and his extreme tenacity of purpose.

These good qualities, each good in itself, and far more excellent in their combination, have been conceded by the foreign press—not in the main friendly to us—and indirectly allowed by his bitter enemies, the rebel editors, who have usually ransacked the chronicles of Billingsgate to find proper titles for our Yankee generals.

But a far higher greatness it required time to develope. Let us attempt to explain this.

By reason of his important successes at the West, which had achieved great popularity and influence throughout the land, he was brought to Washington, no one dissenting, as lieutenant-general. This would have turned the heads of most men. Many generals, easily satisfied with such unprecedented greatness, would have remained in Washington, surrounded themselves with a brilliant staff, and, most inadequately, directed, by telegraph, staff, and courier, the movements of our armies in this vital exigency.

What does Grant do? He takes no easy post, in or out of the field; he does not touch Ralph de Vipont's shield, because he has the least sure seat and is the cheapest bargain, but he strikes that of the dreaded Templar, with the sharp end of his lance, until it rings again. Lee and his veterans are his aim; success, be sure, will gain him the highest glory; but who will succeed against the best general in the Confederacy? The Army of the Potomac had indeed won battles, and lost no honor; but they had gained no signal strategic advantage against "the decisive point"—Richmond. Until this was done, nothing decisive was done.

Follow Grant's course. He moves across the Rapidan, attacks and is attacked in the frightful Wilderness. He finds "a foeman worthy of his steel." Dreadfully handled there, many, nay, most generals would have recrossed the river, and, by admirable strategy, reassured the safety of Washington, and then tried some new circumambulation. Not so Grant. Inflexibly he pushes his skilful antagonist towards the great goal. No power, human or Satanic, can shake him off in the deadly wrestling-match; sometimes down, he is up again with a new clutch, and slowly but surely encircles Lee. The warfare is Titanic.

His great plans, undisclosed to the public eye, often modified by events, require, that while the splendors of victorious battle, for a time dimming his own, shall shine around his skilful lieutenants at the South and West, he should remain in front of Petersburg, winning no laurels in fight, and playing to the world, at home and abroad, a secondary part. Not a few began to shake their heads and wonder if he was the man, after all.

At length, as the confused plot of the drama progresses, light begins to shine upon him: his great argument is developed. Sherman, *nobilis frater*, moves northward, brushing away the slight spider-webs of Johnston, Bragg, and Hardee. Schofield, *benemeritus* for a score of battles, a tried and true soldier, comes up at the appointed time; other combinations are ripe; the hour approaches; and in the words, familiar but immortal, with which the great Captain commanded the great assault—" Up, Guards, and at them !" Grant pours his whole line upon the rebel works. Petersburg falls; Richmond, the great blazing centre, gives up; the humiliating retreat and unrelenting pursuit begin; Lee, the invincible, surrenders his army; and Grant stands forth, after a year of unrequited labors, to claim the issues of his secret plans, the reward of his toils, the greatest of all glories—the conquest of Richmond, and the capture of Lee's proud host. First in rank and station, he is first in fame, and History will seek in vain for his superior.

We are no bestowers of indiscriminate praise; we give him only his just tribute; we acknowledge his surpassing merits.

Sagacious in choosing men, without jealousy or comradeship, he has brought out our best talent, used it just where it was needed; no nepotism; no corps of flatterers; no henchmen surround his person; and yet he is a "good fellow," sensitive to all the just claims of friendship.

Imperturbable in manner, and reticent by habit, he has been content to wait until time should vindicate his plans by according them success.

Of wonderful endurance, mental and physical, his devotion to duty, even in its details, surpasses that of most generals who have been famous in this respect.

Not puffed up by his honors; not "prurient of fame not earned," he has been modest and generous, and indulged in no vainglorious prophecies or oracular declarations.

In a word, a patriot, a soldier, a leader, and a gentleman, he works and fights, placing his best and noblest energies at the disposal of his country, leaving all results to take care of themselves. There will be but one verdict in the high court of History. He will need no title to enduring fame but that name which his father gave him,—GRANT.

RICHMOND AND THE END.

BY THE EDITOR.

"While stands the Coliseum, Rome shall stand:
When falls the Coliseum, Rome shall fall;
And when Rome falls, the world!"

WITH similar boasting have the rebel leaders announced in time past to the world, that upon the impregnable defences of Richmond the fate of the Confederacy depended. With a similar belief, the loyal armies of the Republic, victorious on all other theatres, have been unsatisfied until that stronghold should fall. The first Bull Run was fought with the hope that we might follow the discomfited enemy into Richmond. "On to Richmond!" was the continued and often-derided cry. To guard it, Beauregard's outlying pickets directed their field-glasses upon Washington from Munson's Hill. To conquer it, and annihilate the treason, the Peninsular Campaign "dragged its slow length along." Once more, the furious fight of Fredericksburg found, but could not remove, the lion in the path. Chancellorsville, had we been successful, would have been the usher to Richmond. The terrible battles of the Wilderness, Spottsylvania, the North and South Anna, Cold Harbor, were all most determined efforts to take the rebel capital; and even when beleaguered and almost surrounded by our armies, it resisted all our efforts, and laughed derisively as it declared, "Richmond can never be taken!" So fully were the rebels convinced, by their four years of success, that the strength of the rebellion lay in Richmond, and that Richmond was unconquerable, that they have constantly given us our text, and we can only quote them when we say, that with the splendid campaign of Grant, and the occupation of Richmond, comes, at last, the beginning of the END.

1. It renders the people of the South hopeless: thousands of prisoners are taking the oath of allegiance, saying that as long as there was a cause to fight for, they would fight; but now, with the fall of Richmond, the cause is hopelessly lost. In every captured city, Richmond not excepted, shouts of joy arise as our liberating armies enter. The rebel soldiers in arms will throw down their muskets; will desert in crowds; will seek to be made prisoners: the danger of disintegration is imminent. The leaders will despair; the lesser fry will give themselves up in the hope of amnesty; the arch-traitors, Moloch, Belial, Beelzebub, Mammon, even Satan himself—now sadly out of repute in Pandemonium—will seek some more tropical clime, if they can escape.

The great tide, now and for a long time checking its flow,

will turn with a mighty ebb towards Union and peace, submerging and sweeping away the wrecks of the rebellion, and thus becoming the most formidable of our own allies.

2. The influence of the fall of Richmond upon the loyal people of the country cannot be estimated. Upon the announcement, the great cities were crazy with joy; the streets were thronged with eager and enthusiastic men, women, and children, ready to make new sacrifices for a holy cause now so demonstrating its triumphant success.

Our soldiers cannot be restrained; the *prestige* of victories leads them to perform greater marvels; and, like the avalanche, of enormous proportions and ever-increasing velocity, our great army carries rapid ruin wherever it strikes.

3. Our recent victories forever shut the door upon foreign intervention. As much as the great nations of Western Europe may have desired our ruin, that no American rival might share their greatness or shock their historic dignities; as freely as they would have trampled upon us, had the barbarous treason accomplished its hellish purpose,—they will now conciliate the mighty nation, which has "purged off the baser fire" so gloriously; which has achieved a history in five years which rivals, in feats of arms, the Old World chronicles of five hundred; and which, if not treated with proper respect, will fulminate her eagle lightnings in the "four seas," the Channel, the Bay of Biscay, and the Mediterranean.

The fall of Richmond, then, foreshadows the end; but when will the end be? Let us neither cherish fond fancies nor abate one jot of energy and action. It may yet take "ninety days," and more. Spring and summer are not the seasons when veteran armies are most willing to disband themselves, even when the cause seems hopeless. The bivouac does not pinch; the growing grain still furnishes food.

And when they do break up, we shall not end the war as war is ended between *two nations*, by a treaty of peace, which at once puts an end to all acts of hostility and to all causes of war. Small armed bodies will yet hold out in mountains, in Texas, and elsewhere. There is amnesty to arrange, high justice to be executed; State governments to frame or readjust, financial questions to decide, discordant and belligerent factions to punish or pacify. And thus, even when the great rebellion has its principal collapse, peace will come gradually, prosperity rise sun-like from a new dawning, and America, "Time's noblest offspring," spring from the dust and battle-clouds of the deadly struggle, like a giant, to run her course in future history.

Not long ago, such statements were considered as doubtful prophecies. No prophet is needed now to tell the glorious end. It shines in no dubious light, and the road to it is clearly discerned by him who stands upon the mount of vision, like a line of silver, unbroken and unobstructed. In one way we may anticipate it: by giving thanks to the God of hosts and the God of nations, and by a devout purpose so to use His great goodness, that no such war shall again be needed to punish our sins or purge our errors.

Since the above was written, the country has been kept in a continual state of joyful agitation, by the famous advance of Grant, the interception of Lee, and the surrender of his whole army, fifty thousand strong. Surely the end is very near.

MAJOR-GENERAL PHILIP HENRY SHERIDAN.

PHILIP HENRY SHERIDAN was, we believe, born in Perry County, Ohio, in 1831, although the Army Registers have always given him the credit of being a native of Massachusetts.

At the age of seventeen, through the influence of friends, young Sheridan obtained an appointment as Cadet at West Point, and, passing the preliminary examination with credit, he was enrolled in the fourth class, in 1848. He graduated with honor in 1853, being in the class with McPherson, Schofield, Terrill, Sill, Tyler, and the rebel Lieutenant-General Hood. There being no vacancy, he was appointed brevet second lieutenant in the 1st Regiment Infantry, and ordered to Texas, where his regiment was then serving. The Apaches and Comanches were at that time very troublesome and bold, often venturing into the immediate vicinity of Fort Duncan, where he was stationed, and picking off the men. On one occasion, Sheridan and two of the soldiers were a short distance from the fort, when a band of Apaches attacked them. Sheridan was without arms, but the soldiers had their guns. The Apache chief had just dismounted from his fiery Mustang, to creep up nearer the soldiers, when Sheridan sprang upon its back, galloped to the fort, gave the alarm, seized his own pistols without dismounting, and rode back at full speed to the point where the two soldiers were still fighting, shot the chief dead, and then the other soldiers, having come up, rode down and killed most of the other savages. In the spring of 1855 he was, at his own request, transferred, as full second lieutenant, to the 4th Infantry, then serving in Oregon. He returned to New York to sail for the Pacific, and, while waiting for the recruits who were to go out under his charge, was for two months in command of Fort Wood, in New York harbor. On his arrival at San Francisco, in August, 1855, he was at once selected to command the escort of the surveying party who were exploring the route of the branch of the Pacific Railroad, which was to connect

San Francisco with the Columbia River. For the next six years he was constantly on duty among the Indian tribes of the Pacific coast, and succeeded in winning their confidence and esteem beyond any other officer who had been stationed among them: He built posts among the Yakimas, at Seletz Valley, on the Indian Reservation, and at Yamhill. For his skill and success in conciliating the Coquelle and Yakima Indians, he received high compliments from Lieutenant-General Scott.

In the winter of 1861, in consequence of the resignation of several of the Southern officers on the Pacific coast, Sheridan was advanced to the rank of first lieutenant, and ordered to return to the East. The regular Army was increased at the opening of the war by the addition of several regiments, and Lieutenant Sheridan was promoted to a captaincy in the 13th, one of the new regiments, his commission bearing date May 14th, 1861. In September, 1861, he was ordered to join his regiment at Jefferson barracks, near St. Louis, and at the same time directed to audit the claims against the War Department, arising from the campaign in Missouri. When this was completed, he was appointed Chief Quartermaster and Commissary of the army then organizing for operations in Southwestern Missouri; and in March, 1862, General Halleck made him Chief Quartermaster of the Western Department, with the rank of major: but his known ability as a cavalry officer, and the absolute necessity for an efficient officer in that arm of the service, led General Halleck, much against his will, to release him, to take command of the 2d Regiment Michigan Volunteer Cavalry. He assumed command on the 27th of May, and immediately joined in the expedition to cut the railroads south of Corinth. Immediately on his return, his regiment was ordered to join in the pursuit of the rebel army which was, at this time, retreating from their stronghold at Corinth. In this pursuit, Colonel Sheridan's regiment encountered the rebel left wing, and repulsed their attack, capturing Powell's rebel battery. On the 11th of June he was put in command of a cavalry brigade, and on the 26th he was ordered to take an advanced position at Boonesville, twenty miles in front of the main army, whose front he was to cover, watching at the same time the movements of the rebels who were near him, and bent on mischief. On the 1st of July he was attacked by a rebel force of nine regiments (numbering about six thousand men), under the command of General Chalmers. After skirmishing for awhile, he fell back toward his camp, which was situated on the edge of a swamp, an advantageous position, where he could not readily be flanked, and could hold the enemy at bay for some time. Finding that the enemy, with their greatly superior numbers, were likely to surround him, he had recourse to strategy. Selecting ninety of his best men, armed with revolving carbines and sabres, he sent them around to the rear of the enemy by a *détour* of about four miles, with orders to attack promptly and vigorously at a certain time, while he would make a simultaneous charge in front. The plan proved a complete success. The ninety men appeared suddenly in the enemy's rear, not having been seen till they were near enough to fire their carbines, and, having emptied these, they rushed with drawn sabres upon the enemy, who, supposing them to be the advance-guard of a large force, were thrown into disorder; and, before they had time to recover, Sheridan charged them in front with such fury, that they fled from the field in complete disorder, utterly routed. Sheridan pursued, and they continued their flight, utterly panic-stricken, to Knight's Mills, twenty miles south from Boonesville, throwing away their arms, knapsacks, coats, and every thing which could impede their flight. General Grant reported this brilliant affair to the War Department, with a recommendation that Colonel Sheridan should be promoted, which was done; he was made a brigadier-general July 1st, 1862.

We have not space to record all the young general's *rencontres* with the rebels at Boonesville, Rienzi, and other points in the vicinity. Suffice it to say, that in each he was successful, driving the enemy before him, and taking many prisoners.

Early in September, General Grant detached a portion of his own troops, and among them Brigadier-General Sheridan, and his old command, the 2d Michigan Cavalry, to re-enforce Buell, who was moving northward in pursuit of Bragg. General Buell at once assigned Sheridan to the command of the Third Division of the Army of the Ohio, and he entered upon his duties on the 20th of September. In the reorganization of Buell's army, which followed on his return to Louisville, General Sheridan was transferred to the command of the Eleventh Division; and in the battle at Perryville, on the 8th of October, handled his troops with such skill as to save the Union army from defeat.

On the 30th of October, General Rosecrans succeeded General Buell; and the department, with its territory enlarged, was thenceforth known as the Department of the Cumberland, and the army as the Army of the Cumberland. In this army Sheridan was assigned to the command of one of the divisions of McCook's Corps, which constituted the right wing of the army. After some weeks of preparation, the army moved from Nashville toward Murfreesboro on the 26th of December, skirmishing with the enemy all the way. On the morning of the 31st of December, 1862, commenced the battle of Stone River; and in the disastrous fortunes of the morning of that day Sheridan was involved, but not to his discredit. To the right wing of the Army of the Cumberland (McCook's Corps) had been assigned the duty of repelling the first onset of the enemy; but when Bragg massed his forces, and hurled them upon the flank of McCook, the division on the extreme right (Johnson's) was unable to resist the shock, and crumbled to pieces before the fierce onset of the rebels. Davis, who came next, after a brief resistance, yielded also; and as the victorious foe rushed upon Sheridan and Negley, whose divisions came next, they anticipated an easy triumph: but Sheridan, wheeling in the face of the foe, changed front so as to avoid being flanked on the right, and his men stood like a rock, repulsing the assaults of the enemy, though made with five times his numbers, and four times hurling them back with heavy loss. It was not until the rebels had crushed Negley's Division on his left, and were threatening to surround him, two of his brigade commanders and nearly every colonel in his division having been killed, and his ammunition exhausted, that Sheridan would fall back, and when he did so it was in good order; and he joined Rousseau's Division, which, thus re-enforced, held the enemy at bay, while General Rosecrans re-formed his lines, and on the subsequent days turned this temporary defeat into a glorious victory. General Rosecrans, in his report, complimented in the highest terms the generalship and gallantry of Sheridan, and recommended his promotion to the rank of major-general of volunteers. The President approved the recommendation, and nominated him for that rank to the Senate, who at once confirmed his promotion, his commission dating from December 31st, 1862.

When the advance of the Army of the Cumberland, so long expected, took place on the 23d of June, 1863, to Sheridan was assigned the duty of driving the rebels out of Liberty Gap, a strong mountain-pass, which was one of the keys to the rebel position. After the delay necessary for the repair of the railroads and the bringing forward supplies sufficient for the campaign, the Army of the Cumberland advanced, Sheridan's Division moving to Bridgeport, crossing the Tennessee on a pontoon-bridge, and thence passing by way of Trenton to Winston Gap of Lookout Mountain, thus flanking the rebel position at Chattanooga, and compelling them to evacuate that position.

But, though Rosecrans had obtained possession of Chattanooga, he knew very well that he could not hope to hold it without a battle; and ascertaining that Bragg had been largely re-enforced, and was moving upon Thomas's Corps in McLemore's Cove, in the hope of defeating the several corps in detail, he ordered up the other corps in great haste—McCook's Corps, except Sheridan's Division, coming from Alpine, nearly fifty miles south, and Sheridan crossing Missionary Ridge from Trenton, through Frick's Gap into McLemore's Cove. The battle of Chickamauga followed, on the 19th and 20th of September, in which Sheridan bore an honorable part.

In the grand assault on Lookout Mountain, Orchard Knob, and the forts in front of Chattanooga, General Sheridan and his division were nobly conspicuous. He had felt keenly the breaking of his division at Chickamauga, though it was so nobly atoned for in its subsequent support of General Thomas; and riding in the advance, he called in thunder-tones to his men: "Show the Fourth Corps that the men of the old Twentieth are still alive, and can fight! Remember Chickamauga!" Ever in the front, and always coolest in the moment of the greatest peril, he took a flask from one of his aides, filled the pewter cup, and raising his cap to the rebel battery, drank it off with a "How are you?" never checking for a moment the speed of his advance. The rebels most ungenerously responded by firing the six guns of one of their batteries at the daring rider, and showering him with earth, but doing no other damage. Cheering his men forward to the charge, he now put spurs to his noble steed, and was speedily on the summit, dashing after the rebels. For a few minutes there was sharp fighting; General Sheridan's horse was killed under him, and he leaped at once upon a rebel cannon; but, as he could not keep up with his men on this, he soon found another horse, and pushed on down the eastern slope of Mission Ridge after the now fast-flying enemy, driving them as far as Mission Mills, where, the next day, other troops took up the pursuit. Two days later, he was on his way with his division, under General Sherman's command, to raise the siege of Knoxville, and this accomplished, returned to Chattanooga.

In March, 1864, General Grant, having been promoted to the lieutenant-generalship, called a special conference of the leading officers of the Western Army, at Nashville, and at its close ordered General Sheridan, who had been one of its members, to report at Washington. On his arrival, he was assigned to the command of the Cavalry Corps of the Army of the Potomac, and at once proceeded to organize and train it for efficient service. At the commencement of the campaign, on the 4th of May, 1864, the corps was engaged in protecting the flanks of the Army of the Potomac, and reconnoitring the position and movements of the enemy. On the 9th of May, under General Meade's orders, General Sheridan selected the best-mounted troops of his command, and started upon an expedition to the rear of Lee's army, to cut off his communications and supplies. We have not space to give the details of this expedition, which in the history of cavalry raids has been surpassed only by Sheridan himself in some of his subsequent movements. On the 8th of June he set out on a second cavalry expedition into the heart of the enemy's country, destroying railroads, and routing the enemy wherever encountered. He then made his way, by Spottsylvania Court-House, Guinness' Station, and White House, to Grant's army, at this time south of the James, where he busied himself for the next thirty days in cutting the railroads to the south and southwest of Petersburg. On the 28th of July he fought a severe battle with the rebels near Malvern Hill. He was now called to a higher and more responsible command. The rebel General Ewell and his lieutenant, Early, had moved down the Shenandoah Valley, invaded Maryland and Pennsylvania, burned Chambersburg, captured Frederick and Hagerstown, threatened Washington and Baltimore, and finally recrossed the Potomac with a vast amount of plunder. The four military departments of the Susquehanna, the Monongahela, Washington, and West Virginia, each under the command of independent generals, did not co-operate successfully; and while General Grant would not be lured from his grasp on Richmond and Lee's army, it was necessary that efficient measures should be taken to cripple the rebel army in the Shenandoah Valley. The Middle Military Division, comprising the four departments we have named, was accordingly created, and Major-General Philip H. Sheridan appointed to the command of it, on the 7th of August. The Army of West Virginia, some Pennsylvania and Maryland troops, the Nineteenth Corps, from Louisiana, and the Sixth Corps, from the Army of the Potomac, constituted his army. To afford time to concentrate his forces and to ascertain fully Early's strength, Sheridan began almost immediately to make feints of an advance, and thus compel Early to keep the field and not return toward Richmond. When Early advanced in turn, he would fall back toward Harper's Ferry, and thus draw Early toward the Potomac. Having accumulated and organized a sufficient force to justify his making a permanent advance, he watched the opportunity of some injudicious movement on Early's part, to strike a severe and crushing blow. He had not occasion to wait long. Early, believing that Sheridan feared him, and that by good management he might succeed in flanking him, and again enter Maryland to plunder and destroy, moved east to Berryville, on the 16th of September. Sheridan was ready. On the 18th of September he sent his cavalry to attack the rebels at Darksville, on Opequan Creek, north of Winchester, while his infantry drove the main rebel force from Perryville toward Winchester. By this manœuvre, he not only defeated them with considerable loss, but crowded them west of Opequan Creek, and interposed his own army between Early's forces and their true line of retreat towards Richmond, southeast through the gaps of the Blue Ridge. His policy was now, by quick and heavy blows, to drive them, routed, toward the southwest. On the 19th of September, he flung his cavalry on the rebels on the west bank of Opequan Creek. By some misunderstanding, the infantry were not brought into action till near noon; and though the rebels made stubborn resistance, by five P. M., they were, in Sheridan's expressive language, "sent whirling through Winchester," and pursued relentlessly till they reached their defences at Fisher's Hill, thirty miles below, where they succeeded in rallying for another stand. Bringing his troops up to this new and strong position, with his usual promptness, he made such disposition of them as to flank the rebel force on both sides; the Eighth Corps being sent far to the right, and sweeping about their left, attacked them in rear and drove them out of their intrenchments. The Nineteenth pressed their right flank, and Averill's Cavalry Division was arrayed at the base of South Mountain to attack them as they attempted to fly; while the Sixth Corps made a feint of assailing them in front. Confused and disorganized at being attacked at so many points, the enemy broke at the centre, and the Sixth Corps, separating the two wings, pursued them as they fled in utter rout toward Woodstock; the cavalry soon took up the pursuit, and continued it until the remnant of the rebel army was driven below Port Republic and scattered in the mountains, whence many of them would never return to the ranks. The rebel loss, from the 19th to the 25th of September, in killed, wounded, and missing, was not less than ten thousand men, and a large amount of artillery, ammunition, and stores.

For this brilliant victory General Sheridan was appointed by the President a brigadier-general in the regular Army, in place of the gallant McPherson, killed near Atlanta.

On the 8th of October, as Sheridan, who had been destroying the grain, hay, and forage of the Shenandoah Valley, to prevent Early from subsisting there, was moving back toward Woodstock, the rebel General Rosser, who had just been put in command of a cavalry division, attempted to attack Sheridan's rear. Sheridan instantly faced about, gave him battle, defeated him with very heavy loss, and pursued him "on the jump" for twenty-six miles. "I thought it best," said Sheridan, in his report, "to take one day to settle this new cavalry general." General Early having been re-enforced, and smarting under his defeat, resolved to surprise Sheridan and take his revenge. For this purpose he crept quietly up, under cover of the forest, to the wooded slope south of Cedar Creek, on the 12th of October, and opened a heavy and rapid artillery fire on the Union lines. Sheridan had become aware of his movements, and after replying for a time promptly to his artillery fire, sprang out upon him, and, after a sharp action of three hours, again sent him "whirling" up the valley. Believing that Early had been too severely punished to attempt to attack him again, General Sheridan now made a flying visit to Washington, and to his outposts. But Early, though unsuccessful as a general, was tenacious and revengeful; and learning of Sheridan's absence, and having received still further re-enforcements, he resolved once more to attempt the destruction of the Union army. He determined, by a nocturnal movement, attended with such imminent hazard that it could only have been prompted by desperation, to turn the left flank of the Army of the Shenandoah. To do this, it was necessary that he should pass with about one-half of his army along a gorge, very near, in some places not more than four hundred yards distant from, the Union troops. Discovery at any point of this advance would have been his utter ruin. He accomplished it, however, without detection, and at dawn struck the left flank, and poured a destructive fire into it; his own right, meanwhile, pushing on, and outflanking the Union troops more completely at every step. The Eighth Corps (Crook's) were taken completely by surprise, and, after some ineffectual resistance, compelled to fall back, losing heavily in wounded and prisoners; the Nineteenth Corps (Emory's), in its turn, was also flanked and forced back; and the Sixth, after a somewhat longer struggle, found itself compelled to retreat.

The Army of the Shenandoah had thus been driven back, with heavy loss, about three miles, and forced off the turnpike, while the stragglers were scattered all the way toward Winchester, twelve miles distant, when, about two o'clock, Sheridan, who was on his return from Washington, and had reached Winchester the night before, came up the pike at full speed, his noble horse completely flecked with foam, swinging his cap, and shouting to the stragglers, "Face the other way, boys! We are going back to our camps! We are going to lick them out of their boots!" The effect was magical. The wounded by the roadside raised their voices to shout; the fugitives, but now hurrying forward to Winchester, turned about, at sight of him who had always led them to victory, and followed him back to the battle-ground as hounds follow their master.

Still riding rapidly, he reached the main army, ordered it to face about, form line, and advance to the position it had last quitted. He was obeyed without hesitation, and for two hours he rode along the lines, studying the ground and encouraging the men. "Boys," he said, in his earnest, animated way, "if I had been here, this never should have happened! I tell you, it never should have happened! And now we are going back to our camps. We are going to get a twist on them—we are going to lick them out of their boots!"

Forming his troops in a good position, and ordering the erection of rude temporary breastworks, which were thrown up in an incredibly short time, he notified the Nineteenth Corps that the enemy were advancing against them in column. They came, and were received with so deadly a fire of artillery and musketry, that they awaited no second volley, but fell back out of sight. At half-past three, Sheridan ordered an advance along the whole line, and swung his right (the Nineteenth Corps) around upon the left, so as to flank the enemy, and push them off the crests on to the turnpike and the Middletown Meadows, where he could hurl his cavalry upon them. The movement was successful; and though at first Early's troops held their position with great tenacity, yet under Sheridan's own eye the Union troops, who had neither eaten nor drunk since the previous day, and in the morning had retreated, forgetting their hunger and thirst, forgetting every thing except that they were Sheridan's soldiers, fought like tigers, and drove the enemy back, forcing his first line, carrying his second with a charge which swept all before it, pushed his columns into confusion, and, in spite of the frantic efforts of Early and his officers, sent his utterly routed legions again on their travels up the valley; while the cavalry, taking up the pursuit, pushed them through Strasburg, past Fisher's Hill, and on to Woodstock, sixteen miles distant, abandoning their cannon, small-arms, clothing, every thing, in their mad haste to shake off their pursuers. Forty-nine cannon, fifty wagons, sixty-five ambulances, sixteen hundred small-arms, and fifteen hundred prisoners, were the trophies of this victory. Battles have been lost and won on the same day before now, but in all the cases on record, the retrieval of the misfortune was due to the arrival of re-enforcements at a critical moment; but here, the only re-enforcement which the Army of the Shenandoah received or needed to recover its lost field of battle, camps, intrenchments, and cannon, was one man—SHERIDAN. Well might the Lieutenant-General, ever prompt to notice a gallant action, say of this battle, "It stamps Sheridan, what I have always thought him, one of the ablest of generals."

As an evidence of the appreciation of his extraordinary ability in this and other engagements, General Sheridan was, upon the resignation of General McClellan, on the 8th of November, promoted to fill the vacancy as major-general in the regular Army.

Six weeks after this battle, the Sixth Army Corps returned to the Army of the Potomac; and Early, hopelessly disabled, did not again venture far down the valley. Late in February, 1865, General Sheridan, with his cavalry force of about fifteen thousand men, the finest single body of mounted troops ever assembled on this continent, moved up the Shenandoah Valley, captured Staunton, attacked Early near Waynesboro, and completely annihilated the small remnant of his army, taking thirteen hundred prisoners, and narrowly missing the general himself; and thence moving southeastward, destroyed the Lynchburg and Virginia Central Railroad for nearly thirty miles, and the James River Canal for fifteen or twenty, completely destroying its locks, and breaking its banks beyond the possibility of repair for months, thus cutting off the channels of supply for Lee's army at Richmond, and inflicting injury, to the value of more than fifty millions of dollars, upon rebel property: this accomplished, he marched to White House, and thence crossing the James River, on a pontoon-bridge, on the 27th of March, joined Grant's army.

On the 29th of March, with his cavalry and the Fifth Army Corps, he moved towards Dinwiddie Court-House, threatening, at the same time, the Southside Railroad in the direction of Burkesville. After three days of continuous fighting, culminating on Saturday, April 1st, in the battle of Five Forks, he succeeded in flanking Lee's army, and obtaining possession of the Southside Railroad; the remainder of the Army of the Potomac and the Army of the James engaging, at the same time, the centre and left of the rebel army. The fighting was continued, though more feebly, on Sunday, April 2d; but on Sunday night both Petersburg and Richmond were evacuated, General Lee and his army attempting to escape to Danville. The pursuit was continued with unrelenting activity, Sheridan being always in the advance. On the 6th of April, Sheridan attacked Lee's forces at Deatonville, near Amelia Court-House, and defeated them with great slaughter, capturing Lieutenant-General Ewell and six other generals, and about ten thousand prisoners. On the 8th of April, he brought them to a stand again at Farnville, where, after a brief fight, Lee requested a cessation of hostilities, and the following day, April 9th, surrendered his entire army to General Grant. Such has been the military career of "Little Phil.," as his soldiers affectionately call him. Daring, yet cautious; bold, but not rash; fertile in resources, and knowing no fear, he has never yet lost a battle, or rested satisfied with an indecisive one.

SEEKING THE BUBBLE.

III.

* * * Then a soldier,
Full of strange oaths and bearded like the pard;
Jealous in honor, sudden and quick in quarrel;
Seeking the bubble reputation,
Even in the cannon's mouth * * *
    As You Like It.—Act II., Scene VII.

UNDER CANVAS.

THE rain dripped down the back of our necks.

When I have said that, I have described the most disagreeable of the little miseries that render life intolerable.

I have missed express trains; I have caught accommodation

trains; I have visited insane asylums; I have dined in the country, green in my imagination with fresh fruits and vegetables, upon salt pork and beans and geoponic pies; I have got into a Broadway stage and found my pocket-book left in my other trousers; I have been sea-sick! I have ridden to Harlem in the Third Avenue cars; I have waited "just a minute" while a friend played six or seven games of billiards; I have waited dinner, hungry nigh unto starvation, while my wife finished dressing; I have had my pocket picked; my trunk has been sent to Montreal when I had stopped at Saratoga; I have been in Washington during a dust-storm, and slipped up in Broadway during the muddy season; tall parties have sat in front of me at the theatre, and dexterously wriggled about so as to shut off all the funny parts from my anxious gaze; once I ate a green persimmon; often have my teeth sunk into a w——y chestnut. But what is any one of these things, what all combined, compared with the drip, drip, drip, of a cold rain macerating the back of your neck? Ugh! At most miseries you can grin, and bear them; but if that man lives who can grin with the back of his neck cold and wet——but pshaw! The pachyderm is impossible!

Drizzly over head, soggy all about you, slushy under foot; with wet knees and saturated boots, dampening a damp saddle, you flounder on a steaming horse, shiny and trickling, slop, keslip, keslip keslop, slip slop, slop slop, slip keslop, slop slop slop; and hoosh, serlush, che-wallop, che-bouk, ker-slussssh, gallops up behind you in mad haste one of those aides-de-camp that flourish at head-quarters and sends bucketfuls of the nasty mess of mud into your face and eyes and ears. "Damned Dutchman!" you think, perhaps shriek, according to your rank or irascibility, for all bulgers are Dutchmen to the army mind. You have scarcely time to scoop the mud out of your blinded eyes and smear the surplus alluvion from your mustache, before another great floundering in the sea of mud heralds the approach of the General himself, mounted on a clay horse which cleaves the mud right and left at a swinging trot, followed by an enormous staff coated with mud, tearing along at a full gallop, with a couple of score of mad orderlies racing after these last like mad demons, head down and hand on cap, their poor jaded, soaked beasts, ploughing like so many low-pressure engines. Out of the way, you infantry, up the hillside, behind the trees, into the ditch, into the swamp, for your lives! Clear the track, you artillery, while horses plunge and kick and twist your trace-chains! 'Way to the right, you cavalry! Hoi! hoi! everybody; get out of the way, and curse!

Tantaran-tra-ra-ra, sounds the bugle as a signal to the dirty, tired, wet column, to halt in the mud. Toot-tetootee-toot-tetootee-toot-tetootee-toot, it blows, for "column forward," and on we splash again. The halt and forward sound alternately through the long day as the long wagon-train strings out or closes up, until we think the bugle possessed of a devil. Night falls upon the column still in march, and darkness sits atop our other woes innumerable, the chief whereof is universal wetness. The head-quarters fires blaze up joyously as we toil wearily past the big camp, and the head-quarters bugles snore out a comfortable tattoo, driving us nervous ones to desperation. For what know we now of the night-long labor, the incessant toil, the sleepless responsibility, that fret away the brains of officers, behind those glowing guard-fires, despite that snoring tattoo? Later we found out many other things than luxurious ease under the head-quarters canvas, but to-night felt only tired, miserable, and wet, and indisposed to justice, or indeed any thing but getting into camp and to sleep. At length the column files right and halts in a ploughed stubble-field, with a plentiful garnish of stumps; the brigade forms into line; the regiments break into column by division; arms are stacked; ranks broken; the company officers and the men pitch their shelter-tents; the mounted officers hold their dripping horses till their sleepy, moist contrabands stumble up and relieve them, when they, too, seek shelter in the staff tents, there to flop themselves down on their rubber blankets, and wait, achingly, for supper. Finally, after much hacking and pulling and tearing down of wet fence-rails and picking up of stray logs, the fires blaze merrily, flaring up saucily, full in the face of the sulky Night, and setting even its sullenness aglow, in spite of itself; the inevitable frying-pan sizzles away, very much in earnest, suggestive enough of fried bacon and, after, dyspepsia, if we thought of afterward; and mingling with the savory odor of the fry puffs up the welcome aroma of the soldier's boon companion, coffee. "Supper ready, sah," grins the shiny contraband, leaning his unctuous cheek against the tent-pole, whereat a gleam of joy shoots through the damp and penetrates five human hearts beating under that canvas. Such is the general satisfaction, that even the melancholy Smallweed relaxes so far as only to vent a "Why the devil don't you bring it in, then?" at the head of the smiling African, punctuated by a slice of wet sole just torn from an unfortunate boot. The wool-topped disappears suddenly, in a streak of chuckles, but presently returns, grinning more than ever, bearing a greasy board, part of some abominable patent mess-chest, laden with a steaming freight. We are gastric enough by this time to gulp down in silence, or between spluttering sentences spoken with full mouths, unutterable quantities of coffee, fried grease (bacon, by brevet), soaked hard-tack, hard hard-tack, all except the latter boiling hot, and to our ravenous emptiness exceeding in savor all the delicacies of Delmonico. And from this luxurious repast it is an easy task for all except the poor Adjutant to turn away and roll over into a sound sleep and loud snoring. As for the Adjutant, he tries the same familiar dodge, vainly hoping that no orders will come, or that the Colonel will forget him. Vainly indeed; for he has hardly slept an hour by his big silver watch—the time seems to his sleepy mind less than a dozen seconds—when he is jerked out of his nap by the Colonel's orderly. The orders have come. "What time is it?" "Half-past eleven?" "Why can't they wait till morning?" But they can't, and so, rumpling his dishevelled hair with his hands, and buckling his sword-belt, which has lain beside him, unloosed in the interest of digestion, he rolls stiffly between a yawn and groan, into the raw, dark midnight. Such a night! You cannot see your hand before you. Slush, muck, slosh, slop, slip—"Ouch! D—n that tent-cord!" He kicks at it, in spite, half laughing at himself, half inclined to cry with the pain of a rope-barked shin, and the misery of finding himself off in some undiscovered part of the camp. This is the brigade wagon-master's tent; where's the Colonel's? Take care! a horse! And another—horses all round. No, here is a wagon, as he discovers from tripping over the pole backwards, in the vain attempt to get out of the way of the horses. The pole-chains rattle dismally, the single-trees clank, several horses kick out promiscuously; a mule, excited by the unwonted commotion, sets up his mellow whinny, and ockee, ockee, ockee, ock, ock, ockee-e-e-e-e, a score, ay, a myriad of his long-eared half-brothers swell a direful chorus. Whereat the irate teamster, against whose wagon the Adjutant's unlucky legs have carried him, emerges from his hooded home of dirt and barrels, and, swearing horribly all the while, commences to lay about him with a double-tree, a proceeding which, strange to say, seems not to exercise a quieting effect upon the world of mules, who, from merely yelling, take to kicking, plunging, and turning such somersaults as only mules can turn and live. From this din and confusion the Adjutant is glad enough to escape by asking questions of the infuriated teamster, who, of course, leads him astray and through many unnecessary ditches, against many impenetrable guard-lines, until finally, blinded by the glaring camp-fires, dazed by repeated blunders, and shaken by his unhappy tumbles, he comes home again by accident, to discover that he has been walking round and round his own camp a good half-hour, during which time the Colonel has been cursing him sturdily, and sending poor bedevilled orderlies on a mad game of hide-and-seek all over the camp. But army oaths are never more than chin-deep, and old Colonel Heavysterne is too fat and good-natured to bear too heavily on the unlucky Jenkins, or to dissect too mercilessly what he evidently considers a sorry excuse.

Finally, long after midnight, every thing gets done somehow; the last quibbles of the company commanders are settled, the last impossibility of the quartermaster is disposed of, and I, Jenkins, stumble off to sleep in wet blankets on the wet ground, with my back divided by an incorrigible root. And oh! with such a headache!

Now of all merely temporary peskinesses, a headache is the peskiest.

Did you ever have a headache?

I do not mean a pain in the head simply, but a *headache*. If you ever had one, you will recognize the distinction at once. All the blood in your body collects in your skull, and scrouges your brain until it throbs again. Your feet are icy cold, your fingers are blue and shrivelled into goose-flesh; there is a creepiness along your spine, and an ugly, rubbing noise in the back of your neck. Pump, pump, pump, go your carotid arteries; throb, throb, throb, beats your brain; every pump a stab, every throb a splitting ache. Things take curious shapes, and strange fancies tread upon each other's heels as they chase each other through your head. You think of wild jokes that make you chuckle, until a flush of pain checks the grin, and makes you hold your head for misery. Wonderful black specks and blotches—like nothing so much as the blotches we used to make at school by dropping a penful of ink on a bit of paper, and neatly folding it—appear suddenly before your sight, and wilfully float away into space, luring your eyes to strain themselves in compelled pursuit till, turning again to the right or left, only to meet a new blot and follow it also, they become red, and hot, and tired, and you realize your optic nerve as a darning-needle, skewered through a restless ball and scratching ceaselessly against the tender lining of your brain. You fight the demon to the last, although you know he is sure to win; as finally he does, and you go to bed to sink into helpless wretchedness. You only want to be alone. Nothing does you any good. You try to sleep. Pump, pump, pump, go those arteries in your neck as before; throb, throb, throb, goes your brain always, until you half fancy you can feel the seams of your poor skull gaping and again grating their sides together with every throb. How mercilessly the sun shines in through the cracks you closed so carefully! Hear that canary sing until his shrill pipe bores through your sore nerves like a gimlet; and now the pet mocking-bird in the next room hops to and fro, accompanying each skip with a noise like the sound made by scratching a varnished surface with a nail. Tink-ee, tum-tee, too-tee, tar-tee; that's your little sister banging her favorite exercise on the piano. The house shakes and rumbles as the stages and carts and carriages go by; now an unintelligible dialogue is shrieked between the cook in the basement and the maid in the attic; do they always run up and down stairs like this, and does little Tommy never stop bouncing his ball on the floor overhead? You thought he went to school! And now fretted out, you sink into a kind of lethargy, in which nothing is present to your half-dormant mind but one stupendous ache, crossed by wild dreams of black and shapeless monsters, from which you cannot escape, perpetually rushing at you, through dark tunnels, and by nightmares of falling from immense heights or being pursued by strange animals, or bobbing about helplessly in the sea with an old man sticking to you like a wet sheet and pulling you under, or of fire! At this alarm you start up, broad awake, with a pang and glare at your little wife, who has stolen gently to your bedside to ask if you will have a cup of your beloved tea. Yes, blessings on the flowery kingdom that grew it,—you will!

Why, this is the very poetry of pain. Ache with me, my dear (sir or madam), this raw night, stretched in a roll of coarse blankets upon the damp ground, with my clothes still on and only loosened for half comfort, my racked head pillowed upon a hard, wet saddle, with only a thin saddle-cloth between the aching ball and the hard seat, and a dirty silk handkerchief laid across to keep the *fuz* off; four other officers snoring dismally under the same canvas; mules screaming, teamsters talking; a horse getting loose, rampaging about the camp for an hour or more, and stumbling over your tent-cords with a pertinacity worthy of a better cause—*your* horse, as you presently discover, when your servant comes to report him gone! And so with your other torments mingles a horrible fantasy of the scene that you feel in your aching bones will take place in the morning, when you find your noble charger, freshly branded and bobbed in the tail, in the nearest battery!

Reveillé! Why, you have been asleep! How the canvas bulges and flaps, and the loose tent-cords crack under the roystering nor'wester! Such a change from last night. Pitch dark still. "There was a sound of reveillé by night," you chatter out, shivering into your overcoat and gathering in the slack of your garments, as you hurry out to the morning parade under arms, which old Colonel Heavysterne persists in having, rain or shine (especially rain), just after daybreak, as he says, but just before, as you feel convinced. A dash into the basin of floating icicles, furious scraping with a rough towel, a tug at your hair with Smallweed's pocket comb—yours was "gobbled" long ago—a swallow of scalding coffee, on with your sword, and away you scud against the driving gale, across the frozen camp-ground, tumbling over frozen ridges, slipping across sleety furrows, to form the parade, as is your duty. Early as you think yourself, the old Colonel is there before you, his iron-gray beard fringed with a frosty rime, his fat cheeks in a ruddy glow, smiling vigorously as if he liked it! Smallweed insists that the Colonel uses his authority over the bugler in such wise, that reveillé is never sounded until he, the Colonel, having shaved his upper lip to a smooth purple, gives the signal for it. The parade is over, and it will be a gastric hour to breakfast. We crowd around the cook-fires, greatly to the muttered indignation of our trusty African, Cyrus.

Presently comes an order from brigade head quarters. We are to march at nine o'clock, instead of seven; a great improvement, we all think, except our melancholy quartermaster, who is of the opinion that whatever is, is wrong, if we may judge by his words, as I often think we should not. Smallweed doesn't believe we will move at all, wonders why "they"—not stating whom—couldn't say so at once; "they" were always countermanding orders; issued them just on purpose to have the pleasure of countermanding them, he believed. He would bet five hundred thousand dollars, that we would be here a month. The enemy were not going to run away, and we were not going to attack them. He was d——d tired of this shilly-shally way of carrying on a war; and much more to the same purpose, until breakfast was announced, and we all squatted down around the fire, upon logs, or saddles, or rubber blankets, or what not, to eat it. Oh! what a heavenly thing is breakfast in camp! To the empty and worthless soldier, half collapsed with hunger, his gastric juice fiercely gnawing at his vitals, it comes hot and steaming, like a blessing from above; the first swallow of hot coffee courses down your throat, leaving pleasant memories in its wake, and leaping along your quickened veins, trices up your nerves, and warms into gladness the very cockles of your heart. "Ah!" you exclaim, with rapture. "That goes to the right spot," says young Fippany; and "That's so," echoes everybody, even Smallweed, who, however, cannot quite refrain from asking Lieutenant Fippany why he makes such a fuss about it, as if he had never breakfasted before. "I feel," says little Fip., "as if I never had!" Whereat the mess shakes its cold sides with merriment, even Smallweed grinning, in spite of himself, and the young swell colors scarlet even to the roots of his hair and the curled tips of his English whiskers, having never before, or, indeed, since, perpetrated a remark possessing so much pretension to be considered witty. And so the tongues, until now tied fast by the raw morning hunger—who can talk before breakfast?—are unloosed, and begin to wag merrily enough. Now that their bellies are fast being filled with the warm food, those of the mess who, when empty, had preserved a grim silence under Smallweed's skepticism, launch forth into the most sanguine predictions of the future career of this army. The rebels will make no stand at Yorktown, that is very evident; and if not at Yorktown, where can they resist our advance, this side of Richmond? Richmond! why, they are already preparing to evacuate it. The Confederacy is evidently played out. The young doctor, Assistant-Surgeon Launcelot Cutts, who has come to breakfast with us (liking our fare, probably, better than the fried hard-tack, brine-salted herring, and stiff gin-cocktail, which constitute the matutinal repast of his chief, Dr. Peacack), invents wonderful combinations of strategy, and the grandest of grand tactics, remarkable rather for brilliancy than for their likelihood of adoption by our commanding generals. "Say, Deputy Sawbones, what corps do you expect to command?" asks the incorrigible Smallweed; "stick to your pills, old fellow; stick to your pills and your green sash, and leave fighting to your betters." Which the finnikin little doctor swallows as it were so much aloes, trying to look all the while as if he enjoyed the joke hugely.

The regiment gets under arms at nine, and the rest of the brigade falls in also, as far as we can see, for the woods that skirt our little clearing. A weary hour in the cold wind, and then comes word to remain under arms till further orders. About noon, the sky clouds up again, and the raw easterly storm of yesterday presently settles down to its work once more; its work of wetting us through, and making us thoroughly wretched. And so we yawn, and gape, and shuffle through the livelong day, tediously enough, waiting in the drenching, driving rain, and the thick, adhesive mud, for those orders to move, which never come. For, about dark, up dashes one of the brigade staff, with orders to go into camp, and await further instructions, ready to move at a moment's notice. "What was the firing?" the Colonel asks, alluding to a dull sound, like the distant slamming of big doors, that has been beating upon our ear-drums, at intervals, during the day. "Reconnoissance on the right," the A. D. C. explains briefly, knowing, probably, no more about the subject, and gallops off again, as well as he can, through the sticky soil. And so, in uncertainty, begins the siege of Yorktown.

Siege? That word was never mentioned among us for ten days after we stopped still in our triumphant advance, and took up the spade, except, indeed, by the melancholy Smallweed, who persisted, from the very start, that the General-in-Chief had made up his mind that this was just the place for a siege, and was determined to have one, or perish miserably in the attempt. General Washington had had a siege here; why should not we? With much more bile to the same purport.

It would not have been so bad, we all thought, and many of us still think, if "they" (meaning the indefinite superiors who are supposed to do things) had only told us frankly that we were in for a siege, instead of keeping up the sickening pretence of "forward movements," "assaults," "surprises," "coups de main," "night attacks," "flankings," "waiting for re-enforcements," "waiting for the roads to dry," "waiting for supplies," and who knows how much more rubbish of the same nature! Ah! well. Perhaps "they" couldn't help it, after all. Who is it that invents all the formulas we use every day, to half conceal things we cannot hide; those formulas that nobody ever thinks of believing, that we know nobody ever thinks of believing, and that everybody knows we know they never think of believing? "*Nolo Episcopari*," says the newly-appointed bishop, trying on his episcopal robes and practising his episcopal signature. "Mrs. Brown ain't at home," says Biddy to Jones, who has just seen her whisk away from the parlor window. "I don't want any office," smirks the professional office-seeker, licking his daily boot in the antechamber, in company with a dozen brother-adventurers, each of whom sees through the others, and knows he is seen through. "Forward!" cry the flaming General Orders, and the army incontinently—marks time! Now, a lie may be a very good thing in itself; far be it from me to underrate the value of so useful a member of society; but a lie, for the sake of lying, a lie unbelieved, and the inventor knowing as much—— Go to! No, my dear General, A or B, or C, Canute's facile aides-de-camp might as well have tried to fawn back the North Sea, as you to attempt to deceive your soldiers by an address.

One morning we come back from building a corduroy road to find the crest of the hill beyond our camp adorned by a jagged line of fresh dirt. The men salute the discovery with many a half-laughing, half-derisive cry of "How are *you*, grave-diggers?" "Spades is trumps," "More ditches," and the like. And so for a month we divide our time pretty evenly between digging trenches, making corduroy, standing picket, and idling away the off-days, with the usual amount of getting under arms in the middle of the night to repel imaginary sorties, of getting ready to assault at daylight, of "stampedes," and mud and rain. I sometimes wonder which is the worst—to build a corduroy road, or to travel over it. Such a tramping through mud, knee-deep, with the detestably-cooked rations, under a guide who don't know the way, to a place where some young engineer officer was to have met you, and therefore has not; such a standing around, soaking into the mire until the young engineer finally arrives, several hours late, cursing the "d——d volunteers" for not being at some other place they have never heard of, at a time not mentioned in their orders; such a jabbering and confusion of orders, in regard to the work and the manner of doing it; such a sulking of rejected suggestions! Finally, towards noon, when everybody is worn out with sheer waiting, we at last begin: such a hacking down of trees much too large to move; such a lopping off of saplings much too small to be used; such a felling, and chopping, and lifting, and pulling, and hauling of big logs; such a splashing into the loose mire, making believe to dig ditches; such a gathering of pine-brush; such a piling on of heavy dirt; and all the while such a cursing, and shouting, and grumbling, and getting in one another's way, and stumbling out again; such a fault-finding by the young engineer at the paltry result of the day's work; such a going home wet, and fagged, and muddy, to stretch out supperless and try to sleep! all this, with how much more I cannot tell, rises before my eyes at the very mention of the word corduroy. And so I say it is hard to decide whether it is pleasanter work to build or to travel on one, lurching to and fro, forward and back, hardly two miles an hour, at the risk of your horse's knees and your own neck, scrambling from log to log, getting your poor brute's legs jammed between them, slipping and floundering wearily to your journey's end; with all the while such a smell—nay, such a diabolish stench!—chiefly compounded of dead horse, decayed leaves, and water-rotting roots, as serves to make your misery complete and spherical.

We are still speculating, in our mess, whether we are engaged in a siege or not, when there comes a little cocked hat from brigade head-quarters, which upon being opened is found to contain the following pithy words:—

"HEAD-QUARTERS ARMY OF THE POTOMAC,
"CAMP WINFIELD SCOTT, BEFORE YORKTOWN,
"*April* 17, 1862.

"ORDERS.

"*Detail for To-morrow*
"GENERAL OF THE TRENCHES,
"Colonel Johnson Heavysterne, 3d D. C. Vols.
"By command of MAJOR-GENERAL McCLELLAN:

(Signed)   S. WILLIAMS, *Assistant Adjutant-General.*
"OFFICIAL COPY.

"By order of Acting Brigadier-General FUSSE:
"VERUEL HICK, *Capt. and A. A.-G.*"

And in a few days followed another cocked hat, from division head-quarters, to this effect:—

"HEAD-QUARTERS SECOND DIVISION,
"TWENTY-SIXTH ARMY CORPS,
"BEFORE YORKTOWN, April 19, 1862.

"ORDERS.

"*Detail for To-night*
"GUARDS OF TRENCHES,
"3d Regt. Dist. Col. Vols.—Col. J. Heaveystearns.
"Report at 7 P. M. to Brigadier-General Sturgeon, Gen. of Trenches.
"By order Brigadier-General PIKE, *Com. Division.*
"WASHINGTON SMITH, *Assistant Adjutant-General*

"OFFICIAL COPY.

"By order Act. Brigadier-General FUSSE;
"VERUEL HICK, *Capt. and A. A.-G.*"

I print as they wrote, remember.

Guards of the trenches! welcome detail! welcome any thing

for a change. The muttered growls change to a hum of cheerful chattering; men slough off their moody sullenness, and begin to look alive once more. Officers pass the customary banters, and the inevitable "How are *you?*" resounds throughout the camp. The night comes at last. Full of joy and supper, we march out with a lively step, we mount the hill, descend its farther slope, cross the pontoon-bridge—then a new plaything with us, though now stale enough!—and so to the old mill where we are to report to the engineer officer, who again, as a matter of course, is not to be found there, having somehow gathered an impression that he is to look for us somewhere else. As Smallweed philosophizes, "some pork *will* bile so," though indeed it strikes us as a little hard that after squatting for an hour in the mud and darkness, and exhausting all possible means of discovering the juvenile lieutenant, fresh from the shell (Fassin, I believe his name is), he should suddenly make his diminutive appearance from nowhere in particular, on a gigantic horse, and incontinently begin double-dashing the Colonel and the "dashed volunteers," after the authentic fashion for the case made and provided. I suppose some pork will bile *so*, also; and now we are off for the trenches at last. Here we are. "File right," and we pass along the reverse of a big ditch in which a number of other soldiers are working with that slow and steady dig that soldiers use, and presently we halt and, sitting or lying on the ground, begin our important functions as guards of the trenches, while the old guards, with many an expression of mock sympathy, and many a "Good-by, boys," after the courteous manner of the time, trudge rather gladly rearward by the way we have just come. How quiet it seems! A death-like silence prevails, broken only by men speaking in a half-whisper, by the crack of the sharpshooter's rifle as he sends his occasional greeting to his *vis-à-vis*, or by the metallic click of the pick as it strikes some stray stone that has found its way into this vast bed of sand by mistake. Those of us who are conscious of possessing the faculty of being able to sleep without detection under adverse circumstances, take naps; the others "gas," or think in silence of home and distant scenes, and bygone days that seem, oh! so far away! Suddenly, the dark silence is rent by a shriek and a roar, and more shrieks and more roars, and the thunder of many guns; the enemy are shelling the working parties! On the instant the sleepers wake up, and the most of us drop flat on the ground, by an irresistible impulse, but presently sit up once more and peer round half-laughing, half-ashamed, each pleased to think he has done no worse than his neighbors. From a score of guns the horrid belching goes on for a half hour, and the shells shriek harmlessly over our heads, or, bursting in the air, make the scene ghastly with their glare for one instant, and the next hurtle their fragments with a *hum-m-m-m* among us. All quiet again. Anybody hurt? Nobody hurt! Good! Young Fippany jumps to his feet at my side, whirls his cap over his head, and pretends to give three cheers. Just as he gets to the inevitable "tiger," I am blinded by a streak of light, deafened by a terrible noise, and stunned by what seems an earthquake. When I come to myself my face is full of sand, and somebody is trying to make me drink out of a canteen which tastes weakly of bad whiskey. What has happened? Shell. Any one hurt? Am I? No, I'm all right, I find. What have they done with my blanket? Ah, well! They have taken it to carry off poor Fippany to the surgeon; a needless task, for Harry is already far beyond the leech's skill, having had the top of his skull blown off by the explosion. The first man killed in our regiment.

For five minutes, it may be, or perhaps not so long, everybody is solemn, and then every thing goes on as before. A ripple, and the surface is smooth again!

As for Lieutenant William Jenkins, his nerves are so completely unstrung by the shock, that young Dr. Cutts thinks it necessary to muddle him with brandy, so that he knows nothing more till daylight.

SHERMAN'S GEORGIA CAMPAIGN—FROM ATLANTA TO THE SEA.

BY COLONEL S. M. BOWMAN.

The capture of Atlanta was a terrible blow to the Confederacy; it was as unexpected to the rebel leaders at Richmond, as "a clap of thunder from a cloudless sky." The failure of Johnston to arrest the victorious advance of Sherman had caused universal alarm, and much dissatisfaction, and now Hood also had failed disastrously. It seemed impossible to stay Sherman's victorious progress. President Davis immediately left Richmond, and proceeded with all possible haste to Georgia. At every stage of his journey he was met by a dejected and suffering people, who, now truly alarmed, plied him with anxious inquiries. At Columbia, South Carolina, and other places on his journey, he addressed the people, but in attempting to allay their apprehensions, he only disclosed his own. He seemed only to labor to get rid of his own fears, as if struggling with destiny; the war was getting beyond his control; he saw that in relieving Johnston and appointing Hood, he had only made matters worse, and that his cause was well-nigh lost; and, losing his accustomed equanimity, he launched forth torrents of invective against the Yankees, and hurled defiance at Sherman, as if he thought to accomplish by the force of his rhetoric what Johnston and Hood could not

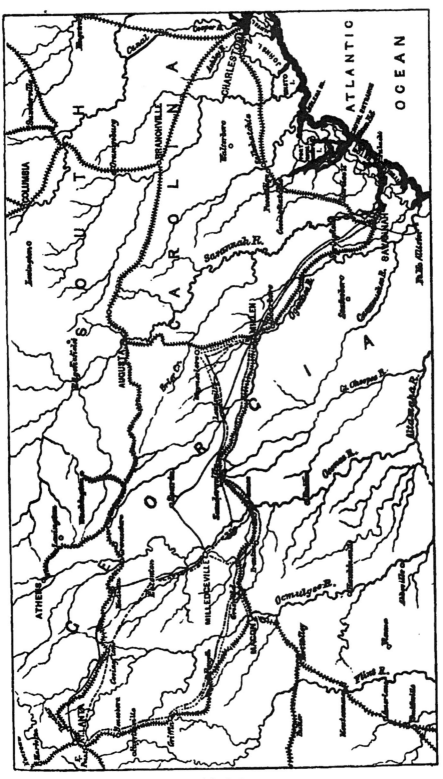

——— Slocum (left wing).
- - - - Davis's Fourteenth Corps, when separated.
—·—·— Howard (right wing).
········ Cavalry.

do by force of arms. His efforts were calculated, nevertheless, to "fire the Southern heart," but, alas! that heart had been too often fired to be easily fanned into flame by boastful words. Still his presence in Georgia, and his speeches at Augusta and Macon, had the effect to arrest the progress of public sentiment, now strongly tending in that State towards reunion. Some of the public journals had already ventured to hint in favor of giving up the war as useless, and it was understood that the Governor of Georgia was himself exchanging views on the subject with Sherman. It was also well known that many influential citizens were in favor of immediate reconstruction, by State action alone, and without the concurrence of the other Confederate States, thus taking Georgia back to the Union by the same road she had left it. But Davis nipped all such plans in the bud. It was not convenient to abide by his own favorite dogma of *State rights* under the present circumstances. Sherman, on witnessing the effect of Davis's presence in Georgia, declared, "Jeff. Davis holds the Southern Confederacy in his hands, and wields it like an army. Before he came down here Governor Brown thought he had some *State rights*, but Davis took that notion out of him quick."

By the last of September, Hood had sufficiently recovered from the stunning blows dealt by Sherman to take the initiative. His plan was, to march to Sherman's rear and break his long line of communication, and by this means compel him to evacuate Atlanta. This, he thought, would undo the work of many months, would force the Union flag back from its proud, advanced position on the ramparts of Atlanta, to where it started from in May. He had recruited his army at Lovejoy's to near forty thousand men, from the Georgia militia, and being all ready, he swiftly threw his whole army upon the railroad between Atlanta and Chattanooga, breaking it up in sundry places, and taking possession of several of our stations on the road. During the entire month of October our communications were interrupted, and then they were re-established. Our secondary base, however, Allatoona, was held against French's entire division by the gallant Corse with seventeen hundred men. The enemy, after five hours' fighting, retreated, leaving two hundred dead on the ground and four hundred prisoners in our hands. Sherman, with all his force, except the Twentieth Corps, was pursuing Hood, and witnessed the action from the top of a distant mountain, from which he signalled Corse to hold on at all hazards, that he was coming to his relief. The signal was not recognized. It was repeated again and again. "I am confident," said Sherman, "that Corse is there, and will hold the place." At length the signal was answered, and Sherman hastened on; but the contest had ended, and the enemy gone before his arrival. Sherman's order of thanks declared:—

"This handsome defence illustrates a most important principle of war—that fortified places should be defended to the last, regardless of the relative numbers of the party attacking and attacked."

Following up the railroad as far as Dalton, where he broke it again, Hood then struck off westerly to Lafayette, and thence southwesterly to Gadsden, Sherman following sharply as far as Gaylesville, Alabama, where he halted.

And now commenced the development of a campaign, originated by Sherman in the exigencies of the moment, and for a specific end, but destined to form the grandest movement of the war, and to exercise a marvellous influence on its destinies. Hood's plan was quickly comprehended by Sherman. It was to gather his forces at Gadsden, increase them by the forces of Dick Taylor and other troops, throw them across the Tennessee at Florence, and march on Nashville. Long before this plan was carried out, Sherman had followed it, and seen its dangerous consequences. It would have thrown him on the defensive, and given his beaten adversary the advantage of the offensive. It would have undone the prospective work of the year, by keeping our troops always busy defending communications and in protecting Tennessee. Any other commander but Sherman would have massed his troops to hurl them against Hood, pursuing him from point to point until he was overtaken. Sherman, however, followed no plan but that dictated by his own genius. Instantly comprehending all the necessities and all the possibilities of the situation, he astonished Europe and America by one of the boldest strokes ever attempted in military history. While Hood and Beauregard, and their corps commanders, S. D. Lee, Cheatham, Cleburne, and Bate, were making windy speeches at Gadsden, promising all sorts of success to their troops, and pledging themselves, as one of them said, "to wipe Sherman from the list of Yankee generals," that General was preparing a scheme that must have suddenly changed their views, and dampened their ardor.

He divided his forces into two parts, and made the Fourth and Twenty-third Corps a nucleus around which his ablest lieutenant, Thomas, should collect troops from the whole Department of the Mississippi, and from re-enforcements on the way, according to directions from Sherman, and with them should resist, check, and finally drive back the advance of Hood into Tennessee. Next he made elaborate dispositions of forces for Bridgeport, Chattanooga, Murfreesboro, and other points to be held, and directed the abandonment of those which could not be well held. Finally, he prepared and mobilized an army of about fifty thousand men for a march across the broad State of Georgia to the sea. Of the admirable manner in which he equipped this column, the perfection of its arrangements—not only in the disposition of its forces and the entire perfection for practical use of the three arms of the service, but also in the Ordnance, Quartermaster, and Commissary Departments, and in all its transportation—of this we cannot speak. But when it is remembered that not one gun or one wagon of all his immense trains was lost or abandoned during the prolonged march which ensued, the skilful preparation of the expedition can be appreciated.

So rapidly and secretly were all these things effected, that long before Hood was ready to leave Florence, entirely ignorant of the scheme of Sherman—the latter was far away on his march towards Savannah. The main outlines of the plan were by Sherman communicated to the Lieutenant-General, and approved by him.

And now Sherman had every thing ready for the start. All wagons, supplies, and extra baggage not needed and tending to impede the most rapid movements, were sent back to Chattanooga. His trains were all in complete order; sixteen days' rations were in the wagons and five days' rations in haversack; the men had all received their back pay and were in fine spirits, and all entertained an enthusiasm for their leader unequalled since the days of Napoleon. On the 3d of November, Sherman telegraphed to Captain Pennock, United States Navy: "In a few days I will be off for salt water, and hope to meet my old friend D. D. Porter again. Be kind enough to write to him and tell him to look out for me about Christmas from Hilton Head to Savannah." He also wrote home to Mrs. Sherman: "This is my last letter from here, you will only hear from me hereafter through rebel sources." Orders had been given for the destruction of the railroad in his rear, and of all public property in Atlanta, and now the march began—a perilous march of three hundred miles through the heart of the Confederacy, from the mountains to the sea. And here we have the order of march and the law of the campaign:—

"1. For the purpose of military operations this army is divided into two wings, viz.: The right wing, Major-General O. O. Howard commanding, the Fifteenth and Seventeenth Corps; the left wing, Major-General H. W. Slocum commanding, the Fourteenth and Twentieth Corps.

"2. The habitual order of march will be, whenever practicable, by four roads, as nearly parallel as possible, and converging at points hereafter to be indicated in orders. The cavalry, Brigadier-General Kilpatrick commanding, will receive special orders from the Commander-in-Chief.

"3. There will be no general trains of supplies, but each corps will have its ammunition and provision train distributed habitually as follows:—Behind each regiment should follow one wagon and one ambulance; behind each brigade should follow a due proportion of ammunition wagons, provision wagons, and ambulances. In case of danger, each army corps should change this order of march by having its advance and rear brigade unencumbered by wheels. The separate columns will start habitually at seven A. M., and make about fifteen miles per day, unless otherwise fixed in orders.

"The army will forage liberally on the country during the march. To this end, each brigade commander will organize a good and sufficient foraging party, under the command of one or more discreet officers, who will gather, near the route travelled, corn or forage of any kind, meat of any kind, vegetables, corn, meal, or whatever is needed by the command; aiming at all times to keep in the wagon trains at least ten days' provisions for the command and three days' forage. Soldiers must not enter the dwellings of the inhabitants, or commit any trespass; during the halt or a camp they may be permitted to gather turnips, potatoes, and other vegetables, and drive in stock in front of their camps. To regular foraging parties must be intrusted the gathering of provisions and forage at any distance from the road travelled.

"5. To army corps commanders is intrusted the power to destroy mills, houses, cotton-gins, &c., and for them this general principle is laid down:—In districts and neighborhoods where the army is unmolested, no destruction of such property should be permitted; but should guerrillas or bushwackers molest our march, or should the inhabitatants burn bridges, obstruct roads, or otherwise manifest local hostility, then army corps commanders should order and enforce a devastation more or less relentless, according to the measure of such hostility.

"6. As for horses, mules, wagons, &c., belonging to the inhabitants, the cavalry and artillery may appropriate freely and without limit; discriminating, however, between the rich, who are usually hostile, and the poor or industrious, usually neutral or friendly. Foraging parties may also take mules or horses to replace the jaded animals of their trains, or to serve as pack mules for the regiments or brigades. In all foraging, of whatever kind, the parties engaged will refrain from abusive and threatening language, and may, when the officer in command thinks proper, give written certificates of the facts, but no receipts; and they will endeavor to leave with each family a reasonable portion for their maintenance.

"7. Negroes who are able-bodied and can be of service to the several columns, may be taken along; but each army commander will bear in mind that the question of supplies is a very important one, and that his first duty is to see to those who bear arms.

"8. The organization at once of a good pioneer battalion for each corps, composed, if possible, of negroes, should be attended to. This battalion should follow the advance guard, should repair roads and double them if possible, so that the columns will not be delayed after reaching bad places. Also, army commanders should study the habit of giving the artillery and wagons the road, and marching their troops on one side; and also instruct the troops to assist wagons at steep hills or bad crossings of streams.

"9. Captain O. M. Poe, Chief Engineer, will assign to each wing of the army a pontoon-train, fully equipped and organized, and the commanders thereof will see to its being properly protected at all times.

"By order of Major-General W. T. SHERMAN.
"L. M. DAYTON, *Aide-de-Camp*."

On the 15th day of November, the march began. There were four full and strong corps of infantry; two strong and excellent divisions of cavalry; a brigade of artillery for each corps, and a battery of flying artillery for the cavalry. Each battery had twelve reserve horses, so that not a gun might be lost.

To Slocum's wing was assigned the task of marching down the Atlanta and Augusta Railroad, or the Georgia Railroad, and destroying it, while Howard's wing was to do the same work for the Atlanta, Macon, and Savannah, called the Georgia Central Road. Each wing was covered entirely from molestation, and even from view, by a column of Kilpatrick's Cavalry, which marched, the one on Slocum's left flank, and the other on Howard's right. The railroad to Augusta, or Slocum's route, was one hundred and seventy-one miles long; the railroad from Atlanta to Savannah was two hundred and ninety-one miles. Slocum moved out on separate roads, and immediately began his work of destruction; he destroyed the railroad inch by inch; burned dépôts and public buildings of all sorts useful to the enemy, cotton-gins with their cotton, blacksmith-shops, tanneries, factories, and all similar structures. Private property was always spared, except when it had been or would be used against the Union, or was needed for actual use. In this way Slocum moved along the railroad. Williams's Twentieth Corps took the northerly road, and entered in succession the villages or hamlets of Decatur, Stone Mountain, Social Circle, Rutledge, and Madison. From Madison, Geary's Division of the Twentieth Corps pushed on to the Oconee River, destroying many supplies, much cotton, many shops and mills, and burning the valuable railroad bridge over the Oconee, a structure about fifteen hundred feet long. This was on the 20th. A part of the cavalry went across the Oconee and reached Greensboro, a point eighty-four miles west of Augusta, but returned to cover Geary's Division. The latter, its work accomplished, moved down the west bank of the Oconee to join the rest of the Twentieth Corps, which, like itself, had changed direction from east to south, and was now heading towards Milledgeville.

Meanwhile, Davis's Fourteenth Corps had moved simultaneously on the Covington Road, inside the Twentieth Corps' track, and had passed successively through Lithonia and Conyers to Yellow River, and thence to Covington. From Covington it moved southerly to Eatonton, and there approached the track of the Twentieth Corps, which had turned off from Madison. Both corps now pushed down to Milledgeville, and on the 21st entered the capital of Georgia, and now once more the flag of the Union floated over this rebellious State. The Legislature and all State officers, and the few troops there, had already taken flight, and Sherman rode up to the executive mansion and took possession of it, without firing a gun; and, indeed, all Slocum's advance, thus far, had been made without material opposition. Trifling skirmishes with the videttes of cavalry, sent out from Augusta, was all the fighting he experienced.

Milledgeville had been hastily abandoned. The enemy had destroyed great quantities of stores; but our troops, coming upon them before their work was completed, were forced to finish the labor themselves. Twenty-five hundred stands of small-arms, a great stock of artillery and infantry ammunition, nearly two thousand bales of cotton, and all the railroad dépôts, freight-houses, &c., were left for us to burn and destroy. The State Prison had been emptied of its inhabitants, the convicts having been put into the enemy's ranks, receiving a pardon for their bounty. The executive mansion had been stripped of its furniture so completely, that not a chair or piece of carpet could be found in it; and the lodging-room appropriated by the Union General was ornamented with no furniture save a pair of blankets spread out on the floor, upon which he reposed, perhaps, more comfortably than his Excellency who had just vacated it had done for many months before.

While Slocum was thus marching on Milledgeville, after a feint on Augusta, Howard was moving in the same direction, after a feint on Macon. He had moved his column out of Atlanta on the 14th, and on the 15th took up his march. His two corps marched on different roads as far as practicable, and a cloud of Kilpatrick's cavalry covered, as by a curtain, all our operations on the Macon Railroad. From the very departure from Atlanta this fine body of cavalry commenced driving in the pickets of the enemy who had been "besieging" Atlanta, according to their accounts. Pressing them through Eastport and Jonesboro, Kilpatrick found a cavalry brigade and some Georgia militia, two or three thousand in number, occupying strong earthworks at Lovejoy's. Our men charged and scattered this force, carrying the works, and capturing two guns which had been turned against us. The enemy's loss was about fifty.

From Lovejoy's the cavalry moved down the railroad to Griffin and thence to Forsyth, visiting also McDonough. The infantry columns followed leisurely, destroying the track, &c., as in Slocum's march. Ten miles north of Griffin, at Bear Creek, Wheeler's cavalry once more were encountered, and again routed and driven back, this time to Barnesville, whence once more, on the following day, they were forced back through Forsyth to Macon. But now, having approached the Ocmulgee, it was necessary to cover Howard's wing in its passage across the river. To effect this, Kilpatrick made a demonstration against Macon, which the enemy, all this time, had believed to be our main point of attack. He pushed his cavalry through Forsyth, across the Ocmulgee to Clinton, and from Clinton to Griswoldville, ten miles east of Macon. From Clinton, on the 20th, a column of cavalry turned abruptly against Macon. In that city was a large confederate army, and many generals, all enclosed by formidable breastworks, carrying no little artillery. In a series of rapid advances, our small cavalry column went over the outlying picket-posts, driving the enemy to East Macon, two miles from the city. There a brigade briskly charged, and one regiment, the 10th Ohio, crossed the creek, burst up the hill on which the earthworks were, and actually captured and held a full battery, driving off all artillerymen and infantry supports. As a feint only was intended, our troops were soon withdrawn. While it was proceeding, the rest of the cavalry went to Griswoldville and Gordon, and destroyed dépôts, a foundry, chemical-works, and other public property, according to the plan pursued in the entire march, of which we cannot always give details. They there resumed, at this short distance from Macon, the destruction of the Georgia Central Railroad, which had been suspended, of course, a few miles west of Macon.

Under cover of this cavalry *détour*, Howard, having carried his infantry column as near to Macon as he could without provoking a skirmish, turned thence easterly, and crossed the Ocmulgee, without opposition, at Planter's Factory, on the 20th; for Kilpatrick's demonstration had concentrated all of Cobb's infantry in Macon, whose capture he feared. Then he pursued rapidly on to Milledgeville, having visited successively the towns of Jackson, Indian Springs, Monticello, and Hillsboro. Slocum's advance had entered the State capital on the 20th, and Howard's the day after. The troops, therefore, had marched more rapidly than the moderate orders of Sherman had imposed, the distance being about one hundred miles, and the time less than one week.

At Milledgeville, Sherman halted his principal columns a few days, and gathered from the surrounding country a full supply of forage and provisions, in anticipation of future need.

Meanwhile, his troops luxuriated amid a region of plenty. They were in the most productive part of Georgia, and to the soldiers it was, literally, "a land flowing with milk and honey." Salt pork and hard-tack were now at a discount, for corn bread, sweet potatoes, tomatoes, sorghum, and fruits, were abundant, and to be had without the asking; and, for the first time in the history of the war, a whole army kept Thanksgiving Day after the style at home—dining on chickens and turkeys.

The soldiers, in the exuberance of their enjoyment, entered the State-House, and organized a mock Legislature, appointed a Speaker, "and proceeded to business," when "honorable members" made amusing speeches, to the infinite delight of all concerned. Thus are the terrible realities of war often relieved by scenes of mirthfulness and joy. There was no wanton destruction of property, no act of violence; the remaining inhabitants were not unnecessarily disturbed; and on that memorable Thanksgiving Eve, 1864, the Union soldiers gathered around their cheerful camp-fires, on the plains of Georgia, and around its capital, as happy and joyful as though that glorious army were on a grand fishing-excursion or a fox-chase, not seeming to think of Cobb and his corps of generals, then safely ensconced behind the earthworks at Macon, nor fearing that terrible fate predicted by the rebel press at Richmond.

A part of the Fifteenth Corps, with some of the cavalry, had been left at Gordon and Griswoldville, to complete the work there, and to protect our rear. The enemy, finding himself deceived into concentrating at Macon, burst upon Howard's rear at Griswoldville, on the 22d, with three full militia brigades and four other regiments, under General Phillips. At first he drove in and captured a few pickets, but he soon came to where our troops were handsomely intrenched, and charged them with great vigor repeatedly. Our men, consisting chiefly of Walcott's Brigade, received the enemy as veterans accustomed to triumph on every field receive, from strong parapets, raw militia. He was repulsed with the loss of more than one thousand men, it is said, his own accounts confessing it to be six hundred and fourteen, including General Anderson. Our loss, of course, was trifling.

This battle of Griswoldville was the heaviest engagement of the march. The enemy's attack was certainly a singular mode of attempting to oppose Sherman's advance, especially considering he had no troops to waste or demoralize. But, in truth, the enemy knew not what to do. He threw himself on us at Griswoldville for very shame for suffering the march to pass without a resolute blow. Where he had massed his troops and arranged for battle—at Augusta and Macon—Sherman declined to go; he snapped his fingers at the breastworks and passed by, cutting the enemy's railroads so he could not transport his troops again in season to head him off, and leaving the enemy at a convenient distance in the rear.

The enemy had for three years been used to picking out his own battle-fields and drawing us to them, especially in the East. Sherman inaugurated the system of going where the enemy did not expect us and did not want us to go, and of attacking him where he was not prepared to resist. He was not on a raid for trophies merely—he had no occasion for the enemy's fortifications in the interior of Georgia; he was after his means of subsistence—his railways, his dépôts of supplies, his factories and work-shops—the means by which the rebellion lived. And, in truth, Sherman managed his campaign so adroitly, that the enemy was completely blinded and mystified by his perplexing moves. At Richmond, as well as at Augusta and Macon, they acted like people in a trance. They pursued him where he was not, and when they struck at him it was as one strikes in the dark; and when they thought to strike a heavy blow at his head, they found it was only aimed at his rear. It was not until he had reached Savannah, that it was ascertained how he got there, and then only by tracing out the terrible track he had left behind.

Slocum's left wing moved out of Milledgeville on the 24th, crossed the Oconee without opposition, and marched on Sandersville. The 25th was occupied in driving Wheeler's cavalry, who now in pretty strong numbers made a stand behind some hasty works near the town. They were expelled after a sharp skirmish, and were driven through the town. The town-people fired upon our troops from their houses, but the place was soon occupied. The next day Slocum struck the Georgia Railroad at Tennille, and, moving on, destroyed every thing of public value as far as the Ogeechee. Meantime, Davis's Fourteenth Corps had driven the enemy back towards Waynesboro, and entered Louisville, and threatened Augusta. Kilpatrick's cavalry operated on the Waynesboro Road, greatly alarming the people of Augusta. Howard's wing having destroyed the important railroad junction at Gordon, moved down the railroad to the Oconee, to cross it there while Slocum was crossing at Milledgeville. Howard found that Wheeler had made a wide *détour* from Macon, and had got his forces into position to oppose our crossing at the railroad bridge and the neighboring ford. On the 23d and 24th, our cavalry had some sharp skirmishing with Wheeler and Wagner, but on the latter day carried the bridge and ford, and swept away all opposition. Howard then pressed on successively to Sandersville and Davisboro, while the cavalry were everywhere, as has been said, driving back and flanking the cavalry of Wheeler and Wagner. It being clear that Macon was not to be attacked, the enemy was now apprehensive of Augusta again. Wheeler, after disputing our advance at Sandersville, fell back towards Waynesboro. Our cavalry, which had cleared the advance of both wings across the Oconee to Sandersville and Tennille, had moved forward, as has been said, on Louisville and Waynesboro. The latter is an important point on the Augusta and Savannah Railroad, just north of which, twenty-two miles from Augusta, is Walker's Bridge, where the railroad crosses Brier Creek. A small detachment was sent out to destroy that bridge, while the main body of cavalry moved on Louisville, and then divided again, a part moving on Waynesboro, and the rest down toward Millen. On the 27th, 28th, and 29th, Kilpatrick had severe skirmishing with Wheeler, who resisted his movement on Waynesboro. On the latter day, Wheeler attacking, was repulsed with the loss, probably, of two hundred men, a part of our forces using the Spencer rifle, and thus inflicting double their own loss on the enemy. But Kilpatrick fell back to Louisville, where the Fourteenth Corps now was. On the 1st he moved once more against Waynesboro, supported by one infantry division, and had a sharp encounter with the enemy the same day. He struck the railroad at Thomas's Station, below Waynesboro, and tore it up. Once more he missed Waynesboro, and, after a severe fight on the 3d and 4th, in which our loss was about sixty, and the enemy's, according to his report, seventy or eighty, our forces broke up the railroad successfully, and then returned to Millen, where the main army was. During these operations against Waynesboro, the station buildings and the bridge at Brier Creek were burned.

And now the second stage of the grand march had been accomplished. As the movement from Atlanta to Milledgeville was the first, so the movement from Milledgeville to Millen may be reckoned the second. The distance in the latter case was about seventy-five miles, and the time eight days, from November 24th to December 2d. But during this period much had been accomplished. Our troops left Milledgeville, according to the enemy, "admirably clothed and equipped. Each man had eighty rounds of ammunition, while their wagons contained fixed material without stint. Rations for forty days had been prepared, and they suffered for nothing." The cavalry with the left wing, on crossing the Oconee, had visited Sparta, which is on a line between Warrenton and Milledgeville, about equidistant from both. On the evening of the 24th, General Slocum's advance encamped at Devereux, seven miles west of Sparta, and the cavalry scoured the whole country, one of the most fertile and thickly settled in the whole State, and vast quantities of forage and provisions, many horses, and mules were obtained, and much cotton burned. For several days our cavalry raided through the entire country between the two railroads in the vicinity last described. Abundance of food and forage was secured, and every thing was destroyed which could be useful to the enemy. The march was leisurely—Sherman evidently finding himself master of the situation. He did not start directly for the seaboard until he had all the provisions he desired, and had inflicted great loss on the enemy.

The enemy now began to look on Sherman's progress with some despair; for he was ready to enter upon the third and last stage of his march. Behind him the Georgia Central lay destroyed for more than a hundred miles, and the Georgia road for full sixty. The railroad bridge over the Oconee and the Ogeechee, on the Georgia Central, had been destroyed, and also those over Brier Creek and Buckhead Creek on the Waynesboro Branch connecting Augusta with Millen. Incalculable damage had been done to the enemy. His troops were driven off. Ours were fresh and enthusiastic. It only remained to move down to the Atlantic, and add the crowning glory to the campaign in the capture of Savannah.

From Millen, then, on the 2d of December, the army swung southerly down on the final stage of its journey to Savannah, in half a dozen columns, moving over as many different roads for the sake of convenience and speed. The enemy massed at Augusta was left hopelessly in Sherman's rear. The army was protected on either flank by a large river, and cavalry formed the van-guard and rear-guard. Its mission as a curtain for the concealment of infantry operations had now been accomplished. The country traversed was covered with pine forests, cut up by numerous creeks, and intersected by wide stretches of swamps;

and farther on, the coastwise swamps and the low rice-fields became the prevalent character of the region. West and south of the Ogeechee, Osterhaus's Fifteenth Corps moved on in advance, and meanwhile the Georgia Central Road was steadily destroyed, mile after mile. This was partially laid with the U-rail and partly with a light T-rail, fastened to parallel stringers fixed to the ties. The Augusta and Atlanta Road was of a heavier T-rail. Many of the station-houses destroyed were substantially built of brick. The destruction of the Georgia Railroad was absolutely *thorough*. It was accomplished by devoting all the time to it which it required. Usually, rails are destroyed by armies by laying them across piles of burning sleepers, when their own weight will bend them. But, lest this should not be effectual, other methods have been devised, of which an officer gives this account:—

"Instruments have been made; one is a clasp which locks under the rail. It has a ring in the top into which is inserted a long lever, and the rail is thus ripped from the sleepers. When the rail has become heated, a wrench is applied which fits close over the ends of the rail; by turning them in opposite directions the rail is so twisted that even a rolling machine could not bring it back into shape. In this manner have been destroyed some thirty miles of rails which lay in the city of Atlanta, and also all the rails on the Augusta and Atlanta road from the last-named place to Madison; and thus far the Georgia Central road, from a few miles east of Macon to Terryville Station, where I am now writing."

Near Monteith Station, ten miles from Savannah, the left wing struck the Charleston Railroad, and encountered the enemy's skirmishers strongly posted in a swamp near by, which indicated the presence of the enemy's forces under Hardee for the first time. The right wing had also reached this outer line of the enemy's Savannah works, and it was swept away at all points. Torpedoes, concealed in the road by the enemy, wounded some of our men in approaching the city. On the 8th, the advance heard the signal guns of our gunboats in Ossabaw Sound. On the 9th, Captain Duncan started down the Ogeechee, and reached Admiral Dahlgren on the morning of the 12th. On the 10th, Sherman lay in line of battle confronting the outer works of Savannah, about five miles distant from the city.

The army now gradually closed in upon Savannah, driving the enemy before them in sharp skirmishing, for he resisted our advance with pertinacity. Howard had already gained, on the 8th, the canal on the west of the city. As we drew our lines in, the natural and artificial obstructions to our approach increased. The rice-fields below the city had been flooded from the canals, and west and north of it were impenetrable swamps. The openings between the morasses and the roads traversing them were defended by heavy guns, and were vigorously contested. But nothing could resist the *élan* of our troops, who, fresh, vigorous, and enthusiastic, vied with each other for the honor of being first in the city, and crawled forward at every point a little nearer each day. But Sherman's eye had seen instantly that we must open communication with the fleet. Fort McAllister, an earthwork of great strength on the Ogeechee, six miles from Ossabaw Sound, interfered with the project. Sherman at once ordered it to be carried by assault; and while Admiral Dahlgren was working his way slowly up, to attack Savannah by water, he was surprised, on the 13th of December, to find, as he expressed it in his dispatch, that Sherman "had just walked over the fort."

On the 12th, Hazen's (Second) Division of Osterhaus's Fifteenth Corps (Sherman's own old corps) was selected for the important work of carrying Fort McAllister. Having marched the previous day and night a distance of fifteen miles, at half-past four o'clock of the 13th the division went forward to the assault, another division supporting, over an open space of more than five hundred yards, swept by the fire of many heavy guns. Through a thick and extended abatis, and across a deep ditch with its bottom planted with sharp palisades which they wrenched away, Hazen's troops rushed with great gallantry at the double-quick. The fort was approached and stormed from all sides. It was most desperately defended by its gallant handful of troops. But had their numbers been tenfold, they could not have checked the enthusiastic rush of our troops, who had gone to the attack sure of success, for Sherman himself had ordered the assault, and witnessed the execution of the order from the top of a house not far distant; and as soon as he saw our gallant men on the parapets, he exclaimed to his staff, "The fort is ours! Order me a boat—I am going down to the fleet."

Torpedoes had been spread along the approaches but they did not check the advance. In less than thirty minutes from the start our flag was waving on the ramparts of the fort, with its garrison of about two hundred men, its full complement of heavy guns, its stores of ordnance and subsistence, and its camp and garrison equipage in our hands.

The navigation of the Ogeechee was secured, and Sherman was able to open a water base at any point on that river. He chose naturally King's Bridge, which Howard held, on the right. Such were the advantages of the prompt assault of Sherman. He took it at a moment when it had not half its proper garrison, a single day's delay might have so re-enforced it as to render its capture a bloody affair. The slow process of regular approach would have been no less fatal to us. As it was, our loss was less than one hundred men.

This successful achievement inspired the whole army with the greatest spirit. Sherman on reaching the fleet sent off the following dispatch:—

"ON BOARD DANDELION, OSSABAW SOUND,
"*December* 13, 11.50 P. M.

"To-day, at 5 P. M., General Hazen's Division of the Fifteenth Corps carried Fort McAllister by assault, capturing its entire garrison and stores. This opened to us the Ossabaw Sound, and I pushed down to this gunboat to communicate with the fleet. Before opening communication, we had completely destroyed all the railroads leading into Savannah, and invested the city. The left is on the Savannah River, three miles above the city, and the right on the Ogeechee, at King's Bridge.

"The army is in splendid order, and equal to any thing. The weather has been fine, and supplies were abundant. Our march was most agreeable, and we were not at all molested by guerrillas.

"We reached Savannah three days ago, but, owing to Fort McAllister, could not communicate; but now, having Fort McAllister, we can go ahead. We have already captured two boats on the Savannah River, and prevented their gunboats from coming down.

"I estimate the population of Savannah at twenty-five thousand, and the garrison at fifteen thousand—General Hardee commands.

"We have not lost a wagon on the trip, but have gathered in a large supply of negroes, mules, horses, &c., and our teams are in far better condition than when we started.*

"My first duty will be to clear the army of surplus negroes, mules, and horses. We have utterly destroyed over two hundred miles of rails, and consumed stores and provisions that were essential to Lee's and Hood's armies. The quick work made with McAllister, and the opening of communication with our fleet, and the consequent independence for supplies, dissipates all their boasted threats to head me off and starve the army.

"I regard Savannah as already gained.

"Yours, truly,
"W. T. SHERMAN, *Major-General.*"

The capture of Savannah was now assured—and the promises of Sherman, confident as they seemed, were received with entire faith by his government and by the people of the North. Indeed, he had now invested the city on all but the eastern side. His right held King's Bridge, far in the rear of Savannah, and controlled the Ogeechee, whence his lines stretched across to the Savannah River, his left being about three miles above the city. He had cut off all the railroad supplies of Savannah. On the south, he had struck the Savannah, Albany, and Gulf Railroad, which formerly had transported large supplies of cattle and provisions from Florida to Savannah. The railroads from Augusta and Macon were thoroughly broken. Foster's batteries had gotten within shelling distance of the Charleston Railroad, and prevented the passage of trains. It only remained to move regularly upon the city by systematic approaches. It could not hope for outside succor of any kind. G. W. Smith, with eight thousand men, had, indeed, been on the other side of the Ogeechee, approaching the city, but Sherman's prompt seizure of Fort McAllister and of the command of the river prevented

---

* The mention of *negroes* in the same sentence with *mules* and *horses*, in this dispatch, gave some offence, and also occasioned sharp criticism in some Northern journals. But no offence was intended. Moses committed a similar blunder:—
"*Thou shalt not covet thy neighbor's house, thou shalt not covet thy neighbor's wife, nor his man-servant, nor his maid-servant, nor his ox, nor his ass, nor any thing that is his.*"
—EXODUS xx. 17.

these re-enforcements from reaching the beleaguered garrison. Rapidly our lines moved forward. The swamps and flooded rice-fields in our front made the approach difficult, while the enemy's gunboats and heavy batteries on the Savannah River, and the peculiar character of the river-banks, kept that side of the city open to him. From the 10th to the 16th, heavy artillery firing and skirmishing went on all along our lines, but no regular engagement occurred. On the 16th, Sherman formally demanded the city from its commander, Hardee, who declined next day to accede to the demand. Sherman instantly hurried more heavy siege-guns upon his lines, and on the 20th was prepared to bombard the city and assault its works. But Hardee had already taken the alarm. Finding that only the eastern exit was open to him, and on that Sherman was already cannonading, and soon might capture it by assault, Hardee resolved to evacuate Savannah. On the afternoon of the 20th his iron-clads and batteries opened a tremendous fire, lasting into the night, and, under cover of the demonstration, which served at once to expend ammunition and to allow the withdrawal of all but his artillerists from his outer lines, the Confederate general crossed his fifteen thousand men and his large force of negro laborers upon a pontoon-bridge, laid below his rear batteries, to the South Carolina side, and marched them off towards Charleston on the Union causeway. The night was exceedingly favorable for such a movement, it being very dark, with a west wind blowing. Next morning, at break of day, the pickets of Geary's Division crept forward, advanced still farther, and went over the works; and Geary himself, marching into Savannah, received, on the morning of the 21st December, 1864, its formal surrender at the hands of its Mayor. The troops were gone. The navy-yard, two iron-clads, many smaller vessels, and a vast amount of ammunition, ordnance stores, and supplies, had been destroyed before the evacuation, but all the rest of the uninjured city was ours. With characteristic terseness and *finesse*, Sherman announced his achievement in the following brief dispatch to the President:—

"*I beg to present you, as a Christmas gift, the city of Savannah, with one hundred and fifty heavy guns and plenty of ammunition, and also about twenty-five thousand bales of cotton.*"

Subsequently, on a more careful estimate, General Foster sent a fuller account to the War Department, which explained that Sherman had underestimated his captures. This account shows the captures to have been *eight hundred prisoners, one hundred and fifty guns, thirteen locomotives in good order, one hundred and ninety cars, a large supply of ammunition and materials of war, three steamers, and upwards of thirty-eight thousand bales of cotton.*

So gloriously ended the campaign through Georgia—from the

mountains to the sea. Long before its conclusion, it had placed Sherman at the head of American soldiers, not only in our opinion and in the opinion of our enemies, but in the opinion of Europe as well. History was ransacked, and ransacked in vain, for parallels to this audacious enterprise. The London *Times* pronounced Sherman " beyond a doubt, both an able and resolute soldier." The capture of Atlanta it styled "a remarkable success." It predicted, on his start for Savannah, "it would either make him the most famous general of the North, or be the ruin of his reputation and his cause." And while doubting the success of "this unparalleled march," it said, in still more pointed terms: " Since the great Duke of Marlborough turned his back upon the Dutch and plunged heroically into Germany, to fight the famous battle of Blenheim, military history has recorded no stranger marvel than the mysterious expedition of General Sherman on an unknown route against an undiscoverable enemy."

The *British Army and Navy Gazette* said of him:—

"It is clear, that, so long as he roams about with his army inside the Confederate States, he is more deadly than twenty Grants, and that he must be destroyed if Richmond or any thing is to be saved."*

And again it said —:

"If Sherman has really left his army in the air, and started off without a base from Georgia into South Carolina, he has done either one of the most brilliant or one of the most foolish things ever performed by a military leader. His success or his failure will not determine the question one way or the other. The data on which he goes, and the plan on which he acts, must really place him among the great generals or the very little ones, and, as yet, he has assuredly given indications that he is more likely to be found in the first than in the second category."

"We are still incredulous," says the *Richmond Examiner*, "but if it be true that Sherman is attempting this prodigious design, we may safely predict that his march will lead him to the Paradise of Fools,† and that his magnificent scheme will hereafter be reckoned

'With all the grand deeds that never were done.'"

The *London Herald*, in the words of its New York correspondent, said :—

"The name of the captor of Atlanta, if he fails now, will become the scoff of mankind and the humiliation of the United States for all time. If he succeeds, it will be written on the tablet of fame, side by side with that of Napoleon and Hannibal."

Still later, the London *Times* argued, from the insuperable

---

* But it was the purpose of Grant that Sherman should not run any risk of being destroyed, and hence he held Lee with his great army, as by a vice, at Richmond.
† Paradise of Fools!—he could hardly go amiss within the limits of the Southern Confederacy. Surely, a people who could lash themselves into fury and go to war against a benign government without cause, and against their best friends, far superior to themselves in power and resources, must inhabit that delectable Paradise.

difficulties in Sherman's course, that they were such as no general, however great, could be expected to overcome. It declared that Sherman's march seemed " to resemble the celebrated march of Napoleon in 1814 to St. Dizier, by which he threw himself upon the communications of the allied armies, then advanced upon Paris, and would, it is said, except for the intervention of Lord Castlereagh, have compelled their retreat at the very moment when the object of all their labors seemed to be within their grasp." It added:—

" If this enterprise be brought to a successful termination, General Sherman will undoubtedly be entitled to the honor of having added a fresh chapter to the theory and practice of modern warfare. But history also records very few instances indeed where operations of this kind have been crowned with success."

Finally—for of such speculative and laudatory opinions only examples can be given—Lieutenant-General Grant, before the news of the fall of Savannah had been received, and while Sherman was supposed to be still " floundering about " in the interior of Georgia, on the 22d of December wrote of him:—" The world's history gives no record of his superiors, and but few equals."*

And, indeed, a little reflection on the actual results of this wonderful campaign of a week and a month will show that no laudation yet lavished upon Sherman and upon his splendid army has surpassed their merits. Whether we look at the daring, the promptitude, and the originality of the strategic plan of the march; or to its wonderfully skilful detail of preparation; or to the admirable practical handling of the great columns all through the march, and the tactics displayed during the few times our troops met the enemy; or to the skilful opening of communication at Savannah; or to the vigor and ability of the final siege; or, greatest of all, to the astonishing results of the campaign upon the rebellion—results clearly defined, promptly developed, and absolutely fatal—we shall pronounce this march not only the greatest achievement of our American war, but one of the greatest achievements in the world's military record. Since William of Normandy crossed the English Channel to the conquest of the island, and burned his boats upon the shore; since Hernando Cortéz plunged into Mexico on that most astounding of expeditions, and stranded his ships at Vera Cruz, " thus taking away," as his published dispatches read, " all hope of leaving the country" from his handful of men, there has hardly been a parallel to Sherman's audacious plunge into Georgia, as he burned his base behind him, and cut the railroad chain that bound him to the North.

---

* And in this the Lieutenant-General shows his own greatness more conspicuously than Sherman's. In truth, our successes of the present and past year are attributable, in a great degree, to the fact that the two commanders of the two Union armies understand, appreciate, and have faith in each other.

But did Sherman do well or ill in this eccentric movement, that so attracted the attention of all America and Europe? Let us glance for a moment at the actual results already developed by the campaign. Its first and most striking result is the entire change of position wrought in the field of war. A large army had been advanced by Sherman into the heart of the enemy's country; but a great part of its force was rendered almost useless by guarding a line of supply of extraordinary and impracticable length. Whole regiments of this army had been discharged, their time having expired, and others were going home as fast as discharge-papers could be made out; and the Presidential election prevented re-enforcements from being promptly sent to take their places. The enemy, defeated and pushed back, had rallied again, had resumed the offensive, and had thrown himself on Sherman's communications. Sherman's situation was perplexing in the extreme. But with that quickness of perception for which he is so remarkable, and with that rapidity of execution which has characterized all his movements, Sherman snatched from the enemy the *prestige* of the offensive, and balked all his plans. He divided his army: with one-half, he beat and almost destroyed the entire forces of his opponent; with the other, amid the awe-struck gaze of two continents, he boldly plunged along a line of march of full three hundred miles to the Atlantic coast, without a possibility of succor in case of disaster, with no means of communication with his government, and with no attainable base except such as he could conquer at the far end of his projected route. With deliberate tread he descended from the Alleghany Mountains into the plains, and swept through Georgia with the sweep of a hurricane—a State much larger than England, nearly as large as England and Scotland together, more than twice as large as Prussia proper, one-third as large as Spain, and more than one-fourth as large as France. He bisected the Confederacy. He severed its railroad communications between East and West, not only for a time, but for the wars—absolutely and irreparably destroyed, rail by rail, the iron twisted and broken at the twist. All along his track, fifty miles in width, not a dépôt, locomotive, car, workshop, factory, foundry, storehouse, bale of cotton, or other thing of value to the enemy, was left. Fifteen thousand cattle and five thousand horses and mules were captured, and the country gleaned of its subsistence, and the army reached Savannah with its wagons full. To use the pithy phrase of a soldier after the march: "A jaybird couldn't now travel from Atlanta to Savannah without a haversack."

Arrived at Savannah, a city containing twenty thousand inhabitants, fortified and garrisoned, filled with supplies, ordnance stores, and cotton, he compelled its evacuation without a battle, and captured nearly one thousand prisoners, one hundred and fifty-two guns, thirty-eight thousand bales of cotton (valued at twenty-five million dollars), three fine steamers, thirteen locomotives in good order, one hundred and ninety cars, and an immense supply of ammunition, provisions, and materials of war; and compelled the enemy to blow up his navy yard, his ironclads, and many smaller craft, and compelled the destruction of other public property of the enemy to the value of many millions of dollars. Finally, he brought with him to Savannah twenty thousand slaves, the "owned labor" of the Confederacy—the hands that cleared the forest, planted the corn and cotton—the blacks who raised the bread upon which white rebels "waxed fat and kicked" themselves out of the Union—slaves, worth before the war, in hard cash, not less than twenty million dollars —an item of vast importance, since a people long accustomed to live by the labor of slaves alone are not themselves likely to raise the necessary subsistence for carrying on the war.

All these results were accomplished, not only with perfect order and system, but with an incredibly small loss of men and material. Our loss from all causes during the march was less than one thousand men, while the enemy's at the same time was more than double that of our own. Our loss at Fort McAllister was less than one hundred men, while the enemy's was much greater, omitting the prisoners. Finally, our loss during the siege was not more than six hundred, while the enemy's was nearly as great, and far exceeded ours, counting the prisoners captured at the taking of the city. Two thousand men will cover our whole loss for the campaign.

But this is not all. The army, so far from being exhausted by its efforts, arrived at Savannah, to use Sherman's own language, "in splendid order, and equal to any thing. The supplies were abundant; our march was most agreeable, and we were not at all molested by guerrillas." The march actually *saved* the country supplies, for the army lived on the enemy, and brought off new wagons and horses in plenty. "We have not lost a wagon on the trip, and our teams are in far better condition than when we started." Such was Sherman's style of campaigning. He lived upon the enemy during his route, destroyed what he could not bring away, easily beat the enemy with great loss whenever the latter attacked him, avoided the positions which the latter invited him to assault, except when necessary to his purpose, and brought off slaves enough to supply fourfold the gaps made in his ranks by service. Quartermaster-General Meigs says:—

"During this remarkable march, the cavalry and train found an abundance of forage and remounts, and the Chief Quartermaster, Brevet Brigadier-General Easton, reports from Savannah that the transportation is even in better condition than when the march commenced—better than he had ever before seen it. No horses or mules are required to refit the army after a march of near three hundred miles through a hostile district."

Even yet we have not reached the end of this wonderful story. The part of this double campaign, which Sherman had intrusted to Thomas, was admirably performed. Hood's army was thoroughly beaten, and his invasion of the North checked and repelled. In the two battles of Franklin and Nashville, and the subsequent retreat, the enemy lost, according to official count, from eighteen to twenty thousand men, while our loss was less than ten thousand, leaving a balance of eight to ten thousand men on our side of the account. Of prisoners alone we captured from him thirteen thousand one hundred and eighty-nine, including seven general officers and nearly one thousand other officers of inferior grades. By official count, Hood left seventy-two pieces of artillery in our hands. He lost nineteen general officers killed, besides a proportionate number of the field and line. About two hundred wagons and large stores of ammunition and supplies are to be added to the loss. He barely escaped entire destruction, with a ruined army which now is isolated from the grand field of operations, almost harmless, in Mississippi.

Sherman, on receiving the congratulations of the President, and also of his personal friends, on account of his wonderful success, and seeing himself greatly praised in the public journals at home and abroad, wrote:—

"I am now a great favorite because I have been successful; but if Thomas had not whipped Hood at Nashville, six hundred miles away, my plans would have failed, and I would have been denounced the world over."

And, when we consider the many vicissitudes of war, how often the speed of one corps or the inactivity of another mars the best-concerted plans, it will be seen how easy it is, by a slight change of circumstances, to convert a prospective hero into a ruined general. But the important trust had been confided to able hands. Sherman added:—

"But I knew General Thomas and the troops under his command, and never for a moment doubted a favorable result."

In his order of congratulation, Sherman counted the "honors even" with Thomas, and declared that any regiment in either army might inscribe on its banners either Nashville or Savannah, showing that he appreciated equally the armies of both, and recognized himself as commander of both.

And, finally, this double campaign, so happily devised by Sherman, and so admirably executed in all its parts, added new *prestige* to our arms, changed the whole theatre of the war, put a totally new phase on the rebellion, greatly influenced in our favor the public sentiment of Europe, carried dismay into the camps and firesides of the enemy, raised up a formidable peace party in the South, set Davis and his Confederate Congress by the ears, and inspired the whole North with renewed hope and confidence.

Nor does it end with the capture of Savannah. More wonderful still, at the moment of this writing, Sherman has led his victorious army on through the very heart of the State of South Carolina, driving all opposition before him; Columbia, its beautiful capital, is fallen; Charleston, that famous city at which we have been pounding away, day and night, for four years, has yielded to his matchless strategy without a blow; and, as yet, without a single disaster, he plants the Union standards almost within sight of Raleigh, the capital of North Carolina, and has largely aided Grant in the consummation of that campaign which has captured Richmond, conquered Lee, and given the death-blow to the great rebellion.

A WORD FOR THE QUARTERMASTER'S DEPARTMENT.

IV.

THESE remarks on water transportation conduct us naturally to the consideration of the whole system of *employés*, as now existing in the Quartermaster's Department. We are constrained to say, that from what observation and experience of it we have had, we deem the system both faulty and bad, for a variety of reasons, but chiefly because, first, it results in such short periods of service—seldom more than six months, and usually less than three—and chronic discharges, with the consequent burden and cost to the Government of such multiplied transportation and subsistence; and, secondly, because, after all, it gives to the Government a man who, in truth, is neither a soldier nor yet a civilian, possessing the vices of both to a very great extent, with no assurance of the virtues of either. True, the Articles of War declare that all persons serving with the army, in whatever capacity, shall be held amenable to "the rules and discipline of war;" but experience shows that this provision is mostly a mere *brutum fulmen*—practically a dead letter—at all posts and dépôts, and that Government employés, as a class, are the most unruly, improvident, not to say vicious and insubordinate men, within the lines of the army. When serving with troops in the field, as laborers, teamsters, or otherwise, they are often a source of perpetual trouble and annoyance to the officer in charge of them. Being better paid than the common soldier, without his direct liability to danger, there is always a festering quarrel between them that is continually breaking out into brawls and fights, where the employés, of course, as the feebler party, usually get worsted. In camp, on the most frivolous of pretexts, they are constantly seeking furloughs and discharges, especially if any active campaign, with its heavy marches and continual changes, appears to be impending. In time of danger, they are practically worthless, *vide* Bull Run, as they are sure to become demoralized at the first sight of cavalry, and to stampede for their lives at the first shriek of shell. Indeed, the concurrent testimony of officers, who have studied the subject at all, is that the best employé by far, for most ordinary duties, whether at post or in the field, is the detailed soldier; the next best, the "intelligent contraband;" and the worst of all, infinitely and in all respects, except where required as *exports*, the hired civilian. The result is a constant fight, in most commands, between the Quartermaster and the Inspector-General—the one, with his eye keen to his own success, *resolved* that he will have all the detailed soldiers he can get, for the current purposes of his bedevilled department, as mechanics, teamsters, laborers, &c.—the other, with his mind bent on keeping the fullest ranks possible, equally *resolved* that "the d——d Quartermaster" shan't have any."

Now the natural escape from all this, and the true solution, as we believe, of the vexed *employé* question, lies undeveloped as yet in the new "Organization of Quartermaster's Employés into a Military Force." This organization, as yet, is in its infancy, and, therefore, necessarily but rough and imperfect; but it contains, we believe, the seeds of great and lasting results, if only logically developed and enforced, as to us seems possible enough anywhere, without much real difficulty. Some idea of such an organization, but of all civil employés in the Government, for military duty in cases of emergency, appears to have occurred to the people at Washington, so long ago as 1862; but it was without much practical result, until the summer of 1864, when Early crossed the Potomac and one fine morning menaced the capital from the north. Then the employés of the Quartermaster's Department there, and perhaps of some others to a limited extent, though we are without sufficient data to speak intelligently of any others, were hastily organized into two brigades, and incontinently hurried to the trenches. They were kept there several days, and, it is reported, behaved very well under fire, all things considered; at least so much was the Secretary pleased with their conduct, that he ordered the organization to be maintained, and soon after he tendered to its officers honorary commissions in the service of the United States. About the same time, but long after Sherman had moved out from Chattanooga, a similar military organization of Quartermaster's employés, by the direction of General Thomas, was begun at Nashville, for local defence of the dépôt there against outbreaks or attack in case of necessity, the usual garrison at Nashville, and everywhere else throughout the Military Division of the Mississippi, having been depleted to the utmost by General

Sherman before starting for Atlanta, in order to swell the aggregate of his actual army in the field. By a general order from the Chief Quartermaster there, all able-bodied employés of the department, fit for military duty, were required to be organized into companies and regiments; and these were afterwards reduced to one division of three brigades, because of certain local peculiarities of the regimental organizations. Subsequently, when, late in August, Wheeler turned Sherman, then before Atlanta, and passed north by Chattanooga, and so around to near Nashville about the middle of September, this organization, on an hour's or so notice, put five thousand (5,000) men under arms, and of itself could have held Nashville against any force that Wheeler could then have brought against it. Later, in November, when Forrest attacked Johnsonville, and reenforcements for that post were not to be had elsewhere, it sent nearly one thousand (1,000) infantry and a section of artillery, all volunteers, to aid in its defence. Later still, when Hood appeared before Nashville, it promptly put over four thousand (4,000) men at work on the fortifications, and would have mustered fully seven thousand (7,000) strong, had not one brigade been excused from duty, for special reasons. It kept them there nearly a fortnight, off and on; and so well did Thomas appreciate their worth and services, that when preparing for battle at Nashville, he specially assigned this organization of Quartermaster's forces, the same as any other body of troops, to hold a portion of his interior line. It happened that the organization was not brought further than this into action at Nashville; but had occasion required, it would, no doubt, have acquitted itself at least creditably, as fully one-half of its men, and more of its *quasi* officers, were old soldiers, or officers of the Army, honorably discharged or mustered out after due term of service.

If, then, such a military organization of Quartermaster's employés is possible at Washington and Nashville, why is it not also possible at other dépôts and posts, and, in short, everywhere? The working force of employés at any post or dépôt is, of course, always proportioned to its importance; and so, the importance of a post or dépôt always determines the strength of its garrison. The force of employés at Washington and Nashville during the past year was varied from ten thousand (10,000) to fifteen thousand (15,000), with a preponderance usually of a thousand or two in favor of Nashville. Of these, fully one-third, and generally one-half, have been ordinary able-bodied men, fit at least for such light military duty as mere local defence usually requires. The same is, of course, true, relatively, of all other posts and dépôts throughout the Union. If, then, these men were thoroughly organized, and tolerably drilled, so as to be fairly reliable, why might they not take the place of permanent garrisons everywhere, to all intents and purposes, except so much of the same as might be required for care of forts, and for special guard and provost duty? The number of troops thus specially required, as everybody knows, is comparatively small anywhere, and thus the swarms of our non-combatant soldiery, the opprobrium of our muster-rolls nowadays, though withheld necessarily from duty in the field under existing circumstances, would soon be reduced at all points to the minimum. In other words, to state the case a little differently, the force of civil employés, at any given place, has to be always sufficiently large to make almost an adequate garrison for that place, if only fit to serve as soldiers. They *can* be made *fit* to serve as soldiers, as experience has demonstrated, if only well organized and tolerably drilled; and thus you would save to the army the bulk of our scattered garrisons, while at the same time you would secure to the public service the trusty soldier, instead of the nondescript insubordinate hybrid, yclept " Government employé."

In point of economy, we think it could be demonstrated, without difficulty, that the adoption of some such plan (details are not important) would result in a decided, not to say vast, saving to the Government. We have not the data by us now to give actual figures, but the facts involved can be readily illustrated. For example, suppose an important post or dépôt requires ordinarily a garrison of say five thousand (5,000) men. Such a post or dépôt, experience shows, would usually have a working force of from ten thousand (10,000) to twelve thousand (12,000) civil employés in the Quartermaster's Department alone. At least one-half of these may be relied on as fit for local military duty, and thus you have your garrison at once, composed of men who are convertible into either troops or operatives, as the occasion requires. One good regiment of infantry, a thousand or so strong, and a company or so of artillery, would ordinarily suffice at such a post or dépôt, for guard and provost duty, and necessary care of forts, and thus you release some four thousand (4,000) men instantly for duty in the field. Now, " a penny *saved* is a penny *gained*," and so four thousand (4,000) men saved by any means for field duty, are practically four thousand (4,000) men recruited for the army, with all the cost of recruiting, in the way of bounties, transportation, clothing, subsistence, pay, &c., the most of which items continue to run on throughout the entire term of enlistment, saved altogether to the Government. Of course, we would have clothing, subsistence, pay, &c., to provide for our employé force, if thus militarily organized; but all this, in some form or other, has to be provided for employés now, without any return of military services, and the usual pay of clerks, superintendents, foremen, &c., in the various staff departments, quite equals on the average, if it does not exceed, the established pay and allowances of commissioned officers of the line. In other words, to put the case a little differently, the same men that now, as civilians, do the work of artisans, mechanics, teamsters, laborers, &c., would, as soldiers, at the same or less cost of wages, perform even better service, and at the same time would be available as an almost equivalent body of troops in case of emergency or necessity. From this approximation, however, the reader will recollect is to be deducted, of course, the value of the time spent in occasional drills, reviews, &c.; but this is a mere driblet, compared with the immense saving thus rudely indicated.

Holding these facts to be substantially indisputable, we return to the proposition we set out with, namely, that in some such a military organization, and only in *such*, lies the true solution of the vexed employé question, as now existing in the Quartermaster's Department, and, for that matter, in all the other staff departments as well. In other words, instead of employés being *hired*, as now, oftentimes at exorbitant wages, and generally for such short periods of service that usually their "time is out" before getting to be really worth much to the Government, we insist that all employés, of whatever Staff Departments, should be regularly enlisted or drafted, the same as soldiers—organized, clothed, armed, equipped, and drilled, the same as soldiers—collected in convenient and central depôts, for transfer on call, the same as soldiers—required to work ordinarily as employés, as now, with designated days or hours for drills and reviews, but held ready to shoulder the musket and fight as soldiers also, if necessary; in short, the same, in all proper respects, for all current purposes of the army, except positive field duty, as ordinary American soldiers. They might require a special uniform, or at least badge, to distinguish them from ordinary soldiers of the line, and the same proficiency in drill, &c., would not, of course, be expected of them; but these and other minor conditions are merely matters of detail, and would readily adjust themselves.

These remarks on the employé question have already been extended too far, in our eagerness thoroughly to elucidate the subject, and we have only to add further, by way of summing up, that the proposed reform, in our judgment, carries with it the following practical arguments: First, subordination and discipline among Government employés, now confessedly a sham in most instances; second, uniformity in time and wages, the depôts of the army over, instead of the strangest and most incongruous variety, as now; third, the abolition of non-combatant garrisons, to a great extent, everywhere, and the keeping of almost the total effective strength of our armies constantly in the field, instead of frittering them away, as now, piecemeal by piecemeal, *pari passu*, as we penetrate into Rebeldom; and fourth, increased economy in the public expenditures, in a variety of ways, not only in the first cost of such a force, as against the combined cost of *both* employés and soldiers, as now, but also in the better attention to duty, and less wear and tear of public property on the part of men long enough and tight enough in the public service to acquire the habits and instincts of the "set-up" soldier. We need scarcely say that we deem the subject one of great importance, and as such commend this discussion of it to the attention of brother officers.

In taking up, next, the *appointment* of officers, we feel that we are entering on delicate ground. But the best friend of the department will scarcely deny that here also there is some room for improvement. In the first year or two of the war especially, many officers crept into the department, who, in our judgment, had much better have remained elsewhere. Not that the Quartermaster's Department, in the main, suffered any more in this respect, perhaps, than other staff departments, or than the line either, for that matter; nevertheless, it *did* get some incompetents and *imbeciles*, not to say worse, that were, to say the least, very poor timber to make a quartermaster out of. We remember an amusing instance of one who, it is reported, after quartermastering for some months, being called on from Washington for some rendition of his accounts, after puzzling his brains with the forms in the regulations for weeks without mentionable success, finally chucked his returns, invoices, receipts, special regulations, and every thing else of that nature, into a barrel, and, heading it up, forwarded it to the Quartermaster-General, with a letter of transmittal about as follows: "Herewith General Meigs will please find my accounts. He can open the barrel at either end, and go through either way; but, if he can make any thing out of its contents, it is a thunderin' sight more than I can do!" We have heard of another, who forwarded his mixed-up accounts to Washington, with a polite request to General Meigs personally "to please make out (his) first set of papers" for him, and he would compensate him liberally.* We know of another, of our own acquaintance, a pretty good sort of an individual, but of great innocence and stupidity, who, after a twelvemonth or so of much tribulation, because overwhelmed with a business he did not know any thing about, finally tendered his resignation, and as explanatory thereof used to discourse to his acquaintances as follows: "I have been a teacher, and a minister of the Gospel for nearly twenty years, and know that I, of all others, ought not to speak so; and yet, after twelve months' hard experience of quarter-

---

* A somewhat similar story is told of the rebel General Marmaduke, when serving as a quartermaster in the old army.

master's affairs, I must be allowed the expression, d—n the Quartermaster's Department!"

Neither do we suppose, to return to our subject, that the officers appointed for the volunteer corps were as a class much poorer, if any, than those appointed for the regular corps; for, we have in our mind, as we write, at least three officers of the volunteer force who began the war as regimental quartermasters, and since then have passed successively up, through brigade, division, corps, and army, to Department Head-quarters, and have maintained themselves at least creditably everywhere; while we know at least two regular officers of several years standing who began the war at Army Head-quarters, in some capacity or other, but who have since dropped down successively, through all the intermediate grades, until now the Chief Quartermasters of their departments would not intrust either of them with even a petty post or brigade. But the facts as to much carelessness in the past, in the appointment of quartermasters, nevertheless are as we have above stated them to be, and Congress fairly surpassed itself last summer when it passed an act providing for an Examining Board for all officers of the various Staff Departments, *now in the service.* This law is good, as it now stands, and we thus heartily commend it. But, in our judgment, it should go a step farther, and prohibit all staff appointments, no matter on whose recommendations, except after a satisfactory examination as to character and qualifications, first had before a board of competent officers.

We think Congress would do this thing if it would divest itself somewhat of politics, and look just a little into the heavy responsibilities, both pecuniary and otherwise, that are liable to devolve any moment upon officers of the Quartermaster's Department. Their direct *money* responsibility alone, in many instances we could name, amounts frequently to millions of dollars monthly; while their *property* responsibility, in the way of equipage, clothing, forage, animals, &c., pretty much always runs up into almost the incalculable. All this alone, mark you, apart from the fearful responsibility of sustaining or ruining an army, according as the Quartermaster's Department bears itself well or ill. Now, in civil life, we all know, such grave responsibilities, such "heavy jobs of work," to be a little Carlylean, would be intrusted only to men of approved ability and unsullied character. Why, then, should not the same rule hold equally good, or rather, *more* so, in military life? Not that we think officers of the Quartermaster's Department any worse than other army officers, nor nearly so bad as men in civil life, of equal standing, intrusted with the same opportunities for "bribery and corruption." But, we submit that, at this stage of the war at least, when good men to choose from are plentiful as blackberries in August, no man should be appointed an assistant quartermaster, no matter what the influence of himself or friends, unless he can show a reputation, like Cæsar's wife, "above suspicion," and has been amply tested as to his capacity, either as a regimental quartermaster in the field, or as leading clerk at some important post or dépôt. Many of these last, from their varied and wide experience in the heaviest of Government transactions, possess splendid qualifications for making dépôt officers; and the department could not do a wiser thing than to recruit its dépôt officers, to a very great extent, from this ready source. We know many chief clerks, faithful and able men, to whom their officers owe almost all the reputation they have as quartermasters, and who are the best of assistant quartermasters to-day in all but the name, "ready made" to its hands, if the Government were only shrewd enough to issue them commissions. In every thing but commissions, they are *de facto* quartermasters to-day, and of themselves pretty much "run the machines" of the officers they are serving with, except the mere mechanical signing of papers. If Mr. Lincoln and Congress do not know this, we think "the time has come" for quietly telling them of it; and we know that Meigs and the Third Auditor would thank them ten thousand times a day, and every hour in the day, if, in making their future appointments, they would both only "govern themselves accordingly." A quartermaster manufactured from either of the classes above indicated would be iron-clad to begin with, well posted in the vast and intricate machinery of the most complex department of the Government, and in nine cases out of ten, not to say ninety-nine out of a hundred, would be worth at least a brigade of new appointees, fresh from the wards of New York or the prairies of Illinois.

In the matter of *rank*, concerning which the department had hitherto been badly off, Congress last summer did something, and will probably do more, when it fairly wakes up. It did the right thing, when it constituted Bureaus in the Quartermaster-General's office, thus dividing and distributing the work, that no one human brain could possibly digest and dispose of promptly; and the good results are already apparent in greater system and much quicker work there. It also was a wise thing to create inspectors with the rank of colonel, though it should have at least double the number, and also to give increased rank to officers charged with the care of divisions in the field, important dépôts, armies, or departments. It had already, some two years before created sufficient rank for chief quartermasters of army corps. But it should also now at once proceed to provide additional rank for ALL officers serving at important dépôts, as well as the chief quartermasters thereof, and the department will never rest content until this simple measure of justice is done. As it is now, subordinate officers at the largest dépôts, though charged in frequent instances with the care and responsibility of millions of dollars, of both money and property, are only entitled to the rank of captain; and for the absolutely priceless services thus rendered, they receive from the Government the petty pay and allowances of one hundred and twenty-five dollars and fifty cents ($125.50) per month, tax off—*less*, by at least one-fourth, than they are allowed and usually compelled to pay their chief clerks and cashiers, neither of whom, of course, has any direct responsibility whatever. Now all right-minded men will allow that this is simply infamous; and Congress, we submit, *must* set the matter right without unseemly delay. Otherwise the Government will soon lose many of its best and worthiest officers, who are too proud to steal, and yet who will not consent much longer to starve. Indeed, it has already lost several that we could name, who have quit the service in disgust, while serving at important posts or dépôts, because of their humiliating rank and pay, so meanly disproportioned in all respects to the labor and responsibility exacted at their hands.

In this connection, while treating of *rank*, we must not forget to notice that the rank created by this recent legislation, above referred to, is, however, only temporary rank, and, *as such*, liable to lapse with change of position. Nevertheless, even with this proviso, it is a real step in the right direction, because of its future promise; for time will no doubt bring with it further legislation, to make absolute the rank thus conferred. It is a proverb, that "great bodies move slowly," and so "great" a body as our modern Congress, must be given ample time for cogitation and reflection, before it can be brought to see what is just and right, where increase of rank or pay to officers is involved. No further action by Congress in the premises would be simply illogical, and, without additional legislation, its action already had would be the merest of mockeries and the cruelest of shams. Because, from the very nature and constitution of things, no officer can hold rank in the army, and be afterwards deprived of it, without being in a measure disgraced, no matter what his personal merit; and it is as cruel and unjust to expect a chief quartermaster, or an inspector with the rank of colonel, to relapse to his captaincy again, when, in the course of events, by the whim of a new commanding or quartermaster general, or the decrease of his dépôt, or the dissolution of his command, he falls to a division or a brigade again, as it would be for a brigadier-general to relapse to a colonelcy, when his commanding general prefers some other brigadier, or, by the fortune of war, his original brigade becomes depleted to the ordinary aggregate of a marching regiment. Rank, if *any* thing, and in the army it is *every* thing, must be fixed and absolute. You may adopt, but cannot possibly maintain any other rule. It is all very well for Burns to say:

> "Rank is but the guinea's stamp,
> A man's a man for a' that!"

But it is not *true* in army life, and in the very nature of things cannot be. A brigadier may be an ignoramus, and in many cases *is;* but he is a brigadier still, and all officers of inferior rank, no matter what their parts, must yield in every thing to the glitter of his stars. "A man," in the army, is not "a man," is simply nothing without rank; and therefore, if you give it to him once, you cannot reduce him without inflicting the keenest of cruelties. The remedy is plain: and that is, give to every officer the rank he seems fairly entitled to; and if he proves incompetent, or you have no further use for him, no matter what his position, whether chief quartermaster or major-general, muster him out, or dismiss him incontinently. But, in the name of common sense, as well as common justice, do not reduce him, if you intend him to continue on in the service; for you cannot reduce an officer, no matter what his grade, without fixing upon him a seeming stigma, that will goad, and harass, and annoy, if not—in the end—for all army purposes, ruin him forever. Better by far, a thousand times, return him to civil life at once, and let him begin anew.

We make these remarks thus earnestly, because we happen to know several excellent officers already who have been deeply injured for life by the working of this anomalous rank, without fault or cause on their part, in any way, but solely from the accident of an accident, so to speak, such as a change of commanding generals, or the dissolution of the command; and therefore we think the law referred to calls for speedy correction in the features indicated. But we have faith in the good sense and the justice of Congress, to set this anomaly all right ultimately, and that right soon, and cannot believe we are going to be disappointed. Meanwhile, let the Quartermaster's Department thank our Solons for even this "half a loaf," which is evidently better than no bread at all, when a man is actually starving; especially, if it be but the *first fruits* of better things to come.

We have thus run hastily through the Quartermaster's Department, distributing praise or censure, as we judged it due, and now conclude. There are several other topics we would like to discuss, especially the subject of United States Military Telegraphs and Railroads, but have no time for them now. Our work, we know, has been done inadequately, and very imperfectly; but we have done the best we could in the press of daily duty, and are wholly satisfied, if, by any thing we have said, the reader has been brought to a juster and truer appreciation of the worth and dignity of mere Bureau work.

MILITARY SURRENDERS AND PAROLES.

We propose to discuss in this article the subject of military surrenders and paroles, in their relations to the laws, military regulations and orders of the United States, and to the rules and usages established by International Laws and the Laws of War.

I. SURRENDERS.

Military surrenders are of two kinds: those which are the immediate result of force, and made unconditionally, and those which are upon conditions agreed upon between the parties.

Publicists apply the term capitulation to the formal agreement entered into by a commanding officer for the surrender, on certain specified conditions, of an army, a fortress, a town, or a district of country; and they say, in general terms, that the authority to make such agreements falls within the implied powers of such chief commander. This is true, inasmuch as regards the captor, and the forces, places, and things, of which he actually possesses himself under the conditions of such capitulations. They are to him legal *captures*, not by virtue of the capitulation, but by virtue of actual military possession. The title to military captures of this kind does not depend upon the mode or means of getting possession of them, whether by force of arms, by surprise, or by surrender, but rather to the actual possession itself.

But this supposed or implied power of the commander who capitulates, binds his own government and those whom he agrees to surrender only in a very limited degree. If he has exceeded the powers actually conferred upon him, or acted in violation of the instructions given him, or of the laws and regulations of his government and service, he may be punished, and his acts disavowed. It should be observed, however, that if his government takes advantage of, or willingly profits by, any one part of the agreement, it is bound by the whole instrument, and must execute all the other parts. But even where the capitulation is within the usually implied powers of the commander, if the orders or instructions of his government, not to agree upon certain specified conditions, are brought to the knowledge of the captor before the surrender, he cannot claim the performance of these conditions from the opposing belligerents, nor can the captured claim the benefit of stipulations which he knew the captor had no authority, express or implied, to grant.

In regard to the persons immediately affected by the capitulation, they are, in general, at liberty either to accept or to reject the conditions agreed upon, for no commander has a right to enforce the surrender of those under him. For example, suppose a general commanding a district of country enters into a capitulation for the surrender of his own immediate post, and also of other posts within the same district under the direct command of his subordinate officers, they being permitted to retain their arms, baggage, &c., and to march out " with all the honors of war," but not again to bear arms against the captor till duly exchanged, &c., &c. The commander of the subordinate and detached post is under no obligation to accept these conditions. He is at perfect liberty to repudiate the capitulation of his superior, and to refuse to surrender his post. By doing so, he subjects himself to no punishment, to no pains or penalties, but simply to the ordinary chances of war and siege. But, in refusing to surrender under the capitulation, he deprives himself and his command of all the benefits of that capitulation, and cannot claim its conditions in favor of himself or his command. His final surrender is a separate and distinct affair, having no necessary relation to the previous capitulation which he has repudiated or refused to accept.

By the Roman law, whosoever surrendered a fort, castle, garrison, or place committed to his trust, incurred capital punishment; " which, nevertheless," says Bruce, " is undoubtedly to be taken with this limitation, that he is not thereto pressed by extreme and invincible necessity. For, in that case (as when provisions fail, or such breaches are made in the fortifications as threaten a sudden storm, &c.), it is surely far better service to a prince or state to yield a little to necessity, and reserve their persons to serve more successfully at another time, than to madly run the risk of utter excision, by the conquering swords of an enraged enemy."

The English law under Queen Elizabeth on this subject was, "That whosoever shall surrender any Town or Fortification, which they are commanded to defend, or speak Words, or make a Shew towards a Surrender, or dispute the Order of the Garrison, they shall dy for it." "But," says Bruce, "all this is to be understood with the above exception of extreme necessity. And therefore it was that those gallant men who sustained a three years and a half's siege of Ostend, were after the surrender, upon very honorable terms, received by that great Captain, Maurice, Prince of Orange, not as vanquished, but as men wearied with repeated victories."

The authority of a general in actual campaign, or on the battle-field, to enter into stipulations for the surrender of the several portions of his command, is much more limited than that of a governor of a town or fortress, or of a commander of a distant and isolated district of country. Here there are no supposed or implied powers; all the authority he can exercise is direct, immediate, and limited. Unlike the case of investment and siege, with a threatened bombardment or assault, he cannot command the surrender either of his officers or of is troops without their consent. A general who surrenders or his taken prisoner has no right to control the conduct of those who do not surrender and are not taken prisoners. He can merely negotiate terms for those who actually surrender or are taken prisoners with him. Others may accept or reject these terms as they deem proper.

In the campaign of 1756, the Prussian general, Finck, was surrounded at Maxen, and capitulated for the surrender of himself and his entire army. His cavalry had forced a passage, but as it was included in the capitulation, it returned and laid down its arms. General Finck was subsequently tried for making this capitulation, found guilty of improper conduct, and sentenced to be deprived of all his military dignities, and to two years' imprisonment.

Napoleon's remarks on this affair, in Chapter V. of his Commentaries on the Wars of Frederick the Great, are interesting and instructive, and should be read again and again by every military student. We make some extracts from these Commentaries:—

"A question of the utmost importance arises here. Do the laws and principles of war authorize a general to order his soldiers to lay down their arms and yield to their enemies, and to constitute a whole corps prisoners of war? There can be no such doubt with respect to the garrison of a fortified place; but the governor of a place is in a peculiar situation. The laws of all nations authorize him to lay down arms when his provisions fail, when the defences of the place are demolished, and when he has sustained several assaults. In fact, a fortified place is a military machine which forms a whole, has peculiar functions, and a prescribed, definite, and known destination. A small number of men, protected by this fortification, defend themselves, stop the enemy, and preserve the deposit intrusted to them against the attacks of a great number of men; but when these fortifications are destroyed, and no longer afford protection to the garrison, it is just and reasonable to authorize the commandant to do what he judges most for the interest of his troops."

* * * * * * * *

"In proof that the laws and practice of all nations have specially authorized commandants of fortified places to surrender their arms on conditions stipulated for their benefit, and that they have never authorized any general to order his men to lay down their arms in any other case, it may be advanced that no prince, no republic, no military law, has ever authorized them to do so. The sovereign or the nation prescribes to the soldiers and to the inferior officer, obedience towards their general and their superiors for all purposes conducive to the interest or the honor of the service. When the soldier receives his arms, he takes the military oath to defend them till death. A general has received orders and instructions to employ his troops in the defence of his country; how, then, can he be empowered to order his soldiers to give up their arms, and to submit to chains?

"There is seldom a battle in which some companies of light infantry or grenadiers, and frequently whole battalions, are not for a short time surrounded in houses, cemeteries, or woods. Any captain or lieutenant colonel who should enter into a capitulation as soon as it became evident that he was surrounded, would betray his prince, and forfeit his honor. There have been few battles in which the conduct of men in analogous situations has not decided the victory. Now a lieutenant-general is to an army what a lieutenant-colonel is to a division. Capitulations made by corps which are surrounded, either during a battle or an active campaign, are contracts of which all the advantageous clauses are in favor of the parties making them, and all the burdensome clauses attach to the prince, and to the other soldiers of the army. To fly from danger in order to render the situation of one's comrades more perilous, is evidently a piece of cowardice. Should a soldier say to a commander of cavalry, 'There is my musket, let me go home to my village,' he would be deserting in the presence of the enemy, and the laws would condemn him to death. But what difference is there between his conduct and that of the general commanding a division, the lieutenant-colonel of a battalion, or the captain, who says, 'Let me go home, or receive me in your country, and I will surrender my arms?' There is but one honorable way of being made prisoner, which is, to be taken alone, with arms in one's hands, when one can no longer use them. It was thus that King John, Francis I., and many other brave men of all nations, were taken. In this manner of surrendering there is no bargain, nor can there be any, consistently with honor; life only is accepted, because the party has no power to take that of his enemy, who spares him on condition of similar lenity, because such is the tenor of the law of nations.

"The danger of allowing officers and generals to lay down their arms on a private capitulation, in any other case than that of the garrison of a fortress, is incontestable. It destroys the military spirit of a nation, and weakens its sense of honor, to open this door to cowardice and timidity, or even to the errors of the brave. If military laws decreed corporal and infamous punishment against all generals, officers, and soldiers, laying down their arms by virtue of a capitulation, this expedient for extricating themselves from a perilous situation would never occur to the soldiers' minds; they would have no resource but their valor and perseverance; and what prodigies have they not performed?" * * *

"But what should a general do, when surrounded by superior numbers? We can give no other answer than that of old Horace. In extraordinary situations, extraordinary resolutions are necessary; the more obstinate the resistance made, the greater will be the chance of being relieved, or of forcing a passage. How many things, which at first appeared impossible, have been performed by resolute men, with no other resource than death! The more resistance you make, the more of the enemy you will kill, and the fewer men he will have to attack the other corps of the army. This question does not appear to us capable of any other solution, without destroying the military spirit of a nation, and exposing it to the greatest calamities.

"Ought the laws to authorize a general, who is surrounded by very superior forces, at a great distance from the army to which he belongs, and who has sustained an obstinate conflict, to disperse his army by night, intrusting every individual with the care of his own safety, and fixing a rallying point more or less distant? This question may be doubtful, but there is certainly no doubt that a general who should take such a measure, in a desperate situation, would save three-fourths of his men, he would save himself from the dishonor of surrendering his arms and colors in pursuance of a contract stipulating advantages for individuals, to the detriment of the army and the country.

"In the capitulation of Maxen there was a very singular circumstance. General Wunsch, with the cavalry, had opened himself a passage at daybreak. One of the conditions of the capitulation was, that he should return to the camp and lay down his arms. This general had the simplicity to obey the order given him by General Finck; this was a misconception of military obedience. A general in the power of the enemy has no right to give orders, and those who obey him are criminal. And here one cannot but observe that, since Wunsch had made his way with a large body of cavalry, the infantry might also have penetrated; for, in a mountainous country like Maxen, it was more easy for the infantry to escape by night than the cavalry.

"The Romans disavowed the capitulation made with the Samnites, and refused to exchange or ransom the prisoners. All that is great was instinctive with them; nor was it without reason that they conquered the world."

The principles enunciated in the foregoing extracts seem to have been adopted by Napoleon as the rule of his conduct towards his own generals. He did not judge them by the victories which they won, but by the measures which they adopted to secure victory. This was right, for success in war, as in any other profession, does not always depend upon the ability of the chief who directs it. The standing of a lawyer is not determined by his success in any particular case, nor, indeed, by the number of decisions in his favor, but by the skill and ability which he displays in the conduct of his causes. Thus, Soult and Massena, although not successful generals when intrusted with separate commands, enjoyed the full confidence of their chief, because he knew that they would always adopt the very best measures of which the circumstances admitted. On the other hand, Ney and Murat, though more successful in the field, often committed the most serious military errors. But while thus considerate towards those who failed of success in spite of human agencies, he was exceedingly severe towards those who, in his opinion, unnecessarily surrendered an army or a place.

One of the most important capitulations made during his wars was that of Genoa, by Massena, in 1800. Although premature and unfortunate, as subsequent events proved, Massena was not blamed for making it, but was fully justified by his chief. Not so with Dupont's capitulation of Baylen, in 1808. He was not only censured by Napoleon, but tried and condemned by a high court of honor. The reason of this was, that he not only capitulated for the troops under his immediate direction, but for others which could readily have escaped (*vide* "Jomini's Life of Napoleon," "Napier's Peninsular War," "Thiers's Consulate and Empire").

A capitulation includes all property and persons in the fort or place surrendered not expressly excepted by its terms; and a commander who destroys military stores or other property, or clandestinely sends away important personages, after entering into such agreement, not only forfeits all its benefits, but subjects himself to severe punishment for his perfidy. So, after a capitulation for the surrender of troops in garrison or the field, any officer who destroys his insignia of rank deprives himself of all the privileges of that rank, and may be treated as a private soldier. All individual violations of the conditions, expressed or implied, of a capitulation, may be punished by a forfeiture of all its benefits, or otherwise more severely, at the discretion of the captor. Such conduct not only deprives the victor of rights to which he would otherwise be entitled, but is, in itself, dishonorable.

II.—PAROLES.

We will next consider the subject of Military Paroles, as immediately connected with military surrenders and capitulations.

Sometimes, prisoners of war, after surrender or capture, are permitted to resume their liberty and to return to their own country, upon the condition or pledge that they will not again take up arms against their captors, either for a limited time, or during the continuance of the war, or until duly exchanged. Such pledges are called *military paroles;* and when agreements of this kind are made within the limits of the actual or implied powers of the parties making them, they are obligatory upon such parties and upon the states to which they belong. Nevertheless, there are certain limits to the conditions which the captor may impose on the release of prisoners of war, and to the stipulations or pledges which an officer is authorized to enter into, either for himself or for his troops. For example, no prisoner of war can enter into engagements inconsistent with his character and duties as a citizen or subject of his state, or in violation of the laws of his government, or of the orders of his military superiors. Moreover, where such laws and orders, or the usages of the particular war, authorize him in general terms to give his parole, he can only bind himself not to bear arms against his captors for a limited period, or until he is exchanged; he cannot pledge his parole that he will never bear arms against such captors, or that he will not bear arms against any other enemy of his own government, not at the time an ally of his captors. All such agreements have reference only to the existing enemy, to his allies, and to the existing war; they cannot include future belligerents or future wars.

Again, when it is said by writers on international law that there is an "implied power in commanders to stipulate the conditions of capitulations and paroles," it is meant that such powers are implied in the particular individual, where his own government permits, or does not forbid, the giving of such paroles, and has not specified by cartel, law, or order, when and by whom they may be given, and what must be their purport and limits. Cartels in regard to paroles are special agreements or contracts between the belligerent states, and, *quo ad hoc,* supersede any rules or usages established by international law. So, any law or published order of one party, prohibiting or limiting the exercise of any particular authority by its officers, is a sufficient notice to the other belligerent that he cannot imply the existence of any power so prohibited. And should this other belligerent release his prisoners on such prohibited paroles, he can neither demand the execution of stipulations thus illegally entered into, nor the return of the prisoners. He can claim no advantages from his own wrong.

It is also proper to remark in this place, that the giving and receiving of paroles not to bear arms or engage in military service until duly exchanged, is a practice of very recent origin, and is by no means a positive law of nations. It has not been generally adopted in European wars, and even where adopted, its application has been usually limited to special cases provided for by special agreements. No state is, therefore, bound to permit its subjects to stipulate any such conditions for their release as prisoners of war. Nevertheless, the practice is sufficiently established to justify one belligerent to infer its adoption by the other, if, in the absence of any direct averment, the acts of the latter imply such adoption. Thus, if, at the beginning of the war, prisoners who have been released on such parole, are received and exchanged without protest or objection, the party receiving the paroles is justified in implying the authority to pledge them, until duly notified to the contrary. In the beginning of the war between the United States and Mexico, many Mexican prisoners of war were paroled and permitted to return to their homes; and such paroled prisoners on both sides were afterwards exchanged without protest or objection in regard to the paroles. But, at a subsequent period of the war, the Mexican authorities attempted to force their paroled and unexchanged prisoners to re-enter the ranks and fight. Accordingly, General Scott announced his intention to hang every one who should be retaken after thus violating his parole of honor.

At the beginning of the present war of rebellion, paroles were given and received in a few special cases, the paroled parties effecting their own individual exchange; but the practice was not generally adopted by either belligerent. On the 22d of July, 1862, a general cartel was entered into, by which it was agreed that prisoners of war should, for purpose of exchange, be delivered on *parole* at certain specified points. It was stipulated in this cartel what particular interpretation should be given to such *paroles*, and what such paroled prisoners, prior to exchange, might and might not do. This special agreement, so far as it was applicable, necessarily superseded all general usages and all implied authority of commanders and their captured commands. Nevertheless, some rebel officers continued to demand and receive paroles to render no service to the United States till duly exchanged, of the sick in our hospitals whenever they fell into their hands, and of stragglers and detachments on the field of battle, without ever reducing such pretended prisoners to actual possession. Citizens were picked up, paroled, and immediately released, in the same manner. The enemy evidently intended, by this mode of proceeding, to gain the double advantage of avoiding the guarding, transportation, and subsistence of prisoners to the appointed place of delivery, and of inducing our men to voluntarily surrender and be paroled on the field, so that, by returning to our camps under parole, they would avoid the fatigues of the march, the dangers of the battle, and the sufferings incident to the rebel prisons. This proceeding was not only illegal, but amounted to an inducement to our men to desert the ranks on the battle-field, in order to surrender to the enemy. So great had the abuse become, that in the latter part of that campaign, whole companies and regiments, at the second battles of Bull Run, straggled from the lines and were paroled by the rebels. It is true that this was due in part to disaffected officers, who, for political purposes, desired to see General Pope defeated and removed from the command.

Notice was afterwards given to the rebel authorities that no paroles given by either party, not in compliance with the stipulations of the cartel, would be recognized or enforced; and orders were issued declaring such paroles to be null and void, and that those giving them should be immediately returned to duty. Nevertheless, the practice was found so advantageous to the enemy, and so convenient to our officers and men who wished to avoid, at the same time, the dangers of battle and the horrors of rebel prisons, that it was repeated again and again, notwithstanding the most stringent orders against it.

We give here a synopsis of the several "Instructions" and "Orders," in regard to military paroles, which have been issued by our Government during the present war.

The pledging of a military parole unauthorized by the common laws and usages of war, or forbidden by the prisoner's own government, is a military offence, punishable under the common laws of war. While the pledging of a military parole is a voluntary act of the individual, the capturing power is not obliged to grant it, nor is the government of the individual paroled bound to approve or ratify it. But if such parole is given with the implied consent of his government, that is, not contrary to its laws or orders, and in accordance with general usages, and his government disapproves it, he is bound to return and surrender himself as a prisoner of war. His own government cannot, at the same time, disown an engagement made under such circumstances, and refuse his return as a prisoner. Where the parole is unauthorized or unlawful, the prisoner is not returned to his captors, but is punished or put on duty without exchange; for the prisoner cannot claim the benefit of an invalid agreement, and the captor cannot enforce a condition which he had no right to impose.

Paroling usually takes place by the exchange of signed duplicates of a written document, in which the names and rank of the parties paroled should be correctly stated. Any one who intentionally mistates his rank forfeits the benefit of his parole, and is liable to punishment. None but commissioned officers can give paroles for themselves or their commands, and no inferior officer can give a parole without the authority of his superior, if within reach. For the officer, the pledging of his parole is an individual act, and no wholesale paroling by an officer for a number of inferiors in rank, is permitted or valid. No non-commissioned officer or private can give his parole except through an officer. Individual paroles not given through an officer are not only void, but subject the individuals giving them to be punished as deserters. The only admissible exception is where individuals, properly separated from their commands, have suffered long confinement without the possibility of being paroled through an officer. Stragglers who give their paroles are to be treated as deserters. No paroling on the battle-field, no paroling of entire bodies of troops after a battle, and no dismissal of a number of prisoners, with the general declaration that they are paroled, is permitted or of any value. An officer who gives a parole for himself or his command on the battle-field is deemed a deserter, and punished accordingly. No prisoner of war can be forced by the hostile government to pledge his parole, and any pledge or parole extorted by threats, ill-usage, or cruelty, is not binding, nor are those extorted from the sick and wounded in hospitals, or on the battle-field. The reason of this is obvious. It is the business of the captor to reduce his prisoners to actual possession, and to guard and take care of them; and if, through necessity or choice, he fail to do this, it is the duty of the prisoner, on the first opportunity, to return to the service of his government. He cannot avoid this duty by giving an unauthorized parole.

The foregoing remarks on *military paroles* not to serve for a limited time or till exchanged, do not apply to *paroles of honor* to do or not to do a particular thing not inconsistent with the duty of a soldier. Thus, a prisoner of war actually in the possession of the enemy and held by him, may, in order to obtain exemption from close guard or confinement, pledge his word of honor that he will not attempt to escape. Such pledges are binding upon the individuals giving them; but they should seldom be given, for it is the duty of a prisoner to escape, if able to do so.

Unless otherwise agreed upon, in a cartel, the general military parole not to serve against the paroling belligerent till exchanged does not refer to internal service, such as police or camp duty, in municipal guards, in manufactories and transports, on railroads, &c., and even on fortifications, if not within the general theatre of war, or to be used against the paroling enemy. Persons under such paroles may also serve in any civil or diplomatic capacity.

The commander of an occupying or besieging army may require of the civil officers of the enemy, and even of private citizens, such pledges or paroles as may be deemed necessary for his security; and if such persons fail to give them, he may arrest, confine, or detain them. But the obligations imposed by the general laws and usages of war upon the non-combatant inhabitants of a section of country passed over by an invading army, cease when the military occupation ceases; and any pledge or parole given by such persons, in regard to future service, is null and of no effect. Thus a parole exacted of or given by a non-combatant that he will not bear arms if he should hereafter be enlisted or conscripted into the military service, cannot prevent or exempt him from the performance of such service.

Another case not yet alluded to is, whether an officer at sea may lawfully pledge his parole not to serve again till duly exchanged. By doing so, he relieves the captor from guarding and subsisting him, and, if placed on a neutral or friendly vessel, or landed in neutral or friendly territory, he deprives himself and his government of the rights of recapture. Our Government has decided that the capturing vessel must retain and guard its prisoners till they are duly exchanged or landed in its own territory. If placed on our own or neutral territory or vessels, they are no longer prisoners of war, and any paroles to the contrary will not be recognized as binding. The regulations of the United States Navy, in regard to paroles, are, therefore, nearly the same as those for the Army. These, of course, apply to army officers captured in naval vessels, transports, or passenger-ships.

In further illustration of the views of our Government on the subject of paroles, we refer to the result of a Court of Inquiry, ordered by the President, by Special Orders 288, June 30, 1863.

It appears that two officers, Major D. and Captain M., were captured just outside of the lines of Washington by a rebel cavalry raiding party. The captors, then on their way to the battle-field of Gettysburg, could not conveniently carry with them their prisoners; so they paroled them not to serve till duly exchanged, and sent them into Washington, in order to avoid the necessity of guarding and subsisting them. The court decided that the paroles, being in violation of general orders, were not binding, and that, as the rebel authorities had been previously notified that such paroles would not be recognized, the Government was free to place these officers on duty without exchange.

At the battle of Gettysburg, General Lee proposed an exchange of prisoners, but General Meade declined the offer. Nevertheless, the former, in order to free himself from guarding them, released many of his prisoners on parole, and sent them into our lines. Some, very properly, refused to give any such parole, and afterwards escaped. Those who gave the unauthorized paroles were returned to duty without exchange.

We have been thus particular in pointing out the general laws of war and the orders and instructions of the Government of the United States in regard to surrenders and paroles, for the reason that many of our officers, both of the regular Army and volunteers, seem to be most lamentably, if not wilfully, ignorant on this subject. Notwithstanding repeated orders against the pledging of paroles, except in the manner agreed upon in the cartel, and the return of those who take them to duty without exchange, we frequently hear of the surrender of our troops in the field and of their release on parole not to serve till exchanged. As this practice is so manifestly to the advantage of the rebels, and so very demoralizing to our armies, it is suggested whether officers, who may, hereafter, be guilty of so notorious a violation of orders, should not be summarily dismissed.

It is alleged that they thus pledge their paroles in order to avoid the cruel and barbarous treatment they would otherwise receive in the Southern prison-pens from their merciless and savage captors. On the same grounds might the commander of a fortress justify his surrender without a proper defence, when summoned with a threat that he and his garrison would be put to the sword unless they laid down their arms! No officer is justified in violating the laws of his country through fear that the enemy may treat him in violation of the laws and usages of war. He must do his duty, and leave to his government the task of vindicating the outraged law of nations and the laws of humanity.

THE THIRD OF APRIL, 1865.

BY MRS. LUCY H. HOOPER.

Ring out, O bells, in gladsome peals!
  Wave forth, O flags, in bright array
Speak, cannon, in your thunder-tones,
  Too weak to tell our joy to-day!

Flash out, O lights, in every home!
  Blaze forth in splendor from each spire,
Till, changed into a brighter day,
  The glad night dies in festal fire.

But from our lips what words shall greet
  This hope fulfilled, deferred for years?
The mighty gladness of this hour
  We greet in silence and in tears—

Tears such as angels well might shed,
  Seeing earth freed from sin and pain;
Oh, he who once has shed such tears,
  Need never care for smiles again!

Hereafter, song and speech may come,
  But now this gladness lies too deep;
O friends, forgive, if in this hour
  We have no words—we can but weep!

HETTY McEWEN.
AN INCIDENT OF THE OCCUPATION OF NASHVILLE.
BY LUCY HAMILTON HOOPER.

O Hetty McEwen, Hetty McEwen!
What were the angry rebels doing,
That autumn day, in Nashville town?
They looked aloft with oath and frown,
And saw the Stars and Stripes wave high
Against the blue of the sunny sky;
Deep was the oath, and dark the frown,
And loud the shout of "Tear it down!"

For over Nashville, far and wide,
Rebel banners the breeze defied,
Staining heaven with crimson bars;
Only the one old "Stripes and Stars"
Waved, where autumn leaves were strewing,
Round the home of Hetty McEwen.

Hetty McEwen watched that day
Where her son on his death-bed lay;
She heard the hoarse and angry cry,—
The blood of "'76" rose high.
Out-flashed her eye, her cheek grew warm,
Uprose her aged, stately form;
From her window, with steadfast brow,
She looked upon the crowd below.

Eyes all aflame with angry fire
Flashed on her in defiant ire,
And once more rose the angry call,
"Tear down that flag, or the house shall fall!"
Never a single inch quailed she,
Her answer rang out firm and free:
"Under the roof where that flag flies,
Now my son on his death-bed lies;
Born where that banner floated high,
'Neath its folds he shall surely die.
Not for threats nor yet for suing
Shall it fall," said Hetty McEwen.

The loyal heart and steadfast hand
Claimed respect from the traitor-band;
The fiercest rebel quailed that day
Before that woman stern and gray.
They went in silence, one by one,—
Left her there with her dying son,
And left the old flag floating free
O'er the bravest heart in Tennessee,
To wave in loyal splendor there
Upon that treason-tainted air,
Until the rebel rule was o'er
And Nashville town was ours once more.

Came the day when Fort Donelson
Fell, and the rebel reign was done;
And into Nashville, Buell, then,
Marched with a hundred thousand men,
With waving flags and rolling drums
Past the heroine's house he comes;
He checked his steed and bared his head,
"Soldiers! salute that flag," he said;
"And cheer, boys, cheer!—give three times three
For the bravest woman in Tennessee!"

A VISION OF DEATH.

Down the vast abyss of ages,
  Gazing through a mist of tears,
Here and there a bloody spectre
  Looms athwart the lessening years.

Phantoms swathed in regal purple,
  Gashed with wounds, and streaked with gore,
At dim intervals are scattered
  On the everlasting shore!

Of these grim and ghastly shadows,
  Through the cycles stricken down,
Every red hand wields a sceptre,
  Every dark front wears a crown!

These were Tyrants; reckless smiters
  On the necks of prostrate hordes,
In a suicidal frenzy,
  With the edges of their swords!

Ay! but on the twilight margin
  Where the Past and Present meet,
Sits a solitary spectre,
  With the sunshine round its feet!

On its brow no crown is burning;
  In its grasp no sceptre lies;
Freedom glitters on its forehead;
  Peace looks sadly from its eyes!

In this spirit's mortal mission,
  On the sacred blade it bore,
Say, O people! was there ever
  One unrighteous stain of gore?

Never! Why then doth the Future
  For this fearful lesson call?
Do the record's sombre pages
  Need this blackest stain of all?

Dead? the pure, the true, the constant!
  Wise—who saith he was not wise
With his generation's wisdom?
  Speak him fairly,—here he lies!

Come and look upon him, foemen!
  Place your hands upon his brow!
Living, ye reviled him, scorned him;
  Say he was a Tyrant, now!

Well for you, if, ere the flowers
  Round his rest shall shrink with frost,
Ye shall not in hopeless sackcloth
  Mourn the saviour ye have lost!

April 16, 1865.   C. D. G.

THE SOLDIER'S LOVE.

BY GEORGE COOPER.

Since I have seen my darling May
  It seems a weary while;
But war will end, and then no more
  I'll march in single file.

Friend Tom, you never saw my love,
  Or else you'd never cease
To sing her praise; for, oh, she is
  A splendid little piece!

You would avow, all other maids
  She throws quite in the shade,
If you could only see her once
  Come out on dress-parade.

Her downy cheeks are rosy Red,
  Her hands are small and White,
Her eyes are Blue,—the colors, Tom,
  For which I'll ever fight!

Surrender, was the word with me,
  Before such lovely charms;
And when we marched, you should have seen
  How she presented arms!

Ah! when we wed, I pray that Fate
  For her sake will be kind,
And in the ranks of happiness
  Will keep us well aligned.

For, Tom, you know, old Care sometimes
  Plays many a wanton trick;
And sends his imps—an awkward squad—
  Oft on the double-quick.

But, then, a noble woman's love!—
  Though every hope be gone,
Where will you look for such reserve
  As this to rally on?

For minor ills, why we will learn
  To fight them as they come;
I'm sure I wouldn't mind at all,
  A little charge at home!

Oh! joy to go a-down the years,
  May's head upon my breast,—
To bide in peace, till Captain Death
  Shall give the order, "Rest!"

April, 1865.

LITERARY INTELLIGENCE
AND
NOTES ON NEW BOOKS.

"The Autobiography of a London Detective," just republished in pamphlet form, by Dick & Fitzgerald, of New York, is an intensely interesting book, displaying the extreme skill and acuteness to which such police officers attain, and a wretched stratum of English society, in which literally they live and move and have their being. We did not lay down the book until we had read the last adventure. pp. 187.

"Die Feldherrnkunst des Neunzehaten Jahrhunderts. Von W. Rüstow. Zürich 1857." (8vo, pp. 795.) The object of the author is to exhibit the development of the Principles of Strategy from the beginning of the wars of the French Revolution to those of the European insurrections of 1848–9. To do this, he begins with preliminary information on Strategy and Tactics, and then proceeds to give succinct accounts of the battles of the several periods in the order of time, but interposing, at appropriate stages in the series, masterly abstracts of the reigning strategic systems—those of Bülow and Jomini, of Clausewitz and of Willison; and then—to enable the reader to study the battles in reference to the tactical principles which they illustrate—he annexes an Index of "Operations" with the appropriate exemplifications classed together. The author—a Prussian officer in the Swiss service—has gained the highest distinction among military writers by his theoretical works on Strategy and Tactics, and by his various military histories—of the War in the Crimea, of the Hungarian War of 1848–9, of the Italian Wars of 1859–60, and of the late Danish War. He also co-operated with Professor Köchly in producing the only satisfactory History of the Art of War among the Greeks.

The "Journal Des Armes Speciales" (December, 15 1864), is a technical magazine which contains the fullest information on special arms. The principal papers are "New Studies on Rifled Arms for Infantry" (*continued*); "Breech-Loading Arms," which presents the Russian and Norwegian experiments; "Rifled Cannon," and "The Profession of Arms." Lucid diagrams explain the first paper.

From T. H. Stickney, Esq., we have received a pamphlet entitled "The Navy in Congress," containing speeches of Senators Grimes, Doolittle, and Nye, and Representatives Rice, Pike, Griswold, and Blow. They form together a defence of Mr. Welles and the Navy Department; a word for the Monitors, and many for fifteen-inch guns.

"The Beautiful Widow," by Mrs. Percy B. Shelley, is republished by Petersons of Philadelphia. It is original and entertaining, but unnatural; the lady falls in love with her husband's natural son, and the husband, taking his only child, a daughter, expatriates himself, and is lost to view in America. At length they return, when he is killed in a duel; mother and daughter are reunited, and the beautiful widow is repaid for her generosity by a happy life after all. 12mo., 244 pp.

Want of space compels us to defer many notices until next month

EDITOR'S SPECIAL DEPARTMENT.

It is recorded of Tiberius Cæsar, in the worst days of the imperial court of Rome, that he "invented evil things," so foul that there were no names for them. Names also had to be invented. Such is the shocking deed which first stunned, and then awoke to horror the people of this land. It is as yet a nameless crime: let us not dignify it with a name; for it can never again occur.

At the sublimest moment of his fame, when his cheerful and unaffected demeanor, not without an increasing dignity, had endeared him to the masses; when his sense of high justice was so tempered with a God-like mercy that even rebels were astonished and won over, and the whole country was being borne along with him in a glorious tide of amnesty and generosity; when the goal for which he had striven was in sight, and he stood the happy leader and representative of a restored nationality, Abraham Lincoln, the good, sagacious, laborious, and merciful President, fell dead by the hand of a cowardly assassin: the first, and to be, we hope and believe, the only president-martyr on the august roll.

First, let us mourn; let our tears fall unchecked upon his martyr-tomb. Let history record that men and women, young and old, wept in a unison of sorrow, without a discordant voice; that a nation was struck at once into the marble grief of Niobe; let a national monument of colossal proportions tell the sad story to after times, and nerve coming statesmen for future perils, even if they hold out the crown of martyrdom.

But if silent grief is our first emotion, as it is our first duty, let us then remember that we are to rise and act. His death should incite us to new deeds and new sacrifices, and should rather hasten than delay the end which seems so near.

As much as we mourn, let the world see that the Great Republic is not struck helpless by the blow. Like the sons that surrounded Torquil of the oak, we cry "Another for Hector;" and by whatever fate they fall, even to the seventh, we shall not want a man to stand before the Lord as the American President forever. Great as he was, noble as were his services, we give him up at the Almighty fiat, and march right onward under his successor.

If the thrice-slain rebellion needs another death-blow, it has received it by this foul murder. Many at the North who have sympathized with it thus far, start back in holy horror now, and part company with it forever. The people of the country have a new bond stronger than any before.

Even in rebel purlieus, there are many who have not so utterly lost all honor and manliness, as not to denounce this wicked deed, and feel less zeal in a cause which could prompt it.

Its effect upon our armies will be to excite an instant spirit of vengeance, which will make their onset terrible beyond the power of words to express. We do not mean the "black flag" and "no quarter" vengeance, but a stronger determination than ever to destroy the armies of treason.

We have called it a nameless crime. History presents no parallel to it. Philip of Macedon was slain for incontinence. Julius Cæsar was the man of a party, and was slain by a rival. Foul as was the murder of William of Orange, by Gerhard—at least the Spanish Government had set a price on his head. Jacques Clement who murdered Henry III. of France, and Ravaillac who assassinated Henry IV., were fanatical ecclesiastics who fancied they were slaying antichrist. Ankerström, who slew Gustavus III. of Sweden, had a private pique, and slew a despot. Such were some of the regicides; but which of them can compare with the foul miscreant, who, in aid of a foul treason, or rather in a demoniac spirit because the treason was past all aid, shot, from behind, as he sat by his wife and friends, in a moment of relaxation from the burdensome cares of State, a ruler whom all had learned to love and to respect; an honest, able, and clement statesman, an incorruptible and kind-hearted man! Our assassin stands upon a pinnacle of infamy which none of the historic miscreants have been able to reach. If there be in the lowest depths of dastard degradation and coward crime a lower deep, it may perhaps be found in him who penetrated the sick chamber of Secretary Seward, and thrice stabbed a man whose life already hung upon a hair.

While we mourn and avenge—upon all *guilty* parties who may be brought to light—our president; while we keep him in fresh and immortal remembrance; let us find means hereafter—so God in His mercy spare him to us—to recompense our noble secretary for his labors, his sufferings, and his perils. Honored and beloved sons of the Republic, who have served and labored and suffered and died for her, in camp or cabinet or Congress or field—to you a grateful nation will pay its fullest tribute in all time to come.

THE FALL OF RICHMOND.

From the heart-rending calamity which has fallen upon the nation, let us turn to the glorious victories which our armies have recently achieved, and which have come in so rapid a torrent of intelligence, that the contemplation confuses and bewilders us. The great event of Lee's surrender which reached us on Sunday night, the 9th of April, and which occasioned a new burst of national enthusiasm, for a moment seemed even grander than the fall of Richmond; while the capture of Richmond, in truth the greatest event of all, so far outshone all the precedent conflicts, that they have fallen into temporary obscurity. The first impulse of the writer is to begin with the last news, taking advantage of his readers' interest, and to work backward to those which have lost the keen edge of present wonder. But this is not a logical plan.

When we last went to press, Grant was preparing, and concentrating his forces, for a general and final movement, for which Lee and the Richmond editors were daily waiting. Grant's plans, however, were not intended for their pleasure, and he, no doubt, disappointed them by not attacking just when and where they wanted him to. But, although his long line of nearly thirty miles still extended from Fort Harrison, across the James, in front of Bermuda Hundred, across the Appomattox, and around Petersburg to Hatcher's Run, the rebel commander was well aware that his troops were strongly massed on the left, and even fancied that our lines were so weak near the Appomattox that he could make an impression, and either break through so as to strike our rear at City Point, or at least inflict such a stunning blow that he could make other attacks with increase of *morale*, or in any event save his army by evacuating, before Grant, thus beaten, could recover his senses to follow and cut him off.

This was the meaning of his attack on Hare's Hill, which immediately resulted in the capture of Fort Steadman, on the 25th of March. To understand the movement, let the reader call to mind that the rebel works run around Petersburg from the Appomattox, on the east, to the Weldon Railroad. At the point where the line of works strikes the railroad, the Boydton Plank-Road runs southwesterly, crossing Hatcher's Run and Gravelly Run, and so down to Dinwiddie Court-House, a distance from Petersburg of about eighteen miles. This plank-road then, or rather the prominent points upon it, may be considered a first line of their works, guarding the South Side Railroad. From or near the point where the Boydton Road crosses Hatcher's Run, the White Oak Road diverges, running westward to the *Five Forks*, a place where five roads meet, three of which run directly to the South Side Road.

With this elucidation of the general field and the purposes of the rebels, let us come back, for a brief moment, to Hare's Hill, upon which Fort Steadman stands: flanked on one side by Fort McGilvery, nearest the river; on the other, by Forts Hascall and Morton, and surrounded in several directions by mortar batteries 8, 9, 10, 11, and 12. It needed not much sagacity to prompt Lee's attack upon Fort Steadman with its commanding position. It needed, however, secrecy, skill, and valor to take it, and these were not wanting. Two columns are organized. The hostile works at this point are very near each other; and they are in readiness to march, before our men dream of it. Some of the commands at least are lulled into the security of strength. The rebel attack, under General Gordon, is eminently successful. The first column cutting gaps through the *abatis*, storm the fort, capture three of the batteries mentioned, and turn the guns at once upon our troops and other works. The second column is ready to pierce its way through to the rear. But here ends the rebel success; it becomes hideous disaster. The other Union works pour sheets of fire through the brightening twilight upon those captured. The rebel attack on Fort Hascall is repulsed with loss; Hartranft, seconded by Potter and Willcox, all of the Ninth, forms into column of attack; the front of Fort Steadman, for a brief moment the rebel rear, is swept by a storm of shot, so that they cannot all get back: a shattered remnant fly back through the gaps they had made, while the remainder surrender, two thousand strong, to Hartranft's glorious recapturing column.

In the mean time, Humphreys, of the Second Corps, far to the left, hearing the battle, and believing that the rebels have weakened their lines in his front for the attack on Steadman, pushes forward, captures their lines, and makes many prisoners. Lee has failed, and is now fairly nonplussed. He has played his strong card and it is lost. Grant sees the game; what had been conjecture before, becomes certainty. He no longer concerns himself about the capture of Richmond; that is sure. He must now make plans which shall eventuate in the capture of Lee. Those plans are rapid and clear. Sheridan, from his magnificent raid, joins him, and marches, at once, with his strong cavalry corps to the left. Every corps is under arms. The Ninth, with Willcox, Hartranft, and Potter, is still to confront Petersburg; the Sixth and the Twenty-fourth on their left; then, without gap on the left, Humphrey's Second Corps, consisting of Hays', Mott's, and Miles's Divisions; still further, the Fifth, and, guarding the left flank, while it seeks to find the rebel right flank and turn it, is Sheridan's Cavalry. Thus our immediate lines, south and west of the Appomattox, were from fifteen to eighteen miles, and every foot of it under fire, in the irregular arc of a circle from Petersburg to Dinwiddie Court-House.

To go a little more into detail: Sheridan moved, on the 29th, to Dinwiddie Court-House; Meade, with the Second and Fifth, moved across the run, by the Vaughn and Halifax Roads. The resistance at Gravelly Run was slight, and easily overcome by Griffin's Division of the Fifth, aided by Ayres and Crawford. The 31st was chiefly employed in manœuvring to unite and advance our lines, which was not accomplished without terrific fighting. Indeed, the struggle of that Friday may be regarded as the battle to which the capture of the Five Forks on the next day was only the glorious sequel. From the Boydton Plank-Road, Warren moves up towards the White Oak Road, thus threatening to cut the rebel line; but the enemy is fully prepared to meet him. A little more than a mile below the White Oak Road, Ayres's Division was charged and driven back; Crawford, who came to the rescue, was overpowered by the numbers and fierceness of the enemy, and the same fate awaited Griffin. Our whole line was thus driven back at that point to the plank-road. And besides, this repulse endangered the cavalry on the left; for, encouraged by their partial and temporary success, the enemy now attacked Sheridan with great vigor, and caused the advance cavalry to retire. But these retrograde movements were but for a brief period. Merritt and Custer pour upon the advancing rebels. The Fifth Corps, re-formed, moves forward, and the lost ground is entirely regained. In this condition of things, Sheridan was placed in command of the cavalry and Fifth Corps, and set to work vigorously to complete the plan, thus temporarily checked. With four divisions of cavalry and the Fifth Corps, he marches forward as the rebels retire, upon the Five Forks, which he determines to flank, isolate, and capture. Our space will not permit the details of this fierce and glorious battle. Sheridan directs and attacks in person. Relieving Warren, for reasons undivulged, and putting Griffin in command of the infantry, he dashes over the field, his form dilating, his sword whirling, his voice thundering appeals, praises, and denunciations. Those who saw him speak in wonder and admiration of his valor. To his individual exertions much of the success is due. The capture of the Five Forks was the signal for a general advance. On Sunday morning, at four o'clock, the Sixth, Second, and Twenty-fourth start for the South Side Railroad, directly in their front. Seymour's Division, of the Sixth, has just reached it through a terrible storm of fire, when, almost simultaneously, the Twenty-fourth is there, tearing up the track; and then they make a grand sweep to the right, inclosing Petersburg.

The Ninth Corps moves up to the works in front, and captures Fort Mahone; to retake this important point, A. P. Hill pushes forward, and is on the point of succeeding, when the Sixth, in its grand wheel, comes up. Hill falls, while trying to rally his troops, and the great battle is over. Our old comrade, gallant soldier, and gentleman, of the former light artillery days in Mexico, we try always to remember him, as then, with the dews of youth upon his curls, and to forget that he turned his arms and his training against his country. Foremost in every battle, the fall of Hill seemed but a question of time, and we mourn that such a man should have given up his life in the cause of treason and after the treason was hopeless and dying.

That Sunday's fighting solved the problem. Lee evacuated both Petersburg and Richmond; Jefferson Davis packed his trunk with archives and gold, and fled to Danville, Hillsboro', and elsewhere. Weitzel, standing ready on the north side, went into the famous capital, and the country was intoxicated with the joy of a captured Richmond and a fearful Libby crowded with rebel prisoners.

Then began a race between Lee and Grant; but Grant had the inside track, and Lee's army knew it.

We pause for a moment to look at the grand tactics which followed the evacuation, and ended in the surrender of Lee. No sooner was he off for Danville, as he fondly hoped, or for Lynchburg as his alternative, than our whole force was put in motion to intercept him. Bear in mind that he was moving on the left bank of the Appomattox, and our force on the right. The cavalry took the rapid advance, followed by the Fifth Corps, across the Namozine, Deep Creek, and other southern tributaries of the Appomattox, and while Lee was pushing on to Amelia Court-House, our cavalry had reached Burkesville, and the Fifth Corps was encamping and intrenching right across the Danville Railroad at Jettersville. For once the tables were turned,—the lion was in Lee's path. The Second Corps followed in supporting distance, and soon joined the Fifth, forming, with it, in line of battle on the 5th of April. Then came the detachments of the Twenty-fourth and Twenty-fifth from Ord's army, marching up the Cox Road, and forming on the rear and left. Two divisions of the Ninth were marched to Burkesville, and on April 6th, Lee was expected to attack. But Lee was still making hopeless efforts to get off, and so being caught at Deatonsville, while our cavalry had reached Payneville in one direction, and routed his reconnoissance at Fame's Cross Roads in the other, the invincible Lee saw that the game was up. Lynchburg had fallen; Grant had hemmed him in; Hancock's trumpets were heard coming up the Valley; Stoneman was across his western path, and Sherman was beginning to deal with Johnston.

And so Lee did, what the wisest man would have done, under the circumstances,—made terms for surrender. Uncommonly good terms they were, prompted by generosity and mercy on Grant's part. Let us hope that he has not miscalculated rebel honor and sentiment.

While we write, the news comes, without details, that Mobile has been captured. All honor to Canby and his army. We expected this result, but, knowing the strength of the defences, the character of the rebel commanders, and the topographical difficulties to overcome, we did not expect it so soon. A few words must present the outline of the movement. To understand it, our readers must remember that, at the head of Mobile Bay, on the western shore, is the city, from which the Mobile and Ohio Railroad runs a little west of north to meridian. East of the city is a difficult country, intersected by the delta of the Mobile River, the Tensaw, the Minette, and other streams, each flowing into a little bay of the same name. Along the eastern shore of Mobile Bay, we find Blakely, near the head of the bay. South of this a few miles, is the old Spanish Fort, the principal defence of Mobile in that direction. From Tensaw Station, north of Blakely, the Mobile and Northern Railroad, running a little north of east, joins the Alabama and Florida Road at Pollard. Still going down the eastern shore, we come to Fish River, and farther south, forming the southeastern corner of the bay, is Bon Secour's Bay. On the western shore, about midway between Mobile Point and the city, is Dog River, and the famous bar which formed the first obstruction to our fleet. We can only indicate the movement of the troops. Gordon Granger's Thirteenth Corps was concentrated at Mobile Point. At Dauphin's Island was A. J. Smith's Seventeenth Corps, which had been shipped from New Orleans. Steele was at Pensacola with a co-operating force. Granger and Smith marched by the eastern shore, along Bon Secour's Bay, across Fish River, to the siege of the Spanish Fort. Steele came up, using the railroad to Pollard, and so to join Granger and Smith. The iron-clads cross the bar, and invest the fort by water, and it is soon cut off from Blakely and Mobile. Torpedoes sink the Milwaukie and the Osage, but the fort, notwithstanding its *feu de joies*, gains nothing thereby. We have not yet the details of its capture, but are content to know that it has fallen, and Mobile is also in our hands.

We must not forget to record the magnificent march of Wilson from Eastport through Russelville, threatening Mobile, Selma, and Montgomery. At Selma he encounters the famous Forrest and Roddy, but dismounting his men, he charges their works, and captures them with their entire command. Montgomery has also fallen.

Sherman, by the last advices, was at and beyond Raleigh. It was rumored that he was offering terms for the surrender of Johnston's army, but Jefferson Davis, who had ventured quite near the army at Hillsboro', has perhaps another plan, equal to those at Vicksburg and Atlanta, and has made a pause in Johnston's movements. The organization of Sherman's army on April 1st is thus given in a general order:—

"Right wing—Army of the Tennessee, Fifteenth and Nineteenth Corps, Major-General O. O. Howard, commanding.

"Left wing—Army of Georgia, Fourteenth and Twentieth Corps, Major-General H. A. Slocum, commanding.

"Centre—Army of Ohio, Tenth and Twenty-third Corps, Major-General J. W. Schofield, commanding.

"Cavalry—Brevet Major-General J. Kilpatrick, commanding.

"8. Each of these commanders will exercise the powers prescribed by law for a general commanding a special department or army in the field.

"9. Major-General Jos. A. Mower is hereby, subject to the approval of the President, appointed to command the Twentieth Corps, *vice* Slocum promoted to a command of an army in the field.

"10. Brigadier-General Charles Walcott is hereby transferred from the Army of the Tennessee to the Army of Georgia, for assignment to the command of a division made vacant.

"11. Brigadier-General Charles Ewing, having been promoted, is hereby relieved from staff duty at these head-quarters, and will report to Major-General Howard, for assignment to duty according to his rank."

A day of triumph and a day of sorrow, a memorable day in all time, is the 14th of April, 1865. On that day fell Good Friday, when Christians commemorate, in a peculiar manner, the death of Him who came to restore the world. On that day our President fell; on that day the old flag lowered four years ago from Fort Sumter, amid hellish shouts, was again flung to the breeze, amid shouts and tears of joy. Some great painter should attempt the glorious picture: the circle of thundering ships; the immense crowd of interested spectators; the diamond-shaped platform, decked with myrtles, evergreens, and flowers; the staff, towering one hundred and fifty feet high; General Anderson, in joy and tears; Beecher's temperate, humane, and happy address; and, in splendid climax, the stars and stripes running up amid the sobs and frantic embraces of those who will never see a more glorious sight.

Our readers are informed that, under the head of SACRED MEMORIES, we shall be glad to publish such brief obituaries of gallant officers as may be sent us; the length of the notice in each case, being regulated by the character, station, and valor of the individual thus noticed. We hope thus to form a valuable corner for future reference.

HOW SHALL BOYS BE SELECTED FOR THE MILITARY AND NAVAL ACADEMIES?

SIR: The present system of presenting candidates for appointments as Cadets and Midshipmen to the Military and Naval Academies of the United States, is through the nominations made by members of Congress, who select whom they please from among the young men of their districts. The objections to this practice are mainly these: that it is not an impartial method—only families having political influence being able to secure the favor; that, taking boys at random, without regard to fitness, results in the failure of large numbers of them (from one-half to three-fourths) to come up to the rigid standard required in those institutions; and that, so many failures not only subject the Government to a heavy and unnecessary expense in endeavoring to train young men to duties which they can never perform, but cripple the Army and Navy by not supplying it with the needed infusion of young men capable of becoming officers.

These appear to be very serious defects of the system. They seemed to me so last June, when I had the honor of being a member of the Visiting Board of the Naval Academy at Newport; and in the little time there was for giving thought to it, I joined in a recommendation for the adoption of the plan of "competitive examinations" as a remedy. Without going too much into detail, that plan looked to competition among all the boys in the country, grouped into Congressional districts, for the privilege of admission: in other words, its operation would send there the very *élite*, so far as scholarship is concerned, of the land. It would, besides, do away with the complaint of favoritism, and open the doors of those Academies to every boy, high or low. In giving the subject more thought, I am not sure that that recommendation, in its main intent—that is, to give efficiency to the service—was a good one.

The movement of an army or a regiment; the sailing of a vessel; the handling of men; the attack or defence of a fortification; the varied requirements of a soldier or a sailor in active service, are not the matters of algebraical, of historical, of logical of rhetorical, solution. They do not require those accomplishments necessary for professorships in colleges. They require executive qualities; aptitude for dealing with men and things; an acquaintance and a faculty for coping with the elements—earth, air, fire, and water;—all based on the indispensable groundwork of a sensible, practical mind, and a strong, healthy body. That is one thing a man should be. If he be that, it will be no disadvantage, but probably an advantage, if he add another thing to it, that is, the highest possible educational accomplishments. But, if he cannot be both, we think that Yale and Harvard will agree with us in choosing, between the conditions with which he shall be endowed. There are men, probably, who combine all these; but they cannot be picked up in every Congressional district, nor in every State, nor, I will venture to say, in every nation. Napoleon, Wellington, Nelson, Paul Jones, Decatur, Perry, were not among them. Grant, Sherman Sheridan, Kilpatrick, Farragut, Porter, are not. It is possible that Washington and Lafayette were, and that Scott is. Of that, I only give way to the possibility. Farragut, beyond all doubt, can sail his ship through the untracked wilderness of the ocean and know exactly each day her position on the face of the great deep; but I doubt whether he can calculate for you the weight of the earth, or the moment when, ages hence, a new comet shall blaze upon the horizon. Sherman, we all know, can lead a host defiantly through the length and breadth of a hostile country; but we know as well that he writes crude if not illogical letters, though forcible and to the mark. And Cushing, whose splendid courage and shrewd enterprise rendered the country a service equal to a naval victory, I am told, "bilged" at one or more of the examinations at the Naval Academy.

As a general rule, excessive mental endowment is not allied to great energy of character and robust physical organization. Of course there are many exceptions to this; but, I believe, not more than enough to prove the rule. They lead to tastes literary and scientific, and seek quiet and peaceful paths of life. Let the reader call up to his remembrance the finished scholars of whom he has any knowledge, and see if what I have asserted is true or not.

It is my belief, then, that the evils complained of in those Academies—that is, the great number of failures to pass the examinations, and the consequent wasting of the public money in carrying along for one or more years so many incompetent students —are really evils engendered by the Academies themselves. The standard of abstruse studies is placed too high. Too much importance is attached, for instance, to excellence in mathematics; and young men who are capable of developing all the qualities needed for the service, but who have not "mathematical minds," are thrown overboard. A system of basing admittance to these Academies upon "competitive examinations," would fill their study-rooms with young men who would come up to the rigid standard now in force, and make failures almost impossible—but, I believe, would tell disastrously upon our future Army and Navy.

The Board of Visitors to the Naval Academy for 1864, report that only about one-fourth or one-third of all the midshipmen are successful enough to graduate. Would the Navy be worse off, if the standard of study were so lowered as that three-fourths could pass? Make a liberal slaughter of dunces; but, for the honor of the race, let us not declare officially that three-fourths of our sons, taken at random through the land, are blockheads. Devise some way, if you please, to get rid of the partiality which now afflicts the system of appointments, but take the boys who seek the service and have a taste for it, and promise to be an honor to the flag. Take a hundred boys at random from every part of the country, and seventy-five of them at least will develop, under liberal and intelligent training, into all that we want of them. A fraction of this number will prove a capacity for reaching the inner temple of mathematical science; they will preside at our astronomical observatories, and fill the places of such men as Gilliss, and, I had almost said, Maury. Some will scarcely make their way through the outer entrance; but give them a chance at "Albemarles" and they will be Cushings. More of them will gain access to the body of the sanctuary, neither halting short, nor penetrating beyond, and come out successors to Farragut, and Foote, and Porter, and that host of gallant men who are making the name of the nation glad upon the face of the waters. R.

LETTER FROM RICHMOND.

(*From our Special Correspondent.*)

RICHMOND, VA., April 11, 1865.

A SAIL up the James to Richmond is not yet so common an occurrence as to be without a lively interest. As one quietly sails past Varina Landing, with its sad memories of haggard, dying prisoners,—Dutch Gap Canal, a present failure, but destined some day to save a sail of eight tedious miles,—Chapin's Bluff, with its neatly turfed but seemingly impregnable earthworks, into the silent mouths of whose grim and formidable tier of guns we now fearlessly look,—Drury's Bluff, surmounted by the historic Fort Darling frowning down its sixty feet of embankment, and whose guns command ten miles of river approach,—on through the partially removed river-obstructions of sunken vessels, closely driven piles, &c., up the newly buoyed channel, the shore of which is lined by torpedoes removed by our forces from the river,—through the open draws of the three bridges that Lee had used instead of more temporary pontoons, to a safe landing at "Rocketts,—"the thought of how different all the attending circumstances of such a sail would have been if made eight days earlier, constantly recurs to mind, and the memory recalls all the history of our four years' struggle over this fiercely contested territory.

Richmond itself—its best business section in ruins and its streets unlighted—is a sad sight, and the first impression is made only sadder when one learns the widespread distress existing among the inhabitants. Our authorities began, at once, the alleviation of this distress by the distribution of rations among the people; and it is a heart-touching sight to notice at every dépôt of distribution ladies of most evident refinement standing in the line, closely veiled and waiting by the hour for their turn to come. As I walked down the street from one of these dépôts, I passed a little group of a mother and her three little daughters, and as one who was carrying a basket, half hidden under her scanty shawl, and had been watching the slowly shortening line at the dépôt, urged her mother on with the remark, "Mamma, there are not many there now," I could not restrain a moisture of the eyes, as I thought of the experience of privation and suffering from which such a remark and such an errand were wrung. Many families who have not been reduced to such deep distress have quietly solicited our officers to board with them, that means of living may in this way be obtained.

It does honor to the hearts of our officers that the knowledge and sight of all this distress produce no word or thought of exultation, but rather an honorable sympathy.

The following actual quotations will show the almost utter worthlessness of the Confederate currency: Flour, $1,200 per barrel; commonest brown sugar, $20 per pound; boots, $500 per pair; felt hats, $500; children's shoes, $100 per pair; kid gloves, $100 per pair; common calico, $30 per yard; coarsest unbleached muslin, $6.50 per yard; spool of cotton, $6, &c., &c.

The people have considered the currency well-nigh worthless for a long time, and now one can get as much of it as he chooses to carry away for the asking. The boys on the street will sell you a large lump of tobacco, wrapped in a one thousand dollar Confederate bond, for a one dollar greenback.

The mercantile community is well-nigh ruined, for almost all merchants had invested largely in cotton, tobacco, &c., which they knew would always be worth real money—and in the conflagration they have lost not only their buildings and stocks, but all such outside accumulations also.

The citizens all unite in warmest praise of the conduct of our troops—they have been entirely exempt from all annoyance or insult, and freely admit their relief at the deliverance from the petty despotism of subordinate officers under which they have lived. A most intelligent lady remarked that she did not understand how we could maintain such perfect discipline—they had known nothing like it. The rebel press and leaders had so constantly reiterated the assertion that our army would sack the city if they ever entered it, that almost all had come to believe the lie—and their present gratified astonishment is easily understood. I could then fully appreciate the tale told by many ladies of the horror of the announcement made amidst the fearful fire lighted by the retreating army on the 3d instant, accompanied as it was by the indiscriminate plundering committed by their rear-guard, that "the Yankees are coming."

In regard to the feeling of the people here, I imagine real Unionism to be in scant supply. Almost every man has been connected with the rebel armies in some way—for their conscription included all classes and almost all ages—and their sympathy is all in that direction. But they are now very quiescent; they freely acknowledge that they have been thoroughly whipped in a fair fight, and are quite willing to give up the contest. One cannot fail to see, however, that they are thus tractable only because they are whipped, and not from any returning love for the old Union, or regret for their recent course. Still the universal sentiment is that the war is virtually over, and that we are again—or soon will be, the "United States." All are hourly expecting to hear of Johnston's surrender, which is considered inevitable.

The question of reconstruction, surrounded on all sides by difficulties, begins to assume the most august proportions, and will require for its proper solving all the wisdom and judicious firmness that our authorities can command. God guide us to a peace, that, in the words of President Lincoln, shall come to stay. H.

MILITARY NOTES AND QUERIES.

Your correspondent, "10th Illinois," from the Army of the Cumberland proposes, in your August number, a method of forming square to the rear from line of battle. This method seems to expect too much individual action from the soldiers of a majority of the companies of the regiment. I propose the following method as better:

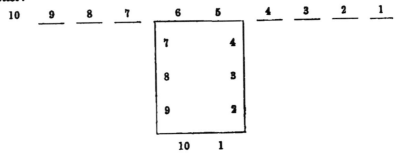

Let the commands be, *To the rear, on Third Division, form square.* At this command, the chief of Third Division will cause it to stand fast. The captains of companies 2, 3, 4, 7, 8, and 9 face them to the rear; 1 and 10 are faced inwards by the flank. At the command, *March*, of the colonel, 4 and 7 wheel and form perpendicularly to ends of Third Division; 2, 3, 8, 9 make a half wheel, and then march forward till they come near their places in the square when they are dressed upon the lines of 4 and 7; 1 and 10 march by the flank to their places to form the rear face of the square, the file-closers of these companies passing inside the square. The lines for 4, 3, and 2, and for 7, 8, and 9, should be established by the guides of those companies throwing themselves out in advance of their companies, and being placed by the lieutenant-colonel and major WEST POINT.

COMMENT.—(*From a distinguished Correspondent and Tactician.*)—There would be no particular necessity for forming square forward on the centre, unless imminently pressed by cavalry, and if so pressed, the moral effect of facing about, back to the enemy, would be bad. This, together with the greater intricacy of the movement is sufficient to reject the proposed method.

In answer to our California correspondent, J. W. McK.'s inquiries, we would state:—

I. Bayonets should be unfixed after the inspecting officer has passed, in accordance with paragraph 239, page 60, Vol. I., Casey's Tactics.

II. The following is the manner of posting the companies of a regiment:—

	R	*		L
Ten companies	1 . 6 . 4 . 9 . 3 . 8 . 5 . 10 . 7 . 2			
Nine companies	1 . 6 . 4. 8* . 3 . 7 . 5 . 9 . 2			
Eight companies	1 . 5 . 4 . 8* . 3 . 7 . 6 . 2			
Seven companies	1 . 5 . 3* . 6 . 4 . 7 . 2			
Six companies	1 . 4 . 3* . 6 . 5 . 2			
Five companies	1 . 4* . 3 . 5 . 2			
Four companies	1 . 3 . 4 . 2			
Three companies	1 . 3 . 2		The star signifies	
Two companies	1 . 2		color-company.	
One company	1			

III. At a military funeral, the music should be at the head of the column.

Editor U. S. Service Magazine:

SIR:—I read with interest your answers to the questions of "J. L., 128th Ohio Vols.," in the "Military Notes and Queries" of the MAGAZINE for July, and have since been waiting with the expectation that some other person would offer further comments upon those questions that have proved so puzzling to many volunteer officers. Permit me to ask for the authority for the rules you lay down in answer to the queries of "J. L." You make no distinction in your rules, between salutes made during the daytime and after sunset; but it is noticeable that the "facing to the proper front," concerning which "J. L." inquires, is prescribed only *after sunset*, and then not as a salute, but only as a mark of *attention*, showing that the sentry is attending properly to his duties. Under the rule that a sentinel, on any one of the four sides of a camp, shall face outward and present arms, when a general or field officer approaches, if the officer approached from within the camp, the sentinel would be presenting arms to an officer behind his back; or rather would be committing the glaring impoliteness of turning his back to the officer he is required to salute, and then gravely presenting arms to nothing! which is hardly consonant with the customary *courtesy* required of all officers and soldiers toward their superiors. In the salutes prescribed in paragraphs 256 and 257, the inferior is required to direct his attention in a respectful manner towards his superior. In paragraph 248, salutes to officers who pass in the rear of a guard, are prohibited. Is there any good reason why the salute of a single sentry should not be made in a like respectful and courteous manner, facing toward the officer saluted? It is very clear, from paragraphs 251 and 423, that no salutes are paid after retreat, and therefore the "facing to the proper front," required by paragraph 423, is prescribed only between *retreat* and *reveillé*.

I understand the second question of "J. L." to be this: "Does the last sentence of paragraph 420, requiring sentinels to 'carry arms' to all officers below field officers, include the usual salute with the left hand brought to the shoulder, or not?" The inference from the language of that paragraph is, that the sentinel should stand at shouldered arms; but the common practice in the volunteer army is otherwise. This practice is doubtless derived from the requirements as to salutes in other cases. Indeed, it is hardly consistent that the single sentry should simply carry arms to a line officer, when walking on a beat; because the same sentry, if in a sentry-box, would salute the same officer by raising the left hand; and if not a sentry, but simply a soldier under arms, and not on duty, he would offer the same salute under paragraph 255. From these facts has originated the custom of interpreting the language of paragraph 420, "carry arms," to mean "carry arms and salute as a sergeant."

If you or your contributors will give more extended opinions upon these subjects with references to authorities, it will, I think, be a great aid to many inquiring volunteer officers. INSPECTOR.

MEMPHIS, TENN.

ANA OF THE WAR.

We have received from a correspondent the following *ana* of the war, which illustrate the relations of the soldiers in the contending armies in a novel manner:—

"The savage picket-firing last summer, along the whole line, especially in front of the Ninth Corps, is known to all the world. To those who were eye-witnesses, to those who were ear-witnesses, and to those at home, who read accounts of the inhuman practice, it may be interesting to know how these matters were managed by the cavalry on the left, on the 'Jerusalem Plank-Road.'

"The most friendly feeling was displayed by the cavalry-pickets of the two armies, and no firing was indulged in. Most positive orders were issued against intercourse and *trade*, but did not prevent either. Papers were exchanged; tobacco, coffee, every thing which a soldier had could be bartered. The matter was thus understood, viz., 'No firing. No advantage shall be taken of each other. If we are ordered to advance we will fire over your heads—and you shall do the same.' A strange regiment coming on to the line was soon *indoctrinated* with these principles, and all went on well.

"When the Second Corps crossed at Deep Bottom, the cavalry was withdrawn for a time. On returning, the old line was to be re-established. Mr. Reb seeing no Yank in his front, had advanced so as to occupy our line. As our boys came up, 'Hello, Yank, what's this?'—'Nothing, only we want our old ground.'—'All right,' and reb goes back to his old position.

"On one occasion the 'call' was answered by a Yankee, and each rode out to exchange papers, when, not more than a hundred yards apart, the Yankee either purposely or accidentally fired his carbine. The Reb halted, looked at him a moment, then said, with an air of disgust, 'You d—d infernal scoundrel!' wheeled his horse and rode back.

"The rebels swore they would kill every man of *that* regiment they could catch; still they did not take revenge by firing at *him* even.

"Officer of the picket came in one day, saying, 'There is no use of a picket out here.'—'Why not?'—'Our boys and that Georgia regiment have consolidated.'—'How so?'—'Well, I was out there just now and found a rebel up a tree shaking down the apples, and a Yankee below picking them up—guns leaning against a stump.'

"May I relate a story illustrative of discipline?

"While reading your 'Ana of the War,' in the February number, this evening, heard a rap at the door. 'Come in.' A tall corporal enters, salutes properly, and remarks, 'Major, I believe your tent is on fire.' True enough; a few shakes of the 'D'Aubree' overhead soon makes all right. I thanked the corporal for his trouble; and he repeated his salute and withdrew.

OFFICIAL INTELLIGENCE.

The Army.

Dismissals,
For the Week ending March 4, 1865.

The following officers, as of the dates set opposite their respective names, for the causes mentioned, having been published officially, and failed to appear before the Commission:—

Desertion.

Second Lieutenant Alexander Wilkie, 10th Vermont Volunteers, to date December 31, 1864.

Absence without leave.

Major George W. Van Beek, 33d Missouri Volunteers, to date February 6, 1865.
Surgeon Ernst Weiler, 52d New York Volunteers, to date February 6, 1865.
Captain Joseph B. Homan, 99th Indiana Volunteers, to date February 6, 1865.
Captain Samuel Moore, 99th Indiana Volunteers, to date February 6, 1865.
Captain Charles M. Scott, 99th Indiana Volunteers, to date February 6, 1865.
Captain George H. Tracy, Company I, 33d Missouri Volunteers, to date March 1, 1865, for disobedience of orders, conduct unbecoming an officer and gentleman, and absence without leave, as reported upon the rolls of his regiment.
First Lieutenant Samuel F. Curtis, Quartermaster 20th Pennsylvania Cavalry, to date March 1, 1865, for absence without leave.
First Lieutenant Robert M. Reed, 33d Missouri Volunteers, to date February 6, 1865, for absence without leave, having been published officially, and failed to make satisfactory defence before the Commission.

For the Week ending March 11, 1865.

The order heretofore issued honorably discharging Second Lieutenant Edward Wheeler, 17th Michigan Volunteers, is amended so as to dishonorably dismiss him as of date of order of discharge.
Lieutenant-Colonel J. J. Hammill, 66th New York Volunteers, to date March 2, 1865, for leaving the post at Annapolis, Maryland, in an irregular way, thereby absenting himself without leave, and attempting to visit Washington (in citizen's clothes), without authority from the War Department.
Captain R. J. Wright, 6th Ohio Cavalry, to date March 2, 1865, for absence without leave, and attempting to visit the city of Washington (dressed in citizen's clothes), without authority from the War Department.
Captain A. Hyde, 16th Kansas Cavalry, to date March 6, 1865, for, while a Lieutenant, holding out false inducements to men to enlist in the service of the United States.
Captain A. J. Marsh, Veteran Reserve Corps, to date March 7, 1865.
Captain James E. Philpot, 186th Ohio Volunteers, to date March 8, 1865, for fraud in local bounties, in requiring $1,050 to be given him as a consideration for procuring commissions for two men as lieutenants in his company.
First Lieutenant Peter Meyers, 1st United States Veteran Volunteers (Engineers), to date October 26, 1864, for absence without leave.
First Lieutenant Hiram Malott, Company F, 16th Kansas Cavalry, to date March 8, 1865, for disobedience of orders, drunkenness, encouraging enlisted men to get drunk, and conduct unbecoming an officer.
Second Lieutenant George H. Boyd, Company H, 11th Ohio Cavalry, to date March 6, 1865, for intemperance and inefficiency.

Second Lieutenant Eugene Clyde, Signal Corps, to date March 8, 1865.

The following officers, to date February 11, 1865, for the causes mentioned, having been published officially, and failed to appear before the Commission:—

Absence without leave.

First Lieutenant Willard W. Hubbell, 15th Michigan Volunteers.
Captain George D. McClure, 57th Ohio Volunteers.
Second Lieutenant Edward A. Gordon, 57th Ohio Volunteers.

For the Week ending March 18, 1865.

The following officers to date March 10, 1865, for neglecting their duties and violating orders and regulations by going to bed and sleeping during their tours of duty when Officers of the Day. This while their commands were in the field, and liable to attacks from the enemy:—

First Lieutenant William J. Anderson, Battery F, 1st New York Light Artillery.
Second Lieutenant John W. Jacobs, Jr., Company C, 1st Virginia Light Artillery.
First Lieutenant L. B. Richards, Company I, 1st Pennsylvania Light Artillery.
Second Lieutenant S. S. Allen, Battery D, 1st Maryland Light Artillery.

The following officers to date February 20, 1865, for the causes mentioned, having been published officially, and failed to appear before the Commission:—

Disobedience of orders, and absence without leave.

Captain Frederick S. Gimber, 109th Pennsylvania Volunteers, now consolidated with the 111th Pennsylvania Volunteers.

Absence without leave.

Captain W. W. Watts, 46th Ohio Veteran Volunteers.
Captain Nathaniel Crane, 97th Indiana Volunteers.
Captain B. W. Harrelson, 40th Illinois Veteran Volunteers.
Additional Paymaster Benjamin L. Martin, United States Volunteers, to date February 25, 1865, in accordance with section four of Act of June 25, 1864.

For the Week ending March 25, 1865.

Captain M. T. Sappington, Assistant Quartermaster United States Volunteers, to date March 23, 1865.

First Lieutenant J. J. Kelly, 14th Michigan Battery, to date March 13, 1865, for bringing up frivolous charges against a brother officer, on account of enmity existing between them.

First Lieutenant Silas D. Kain, 62d Ohio Volunteers, to date March 17, 1865, for absence without leave.

First Lieutenant August Buddenbrook, Company H, 181st Ohio Volunteers, to date March 17, 1865, for absence without leave, breach of arrest while under charges, and desertion.

First Lieutenant Emerick Knowles, 21st Pennsylvania Cavalry, to date March 20, 1865, for conduct prejudicial to good order and military discipline.

First Lieutenant Samuel A. Armstrong, 5th Indiana Cavalry, to date March 21, 1865, for absence without leave.

The following officers, to date March 18, 1865, for defrauding certain enlisted men of a portion of the bounties paid them by the United States:—

First Lieutenant George T. Welch, 98th United States Colored Infantry.
Second Lieutenant Sumner W. Lewis, 98th United States Colored Infantry.

The following officers, to date February 27, 1865, for the causes mentioned, having been published officially and failed to appear before the Commission:—

Absence without leave.

First Lieutenant O. G. Smith, 17th Michigan Volunteers.
First Lieutenant Nathan Branson, Quartermaster 8th Indiana Volunteers.
Captain Sanford H. Platt, 126th New York Volunteers.
First Lieutenant Harrison H. McMichael, 46th Ohio Veteran Volunteers.
Second Lieutenant Frederick Gutterman, 7th New York Volunteers.
Second Lieutenant Thomas J. McHale, 170th New York Volunteers.

First Lieutenant James H. Walker, 81st Pennsylvania Volunteers.
Captain Alexander Watts, 63d New York Volunteers.
Second Lieutenant Jacob G. Lowry, 99th Pennsylvania Volunteers, to date March 18, 1865, for absence without leave.
Second Lieutenant William Closter, 52d New York Volunteers, to date February 27, 1865, for absence without leave, having been published officially, and failed to make satisfactory defence before the Commission.
Captain Samuel W. Yearick, 69th United States Colored Troops, to date March 1, 1865.
First Lieutenant James A. Wallace, Quartermaster 10th Indiana Cavalry, to date March 4, 1865, for having tendered his resignation "by reason of incompetency."

Dismissals Amended.

The order heretofore issued dismissing First Lieutenant A. C. Salisbury, 14th United States Colored Troops, has been so amended as to honorably discharge him as of the date of the order of dismissal.

The order heretofore issued dismissing Second Lieutenant Michael H. Kenneally, 63d New York Volunteers, had been so amended as to read, Captain Michael H. Kenneally, same regiment.

The order heretofore issued dismissing First Lieutenant Horace K. Stille, 13th Pennsylvania Cavalry, for "desertion" has been so amended as to dismiss him for absence without leave.

The orders of dismissal heretofore issued in the following cases have been so amended as to honorably discharge them as of date of order of dismissal:—
Major Lyman W. Brown, 11th Wisconsin Cavalry.
First Lieutenant Joseph R. Vail, Adjutant 47th Illinois Volunteers.

Dismissals Revoked.

The orders of dismissal heretofore issued in the following cases have been revoked:—
First Lieutenant William G. Anderson, Adjutant 4th Indiana Cavalry, and he has been honorably discharged, to date April 24, 1864.
First Lieutenant Michael McIntire, 3d Michigan Cavalry, and he has been discharged as of the date of the order of dismissal.
Major George N. Van Beek, 33d Missouri Volunteers, he having been previously discharged upon tender of resignation.
Captain Thomas M. Gibson, 33d Missouri Volunteers, he having been previously discharged upon tender of resignation.
Lieutenant Matthew H. Ward, 9th Michigan Cavalry, and he has been honorably discharged as of the date of the order of dismissal.
Captain G. B. Harrington, 2d Iowa Cavalry, and he has been honorably discharged as of the date of the order of dismissal.
First Lieutenant Sumner Howard, 17th United States Infantry, and his resignation has been accepted to take effect as of the date of the order of dismissal.
Surgeon George Burr, United States Volunteers.
Assistant Surgeon J. P. Siddall, 22d Indiana Volunteers, he having been previously honorably discharged.
Assistant Surgeon Charles E. Goldsborough, 5th Maryland Volunteers, and he has been honorably discharged as of date of the order of dismissal.

Dishonorably Discharged.

First Lieutenant W. D. Pearne, 15th New York Cavalry, to date March 9, 1865, having tendered his resignation while under charges for "disobedience of orders, conduct prejudicial to good order and military discipline, and absence without leave."

Dishonorable Discharge Amended.

The order heretofore issued, dishonorably discharging Second Lieutenant D. R. S. Wells, 126th Ohio Volunteers, has been so amended as to discharge him upon tender of resignation.

Restored to Commission.

The following-named officers heretofore dismissed have been restored with pay from the date at which they rejoin their regiments for duty, provided the vacancies have not been filled by the Governors of their respective States:—

Captain C. W. Edward Weltz, 14th Pennsylvania Cavalry.
First Lieutenant William McIlwraith, 9th Cavalry, Missouri State Militia.
Captain Robert A. Halbert, Company H, 117th Illinois Volunteers.
First Lieutenant L. W. Hover, 12th Kansas Volunteers.
Lieutenant-Colonel J. J. Hammill, 66th New York Volunteers.
Lieutenant-Colonel N. B. Knight, 1st Delaware Cavalry.
Lieutenant L. H. Hamlin, Adjutant 123d Illinois Mounted Infantry.

Second Lieutenant James E. C. Covel, 16th Iowa Volunteers, heretofore dismissed, has been restored to his command as of date of order of dismissal, provided the vacancy has not been filled.

First Lieutenant P. A. O. Malley, 13th New York Artillery, heretofore dismissed, has been restored, with pay from the date at which he rejoins his regiment for duty, provided the vacancy has not been filled, evidence of which must be obtained from the Governor of his State.

Second Lieutenant Henry M. Field, 36th United States Colored Troops, heretofore dismissed, has been restored, with pay from the date on which he rejoins his regiment for duty, provided the vacancy has not been filled, evidence of which must be obtained from Major-General Ord, commanding Department of Virginia.

Exempt from Dismissal.

WAR DEPARTMENT,
ADJUTANT-GENERAL'S OFFICE,
WASHINGTON, March 14, 1865.

Assistant Surgeon Hugh McG. Wilson, 2d Mounted Rifles, New York Volunteers, charged with offences, and heretofore published, is exempt from being dismissed the service of the United States, the Military Commission instituted by Special Orders, No. 53, series of 1863, from the War Department, having reported that satisfactory defence has been made in his case.

March 20, 1865.

The following-named officers, charged with offences, and heretofore published, are exempt from being dismissed the service of the United States, the Military Commission instituted by Special Orders, No. 53, series of 1863, from the War Department, having reported that satisfactory defence has been made in their respective cases, namely:—

First Lieutenant Henry Kottweitz, 7th New York Volunteers,
First Lieutenant John D. Mercer, 119th Pennsylvania Volunteers.

E. D. TOWNSEND,
Assistant Adjutant-General.

Dropped from the Rolls of the Army.

First Lieutenant John L. Coppock, 46th United States Colored Infantry, to date January 19, 1865, for desertion.

Captain Thomas B. Alexander, 4th United States Cavalry, to date March 14, 1865, for desertion.

Second Lieutenant Robert Morrison, 1st Arkansas Volunteers, to date May 31, 1864, for absence without leave.

Regular Navy.

Orders, &c.

March 25.—Vice-Admiral D. G. Farragut, ordered to return to his residence, the special duty to which he was ordered being completed.

March 1.—Rear-Admiral Samuel F. Du Pont, ordered to report to Vice-Admiral Farragut at Washington, D. C., for duty as member of a Board of which he is the presiding officer.

March 23.—Rear-Admiral Hiram Paulding, detached from command of the Navy Yard, New York, to take effect on the 1st proximo.

March 25.—Rear-Admiral S. F. Du Pont, ordered to return to his residence, the Board of which he was a member being dissolved.

March 23.—Commodore Charles H. Bell, ordered to take command of the Navy Yard at New York, on the 1st proximo.

March 6.—Captain William M. Walker, detached from special duty at New York, and ordered to command the De Soto.

March 7.—Captain Joseph F. Green, ordered to Ordnance duty at Boston, Mass.

March 14.—Captain R. W. Meade, detached from command of the (late) San Jacinto.

March 6.—Commander A. D. Harrell, detached from special duty at New York, and ordered to command the Kearsarge.

March 8.—Commander George B. Balch, ordered to duty at the Navy Yard, Washington, D. C.

March 10.—Commander Louis C. Sartori, detached from command of the Portsmouth, and ordered North.

March 15.—Commander George H. Preble, detached from command of the St. Louis, and ordered to command the Cambridge.

March 17.—Commander E. R. Calhoun, ordered to report to Rear-Admiral Gregory for duty.

March 21.—Commander Selim E. Woodworth, detached from command of the Narragansett, and waiting orders.

March 22.—Commander Henry Rolando, detached from command of the Keystone State, and ordered to temporary duty at Baltimore, Md.

March 27.—Commander J. B. Creighton, detached from the command of the Mingoe, and ordered to temporary Ordnance duty at Boston.

March 1.—Lieutenant-Commander Leonard Paulding, detached from the Navy Yard, New York, and ordered to command the Monocacy. Lieutenant-Commander John H. Upsher, detached from command of the A. D. Vance, and ordered on special duty at the Navy Department, Washington. Lieutenant-Commander James E. Jouett, ordered to the Navy Yard, New York.

March 6.—Lieutenant-Commander John Madigan, detached from Ordnance duty at Boston, and ordered to command the Paul Jones.

March 8.—Lieutenant-Commander John H. Upsher, orders to special duty at the Department revoked, and he will resume command of the A. D. Vance.

March 13.—Lieutenant-Commander Joseph D. Danels, detached from the Vanderbilt, and waiting orders.

March 14.—Lieutenant-Commander J. N. Quackenbush, detached from the (late) San Jacinto, and waiting orders. Lieutenant-Commander E. K. Owen, detached from the North Carolina, and ordered to command the Seneca. Lieutenant-Commander Montgomery Sicard, detached from the command of the Seneca, on the reporting of his relief. Lieutenant-Commander James W. Shirk, detached from special duty at Philadelphia, and ordered to the Vanderbilt.

March 18.—Lieutenant-Commander J. M. Pritchett, detached from the command of the Eutaw, and ordered to the Vanderbilt. Lieutenant Commander Jonathan Young, detached from command of the Sangamon, and ordered to command the Saginaw. Lieutenant-Commander James W. Shirk, orders to the Vanderbilt revoked, and he will remain attached to the Philadelphia Navy Yard.

March 24.—Lieutenant-Commander O. F. Stanton, detached from Ordnance duty at New York, and ordered to the Powhattan.

March 27.—Lieutenant-Commander S. P. Quackenbush, ordered to command the Mingoe. Lieutenant-Commander J. C. Chaplin, detached from command of the (late) Dai Ching, and waiting orders.

March 28.—Lieutenant-Commander Jonathan Young, orders to command the Saginaw revoked, and he will wait orders. Lieutenant-Commander R. W. Scott, detached from command of the Catskill, and ordered to command the Saginaw. Lieutenant-Commander Richard L. Law, ordered to command the Naval Rendezvous at Chicago, Ill.

March 30.—Lieutenant-Commander Byron Wilson, ordered to the North Atlantic Squadron. Lieutenant-Commander Leonard Paulding, detached from command of the Monocacy, and ordered to command the Eutaw.

March 31.—Lieutenant-Commander R. S. Phythian, detached from the New Ironsides, and waiting orders.

March 1.—Lieutenant Beatty P. Smith, ordered to the Susquehanna. Lieutenant George M. Brown, detached from the Susquehanna, on the reporting of his relief, and waiting orders.

March 6.—Lieutenant George Dewey, ordered to the Kearsarge.

March 7.—Lieutenant M. W. Sanders, detached from the Malvern, and ordered to the Pacific Squadron.

March 9.—Lieutenant R. H. Lamson, detached from command of the Gettysburg, on the reporting of his relief, and ordered to the Colorado. Lieutenant Edwin T. Woodward, ordered to the Kearsarge. Lieutenant Stephen A. McCarty, ordered to the Wyoming.

March 16.—Lieutenant M. L. Johnson, detached from the Colorado, and ordered to the West Gulf Squadron.

March 20.—Lieutenant C. M. Schoonmaker, detached from the De Soto, and ordered to the Catskill. Lieutenant G. C. Wiltse, detached from the St. Louis, and ordered North. Lieutenant C. W. Tracy, detached from the Catskill, on the reporting of his relief, and ordered North.

March 22.—Lieutenant J. P. Robertson, detached from the Keystone State, and waiting orders.

March 24.—Lieutenant R. S. McCook, detached from the Canonicus, and waiting orders.

March 27.—Lieutenant N. W. Thomas, detached from Ordnance duty at Boston, and ordered to the Susquehanna.

March 30.—Lieutenants George M. Bache and Henry C. Tallman, ordered to the North Atlantic Squadron.

March 31.—Lieutenant Henry J. Blake, detached from the New Ironsides, and ordered to the Ticonderoga. Lieutenant A. R. McNair, detached from the New Ironsides, and waiting orders.

March 6.—Acting Ensigns Charles J. Barclay and William H. Whiting, ordered to the Kearsarge.

March 7.—Acting Ensign George T. Davis, detached from the Malvern, and waiting orders.

March 3.—Assistant Surgeon David F. Ricketts, detached from the Naval Rendezvous at New York, and ordered to the New National. Assistant Surgeon Henry C. Eckstein, detached from the Naval Rendezvous at Philadelphia, and ordered to the General Lyon.

March 6.—Assistant Surgeon E. D. Payne, ordered to the Naval Rendezvous at Philadelphia.

March 8.—Assistant Surgeon William P. Baird, ordered to the West Gulf Squadron. Assistant Surgeon Robert Willard, detached from the Colorado, and ordered to the West Gulf Squadron. Assistant Surgeon Thomas Hiland, detached from the West Gulf Squadron, on the reporting of his relief, and ordered North.

March 14.—Surgeon Charles Eversfield, ordered to the Navy Yard at New York. Surgeon Delavan Bloodgood, ordered to the Michigan. Surgeon William M. Wood, detached from the Michigan, on the reporting of his relief, and waiting orders. Surgeon John M. Brown, detached from the Navy Yard at New York, and ordered to the Navy Yard at Mare Island, Cal.

March 15.—Assistant Surgeon John D. Murphy, detached from the Santiago de Cuba, and waiting orders.

March 17.—Surgeon Arthur Matthewson, detached from the Shawmut, and waiting orders.

March 18.—Surgeon Benjamin Vreeland, detached from the Naval Hospital at New York, and ordered to the Kearsarge. Surgeon James Suddards, ordered to the Vermont. Surgeon T. W. Leach, ordered to the Naval Hospital at New York. Surgeon H. F. McSherry, ordered to the Wyoming.

March 21.—Assistant Surgeon Joseph A. Bubier, detached from the Narragansett, and waiting orders.

March 22.—Assistant Surgeon F. M. Dearborne, detached from the Ohio, and ordered to the Octarora. Passed Assistant Surgeon Walter K. Scofield, detached from the Naval Hospital at Norfolk, Va., and ordered to the Bienville. Surgeon B. F. Gibbs, detached from the Ossipee, on the reporting of his relief, and ordered North. Assistant Surgeon Samuel F. Shaw, detached from the Sonoma, on the reporting of his relief, and ordered North. Assistant Surgeon L. Zenzen, detached from the Octarora, on the reporting of his relief, and ordered North. Assistant Surgeon H. M. Rundlett, ordered to the Ohio. Surgeon A. C. Rhoades, detached from the Bienville, and ordered to the Ossipee.

March 28.—Assistant Surgeon Theoron Woolverton, detached from the West Gulf Squadron, on the reporting of his relief, and ordered North. Assistant Surgeon Elwood Corson, detached from the Nantucket, on the reporting of his relief, and ordered North. Assistant Surgeon John T. Luck, detached from the Saranac, and ordered home. Assistant Surgeon L. M. Lyon, detached from the Vanderbilt, on the reporting of his relief, and waiting orders. Assistant Surgeon James Wilson, detached from the Monadnock, and ordered to the Vanderbilt.

March 29.—Surgeon S. Wilson Kellogg, detached from Naval Rendezvous, Burling Slip, New York, and waiting orders.

March 30.—Assistant Surgeon Charles L. Green, ordered to duty as Assistant to the Fleet Surgeon of the West Gulf Squadron. Assistant Surgeon Charles H. Perry, detached from the Susquehanna, on the reporting of his relief, and waiting orders.

March 31.—Assistant Surgeon F. B. A. Lewis, detached from the Mahopac, on the reporting of his relief, and waiting orders. Assistant Surgeon William J. Simon, detached from the Sangamon, and ordered to the Susquehanna. Surgeon Edward Shippen, and Assistant Surgeon George A. Bright, detached from the New Ironsides, and waiting orders.

Appointed Assistant Paymasters.

March 11.—James E. Tolfree, Luther J. Billings, James F. Hamilton, and Charles P. Thompson.

March 7.—Assistant Paymaster W. M. Watmough, ordered to the De Soto.

March 14.—Paymaster Rufus Parks, detached from the (late) San Jacinto, and waiting orders.

March 17.—Assistant Paymaster Theron Merritt, detached from the Kansas, on the reporting of his relief, and his resignation accepted.

March 18.—Paymaster J. C. Eldridge, detached from duty as Superintendent of the Purchase of Flour, &c., at New York Yard, and ordered to assume the duties of Paying Agent at the New York Navy Agency. Paymaster Henry Etting, detached from special duty at the New York Navy Agency, on the reporting of his relief, and waiting orders. Paymaster William Meredith, ordered to duty as Superintendent of the Purchase of Flour, &c., at New York Yard.

March 20.—Assistant Paymaster W. N. Watmough, detached from the De Soto, and ordered to the Kearsarge.

March 21.—Assistant Paymaster Charles E. Chenery, detached from the Narragansett, on completion of transfer, and ordered to settle his accounts.

March 27.—Assistant Paymaster C. F. Guild, detached from duty under Rear-Admiral Porter, and ordered to the Frolic (A. D. Vance).

March 29.—Paymaster Elisha W. Dunn, detached from duty as Fleet Paymaster of the Mississippi Squadron, and ordered to settle his accounts. Paymaster John S. Gulick, detached from duty at Philadelphia, on the reporting of his relief, and ordered to duty as Fleet Paymaster of the Mississippi Squadron. Paymaster Henry Etting ordered to Navy Yard at Philadelphia.

March 31.—Paymaster George Plunkett, detached from the New Ironsides, on completion of transfer, &c., and ordered to settle his accounts.

March 3.—Chief Engineer George S. Bright, ordered to Philadelphia for duty, as Superintendent of all Government work at the establishment of Merrick & Sons.

March 9.—Chief Engineer William J. Lamdin, detached from special duty at Baltimore, and waiting orders.

March 14.—Chief Engineer William J. Lamdin, ordered to the Dacotah.

March 31.—Chief Engineer Alexander Greer, detached from the New Ironsides, as on "sea duty," and ordered to duty in charge of the machinery of that vessel.

Promoted.

March 11.—Lieutenant-Commanders Henry N. T. Arnold, Thomas Pattison, Wm. N. Jeffers, Edward Simpson, and William G. Temple, to Commanders on the Active List, to date from March 3d, 1865. Ensign Edward E. Preble, to Lieutenant, to date from February 22d, 1865. Lieutenant George W. Doty, to Commander on the Retired List, to date from July 16th, 1862.

March 21.—Assistant Surgeon Archibald C. Rhoades, to Surgeon, to date from the 19th of March, 1865.

March 22.—Acting Volunteer Lieutenant-Commander Joseph D Danels, to Lieutenant-Commander on the Active List, to date from July 16th, 1862.

March 27.—Assistant Paymaster Albert S. Kenny, to Paymaster, to date from March 9th, 1865. Acting Assistant Paymaster Francis H. Swan, to Assistant Paymaster, "for meritorious services in connection with the destruction of the ram Albemarle," to date from March 9th, 1865. Commander John J. Young, to Captain on the Reserved List, to date from August 12th, 1854. Lieutenant-Commander Richmond Aulick, to Commander on the Retired List, to date from March 3d, 1865. Acting Lieutenant Edgar C. Merriman, to Lieutenant on the Active List, to date from July 16th, 1862.

Resigned.

March 1.—Assistant Surgeon Heber Smith.
March 13.—Surgeon John A. Lockwood.
March 17.—Assistant Paymaster Theron Merritt (to take effect on the reporting of his relief).
March 18.—Surgeon J. W. Shively.

Placed on the Retired List.

March 2.—Lieutenant-Commander Richard L. Law.
March 18.—Lieutenant-Commander Greenleaf Cilly.

Volunteer Navy.

Orders, &c.

March 3.—Acting Volunteer Lieutenant-Commander Pierre Giraud, detached from command of the Huntsville, and ordered to command the Monticello.

March 13.—Acting Volunteer Lieutenant-Commander E. F. Devins, detached from Navy Yard, Boston, and ordered to command the Huntsville.

March 15.—Acting Volunteer Lieutenant E. F. Devins, orders to the command of the Huntsville revoked.

March 22.—Acting Volunteer Lieutenant-Commander Pierre Giraud, detached from command of the Monticello, and ordered to command the Lady Stirling.

March 1.—Acting Volunteer Lieutenant Samuel B. Washburne, detached from the Newbern, and ordered to command the A. D. Vance.

March 8.—Acting Volunteer Lieutenant Samuel B. Washburn, orders to the A. D. Vance revoked, and he is ordered to report to Rear-Admiral Porter for duty.

March 11.—Acting Volunteer Lieutenant Thomas F. Wade, ordered to the North Carolina for temporary duty.

March 15.—Acting Volunteer Lieutenant J. F. Nickels, detached from command of the Cambridge, on the reporting of his relief, and ordered to report to Rear-Admiral Dahlgren for duty.

March 29.—Acting Volunteer Lieutenant E. D. Bruner, detached from command of the Lillian, and waiting orders. Acting Volunteer Lieutenant Henry Brown, detached from command of the Dumbarton, and waiting orders.

March 31.—Acting Volunteer Lieutenant C. J. Van Alstine, detached from the Stettin, and waiting orders.

March 1.—Acting Master William Tallman, detached from the Flag, and waiting orders. Acting Master John B. Childs, detached from the Memphis, and waiting orders. Acting Master R. O. Patterson, detached from command of the Memphis, and waiting orders. Acting Master Robert Y. Holley, ordered to command the Newbern.

March 3.—Acting Master R. B. Arrants, ordered to command the Currituck.

March 6.—Acting Master Charles Huggins, detached from the Fort Morgan, and ordered to the Paul Jones. Acting Master H. C. Wade, ordered to command the Yucca. Acting Master L. B. King, ordered to the Kearsarge.

March 7.—Acting Master T. W. Steer, detached from command of the Wyandotte, on the reporting of his relief, and ordered to report to Rear-Admiral Porter for such duty as he may assign. Acting Master J. A. Jackaway, detached from command of the Dawn, on the reporting of his relief, and ordered to report to Rear-Admiral Porter for such duty as he may assign. Acting Master William G. Nutting, detached from command of the Samuel Rotan, on the reporting of his relief, and ordered to report to Rear-Admiral Porter for such duty as he may assign.

Appointed Acting Master.

March 7.—E. S. Shurtliff, Potomac Flotilla.

Appointed Acting Master and Pilot.

March 1.—B. F. Clifford, East Gulf Squadron.

March 8.—Acting Master H. A. Phelon, detached from command of the Daylight, and ordered to report to Rear-Admiral Porter for such duty as he may assign. Acting Master Robert G. Lee, detached from command of the Commodore Morris, on the reporting of his relief, and ordered to report to Rear-Admiral Porter, for such duty as he may assign.

March 9.—Acting Master E. B. Mallett, detached from the Wyoming, on the reporting of his relief, and ordered to the Potomac Flotilla.

March 13.—Acting Master E. D. Percy, ordered to the Huntsville. Acting Master W. G. Wright, detached from the (late) San Jacinto, and waiting orders. Acting Master and Pilot, William Richardson, detached from the (late) San Jacinto, and ordered to report to the Department when discharged from the Court.

March 15.—Acting Master James L. Plunkett, detached from the North Carolina, and granted sick leave.

March 18.—Acting Master William Hedger, ordered to the Vanderbilt. Acting Master A. M. Keith, detached from the Vanderbilt, and waiting orders.

March 20.—Acting Master A. K. Jones, detached from the East Gulf Squadron, and ordered North.

March 21.—Acting Master Stephen H. Cornell, detached from the Narragansett, and waiting orders.

March 22.—Acting Master George W. Caswell, ordered to the East Gulf Squadron. Acting Masters W. T. Buck and L. E. Degn, detached from the Keystone State, and waiting orders.

March 25.—Acting Master William Tallman, ordered to the Lady Stirling.

March 27.—Acting Master W. N. Griswold, detached from the J. L. Davis, on the reporting of his relief, and ordered North. Acting Master A. K. Jones, detached from the Pursuit, on the reporting of his relief, and ordered North. Acting

Master Alfred Everson, detached from the De Soto, and ordered to the Conemaugh. Acting Master, R. O. Patterson, ordered to the J. L. Davis. Acting Master W. L. Howarth, ordered to the Conemaugh.

March 29.—Acting Master G. H. Pendleton, detached from the Lenapee, and granted sick leave. Acting Master G. C. Schulze, ordered to the Potomac Flotilla.

March 30.—Acting Master Henry O. Porter, detached from the Susquehanna, and ordered to the West Gulf Squadron. Acting Master and Pilot William Richardson, ordered to the Powhattan.

March 31.—Acting Master J. M. Butler, detached from the Stettin, and waiting orders. Acting Masters Walter Pearce and Henry P. Conner, detached from the New Ironsides, and waiting orders. Acting Master Joseph S. Gelett, detached from the Lillian, and granted sick leave. Acting Master G. H. Leinas, ordered to command the Squando.

Appointed Acting Ensigns.

March 1.—William K. Engell, and ordered to the Santiago de Cuba.
March 7.—Sydney B. Cline, Potomac Flotilla.
March 9.—Alfred Staigg, U. S. S. Winona; William A. Stannard, U. S. S. Saratoga.
March 10.—H. C. Eldridge, Potomac Flotilla.
March 11.—William B. Spencer, U. S. S. Nereus; William H. Hardison, and ordered to the Nahant; Charles Clark, James M. Jackson, and Charles B. Boutelle, and ordered to the Camanche.
March 16.—Charles A. Stewart, and ordered to the Muscoota; William L. Howarth (paroled prisoner).
March 18.—Abraham Leach, U. S. S. Camelia.
March 20.—N. B. Walker, U. S. S. Daffodil.
March 27.—R. L. M. Jones, U. S. S. Brittania; C. H. Burner, U. S. S. Glaucus.
March 29.—James West, U. S. S. Kensington; William Flood, Potomac Flotilla; Thomas C. Tinker, U. S. S. Arkansas.

Appointed Acting Ensign and Pilot.

March 18.—L. B. Kelley, U. S. S. Wissahickon.
March 25.—William Chapman, U. S. S. Albatross.

Appointed Acting Ensigns, and ordered to the School-Ship Savannah.

March 7.—George W. Lord, Henry B. Morton, Lewis H. Moore, and Francis A. Dean.
March 15.—Peltiah Perkins.
March 16.—William W. Hatch, and John W. Chase.
March 18.—William Mullen.
March 21.—John H. Marshall.
March 22.—Henry J. Trivett.

March 1.—Acting Ensigns Samuel A. Gove, E. W. Watson, and C. V. Kelley. detached from the Flag, and waiting orders. Acting Ensigns Seth W. Cowing, B. D. Reed, and George Chamberlain, detached from the Memphis, and waiting orders.

March 3.—Acting Ensign C. R. Fleming, detached from the Trefoil, and ordered to the Ohio. Acting Ensign Charles Moore, detached from the Ohio, and ordered to the Trefoil.

March 6.—Acting Ensign M. P. Powers, detached from the Fort Morgan, and ordered to the Yucca. Acting Ensign S. C. Hill, ordered to the Paul Jones. Acting Ensign W. B. Rankin, ordered to the Paul Jones. Acting Ensign W. J. Kirby, ordered to the Kearsarge.

March 8.—Acting Ensign F. B. Allen, detached from command of the J. N. Seymour, and ordered to report to Rear-Admiral Porter for such duty as he may assign.

March 10.—Acting Ensign Simpson Jenney, ordered to the Ottawa. Acting Ensign Jacob Cochran, detached from the Ottawa, on the reporting of his relief, and ordered North. Acting Ensign W. J. Kirby, orders to the Kearsarge revoked; he is detached from the (late) Merrimack, and ordered to the Bermuda. Acting Ensign Henry Heamre, detached from the (late) Merrimack, and ordered to the Bermuda.

March 11.—Acting Ensign C. J. Rogers, detached from the Nahant, on the reporting of his relief, and ordered North.

March 13.—Acting Ensigns S. T. Bliss, B. P. Trask, and C. V. Kelley, Jr., ordered to the Huntsville.

March 14.—Acting Ensign H. D. Foster, detached from the Constellation, on the reporting of his relief, and ordered to the Potomac Flotilla.

March 16.—Acting Ensign and Pilot Oliver Lasher, ordered to the North Atlantic Squadron.

March 17.—Acting Ensign F. A. Gross, detached from the Gettysburg, and ordered to the Advance. Acting Ensign James McVey, detached from the East Gulf Squadron, and waiting orders. Acting Ensign W. B. Rankin, to regard himself as detached from the Paul Jones, on her arrival in the Squadron to which she is ordered, and to report to the Commanding Officer of the Squadron for duty. Acting Ensign W. J. Eldridge, detached from the Advance, and ordered to the Gettysburg.

March 18.—Acting Ensign O. B. Holden, ordered to the East Gulf Squadron.

March 20.—Acting Ensign Henry F. Cleverly, detached from the Mount Vernon, and granted sick leave. Acting Ensign C. F. Ware, detached from the Frolic (Advance), and ordered to the Horace Beals. Acting Ensign Albert Melchert, detached from the Horace Beals, and ordered to the Frolic (Advance). Acting Ensign C. M. Bird, detached from the Keystone State, and ordered to the Sassacus.

March 21.—Acting Ensigns Jeremiah Mitchell and Cornelius Bartlett, detached from the Narragansett, and waiting orders. Acting Ensign E. W. Watson, ordered to the Frolic.

March 22.—Acting Ensign C. V. Kelley, Jr., ordered to the Huntsville.

March 23.—Acting Ensign Samuel A. Gove, ordered to the Union. Acting Ensign Joseph H. Clark, detached from the St. Lawrence, and ordered to report to Rear-Admiral Porter for duty.

March 25.—Acting Ensign A. R. Hazard, detached from the De Soto, and ordered to the Huntsville. Acting Ensign C. V. Kelly, Jr., detached from the Huntsville, and ordered to the Wyoming. Acting Ensigns George Chamberlain, A. P. Bashford, S. W. Cowing, and H. B. Francis, ordered to the Lady Stirling.

March 27.—Acting Ensign C. F. Palmer, detached from the Fort Henry, on the reporting of his relief, and ordered North. Acting Ensign H. S. Bunker, detached from the Stonewall, and ordered North. Acting Ensigns James McVey and B. D. Reed, ordered to the Conemaugh.

March 28.—Acting Ensign Thomas S. Gay, ordered to the Vandalia.

March 29.—Acting Ensign W. C. Underhill, detached from the Lillian, and waiting orders. Acting Ensign John A. Williams, detached from the Dumbarton, and waiting orders. Acting Ensign J. H. Jenks, ordered to the North Carolina.

March 30.—Acting Ensign Peter Howard, detached from the Vermont, and ordered to the Agawam. Acting Ensign Frederick O'Connor, ordered to the Ohio.

March 31.—Acting Ensigns J. C. Staples, C. B. Pray, and William Jenney, detached from the Stettin, and waiting orders. Acting Ensigns William A. Duer and John W. King, detached from the New Ironsides, and waiting orders. Acting Ensigns J. Mitchell and A. A. Franzen, ordered to the Squando. Acting Ensign C. V. Kelley, Jr., detached from the Huntsville, and ordered to the Wyoming. Acting Ensign C. R. Fleming, detached from the Ohio, and ordered to the Squando.

Appointed Acting Assistant Surgeons.

March 1.—Linnæus Fussell, and ordered to the Princeton.

March 3.—Henry Richardson, and ordered to the Alleghany. Edward C. Thatcher, and ordered to the Princeton. Charles E. Hosmer, and ordered to the Mississippi Squadron.

March 6.—Lyman Dow, and ordered to the Mississippi Squadron.

March 8.—Henry C. Young, Asa H. Zeigler, James N. Young, and John Mallam, and ordered to the Mississippi Squadron.

March 9.—Ernest D. Martin, and ordered to the Princeton.

March 10.—Frederick H. R. Phillips, and ordered to the Ohio. Nicholas H. McGuire, and ordered to the Mississippi Squadron. P. Wadsworth, and ordered to the Navy Yard, Washington, D. C.

March 11.—Frederick P. Sheppard, and ordered to the North Carolina. William P. Davis, and ordered to the Princeton.
March 14.—George W. Marsters, and ordered to the Ohio.
March 20.—Alvan Dodge, and ordered to the North Carolina.
March 21.—Jared W. Dillman, and ordered to the Princeton.
March 22.—Gilbert Balfour, and ordered to the Princeton.
March 24.—Ira L. Davies, and ordered to the Navy Yard, Washington, D. C.
March 25.—William J. Brofey, and ordered to the Mississippi Squadron.
March 28.—James T. Whittaker, and ordered to the Mississippi Squadron.

March 1.—Acting Assistant Surgeon William J. Burge, detached from the Flag, and waiting orders. Acting Assistant Surgeon W. H. Bates, detached from the Memphis, and waiting orders. Acting Assistant Surgeon Benjamin G. Walton, detached from the Gem of the Sea, and waiting orders.
March 2.—Acting Assistant Surgeon G. F. Brickett, detached from the Ohio, and ordered to the South Atlantic Squadron. Acting Assistant Surgeon Lewis Darling, Jr., detached from the North Carolina, and ordered to the South Atlantic Squadron. Acting Assistant Surgeon J. J. Sowerby, detached from the (late) Merrimack, and waiting orders.
March 3.—Acting Assistant Surgeon S. C. Johnson, ordered to the Mississippi Squadron.
March 9.—Acting Assistant Surgeon William H. Faxon, detached from the North Carolina, and ordered to the Galena. Acting Assistant Surgeon H. I. Babin, detached from the Ohio, and ordered to the Mercedita. Acting Assistant Surgeon Ed. Macomb, detached from the North Carolina, and ordered to the Tahoma. Acting Assistant Surgeon Linnæus Fussell, detached from the Princeton, and ordered to the Sagamore.
March 11.—Acting Assistant Surgeon Edward C. Thatcher, detached from the Princeton, and ordered to the Governor Buckingham. Acting Assistant Surgeon Henry C. Meredith, detached from the Princeton, and ordered to the Miami.
March 14.—Acting Assistant Surgeon P. Wadsworth, detached from duty at Washington Navy Yard, and ordered to the Potomac Flotilla.
March 15.—Acting Assistant Surgeon D. J. Harris, detached from the Commodore McDonough, on the reporting of his relief, and ordered North. Acting Assistant Surgeon F. P. Sheppard, detached from the North Carolina, and ordered to the Commodore McDonough.
March 17.—Acting Assistant Surgeon J. J. Sowerby, ordered to the Shawmut.
March 18.—Acting Assistant Surgeon George W. Shields, ordered to the Fort Henry. Acting Assistant Surgeon B. F. Hamell detached from the Frolic (Advance), and ordered to the Neptune. Acting Assistant Surgeon George Doig, detached from the Emma, and ordered to the South Atlantic Squadron. Acting Assistant Surgeon J. F. Fourtellotte, detached from the Fort Henry, on the reporting of his relief, and ordered North.
March 22.—Acting Assistant Surgeon Henry Richardson, detached from the Alleghany, and ordered to the Sonoma.
March 25.—Acting Assistant Surgeon E. D. Martin, detached from the Princeton, and ordered to the Fort Henry. Acting Assistant Surgeon G. W. Shields, orders to the Fort Henry revoked, and he is ordered to the Mississippi Squadron.
March 30.—Acting Assistant Surgeon F. H. R. Phillips, detached from the Ohio, and ordered to the Paul Jones.
March 31.—Acting Assistant Surgeon R. Stone, detached from the Stettin, and waiting orders. Acting Assistant Surgeon W. P. Davis, detached from the Princeton, and ordered to the Sangamon. Acting Assistant Surgeon Nelson Ingram, detached from the Ohio, and ordered to the Mahopac. Acting Assistant Surgeon Charles A. Manson, ordered to the Nantucket.

Appointed Acting Assistant Paymasters.

March 2.—David S. Knapp, and waiting orders.
March 6.—William W. Castle, and waiting orders.
March 15.—Dominick Batione, and waiting orders.
March 16.—Eugene Littell, and waiting orders.
March 20.—George W. Brown, and waiting orders.

March 27.—C. S. Dickerman, and waiting orders. Henry M. Upham, and waiting orders.

March 29.—William J. Thompson, and waiting orders. Frank K. Balch, and waiting orders.

March 30.—J. W. Meacham, and waiting orders.

March 31.—C. W. Armstrong, and waiting orders.

March 1.—Acting Assistant Paymaster O. B. Seagrave, detached from the Flag, on completion of transfer, and ordered to settle accounts. Acting Assistant Paymaster Henry G. Colby, detached from the Gem of the Sea, on the completion of transfer, and ordered to settle accounts.

March 6.—Acting Assistant Paymaster J. T. Wildman, ordered to settle accounts of the (late) Merrimack.

March 7.—Acting Assistant Paymaster George A. Ferre, detached from the Morse, on the reporting of his relief, and ordered to settle accounts. Acting Assistant Paymaster Charles A. McDaniel, ordered to the Morse.

March 9.—Acting Assistant Paymaster S. Anderson, ordered to the Lodona. Acting Assistant Paymaster Myron M. Hovey, ordered to the E. B. Hale. Acting Assistant Paymaster Granville Bacon, ordered to the Honduras. Acting Assistant Paymaster Henry Russell, ordered to the Ethan Allen.

March 9.—Acting Assistant Paymaster William R. Woodward, detached from the Ethan Allen, on the reporting of his relief, and ordered to settle his accounts. Acting Assistant Paymaster O. B. Gilman, detached from the E. B. Hale, on the reporting of his relief, and ordered to settle his accounts. Acting Assistant Paymaster A. Murray Stewart, detached from the Lodona, on the reporting of his relief, and ordered to settle his accounts. Acting Assistant Paymaster John C. Stoever, ordered to the Mississippi Squadron. Acting Assistant Paymaster T. L. Tullock, Jr., ordered to the Paul Jones.

March 10.—Acting Assistant Paymaster John Read, ordered to the Kearsarge. Acting Assistant Paymaster Edward Sherwin, detached from the (late) Dai Ching, and ordered to settle his accounts.

March 13.—Acting Assistant Paymaster D. L. Ruth, ordered to the Forest Rose.

March 14.—Acting Assistant Paymaster T. A. Swords, detached from the Niphon, and ordered to settle his accounts.

March 17.—Acting Assistant Paymaster Frank H. Arms, detached from the Memphis, and ordered to settle his accounts. Acting Assistant Paymaster C. H. Lockwood, ordered to the Kansas. Acting Assistant Paymaster Charles W. Slamm, ordered to the Huntsville.

March 20.—Acting Assistant Paymaster William W. Castle, ordered to the Yucca.

March 22.—Acting Assistant Paymaster J. W. Fairfield, detached from the Keystone State, on the completion of transfer, and ordered to settle his accounts.

March 23.—Acting Assistant Paymaster George W. Brown, ordered to the Lillian.

March 24.—Acting Assistant Paymaster C. H. Lockwood, orders to the Kansas revoked, and waiting orders. Acting Assistant Paymaster Eugene Littell, ordered to the Kansas.

March 27.—Acting Assistant Paymaster Franklin Miller, detached from the Frolic (Advance), on the reporting of his relief, and ordered to settle his accounts. Acting Assistant Paymaster C. H. Lockwood, ordered to the Lady Stirling.

March 28.—Acting Assistant Paymaster Dominick Batione, ordered to the Calypso.

March 29.—Acting Assistant Paymaster Charles W. Crary, detached from the Dumbarton, on the completion of transfer, and ordered to settle his accounts. Acting Assistant Paymaster R. B. Rodney, ordered to the Conemaugh. Acting Assistant Paymaster W. W. Castle, orders to the Yucca revoked, and waiting orders. Acting Assistant Paymaster George W. Brown, orders to the Lillian revoked, and he is ordered to the Yucca. Acting Assistant Paymaster Benjamin Abrahams, detached from the Stettin, and ordered to settle his accounts.

Promoted for Good Conduct, &c.

March 7.—Acting Volunteer Lieutenants John MacDearmid and L. W. Pennington, to Acting Volunteer Lieutenant-Commanders. Acting Masters Alfred Weston,

W. H. Woods, Thomas G. Grove, Charles Norton, and S. Nickerson, to Acting Volunteer Lieutenants. Acting Ensign C. L. Wilcomb, to Acting Master.

March 11.—Acting Volunteer Lieutenants William S. Cheeseman and William P. Randall, to Acting Volunteer Lieutenant-Commanders. Acting Ensign Albert Taylor, to Acting Master.

March 13.—Acting Masters J. A. Pennell and W. T. Gillespie, to Acting Volunteer Lieutenants. Acting Ensign N. A. Blume, to Acting Master.

March 15.—Acting Ensign Sanford S. Miner, to Acting Master. Acting Master Francis Josselyn, to Acting Volunteer Lieutenant.

March 17.—Acting Master E. M. Stoddard, to Acting Volunteer Lieutenant.

March 20.—Acting Ensigns Thomas F. Lacock and George W. Bourne, to Acting Masters.

March 23.—Acting Ensigns J. J. Brice and Eugene Biondi, to Acting Masters.

March 24.—Acting Ensign Walter Pearce, to Acting Master.

March 27.—Acting Volunteer Lieutenant C. H. Rockwell, to Acting Volunteer Lieutenant-Commander. Acting Ensigns Thomas Nelson, C. F. Hodgkins, and Hans J. Ipsen, to Acting Masters.

March 28.—Acting Ensign William Jennings, to Acting Master.

March 29.—Acting Ensign G. E. McConnell, to Acting Master.

March 30.—Acting Assistant Surgeon N. L. Campbell, to Acting Passed Assistant Surgeon.

Resigned.

March 2.—Acting Volunteer Lieutenant-Commander Edgar Brodhead.

March 3.—Acting Ensign Alfred Hornsby.

March 7.—Acting Master W. Wright; Acting Master Charles Potter; Acting Volunteer Lieutenant W. D. Roath.

March 8.—Acting Ensign and Pilot I. H. Puckett; Acting Assistant Surgeon William S. Parker.

March 9.—Acting Assistant Paymasters Jonathan Chapman and Thomas B. Cushing.

March 11.—Acting Assistant Surgeon G. H. Marvin.

March 13.—Acting Assistant Surgeon A. Shirk; Acting Master D. P. Heath; Acting Ensigns D. B. Corey, Charles T. Somes, and George T. Miller. Acting Assistant Paymaster A. J. Myers.

March 14.—Acting Assistant Paymaster H. Y. Glisson.

March 15.—Acting Assistant Paymaster Herman Dorr. Acting Master Frank H. Wilks.

March 16.—Acting Masters H. S. Borden and John M. Skillings. Acting Ensigns Lewis P. Cassan and Thomas McLevy.

March 17.—Acting Master P. J. Hargous. Acting Ensign Charles E Clark.

March 18.—Acting Master W. N. Griswold. Acting Ensigns Edwin McKeever and A. H. Mandell. Acting Assistant Surgeons George W. Hatch and M. C. Drennan.

March 20.—Acting Assistant Paymasters J. R. Morris and John Read.

March 21.—Acting Assistant Paymaster Clifford S. Sims. Acting Ensign Joseph T. Ridgway.

March 22.—Acting Volunteer Lieutenant William H. Latham.

March 23.—Acting Ensign P. A. Seabury.

March 25.—Acting Masters S. H. Cornell and Lewis West.

March 27.—Acting Master and Pilot Samuel J. White. Acting Master Francis E. Ellis. Acting Ensigns William H. Gibson and Charles J. Walstrom.

March 28.—Acting Assistant Paymaster A. H. Nelson, to take effect on the reporting of his relief. Acting Ensigns William H. De Grosse and Charles D. Duncan.

March 30.—Acting Ensign Clinton Wiley. Acting Master Charles Potter. Acting Ensign Abram H. Hicks.

Revoked.

March 6.—Acting Assistant Surgeon R. E. Woodward.

March 9.—Acting Masters and Pilots, George Look, Thomas Smith, G. F. Bowen, J. S. Furlaw, James W. Taylor, John W. Sayres, T. A. Wyatt, E. A. Elliott.

March 14.—Acting Ensign T. F. De Luce.
March 16.—Acting Assistant Surgeon Ira C. Whitehead.
March 24.—Acting Master W. G. Nutting.
March 28.—Acting Volunteer Lieutenant John D. Harty, to take effect on the reporting of his relief.
March 31.—Acting Master and Pilot Benjamin R. Dorey.

Dismissed.

March 8.—Acting Master E. Herrick.
March 25.—Acting Assistant Paymaster, George W. McLane.

Miscellaneous.

March 8.—Order dismissing Acting Ensign Arnold Harris revoked, and his resignation accepted from Feb. 21st, 1865.
March 9.—Order of Feb. 24th, 1865, dismissing Acting Master George W. Frost, revoked.
March 18.—Acting Master G. W. Caswell, term of suspension having expired, he is ordered to report to the Department by letter.
March 30.—Acting Master and Pilot William Jones, order of Dec. 29th, 1864, revoking his appointment revoked, and his resignation accepted from that date.

Mississippi Squadron.

Appointed Acting Ensigns.

March 22.—Joseph Graham, U. S. S. Daisy; Hiram Simonton, U. S. S. Grosbeak; William Kesner, U. S. S. Naumkeag; Benjamin W. Herr, U. S. S. Tempest.
March 25.—E. F. Crane, U. S. S. Chillicothe.
March 29.—Edward C. Urner, U. S. S. Lexington.

Promoted.

March 25.—Acting Ensign M. B. Muncy, to Acting Master.

Resigned.

March 1.—Acting Ensign George J. Hazlett.
March 2.—Acting Ensign H. B. O'Neill.
March 3.—Acting Master George D. Little; Acting Ensign E. C. Van Pelt.
March 13.—Acting Ensign W. K. Owen.
March 16.—Acting Ensign Charles C. Briggs.
March 21.—Acting Ensign W. L. Constantine.
March 22.—Acting Ensign Charles W. Spooner; Acting Master Benjamin Sebastian.
March 25.—Acting Volunteer Lieutenant Charles G. Perkins.

Personal Items.

Brigadier-General Jas. F. Hartranft has, on General Grant's recommendation, been promoted major-general by brevet, "for conspicuous gallantry in repulsing and driving back the enemy from the lodgment made on our lines, March 25th, 1865."

Major-General N. P. Banks, accompanied by Colonel Wilson and Captain Crosby of his staff, has returned to New Orleans, and assumed command of the Department of the Gulf.

Brevet Colonel F. T. Dent, of Lieutenant-General Grant's staff, has been appointed brigadier-general, and assigned to command as military governor at Richmond.

Colonel Schofield has been appointed brigadier-general and chief of staff to his brother, Major-General J. M. Schofield.

Colonel Kendall (33d New Jersey) has been appointed brigadier-general and chief of staff to Major-General H. W. Slocum.

THE UNITED STATES SERVICE MAGAZINE.

VOL. III.—JUNE, 1865.—NO. VI.

SHERMAN'S TRUCE.

We have been at some pains—a labor tenfold repaid by the pleasure—to present to our readers, both in our special editorial pages, and in the essays of distinguished contributors, full accounts of the wonderful strategy, magnificent marches, and victorious battles, of this illustrious general. To him, more than to any other man, except Grant, the country owes the dissolution of the rebel armies, the collapse of the rebellion, and the spring harbingers of the grandest peace ever conquered and established. After marvels at which the world will never cease to wonder, he followed Johnston's shattered army to Durham Station, and there, removed from immediate communication with the Department, made with the rebel general the basis of an agreement for a disbandment of the rebel armies, the re-establishment of the Federal and State authorities, and a general amnesty. The truce was to hold until the required authorities should express their willingness to carry out the programme. That Sherman's action was not final, it hardly seems necessary to say; for in the *seventh* article of the "basis of agreement" it is distinctly stated.

It is neither unjust nor ungenerous to Sherman to state that these terms, prompted by a warm heart and a vivid vision of instant peace even " to the banks of the Rio Grande," were not satisfactory to the Government or to the people. What then? Simply disapprove them, and order a resumption of hostilities. The President rejected them, the Department disallowed them, and General Grant, one of Sherman's warmest friends, disapproved them. The latter went in person to the scene, dictated other terms, and left Sherman to carry them out. Here the matter ends. The policy of Sherman, which was disapproved by the Government, so far from impeaching his patriotism, gives proof of an ardent desire for the immediate restoration of the Union, and Peace; so far from charging him with ambition, it shows a readiness to give generous terms to a foe whom he might have routed to the winds, and to finish, by a convention, a contest every day of which caused his name to be sounded with new sonorous harmony all over the civilized world. Many thought the kind-hearted and revered Lincoln too lenient; not a few growled and snarled at Grant for his terms to Lee; Sherman only went a little farther, and his action needed not reprehension but modification. These his agreement allowed for, and these were at once set forth. Detraction, more hateful than death, "loves a shining mark." Little critics, like Egyptian boys who pelt the pyramids with balls of sand, have had, for a day, rich sport. One says, in the emphatic language of Webster when speaking of the murderer's secret: "Ah, gentlemen, it was a fatal mistake!" Another speaks—with high-tragedy air—of "Sherman's fall," as long and terrible as that of Satan from heaven! And yet another caps the climax by saying: "Sherman voluntarily committed a fault the country can never forget."

Now, this is all simply ridiculous; the high tragedy is rich farce. Sherman has not fallen at all; his mistake was not fatal; his truce was submitted and disallowed. Without a murmur, even of disappointment, but doubtless with a feeling of insulted dignity at the manner of the disavowal, he prescribes the new terms brought by Grant, and Johnston's army is surrendered at once.

If Sherman made a mistake, he did not commit a crime; and when the convention of Durham Station, its issue, and the carping voices of the little critics are entirely forgotten, the patriot, the great captain, the honest man, the hero of a hundred fights, will shine with ever-increasing lustre and diameter. History will deal with his "crazy" but far-seeing call for two hundred thousand men, with Pittsburg Landing, Vicksburg, the march to Meridian, Chattanooga, Missionary Ridge, the bold move from Atlanta to the sea, the fall of Savannah, Charleston, Wilmington, Raleigh, and the *surrender of Johnston's army.*

General Sherman has, with commendable spirit, said nothing as yet in regard to the truce; the time will come for him to speak, and he will speak with no truckling, no uncertain sound. Until then we express what ought to be, and we believe are, the views of our whole people. Whatever he may find in the retrospect to forgive himself for—if any thing—we owe him rather too much to humiliate him either with reproach or forgiveness; for if we come to compare accounts, we shall find that we are bankrupt debtors, who can never repay him for a thousandth part, even if we load the scale with "*unconditional forgiveness.*" We hope Sherman will *not forget* those who have so boldly asserted that *they cannot forget.* He may, however, bear up under the admiring friendship and entire confidence of General Grant, the enthusiastic gratitude of the whole country, and such an unsolicited opinion as is contained in the following letter from Chief-Justice Chase:—

"WASHINGTON, *April* 29, 1865.

"WILLIAM G. DESHLER, Treasurer Sherman Testimonial Fund:—

"MY DEAR SIR:—Enclosed is a contribution to the Sherman Fund. I take this moment for making it, because just now many seem disposed to forget his great deservings, and remember only his recent convention with Johnston. But that act, however regretted and disapproved, must not cancel in our memories, or even obscure his splendid services. His patriotism is no more doubtful than his courage. No man's achievements have contributed more to the grand triumph of Union and freedom over rebellion and slavery. His deeds are among the choicest treasures of our own Ohio, as well as of our whole country. And we, the children of Ohio, are bound especially, and by the most sacred obligations, to defend and protect the good name of every brave and loyal son she has. She has none braver or more loyal than Sherman.

"Yours most truly,

"S. P. CHASE."

WHAT THE COAST SURVEY HAS DONE FOR THE WAR.

WHEN men are aware of the existence of a certain thing, if they do not perceive its results, they not unfrequently assume that there are none.

There is probably nothing to which this observation is more applicable than to the Coast Survey of the United States. Although it has been in operation for a number of years, and has been prosecuted with zeal, fidelity, and success, unsurpassed in the history of natural enterprise, the knowledge of its merit has been confined to a limited number of persons beyond those employed in its labors. Yet, during that time, the country at large has been benefited, to an incalculable degree, by operations which embrace a range including the most scientific methods known to geodesy, as well as the infinite and infinitesimal details that bring the practical results of the survey within the comprehension of the least skilful navigator. Stated simply, without reference to scientific investigation, the Coast Survey has been the agency which has saved to the country millions of dollars and thousands of lives. But it was not appreciated, because its results are intangible. Men seldom realize the worth of that which benefits them indirectly.

The rebellion came, and the Coast Survey, and, indeed, all

other public interests, dwindled into insignificance before the vital one attached to the restoration of the integrity of the Republic. There were comparatively few who were aware that the Coast Survey could aid the Government in its efforts to suppress the rebellion. Yet the Survey has never rendered to the country more important service than that performed since the commencement of the war. Independently of the vast amount of information which it put into the possession of the Army and Navy, when the country was forced to the arbitrament of arms, it has never ceased to take an active part in connection with actual hostilities.

It is not within the scope of these papers to give a history of all the various means by which the Coast Survey has aided the military authorities. This would require far more space than the narrow limits within which they are necessarily confined. Were it possible to do otherwise, the account would prove a mass of dry details, as uninteresting in comparison with active movements, as the daily drill and camp routine of an army are to the hostile shock upon the day of battle. For these reasons, it is intended to descant only upon those services which are indissolubly linked with some grand operation of the war.

All of the military surveys executed have been valuable to the commanders of our land and naval forces; but an account of all, forms no legitimate part of a narrative intended for the general reader. Had a battle or a bombardment happened along every league of the coast which the rebels attempted to wrest from the United States, the labors of the Survey in each place would not have failed to become manifest.

We cannot overestimate the value of the operations undertaken with special reference to military and naval movements—reconnoissance, sounding, buoying, piloting—that have aided our armies and fleets. Some of these labors must, of course, forever remain in comparative obscurity, for their full value could be brought to light only in the progress of military enterprise. But, whenever movements have taken place upon land or sea, the material aid derived from these labors has awakened the admiration of both Army and Navy, and they have rivalled each other in avowing their indebtedness, and in awarding unqualified praise.

The people, also, will appreciate these services, which, however humble they may appear when contrasted with the vast operations to which they contributed, have proved largely conducive to the brilliant achievements of our arms. The most acceptable form which this account can take for the public, will be a recital of the general services rendered by the Coast Survey in the field, but more particularly of those in which it enacted a conspicuous part in the battles of the war.

At the beginning of the year 1861, all the usual arrangements had been made for the continuation of the survey on the Southern sea-board of the Atlantic, and on the shores of the Gulf of Mexico. The angry cloud which was so soon to darken the land, had already commenced to gather and to assume an alarming significance; but the wisest were not without hope that the danger portended would pass harmlessly away. At all events, it was not proper that the premature action of any department of the Government should lend countenance to the rebellion, even by so much as tacitly ackowledging it to be a possibility. Accordingly, the parties of the Coast Survey resumed work in the various fields suitable for their operations.

Although it was ascertained that they were well received, events soon took such a course as to induce Professor A. D. Bache, the Superintendent of the Coast Survey, to dispatch a vessel for the purpose of conveying secret instructions to each party in order to insure the safety of the Government property, in the event of hostile demonstration on the part of the South. To this precaution the Survey is indebted for the exemption of most of its property from capture by the enemy. The officers were upon the alert, and except the seizure of three small vessels, and a small amount of property stored in remote places, nothing was lost. Two of the vessels were seized as they lay in ordinary at Charleston, and the other was seized while engaged in stationing tidal observers along the shores of the Gulf. The loss entailed by their capture was inconsiderable; for two were schooners, of which one had been long in the service, and the third vessel was a steam-tender, so small that she was not considered fit to make voyages from Charleston to New York. This vessel, when in possession of the rebels at Savannah, was burned by accident. One of the schooners, the *Petrel*, was the first vessel which the rebels sent out as a privateer. In the mist and gloaming she mistook the frigate *St. Lawrence* for a merchantman, and fired a shot across her bows. In an instant, the ports of the frigate flew open, and a well-aimed broadside sent the schooner to the bottom.

The spring of 1861 saw almost all of the officers of the Coast Survey engaged on duty in the Northern States, either in continuing the regular surveys, or in aiding the Government wherever their services were available within the field of military operations. The new exigencies of the Government found them conversant with duties which they were needed to perform. The Engineers and the Topographical Engineers,[*] two corps of the regular Army, had been created with reference to the scale upon which the old Army was based. They were now numerically insufficient for the performance of all the duties of reconnoissance, surveying, etc., devolving upon the

---

[*] These two corps have since been merged into one, called the Corps of Engineers.

immense forces in the field. Besides, they were needed more especially for the duties of military engineering, and some were withdrawn from these by the attainment of high command. Thus, they were soon absorbed by the demands of a service to which all that the Nation had previously experienced of war was like playing soldiers. It was under these circumstances that the Coast Survey soon proved its usefulness.

Relative to the state of affairs on that work, in the spring of 1861, the Superintendent, in his Report for the year, said:—

"The call for the services of the officers of the Army and Navy being imperious, the operations, generally, have been executed by civilians. The advantages of the organization of the work, which have often been stated, were never so fully displayed as in this exigency. The regular work was carried on systematically, though upon a reduced scale. The Navy found on its roll, officers who had knowledge of the harbors and coasts, from service on the survey. To the army list were returned officers skilled in reconnoissance, and in the other various operations of the survey, and familiar with the coast and its shore-lines. The vessels of the survey, both steam and sail vessels, were ready in the emergency for the revenue and naval services, and were freely yielded to their use.

"The material in the Coast Survey office was rapidly put in the shape of hydrographic notes, and, by lithographic and photographic processes, the unpublished maps and charts, and memoirs of the coast, were placed at the disposal of the departments of the Government, and of the officers engaged in consultations in regard to, or the executions of, operations along the coast."

In the year 1860, there had been twelve officers of the Army, and eleven officers of the Navy, serving on the Coast Survey. Of these, in 1861, eleven were detached from the work, and eight resigned. Two officers of the Army and two of the Navy remained temporarily. Of the civilians of the Survey, only seven were recreant to duty. All the rest proved their devotion to the Union.

One officer of the Survey accepted a colonelcy on the staff of Major-General Halleck, which position he still occupies, having accompanied General Halleck to the various military departments in which he has been engaged since the beginning of the war. Another officer of the Survey accepted the lieutenant-colonelcy of the 24th Ohio Regiment, and afterwards became colonel of the 44th Ohio Regiment. It was he, who, when commanding at Lexington, Ky., notified the disloyal convention there assembled, that it might consider itself dissolved. Another officer became assistant quartermaster in the Army. He is now in charge of ocean transportation for the Army.

When the rebellion broke out, one of the assistants on the Coast Survey happened to be in Virginia with his family. Cut off from communication with the office, he was not only without his usual means of support, but, at the same time, exposed to solicitations to join the insurgents. Although in such a strait, he repelled the offers which were made to him, and managed to maintain himself and his family by keeping store in Brentsville, Va., where he was found when our lines were extended to that town. He immediately submitted to the Government proof of his loyalty, and delivered the maps which he had secreted during the time that he was liable to be plundered of them. Since that time he has been constantly engaged, with the rank of captain, in making surveys for the Corps of Engineers.

The only person on the Coast Survey, who, upon the breaking out of hostilities, was so unfortunate as to fall into the hands of the insurgents, was a tidal observer, stationed at Calcasieu Entrance, Louisiana. About the beginning of April, 1861, he was questioned in regard to the nature of his occupation, and having satisfied his interrogators as to its harmlessness, he was allowed to continue his duties until the 11th of July, at which time he was arrested, in consequence of an order dispatched from New Orleans. At first, it was intended to try him as a spy, at Lake Charles City; and he was confined there until the 15th of August, when a detachment of soldiers sent from New Orleans carried him to that city as a prisoner of war. He was finally brought before the military commander, General Twiggs, who silenced his explanations by personal abuse, remanded him to prison, and ordered his trial as a spy. He was first sent to the common "lock-up," and then, after an examination by a recorder, he was placed in the parish prison, subject to the order of the military commander. In that place of confinement he spent three months, and at last obtained his release through the interposition of the British consul. He immediately left New Orleans, and reported in person at Washington, where he gave an account, from which these statements are taken.

In May, 1861, a hydrographic reconnoissance of the Potomac, between Blakistone Island and Georgetown, D. C., was executed by the Coast Survey. The results of the reconnoissance were immediately plotted and furnished to the military and naval authorities.

In the first week of June, a topographical and hydrographical reconnoissance was made at White House Point, Mathias Point, and Lower Cedar Point. The results of the reconnoissance were immediately furnished to the Government.

By request of Lieutenant-General Scott, arrangements were at the same time effected to make a detailed survey of the ground occupied by Brigadier-General (now Major-General) McDowell's army, and of the country to the north and west of his pickets, in the direction of Fairfax Court-House, including the Upper Potomac, as far as the point known as the Chain Bridge.* As the survey progressed, tracings of it were furnished to Generals McDowell and Tyler, and to Colonel (now General) Heintzelman. The two Corps of Engineers were also supplied with copies. Subsequently, the survey was photo-

---

* That bridge has long been superseded by another kind of structure.

graphed, and placed at the disposal of the officers for whose purposes it had been ordered.

In the middle of August, at the request of Major-General McClellan, the northwestern approaches of the city of Washington were surveyed. In October, the surveys were extended toward the northward and westward, from Fall's Church and the Chain Bridge.

Early in November, the topography of the Potomac was executed from below Alexandria to Mount Vernon, and from the southern shore of the Potomac to within three miles of Fairfax Court-House.

These surveys, in the aggregate, embraced two hundred and twenty-three square miles.

After the month of August, the parties engaged in these operations were under the general direction of Lieutenant-Colonel Macomb, Topographical Engineer-in-Chief of the Army of the Potomac.

In the Report of Major-General McClellan, where he refers to the Peninsular Campaign, after enumerating certain officers of the Topographical Engineers, he says:—

"This number, being the greatest available, was so small, that much of the duty of the department devolved upon parties furnished by Professor Bache, Superintendent of the Coast Survey, and other gentlemen from civil life."

Towards the last of August, two ships, the Express and Orizimba, were seized in Maine, by a Coast Survey party on board of the Arago. This vessel was engaged in hydrography on the coast of Maine, and the seizure alluded to was executed under the authority of the Collector of Customs at Eastport, Maine. In September, the Arago, which, by request of the same collector, was cruising in the Bay of Fundy, captured the ship Alice Ball, of New Orleans.

While reconnoissances and surveys were in progress within the theatre of active military operations, other reconnoissances and surveys, for military purposes, were executed in places more remote. The Delaware, opposite Philadelphia, was surveyed, and also near Fort Mifflin and Fort Delaware. Military surveys were executed in Accomac and Northampton Counties, Virginia. In fact, wherever a prospective need of defence called for information which the Coast Survey could provide, or wherever a military movement demanded the aid which it alone had the power to give, there the Coast Survey was found.

To facilitate the operations of blockading squadrons, hydrographic notes were prepared for the use of the War and Navy Departments, and furnished to them and to the commanders of expeditions. The first copies were referred to an advisory commission composed of Brigadier-General (now Major-General) Barnard, Captain (now Rear-Admiral) Du Pont,

Commander (now Rear-Admiral) Davis, and the Superintendent of the Coast Survey. In the Report of the Secretary of the Navy for 1861, he referred to the importance of this Commission. The estimation in which the material, submitted by the Coast Survey, was held by the naval officers who composed the Commission, is shown by the following letter:—

"WASHINGTON, *October* 2, 1861.

"SIR:—On closing, for the present, the labors of the mixed conference, in which I have presided, I cannot but express the high opinion I have been led to entertain of the usefulness of the Coast Survey to our knowledge of the sea-coasts, sounds, and bays of the Atlantic and Gulf borders of the United States, without which the deliberations of the conference could not have been successfully conducted.

"Very truly, your friend and obedient servant,
"S. F. DU PONT,
"*Flag-Officer, President.*

"A. D. BACHE, LL. D.,
"*Superintendent United States Coast Survey,*
"*Washington, D. C.*

"C. H. DAVIS,
"*Commander, Secretary.*"

The name of Admiral Du Pont naturally brings us to the consideration of the most important service which the Coast Survey rendered to the Government in the course of the year 1861.

The reader will recollect that, for a long period after the battle of Bull Run, the war seemed to languish. The forces opposing each other near the Potomac presented the strange spectacle of two hostile armies, both of which were upon the defensive, and neither of which seemed inclined to take the initiative.

Although Western Virginia continued to witness the uninterrupted triumph of our arms, and the expedition to Hatteras Inlet, North Carolina, and the lodgment on Ship Island, Mississippi Sound, had been successful, yet the general result of operations since the commencement of the war had been manifestly in favor of the South. Since the battle of Bull Run, no decisive conflict had taken place but the rebel armies, from East to West, had closed around the line which had become a frontier; while the Government of the United States, trammelled by the necessity of consulting political expediency as well as military exigency, seemed almost paralyzed in confronting a force precipitated with the volcanic energy characteristic of rebellion.

The country was despondent. The cause of this feeling originated less in the belief that the South had accomplished much, than in the experience that the United States had given little evidence of that great military power, which, despite the most stubborn resistance, was eventually to overwhelm the rebellion. True, this dark hour was not like that when the Army of the Potomac, baffled in its purpose, returned from Richmond, joined the shattered ranks of General Pope, and barely saved the capital. But it was dark enough, for then the Nation was doubtful of its untried strength; whereas, when it welcomed back its army from the Peninsula, its sadness was redeemed by the thought that it possessed a force of veterans so tried, that, even in retreat, they had often snatched victory from the enemy.

At this period, however, the people sorely needed some military success to cheer their drooping spirits, and inspire them with confidence in the administration of affairs. The victory at Port Royal had that effect.

A mysterious fleet, a mixed military and naval expedition, assembled in Hampton Roads. On the 29th of October it sailed towards the South. The naval part of the expedition was commanded by Commodore Du Pont, the land-forces were commanded by Brigadier-General T. W. Sherman. Scarcely had the fleet put to sea, when it encountered a violent gale, which scattered the vessels in every direction. The public mind was much excited lest the storm should prove fatal to the success of the expedition, for it was known that the fleet comprised many craft that were entirely unfit to meet heavy weather.

The crew of the transport *Peerless* were removed when she was in a sinking condition. The marines on board of the steamer *Governor* were with difficulty rescued. But the fleet, although shattered, was not wrecked. As soon as the vessels assembled, operations commenced.

In his Report to the Superintendent of the Coast Survey, Assistant Boutelle, speaking of the preliminaries of the attack, says:—

"The *R. B. Forbes* came to me to say that the *Augusta* and *Dale*, steam sloop and gunboat, were outside. I reported the fact to the commodore, and he expressed so earnest a wish to get them in before the attack, that I determined to bring them in at once, though night had already come on. * * *
The *Augusta* took the *Dale* in tow, and we passed in without trouble, having no cast less than nineteen feet, and I had the satisfaction of reporting to the flag-officer their arrival at half-past eleven P. M. Running outside again, I anchored the *Vixen* at the entrance, in readiness to bring in the *Ericsson* and the *Baltic*, drawing twenty and twenty-two feet. * * *

"At sunrise we anchored a large spar-buoy at the entrance of the south channel. Mr. Platt and Mr. Jones, first and second officers of this vessel, were then sent on board of the *Baltic* and *Ericsson*, respectively, and I led in with the *Vixen* at half flood." * * *

"After anchoring the *Baltic* and *Ericsson*, I went on board of the *Atlantic* with General Sherman, and witnessed the fight." * * *

The attack was made on the morning of the 6th of November. The vessels steamed slowly around, describing the figure of an ellipse, and delivering their broadsides as they passed within short range of Fort Beauregard and Fort Walker, which are on opposite sides of the harbor. The fire of the vessels was so rapid and well-directed, that, as they approached to make their third revolution, the flag of Fort Beauregard was hauled down, and the enemy hastily abandoned both works.

In the Report of Commodore Du Pont to the Navy Department, he remarks:—

"The Department is aware that all the aids to navigation had been removed, and the bar lies ten miles seaward, with no features on the shore-line sufficient to make any bearings reliable. But, by the skill of Commodore Davis, the Fleet-Captain, and Mr. Boutelle, the able Assistant of the Coast Survey, in charge of the steamer *Vixen*, the channel was immediately sounded out and buoyed. On the evening of Monday, Captain Davis and Mr. Boutelle reported water enough for the Wabash to venture in." * * *

In the Report of General Sherman to the War Department, he says:—

"It is my duty to report the valuable services of Mr. Boutelle, Assistant in the Coast Survey, in assisting me with his accurate and extensive knowledge of this country." * * *

On the Pacific coast, upon the breaking out of hostilities, the Coast Survey steamer *Active* took measures in concert with the military and naval authorities. The vessel was once anchored off Mare Island Navy Yard, for the purpose of protecting the Government property there, which there was reason to believe was endangered. This vessel performed other service, in transporting troops and supplies. The Pacific coast was only temporarily involved in the general disorder which pervaded the country, and there will be no further occasion to notice events in that section.

In the course of the year 1862, of forty-nine officers of various grade on the Coast Survey, thirty-two, in addition to their usual duties, rendered service in military operations. Sub-Assistant Dorr narrowly escaped being killed before Yorktown. The instrument with which he was working was shivered into atoms by a shell thrown by the enemy, and a soldier on picket near by was killed outright. The same shell mortally wounded Lieutenant Wagner, of the Topographical Engineers, and a soldier named Lacter, of the 2d Rhode Island Regiment, who was attached to the surveying party. Messrs. Bradford and Boyd, while surveying on James Island, South Carolina, were surprised by a party of the enemy, but instead of being captured, took the rebels prisoners. Sub-Assistant Oltmanns was dangerously wounded, while on a reconnoissance up Pearl River, the stream which for some distance forms the boundary between Mississippi and Louisiana.

During this year, Major Palmer, who for a long time had been Assistant in charge of the Coast Survey Office, died in consequence of disease contracted from exposure during the Peninsular campaign. He was succeeded in the office by J. E. Hilgard, Assistant on the Coast Survey.

The reconnoissances and surveys for military purposes, executed during the year 1862, were so numerous, that it will not be possible to give more than a synopsis of them. This will be best afforded by the following transcript of portions of Appendix No. 1 of the Superintendent's Report for 1862:—

"Reconnoissance for defensive purposes, and mapping of the environs and southern approaches of the city of Portland, Maine."

"Special hydrographic examination made in the vicinity of Pea-Patch Island, Delaware River, and development of changes by comparison with previous surveys."

"Triangulation and plane-table survey of the banks of the Potomac, completed, from Blakistone Island to Washington."

"Detailed survey of the environs of Williamsport, Maryland, for military purposes. Topography, for military use, of the ground north and west of Bladensburg, Maryland, along the line of the District of Columbia."

"Plane-table survey commenced of the site and approaches of Fort Lincoln, and other defensive works, near Washington City."

"Extension of the Topographical survey in Fairfax County, Virginia, from Falls Church towards Fort Marcy and Lewinsville."

"Topography of Manassas Junction, Virginia, and its vicinity, including, with other surface details, the intrenchments erected in 1861."

"Plane-table survey on the north side of the Rappahannock River, opposite Fredericksburg, including Falmouth and its environs, and the roads leading to Belle Plain and the upper part of Potomac Creek."

"Special topographical service in the Army of the Potomac, on the peninsula between York and James Rivers, including local surveys and general reconnoissance."

"Topographical survey of Drummondtown and its vicinity, for military purposes."

"Special plane-table surveys of redoubts, forts, and intrenched camps, on the banks of Elizabeth River, Virginia, and in the neighborhood of Norfolk."

"Hydrography of the Potomac River, extending upward from Blakistone Island to the vicinity of Indian Head."

"Hydrographic survey of the Potomac from Alexandria to Georgetown, including the Eastern Branch to the vicinity of the Navy Yard."

"Special service with North Atlantic Blockading Squadron before Yorktown, Virginia; in York River and its branches; extending reconnoissance up the Mattapony River, and guard duty at West Point."

"Hydrographic resurvey of Metomkin Inlet, Virginia, including also Metomkin Bay, and development of changes in the shore-line of the entrance, for military purposes. Buoys set to mark the channel into the inlet."

"Complete hydrographic resurvey of Hatteras Inlet, including its approaches from seaward and the channels leading into Pamlico Sound. Observations on the tides and currents of Hatteras Inlet, North Carolina, with reference to their effect in changing the shore-lines outside and inside of Pamlico Sound."*

"Special service at Hatteras Inlet with North Atlantic Blockading Squadron. Hydrography of Oregon Inlet, and hydrographic reconnoissance in Neuse River, N. C. Stakes set to mark the channels, and buoys placed on the Middle Ground."

"Shore-line survey to determine changes, and hydrographic resurvey of the entrance, approaches, and harbor of Beaufort, N. C."

"Special and general service on the coast of South Carolina and Georgia, with the South Atlantic Blockading Squadron"

"Shore-line survey, for military purposes, of Stono, Folly, and Kiawah Rivers, and of John's, James's, Cole's, Kiawah, and Folly Islands, including the intrenchments found on their banks."

"Shore-line survey, for military purposes, of Beaufort River, S. C., and of the upper part of Broad River, etc."

"Hydrography of Stono, Folly, and Kiawah Rivers, and supplementary soundings in Broad and Beaufort Rivers, S. C., etc."

"Plane-table surveys, for military purposes, of the ground commanded by the defensive works erected at St. Louis, Mo., in 1861."

---

* This survey was made on account of the encroachment of the sea upon Fort Hatteras.

The preceding list gives the nearest outline of the amount of service which the Coast Survey rendered to the military authorities during the year 1862. The occasion during that year, upon which it most signalized itself by its connection with military operations, was at the forcing of the passage of the Mississippi, an exploit which resulted in the rendition of the city of New Orleans.

In April, 1862, Captain (now Vice-Admiral) Farragut attacked Fort St. Philip and Fort Jackson, situated near the mouth of the Mississippi. Captain (now Rear-Admiral) D. D. Porter commanded the bomb-flotilla, and to that was attached the *Sachem*, in charge of Assistant Gerdes, of the Coast Survey.

During the season immediately preceding the rebellion, the regular triangulation of the Survey had established the positions of certain points near the mouth of the Mississippi. It was, therefore, easy to determine other points, from those whose positions had been calculated. The use to which this process could be applied, was soon exemplified in the bombardment.

By the morning of the 18th of April, when the mortar-vessels, twenty-one in number, took position, the exact distance from each one of them to Fort Jackson had been correctly determined. Some of the vessels lay along the shore of the river, where it is covered with a sparse growth of timber. These were concealed as much as possible from the observation of the enemy, by dressing the masts with foliage, so as to render them undistinguishable from the trees which they overtopped.

The bombardment of Fort Jackson opened immediately after each vessel had been placed in its allotted position; and during the following three days, whenever a vessel was obliged to change its place, the distance from its new position to the fort was redetermined by Coast Survey officers who remained with the flotilla.

Some of the party were in the mean time engaged in making maps of the Mississippi, in the vicinity of the defences. An examination was made of the channels which commence near Fort Jackson and connect the Mississippi with the Gulf of Mexico. The *Sachem* was also employed in transporting the wounded of Commodore Farragut's fleet to the hospital at Pilot Town.

On the 24th of April, Assistant Gerdes accompanied Major-General Butler, and piloted his boats, in an attempt to turn the forts from the direction of the waters to the northward of Fort St. Philip.

In relation to these operations, Commodore Porter, writing to the Superintendent of the Coast Survey, under date of April 29th, says:—

"Amid the exciting scenes here, and the many duties that are imposed on me, I must steal a few moments to tell you something of the share the Coast Survey has had in our doings, and to thank you for the valuable assistance rendered me by the party you sent here. . . . . The results of our mortar-practice here have exceeded any thing I ever dreamed of; and for my success, I am mainly indebted to the accuracy of positions marked down, under Mr. Gerdes's direction, by Mr. Harris and Mr. Oltmanns. They made a minute and complete survey from the 'jump' to the forts, most of the time exposed to fire from shot and shell, and from sharpshooters from the bushes. . . . . The position that every vessel was to occupy, was marked by a white flag, and we knew to a yard the exact distance of the hole in the mortar from the forts, and you will hear in the end how straight the shells went to their mark. Mr. Oltmanns and Mr. Harris remained constantly on board to put the vessels in position again when they had to haul off for repairs, or on account of the severity of the enemy's fire. . . . I cannot speak too highly of these gentlemen. I assure you that I shall never undertake a bombardment, unless I have them at my side. Mr. Gerdes has been indefatigable in superintending the work, laboring late at night in making charts and providing the officers in command of ships with them, marking the positions of obstructions in the channel, and making all familiar with the main way."

On May 16th, Commodore Porter again wrote to the Superintendent of the Coast Survey, as follows:—

"I forward to you, by the Baltic, a plan of Fort Jackson (or the remains of it), faithfully drawn, under the direction of Mr. Gerdes, by Messrs. Harris and Oltmanns, Assistants of the Coast Survey. It is a striking specimen of the effects of mortar-practice, showing what can be done when distances are accurately determined, as they were in this case by the gentlemen belonging to the Coast Survey."

During the years which preceded the war, the demand for charts did not average ten thousand annually. In the year 1861, however, the Coast Survey issued twenty-one thousand copies of charts, and in the following year forty-four thousand.

Of course, the general issue of all maps by which the enemy could profit, if they fell into their possession, was suspended from the commencement of hostilities. Issues of such maps were made only to those who were clothed with the proper authority.

Totally distinct from the charts, is another class of maps, universally called war maps. These have been in great request. The Superintendent, in his Report for 1862, says: "Color printing has been introduced for maps of the seat of war, and has proved very acceptable, the sale of the maps more than reimbursing the cost of their production."

Let us for a moment revert to the postulate with which this paper commences. To establish its truth, at least with reference to the special application, to the subject under consideration, it is only necessary for the reader to be informed, in addition to what has already been learned, that as late as February, 1863, after all the important services which have been detailed, some newspapers in the United States urged that the Coast Survey should be discontinued during the war. This view was rendered still more singular by the fact that one of the principal reasons assigned for its discontinuance was, the consequent release of a comparatively small number of persons, who could thenceforward take an active part in the prosecution of the war. They might, perhaps, form a company of soldiers. Fortunately, most of the influential newspapers, as well as most of the influential men of the country, took a very different view of the manner in which the Coast Survey could be instrumental in aiding the Government, but none knew what these few pages have imperfectly set forth.

SHERMAN'S SIXTY DAYS IN THE CAROLINAS.
BY J. E. PARKER DOYLE, VOLUNTEER AIDE-DE-CAMP.

SCARCELY had the intelligence of Sherman's triumphant march to the sea reached the capitals of Europe, and created a lively discussion in the military circles of foreign powers, ere his battalions were in motion again upon a new campaign, even more dangerous and marvellous than that which gave him Savannah and a new base upon the coast.

The press of the country has spread broadcast the glad tidings of the capture of Wilmington and Charleston, and the repossession of the entire coast, from Mobile to Virginia; and ere Sherman had reached his new base at Goldsboro, the European press proclaim the Hero of the West among the greatest military strategists of the age.

The public pulse has now had time to regain its wonted regularity, and while the glad nation is singing hallelujahs over the fall of Richmond, that has cost so much blood and treasure, as a result of Grant and Sherman's remarkable strategy, it may not be inopportune for one who has marched with Sherman through the heart of the enemy's country, and watched his feints and strategy with an enthusiasm bordering upon idolatry, to briefly review his campaign in the Carolinas, as he has already reviewed that through Georgia.

About the 16th of January, hardly a month from his triumphant entry into Savannah to the music of the Union, Sherman had reviewed and reorganized his command, but only partially refitted it, owing to delays in forwarding the necessary supplies. To delay his movement until clothing and the necessary refitment was obtained would have given the enemy time to concentrate his forces against him, and rendered his march difficult, if not disastrous. Sherman consequently hurried forward his preparations, and dispatching Howard's wing by water to Beaufort, from whence it penetrated up the Pocotaligo, deceived the enemy into the belief that this force was the advance of his army, moving upon Charleston. The interval between the embarkation of Howard at Savannah and his arrival in front of the Branchville and Charleston Railroad was well employed by Sherman, who marched Slocum's wing towards

Augusta, Davis's Corps on the Georgia side, and Williams's on the Carolina side of the Savannah River, to Sister's Ferry. Here, the incessant rains, that had somewhat impeded Howard, delayed Slocum several days in crossing the river, the banks of which were overflown, and the low, swampy country bordering on the river inundated for many miles to an extent greater than it had been known since 1840. Eventually, the crossing was effected in safety, and the laborious duty of the campaign at once commenced. The enemy had concentrated all his available force at and near Branchville, guarding all the approaches to the railway that connected Charleston with the interior. The fate of the city, the enemy was quick to see, depended upon his holding that line; and not until the left wing, by rapid marches of eighteen miles per day, constantly harassed by cavalry in front, and impeded by fallen timber, rain, and swollen streams, had made a détour far to the left, within thirty miles of Augusta, gained a lodgment upon the road, and severed communications, did Sherman's adversary discover how thoroughly he had been deceived. Here was a dangerous position for the enemy; his whole force of cavalry, militia, and veterans, at Branchville, and Augusta open to capture by a sudden swoop of Kilpatrick's horse. That city, with its arsenals, laboratories, machine-shops, rolling stock, and cotton, was too valuable to be neglected; and Cheatham's Corps, of Hood's army, was marched night and day to its relief, arriving there in time to find that Sherman had turned the cold shoulder upon Augusta, and by a dexterous movement thrown his left wing between Hill and the main force in his front. While Slocum was sweeping unopposed through the upper portion of the State, Howard was quietly possessing himself of the railroads connecting Columbia with Charleston; and Hardee, flanked at Charleston, made all haste to join the main rebel column, leaving the birthplace of Treason to its fate.

Rapid marches by day and night gave us Columbia, the State capital, before the enemy could concentrate to prevent the catastrophe; and Slocum had the satisfaction of knowing that when he crossed the Broad River and burned the bridges, Cheatham, destitute of a pontoon-train, was cut off far in his rear, and unable to get in his front, except by making a long détour and crossing on the river above.

Remaining at Columbia but one day, Sherman once more put his columns in motion towards Charlotte, where all the rolling stock of the railroads destroyed had been run, and from which it could not be removed on account of the railroad beyond that being of a different guage.

By this time Johnston had got his command well in hand, and, strengthened by Hardee, who had joined him, made all haste to defend Charlotte, the door to Virginia. Had Sherman chosen, he could no doubt have brought Johnston to battle and rout at Charlotte; but he would have been further from the accomplishment of his object—the destruction of the enemy's interior line of railway, and the possession of a new base near the coast, where he could more successfully co-operate with Grant for the defeat of Lee.

Slocum again made a détour toward Charlotte, where Johnston waited and watched, confident that *this time*, at least, he correctly interpreted the singular movements of Sherman. This feint had a very important effect upon the result, for it uncovered Fayetteville to Sherman and Goldsboro to Schofield, who, with a large and victorious army, was sweeping up from the coast with re-enforcements for Sherman, establishing a line of supplies as he moved.

The feint upon Charlotte gave us Fayetteville and Wilmington, and enabled Sherman to disencumber his command of the thousands of black and white refugees, and obtain supplies necessary to subsist his army until he had reached his base.

Leaving Fayetteville to its fate, Sherman swept up towards Raleigh, and cleared the way for Schofield to possess Goldsboro, which he accomplished with skill and alacrity.

The battle of Bentonville could have been avoided by Sherman, had that been his programme; but he was now near his base, and the vaunting Johnston, to whom the rebels looked to wipe Sherman out, could not receive a lesson at war at a more opportune moment. Carlin and Kilpatrick ran into the celebrated general on the 19th, and, as Johnston's whole army stood in Sherman's road, from which he did not care to diverge, the victorious leader, reposing implicit confidence in the heroes of twoscore battles, ordered them forward to brush the rebels from his path.

Skirmishing with the enemy for half an hour developed the fact that the wily Johnston had massed his whole force of infantry, artillery, and cavalry, on General Davis's front, evidently intending to crush the left wing by sudden and vigorous assaults before it could be re-enforced from the right. In this he was most wofully deceived. Davis's corps, that at Chickamauga, under Thomas, placed itself like a rock in the path of the exulting rebels, and rolled back column after column upon their reserve, had not forgotten how to fight; and while Davis looked on, confident of the issue, Carlin and Morgan, and their brigade commanders, rode amidst the smoke and bullets, and held the enemy handsomely in check until re-enforcements arrived, when a new line was formed, which Johnston charged in vain, and at night withdrew, leaving his dead and wounded and several thousand prisoners in Davis's hands. This battle was among the most terrific and bloody since Chickamauga, for the time it lasted; and although the enemy succeeded in breaking the line, he was repulsed at all points, and surrendered the blood-stained field to the victors, less than half his own numbers, and Sherman, with his victorious and ragged veterans, marched unopposed to his new base with buoyant heart and measured tread.

With the combined forces of Bragg, Johnston, Hardee, Hampton, Wheeler, Hill, S. D. Lee, Cheatham, and Butler, numbering over forty thousand, scattered over North and South Carolina, from Charleston to Augusta, with ample railways to enable them to concentrate and deliver battle, it is a marvel how Sherman could have avoided a decisive encounter in South Carolina, and safely conducted his army to a base after a campaign of sixty days, through a country swarming with guerrillas, and over the worst roads ever encountered by an army. Yet the fact is now patent that he has more than accomplished the objects of the campaign, and the world looks on in wonder and admiration of the man and the army that has never known defeat.

By his mysterious strategy he has wrested from the enemy's grasp the entire coast, deprived them of their blockading advantages, destroyed most effectually their interior network of railways, compelled the enemy to concentrate on the border of North Carolina, laid waste one-third of South Carolina, and, destroying all the railway routes over which Lee supplied his army from the Southwest, efficiently aided Grant's brave army in forcing the evacuation of the rebel stronghold in Virginia that for four years has been impervious to shot and shell.

Looking back over a period of six months to the time when Sherman cut loose from Atlanta, and recalling the movements that he has made, the student of military strategy must have long since arrived at the conclusion that to Sherman's policy of carrying the war into the enemy's country, destroying his railways, burning his public works, consuming his subsistence, and rendering the country uninhabitable, much of the success that has attended our arms this winter must be ascribed; and that by this policy, marked by profound wisdom and indomitable energy, more has been accomplished, with the loss of less than five thousand men, than could have been worked out in direct assaults upon fortified positions, with the sacrifice of many thousands of noble-hearted patriots.

A glad nation may well thank God for raising up a Grant and a Sherman, a Thomas and a Sheridan, whose names will live so long as the earth shall perform its revolutions, and men make and write history. To Sherman himself the thought must be indeed gratifying that he has triumphed over the calumny of his enemies, who, less than four years ago, pronounced him insane, and that to-day he stands before the world's eye among the master military minds that the fortunes of war have rescued from oblivion.

SEEKING THE BUBBLE.

IV.

* * * * "Then a soldier,
Full of strange oaths and bearded like the pard;
Jealous in honor, sudden and quick in quarrel;
Seeking the bubble reputation,
Even in the cannon's mouth." * * *

As You Like It.—Act II., Scene VII.

UNDER FIRE.

IF the grave-digger in *Hamlet* will communicate, in person or by post, with First Lieutenant William Jenkins, Adjutant, 3d Regiment District of Columbia Volunteers, he will hear of something very much to his advantage. I can teach him a thing or two. Shakspeare knew all about digging, as well as every thing else. I found this out at Yorktown.

Now, this operation of digging seems a very simple one, but it is really most complex. Spitting on the hands, hefting the spade, the thrust, the jam, the pry, the lift, the heave, and finally, patting the clod of fresh earth with the back of the spade before beginning anew, is really quite a mystery, you see. * * * * * Nonsense? Well, perhaps. But this is one of the many wild, undigested fancies which my memory hiccoughs forth whenever I think of the night of May 4th, 1862. Such thoughts waltzed through my tired brain all night, as our regiment dug away on the boyau of the second parallel. It was an exciting night, what with the cracking of rifles from the enemy's advanced posts, scarce fifty yards distant, the incessant roar of the enemy's big guns, and the bursting of shells over our heads. Never before had I heard such a cannonade. We had become so used to these sights and sounds, that the extra firing only seemed to serve as a nervous stimulant, making the pick and spade more nimble, and bringing out the playful wit of the officers and men in stage whispers. It was dismal enough, though, to be so thundered at, and to hear no answer from behind us. It was rumored by the sanguine men, that our batteries were to open early in the morning, all along the line, hundred and two hundred pounder Parrotts, thirteen-inch mortars, little guns and all, when we should see things smashed generally. Some of the incredulous were pleased to inquire whether the back-bone of the rebellion was to be broken, or the anaconda was to tighten its last coil, and so on, bandying about the hollow comforts that our newspaper friends used to keep standing on their galleys. Why was old Magruder treating us to such a diabolish salute, keeping the pickets out of their natural rest? "Short of transportation," our melancholy Quartermaster suggested, and was unanimously snubbed for his pains.

The first thing we saw when the sun rose, at last (as it will rise even upon working parties in the trenches), was that arch humbug, the balloon, going up on what it used to call a reconnoissance. Well, it came down again presently, and, as I afterwards learned, reported every thing as usual in Yorktown; and sure enough, the very last files of the rear-guard were leaving the place at that very moment, and the works had been already taken possession of by one of the Flop Telegraph men (as we used to call the signal-officers), and claimed for the United States, by right of discovery, as one might say. He was even then flopping his news with his red and white rag to another red and white rag near the corps' head-quarters, where there was a grim rubbing of sleepy eyelids, I dare say, and a weak pretence of having expected the news, and being delighted to hear it. Soon the long-forbidden bands pealed forth their most stirring strains, and waked up the overgrown camp at army head-quarters, whence there presently issued orders for one of those vigorous pursuits for which the Army of the Potomac used to be famous.

Pursuit! Our regiment waded through a sea of mud, knee-deep, till we got to a dense pine-wood, from beyond which came rattling sounds as of distant packs of fire-crackers let off in barrels, and the door-slamming noises which I have already described; and in the morning we heard that that was the battle of Williamsburg! A battle wherein one general ordered to command by the General-in-Chief, without special instructions for the contingency, was superseded in the dead of night by another general detailed by the Chief of Staff, with no particular orders for the emergency; fought, for this reason, without a tactical plan, and in violation of the strategical plans of the Commander-in-Chief; and resulting in the retreat of the enemy's rear-guard, after great loss on both sides, especially on ours. Followed up by going into camp near the battle-field on the next day, and there quietly remaining to await the news of the failure of the operations of another column. Meanwhile, the rebels quietly retired to the Chickahominy, and prepared to defend its crossing. And we trudged slowly after, nursing the idea that this procession was the very " driving to the wall" our General had promised us. We were in sight of Richmond— so the rumor ran round the mess-tables—and, indeed, the *New York Herald* soon brought us, under the very largest headings, the news sent by its faithful correspondent "Scorpio," that a party of our generals (accompanied, we may suppose, by "our reporter," and the inevitable "brilliant staffs, among which we noticed," etc., etc.) had seen, from the top of a tall tree on the extreme front, the very spires of the DOOMED CITY.

But in spite of large headings and the bill-poster literature of our "own correspondents;" in spite of the disgusting anaconda, and the broken back-bone, and the starving out, the flanking, the driving to the wall, the crushing, the telling blows in preparation by General A., as explained by his reporter; the plans for the "speedy suppression of the most wicked and unnatural rebellion ever waged against the best government ever framed by man," always being matured in the brain of General B., as narrated by *his* reporter; the preternatural vigilance of General C., as described by *his* reporter; the great things that Generals D., E., and F., might, could, would, or should have done, as recounted by *their* reporters; in spite of the glowing predictions of the intelligent contraband; the important revelations of the rebel surgeon who had just come into our lines; the valuable information obtained from the rebel major just captured by our pickets in front of such a division; in spite of Jeff. Davis's coachman, and even of the reliable gentleman of Louisville; yea, in spite of general orders to the contrary, the DOOMED CITY obstinately declined to accept the doom prepared for it. And so, as Mr. Murdoch used to say, in the "Inconstant," with his very best comedy manner, after describing the splendid way in which we fellows of the guards, you know, "danced" up to the breach at Badajos or Corunna, or some of those places—("Yes, yes; what did you do then?" interrupts the gruff military uncle, with the big stick), "and so—we danced back again."

Pray do not suppose, my dear Major, that your friend William Jenkins intends to put his head into the lion's mouth this bright spring morning, by launching forth into a description of that memorable campaign. No, no. Do you remember, Major, the thing that used so to disgust F. M. the Duke of Wellington with his soldiers on his Peninsula? *Stealing bee-hives.* You don't catch me at that trick, I promise you.

And so, leaving the strategy and grand tactics, and all the big moves to the Committee on the Conduct of the War, and the editors, and the ward politicians, and the village tavern-keeper, the barber who cuts your hair too short, and the Reverend who cuts your sermon too long, let me tell you what we little pawns did and felt while the Queens, and Castles, and Knights, and Bishops, were working out the game after their mighty fashion, and having their wicked will of us, and the poor Kings were getting in check and getting out again as best they could, to the discomfiture of the other pieces, their friends. Did not Miss Chloe ask you, almost the first thing, Captain Strephon, that time when you went home on a furlough and two crutches: "Were you ever in a battle? How many fights have you been in? How does it feel? How were you wounded? Oh, I should be so frightened!" And then, when you tried to describe to her, bumptiously, and looking as terribly military as you could, how this division came up and that didn't; how the other division moved by the flank, and a fourth—yours, of course—charged splendidly, and drove the enemy through the woods at the point of the bayonet, did she not interrupt you, oh! so innocently, with that enormous question, "How does a battle look?" If she did not, she is not the Chloe I take her for, and you, sir, might as well have saved your postage-stamps and worn your old uniform on furlough, for all the interest she takes in *you*. Those are the questions I mean to answer here for the benefit of whom it may concern; and you, Captain Strephon, are at liberty to ridicule the replies at the mess, and use them for your own behoof, if it should so suit your pleasure, when next you see her; *she* never sees the *Service Magazine*, you may be certain.

We were loafing quietly in camp, smoking, whittling, studying tactics, playing cards, mixing cocktails, writing letters, or what not, when suddenly there broke upon our ears the dull booming with which we had become so familiar as the sound of distant cannonade. Presently followed, in rolls and spirts, the rattling noise of musketry, again reminding us of our Fourth-of-July experiences with fire-crackers under a barrel. How heavy and ominous, and yet how clearly it sounded through the saturated air! Listen! what a roar that was, fellows! We never heard any thing like this before, surely. Now the bugle sounds from brigade head-quarters, and we fall in, under arms, all in a glow of excitement, wondering what is to come next. We have not long to wait, for already the rest of the division is in the muddy road, and soon our regiment files out also and takes its place in the column. The incessant roar of cannon and musketry grates horribly upon our untutored nerves. Where is the fight? Who is engaged? Are we whipping them? Or are we whipped again, as the growlers will have it? I don't half like this galloping past of young A.-D.-C's, and spattering orderlies, in such a hurry that they have never a word of news for us.

And so the croakers make the most of it, and wet down our souls with their forebodings, until they are as heavy as our boots with the soggy mud. How it rains! It does not pour; the sky fairly leaks. Is this the Chickahominy? I thought it was a river. Others thought it was a swamp. It turns out to be a deluged bottom half a mile wide or more, and we are expected to cross it on that thing there they call a bridge. "Sumner's *Upper* Bridge," indeed! What must the lower one be like—the comic men ask—if this raft of big, floating logs, which has almost to be held down as we tumbled over it, is the upper bridge? We are hardly across, when the rising freshet sweeps away a raft of the biggest logs, and breaks up the only mode of communication we know of with the other shore. About a mile or so farther on, through the quicksands and the pine-woods, we come to an opening, and, not far to our left, can see the smoke curling up over the trees, and the occasional flash of a gun from the battery just within the opening. Here we halt and commence that sickening delay which takes the starch out of your enthusiasm, and makes the poetry of war a dreadful prose. It is not all profanity when the men say, "This waiting is hell!" It is; and twice as terrible, too, as the allegorical cauldrons of brimstone. For my part, I think any amount of sizzling preferable to an hour of this horrible suspense. How long it has lasted I hardly know, when suddenly the roar begins to spread our way, the line of smoke from the opposite woods creeps along until it breaks into a sharp, rattling fire on us. The men jump to their feet hardly an instant too soon, and in great confusion. Some start to run one way, some another, even officers give way to the alarm of the moment; others commence firing wildly into the air. But a good deal of shouting and cursing, and some rough handling, and the example of a few energetic officers, and many cool hands in the ranks, and especially the great practical fact that only one or two of us are hit, in a very few seconds brings a wavy line of file-firing out of the confusion; the men cheer, the roar of their own muskets drowns the rattle of the enemy's; suddenly from somewhere, off on our right, joins in the banging of a friendly battery, with that screech of its rifled shells so peculiarly grateful when they are travelling the other way; the firing from the opposite woods patters out like the last of an April shower; the command is given for our regiment to cease firing, and we become aware, from the general silence, broken only by the bursting of a casual shell, that the fight is over: and so ends, for us, the battle of Fair Oaks. Why, or how it began, what has happened except what I have just told you, we officers, non-commissioned officers, musicians, and privates of the 3d District of Columbia Volunteers, know no more than that ignorant myth, the Man in the Moon. And now begins the bragging and chattering. Molony's hit. Where is Ferguson? Where is Jessup? Here,—you fellows! Fight's over; come back! Musician Tappitt, with his great red bosom, wanders back sheepishly, trying to look as unlike as possible the straggler he has been. The skedaddlers return, some three or four score of them, feebly pretending they have been carrying the two killed and thirteen wounded men to the rear. It is remarkable, the *penchant* those big fellows have for running away, while your little runts stick to their work like wax. In his nimbleness of heel, Jack Falstaff is the type of the breed. "Say, Puffy," the funny men will cry, "how about that tree I saw you holdin' up?" "How are you, legs?" And the like. And night falling in the mean time, we fall to work cooking supper and trying to rest in the rain and mud as best we may, after our hard and exciting day. Our tents and knapsacks, you remember, are safe on the other side of the Chickahominy.

This is not very romantic, I know, and not at all like the battles our nimble-penned friends the novelists fight; as witness Victor Hugo's Waterloo, in *Les Miserables*. My only excuse is, that it is true. And if we didn't fight a grand, heroic battle, with gallant charges and immense slaughter and wild enthusiasm, wherein Jenkins cut down the enemy's color-bearer, and, trampling the hated standard under foot, unfurled our own glorious banner to the breeze as alone he scaled the steep parapet, and shouting to our brave boys to follow him, fell bleeding at every pore, and wrapped in his country's flag, and remained unconscious until he awoke in Chapter XXVIII. to drink the lemonade kindly prepared for him by the dark-eyed Southern belle, etc., etc., etc.: if, I say, all this didn't happen, how can I, a faithful historian, with no more imagination than the younger Mr. Willett, be expected to narrate the particulars attractively?

Three weeks or more we stand in bivouac on the spot where we had our little battle, for little enough it had been in our case; although sufficiently terrible off on the left, where, as we presently learned, the fight had raged with a murderous fury all day. Had we suffered a great disaster, or won a great victory? Both. Certain it is, the two corps of our army which had crossed the Chickahominy, most narrowly escaped destruction that morning. Was their rescue the glorious victory that our Generals and the enemy's deserters (backed, of course, by that illustrious trio, the intelligent contraband, the reliable gentleman, and the rebel surgeon) told us? We pawns thanked Heaven for our great deliverance, and incontinently wrote off, in the rain, between burials and trench-digging, such bragging accounts of the affair and our several parts in it, individually and regimentally, as my pen even now blushes to think of; and oh! the sights and smells of that week. A camp-ground trodden hard, and then soaked with the blood of men and horses till it was stained to a dull red, in clots; the bodies of thousands of men half buried; other bodies in the neutral space beyond our lines, not buried at all, but rotting in the damp heat; torn clothing, old knapsacks, abandoned litter of all kinds, the carcasses of horses half buried in huge piles, and then half covered with the soggy earth; and such a stench! 'Twas enough to vomit a vulture! And yet, in this stinking hell our soldiers lived, ate, slept, and dug, for weeks. Pah! The very whiff of recollection chokes me.

Here the yellow demon of malaria joined our bivouac. What with the smell, and the rotting bodies of men and horses, and the decaying mass of leaves and camp-rubbish, and the general decomposition in the damp heat of every thing decomposable, and the poison absorbed by the pools of nasty, filthy water we were compelled to drink and use for cooking,—men's eyes turned gamboge, and their skins became livid, and their flesh shrank as if from contact with such an atmosphere, and their bones ached, and by tens and twenties, and hundreds, and thousands, the strongest of us gave way, fairly broken down by this demon. He is a demon of many nicknames. Some call him Cholera, others Yellow Fever; in the East he trades as the Plague, in the West as the Shakes; to us, he came under the innocent names of Diarrhœa, and Camp Fever, Jaundice, and Typhoid. And he had his hands full. What though we drank commissary whiskey till we were half drunk, or swallowed quinine till our heads buzzed again—what could "antifogmatics" do while we absorbed the terrible poison with every respiration? The living rotted faster than the dead. The dead multiplied like white mice.

Men's minds, too, festered with their bodies. Stragglers loafed to the rear and encamped in pairs or squads on their own hook; officers saw them, but took no note, or only cursed feebly, or pretended to do something. The once jolly mess-tables, that used to ring with jests and laughter, and shine with wit and good-humor, now heard only the continuation of the low, peevish growl that resounded through that camp. A poisoned army lying still in camp has about as much *morale* as you may find in a sheep-fold.

At the battle of Fair Oaks, our regiment numbered twenty-four officers and seven hundred and three men present, of whom twenty-two officers and six hundred and eighty-seven men were fit for duty. At the end of three weeks thereafter we reported seventeen commissioned officers and five hundred and eight men present, of whom nine officers and two hundred and fifteen men were fit for duty, the remainder being "sick in quarters" (*i. e.*, rotting where they were, under the broiling sun), or sick in regimental hospital (*i. e.*, dying a few yards off, in "the piney woods"). Save that the well men looked a reddish sallow, and the sick ones a greenish sallow, I hardly know which were the sallowest.

It was more surprising to me in those days, than amusing, to note the different effects of this state of things on the minds of my mess-mates. To see how the sanguine men degenerated into atrabiliousness, and the quiet ones lighted up with a calm fortitude superior to every terror, and the croakers croaked on! Chaplain Bender, very much to the joy of the whole mess—except Colonel Heavysterne, who thinks it necessary to make allowances for everybody, and that all men are exactly alike—stayed behind when we crossed the Chickahominy, and was not heard of for a week afterward, when we received an order from Head-Quarters, Army of the Potomac, through Corps, Division and Brigade Head-Quarters, detailing him to go North on some loafing billet or other, to take home the men's pay or accompany the wounded, or I know not what invention of clerico-military genius.

> "Bless him, let him go-o-o-o-o!
> And joy go with him, too!"

We shouted in chorus as I announced the order at tea-time;— we always had tea in our mess, for the benefit of Smallweed and myself, whom the others called old maids in consequnence, not that they drank less than we, but that we confessed our weakness first, and the legends of the world must be satisfied. Old Doctor Peacack kept his countenance of an oily ruddiness by means of copious libations of quinine and whiskey—occasionally, I fear, forgetting the quinine; and in this respect it must be confessed that "Old Pills," as he was irreverently called, even to his red face, practised what he preached, for I never met a more steadfast upholder of the alcoholic creed. He believed in the whiskey-cure for every thing and that all the evils currently attributed to that mode of practice sprang from dilution. "Don't drink that water," he would say. "Good God! young man, you'll ruin your stomach!" Naturally enough, the doctor thought every thing was going to the "demnition bow-wows," as Mr. Mantalini says, very fast, but gave himself very little care on this or any other subject. Indeed, I think the gigantic quantities of whiskey he swilled held his ideas on most subjects in constant solution; and I wish I could say as much of his assistant surgeon, young Doctor Launcelot Cutts, who would insist on entertaining us with his opinions upon every subject at prodigious length and without an instant's hesitation. Just now he did the dismal strategy for us, decimated us by fearful and complicated diseases at breakfast, routed us and cut us to pieces for dinner, and drove us in confusion into the James River for tea. The mess used to poke fun at him awfully. "Can I get a copy of those closing remarks of yours?" Smallweed would ask; or "would you favor us with an abbreviated statement of your plan for the reconstruction of the solar system, under the supervision of the medical director?" Even Colonel Heavysterne one day stopped eating—which was his chief occupation at the table, next to laughing at the young men's jokes—to ask him if he had got his orders yet; and on his asking innocently, not suspecting the old gentleman of a joke, "What orders?" answered, "Assigning you to the command of the Army of the Potomac." Whereupon there was a roar, followed by a shout of "How are you, Deputy Sawbones?" from the pit, as we used to call the fellows who thought such slang funny. Lieutenant Peck, formerly our commissary sergeant, who was promoted to be commissary on the death of poor Tiffany, astonished us all by ventilating the most hopeful views of things when every one else desponded, and by desponding when every one else was rejoicing. He seems to have fancied himself a kind of escapement to regulate the flow of our animal spirits; for I am sure he saw things too clearly, and was entirely too steady and cool-headed, to be carried away by either extreme. As for Smallweed, he continued melancholy to the last, and took no comfort save in the general blackness of things; though I am bound to say, to his credit, that his growl was always good-humored and amusing, and more likely to provoke a smile or a laugh than to spread his own melancholy. Indeed, I often think the latter is but skin-deep—a veil assumed to hide a large but too sensitive heart; to screen a generous nature from the vulgar stare. His rind was bitter enough, but the core was surpassingly sweet and mellow. He spied out meanness by intuition, and hated it most energetically. Not Dr. Johnson himself could have been a better hater, and I never knew a better friend. In those gloomy days, it was his quaint, humorous growling that kept me up far more than the froth of the boasters. Indeed, my common sense curdled all such milk-and-water views, and made them sit uneasily on my stomach.

One evening, toward the end of that hot June, after an insufferable day, we were dining languidly under the brush arbor behind the colonel's tent, almost worried to death by the incessant but futile effort to draw a distinction between blow-flies and beefsteak. The complaints had been more than usually loud, the curses at our condition more than ordinarily deep, and Smallweed's growling over his "good, practicable grievances," as he called them, more than commonly funny. The absurdity of another man's grievance will sometimes make you forget your own important sore; and so the mess had become half good-natured again, when an orderly came up and handed the colonel a paper.

The melancholy Smallweed groaned. "'Detail for picket duty, the 3d D. C. Volunteers; working party for the trenches, the 3d D. C. Volunteers,'" he affected to read from his empty plate.

The colonel's honest old phiz lighted up as he gave the orderly a receipt for the dispatch. "Boys," he cried, in a broad grin, "here's news! We're off for Fort Monroe in the morning!"

"For Fort Monroe!" chimed the mess.

"What for?" I ventured to ask.

"Expedition. Don't say where. Whole corps going. Old Bulger's going, too, I suppose. Nice man to command an expedition! D——d glad to get out of this mud, boys, and that's a fact."

"Where do you suppose we are going?" every one asked everybody else. Wilmington, Charleston, Savannah, Mobile, and a dozen other places, were canvassed excitedly, and their merits as the possible objective points of a large expedition eagerly discussed by their respective partisans. The " deputy sawbones," as we used to call Dr. Cutts, leaned back so as to crack his camp-stool and nearly upset himself and the rickety table, and stretching his arms, yawned out complacently, "Gentlemen, you are all wrong."

Cries of "Hear, hear!" "Let's have it, Deputy Sawbones," "Go it, Young Pills," and the like.

"Well, gentlemen," the youth continues, unabashed, "I heard all about it a week ago, from a friend of mine in Washington."

Smallweed walked round the table with his cap over his eyes, and fell into an attitude, after the manner of Dan Bryant in a break-down.

The mess roared, and requested the doctor to "spit it out."

"We are going to Texas."

MILITARY READING.

WE have been often and urgently applied to by officers of our Army to give them, through our pages, such information as would assist them in the selection and purchase of a suitable library of military books. We do not wonder at such applications; for never was an army composed to so large an extent of intelligent and educated men; and no duty could we perform with greater satisfaction than that of assisting such men in the choice of books. We shall proceed, therefore, at once to give the titles of a considerable number of military works of established character, with so much of accompanying remarks as may be necessary to make a list of titles of real practical value—after promising an introductory *caveat* or two to the reader.

First, it should be recollected, that the greater part of the books mentioned by us are such as are said technically to be "out of print"—that is, they are no longer in the hands of the original publishers, but belong to the stocks of "second-hand" dealers (or "antiquarians," as the Germans call them), who furnish themselves at the sales of private libraries and from similar sources. They cannot be purchased, therefore, like the publications of a Van Nostrand, by applying to the nearest bookseller one happens to know. They are not always secured even by sending the titles to a city bookseller; for he must order them from Europe at hap-hazard, trusting to his agent there to look them up. The better way is, to put one's self into communication with one of those city booksellers who make it their special business to import books—not from existing publishers alone—but from the second-hand dealers of London, Paris, and Leipsic. These importers furnish themselves, by every steamer, with the current-priced catalogues of the foreign dealers, which they are ready to distribute to their customers by post, inviting orders from those catalogues. The order should name the catalogue, the number of the article, the title, and the price. The book will then be ordered from abroad, and—if secured—will be charged at rates fixed and published beforehand. It is in this way, and in this way alone, that all important collections of all other than current books are made.

In the second place, our list must embrace a large proportion of works not in the English language. This we regret; although we are aware that many of our officers (nay, privates) are liberally educated men; many of them know, or would readily acquire, French; and a considerable number are Germans by birth or extraction. But the truth is, the English have contributed comparatively little to military literature; they have resorted largely, as we must do, to their neighbors the French, who have long excelled in military learning and in clear, practical military writing. The German language, however, is not less rich in warlike books, original and translated. We shall, therefore, in many cases, give titles in all these languages, always naming English translations, when we are aware that they exist. But we do not find English dealers confining themselves exclusively to military works, as in France and Germany; and we cannot, therefore, report for the knowledge of titles to some one known London catalogue, as we can to those of Dumaine and Corréard for Paris.

And, finally, as we do not aim at giving even a *skeleton*-bibliography of the art of war, we shall omit all new and current American publications and all new text-books, however valuable, and shall aim at little other method than to let one book mentioned open another.

Books of a general character—such as, in some shape, cover a wide field in military literature—naturally come first. Were there any systematic bibliography of war, works in that line would take the precedence. The catalogue of the Library of the United States Military Academy, West Point, prepared in 1853, by (the then) Captain Coppée, now the editor of this Magazine, gives only one title: Doisy—*Essai de bibliologie militaire*. Paris, 1824, 8vo. Captain De La Barre Duparcq, of the St. Cyr Military School, is the author of a pamphlet: *Des sources bibliographiques militaires*. Paris, 1856; and Potzhold has a similar sketch in German: *Uebersicht der ge-*

sammten militärischen Bibliographie. Dresden, 1857, p. 23. The Germans have also three works of considerable value, as systematical military bibliographies, viz.: Schülte—*Repertorium der Militär-Literatur.* Stralsund, 1842, 8vo, p. 208; Witzleben—*Deutschland's Militär-Literatur.* Berlin, 1850, 8vo, p. 248; and Seelhorst—*Deutschland's Militär-Literatur im letzen Jahrzehent,* 1850 *bis* 1860 (a supplement to Witzleben), Berlin, 1862, 8vo, p. 260. For French bibliography we have the catalogues of Corréard, Tanéra, and (especially) of Dumaire.

In this connection, Rocquancourt's *Cours complet d'art et d'histoire militaires* (3d ed., Paris, 1840, 4 vols. 8vo) deserves especial mention. For, besides giving in the first three volumes an uncommonly valuable course of military history, ancient and modern, and in the third a summary of military art, it also furnishes (by way of supplement) a *Littérature militaire* of about one hundred and fifty pages, in which—not the titles merely—but a critical estimate is given of a very large number of military works. In like manner the reader is guided to many books, with a knowledge of their real value, by the mention made of them by Jomini in the preface to his *Précis* (Art of War), by General Dufour, in the list prefixed to his Tactics, by Lecompte in the critical account of recent authors in strategy annexed to his Life of Jomini, &c.

General histories of war have their value, but none have attained any very high rank. That of Carrion-Nisas we have found very unequal. Major von Kausler wrote two or three works of this character: the best, for a book of reference, would be his *Wörterbuch der Schlachten, Belagerungen, und Treffen aller Völker,* in four large octavo volumes, 1825–33, with his magnificent *Atlas der merkwürdigsten Schlachten,* &c., in two hundred sheets (containing plans of battles from those of Grecian history to Waterloo), with explanations in German and French. But, generally speaking, none but special histories and special treatises are really satisfactory.

Certain military writers scoff at these, who seek to learn any thing about war from the ancients. In a certain sense they are doubtless right; but they must also in a certain sense be wrong; or we should not find the greatest captains so generally fascinated by the study of the Grecian and Roman histories— by the story of what was done, with so different a system of tactics, by great strategists, like Alexander, Hannibal, and Cæsar. We may, therefore, safely recommend a few works on the warfare of the ancients. For such purposes—leaving the professed scholar to his original Greek and Latin—we might first take up the ancient historians themselves in approved translations—Herodotus, Thucydides, and Xenophon; Cæsar, Livy, and Tacitus—in Bohn's Classical Library; Arrian's Expedition of Alexander, by Hooke; Polybius, in Hampton's version; Diodorus and Plutarch as we find them in the market; (Lorg's four little volumes, contributed to Knight's shilling series, and entitled the *Civil Wars of Rome*, is by far the best translation of Plutarch, as far as it goes). The best commentary on the Greek historians, down to the death of Alexander, is Grote's *History of Greece* (London, 12 vols. 8vo, with maps and plans, and New York [Harpers], 12 vols. 12mo, without maps and plans); for Grote, although a civilian, was a thorough student of the ancient art of war, and has given proof of possessing superior military judgment. The third volume of Dr. Arnold's *History of Rome* (London, 1840; New York [Appletons], 1846) contains, in its chapters on the career of Hannibal in Italy, at the same time the best commentary (in so far) on Livy and Polybius, and one of the most remarkable pieces of military history, ever written. General Guillaume de Vaudoncourt (of the Napoleonic period) has devoted three quarto volumes (*Histoire des campagnes d'Annibal en Italie*, Milan, 1812) to the same subject. We cannot accept all his criticisms, but by his illustrations (among which is a complete translation of Arrian's Tactics) and by his accurate plans he has made a most important contribution to the knowledge of the ancient art of war. As to the route of Hannibal through the Alps, a more correct view than Guillaume's is given by two Oxford scholars, Cramer and Wickham, in their *Dissertation*, &c. (2d ed., London, 1828, 8vo).

The most instructive work for the comparative study of the Grecian and modern art of war is a recent one, in which a Greek professor with military tastes, and a Prussian officer with literary accomplishments, united, viz.: *Geschichte des griechischen Kriegswesens . . von W. Rüstow und H. Köchly.* Aaran, 1852, 8vo, pp. xviii. and 435, with illustrations. This book supersedes all others of the kind. The same authors have also united to bring out an edition of the chief "Tacticians"—Æneas, Arrian, Hero, Philo, &c.—in the original Greek, with a German translation and German notes:—*Griechische Kriegsschriftsteller—Griechisch und Deutsch mit kritischen und erklärenden Anmerkurgen.* Leipzig (Engelmann) 1853–5, 3 vols. small 8vo (or 12mo) vols. No edition can compare with it. Rüstow and Köchly's labors may be illus, trated, in one important point, by General Dufour's *Mémoire sur l'artillerie des anciens.* Paris and Geneva, 1840, 4to, p. 123, with plates—an essay, in which the learned general (author of the work on Tactics) was assisted by the celebrated Greek Professor Bétant, of Geneva.

The Roman art of war has not been treated so satisfactorily as that of the Greeks. We have missed the hand of a military *collaborateur* in the most recent work: *De la milice romaine, par Cl. Lamarre*, Paris, 1863, 8vo. The book is, however, the most convenient manual to be had. General Rogniat, in his *Considérations sur l'art de la guerre*, Paris, 18—, 8vo, p. —, offers some views of great interest, as coming from a practical soldier—a general of Napoleon's. Gibbon, *ci-devant* captain in the Hampshire militia, has in several places touched Roman tactics with a master's hand; but he has done a still better service in calling attention to the truly admirable works of Guischardt, the Quintus Icilius of Frederick the Great: *Mémoires militaires sur les Grecs et les Romains, avec une dissertation sur l'attaque et défense des places des anciens la traduction d'Onosandre et de la Tactique d'Arrien, et l'analyse de la campagne de Jules César en Afrique.* Lyons, 1760, 2 vols. 4to); and *Mémoires critiques et historiques . . . contenant l'histoire de la campagne de Jules César en Espagne*, &c. Paris, 1774, 4 vols. 8vo. As it is safe to predict, that the work of Napoleon III. will draw the attention of military men anew to "the foremost man of all the world," we think it seasonable to recommend these labors of Guischardt as of incomparable value.

It may be a curious fact—but it is a fact—that the practical soldier finds the study of Greek and Roman warfare far more attractive than that of later periods, down perhaps to the age of Louis XIV. The ancient tactical system was perfect of its kind; and greater strategists than Alexander, Hannibal, and Cæsar, never lived. Whereas, the mediæval fighting was done by untutored soldiers, who had lost the fine training of the phalanx and the legion, without having acquired any adequate substitute; and only very rarely did a true captain arise to study his ground, to adapt his means to his ends, and to bring moral influences to bear, like King Robert Bruce at Bannockburn. In so slight a sketch as this, therefore, we leave our student to read the earlier wars of mediæval and modern Europe in the historical works of unprofessional writers, or in the scientific but brief narrations of Rocquancourt and Carrion-Nisas. Our own great historians may teach him how justly Gonsalvo of Cordova, even in the fifteenth century, was styled the Great Captain; and if he would like to know how a man of genius, of that day, would treat the theory of tactics, let him hunt up one of the many copies of Machiavelli's *Art of War*, which some very sagacious bookseller published for the benefit of our officers at Albany, in 1815. The Thirty Years' War (16— to 1648) developed a great deal of military talent; and a military scholar might be interested in reading the many improvements in arms and in tactics, attempted by the great Gustavus Adolphus, in even such a book as Harte's *History of Gustavus Adolphus* (3d ed. 2 vols. 8vo, London, 1807), as to which Lord Chesterfield "wondered where the devil his son's tutor got his style." Less of such details are found in the beautiful *Gustav Adolph König von Schweden und seine Zeit*, by Gfrover (Stuttgart, 1852, 8vo). Mitchell's *Life of Wallenstein, Duke of Friedland* (London, 1840, 12mo), may gratify the interest with which poetry has invested one of the colossal figures of the time. But the military student's interest will be more naturally concentrated in the deeds of one who began to exhibit his great genius at the close of that war—the French Marshal Turenne, who, in his old age, may be said to have been the tutor of Marlborough. Full justice has not yet been done to this great captain. The brief sketches of the military historians and Napoleon's Notes, in Montholon, are satisfactory as far as they go; but the older works devoted to his life and campaigns are understood to possess no great merit, whether literary or scientific. The most noted of them (in a recent edition) is Ramsay's *Histoire du vicomte de Turenne*, Paris, 1835, 2 vols. 4to.

More fortunate than Turenne, in leaving behind him writings of singular value, was his last great antagonist, Montecuculli, the best edition of whose works is that of Turin, 1821, 2 vols. 8vo: *Opere militari, corrette, accresciute, ed illustrate da Guiseppe Grassi*. He is better known, however, by the more accessible French translation of his *Mémoires*, which have appeared, by themselves, in several editions of one or two small duodecimo volumes—for Montecuculli was the most sententious of writers—or three quarto volumes, overloaded with the Commentaries of Turpin de Crissé, in 1769.

A large body of military literature is devoted to the wars of the period, from the Thirty Years' War to the Revolution: the difficulty is to make a selection. One would like to possess, in honor of a great name, the *Traité de l'attaque et de la défense des Places par le Maréchal de Vauban*, of which we have an edition from the author's MS., by MM. le Général de Valazé et Augoyat, in 2 vols. 8vo, with a folio of plates; and it would be desirable to possess a true military history of so great a captain as Marlborough, instead of the rather heavy *Memoirs* by Archdeacon Coxe, illustrated with maps and plans. London, 1818-19, 3 vols. 4to, or in 6 vols. of Bohn's Standard Library. Alison's *Military Life of John Duke of Marlborough* (Edinburgh, 1848, 8vo, and New York, 12mo), is short and brilliant; and we now have his original *Dispatches*, 1702-12, edited by Sir George Murray. (London, 1845, 5 vols. 8vo.) The French side may be read in Memoirs, of which those of Marshal Feuquières (*Mémoires sur la guerre*, London, 1737, 2 vols. 12mo), are especially commended. The didactic work of Puységur (*Art de la Guerre par principes*, 1748), and the multifarious lucubrations of the Chevalier Folard strung together around his *Histoire de Polybe* (Paris, 1727,

6 vols. 4to), throw light upon the same period. It is a pity that we have no better means of measuring the genius of Charles XII. of Sweden, than one which military men laugh at—his life by Voltaire. The works of Maurice of Nassau (his *Annibal et Scipion*, &c., La Haye, 1675, be it noted, is an *Elzevir*), and the *Rêveries* of the Comte de Saxe (English: Edinburgh, 1759, 8vo), are interesting for their connection with improvements in the art of war.

But the great lessons in war, for the period, were given toward its close, by Frederick of Prussia; and these have fortunately been preserved and illustrated by competent authors. Frederick himself, while silent on the great secrets of his system, appeared as a teacher of detail in certain minor treatises, which form three volumes of his collected works, but are chiefly known by the convenient little French editions, e. g.: *Instruction destinée aux troupes légères*, &c., 32mo; *Instructions à ses généraux*, 12mo; and *Instruction sécrète dérobée*, 12mo. It is hardly necessary to refer, for his campaigns, to the works of Lloyd and Tempelhoff: the great *Traité des grandes opérations militaires* by Jomini (an American edition, of which, in English, we owe to the enterprise of Mr. Van Nostrand), has made it idle to recur to more than one book, unless it be for a more rapid and comprehensive view of the events of his campaigns, which may be got from the clear narrative of Lord Mahon in his History. If the soldier expects to find any illustrations of Frederick's military genius in Carlyle's Life (just completed), we recommend him to seek them there. To a Swiss officer of the King of Prussia (Warnery), we owe a classical work on cavalry: *Remarques sur la cavalerie*, Lublin, 1781, 8vo, and Paris, 1828, 12mo. A French officer of the period composed one of the works, which rank among the classics of the art; we speak of Guibert and his *Essai général de Tactique* (Paris, 1803, 2 vols. 4to), which Frederick recommended to his generals, and which Napoleon spoke of as calculated to form great men.

From Frederick we pass to the period of the French Revolution and our own day—to the system of Napoleon, and its echoes in later wars. Here Jomini covers the ground, to the close of Napoleon's own career, in his *Histoire critique et militaire des guerres de la Révolution* (Paris, 1820-4, 15 vols. 8vo, or Brussels, 4 vols. 8vo), and his *Vie politique et militaire de Napoléon* (Paris, 1827, 4 vols. 8vo., or *Brussels*, 2 vols. 8vo), translated by General Halleck, and published by Van Nostrand. General Halleck worked up into his translation the enlarged account of the Waterloo campaign, which Jomini published as a separate work, under the title of *Précis politique et militaire de la campagne de* 1815 (Paris, 1842). This also exists in a translation by L. V. Benét, United States Ordnance (New

York, 1863). From these works must not be separated, of course, Jomini's *Précis de l'art de la guerre* (Paris, 2 vols. 8vo; Brussels, 2 vols. 8vo); which again is accessible in an English translation by two American officers: *Summary of the Art of War* (New York, 1854). It is difficult to make any selection of the other interesting historical and didactic works of the period, all having the special value of being exponents of a system of war at this moment in actual practice.

We have already mentioned (in our March number) the most important works on the life and character of Napoleon. We add a few titles of such as are more especially addressed to the military student. Such are General Mathieu Dumas' *Préces des évènements militaires depuis le 1er mai*, 1799, *jusqu'en* 1814, in nineteen volumes, with maps and plans. This work enjoys the very highest reputation. Of much the same rank are the *Mémoires* of Marshal Gouvion Saint-Cyr. Paris, 1821-29, 9 vols. 8vo. Napoleonists think the author rather too much disposed to find fault with the Emperor. Jomini ranks very high. General Pelet's *Mémoires sur la guerre de 1809 en Allemagne*, &c., 1824, 4 vols. 8vo. Marshal Suchet proved himself in Spain to be second to none of Napoleon's generals, and his *Mémoires* in 2 vols. 8vo are esteemed in proportion. The Memoirs of others of Napoleon's marshals, as they have been published, at intervals, necessarily possess peculiar value—especially those of Soult and Marmont. The Russian campaign has been written by a legion: Labaume's *Relation circonstanciée* (Paris, 1820, 6th ed.) was approved by Napoleon at St. Helena; Chambrai's *Histoire*, in 3 vols. 8vo, is called the best by Rocquancourt; while Marshal Marmont gave the highest credit to the work of a civilian, the *Histoire de Napoléon et de la Grande Armée en* 1812, by the Comte de Ségur, of which (as well as of Labaume's) an English translation is a current book. There is an English translation of General Clausewitz's critical view of the same campaign (London, 1843, 8vo). Baron Odeleben's *Campaign in Saxony* (Eng. trans., London, 1820, 2 vols. 8vo.), is the source of the best account of Napoleon's behavior while in the field; and the *Commentaries* of the Cathcart who fell at Inkerman, *on the war in Russia and Germany in* 1812 *and* '13 (London, 1850), have uncommon military value.

The part which Great Britain took in these wars has led to the production of many excellent works, in reference to them, in the English language. Napier's *War in the Peninsula*—with all its outrageous faults, the best military history of the day—is too well known to need further mention. Larpont's *Private Journal* in the Peninsula from 1812 (London, 1853, 3 vols. 12mo), brings us as near the person of Wellington as Odelebon's does to that of Napoleon. English literature is so overrun with really admirable books on the Peninsular War, that we must pass the most of them by—such as Gleig's *Subaltern*, Sherer's *Recollections* of the Peninsula, Hamilton's *Annals*, &c., &c.—to particularize, the important scientific works of Colonel Jones: *Journal of the Sieges undertaken by the Allies in Spain, in the years* 1811 *and* 1812, with Notes (London, 1814, 8vo), which the French have translated, although they possess Belmar's *Journaux des siéges faits ou soutenus par les Français dans le Péninsule de* 1807 *à* 1814 (Paris, 1837, 4 vols. 8vo, with atlas in folio).

Men are not yet tired of making and reading books on the great historical battle of Waterloo. It is well, therefore, to name a few of them here. Napoleon's papers (the *Mémoires* by Montholon, &c.) contain three different accounts, all valuable in their way; none of them written with any very strict regard for truth. Grouchy, Gourgaud, Gérard, and other French officers, published their controversial pamphlets. Quinet, Thiers (in his detached chapter), and Charras (lately died in exile), have published volumes. Of these, Thiers's gives the clearest and liveliest view of the plan and progress of the fight, and is as fair and accurate as the Emperor's own; Charras' is controversial and minutely exact, while the style has the piquancy of Tacitus. It has appeared in three editions, the last of which is a 12mo, with a sufficient atlas. Charras is said to have published a most trenchant critique on Thiers' chapter, but we have not yet seen it; and Marshal Grouchy's son has vindicated the memory of his father from this renewed attack. The Prussian history of the battle is given in Plotho's *War of the Allied Powers*, &c. (the German title has escaped us), Berlin, 1818. Damitz's German work, based on the papers of General Grollmann: *Geschichte des Feldzugs von* 1815 *in den Niederlanden und Frankreich* (Berlin, 1838), can be had in French also: *Histoire de la campagne de* 1815 (Paris, 1842, 2 vols. in 8vo, with plans). The English books are in themselves a legion; but the one exhaustive record is that of Captain Siborne: *History of the War in France and Belgium*, &c. London, 1844, 2 vols. 8vo, with a very remarkable atlas of plans engraved in medallion style. With this should be read the articles in the Quarterly (No. cxi., for June, 1842, and No. cli., for June, 1845), ascribed to Lord Ellesmere, written in evident communication with the Duke of Wellington, and that in the Edinburgh Review, for June, 1863 (No. ccxxxix.), which has especial reference to Thiers, Quinet, and Charras. Of course, the *Dispatches of the Duke of Wellington* (London, 1834, &c., 12 vols. 8vo), with the supplementary volumes, now in course of publication, must always recommend themselves to the serious attention of such as would trace the workings of a great captain's mind in all its details and under every difficulty. Brialmont's

Life of the Duke of Wellington, as translated and supplemented by Gleig (London, 3 vols. 8vo), may also be recommended.

The theoretical works of this period, complete in number and value, with its memoirs and histories—Jomini's take the lead—as the recognized exponents of Napoleonic strategy, and need no further mention. Side by side with these—and, in the opinion of some military men, even superior to them—must be placed the works of the truly illustrious Archduke Charles. Captain De La Barre Duparcq has presented in a superb folio volume (Paris, 1851, Tanéra), the Archduke's *Principes de la grande guerre, suivis d'exemples tactiques raisonnés de leur application*—"the most curious work (says the translator) of the worthy adversary of Napoleon." A complete edition of the Archduke Charles's military works, in the original German, is now passing through the press at Vienna. Napoleon's own supreme position as a military author need be mentioned only for the purpose of observing, that his various notes, dictations, &c., are now to be had collected together as his works (*Œuvres*, Paris, 5 vols. 8vo). The *Military Maxims* of Napoleon are, of course, known to everybody. The Marquis de Ternay's *Traité de Tactique*, edited by Koch (Paris, 1832, 2 vols. 8vo, or Brussels, 1 vol., with atlas); Lallemand's *Traité théorique et pratique des opérations secondaires de la guerre* (Paris, 1825, 2 vols. 8vo, with atlas); La Roche-Aymon's *Mémoires sur l'art de la guerre* (Paris, 1857, 5 vols. 8vo, with atlas), as well as his work *Des troupes légères* (1857, 1 vol.), and his great *De la Cavalerie* (1828-9, 2 vols. 8vo); and General Rogniat's *Considérations*, already mentioned, are mere specimens from a field unrivalled in the richness of its production.* The high authority of General Sigel induces us to add certain little essays of Marshal Bugeaud, as of the very highest value, viz.: his *Instructions pratiques: Avant-poste — reconnoissances — stratégie — tactique*, &c., &c. Paris, 1855, 1 vol.

Our own generation has had its interesting military events, and its share of productiveness in excellent military books. The wars of the Hungarian insurrection, in 1848 and 1849, gave specimens of extraordinary strategic talent, especially on the part of Görgei, whose work (known in the English translation by the title of *My Life and Acts in Hungary* (New York and London, 1852, 12mo) enabled Sir Archibald Alison to produce an unusually good military history in the chapters

---

* This work of Rogniat is so particularly mentioned because of the important discussions to which it gave rise. General Marbot attacked some of its positions in his *Remarques critiques sur l'ouvrage du Général Rogniat* (Paris, 1821, 8vo); and Napoleon himself showed his sense of the damage which Rogniat's severe criticism of some of his operations might do him, by dictating certain very copious "Notes" on the *Considérations* at St. Helena; to which Rogniat—nowise abashed at the eminence of his adversary—replied at considerable length in his *Réponse aux notes critiques de Napoléon, &c.* (Paris, 1823, 8vo.)

devoted to that struggle, in his later History of Europe. But this war has been treated with the greatest ability and equal dryness by one whom we have already mentioned as taking the lead among our contemporary military authors, in the *Geschichte des ungarischen Insurrectionskrieges in den Jahren 1848 und 1849, von* W. Rüstow, Zürich, 1860-1, 2 vols. 8vo. The same author closes his most readable production, *Die Feldherrnkunst des neunzehnten Jahrhunderts* (Zurich, 1857, 8vo, p. 795), with a succinct military history of all these wars, including that of Baden, in 1849, in which some of our own able officers of foreign birth bore an honorable part. If, from this circumstance, any of our readers should be interested in that brief struggle (and it was not without its military lessons) we can reccommend as an excellent work, on the republican side, Becker and Essellen's *Geschichte der süddeutschen Mai-Revolution.* (With maps and plans.) Schaffhausen, 1849, 8vo.

The Invasion of the Crimea has found its English historian in Kinglake. The French have General Niel's *Siége de Sébastopol*, published by authority of the War Department, Paris, 1858, 4to, with atlas; while the recent work of General Todleben (made familiar to the English reader by our friend Russell) speaks ably for Russia. An official account of the recent French campaign in Italy has been published under the title of *Campagne de l'Empereur Napoléon III. en Italie, publiée par ordre de Sa Majesté* (Paris, Dumaine, 1863, 4to, with atlas). Baron de Bazancourt has treated the same campaign in *Chronique* of 2 vols. 8vo (Paris, Amyot, 1860). Garibaldi's feats a year later have been treated by Rüstow (who was on the spot), in German: his work has been translated into French (*La Guerre Italienne en* 1860. Paris, Charbulier, 1862, 8vo) And, finally, hardly has the Schleswig-Holstein war been closed, when Rüstow has appeared as its historian.

And here we close our list of such books as we could recommend a well-educated officer to choose from, in forming a general military library. It would take the space of a regular military bibliography to name the works appropriate to the several *special* libraries, which officers of different services might be disposed respectively to form. What we have said is so obviously imperfect, to ourselves as well as to others, that we are forcibly reminded of the pressing demand there is for a reasonably full and accurate *Military Bibliography*, so far and so conscientiously *raisonné* as to be a safe guide to the purchaser of military books in every department and of every period. The close of the war is not to be the extinction of all the interest now felt in military science and military literature; and the booksellers, who hope to import largely for military readers, would find their account in encouraging the preparation of such a "Soldier's Brunet" as we have recommended.

A WORD ABOUT SLANG.

The French use the same word, *argot*, to represent both "slang" and "dead-wood." The connection is natural and plain, the first operating as an impediment to the healthy progress of a language, as the second does to the progress of a vehicle.

Slang is to a language what any gross perversion of a usage of society is to the etiquette of refinement.

It is an excrescence, the visible effect of a disease—a plague-spot, which, striking the eye at every turn, is too common to excite terror, yet is none the less a sign of pestilence, spreading daily and hourly, threatening its victims with corruption and decay. To guard against the growth of the evil is the duty not only of the physician, but of every one who values the health and strength of vigorous manhood, and desires to see no taint transmitted to posterity.

The settlement of the question, "How much slang should be allowed to obtain in a given language?" has never been reached. In this the sages of the world are far behind the driver of the Dutch *trek-schuyt*, who calculates to a nicety the pounds and ounces his conveyance can bear without foundering, before he will consent to bargain for your freight—careful that a ton too much, which pays him certain thalers, does not, in the end, entail upon him an expense of many more broad pieces in the matter of repairs.

More than one philosopher has observed that the degeneration of a people's language marks the degeneration of the people. The history of Greece and that of ancient Italia bear testimony to the truth of the assertion. Purity of thought requires the language of purity; and where the speech is coarse, or brutal, or obscene, the fair inference is that the thoughts of which it is the messenger are fittingly represented. Too little heed is paid to the experience of the past, and it is but rational to suppose that we, as a people, are now suffering, to a certain extent, for this sin of indifference or carelessness.

The corruption of our language—for that impurity is fast becoming the characteristic of ordinary conversation, no one can deny—is the result of many causes, chief among which is the prevalence of a slang style among those who cater for the public amusement in the columns of our papers, and even our more dignified magazines. As these form the circulating libraries of the masses, and as their great aim is originality, the people, glad to greet novelty in whatever form it appears, readily fall into the easy habit of slovenly speech, and adopt it without a protest, forgetful of the precepts of Lindley Murray and the stately rules of Archbishop Whately. "This expression," says one, "is from the pen of a great writer—a man of education and ability. It is forcible, and *piquant*, and *odd*. It is good." The expression becomes familiar, perhaps fashionable, and we may expect to hear it long after the subject to which it was originally applied has passed from the memory. From the pulpit, too, are heard phrases which grate harshly upon the sensitive ear, but which, sanctified by the air in which they are breathed, are soon received, and circulate as lawful mediums of thought. Another cause, too patent to require any more than a passing notice, but too important to remain unnoticed, is the influence of that class of weekly story-papers, whose circulation in our country is one of the wonders of the nineteenth century. The stage lends its aid. Actors delight in tickling the ears of the groundlings with words and phrases of ambiguous character, skilfully introduced into the lines of the text; managers, intent upon the acquisition of wealth, present plays of questionable morality and doubtful purity as to language; and dramatic writers vie with each other in pandering to the vitiated taste of the mob. What wonder, then, that corruption should creep into our daily conversation, and that, at length, the very language, undergoing day by day the changes that time and circumstances never cease in producing, should become impregnated with it, to the shame and sorrow of our race?

With all these influences operating upon a people engaged heart and soul in the greatest undertaking which has ever taxed the energies of a nation, it is not a matter of surprise that, in the Army, where men are debarred the privileges, the comforts, the luxuries of home, and cut off from all those associations which tend to humanize the roughest, so little attention is paid to the use of that pure speech which distinguishes the gentleman from the rowdy. Lucilius complained of the debasement of literature and public taste in his time; but could he visit our earth to-day, particularly that part of it in which the armies of the young Republic are encamped, he could hardly fail to essay one more withering satire on the wilful blindness of mankind. He would find much fault with the colloquial style of modern patriots, and would have abundant cause to wonder that in an age of refinement men can be induced to read the trashy books sent by unscrupulous publishers to be sold at military stations.

The existence of a slang element in the Army cannot, of course, be prevented. It came from home, where the fault lies. But to what is due its increase? We have considered some of the influences bearing upon all alike. There is another, which is confined to the service. The too common use of by-words, words of *argot*, words from the engine-room, the Bowery, the tavern—nicknames, catchwords, on the part of those appointed to positions of honor, many of whom have enjoyed the advantages of education and the refinement of well-ordered homes—gives a stamp of genuineness to this false coin, which less favored subordinates keep in circulation, not because its intrinsic worth is greater, but because there is a glitter about it which the legal tender lacks, and because it passes current with the titled ones. It may be that to the illiterate man slang is a dialect more readily mastered and more easily handled than the *lingua pura;*[*] but by what process does he assimilate his tent-mate to a "skee-sicks" or a "stick-in-the-mud?" It has been remarked that the abecedarian must needs be a natural mnemonician to fix in his mind the letters of the alphabet, apparently so unconnected with any of his material associations; but consider the mental labor required of a soldier who likens a pair of boots to "mud-hooks" or "gunboats," and makes "skedaddle"[†] a synonym for retreat! Perhaps, having been denied the opportunities which most have, in our day, to become acquainted with other means whereby to "conceal his thoughts," and still desirous of enriching his vocabulary,[‡] he has recourse to invention, imitating unconsciously and in an humble way the great lexicographers, who frequently bring their neologisms into life, only to see them die of neglect.

It is easy now to identify those slang words which have

---

[*] The writer was conversing with an army officer at Stoneman's Switch, Va., one day in the fall of '62. The subject of our colloquy was "slang," to which the officer was much addicted. To him the *gaucheries* of the Faubourg Bowery were more familiar than the Gallic accent. About this time Victor Hugo's great book was much sought after in the army.

"By-the-way," said the officer, "there is an excellent thing about slang in Hugo's work. Have you read *Les Misérables?*"

"*I* have," replied a gallant young soldier whom General Hooker delights to honor, "but I'd rather see them whipped."

There was evidently a joke in the wind, but the questioner could only snuff it. Turning a semi-suspicious eye upon the aide, he remarked—

"It's a bully big thing on ice, ain't it?"

[†] *Skedaddle* comes of good Hellenic stock, and in its primitive form may be found in Homer and Hesiod. The original *skedannumi* means to run in a crowd, and is doubtless the parent of our vulgar *skeet* and *scoot*. How the Western widow who first Americanized it, ever came to apply it to the clandestine departure of her liege lord (who was also a landlord) is more than we can conjecture, unless she considered, as we do, that the inconstant one was a *host* in himself.

[‡] Brantome tells us that Charles V. "disoit et repetoit souvent, quand il tomboit sur la beauté des langues (selon l'opinion des Turcs), qu'autant de langues que l'homme sçait parler, autant de fois est il homme."

It is worth while, for those who are destined, when this war is over, to hear of many hair-breadth escapes by flood and field, recited in language strange yet to ears polite, to know that "chin" means talk, report, rumor, just as *gab, tongue, lip,* apply in different degrees to the same idea of garrulity. The slang-speaker is never at a loss for a synonym, and rarely halts in his narration of facts. From the latter faculty of pouring forth his words in a stream, as it were, fluently, he is said to "*blow;*" and, to complete the analogy, for such there undoubtedly is, his discourse, often as lacking in form, always as constant in its flow, often as inflammable, is known, from Maine to California, as "*gas.*"

grown out of this war, but a quarter century hence, who but the antiquary, the collector of odds and ends, will be able to give the pedigree of half of them? "Contraband" is historical, so are "Reb," and "Copperhead," and "Grayback,"—all as much entitled to a long life on the lips of the people as "Methodist," "Tory," "Whig," and "Mob," all slang words, but rendered respectable by age and long residence among respectable people. But, should we not henceforth guard the doors of society against all other nondescripts who would enter surreptitiously, relying upon contact with purity for their future position among the *élite?* The eighty thousand legitimate words which compose our language are surely sufficient for all the purposes of this life,—words brim full of associations of the honored past; bearing upon their face all the attributes of the noble races from which they descended, and possessing in themselves those wonderful principles by which they may be modified to meet the constant demand made upon them in the progress of science, literature, art, and human thought. Whence the need of Billingsgate, of Romanee, of Flash, of Argot, the dregs of a hundred corruptions of as many tongues?

Shades of Milton, Addison, Pope, pardon for the word, but there is a funny side to this subject of slang, and may-be something nearly akin to philosophy in it.

In civil life one man "jews," or cheats another; in the army a trickster "yanks" his fellow. The army teamster "yanks" his wagon from a bad place in the road, or "snakes" it out, both operations requiring the peculiar skill, ingenuity, and tortuous cunning so generally considered the characteristics of the children of Israel, the sons of America, and the tribe to which the first tempter belonged.

In army phrase, a white man, acting as servant to an officer, is a "dog-robber," a term first used at Fort Bridges in 1861. It implies that the man is a consumer of what daily morsels should fall to the lot of some Gelert, Blanche, Sweetheart, or Pompey. He is a "Dead Beat," or "D. B." who is exempt from military duty, as the "Dead-head" is from any pecuniary demand at the ticket-office of Wallack's. To "confiscate" (generally "confisticate") is to put into one's basket what belongs to another. To "snatch bald-headed"* is to do the same thing, but with the difference that "snatching" property "bald-headed" is always accomplished by "strategy."

---

* *Bald-headed.* This is the Latin *calvus.* On the Roman stage it was the fashion to represent clowns and demoralized old men as bald-headed. It came to pass that a new verb was coined from this word *calvus,* viz., *calvio,* to disappoint, shuffle, frustrate, trick, cheat. Even the lovely Venus is called Bald-headed, *quod corda amantium calviat,* because she cheats the hearts of lovers.—(Servius, Virg. Æn. i., 720.)

Query.—How has the modern slang-speaker been enabled to revive this expression.

"Currency" is a new word for money. The familiar "greenback" has for synonyms, "spondulix," "stamps," "shinplasters," and "soap," all which terms may, in the course of years, be as unintelligible as the hieroglyphics on Cleopatra's Needle; but, as according to a great writer, "whatever is popular is worthy of notice," it can scarcely be deemed a waste of time to record these uncouth expressions, and to invite to them the attention of the curious. They spring from the people; they are the humble chroniclers of our national progress; they hint at the character of our national wit; or they serve as additional illustrations of that singular principle of analogy which seems to be common to all the languages of the earth. When was "Currency" ever before a household word? and why should it be so familiar now?—are questions which the historian and the financier may readily answer. "Greenback" is an object word, just as "tin" was before the glitter of the precious metals yielded to the bronze and sad color of our postal notes. "Spondulix" is suggestive. It recalls the wampum of the poor Indian, the cowrie of the Ethiopian, and resuscitates the ancient blackmail man, who, as his kinsman, the dun, does to-day, called upon his victim to "shell out." For "Spondulix" is conchological.*

In the army, as in the walks of civil life, our language loses much by abbreviation and contraction, "letters, like soldiers, being very apt to drop off on a long march, especially if their passage happens to lie near the confines of the enemy's country."† And, "abbreviations and corruptions are always busiest with the words which are most frequently in use."‡ Thus it is that "bombshell" has become "shell;" "Minié rifle," plain "Minnie" without the accent; "Navy tobacco," "navy;" "Commission," "Commish;" and "Secessionist," "Secesh." By the same process and in obedience to the same law, "Colt's revolvers" have been metamorphosed into "Colts," "Spondulix" becomes "Spons;" and "Greenbacks" "Greens." A man who re-enlists is a "Vet;" one who represents another is a "Sub;" and it is no uncommon thing to hear a "D. B." ordered to go to the "Sut's" to get "two botts" of "Whisk" for "Cap and Lute," so strong is the inclination to do away with all vowels and consonants whose utterance impedes business, or lengthens the time between drinks.

Shall we consider this new phase in the growth of our tongue an evidence of health and strength, a symptom of increasing vigor which should be encouraged? or, shall we look upon it as

---

* The *spondylus* (from Greek *spondulos*,) is a shell inequivalve, rough, hinge having two recurved teeth with an intermediate hollow; sometimes eared. One of the valves convex and thick, the other flatten. These shells are attached to rocks, from which they are separated with the greatest difficulty.—*Burrows.*

† Horne Tooke. ‡ Ibid.

an apocatastasis which should be checked by the example of those whose position entitles them to respect? As before remarked, experience teaches us a lesson. There was a time when men of spirit and ability lived in every Greek city; when the Roman Empire governed the whole world; when the language of Athens and that of Rome were the purest. But Greece perished, and Rome fell; and there was not a great man from Britain to the banks of the Euphrates. To-day the language of Virgil is nowhere spoken, that of Homer nowhere heard. They live only in the library of the scholar; to the world they are dead.

Now that literature has given a permanence to our language, no other tongue will ever be spoken on this continent. How important is it that it should be kept free from those influences which tend to debase; that it should be passed down from our generation to the next pure and undefiled; that every new element of its strength should be drawn from a pure source, and applied religiously to the development of a perfect language! We can see no limit to the spread of such a language, nor to that of the literature and laws of the people who speak it. It is in the power of every man to assist in bringing about a consummation so devoutly to be wished. Let the clergyman, the teacher, the editor, and the reporter; the actor, the play-wright, and the novelist, strike out from their vocabularies every vicious word. Let the soldier drop the disgusting obscenities, the useless by-words, the irrational slang, which army life makes so familiar. Let the officer to whom men look for example discourage impure language, bearing in mind that every member of his military family, on returning home, will influence, in a greater or less degree, for good or for evil, the community to which he belongs. It is a duty all these owe to society, to humanity, not to abuse that which is the property of all. Language, like water, is a common necessity. Impure, it causes disease; fresh and sparkling, as it flows from the pure fountain, it adds vigor to life, and in a thousand ways is an instrument of happiness and comfort.

"The sand," says Hugo, "which you trample under foot, when fused in the furnace becomes splendid crystal, and by its aid Newton and Galileo discover planets." R. W. McA.

ARMY MOVEMENTS.

BY LIEUTENANT-COLONEL O. W. TOLLES.

THE ultimate design in the creation and organization of an army is victory. To fight and win battles is the object for which all the intricate sciences and the toilsome processes involved in raising and sustaining a military force have been cultivated and pursued. All military art resolves itself into the elucidation of one question—How can success be made a matter of certainty? To this an incalculable amount of ability has been devoted, and experiments have been made on thousands of battle-fields, and yet to-day accidents (so called) enter so largely into the decision of a contest, that no commander can feel entirely assured, when about to engage his foe, that he will be victorious. Marshal Marmont said, " A battle should be undertaken only when there is no other method of obtaining the desired result. For chance plays a great *rôle* in conflicts. Whatever may be the advantages one has on his side, there are always unforeseen accidents which may determine the victory." These accidents—though such a denomination of them is improper—arise from the comparative abilities of opposing commanders to take advantage of circumstances; the facilities offered by the topographical configuration of the ground for manœuvres; the weather, the relative situation of the masses of troops, &c. Military science has instituted certain general rules concerning the conduct of battles, founded on experience, and as far as practicable devised precautions against emergencies; but beyond there is always a margin in which circumstances have scope for their operation. The consummation of all strategy, tactics, and skill, is the collection of superior numbers upon decisive points at decisive moments. The only surety of victory is the possession of the "strongest battalions."

The character of every battle is determined and controlled largely by the character of the ground on which it is fought. If two armies equal in strength and equipments should be placed on an open plain, victory would become the prize of that one which should fight with the greatest vigor and pertinacity. There would be no opportunity for tactical manœuvres, nor for any of the feints and stratagems and efforts at deception which are part of the operations of battle-fields. For, in pursuance of the rule directing the accumulation of superior forces on decisive points, the object of every commander is to break or turn the lines of his opponents (if he be making an attack) in the centre, or one of the wings, or on a flank, by massing his troops behind the cover of woods or hills, and precipitating them unexpectedly on the place selected; or if he be acting on the defensive, it is his object to defend his most vulnerable points by strengthening them with artificial protection. The shape of lines of battle is therefore invariably governed by the characteristics of the ground. They generally approximate, however, to the shape of one of a half dozen species defined by military writers, which will be noticed hereafter. Meanwhile let us consider the various preliminary processes incident to the initiation of a general engagement.

If an army is acting on the defensive, the chief object of its commander is to establish himself in some position in which he can best repel an attack with as little loss to himself and as great a loss to his opponent as possible, so that by pursuing his success the repulse may be converted into a rout. Such a position must offer facilities not only for actual battle—that, is a defensible position of perhaps five miles long—but also facilities for strong outpost situations for observing the movements of the enemy, or sufficient obstructions to prevent a surprise, and protections for the flanks and rear. Ordinarily, also, a good defensive position must have a strategetical as well as a tactical excellence; it must cover the necessary natural approaches by which the attacking army seeks to reach the objective points of its movement. For, if a position can be flanked, it is of course untenable or useless.

The tactical features which render a defensive position excellent are hills, woods, streams, marshes, &c., sometimes villages or isolated houses; even a sunken road may be of great importance. All these advantages can be greatly assisted by twenty-four hours' labor with intrenching-tools. It may be remarked, in passing, that a great deal of foolish ridicule has been bestowed by the newspapers on the use of the shovel and pickaxe in our warfare, whereas the truth is that they are honorable and important instruments. The Romans never made a camp without fortifying it, going out of their intrenchments to fight, if they were engaged in offensive operations. Their example has been followed in all subsequent periods. All judicious commanders have recognized the propriety of intrenchments, or, what is the same, of availing themselves of natural facilities for strengthening the position of their forces. As between the Northern and Southern armies in our civil war, the latter have been far more diligent with intrenching-tools than the former, since they have mostly acted on the defensive. The works erected by the rebels at Yorktown, Williamsburg, and Richmond, those met by the Army of the Potomac in its present campaign, and those encountered by our armies in the Southwest, have been of the strongest character. The chivalry are as facile with the spade as laborers on a railroad.

Two of the best examples of defensive positions occupied by the contending armies during our war were those held respectively by the rebels at Fredericksburg and by the Union army at Gettysburg. The former could not be flanked and left in the rear by our forces without a battle, except by an abandonment of the base at Acquia Creek; it covered entirely the route of approach to Richmond upon that line; hence, strategically it was perfect. It lay upon a range of bluffs, with an open plain before them, and in front of the plain a river. The hills were wooded, so that all movements of the rebels were concealed, while they had a full view of every movement of the Union forces. The town of Fredericksburg covered their sharpshooters, who interfered with the construction of pontoon-bridges. At the right of the rebel line was a creek with high banks, and on their left the almost impassable country of the Wilderness. With all these advantages, assisted by long ranges of rifle-pits, and high earthen walls covering batteries, it is not surprising that they slaughtered thousands of their assailants in the disastrous battle of December, 1862. One peculiar feature of a defensive position, which has been mentioned, viz., a sunken road, was remarkably prominent in this battle. Behind the city of Fredericksburg, at the foot of the ridge where the rebels were posted, and parallel to the front of their position, was a street of about an eighth of a mile long, the bed of which was some four feet below the surface of the ground. The side of the street toward our army was walled with stone, laid up against the earth. Here stood a line of rebels, with cartridges laid in the crevices of the stones, their ends already bitten off so as to be ready for immediate use, and poured upon our gallant soldiers a continuous fire, before which their ranks melted. Many hundreds fell in front of that deadly line of flame.

The position at Gettysburg, strategically considered, covered several main routes of approach to Baltimore, and offered opportunities of assailing the rebel army in the rear, should it advance northward. It was therefore necessary that General Lee should defeat the Northern army, or retreat. His most prudent course would have been to adopt the latter alternative, but overweening presumption induced him to make an attempt which resulted in a disaster from which his army has never recovered. Tactically the position was very strong, though it had some disadvantages. The crest held by our army was well wooded, while the rebels were obliged to advance over an open plain to the attack. Our chief misfortunes in the conflict occurred when we assumed the offensive, and met them on the plain, where they were able to assail the flank of our attacking forces.

The Union armies in this war have generally made offensive movements, and our battles have been those of attack rather than of defence. It will be more interesting, therefore, to trace the process in which offensive preliminaries to conflicts are conducted.

The commander of an attacking army first thoroughly learns, by all the means at his command—such as spies, scouts, deserters, prisoners, reconnoissances, &c.—the position of his enemy. He then determines the point and mode of attack. Then he chooses, in conformity with this decision, his routes of approach. Ordinarily, the attacking army is brought almost within striking distance of the enemy one or several days previously to the general conflict, the outposts of the defending army are driven in, and, by a number of skirmishes, its position is further developed, and its intentions understood. When the time for the general conflict approaches, the principal commanders are informed in detail of the places of the general, and their relative parts are assigned them. Usually, two attacks are made—one a feint, and the other a real one. These attacks are rarely made with the whole strength of an army, or along its whole line; for this would determine the conflict by the relative endurance of the armies. The most usual course is to concentrate a superior force at one point of the defending line, with the intention of carrying it, and thus destroy the order of battle of the defenders. The latter rely on the natural or artificial advantages of their position to hold this attack at bay, until they can mass their forces so as to be equal to those of their assailants. In relation to the method of attack, we quote some paragraphs from a standard military work.*

The points at which attacks will be made, being selected in accordance with these principles, the commander decides upon the formation of his order of battle. This is usually composed of three lines—the first line, second line, and reserves. The character of the ground modifies their relative positions; but in most cases the interval between the two lines will be from one to three hundred yards, while the reserves will be posted within supporting distance behind the cover of a forest or hill. Each corps will have a reserve of its own, and there may be an entire corps held as a grand reserve. Suppose an army to be composed of four corps, with cavalry and a park of reserve artillery—each corps composed of three divisions. The simplest arrangement will be, therefore, to put three corps in line of battle, with the fourth corps behind the centre, or the weakest point of the line, as a reserve. Each of the three corps will put a division in each of its three lines, with proper artillery. The cavalry of the army will be posted on the flanks.

The positions of the lines of battles of two armies have been designated by military writers as of four kinds. The first is the *parallel* order—that is, when the two armies are arrayed against each other in straight lines, all parts of which are equi-

---

* Duparcq's "Military Art and History," translated by Brigadier-General Cullum:

"The choice of the point of attack will be determined by principles of strategy, tactics, or character of the ground. If the enemy keeps one of his wings in proximity to his lines of communication, or to his frontier, strategy requires that the attack should commence on that wing. Where the enemy is near some dangerous obstacle which covers him, do not, on any account, attack him on the side nearest that obstacle, but direct your blows beyond, so as to penetrate the lines which face you, and drive him headlong on the obstacle. Suppose the order of battle of the enemy presents a void, or any other defect, then you should doubtless throw yourself on this weak point, always guarding yourself by small flanking reserves against any traps he may lay for you. Finally, a topographic reason will determine the choice of a point of attack. When the enemy occupies some elevations, then aim at the highest, and if you succeed, all his other positions must fall. A village or a wood may sometimes perform the same part as such an eminence, and will, for the same reasons, require your attention."

distant. In practice, however, this is rarely the case, for the lines of battle are adapted to the configuration of the ground, and therefore irregular. The second is the *oblique* order, in which one end of the lines approaches more closely than the other. Almost every attacking line of battle approximates to this character, for generally one wing is advanced to fight, while the other is *refused*, as it is called in military parlance. Third, is the *concave* order, in which the centre is refused, or kept back, while the wings are advanced. This was the case with the Union army at Antietam, where the attack was made with both wings, while the centre did not participate. Fourth is the *convex* order, the opposite of the last, the centre being pushed forward, and the wings held back.

It is evident that the character of the order of battle will be governed by the nature of the attack intended.

After the lines have been posted, the rear of the army becomes a busy scene, and continues so until long after the conflict is ended. Ammunition, hospital, and ambulance trains are posted where they will be of most advantage, field hospitals are located, and the reserves take their appointed position. As the battle progresses, regiments and caissons come down to be resupplied with ammunition, exhausted troops march to places where they can rest and reorganize, ambulances are driven to the hospitals conveying wounded, the hospitals themselves become crowded, and present shocking spectacles, detachments of prisoners are marched along under guard, and, to give excitement to the whole, shells from the enemy's batteries, which have failed to burst, or round shot which have *richochetted*, come whizzing along for a mile or two behind the lines where the main conflict is progressing. A military adage, the sagacity of which is proved by experience, directs that a general should always have good roads in his rear, so that retreat in case of disaster may be easy. Many a position for battle, excellent in other respects, is unavailable on this account. Such roads being secured, present busy spectacles for miles in the rear of an army during a long engagement, and become filled with men and horses slightly wounded, disabled batteries, and other wrecks of war, going to the main or temporary base.

All arrangements being made, the anxious moment of suspense previous to the opening of the engagement arrives. This is the time that tests the nerve of the commander. Hitherto he has been busily engaged in maturing his plans and superintending the disposition of his troops. Perhaps all things have been made ready at nightfall, and he knows that he has but to give the order, and at daybreak will commence a strife which will cost thousands of lives, and determine the course of a nation's destiny. If he trembles in those hours of uncertainty, and vainly seeks sleep on his camp-cot, we cannot wonder.

The method of opening and conducting a battle is, of course, varied in all possible respects by the circumstances of the case. Usually, however, there is a more or less general cannonading, particularly upon that part of the defending line selected for the feint attack, so as to prevent movements of troops. Skirmishers are then deployed in the front of the attacking party, who, driving back the skirmishers of the defenders, open the way for the main advance, which pushes on and engages its opponents. The fighting becomes warm, and if the defenders are overpowered, or convinced that the feint is intended as a real attack, they hurry up re-enforcements. Several hours have been consumed in this, when, on another part of the line, where the real attack is to be made, a concentrated fire of artillery is opened on the selected spot, and the attacking columns rush forward. The fighting is now desperate, the advances and retreats, the shouts and yells of the combatants, and the constant rattle of muskets, making a turmoil and a din indescribable. To an unpractised eye, all seems inextricable confusion. Yet there is order in the chaos of horrors. On a battle-field there is not that haste and confusion generally supposed. Movements, except in case of decisive charges, are made with calmness and order; rarely is the fighting at any one spot ended under a couple of hours. If the attack is successful, a rush with bayonets ensues, and the enemy is driven back to his interior defences. If unsuccessful, the attacking columns return to their supports. Now comes a lull, in which not a sound is heard, and one could scarcely imagine that in the woods and behind the hills, and crouched under stone walls, and swarming in rifle-pits, were two hundred thousand men bent on mutual destruction, and that the dark-looking guns, now so quiet, were shortly to open with volumes of flame. Meanwhile, new plans are made, and the positions of the troops rearranged. Perhaps a portion of the reserves are brought up and put in the front. A decisive charge is ordered. The storm recommences. The assailants crowd up the hills held by the defenders, rush over their rifle-pits, capture their cannon, and drive them, pell-mell, out of their defences. The reserves stem the torrent till nightfall, and the beaten army retires, leaving its dead, its wounded, its cannon, its flags, and the *débris* of its morning's splendor, in the hands of the victors. Or perhaps the attack recoils, and the assailants, growing disheartened, steadily yield before the defenders, now become the assailants, and in their turn are driven back and back till the tide of overthrow is stayed, or reverse becomes defeat, and defeat a rout. In our war, a rout has rarely occurred to either party, since the first Bull Run battle, the defeated army being generally able to withdraw in some kind of order. This is owing to the nature of the country, which offers so many facilities for protection, and perhaps to the excellence of the troops on both sides.

One of the most wonderful of the phenomena of a battle, is the disproportion between the number of shots fired and the effects produced. Any one who has visited the scene of a battle will have observed the immense number of bullets in fences, trees, &c. At Antietam this was very remarkable. The fences around the famous corn-field were honey-combed with balls, and the trees contained large numbers of unexploded shells. In his report of the battle of Stone River, General Rosecrans says: "Of fourteen thousand five hundred and sixty rebels struck by our missiles, it is estimated that twenty thousand rounds of artillery hit seven hundred and twenty-eight men, and two million rounds of musketry hit thirteen thousand eight hundred and thirty-two men—averaging twenty-seven cannon-shots to hit one man, and one hundred and forty-five musket-shots to hit one man."

This great waste of ammunition ensues in several methods. Artillery fire is often employed not so much with the expectation of killing and wounding, as to prevent movements of troops. The men lying down, or perhaps sheltered by embankments, can scarcely be touched by the shot. In musketry engagements, even at close quarters, soldiers, except they have become veterans, fire largely at random, and a great proportion of the bullets fly over the heads of the combatants, or strike the ground in front of them. The old proverb, "A miss is as good as a mile," is strikingly appropriate to the experiences of a battle-field. In the miscellaneous whizzing of bullets, a man will perhaps distinguish a dozen which come almost in contact with him, singing in his ears, or grazing his clothing. Some interesting facts on this topic are given in Prof. Mahan's work on fortifications. We quote the following:—

"Beyond two hundred and twenty yards, the effect of the fire (small-arms) is very uncertain. Beyond four hundred and fifty yards, the ball seldom gives a dangerous wound, although the musket fired under an elevation of 4° or 5° will carry from six to seven hundred yards, and under greater elevations over one thousand yards.

"The nature of the surface of the ground has considerable influence upon the efficacy of the fire. In broken or ploughed ground, fire is less effective than on an even, firm surface, since in the former the balls are embedded, whereas in the latter they *ricochet*, and thus attain their mark. It is estimated that under favorable circumstances, about one-seventh of the balls take effect in this way."

TABLE OF THE EFFECTS OF FIRE ON A TARGET FIVE FEET NINE INCHES HIGH, AND NINETY-FIVE FEET IN LENGTH.

Number of Balls out of a hundred that hit the Mark.		Distances to the Target in yards.	Penetration into Pine, &c., in inches, at same distances.	Penetration into Oak, in inches, at same distances.
On even ground, by direct and ricochet shots.	On broken ground by direct shots.		ft. in.	inches.
75	67	85	3 3	4.0
50	38	170	2 2	2.3
27	16	255	1 2	1.2
20	6	340	0 7	0.6
14	8	425	0 4	0.4
7	5	510	0 1	0.1

In rifle practice with the ordinary rifle, owing to the greater length of time requisite to load this arm, there is some compensation for the more uncertain aim of the musket in short ranges and large targets. When the distance is under one hundred and seventy yards, and the mark large, the effects of the two arms are nearly equal; but for distances of two hundred and twenty yards and beyond, the balance is greatly in favor of the rifle. This superiority of the rifle is more particularly observable in the latest improvements of this arm, by Hall, in loading at the breech.

Decker, a German author of reputation, lays down the following as the probable number of balls out of one hundred which will attain their aim when fired by well-instructed troops, making full allowance for the over-estimation of distances in firing on an enemy :—

```
Troops firing in line at  300 paces, out of 100 balls,  1 will touch.
   "      "     "   "    200    "     "   "    "     20    "
   "      "     "   "    100    "     "   "    "     40    "
   "   as skirmishers,   400    "     "   "    "      5    "
   "      "     "   "    300    "     "   "    "     10    "
   "      "     "   "    200    "     "   "    "     30    "
   "      "     "   "    100    "     "   "    "     80    "
Rifle practice, at       400    "     "   "    "     10    "
   "      "     "        300    "     "   "    "     20    "
   "      "     "        200    "     "   "    "     72    "
```

MY CAPTURE AND ESCAPE FROM MOSBY.

BELLE, my favorite mare, neighed impatiently in front of my tent, just as the bright sunrise of early autumn was gilding the hills. The morning was cold and brilliant, and the first crisp frost had just sufficiently stiffened the sod to make a brisk gallop agreeable to both rider and horse.

The bold Shenandoah shook the icy wrinkles from its morning face, and rolled smoothly away before me into the gorgeous forest of crimson and gold below Front Royal.

It is the day of the regular train, and a thousand army wagons are already rolling away from Sheridan's head-quarters down the famous Valley Pike, to bring food and raiment to a shivering and hungry army. I spring into the saddle, and Belle, in excellent spirits, evidently thinks she can throw dust in the eyes of Mosby or any other guerrilla who dares follow her track. It is nine miles to where the train is parked, and before I arrive there, the last wagon has passed out of sight, and the picket-gate of the army has been closed for an hour behind it. My orders are imperative to accompany this train, and military law allows of no discretion. With a single orderly and my colored servant, George Washington, a contraband, commonly called Wash, to constantly remind him of the Christian virtue of cleanliness, I pass out into the guerrilla-infested country.

It is but an hour's work to overtake the train, and mounted as I am I feel great contempt for guerrillas, and inwardly defy any of them to catch *me*, as I give Belle the rein and dash on at a sweeping gallop till I come in sight of the train, a mile ahead, winding its way through the little village of Newtown, nine miles south of Winchester.

"Mosby be hanged!" I said to myself, as I slacken speed and pass leisurely through the town, noticing the pretty women, who, for some reason, appear in unusual force at the doors and windows, and one or two of whom wave their handkerchiefs in a significant manner, which, however, I fail to understand, and ride heedlessly forward. Who would suppose a pretty woman waving a handkerchief to be a sign of danger?

Evidently no one but a cynic or a crusty old bachelor, and, as I am neither, I failed to interpret the well-meant warning.

As I had nearly passed the town, I overtook a small party, apparently of the rear-guard of the train, who were lighting their pipes and buying cakes and apples at a small grocery on the right of the pike, and who seemed to be in charge of a non-commissioned officer.

"Good-morning, sergeant," I said, in answer to his salute. "You had better close up at once. The train is getting well ahead, and this is the favorite beat of Mosby."

"All right, sir," he replied, with a smile of peculiar intelligence, and nodding to his men they mounted at once and closed in behind me, while, quite to my surprise, I noticed three more of the party, whom I had not before seen, in front of me.

An instinct of danger at once possessed me. I saw nothing to justify it, but I felt a presence of evil which I could not shake off. The men were in Union blue complete, and wore in their caps the well-known Greek cross which distinguishes the gallant Sixth Corps. They were young, intelligent, cleanly, and good-looking soldiers, armed with revolvers and Spencer's repeating carbine.

I noticed the absence of sabres, but the presence of the Spencer, which is a comparatively new arm in our service, reassured me, as I thought it impossible for the enemy to be, as yet, possessed of them.

We galloped on merrily, and just as I was ready to laugh at my own fears, Wash, who had been riding behind me and had heard some remark made by the soldiers, brushed up to my side and whispered through his teeth, chattering with fear, "Massa, Secesh sure! Run like de debbel!"

I turned to look back at these words, and saw six carbines levelled at me at twenty paces' distance; and the sergeant, who had watched every motion of the negro, came riding towards me with his revolver drawn, and the sharp command, "Halt—surrender!"

We had reached a low place where the Opequan Creek crosses the pike a mile from Newtown. The train was not a quarter of a mile ahead, but out of sight for the moment over the next ridge. High stone walls lined the pike on either side, and a narrow bridge across the stream in front of me was already occupied by the three rascals who had acted as advance-guard, who now coolly turned round and presented carbines also from their point of view.

I remembered the military maxim, a mounted man should never surrender until his horse is disabled, and hesitated an instant considering what to do, and quite in doubt whether I was myself, or some other fellow whom I had read of as captured and hung by guerrillas; but at the repetition of the sharp command, "Surrender," with the addition of the polite words, "you d——d Yankee son of a b——h," aided by the somewhat disagreeable presence of the revolver immediately in my face, I concluded I was undoubtedly the other fellow, and surrendered accordingly.

My sword and revolver were taken at once by the sergeant, who proved to be Lieutenant C. F. Whiting, of Clark County, Virginia, in disguise, and who remarked, laughing, as he took them, "We closed up, captain, as you directed; as this is a favorite beat of Mosby's, I hope our drill was satisfactory."

"All right, sergeant," I replied. "Every dog has his day, and yours happens to come now. You have sneaked upon me in a cowardly way, disguised as a spy, and possibly my turn may come to-morrow."

"Your turn to be hung," he replied. And then as we hurried along a wood-path down the Opequan, he told me with great satisfaction, how they had lain in ambush in expectation of catching some stragglers from our train, and seeing me coming, had reached the little grocery from the woods behind it, just in time to appear as belonging to our party; that Mosby was three miles back, with a hundred men, and I should soon have the honor of seeing him in person.

They were a jolly, good-natured set of fellows, who evidently thought they had done a big thing; and as I scanned them more closely, the only distinction in appearance between them and our soldiers, which I could discover, was that the Greek cross on their caps was embroidered in yellow worsted.

I was offered no further indignity or insult, and was allowed to ride my own horse for the present, though I was quietly informed on the way, that Mosby had threatened to hang the first officer he should catch, in retaliation for his men who had been hung as guerrillas at Front Royal, and that I would undoubtedly be the unfortunate individual.

With this consoling information, I was ushered into the presence of the great modern highwayman, John S. Mosby, then lieutenant-colonel C. S. A.

He stood a little apart from his men, by the side of a splendid gray horse, with his right hand grasping the bridle-rein, the forearm resting on the pommel of his saddle, his left arm akimbo, and his right foot thrown across the left ankle, and resting on its toe. He is a slight, medium-sized man, sharp of feature, quick of sight, lithe of limb, with a bronzed face, of the color and tension of whip-cord; his hair a yellow brown, with full but light beard, and mustache of the same. A straight Grecian nose, firm-set, expressive mouth, large ears, deep-gray eyes, high forehead, large, well-shaped head, and his whole expression denoting hard services, energy, and love of whiskey.

He wore top-boots and a civilian's overcoat—black, lined with red—and beneath it the complete gray uniform of a Confederate lieutenant-colonel, with its two stars on the sides of the standing collar, and the whole surmounted by the inevitable slouched hat of the whole Southern race. His men were about half in blue and half in butternut.

He scarcely noticed me as I approached, but fixed his gaze on the noble animal I rode, as evidently the more valuable prize of the two. As I dismounted, he said to his servant, "Dick, take that horse;" and I knew the time had come when I must part with my beautiful Belle, whom I had rode nearly three years, through many a bloody field and hair's-breadth escape, and who loved me with an almost human love. Twice during the last three miles, as I came to a space of open country, had I resolved to dash away and trust to her nimble feet to distance their deadly rifles, and twice the sweet faces of home had appeared to scare me back to propriety.

Ah! what will a man not endure for the sweet faces of home!

Beware of tender ties, you who aspire to deeds of desperate daring; for although ennobling and inspiring to all that is duty, you will be either more or less than man, if they fail to compel you to prudence wherever there is a choice of action left. I could not refrain from throwing my arms around Belle's neck and tenderly caressing her for the last time before she was led away.

The lieutenant ventured to protest against Mosby's appropriating the mare to himself, without an apportionment and division of her value, in accordance with the rules of the gang; but he was promptly silenced, and ordered to content himself with his choice of the other two horses he had captured, which he immediately did by taking both of them. While this colloquy was passing, Mosby was quietly examining my papers, which had been taken from my pocket on my arrival; and presently, looking up with a peculiar gleam of satisfaction on his face, he said:

"Oh! Captain B——, inspector-general of ——'s cavalry? Good-morning, Captain. Glad to see you, sir. Indeed, there is but one man I would prefer to see this morning to yourself, and that is your commander. Were you present, sir, the other day, at the hanging of eight of my men as guerrillas, at Front Royal?"

This question pierced me like a sword, as I really had been present at the terrible scene he mentioned; and although I had used my full influence, even to incurring the charge of timidity, in attempting to save the lives of the wretched men, believing that retaliation would be the only result, I could not show that fact, and doubted if it would avail me aught if I could.

I therefore answered him firmly: "I was present, sir, and, like you, have only to regret that it was not the commander instead of his unfortunate men."

This answer seemed to please Mosby, for he apparently expected a denial. He assumed a grim smile, and directed Lieutenant Whiting to search me. My gold hunting-watch and chain, several rings, a set of shirt studs and buttons, some coins, a Masonic pin, and about three hundred dollars in greenbacks, with some letters and pictures of the dear ones at home, and a small pocket Bible, were taken.

A board of officers was assembled to appraise their value, also that of my clothing, and to determine the ownership of each of the articles; the rules of the gang requiring that all captures shall be thus disposed of, or sold, and their value distributed proportionately among the captors.

My boots were appraised at six hundred and fifty dollars in Confederate money; my watch at three thousand, and the other articles in the same proportion, including my poor old servant Wash, who was put up and raffled for at two thousand dollars. Wash was very indignant that he should be thought worth only two thousand dollars Confederate, and informed them that he considered himself quite unappreciable, and that among other accomplishments he could make the best milk-punch of any man in the Confederacy, and, if they had the materials, he would like to try a little of it now. This hit at the poverty of their resources raised a laugh, and Mosby's man, Dick, to show that they had the materials, offered Wash a drink, which, quite to my surprise, and doubtless to that of his own stomach also, he stubbornly refused. On asking him privately why he refused, he replied, " You know, massa, too much freeder breeds despise !"

When all this was concluded, Mosby took me one side, and returned to me the Bible, letters, and pictures, and the Masonic pin, saying quietly, as he did so, alluding to the latter with a significant sign:

" You may as well keep this; it may be of use to you somewhere. Some of my men pay some attention to that sort of thing. Your people greatly err in thinking us merely guerrillas. Every man of mine is a duly-enlisted soldier, and detailed to my command from various Confederate regiments. They are merely picked men, selected from the whole army for their intelligence and courage. We plunder the enemy, as the rules of war clearly allow. To the victors belong the spoils, has been a maxim of war in all ages. I can hang two for one all the year round if your men insist upon it; but I hope soon to have a better understanding. I yesterday executed eight of your poor fellows on the Valley Pike, your highway of travel, in retaliation for my men hung at Front Royal; and I have to-day written to General Sheridan, informing him of it, and proposing a cessation of such horrible work, which every true soldier cannot but abhor. I sincerely hope he will assent to it."

I thanked him warmly for his kindness, as I took his offered hand with a grip known all the world over to the brethren of the mystic tie, and really began to think Mosby almost a gentleman and a soldier, although he had just robbed me in the most approved manner of modern highwaymen.

The sun was now approaching the meridian, and immediate preparations were made for the long road to Richmond and the Libby. A guard of fifteen men, in command of Lieutenant Whiting, was detailed as our escort; and accompanied by Mosby himself, we started directly across the country, regardless of roads, in an easterly direction, towards the Shenandoah and the Blue Ridge. We were now in company of nine more of our men, who had been taken at different times, making eleven of our party in all, besides the indignant contraband, Wash, whom it was also thought prudent to send to the rear for safe keeping.

I used every effort to gain the acquaintance and confidence of these men, and by assuming a jolly and reckless manner, I succeeded in drawing them out and satisfying myself that some of them could be depended on in any emergency. I had determined to escape if even half an opportunity should present itself, and the boys were quick in understanding my purpose and intimating their readiness to risk their lives in the attempt.

Two of them, in particular—George W. McCauley, of Western Virginia, commonly known as Mack, and one Brown, of Blaser's scouts—afterwards proved themselves heroes of the truest metal.

We journeyed rapidly, making light of our misfortunes, and cracking many a joke with our rebel guard, until we reached Howittsville, on the Shenandoah, nine miles below Front Royal, where we bivouacked for the night in an old school-house, sole relic left of a former civilization. It is an old, unpainted, two-story building, with wooden blinds nailed shut, and seems to have been fitted up by Mosby as a kind of way-station, in which to camp with his stranger-guests. Many a sad heart, more hopeless and broken than our's, has doubtless throbbed restless on its naked floors, with premonitions of the dreary Libby. All of the guard confirmed Mosby's statement as to the organization of his band and the execution of our men the day previous; and his letter to Sheridan in regard to it has since been published, and certainly speaks for itself of the business-like habits of its author.

Our party of eleven were assigned to one side of the lower floor of the school-house, where we lay down side by side, with our heads to the wall, and our feet nearly touching the feet of the guard, who lay in the same manner opposite to us, with their heads to the other wall, except three who formed a relief guard for the sentry's post at the door. Above the heads of the guard, along the wall, ran a low school-desk, on which each man of them stood his carbine and laid his revolver before disposing himself to sleep. A fire before the door dimly lighted the room, and the scene as they dropped gradually to sleep was warlike in the extreme, and made a Rembrandt picture on my memory which will never be effaced.

I had taken care, on lying down, to place myself between McCauley and Brown, and the moment the rebels began to snore and the sentry to nod over his pipe, we were in earnest and deep conversation. McCauley proposed to unite our party and make a simultaneous rush for the carbines, and take our chances of stampeding the guard and making our escape; but on passing the whisper quietly along our line, only three men were found willing to assent to it. As the odds were so largely against us, it was useless to urge the subject.

The intrepid McCauley then proposed to go himself alone in

the darkness among the sleeping rebels, and bring over to our party every revolver and every carbine before any alarm should be given, if we would only use the weapons when placed in our hands; but again timidity prevailed, and I must confess that I myself hesitated before this hardy courage, and refused to peril the brave boy's life in so rash a venture, as a single false step or the least alarm, in favor of which the chances were as a thousand to one, would have been to him, and probably to all of us, instant death.

I forbade the attempt, but could not help clasping the brave fellow to my heart and kissing him like a brother for the noble heroism of which he was evidently made. He was a fair boy of but eighteen summers, with soft black eyes, and a rosy, round face as smooth and delicate as a girl's, with a noble forehead and an unusually intelligent countenance. I had picked him out at first sight as a hero, and every hour was increasing my admiration of him. He slept in my arms at last as the long night wore away, till the morning broke dull and rainy, finding us exhausted and thoroughly wretched and despondent.

The march began at an early hour, and our route ran directly up the Blue Ridge. We had emerged from the forest and ascended about one-third the height of the mountain, when the full valley became visible, spread out like a map before us, showing plainly the lines of our army, its routes of supply, its foraging parties out, and my own camp at Front Royal as distinctly as if we stood in one of its streets. We now struck a wood-path running southward and parallel with the ridge of the mountain, along which we travelled for hours, with this wonderful panorama of forest and river, mountain and plain before, us in all the gorgeous beauty of the early autumn.

"This is a favorite promenade of mine," said Mosby. "I love to see your people sending out their almost daily raids after me. There comes one of them now almost towards us. If you please, we will step behind this point and see them pass. It may be the last sight you will have of your old friends for some time."

The coolness of this speech enraged me, and yet I could not help admiring the quiet and unostentatious audacity which seemed to be the prominent characteristic of its author. I could hardly restrain an impulse to rush upon him and

"Try this quarrel hilt to hilt,"

but the important fact that I had not a hilt even, while he wore two revolvers, restrained me, and looking in the direction he pointed, I distinctly saw a squadron of my own regiment coming directly towards us on a road running under the foot of the mountain, and apparently on some foraging expedition down the valley. They passed within a half mile of us under the mountain, and Mosby stood with folded arms on a rock above them, the very picture of stoical pride and defiance, or, as Mack whispered:—

"Like patience on a monument smiling at grief."

We soon moved on, and before noon reached the road running through Manassas Gap, which place we found held by about one hundred of Mosby's men, who signalled him as he approached; and here, much to my regret, the great chieftain left us, bidding me a kindly good-by, and informing me that my last hope of rescue or escape was now gone.

We were hurried on through the Gap and down the eastern slope of the mountain, and turning southward, in a few hours passed Chester Gap, finding it also occupied by Mosby's men in force, and we were only able to approach it after exchanging the proper signals.

This gave me an idea of how Mosby conducts his raids so successfully, by leaving a garrison in each of the gaps behind him before he ventures far into the valley. These garrisons he can concentrate at any desired point by signals almost in an hour, and any of them can communicate with him from the mountain-tops to any part of the valley, and either warn him of danger or direct him where to strike. If pursued, he has but to retreat in such a direction as to draw his pursuers on to this reserve force which he concentrates in some strong position, or in ambush, at his pleasure, and develops with fresh horses just as his pursuers are exhausted with the long chase. He is thus enabled, with about five hundred picked men, to remain, as he has been for two years past, the terror of the valley.

After passing Chester Gap, we descend into the valley and move towards Sperryville, on the direct line to Richmond, the last gate of hope seeming to close behind us as we leave the mountains. Our guard is now reduced, as we are far within the Confederate lines, to Lieutenant Whiting and three men, well mounted and doubly armed, and our party of eleven prisoners have seven horses to distribute amongst us as we please, so that four of us are constantly dismounted. There is also a pack-horse carrying our forage, rations, and some blankets. To the saddle of this pack-horse are strapped two Spencer carbines, muzzle downward, with their accoutrements complete, including two well-filled cartridge-boxes.

I called Mack's attention to this fact, as soon as the guard was reduced, and he needed no second hint to comprehend its significance at once. He soon after dismounted, and when it came his turn again to mount he secured, apparently by accident, the poorest and most broken down horse in the party, with which he appeared to find it very difficult to keep up, and which he actually succeeded in some mysterious way in laming.

He then dropped back to the lieutenant in charge, and modestly asked to exchange his lame horse for the pack-horse, and being particularly frank in his address his request was at once granted, without a suspicion of its object, or a thought of the fatal carbines on the pack-saddle. I used some little skill in diverting the attention of the lieutenant while the pack was readjusted; and as the rain had now begun to fall freely, no one of the guard was particularly alert.

I was presently gratified with the sight of Mack riding ahead on the pack-horse, with the two carbines still strapped to the saddle, but loosened and well concealed by his heavy *poncho* which he had spread as protection from the rain.

These carbines are seven-shooters, and load from the breech by simply drawing out from the hollow stock a spiral spring and dropping in the seven cartridges, one after the other, and then inserting the spring again behind them, which coils as it is pressed home, and by its elasticity forces the cartridges forward one at a time into the barrel, at the successive movements of the lock.

I could see the movements of Mack's right arm by the shape into which it threw the *poncho*; and while guiding his horse with his left, looking the other way and chatting glibly with the other boys, I saw him carefully draw the springs from those carbines with his right hand and hook them into the upper button-hole of his coat to support them, while he dropped in the cartridges one after another, trotting his horse at the time to conceal the noise of their click, and finally forcing down the springs and looking round at me with a look of the fiercest triumph and heroism I have ever beheld.

I nodded approval, and fearing he would precipitate matters, yet knowing that any instant might lead to discovery and be too late, I rode carelessly across the road to Brown who was on foot, and dismounting asked him to tighten my girth, during which operation I told him as quietly as possible the position of affairs, and asked him to get up gradually by the side of Mack, communicate with him, and at a signal from me to sieze one of the carbines and do his duty as a soldier if he valued his liberty.

Brown, though a plucky fellow, was of quite a different quality from Mack. He was terribly frightened and trembled like a leaf, yet went immediately to his post, and I did not doubt would do his duty well.

I rode up again to the side of Lieutenant Whiting, and like an echo from the past came back to me my words of yesterday, "Possibly my turn my come to-morrow." I engaged him in conversation, and among other things spoke of the prospect of sudden death as one always present in our army life, and the tendency it had to either harden or ameliorate the character according to the quality of the individual. He expressed the opinion which many hold that a brutal man is made more brutal by it, and a refined and cultivated man is softened and made more refined by it.

I scanned the country closely for the chances of escape if we should succeed in gaining our liberty, I knew that to fail or to be recaptured would be instant death, and the responsibility of risking the lives of the whole party, as well as my own, was oppressing me bitterly. I also had an instinctive horror of the shedding of blood, as it were, with my own hands, and the sweet faces of home were haunting me again, but this time, strange to say, urging me on, and apparently crying aloud for vengeance.

We were on the immediate flank of Early's army. His cavalry was all around us. The road was thickly inhabited. It was almost night. We had passed a rebel picket but a mile back, and knew not how near another of their camps might be. The three rebel guards were riding in front of us and on our left flank, our party of prisoners was in the center, and I was by the side of Lieutenant Whiting, who acted as rear-guard, when we entered a small copse of willow which for a moment covered the road.

The hour was propitious; Mack looked round impatiently; I wove the fatal signal, "Now's the time, boys," into a story of our charge at Winchester, which I was telling to distract attention, and at the moment of its utterance threw myself upon the Lieutenant, grasping him around the arms and dragging him from his horse, in the hope of securing his revolver, capturing him, and compelling him to pilot us outside of the rebel line.

At the word, Mack raised one of the loaded carbines, and in less time than I can write it, shot two of the guard in front of him, killing them instantly; and then coolly turning in his saddle and seeing me struggling in the road with the lieutenant, and the chances of obtaining the revolver apparently against me, he raised the carbine the third time, and as I strained the now desperate rebel to my breast with his livid face over my left shoulder, he shot him as directly between the eyes as he could have done if firing at a target at ten paces' distance. The bullet went crashing through his skull, the hot blood spirted from his mouth and nostrils into my face, his hold relaxed, and his ghastly corpse fell from my arms, leaving an impression of horror and soul-sickness which can never be effaced.

I turned around in alarm at our now desperate situation and saw Mack quietly smiling at me, with the remark:

"Golly, Cap! I could have killed five or six more of them as well as not. This is a bully carbine, I think I will take it home with me."

Brown had not accomplished so much. He had seized the second carbine at the word, and fired at the third guard on our flank; but his aim was shaky, and he had only wounded his man in the side and allowed him to escape to the front, where he was now seen a half mile away, at full speed, and firing his pistols to alarm the country.

Our position was now perilous in the extreme; not a man of us knew the country, except its most general outlines. The rebel camps could not be far away; darkness was intervening; the whole country would be alarmed in an hour; and I doubted not that before sundown even bloodhounds would be on our track. One half of our party had already scattered, panic-stricken, at the first alarm, and, every man for himself, were scouring the country in every direction.

But five remained, including the faithful Wash, who immediately shows his practical qualities by searching the bodies of the slain, and recovering therefrom, among other things, my gold hunting-watch from the person of Lieutenant Whiting, and over eleven hundred dollars in greenbacks, the proceeds doubtless of their various robberies of our men.

"Not quite nuff," said Wash, showing his ivories from ear to ear, "Dey vally dis nigger at two tousand dollers—I think I ought ter git de money."

We instantly mounted the best horses, and, well armed with carbines and revolvers, struck directly for the mountain on our right; but knowing that would be the first place where we should be sought for, we soon changed our direction to the south and rode for hours directly into the enemy's country as fast as we could ride, and before complete darkness intervened, we had made thirty miles from the place of our escape; and then turning sharp up the mountain, we pushed our exhausted horses as far as they could climb; and then abandoning them, we toiled on, on foot, all night to the very summit of the Blue Ridge, whence we could see the rebel camp-fires, and view their entire lines and position just as daylight was breaking over the valley.

We broke down twigs from several trees in line to determine the points of compass and the direction of the rebel forces and pickets after it should be light, and then crawled into a thicket to rest our exhausted frames and await the return of friendly darkness in which to continue our flight.

The length of this weary day and the terrible pangs of hunger and thirst, which we suffered on this barren mountain, pertain to the more common experience of a soldier's life, and I need not describe them here.

Neither will I narrate in detail how some of our party who scattered arrived in camp before us, and how one feeble old man was recaptured and killed, nor our hopeless despair as day after day we saw the mountain alive with rebel scouts sent out for our capture, and at night blazing with their picket-fires; and how we even ate a poor little dog which had followed our fortunes to his untimely end, and were thinking seriously of eating the negro Wash, when he, to save himself from so unsavory a fate, ventured down in the darkness to a corn-field and brought us up three ears of corn apiece which we ate voraciously; and how we had to go still farther south and abandon the mountain altogether to avoid the scouts and pickets; and how we finally struck the Shenandoah, twenty miles to the rear of Early's army, and there built a raft and floated by night forty miles down that memorable stream, through his crafty pickets, and thereafter passed for rebel scouts earnestly "looking for Yanks" until we found them, and the glorious old flag once more welcomed us to Union and liberty.

These things the writer expects to tell, by the blessing of God, to the next generation, with his great-grandchildren on his knee.

THE FIELD ELOQUENCE OF NAPOLEON.

BY J. G. W.

The sayings of soldiers have been memorable in all ages. Among the great Captains of the past, none has bequeathed to us such a rich store of striking and effective words—such eloquent orders, brimful of magnetism upon his soldiers, as *Le Petit Caporal*, as the Old Guard loved to call their idolized chief, the young hero of Lodi and Marengo. His eloquence of the field has no example in history. The same instinct of improvisation which prompted so many of his strategetical evolutions, was manifested in his language and sentiments. He gained this knowledge from no teacher, for he never had a mentor, nor did he derive it from experience, for he had not the years. He had it as a gift.

To a general officer not eminently distinguished, who solicited from the Emperor a marshal's baton, he said: "It is not I that make marshals; it is victories."

On hearing the first gun at Friedland, he exclaimed: "Soldiers! it is an auspicious day. It is the anniversary of Marengo."

To a troop of artillery, which had failed in their duty, he said: "This flag that you have basely deserted shall be placed in the Temple of Mars, covered with crape; your corps is disbanded."

He presented Moreau, on one occasion, with a magnificent pair of pistols, as a *cadeau*. "I intended," said he, "to have got the names of your victories engraved upon them, but there was not room for them."

A sentinel who allowed General Joubert to enter Napoleon's tent without giving the pass-word, was brought before him:

"Go," said he, "the man who forced the Tyrol may well force a sentinel."

On catching the first sight of the Mamelukes, drawn up in order of battle, on the banks of the Nile, in view of the Pyramids, Bonaparte, riding before the ranks, cried: "Soldiers! from the summits of yonder Pyramids, forty generations are watching you."

The fourth regiment of the line, on one occasion lost its eagle. "What have you done with your eagle?" asked Napoleon. "A regiment that loses its eagle has lost all. Yes; but I see two standards that you have taken. 'Tis well," concluded he, with a smile, "you shall have another eagle."

On the field of Austerlitz, a young Russian officer, taken prisoner, was brought before him. "Sire," said he, "let me be shot. I have suffered my guns to be taken." "Young man," was the reply, "be consoled! Those who are conquered by my soldiers, may still have titles to glory."

When the Duke of Montebello, to whom he was tenderly attached, received a mortal wound from a cannon-ball, Napoleon, then in the meridian of his imperial glory, rushed to the litter on which the dying hero was stretched, and embracing him, and bedewing his forehead with tears, uttered these untranslatable words: "*Lannes! me reconnais tu? C'est Bonaparte; c'est ton ami!*"

On the morning of the battle of Moscow, the sun rose with uncommon splendor in an unclouded firmament. "Behold!" exclaimed Napoleon to his soldiers, "it is the sun of Austerlitz." It will be remembered that the battle of Austerlitz was commenced at sunrise, and on that occasion, the sun rose with extraordinary splendor.

In the celebrated march from Fréjus to Paris, on his return to France from Elba, one of the regiments at Grenoble hesitated before declaring for him. He, with a remarkable instinct, leaped from his horse, and unbuttoning the breast of his gray surtout, laid bare his breast. "If there be an individual among you," said he, "who would desire to kill his general—his emperor—let him fire."

At Montereau, the guns of a battery near his staff were ineffective, owing to being badly aimed. He dismounted from his horse, and pointed them with his own hands, never having lost the skill he acquired as an artillery officer. The grenadiers of the guard could not conceal their terror at seeing the cannonballs of the enemy falling around their chief. "Have no fears for me," he observed; "the ball destined to kill me has not yet been cast."

To reproduce the highly figurative language used by him in his addresses and general orders, after the fever of universal enthusiasm, in the midst of which it was uttered, has passed away, is hazardous and may seem to border on the ridiculous. But let the reader endeavor to transport himself back to the exciting scenes amid which Napoleon acted and spoke. At six-and-twenty he superseded Scherer in the command of the Army of Italy, surrounded with disasters, oppressed with despair, and entirely destitute of every provision necessary for the well-being of a soldier. He fell upon the enemy with all the confidence of victory which would have been inspired by superior numbers, discipline, and equipment. In a fortnight, the whole aspect of things was changed, and here was his first address to the army:—

"Soldiers!—You have, in fifteen days, gained six victories, taken twenty-one standards, fifty pieces of cannon, several fortresses, made fifteen hundred prisoners, and killed or wounded more than ten thousand men! You have equalled the conquerors of Holland and the Rhine. Destitute of all necessaries, you have supplied all your wants—without cannon you have gained battles—without bridges you have crossed rivers!—without shoes you have made forced marches!—without brandy and often without bread you have bivouacked! Republican phalanxes, soldiers of liberty, alone could have survived what you have suffered! Thanks to you, soldiers!—your grateful country has reason to expect great things of you! You have still battles to fight, towns to take, rivers to pass. Is there one among you whose courage is relaxed? Is there one who would prefer to return to the barren summits of the Apnenines and the Alps, to endure patiently the insults of these soldier slaves? No!—there is none such among the victors of Montenotte, of Millesimo, of Dego, and of Mondoir! My friends, I promise you this glorious conquest; but be the liberators, and not the scourges, of the people you subdue."

Such addresses had an electrical effect on the French army. Napoleon passed from triumph to triumph in Italy, with a facility and rapidity which resembles the shifting views of a phantasmagoria. He entered Milan, and then, to swell and stimulate his legions, he again addressed them:—

"You have descended from the Alps like a cataract. Piedmont is delivered. Milan is your own. Your banners wave over the fertile plains of Lombardy. You have passed the Po-the Tessino, the Adda—those vaunted bulwarks of Italy. Your fathers, your mothers, your sisters, your betrothed, will exult in your triumphs, and will be proud to claim you as their own. Yes, soldiers; you have done much; but much more is still to be accomplished. Will you leave it in the power of posterity to say that in Lombardy you have found a Capua? Let us go on. We have still forced marches to make, enemies to subdue, laurels to gather, and insults to avenge. To re-establish the Capitol, and re-erect the statues of its heroes; to awaken the Roman people sunk under the torpor of age, of bondage: behold what remains to be done! After accomplishing this, you will return to your hearths, and your fellow-citizens, when they behold you pass them, will point at you and say: '*He was a soldier of the Army of Italy!*'"

When Bonaparte sailed from the shores of France, on the celebrated expedition to Egypt, the destination of the fleet was confided to none but himself. Its course was directed first to Malta, which, as it was known, submitted without resistance. When lying off its harbor, he thus addressed the magnificent army which floated around him:—

"Soldiers!—You are a wing of the Army of England. You have made war on mountain and plain, and have made sieges. It is still reserved for you to make a maritime war. The legions of Rome, which you have sometimes imitated, but not yet equalled, warred with Carthage by turns on the sea, and on the plains of Zama. Victory never abandoned them, because they were brave in combat, patient under fatigue, obedient to their commanders, and firm against their foes. But, soldiers, Europe has its eyes upon you; and you have great destinies to fulfil, battle to wage, and fatigues to suffer."

When from the mast-heads of the vessels his troops discovered the town of Alexandria, Napoleon first announced to them the destination of the expedition:—

"Frenchmen!—You are going to attempt conquests, the effect of which upon civilization and the commerce of the world is incalculable. Behold the first city we are about to attack! It was built by Alexander."

Bonaparte was remarkable for breaking through the traditions of military practice. Thus, on the eve of the battle of Austerlitz, he adopted the startling and unusual course of disclosing the plan of the campaign to the private soldiers of his army:—

"The Russians want to turn my right, and they will present me their flank. Soldiers! I will myself direct all your battalions; depend upon me to keep myself far from the fire, so long as, with your accustomed bravery, you bring disorder and confusion into the enemy's ranks; but if victory were for one moment uncertain, you would see me in the foremost ranks, to expose myself to their attack. There will be the honor of the French infantry—the first infantry in the world. This victory will terminate your campaign, and then the peace we shall make will be worthy of France, of you, and of me!"

His speech after the battle is a *chef d'œuvre* of military eloquence. He declares his satisfaction with his soldiers—he walks through their ranks—he reminds them whom they have conquered, what they have done, and what will be said of them; but not one word does he utter concerning their chiefs.

The Emperor and the soldiers—France for a perspective—peace for a reward—and glory for a recollection! what a commencement and what a termination!

"Soldiers! I am satisfied with you; you have covered your eagles with immortal glory. An army of one hundred thousand men, commanded by the Emperors of Russia and Austria, has been, in less than four hours, cut to pieces and dispersed; whoever has escaped your sword has been drowned in the lakes. Forty stands of colors, the standards of the Imperial Guard of Russia—one hundred and twenty pieces of cannon, twenty generals, and more than thirty thousand prisoners, are the results of this day, forever celebrated. That infantry, so much boasted of, and in numbers so superior to you, could not resist your shock, and henceforth you have no longer any rival to fear. Soldiers! when the French people placed the imperial crown upon my head, I intrusted myself to you; I relied upon you to maintain it in the high splendor and glory which alone can give it value in my eyes. Soldiers! I will soon bring you back to France; there you will be the object of my most tender solicitude. It will be sufficient for you to say, '*I was at the battle of Austerlitz,*' in order that your countrymen may answer, '*Voila un brave!*'"

On the anniversary of this battle, Bonaparte used to recapitulate with pleasure the accumulated spoils that fell into the hands of the French, and he used to inflame their ardor against the Prussians by the recollection of those victories. Thus, on the morning of another conflict, he apostrophised his soldiers in the following manner:—

"Soldiers! It is to-day one year, this very hour, that you were on the memorable field of Austerlitz. The Russian battalions fled terrified; their allies were destroyed; their strong places, their capitals, their magazines, their arsenals, two hundred and eighty standards, seven hundred pieces of cannon, five grand fortified places, were in your power. The Oder, the Warta, the desert of Poland, the bad weather—nothing has stopped you; all have fled at your approach. The French eagle soars over the Vistula; the brave and unfortunate Poles imagine that they see again the legions of Sobieski. Soldiers! we will not lay down our arms until a general peace has restored to our commerce its liberties and its colonies. We have, on the Elbe and the Oder, recovered Pondicherry, our Indian establishments, the Cape of Good Hope, and the Spanish colonies. Who shall give to the Russians the hope to resist destiny? These and yourselves. Are we not the soldiers of Austerlitz?"

HOME FROM THE WAR.

BY GEORGE COOPER.

ANNIE'S by the garden gate,
  Looking down the lane,
And the amber clouds of sunset
  Pour their golden rain.

Rings the village bell good-night,
  Hushed are all the bowers;
And the birds will soon be dreaming
  Of the sleeping flowers.

Annie's eyes with love are glowing,—
  Somebody she sees
As she clinks the gate behind her,
  Near the way-side trees.

Two are straying in the twilight!
  Three long years ago,

May, 1865

Some one very dear to Annie,
  Went away, you know;—

Went away to fight for Freedom.
  Has he come again?
There's a soldier-boy with Annie,
  Coming up the lane;

And his arm has gently stolen
  Round her pretty waist;
And she never frowned a moment,
  When it there was placed!

But her cheeks are sweetly blushing,
  While he whispers low:
What he's telling in the shadows,
  Would you like to know?

LAUREA DONANDUS.

"Laurea donandus Apollinari."—HORACE.

BY MRS. LUCY H. HOOPER.

O MOUNTAINS, on whose awful crests
  Unfading laurel grows,
We fain would rob you of your wreaths
  To crown far nobler brows!
From the dark pines of frozen Maine
  To Californian corals,
We summon heart, and hand, and will,
  For wreathing of the laurels.

From Lookout Mountain shall we cull
  The meed of Hooker's fame,
And far Antietam yields a wreath
  For him we must not name;
The Carolinas tribute bring
  Of bays for Sherman's crown,
And all the South must laurels yield
  To mark our Grant's renown.

Alas, the field of Gettysburg!
  The breezes, as they pass,
Learn sadder sighs, the while they wave
  The long funereal grass.

Oh, deathless is the bay that springs
  Where patriot heroes bleed!
And here we seek a wreath to crown
  The honored brow of Meade.

What tribute shall our Martyr claim?
  The honored and the dear,
The flowers that should have strewed his path
  We lay upon his bier.
No earthly bay befits *his* brow,
  So holy and so calm;
He does not need the laurel-wreath
  Who wins the martyr's crown.

As changed the serpent to a rod
  The Prophet's touch beneath,
Our heroes clutch Secession's coils,
  And lo! a laurel-wreath.
O come, bright day! whose golden dawn
  The future now discloses,
When Peace, amid those deathless wreaths,
  Shall twine her snowy roses.

LITERARY INTELLIGENCE

AND

NOTES ON NEW BOOKS.

WHAT we have long desired has at length happened. From Messrs. John Wiley & Son, of New York, we have received a new edition of Mahan's "Field Fortification," being now—Part I. of "An Elementary Course of Military Engineering." Instead of the small and contracted form of the old work, it is in octavo, with generous print; instead of plates of figures, which opened out into uncomfortable scrolls, uncomfortable to handle, inconvenient of reference, and soon torn, we have each figure on the page with the letter-press, and immediately illustrating it. Besides, there is very much that is new: the Introductory Chapter; the entire subject of military mining, with illustrations taken from recent wars; siege operations, the formation of parallels, saps, &c., posting of artillery, attacks, with special notices of the sieges in the present war—Vicksburg, Charleston, &c. The book is altogether the best treatise on its subject which we know; lucid, accurate, full, and yet concise, we recommend it to every institution which has introduced the military element, as *the* book, if they use no other whatever, by which the most can be learned about the art of war. Field fortification is in itself an epitome of the military art. Its points and lines are chosen by strategy; engineers build it of dimensions determined by the range of fire-arms; artillery and infantry defend and assault it; cavalry is always a complementary force in the intervals; and thus a student, who learns the contents of this book, has the most varied knowledge, as well as the best basis for future study.

To the new publisher, D. Van Nostrand, we are indebted for the seventh volume of the "Rebellion Record," and also for Parts 46 and 47, which commence Volume VIII. We cannot too highly commend this noble work to our readers. The *Documents* are invaluable; the "Rumors, Anecdotes, Poetry, and Incidents," are scarcely less so: the work forms, from its beginning to the very last number, a storehouse in which are collected all the important materials from which the future historian may edit a philosophic history of the war. The portraits (two in each number) are exact likenesses, from excellent photographs, and are engraved in the most beautiful manner. We are particularly struck with those of Generals Sickles and Foster, in Part 46. No family, the children of which have been growing up during this war, should fail to secure this work, in order to aid their retrospect, in the time to come, of the greatest national crisis known to history. Each part is royal 8vo, of about 120 pages, and the price is 60 cents.

The comparative geography of Carl Ritter, the famous professor in the University of Berlin, has been translated by W. L. Gage, and published by Lippincott & Co., of Philadelphia, in a 12mo, of 220 pages. Of course, the original work is admirable: it treats of the form, atmosphere, and surface; the hills, mountains, and plains; seas, lakes, and rivers, which form the anatomical structure of the great crust, and a comparative consideration of the Old World and the New. The Introduction is long and learned, and perhaps detracts somewhat from the practical usefulness of the book, which is otherwise admirably designed for students in colleges and schools.

"OUR GREAT CAPTAINS" is the title of a volume just issued by Mr. C. B. Richardson, military publisher, of New York. It contains biographies of Grant, Sherman, Thomas, Sheridan, and Farragut. The work is well done, sparkling, and accurate. The portraits are excellent, and it has the great advantage of being brought down to the very close of hostilities, thus including the surrender of the armies of Lee and Johnston. Although our space is small, we cannot help quoting, with pleasure, the following from the biography of General Sherman, illustrating as it does the malice of false reporters, and the beautiful reciprocal estimate of Grant and Sherman:—"It is related that a distinguished civilian began to speak to Sherman of Grant in terms of depreciation. 'It won't do—it won't do, Mr. ———,' said Sherman, in his quick, nervous way, 'General Grant is a great general; I know him well: he stood by me when I was *crazy*, and I stood by him when he was *drunk*; and now, sir, we stand by each other always.'" *Si non e vero e ben trovato*; —no comment is needed. 12mo, 250 pp. $1.75.

It is with real pleasure that we notice the seventh and concluding volume of that most sterling work and splendid specimen of American book-making, "Merivale's History of the Romans under the Empire." It is reprinted from the fourth London edition, and has a copious analytical index. This volume begins with Vespasian and Titus, taking up their history after the fall of Jerusalem; it relates the cruelties and follies of Domitian, and the wise efforts of the "good emperors" to buttress the already tottering empire; incidentally are told the sad and sudden fate of Herculaneum and Pompeii, and the demolition of the "golden house" of Nero; and there is a valuable account of the condition and progress of the Christian Church. The work richly deserves at our hands an extended review, rather than this brief notice, but we can only find space in which to congratulate Mr. Merivale upon his great achievement, and the Appletons upon the noble form in which they have presented it to American readers. 8vo, 596 pp.

From Messrs. Ticknor & Fields we have received two exquisite little blue and gold volumes, in the finest style of typography and book-making—one containing the poems, and the other the essays, of Ralph Waldo Emerson. Being ourselves very matter-of-fact men, in an extremely busy age, and having study enough to do in positive science and practical art, we are not capable of appreciating these dreamy—with occasional starts—visions of Platonic philosophy. To translate from Greek or German is *one* trouble, but we do it cheerfully; to translate from Emersonese into English goes against the grain. Mr. Emerson has, we are sure, great merits, quite in spite of our want of appreciation, and his admirers will find them done up in lavender in the beautiful little volumes to which we refer.

We come at length to a very refreshing book—"The Hand-Book of Dining; or, Corpulency and Leanness Scientifically Considered; translated and adapted from the French of Brillot Savarin, by L. F. Simpson." It is neither a cook-book nor a system of table etiquette; but it aims, by precept and example, to show that good dinners, adapted to the peculiar nature of the diner, have a great influence upon health, morals, society, and even revolutions. The views seem just, and the stories are pleasant. Appletons. 12mo, 200 pp.

EDITOR'S SPECIAL DEPARTMENT.

The hopes with which we opened our editorial of last month were not simply wishes "father to the thought." The murder of President Lincoln has not paralyzed the Great Republic. Still and forever mourning the sad event, the country has yet risen from the blow; the new President, ANDREW JOHNSON, commends himself, by every act and word, as a worthy successor, who will deal right manfully with the chief traitors, even now that the treason is dead; the finances are in the best possible condition, and—to use the President's words—"Armed resistance to the authority of this Government, in certain States heretofore declared to be in insurrection, may be regarded as virtually at an end." The armies of Joe Johnston and Dick Taylor have surrendered. Jefferson Davis is a captive, accused of complicity in the great murder, as well as of high treason. The Great PAN of the Southern Rebellion is dead, dead, dead!

With less scope and less warrant for current, stirring intelligence, the province of our magazine becomes still more important and dignified, as, in closing our Fourth Volume with this number, we proceed to gather up, in the coming issues, the details of the great campaigns, jealous in our historical labors that even of the fragments nothing be lost. Indeed, the value and importance of our magazine are greatly enhanced by the peace opening to us the new material from the pens of distinguished eye-witnesses, who have hitherto been, from prudence and necessity, silent.

Sherman having brought the army of Johnston to a final stand, and having proposed a basis of agreement, elsewhere referred to, which was not approved by the Government, afterwards received the surrender upon the terms dictated by General Grant, which were the same as those offered to Lee. Right generous were those terms, for we are informed that Johnston's army was greatly demoralized, without supplies, and ready upon many pleas to dissolve. The force which should have surrendered was more than thirty thousand, but pending the making out of papers, &c., ten thousand dissolved themselves, making the actual surrender of not more than twenty thousand, composing the remnants of Hardee's, Stewart's, and Lee's corps, and a portion of Hampton's cavalry. The rest of the cavalry, handsomely paid by Jeff. Davis, out of the abstracted gold, went to escort him *in partibus*—towards Texas most probably, whither he had prepared himself a *nidus*, by sending word to Kirby Smith by no means to surrender: *Homme propose!* It is said that the first terms proposed by Sherman were the cause of his capture, for, hoping by them to be a partaker in the amnesty, he lingered too long, and the delay was fatal.

Dick Taylor surrendered to Canby, and the special surrenders were made by detached commands all through the South; General Sam Jones being paroled in Florida by General Vogdes, and Jeff. Thompson surrendering to Captain Mitchell, of the navy.

Only Kirby Smith remains in the field. General Grant sent an officer down to demand his surrender. Whether he will adhere to the spirit of his recent proclamation and still show fight, remains to be seen. He is in a far better position to do so than any of the others were; but if he does, he will be outlawed, and the result is by no means doubtful. Sheridan has gone down to see.

JEFFERSON DAVIS.—The doctrine of punishing ringleaders is as old as history, and if ever it needed the perfection of an illustration we have it now. It will not do to say, he is no worse than others. He is the very head and front of the offending; the most prominent man before the war; a chief among the instigators, and a manifold traitor: a traitor to the memories of West Point and Mexico; a traitor to the Federal Senate-chamber; a traitor to the Federal cabinet; a man upon whom his country had bestowed rank and station, and who turned his arms and his influence against her. We need not go to his family antecedents: we need but take him for himself, to hold him up to the condemnation which he now receives both at the North and at the South. Nor is this all: before his capture, and with remarkable dramatic connection, the President of the United States, declaring that the murder of Mr. Lincoln was incited, concerted, and procured by and between Jefferson Davis and other fugitives from justice, had set a price upon his head, of one hundred thousand dollars. What a horrible antithesis! not long since, he was a dictator out-Heroding Herod; standing out against the world; now none so *base* to do him reverence.

We shall not anticipate the evidence upon which the President's proclamation was based; but merely say, that no cabinet would issue such without strong grounds for commitment to trial. But this is not yet all. The high tragedy was to end in a most ridiculous farce; the great actor, who had played the part of "the king" in a manner to satisfy the critical Partridge in Tom Jones (among whose kingly crimes, by-the-by, was the murder of a brother-king), was fain at last to conceal himself in the petticoats of his wife, and fly to the woods, in the most ridiculous of disguises. If the Confederacy still retained a particle of the esteem of foreign nations, this ludicrous ending must extinguish it forever. It has made thoroughly contemptible that which before was simply execrable and detestable.

We place on record what is now old news to the country—the capture and death of J. Wilkes Booth, the assassin of the President. The vengeance was executed speedily. Colonel L. C. Baker, efficiently aided by Colonel Conger, tracked him in his flight to a barn in Accomac County. The barn was fired, and Booth, thus brought to bay, was shot by Sergeant Boston Corbett, through the head—far too noble a death for one who deserved the extreme of ignominy in the mode of his punishment. The investigation has brought to light a wide-spread conspiracy. Besides Jefferson Davis and the fugitives in Canada, the following persons are now being tried by the military court, of which General Hunter is president—Arnold, Dr. Mudd, Spangler, O'Laughlin, Atzerott, Payne, Harold, and, we regret for the sake of humanity to add, a woman, Mrs. Surratt. But no! If she is declared guilty, she has unsexed herself. She is not a woman.

THE RETURN OF THE HERACLIDÆ.—Reminding us of the march of the Dorians to Peloponnesus, under the conduct of the descendants of Hercules, the great corps of heroic men who have achieved the liberty, vindicated the power, and assured the perpetuity of the Republic, have set out on their triumphant march homeward. Schofield is left for a time in North Carolina; Wright, with the Sixth Corps, remains temporarily at Danville; Sheridan marched through Richmond with his invincible troopers, and is now at Washington; Humphreys with the Second, and Griffin with the Fifth, passed in grand procession up and down the streets of

Richmond, and then moved northward, to the final rendezvous at the Capital. It is said that when our brave fellows first caught sight of the dome of the Capitol at Washington, they broke out into spontaneous cheers, and could not control their emotion.

Howard was at Richmond on the 8th, with the Fifteenth and Seventeenth Corps, constituting the left wing of Sherman's army, which he has so ably commanded, and at the last accounts was moving upon Alexandria.

Gibbons's Twenty-fourth Corps was to remain for the present at Richmond. Weitzel with the Twenty-fifth was to form a camp of instruction at City Point. How far the Army will be disbanded is not yet stated, but we are sure that in the present unsettled state of things, a large force will be kept in the field. Camps of instruction will be formed, thorough system introduced, and strict discipline established and enforced.

Before this number appears, the great reviews, ordered by General Grant, will have taken place at Washington: that of the Army of the Potomac and Sheridan's cavalry, on Tuesday, May 23d, and that of Sherman's army on Wednesday—all passing in review before the President and General Grant, at the White House.

A glorious sight this, to those who are able to see it—the march of two hundred thousand men—not holiday soldiers in "purple and fine linen," but war-worn veterans of a hundred fights, who have redeemed their pledge, and saved their country; now, if never before, "the finest army on the planet," since the planet began its revolutions!

The next step in our progress will be that of reconstruction, which will be accomplished, we think, by the coming in of State after State, upon the terms dictated by the Government. Indeed, this is already begun. Virginia is being reconstructed under Governor Pierpont, and a convention to the same end will be called at once in North Carolina. Others will soon follow.

The pirate *Stonewall*, now indeed a *pirate*, without controversy, if she continue her cruise, left Teneriffe on the 1st of April; was at Bermuda on the 26th; tried to pass the bar at Nassau, and failed; and was reported at Havana on the 11th of May. It is to be hoped our vessels will treat her as the poet did the "last rose of summer," which she closely resembles.

FOREIGN AND INTERNATIONAL.

The news of Mr. Lincoln's death has been received with emotions of profound sorrow and expressions of detestation at the anomalous crime. From France, from Italy, and all the Continental countries, we have messages of sympathy and condolence; but we confess to a particular pleasure in the outspoken and hearty sympathy of the English people, from the Queen on her throne to the humblest subject, who has learned by hearsay what he is not able to read. In Parliament, the Lords speak through Palmerston and Derby, while the refined rhetoric of D'Israeli gives utterance to the feelings of the Commons.

Our loss is but another illustration of that "one touch of nature" which "makes the whole world kin."

The Mexican question is assuming very serious proportions. Maximilian is very unpopular, both at home and abroad. The patriots are gathering thickly around his French skirts, and a cloud is arising in the North, incident to the collapse of our rebellion, which may well give him great concern. When the question is asked, "What is to be done with our disbanded men?" our answer is—

"Mexico!" But to this we shall refer at length hereafter, only hinting now that, as we have never recognised the government of Maximilian, we shall hardly feel obliged to hinder our discharged soldiers from going quietly, even in considerable bodies, to join the Liberals in putting down the Imperialists and destroying the Empire.

PERSONAL ITEMS.

Major-General G. K. Warren has been appointed to the command of the Department of the Mississippi, relieving Major-General N. J. T. Dana.

Brigadier-General E. A. Carr has been brevetted Major-General for distinguished services.

We are glad to learn that Captain James F. Rusling, Assistant Quartermaster, has been promoted to the rank of Colonel and Inspector of the Quartermaster's Department. Colonel Rusling entered the service in August, 1861, as Regimental Quartermaster of the 5th New Jersey Volunteers. He was subsequently appointed Captain and Assistant Quartermaster, and served as Brigade Quartermaster during the Peninsular Campaign. He was then assigned, as Division Quartermaster, to the Second Division, Third Corps, Hooker's old Division. He afterwards served as Corps Quartermaster, with the rank of lieutenant-colonel, with the Third Corps. Afterwards he was assigned to duty at Head-Quarters of the Army of the Potomac, as Inspector of Transportation of the Army. Later he was transferred from the Army of the Potomac and assigned to duty in this city, in the office of General Donaldson, Chief Quartermaster. Colonel Rusling is one of the most talented young officers in the Army. Notwithstanding the heavy drafts upon his time by the pressing duties incident to the great campaigns of Sherman and Thomas, he has contributed a valuable paper to the UNITED STATES SERVICE MAGAZINE, on the Quartermaster's Department of the Army, which will take its place in history, and be referred to for the many important facts it contains. No one can read it without realizing how much the nation owes to the ability and energy with which the Quartermaster's Department has been conducted.—*Nashville Union.*

Colonel Stewart L. Woodford, Chief of Staff to Major-General Gillmore, has been brevetted Brigadier-General.

Colonel N. B. Sweitzer, 16th New York Cavalry, has been brevetted Brigadier-General.

Colonel J. L. Thompson, 1st New Hampshire Cavalry, has been brevetted Brigadier-General.

Colonel R. D. Mussey, 100th United States Colored Troops, has been brevetted Brigadier-General.

Brevet Major-General Merritt, of the cavalry, has been appointed to a full Major-Generalship, to date from the 9th of April.

Colonel Lewis E. Parsons, Assistant Quartermaster at St. Louis, has been promoted to the rank of Brigadier-General, in charge of the Bureau of Transportation at Washington.

OFFICIAL INTELLIGENCE.

The Army.

The Old Flag of Fort Sumter.

[General Orders, No. 50.]

WAR DEPARTMENT,
ADJUTANT-GENERAL'S OFFICE,
WASHINGTON, March 27, 1865.

Ordered,

I. That, at the hour of noon, on the 14th day of April, 1865, Brevet Major-General Anderson will raise and plant upon the ruins of Fort Sumter, in Charleston harbor, the same United States flag which floated over the battlements of that fort during the rebel assault, and which was lowered and saluted by him and the small force of his command when the works were evacuated on the 14th day of April, 1861.

II. That the flag, when raised, be saluted by one hundred guns from Fort Sumter, and by a national salute from every fort and rebel battery that fired upon Fort Sumter.

III. That suitable ceremonies be had upon the occasion, under the direction of Major-General William T. Sherman, whose military operations compelled the rebels to evacuate Charleston, or, in his absence, under the charge of Major-General Q. A. Gillmore, commanding the Department. Among the ceremonies will be the delivery of a public address by the Rev. Henry Ward Beecher.

IV. That the naval forces at Charleston, and their commander on that station, be invited to participate in the ceremonies of the occasion.

By order of the President of the United States:

EDWIN M. STANTON,
Secretary of War.

Opinion

UPON QUESTIONS GROWING OUT OF THE CAPITULATION BETWEEN GENERAL GRANT AND GENERAL LEE.

ATTORNEY-GENERAL'S OFFICE,
April 22, 1865.

SIR—I have the honor to acknowledge the receipt of your letter of the 22d of April. In it you ask me three questions, growing out of the capitulation made betwixt General Grant, of the United States Army, and General Lee, of the rebel army. You ask—

First.—Whether rebel officers who once resided in the city of Washington, and went to Virginia, or elsewhere in the South, and took service, can return to the city under stipulations of the capitulation, and reside here as their homes?

Second.—Whether persons who resided in Washington about the time the rebellion broke out, left the city and went to Richmond, where they have adhered to the rebel cause, entered into the civil service, or otherwise given it their support, comfort, and aid, can return to Washington, since the capitulation of General Lee's army, and the capture of Richmond, and reside here under the terms of the capitulation?

Third.—You state that since the capitulation of General Lee's army, rebel officers have appeared in public in the loyal States, wearing the rebel uniform; and you ask whether such conduct is not a fresh act of hostility, on their part, to the United States, subjecting them to be dealt with as avowed enemies of the Government?

Your letter is accompanied with a copy of the terms of capitulation entered into betwixt Generals Grant and Lee. It is as follows:—

"Rolls of all the officers and men to be made in duplicate; one copy to be given to an officer designated by me, the other to be retained by such officer or officers as you may designate. The officers to give their individual paroles not to take arms against the Government of the United States until properly exchanged, and each company or regimental commander to sign a like parole for the men of their commands. The arms, artillery, and public property, to be parked and stacked, and turned over to the officers appointed by me [General Grant] to receive them. This will not embrace the side-arms of the officers, nor their private horses or baggage. This done, each officer and man will be allowed to return to their homes, not to be disturbed by United States authority so long as they observe their parole and the laws in force where they may reside."

I. In giving construction to these articles of capitulation, we must consider in what capacity General Grant was speaking. He, of course, spoke by the authority of the President of the United States, as Commander-in-Chief of the Armies of the United States. It must be presumed that he had no authority from the President, except such as the Commander-in-Chief could give to a military officer.

The President performs two functions of the Government—one civil, the other military. As President of the United States and its civil head, he possesses the pardoning power. As President of the United States, he is Commander-in-Chief of the Armies of the United States, and is the head of its belligerent power. His power to pardon as a civil magistrate cannot be delegated; it is a personal trust, inseparably connected with the office of President. As Commander-in-Chief of the Armies of the United States, he has, of necessity, to delegate a vast amount of power. Regarding General Grant, then, purely as a military officer, and that he was speaking as one possessing no power except belligerent, and considering that fact to be well known to the belligerents with whom he was making the stipulation, let us come to the consideration of the first question which you have propounded.

It must be observed that the question is not as to the extent of the power that the President, as Commander-in-Chief of the Armies, possesses; it is not whether he, as Commander-in-Chief of the Armies of the United States, could grant parole by virtue of his military authority to rebels to go to and reside in loyal communities, communities that had not been in rebellion against the Government of the United States; but the question is, whether by and under the terms of the stipulations, he *has* granted such permissions.

In the cases in 2 Black., commonly called the Prize Cases, the Supreme Court of the United States decided that the rebels were belligerents; that this was no loose, unorganized insurrection, without defined boundary, but that it had a boundary marked by lines of bayonets, which can only be crossed by force; that south of that line is enemy's territory, because claimed and held by an organized hostile and belligerent power; that all persons residing within that territory must be treated as enemies, though not foreigners; and it is well settled that all persons going there without license, pending the hostilities, or remaining there after hostilities commenced, must be regarded and treated as residents of that territory. It follows, as a matter of course, that residents of the territory in rebellion cannot be regarded as having homes in the loyal States. A man's home and his residence cannot be distinct the one from the other. The rebels were dealt with by General Grant as belligerents. As belligerents, their homes were of necessity in the territory belligerent to the Government of the United States. The officers and soldiers of General Lee's army, then, who had homes, prior to the rebellion, in the Northern States, took up their residences within the rebel States, and abandoned their homes in the loyal States; and when General Grant gave permission to them, by the stipulation, to return to their homes, it cannot be understood as a permission to return to any part of the loyal States.

That was a capitulation of surrender, and not a truce. Vattel lays it down that (p. 411) "during the truce, especially if made for a long period, it is naturally allowable for enemies to pass and repass to and from each other's country, in the same manner as it is allowed in time of peace, since all hostilities are now suspended. But each of the sovereigns is at liberty, as he would be in time of peace, to adopt every precaution which may be necessary to prevent this intercourse from becoming prejudicial to him. He has just grounds of suspicion against people with whom he is soon to recommence hostilities. He may even declare, at the time of making the truce, that he will admit none of the enemy into any place under his jurisdiction.

"Those who, having entered the enemy's territories during the truce, are detained there by sickness, or any other unsurmountable obstacle, and thus happen to remain in the country after the expiration of the armistice, may, in strict justice, be kept prisoners; it is an accident which they might have foreseen, and to which they have, of their own accord, exposed themselves; but humanity and generosity commonly require that they should be allowed a sufficient term for their departure.

"If the articles of truce contain any conditions either more extensive or more narrowly restrictive than what we have here laid down, the transaction becomes a particular convention. It is obligatory on the contracting parties, who are bound to observe what they have promised in due form; and the obligations thence resulting constitute a conventional right."

Now, if the rights of enemies, during a long truce and suspension of hostilities are thus restricted, it would seem evident that their rights under a capitulation of surrender, without any suspension of hostilities, could not, without express words in the stipulation to that effect, be any thing like as large as under a truce and suspension of hostilities.

Regarding General Grant, then, as speaking simply as a soldier, and with the powers of a soldier; regarding this war as a territorial war, and all persons within that territory as residents thereof, and, as such, enemies of the Government; and looking to the language of the stipulation, I am of opinion that the rebel officers who surrendered to General Grant have no homes within the loyal States, and have no right to come to places which were their homes prior to their going into the rebellion.

II. As to your second question. The stipulation of surrender made betwixt Generals Grant and Lee does not embrace any persons other than the officers and soldiers of General Lee's army. Persons in the civil service of the rebellion, or who had otherwise given it support, comfort, and aid, and were residents of the rebel territory, certainly have no right to return to Washington under that stipulation.

III. As to the third question. My answer to the first is a complete answer to this.

Rebel officers certainly have no right to be wearing their uniforms in any of the loyal States. It seems to me that such officers, having done wrong in coming into the loyal States, are but adding insult to injury in wearing their uniforms. They have as much right to bear the traitors' flag through the streets of a loyal city as to wear a traitor's garb. The stipulation of surrender permits no such thing, and the wearing of such uniform is an act of hostility against the Government.

Very respectfully, your obedient servant,

JAMES SPEED,
Attorney-General.

Reduction of Expenses.

[General Orders, No. 24].

QUARTERMASTER-GENERAL'S OFFICE,
WASHINGTON, D. C., April 29, 1865.

I. In carrying out the provisions of General Orders No. 77, from the War Department, Adjutant-General's Office, dated 28th April, 1865, so far as relates to the Quartermaster's Department, all chartered steamers, both ocean and river, which, under the new military situation, can be spared, will be discharged immediately.

II. Ocean steamers, at distant ports, will be loaded with the supplies which are no longer needed at such ports, and returned either to the dépôts of New York or of Washington.

III. Troops under orders to return North will be transported in the returning steamers, or in the steamers which are the property of the Department.

IV. The chiefs of divisions of this office, and the chiefs of the principal dépôts, will immediately report to the Quartermaster-General the extent of the reduction which they are able to make in the force of laborers, operatives, clerks, and agents, under their command.

V. It is understood that troops will be made available for most of the work at the dépôts, and that thus very large reductions in the rolls of employés will be possible.

VI. All railroad construction and repairs, except those needed on lines by which troops are still supplied, or by which troops may be marching, will cease.

VII. Construction and extension of all barracks, hospitals, and other buildings, will cease, unless authorized upon special report, which in all cases of necessity should be made immediately by telegraph.

VIII. Property returns of all property on hand on the 30th April should be made up immediately, and forwarded to this office, with recommendations as to the dispositions to be made thereof, whether to be stored or to be sold, and where to be stored or sold, in each case.

IX. The efforts of all officers of this Department will be directed to the greatest possible reduction of expenditure consistent with the efficiency and comfort of the troops now about to be withdrawn from active operations in the field.

X. Attention of all officers of the Quartermaster's Department is specially called to paragraphs II. and IX. of General Orders No. 77, which are herewith republished, as follows:—

"II. That the Quartermaster-General discharge all ocean transports not required to bring home troops in remote departments. All river and inland transportation, except that required for necessary supplies to troops in the field. Purchases of horses, mules, wagons, and other land transportation, will be stopped; also purchases of forage, except what is required for immediate consumption. All purchases for railroad construction and transportation will also be stopped."

"IX. The chiefs of the respective bureaus will immediately cause property returns to be made out of the public property in their charge, and a statement of the property in each that may be sold upon advertisement and public sale without prejudice to the service."

M. C. MEIGS,
Quartermaster-General, Brevet Major-General.

Dismissals,

For the Week ending April 1, 1865.

Lieutenant-Colonel George K. Bowen, 188th Pennsylvania Volunteers, to date March 27, 1865, for intoxication, gross ignorance of his duties, and allowing a total want of discipline to exist in his regiment.

Captain J. F. Stevens, 146th Illinois Volunteers, to date March 25, 1865, for inefficiency and worthlessness as an officer, as shown by the utter lack of discipline in his company, and the lawless and disorderly conduct of members thereof while on duty at Springfield, Illinois.

Captain Richard R. Corson, Assistant Quartermaster United States Volunteers, to date March 27, 1865.

Captain William D. Earnest, Assistant Quartermaster United States Volunteers, to date March 25, 1865, in accordance with act of June 25, 1864.

First Lieutenant Abram W. Bickley, 6th United States Infantry, to date March 28, 1865, with loss of all pay and allowances.

For the Week ending April 8, 1865.

Captain Orville A. Baughn, 46th United States Colored Infantry, to date November 24, 1864, for desertion.

Captain Albert S. Cloke, 3d New Jersey Cavalry, to date March 31, 1865, for gross neglect of duty, drunkenness, and inefficiency.

First Lieutenant James I. J. Kierstead, 66th New York Volunteers, to date February 9, 1864, for desertion; having been published officially, and failed to make satisfactory defence before the commission.

The following officers, to date March 14, 1865, for the causes mentioned, having been published officially, and failed to appear before the Commission:—

Neglect of duty in allowing a large number of recruits under his charge to desert, while en route to regiments.

First Lieutenant M. J. Petry, 173d New York Volunteers.

Absence without leave.

Assistant Surgeon Nehemiah Osborne, 78th United States Colored Troops.

First Lieutenant Albert Reynolds, 125th New York Volunteers.
First Lieutenant Asa S. Mason, 40th New York Volunteers.
Captain Hezekiah Cullen, 4th Delaware Volunteers.
First Lieutenant Daniel Deno, 81st Pennsylvania Volunteers.

Second Lieutenant Morris H. McNully, 1st United States Colored Artillery (heavy), to date March 31, 1865, for having tendered his resignation while under charges—to wit, disobedience of orders, and using disrespectful language to his superior officer.

For the Week ending April 15, 1865.

Colonel George H. Hanks, 99th United States Colored Troops, to date April 7 1865, having fraudulently and in violation of the trust reposed in him accepted money by way of gratification, and in consideration of the services of certain negro laborers under his charge.

The following officers, to date March 20, 1865, for the causes mentioned, having been published officially, and failed to appear before the Commission:—

Absence without leave.

Assistant Surgeon M. Phillips, 22d United States Colored Troops.
Second Lieutenant William P. Brooks, 29th Connecticut Volunteers.
Captain J. C. Tytle, 115th United States Colored Troops.
Captain Andrew P. Gallagher, 4th Indiana Cavalry.

The following officers of the 40th Iowa Volunteers, to date April 12, 1865, for endeavoring, by intimidation, to cause the resignation of a field officer of their regiment, with a view of securing promotion thereby:—

Captain O. J. Amos.
Captain William M. Blair.
Captain D. C. Jordan.

Captain Sidney W. Lea, 5th Indiana Cavalry, to date April 13, 1865, for absence without leave.

For the Week ending April 22, 1865.

The following officers, to date April 18, 1865, for evading duty and absence without leave:—
Colonel Charles D. Murray, 89th Indiana Volunteers.
Captain F. W. Doran, 35th Iowa Volunteers.
First Lieutenant W. C. Kennedy, 35th Iowa Volunteers.

The following officers, to date March 27, 1865, for the causes mentioned, having been published officially, and failed to appear before the Commission:—

Absence without leave.

Surgeon E. Hutchinson, 137th New York Volunteers.
Second Lieutenant J. L. Styron, 2d North Carolina Volunteers.
Assistant Surgeon Frank White, 31st United States Colored Troops.
First Lieutenant Emmett Stafford, 9th New York Artillery.
First Lieutenant Duncan D. Cameron, 9th United States Colored Troops.
Second Lieutenant James A. Bowles, 9th New York Artillery.

Second Lieutenant John Malloy, 111th United States Colored Infantry, to date April 17, 1865, having tendered his resignation while under charges embracing "drunkenness" and "disorderly conduct," the truth of the former of which he acknowledges.

For the Week ending April 29, 1865.

Surgeon George J. Potts, 23d United States Colored Troops, to date April 21, 1865, for unjustifiably mutilating the body of a deceased soldier in the presence of enlisted men of that command.

Captain A. S. Jackson, 188th Pennsylvania Volunteers, to date April 21, 1865, for having tendered his resignation based upon false statements, and for frequent intoxication.

Captain George May, Commissary of Subsistence, United States Volunteers, to date April 21, 1865.

Captain Abraham O. Wancop, 118th Ohio Volunteers, to date April 24, 1865, for absence without leave.

The following officers, to date April 26, 1865, for absence without leave:—
Captain Charles Hattenhof, 47th Ohio Volunteers.
First Lieutenant Samuel W. Durant, 127th Illinois Volunteers.
Captain William Simpson, First Veteran Army Corps, United States Volunteers, to date April 27, 1865, having fraudulently procured the enlistment in that corps of a man not eligible for enlistment in said corps, knowing such enlistment to be fraudulent.
Captain George W. Claypool, 68th Indiana Volunteers, to date April 27, 1865, for conduct unbecoming an officer and a gentleman in official correspondence with an officer of the United States Treasury.
The following officers to date April 3, 1865, for absence without leave, having been published officially and failed to make satisfactory defence before the Commission:—
First Lieutenant Oscar Rahn, 184th Pennsylvania Volunteers.
Captain John H. Busby, 108th Ohio Volunteers.
The following officers, as of the date and for the causes mentioned, having been published officially and failed to appear before the Commission:—

Desertion.

Second Lieutenant George H. G. Morton, 48th New York Volunteers, to date January 17, 1865.

Disobedience of orders, and absence without leave.

Captain A. G. P. Brown, 24th New York Cavalry, to date April 22, 1865.

Absence without leave.

Captain A. T. Clark, 21st Pennsylvania Cavalry, to date April 22, 1865.
Second Lieutenant Edward Chappell, 5th New Jersey Battery, to date April 22, 1865.
Assistant Surgeon C. D. Case, 180th Ohio Volunteers, to date April 22, 1865.
Second Lieutenant J. C. Appleby, 19th United States Colored Troops, to date March 14, 1865, for absence without leave, having been published officially and failed to make satisfactory defence before the Commission.
Second Lieutenant John H. Brown, 27th United States Colored Troops, to date April 25, 1865, having tendered his resignation, assigning frivolous and improper reasons therefor.
Second Lieutenant John D. Nutting, 7th New York Heavy Artillery, to date February 14, 1865, having tendered his resignation upon false representations.
Second Lieutenant Thomas Saul, 25th Massachusetts Volunteers, to date April 27, 1865, for disobedience of orders and absence without leave.

The order heretofore issued honorably discharging Major I. B. Atherton, 22d Iowa Volunteers, has been so amended as to dishonorably dismiss him as of the date of the order of discharge, which was based on a false statement made to his Commanding General, with the view of avoiding the just consequences of cowardly conduct in the face of the enemy.

Dropped from the Rolls of his Regiment.

Captain W. L. Evans, 91st New York Volunteers, to date October 1, 1864.
Lieutenant J. H. Popp, 18th Indiana Volunteers, to date October 13, 1864, for absence without leave.

Dropped from the Rolls of the Army.

First Lieutenant E. E. Hermans, 4th United States Colored Artillery (heavy), to date December 7, 1864, for absenting himself from his command without authority, since that date.

Dishonorably Mustered Out.

Captain F. Turnt, 103d New York Volunteers, as of date his company was so, mustered, for neglect of duty and violation of the Regulations of this Department.

Exempt from Dismissal.

WAR DEPARTMENT,
ADJUTANT-GENERAL'S OFFICE,
WASHINGTON, April 3, 1865.

Captain James Coey, 147th New York Volunteers, charged with offences, and heretofore published, is exempt from being dismissed the service of the United States, the Military Commission instituted by Special Orders, No. 53, series of 1863, from the War Department, having reported that satisfactory defence has been made in his case.

April 18, 1865.

Lieutenant-Colonel James Brady, 1st Pennsylvania Light Artillery, charged with offences, and heretofore published, is exempt from being dismissed the service of the United States; the Military Commission instituted by Special Orders, No. 53, series of 1863, from the War Department, having reported that satisfactory defence has been made in his case.

April 24, 1865.

Captain Hancock T. McLean, 6th United States Cavalry, heretofore published for absence without leave, and conduct prejudicial to good order and military discipline, is exempt from dismissal from the service of the United States, he having appeared before the Military Commission of which Brigadier-General Caldwell, United States Volunteers, is President, and made satisfactory defence to the charges against him.

Dismissal Amended.

The order heretofore issued, dismissing Lieutenant Richard B. Crawford, 13th Ohio Volunteers, has been amended so as to omit the words "with loss of all pay and allowances."

The order heretofore issued dismissing Captain James Connor, 124th Indiana Volunteers, for desertion, to date October 4, 1864, has been amended so as to dismiss him for absence without leave, to date December 22, 1864.

Dismissals Revoked.

The orders of dismissal heretofore issued in the following cases have been revoked:—

Major Norman M. Finley, 19th Pennsylvania Cavalry, and he has been honorably discharged, as of the date of the order of dismissal.

First Lieutenant Charles S. Hazen, 3d New Hampshire Volunteers, he having been previously discharged.

The order heretofore issued dismissing First Lieutenant Alexander Anderson, 14th New York Cavalry, has been revoked, and he has been honorably discharged, as of the date of the order of dismissal.

The order of dismissal heretofore issued in the case of First Lieutenant Christopher T. Bybee, 6th Kentucky Cavalry, has been revoked, and he has been honorably discharged, to date April 8, 1865.

Restored to Commission.

The following-named officers, heretofore dismissed, have been restored with pay from the date at which they rejoin their regiments for duty, provided the vacancies have not been filled by the Governors of their respective States:—

First Lieutenant William J. Anderson, Battery F, 1st New York Light Artillery.
Second Lieutenant John W. Jacobs, Jr., Company C, 1st Virginia Light Artillery.
First Lieutenant L. B. Richards, Company I, 1st Pennsylvania Light Artillery.
Second Lieutenant S. S. Allen, Battery D, 1st Maryland Light Artillery.
First Lieutenant J. Moore Wirtz, 3d Michigan Cavalry.
Captain Samuel Moore, 99th Indiana Volunteers.
Captain Timothy Pearson, 15th Massachusetts Battery.

The order of dismissal heretofore issued in the case of Additional Paymaster

Benjamin L. Martin, United States Volunteers, is revoked, and he has been restored to his former position and rank in the service.

Captain A. Hyde, 16th Kansas Cavalry.

Captain Frederick S. Gimber, 109th Pennsylvania Volunteers (now consolidated with the 111th Pennsylvania Volunteers).

The order heretofore issued, dismissing Captain W. B. Dugger, 122d Illinois Volunteers, has been revoked, and he is restored to his position unconditionally.

W. A. NICHOLS,
Assistant Adjutant-General.

Regular Navy.
Orders, &c.

April 12.—Rear-Admiral L. M. Goldsborough, appointed to command the European Squadron, with the Colorado (1st rate) as his Flag-Ship.

April 28.—Rear-Admiral Charles H. Davis, detached from duty as Chief of the Bureau of Navigation, and appointed Superintendent of the U. S. Naval Observatory. Rear-Admiral D. D. Porter, detached from command of the North Atlantic Blockading Squadron, and waiting orders.

April 20.—Commodore Charles H. Poor, detached from command of the Saranac, on the reporting of his relief, and ordered North.

April 28.—Commodore William Radford, appointed to command the North Atlantic Squadron, hoisting his flag as Acting Rear-Admiral.

April 29.—Commodore J. L. Lardner, detached from special duty at Philadelphia, and ordered to report to Commodore Engle, for duty on the Board of which he is President.

April 1.—Captain William Rogers Taylor, ordered to report to the Chief of the Bureau of Ordnance for such Ordnance duty as he may assign him.

April 3.—Captain A. M. Pennock, detached from duty as Fleet-Captain of the Mississippi Squadron, and ordered to the Navy Yard at New York.

April 5.—Captain G. H. Scott, detached from command of the Canandaigua, and waiting orders.

April 12.—Captain A. Ludlow Case, detached from the Navy Yard at New York, and ordered to report to Rear-Admiral L. M. Goldsborough, for duty as Fleet-Captain of the European Squadron.

April 20.—Captain Daniel B. Ridgely, detached from command of the Shenandoah, and waiting orders. Captain G. H. Scott, ordered to command the Saranac (Pacific Squadron).

April 21.—Captain H. S. Stellwagen, detached from command of the Pawnee, and granted sick leave.

April 25.—Captain S. B. Bissell, ordered to special duty at Navy Yard, Washington, D. C. Captain S. F. Hazard, detached from the Naval Rendezvous, Boston, Massachusetts.

April 28.—Captain Percival Drayton, appointed Chief of the Bureau of Navigation, Navy Department. Captain T. A. Jenkins, appointed senior member of a Board for the investigation of Bounty Claims of Men in the Mississippi Squadron. Captain William M. Walker, detached from command of the De Soto, and waiting orders.

April 29.—Captain Alfred Taylor, detached from the Navy Yard, Boston, and ordered to command the Susquehanna.

April 5.—Commander James H. Strong, detached from command of the Monongahela, and waiting orders.

April 8.—Commander Nathaniel C. Bryant, detached from Ordnance duty at Mound City, Illinois, and waiting orders.

April 11.—Commander Edward Donaldson, detached from Ordnance duty at Baltimore, and ordered to command the Susquehanna. Commander M. B. Woolsey, detached from command of the Princess Royal, on the reporting of his relief, and ordered North.

April 14.—Commander James H. Strong, ordered to duty with Rear-Admiral Gregory, at New York. Commander Napoleon B. Harrison, ordered to report by letter to Rear-Admiral Gregory, for such duty as he may assign.

April 17.—Commander John Guest, detached from special duty at New York, and ordered to command the Dacotah.

April 18.—Commander J. R. M. Mullaney, detached from command of the Bienville, and waiting orders.

April 20.—Commander M. C. Marin, detached from Court-Martial duty at Philadelphia, on the reporting of his relief, and ordered to command the Receiving-Ship Vandalia, at Portsmouth, New Hampshire. Commander E. C. Bowers, detached from command of the Receiving-Ship Vandalia, on the reporting of his relief, and waiting orders. Commander B. J. Totten, detached from command of the Naval Rendezvous at New Bedford, Massachusetts, and ordered to duty as member of Court-Martial at Philadelphia.

April 22.—Commander Fabius Stanley, detached from the South Atlantic Squadron, and waiting orders.

April 25.—Commander M. C. Marin, orders detaching him from Court-Martial, at Philadelphia, revoked. Commanders Samuel Swartwout and George W. Doty, detached from the Naval Rendezvous at New York, and waiting orders. Commander J. C. Williamson, detached from command of the Naval Rendezvous, Brooklyn, New York, and waiting orders. Commander E. C. Bowers, orders detaching him from command of the Receiving-Ship Vandalia revoked. Commander B. J. Totten, that portion of orders of the 20th instant appointing him a member of a Court-Martial at Philadelphia is revoked, and he will await orders.

April 27.—Commander Edward Donaldson, detached from command of the Susquehanna, and granted sick leave. Commander J. R. M. Mullaney, ordered to duty with Rear-Admiral Gregory, at New York.

April 28.—Commander Robert H. Wyman, ordered to command the Colorado, Flag-Ship of the European Squadron, fitting out at New York. Commander Fabius Stanley, ordered to duty as member of Board under Captain Jenkins, at Mound City, Illinois.

April 7.—Lieutenant-Commander John G. Walker, detached from command of the Shawmut, and waiting orders.

April 10.—Lieutenant-Commander Charles H. Cushman, detached from special duty at New York, and ordered to temporary duty at the Navy Yard, at Portsmouth, New Hampshire.

April 14.—Lieutenant-Commander A. F. Crossman, detached from the South Atlantic Squadron, and ordered to the Naval Academy at Newport, Rhode Island.

April 18.—Lieutenant-Commander James P. Foster, detached from the Mississippi Squadron, and granted leave.

April 21.—Lieutenant-Commander James H. Gillis, detached from command of the (late) Milwaukee, and waiting orders.

April 24.—Lieutenant-Commander James H. Howell, detached from the Ossipee, and ordered North. Lieutenant-Commander George C. Remey, detached from the De Soto, and ordered to the Mohongo.

April 25.—Lieutenant-Commander John G. Walker, ordered to command the Shawmut.

April 26.—Lieutenant-Commander John S. Barnes, detached from command of the Bat, on the reporting of his relief, and ordered to the Naval Academy.

April 3.—Lieutenants William T. Sampson, and J. Crittenden Watson, ordered to the Colorado. Lieutenant Sullivan D. Ames, detached from the Naval Academy, and ordered to the Colorado.

April 5.—Lieutenants Thomas C. Bowers and Oliver A. Bachellor, detached from the Monongahela, and waiting orders. Lieutenant Walter Abbot, detached from the Canandaigua, and waiting orders.

April 6.—Lieutenant Elliott C. V. Blake, ordered to the Juniata.

April 11.—Lieutenant John H. Reed, detached from the Lehigh, on the reporting of his relief, and waiting orders. Lieutenant E. C. Merriman, ordered to the Lehigh.

April 17.—Lieutenant George B. White, detached from the Ticonderoga, and ordered to the Dacotah. Lieutenant G. M. Brown, ordered to the Dacotah.

April 18.—Lieutenant Henry L. Howison, detached from the Bienville, and waiting orders.

April 20.—Lieutenant Henry L. Johnson, detached from the Shenandoah, and waiting orders.

April 21.—Lieutenant James P. Robertson, ordered to the Colorado.

April 22.—Lieutenant Joseph D. Marvin, detached from the Mohican, and waiting orders.

April 23.—Lieutenant R. S. McCook, ordered to the Ossipee.

April 24.—Lieutenant G. C. Wiltse, ordered to the North Carolina.

April 27.—Lieutenant Charles L. Huntington, detached from the Chickasaw, on the reporting of his relief, and ordered North.

April 30.—Lieutenant Joseph D. Marvin, ordered to the Susquehanna.

April 25.—Master Julius S. Bohrer, detached from the Naval Rendezvous at Baltimore, and ordered to duty in the Navy Yard at that place.

April 3.—Ensigns Ira Harris, Jr., and Charles H. Craven, and Acting Ensign Charles H. Pendleton, ordered to the Colorado.

April 17.—Acting Ensigns George T. Davis and D. R. Cassell, ordered to the Dacotah.

April 20.—Ensigns James H. Sands and Yates Sterling, detached from the Shenandoah, and waiting orders. Acting Ensign R. D. Evans, detached from the Powhatan, and granted sick leave.

April 5.—Chaplain Charles A. Davis ordered to the Naval Station, Norfolk, Virginia. Chaplain Joseph Stockbridge, detached from the Naval Station at Norfolk, Virginia.

April 10.—Chaplain George Jones, detached from the Navy Yard at Washington, D. C., and waiting orders.

April 1.—Assistant Surgeon G. S. Franklin, detached from the Onondaga, on the reporting of his relief, and waiting orders. Assistant Surgeon George H. Cooke, detached from the Navy Yard at Philadelphia, and ordered to the Onondaga. Assistant Surgeon William Commons, detached from the Passaic, on the reporting of his relief, and ordered to the Lancaster (Pacific Squadron). Assistant Surgeon J. H. Hazleton, detached from the Lancaster, on the reporting of his relief, and ordered North. Assistant Surgeon C. J. S. Wells, detached from the Mississippi Squadron, on the reporting of his relief, and waiting orders. Assistant Surgeon Henry S. Pitkin, ordered to the De Soto. Assistant Surgeon William S. Fort, ordered to the Navy Yard at Philadelphia. Assistant Surgeon Edward Kershner, detached from the Mississippi Squadron, on the reporting of his relief, and waiting orders. Assistant Surgeon Frank L. Du Bois, detached from the Naval Rendezvous at Chicago, Illinois, and ordered to the Mississippi Squadron. Assistant Surgeon S. N. Brayton, detached from the Pacific Squadron, and ordered North.

April 3.—Surgeon S. W. Kellogg, ordered to duty, as senior member of a Board for the Examination of Candidates for Appointment, and Promotion of Medical Officers of the Volunteer Navy, at New York. Surgeon A. Mathewson, ordered to duty with Surgeon Kellogg, at New York.

April 5.—Surgeon John C. Spear, detached from the Monongahela, and waiting orders. Surgeon Charles H. Burbank, detached from the Canandaigua, and waiting orders.

April 10.—Assistant Surgeon C. E. Stedman, detached from the Circassian, and waiting orders.

April 13.—Surgeon W. S. W. Ruschenberger, ordered to hold himself in readiness for duty on board the Colorado, as Surgeon of the Fleet of the European Squadron.

April 14.—Assistant Surgeon W. H. Wescott, detached from the Saugus, and ordered to the Powhatan. Assistant Surgeon W. H. Johnson, detached from the Powhatan, and waiting orders.

April 20.—Surgeon James McMaster, detached from the Shenandoah, and waiting orders. Assistant Surgeon Edward R. Dodge, ordered to the Navy Yard at Philadelphia.

April 21.—Passed Assistant Surgeon James H. Tinkham, ordered to the Colorado.

April 22.—Surgeon Charles Martin, detached from the Mohican, and waiting orders. Assistant Surgeon George T. Shipley, detached from the Wateree, and ordered home. Assistant Surgeon Charles H. Giberson, detached from the Marino

Rendezvous at New York, and ordered to the Susquehanna. Surgeon Henry O. Mayo, ordered to duty at the Marine Rendezvous at New York.

April 24.—Passed Assistant Surgeon G. H. E. Baumgarten, detached from the Naval Hospital at Memphis, Tennessee, and ordered to the Wateree.

April 25.—Surgeon Robert Woodworth, detached from the Naval Rendezvous at New York, and waiting orders. Surgeon Isaac Brinkerhoff, detached from the Naval Rendezvous at Boston, and waiting orders. Surgeon John Thornley, detached from the Naval Rendezvous at New York, and waiting orders. Surgeon Edwin R. Denby, detached from the Naval Rendezvous at New York, and waiting orders. Surgeon D. S. Edwards, detached from the Naval Rendezvous at New Bedford, Massachusetts, and waiting orders. Assistant Surgeon E. C. Ver Meulen, detached from the Naval Rendezvous at Portsmouth, New Hampshire, and waiting orders. Assistant Surgeon D. McMurtrie, detached from the Muscoota, and ordered to the North Atlantic Squadron. Assistant Surgeon J. W. Boyden, detached from Naval Hospital, Norfolk, Virginia, and ordered to the Muscoota.

April 26.—Passed Assistant Surgeon J. H. Clark, detached from the Navy Yard, Portsmouth, New Hampshire, and ordered to the Mohongo.

April 27.—Surgeon A. C. Rhoades, ordered to the Naval Hospital at New York.

April 29.—Assistant Surgeon E. C. Ver Meulen, ordered to the Naval Hospital at New York.

April 3.—Paymaster John S. Cunningham, ordered to the Colorado. Fleet Paymaster Edward T. Dunn, detached from the West Gulf Squadron, on the transfer of accounts, &c., and ordered North.

April 5.—Assistant Paymaster W. H. Anderson, detached from the Canandaigua, on completion of transfer, and ordered to settle his accounts. Assistant Paymaster Forbes Parker, detached from the Monongahela, on completion of transfer, and ordered to settle his accounts.

April 6.—Assistant Paymaster R. P. Lisle, detached from the Canonicus, on the reporting of his relief, and ordered North.

April 17.—Assistant Paymaster F. H. Swan, detached from the (late) Otsego (detachment to date from February 21st, 1865), and ordered to settle his accounts.

April 18.—Assistant Paymaster J. F. Hamilton, ordered to the Dacotah.

April 20.—Paymaster R. H. Clark, detached from the Naval Station at Pensacola, Florida, on the reporting of his relief, and ordered North. Paymaster Henry H. Pangborn, ordered to duty at the Naval Station, Pensacola, Florida.

April 22.—Assistant Paymaster S. T. Brown, detached from the Onondaga, on the reporting of his relief, and waiting orders.

April 24.—Paymaster Robert Pettit, detached from temporary duty at the Navy Yard, Philadelphia, and ordered to continue his regular duties (to take effect on the 1st proximo).

April 25.—Assistant Paymaster Francis H. Swan, ordered to the Mohongo.

April 26.—Assistant Paymaster F. H. Swan, orders to the Mohongo revoked, and he is ordered to the Frolic. Assistant Paymaster Charles F. Guild, orders to the Frolic revoked, and waiting orders.

April 27.—Assistant Paymaster H. P. Tuttle, detached from the Catskill, on the reporting of his relief, and ordered North.

April 28.—Paymaster A. H. Gilman, ordered to duty, as member of Board under Captain Jenkins, at Mound City, Illinois. Paymaster Gilbert E. Thornton ordered to duty as Inspector in charge of Provisions and Clothing, at Norfolk Navy Yard. Paymaster Washington Irving, detached from duty as Inspector of Provisions and Clothing, at Norfolk Navy Yard, on the reporting of his relief, and waiting orders.

April 5.—Chief Engineer George F. Kutz, detached from the Monongahela, and waiting orders.

April 11.—Chief Engineer Alexander Greer, detached from duty connected with the machinery of the New Ironsides, and waiting orders.

Promoted.

April 1.—Lieutenants Henry W. Miller, Allen V. Reed, George Dewey, Charles L. Franklin, and Joshua Bishop, to Lieutenant-Commanders on the Active List, to date from March 3d, 1865.

April 14.—Assistant Paymaster John J. Philbrick, to Paymaster, to date from March 9, 1865.

Resigned.

April 27.—Assistant Surgeon William H. Wescott.
April 29.—Assistant Surgeon J. H. Gunning.

Volunteer Navy.

Orders, &c.

April 11.—Acting Volunteer Lieutenant-Commander C. F. W. Behm, ordered to command the Princess Royal.

April 6.—Acting Volunteer Lieutenant H. Brown, ordered to command the Great Western (Mississippi Squadron). Acting Volunteer Lieutenant Nathan W. Hammond, notified of his exchange, and detached from the late Velocity, and waiting orders.

April 10.—Acting Volunteer Lieutenant Henry Churchill, detached from Command of the Circassian, and waiting orders.

April 13.—Acting Volunteer Lieutenant Edward Baker, detached from the Kennebec, on the reporting of his relief, and ordered North. Acting Volunteer Lieutenant W. H. Garfield, detached from the Navy Yard, Boston, and ordered to the West Gulf Squadron.

April 18.—Acting Volunteer Lieutenant George E. Welch, detached from command of the Saratoga, and waiting orders. Acting Volunteer Lieutenant George W. Brown, detached from command of the Perry, and waiting orders. Acting Volunteer Lieutenant C. J. Van Alstine, ordered to the Boston Navy Yard.

April 20.—Acting Volunteer Lieutenant E. D. Bruner, ordered to the Mississippi Squadron.

April 22.—Acting Volunteer Lieutenant E. M. Stoddard, detached from the Naval Rendezvous, South Street, New York, and ordered to command the Memphis.

April 27.—Acting Volunteer Lieutenant L. G. Vassallo, ordered to the Chickasaw.

April 29.—Acting Volunteer Lieutenant H. S. Wetmore, detached from the Eolus, and ordered to the Navy Yard, Philadelphia. Acting Volunteer Lieutenant Frederick Crocker, ordered to command the Bat.

Appointed Acting Master and Pilot.

April 5.—Lorenzo Baker, North Atlantic Squadron.

April 3.—Acting Master N. B. Heath, detached from the Augusta, and ordered to the Conemaugh. Acting Master W. L. Howarth, to regard himself as detached from the Conemaugh, on her arrival in the Squadron to which she is ordered, and to report to the Commanding Officer of the Squadron for duty.

April 5.—Acting Masters A. A. Owens and Calvin C. Childs, detached from the Canandaigua, and waiting orders.

April 6.—Acting Master John B. Childs, ordered to the Juniata. Acting Master John S. Watson, detached from the Shenandoah, and ordered to the Conemaugh.

April 7.—Acting Master James T. Rose, detached from the Shawmut, and waiting orders. Acting Master L. E. Degn, ordered to the Princeton.

April 8.—Acting Master W. A. Maine, detached from the Seminole, on the reporting of his relief, and ordered North. Acting Masters George Finney and George H. Holmes, detached from the St. Mary's, on the reporting of their reliefs, and ordered home. Acting Master Albert Cook, detached from the Princeton, on the reporting of his relief, and ordered to the Seminole. Acting Master W. T. Buck, ordered to the St. Mary's.

April 10.—Acting Master W. N. Griswold, detached from the J. L. Davis, on the reporting of his relief, and ordered North. Acting Masters William Williams and Daniel R. Browne, detached from the Circassian, and waiting orders. Acting

Master William Burditt, detached from the Mohican, and ordered to Ordnance duty at the Washington Navy Yard. Acting Master J. L. Plunkett, ordered to the J. L. Davis.

April 11.—Acting Master F. P. B. Sands, detached from the Gettysburg, and ordered to the Frolic. Acting Master and Pilot William Richardson, detached from the Powhatan, and waiting orders. Acting Master E. A. Decker, detached from the Osceola, and ordered to the Gettysburg. Acting Master A. M. Keith, ordered to the Mississippi Squadron.

April 12.—Acting Master W. T. Pratt, ordered to the Receiving-Ship North Carolina.

April 14.—Acting Master Francis G. Osborn, detached from command of the Vicksburg, and waiting orders.

April 17.—Acting Master C. H. Baxter, detached from the North Carolina, and ordered to the Emma Henry. Acting Master T. F. Lacock, ordered to the North Carolina.

April 18.—Acting Master G. F. Hollis, detached from command of the Fernandina, and waiting orders. Acting Master T. N. Myer, detached from the Bienville, and waiting orders. Acting Masters B. S. Melville and Joshua W. Crosby, detached from the Saratoga, and waiting orders. Acting Master Walter Pearce, ordered to the Pacific Squadron.

April 20.—Acting Master William H. Brice, detached from the Shenandoah, and waiting orders.

April 21. Acting Master William Williams, ordered to the Pacific Squadron. Acting Master L. A. Brown, detached from the Vincennes, on the reporting of his relief, and ordered North. Acting Master Walter Pearce, orders to the Pacific Squadron revoked.

April 22.—Acting Masters J. M. Butler and J. S. Gelett, ordered to the Memphis. Acting Master George H. Pendleton, ordered to the Fort Morgan.

April 24.—Acting Master O. K. Bernbum, ordered to return to the Susquehanna. Acting Master Walter Pearce, ordered to the Mohongo. Acting Master H. P. Conner, ordered to the Mohongo. Acting Master H. W. Washburn, ordered to the Sabine. Acting Master D. R. Brown, ordered to the Dacotah.

April 25.—Acting Master and Pilot Edward A. Decker, detached from the Gettysburg, and ordered to the Osceola.

April 27.—Acting Master A. A. Owens, ordered to the Mohongo. Acting Master D. Rodney Brown, ordered to the Dacotah.

Appointed Acting Ensigns.

April 7.—Mason S. Cooper, and ordered to the Frolic.
April 8.—M. J. Nicholson, and ordered to the Arkansas.
April 13.—James Wilber, and ordered to the South Atlantic Squadron.
April 18.—Walter S. Howland, and ordered to the Potomska.
April 21.—J. W. Wallace, Potomac Flotilla.
April 24.—Joseph N. Peabody, U. S. S. Genesee.
April 27.—C. H. Cobb, Potomac Flotilla.
April 28.—H. S. P. Rollins, and waiting orders.
April 29.—John W. Sanderson, U. S. S. Mahaska.

Appointed Acting Ensigns, and ordered to the School-Ship Savannah.

April 5.—Owen S. M. Cone.
April 11.—William J. Dumont.
April 14.—Samuel Atwood.

April 4.—Acting Ensign J. F. Bliss, detached from the Huntsville, and he is granted three weeks' sick leave; on the expiration of which he is to report for duty in the South Atlantic Squadron.

April 5.—Acting Ensigns G. H. Barry and R. P. Leary, detached from the Canandaigua, and waiting orders. Acting Ensigns P. F. Harrington, D. W. Mullan, and C. F. R. Wappenhaus, detached from the Monongahela, and waiting orders. Acting Ensign T. F. Lacock, detached from the Susquehanna, and waiting orders.

April 7.—Acting Ensigns Daniel Friele and James B. Russell, detached from the

Shawmut, and waiting orders. Acting Ensign T. E. Harvey, ordered to command the tug Pilgrim. Acting Ensign Cornelius Bartlett, ordered to the Squando.

April 8.—Acting Ensign James Birtwistle, ordered to the St. Mary's.

April 10.—Acting Ensigns James E. M. Graham, Joseph W. Mulford, G. E. French, and C. H. Danforth, detached from the Circassian, and waiting orders.

April 11.—Acting Ensign Francis H. Brown, detached from command of the Ariel, on the reporting of his relief, and ordered North. Acting Ensign W. B. Browne, detached from the Honduras, on the reporting of his relief, and ordered North. Acting Ensign Israel Halsted, detached from the Princeton, and ordered to the Honduras. Acting Ensign Charles P. Bragg, detached from the (late) Signal, and granted leave. Acting Ensign L. R. Chester, ordered to command the Ariel. Acting Ensign W. C. Underhill, ordered to the Granite.

April 12.—Acting Ensign Edward Pendexter, detached from the Penobscot, and ordered North. Acting Ensign W. W. Smith, detached from the Frolic, and ordered to the James S. Chambers. Acting Ensign James T. Bowling, ordered to the Penobscot.

April 13.—Acting Ensign J. H. Rogers, ordered to the Sweet-Brier.

April 14.—Acting Ensign Robert B. Eider, detached from the Vicksburg, and ordered to the Ottawa. Acting Ensign David P. Cook, detached from the Vicksburg, and ordered to the Catskill. Acting Ensign Frederick Elliott, detached from the Catskill, on the reporting of his relief, and ordered North. Acting Ensign Walter N. Smith, detached from the Ottawa, on the reporting of his relief, and ordered North. Acting Ensigns William H. Otis and G. V. Demorest, detached from the Vicksburg, and waiting orders.

April 17.—Acting Ensign N. R. Davis, detached from the North Carolina, and granted leave. Acting Ensign John Williams, detached from the North Carolina, and ordered to the Emma Henry. Acting Ensign J. A. Williams, ordered to the Emma Henry. Acting Ensign J. C. Staples, ordered to the Emma Henry.

April 18.—Acting Ensigns Edwin B. Cox, Edward H. Sheen, and Rufus R. Donnell, detached from the Perry, and waiting orders. Acting Ensigns Henry G. Seaman, B H. Chadwick, and C. H. Sawyer, detached from the Fernandina, and waiting orders. Acting Ensigns Francis O. Abbott, George H. French, George E. Wing, and Emile Enfer, detached from the Bienville, and waiting orders. Acting Ensigns George O. Fabeus, William A. Stannard, William H. Anderson, and Edward Rogers, detached from the Saratoga, and waiting orders. Acting Ensign P. W. Fagan, ordered to the Pacific Squadron.

April 20.—Acting Ensign Thomas H. Wheeler, detached from the Shenandoah, and waiting orders,

April 21.—Acting Ensign J. H. Rogers, orders to the Sweet-Brier revoked, and granted sick leave.

April 22.—Acting Ensigns Horace Dexter and N. C. Borden, detached from the Braziliera, and waiting orders. Acting Ensigns H. T. Page and B. F. Blair, detached from the Mohican, and waiting orders. Acting Ensign J. H. Bennett, detached from command of the Braziliera, and waiting orders. Acting Ensigns Hazard Marsh and John W. King, ordered to the Memphis. Acting Ensign Daniel Friele, ordered to the Memphis.

April 24.—Acting Ensigns P. F. Harrington and W. A. Duer, ordered to the Mohongo.

April 25.—Acting Ensign S. L. La Dein, detached from the Osceola, and ordered to the Gettysburg. Acting Ensigns G. H. Barry and C. J. Rogers, ordered to the Coast-Survey Steamer Corwin.

April 26.—Acting Ensign P. P. Hawkes, ordered to the Unadilla.

April 27.—Acting Ensign Joseph W. Mulford, ordered to the Huron. Acting Ensign C. F. P. Wappenhaus, ordered to the Mattabesett.

April 28.—Acting Ensign G. E. French, ordered to the Juniata.

Appointed Acting Assistant Surgeons.

April 1.—Edwin A. Forbes, and ordered to the North Carolina.

April 11.—Lewis W. Loring, and ordered to the North Carolina. B. Sernig, and ordered to the Navy Yard at Washington, D. C.

April 17.—George H. Bull, and ordered to the Ohio.

April 20.—Clarence M. Slack, and ordered to the North Carolina.

April 28.—Wilford H. Wetherill, and ordered to the North Carolina.

April 1.—Acting Assistant Surgeon Gilbert Balfour, detached from the Princeton, and ordered to the Passaic. Assistant Surgeon A. Dodge, detached from the North Carolina, and ordered to the Mississippi Squadron.

April 5.—Acting Assistant Surgeon W. H. Bates, orders to the Huntsville revoked, and he is ordered to the Mississippi Squadron. Acting Assistant Surgeon A. Dodge, orders to the Mississippi Squadron revoked, and he is ordered to the Huntsville.

April 7.—Acting Assistant Surgeon J. J. Sowerby, detached from the Shawmut, and waiting orders. Acting Assistant Surgeon G. W. Masters, detached from the Ohio, and ordered to the James Adger. Acting Asistant Surgeon W. W. Myers, detached from the James Adger, on the reporting of his relief, and ordered North.

April 10.—Acting Assistant Surgeon E. D. G. Smith, detached from the West Gulf Squadron, on the reporting of his relief, and ordered North. Acting Assistant Surgeon Jared W. Dillman, detached from the Princeton, and ordered to the West Gulf Squadron.

April 12.—Acting Assistant Surgeon C. W. Knight, detached from the Carrabasset, on the reporting of his relief, and ordered North. Acting Assistant Surgeon E. A. Forbes, detached from the Princeton, and ordered to the Carrabasset.

April 14.—Acting Assistant Surgeon Thomas W. Bennett, detached from the Vicksburg, and waiting orders.

April 17.—Acting Assistant Surgeon John M. Batten, detached from the Valley City, on the reporting of his relief, and ordered North. Acting Assistant Surgeon L. W. Loring, detached from the North Carolina, and ordered to the Valley City.

April 18.—Acting Assistant Surgeon S. B. Kenney, detached from the Fernandina, and waiting orders. Acting Assistant Surgeon Winthrop Butler, detached from the Saratoga, and waiting orders.

April 24.—Acting Assistant Surgeon Nelson Ingram, detached from the North Carolina, and ordered to the Mahopac.

April 26.—Acting Passed Assistant Surgeon N. L. Campbell, ordered to the Mohongo.

April 27.—Acting Assistant Surgeon J. W. Hamilton, ordered to the Conemaugh. Acting Assistant Surgeon A. R. Holmes, detached from the Pembina, on the reporting of his relief, and ordered North. Acting Assistant Surgeon Ira L. Davies, detached from the Navy Yard, Washington, and ordered to the Potomac Flotilla.

April 28.—Acting Passed Assistant Surgeon N. L. Campbell, orders to the Mohongo revoked, and he is ordered to the Memphis.

April 29.—Acting Assistant Surgeon B. Sernig. detached from the Navy Yard, Washington, D. C., and ordered to the Commodore Morris.

Appointed Acting Assistant Paymasters.

April 4.—T. C. Dickinson, and waiting orders.

April 5.—John H. Abell and Frederick Wells, and waiting orders.

April 6.—Wm. Holland, L. C. Woods, Jr., and S. D. Hurlburt, and waiting orders.

April 13.—Nicholas H. Belding, and waiting orders.

April 22.—R. G. Simpson, and waiting orders.

April 24.—Charles F. Abbott, and waiting orders.

April 25.—William A. Gale, and waiting orders.

April 3.—Acting Assistant Paymaster E. Mellach, detached from duty in charge of stores at Newbern, North Carolina, and ordered to settle his accounts. Acting Assistant Paymaster William S. Thomson, ordered to the Squando. Acting Assistant Paymaster George R. Watkins, ordered to duty in charge of stores at the Naval Station, Newbern, North Carolina.

April 6.—Acting Assistant Paymaster Mathew T. Trumbour, ordered to the Canonicus. Acting Assistant Paymaster D. L. Ruth, orders to the Forest Rose revoked, and waiting orders.

April 7.—Acting Assistant Paymaster Bela M. Farnham, detached from the Shawmut, on completion of transfer, and ordered to settle his accounts.

April 8.—Acting Assistant Paymasters C. W. Armstrong, Charles H. Hill, and H. G. Colby, ordered to the Mississippi Squadron.

April 10.—Acting Assistant Paymaster T. H. Haskell, detached from the Circassian, on completion of transfer, and ordered to settle his accounts.

April 12.—Acting Assistant Paymasters Charles S. Dickerman and Frank H. Balch, ordered to the Mississippi Squadron. Acting Assistant Paymaster H. D. Kimberly, ordered to the Sassacus.

April 14.—Acting Assistant Paymaster J. H. Bulkley, detached from the Vicksburg, on completion of transfer, and ordered to settle his accounts.

April 17.—Acting Assistant Paymaster E. B. Southworth, detached from the Grand Gulf, on the reporting of his relief, and ordered to settle his accounts. Acting Assistant Paymaster H. B. Wetherill, ordered to the Grand Gulf. Acting Assistant Paymasters S. D. Hurlbut and J. W. Meacham, ordered to the Mississippi Squadron. Acting Assistant Paymaster L. C. Woods, Jr., ordered to instruction at New York.

April 18.—Acting Assistant Paymaster W. W. Goodwin, detached from the Bienville, on completion of transfer, and ordered to settle his accounts. Acting Assistant Paymaster L. S. Yorke, detached from the Saratoga, on completion of transfer, and ordered to settle his accounts. Acting Assistant Paymaster Thomas A. Emerson, detached from the Perry, on completion of transfer, and ordered to settle his accounts. Acting Assistant Paymaster F. N. Murray, detached from the Fernandina, on completion of transfer, and ordered to settle his accounts. Acting Assistant Paymaster Frederick Welles, ordered to the Emma Henry.

April 20.—Acting Assistant Paymaster C. M. Guild, detached from the Shenandoah, and ordered to settle his accounts. Acting Assistant Paymaster William Holland, ordered to the Mississippi Squadron.

April 22.—Acting Assistant Paymaster J. C. Canning, detached from the Mohican, on completion of transfer, &c., and ordered to settle his accounts. Acting Assistant Paymaster C. H. Longstreet, detached from the Braziliera, on completion of transfer, &c., and ordered to settle his accounts. Acting Assistant Paymaster D. L. Ruth, ordered to the Onondaga.

April 26.—Acting Assistant Paymaster T. S. Dabney, ordered to the Mohongo. Acting Assistant Paymaster Edward Sherwin, ordered to settle the accounts of the (late) Dai Ching.

April 27.—Acting Assistant Paymaster T. A. Swords, ordered to the Catskill. Acting Assistant Paymaster L. C. Woods, ordered to the Nantucket. Acting Assistant Paymaster G. W. Allen, detached from the Nantucket, on the reporting of his relief, and ordered to settle his accounts.

April 10.—Acting Chief Engineer Samuel N. Hartwell, detached from the Circassian, and waiting orders.

April 18.—Acting Chief Engineer William F. Wright, detached from the Bienville, and waiting orders.

April 20.—Acting Chief Engineer Nelson Winans, detached from the Shenandoah, and waiting orders.

April 29.—Acting Chief Engineer Alexander McCausland, ordered to the Juniata.

Promoted.

April 5.—Acting Master Nathaniel S. Morgan, to Acting Volunteer Lieutenant. Acting Ensign Rowland B. Brown, to Acting Master.

April 6.—Acting Masters S. P. Crafts, H. P. Conner, W. H. Maies, and E. H. Keyser, to Acting Volunteer Lieutenants. Acting Ensigns O. C. K. Bernbum and Charles Grieve, to Acting Masters.

April 8.—Acting Masters Jacob Kimball, Joseph E. Stannard, and Leander H. Partridge, to Acting Volunteer Lieutenants. Acting Ensigns W. H. Colley, W. Nyborg, Julius Nilson, David P. Page, John L. Hall, and E. Spedden Lowe, to Acting Masters.

April 11.—Acting Ensign W. H. Mayer, to Acting Master.

April 12.—Acting Assistant Surgeons George B. Todd and John J. Sowerby, to Acting Passed Assistant Surgeons.

April 18.—Acting Ensign Henry W. Mather, to Acting Master.

April 20.—Acting Ensign Jacob Barron, to Acting Master.

April 22.—Acting Master Nehemiah M. Dyer, to Acting Volunteer Lieutenant. Acting Ensign Theodore H. Paine, to Acting Master.

April 24.—Acting Master C. C. Kingsbury, to Acting Volunteer Lieutenant.

April 25.—Acting Ensign Nichols Pratt, to Acting Master.

April 26.—Acting Volunteer Lieutenant Thomas A. Harris, to Acting Volunteer Lieutenant-Commander.
April 27.—Acting Assistant Surgeon A. B. C. Sawyer, to Acting Passed Assistant Surgeon.
April 28.—Acting Master C. C. Bunker, to Acting Volunteer Lieutenant.
April 29.—Acting Volunteer Lieutenant R. B. Smith, to Acting Volunteer Lieutenant-Commander. Acting Master Thomas Chatfield, to Acting Volunteer Lieutenant.

Resigned.

April 1.—Acting Ensigns Samuel Smith and Henry T. Blake.
April 3.—Acting Assistant Surgeon Israel Bushong.
April 4.—Acting Master Henry A. Phelon; Acting Ensigns William H. Metz, D. B. McKenzie, John A. Davis, and Gardner A. Churchill.
April 6.—Acting Master Alfred Everson.
April 7.—Acting Ensign David J. Starbuck; Acting Assistant Paymaster C. E. Taylor.
April 8.—Acting Volunteer Lieutenant John D. Harty; Acting Ensign, Charles Ekman.
April 11.—Acting Assistant Surgeon Edward P. Colby; Acting Ensigns Lewis P. Delan and S. G. Bryer.
April 13.—Acting Ensign D. Dexter.
April 14.—Acting Ensign Alexander S. Gibson.
April 17.—Acting Ensign George Anderson; Acting Assistant Paymaster George M. Burns, Jr.
April 18.—Acting Master B. S. Weeks; Acting Master and Pilot Isaac Sofield; Acting Ensign William Schultz; and Acting Assistant Surgeon J. T. Coates.
April 20.—Acting Volunteer Lieutenant C. Dominy; Acting Ensigns G. H. Barrows and J. W. Grattan.
April 21.—Acting Ensigns P. J. Markoe and William R. Avery; Acting Assistant Surgeons Henry H. Smith and George S. Eddy; Acting Assistant Paymaster J. H. Jenkins.
April 22.—Acting Assistant Surgeon Henry Johnson.
April 24.—Acting Masters Foster Willis and John Wallace; Acting Ensign James H. Barry; Acting Assistant Paymaster George H. Andrews.
April 25.—Acting Master S. A. Waterbury; Acting Ensign Stephen C. Hill.
April 26.—Acting Ensigns John Cullaton and Winslow B. Barnes.
April 27.—Acting Ensigns J. Ryon, Samuel H. Maunder, S. S. Bissell, James W. Fisk, and J. B. Trott; Acting Volunteer Lieutenant D. A. Campbell; Acting Master Walter Pearce.
April 28.—Acting Ensigns George T. Joslin, Andre S. Rounds, Jr., and William D. Price; Acting Assistant Surgeons Benjamin F. Brown, P. H. Pursell, and R. W. Gifford.
April 29.—Acting Ensigns Ralph C. Peck and Charles Millett; Acting Assistant Surgeon Robert W. Clark.

Honorably Discharged; Services being no longer Required.

April 25.—Acting Volunteer Lieutenant Henry C. Keene.

Revoked.

April 1.—Acting Master Gilbert Richmond.
April 4.—Acting Ensign and Pilot Oliver Lasher.
April 10.—Acting Master R. O. Patterson; Acting Assistant Surgeon B. G. Walton.
April 14.—Acting Master and Pilot D. V. N. Wright.
April 21.—Acting Master Thomas H. Ferney; Ensign Charles P. Gifford.

Dismissed.

April 20.—Acting Ensign and Pilot William C. Williams.
April 21.—Acting Ensign E. B. Hunt.
April 24.—Acting Ensign F. S. Leach.

CPSIA information can be obtained at www.ICGtesting.com
Printed in the USA
BVOW07s0912220414

351354BV00011B/823/P